P9-DXO-139

AMERICAN MUSEUM OF NATURAL HISTORY

BIRDS
OF NORTH AMERICA

WESTERN REGION

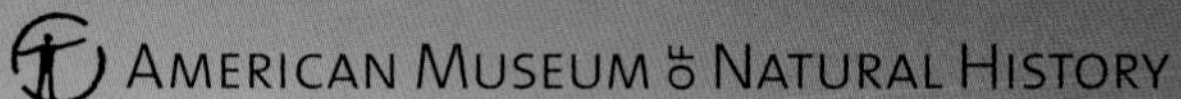

BIRDS
OF NORTH AMERICA

Editor-in-Chief
François Vuilleumier

WESTERN REGION

Content previously published in
Birds of North America

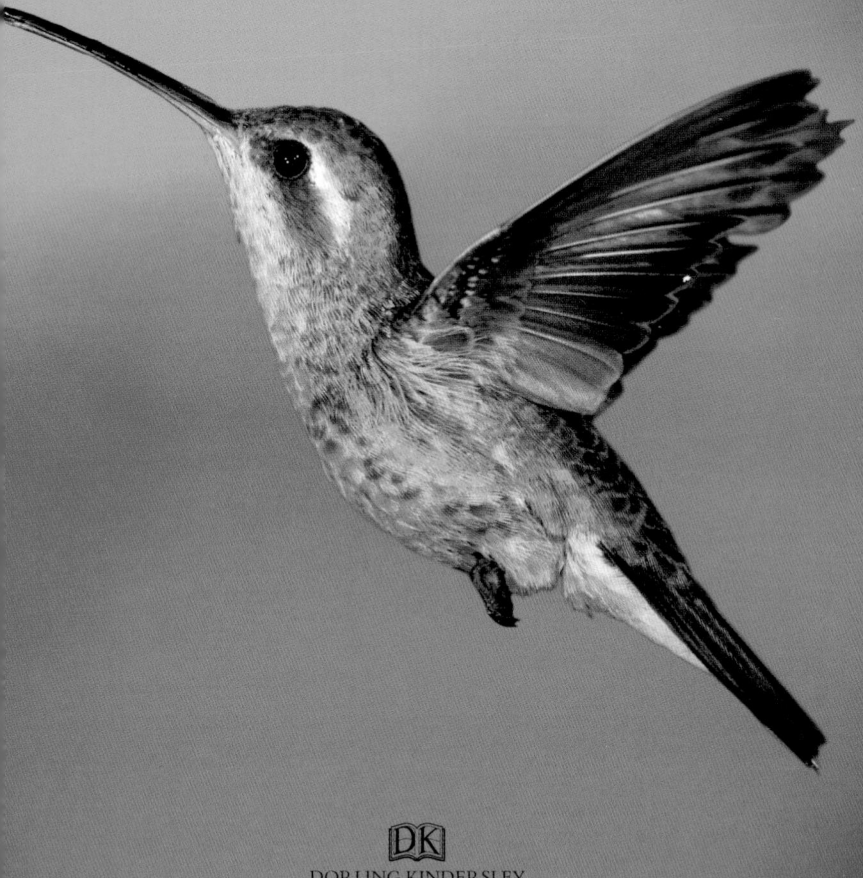

LONDON, NEW YORK, MUNICH, MELBOURNE, AND DELHI

DORLING KINDERSLEY

Senior Art Editors
Caroline Hill, Ina Stradins

Senior Editor
Angeles Gavira Guerrero

US Senior Editors
Shannon Beatty, Jill Hamilton

Project Editor
Nathan Joyce

Designers
Sonia Barbate, Helen McTeer

Editors
Jamie Ambrose, Lori Baird, Tamlyn Calitz, Marcus Hardy, Lizzie Munsey, Patrick Newman, Siobhan O'Connor, David Summers, Cressida Tuson, Miezan van Zyl, Rebecca Warren

Design Assistant
Becky Tennant

Editorial Assistant
Jaime Tenreiro

Creative Technical Support
Adam Brackenbury, John Goldsmid

Production Editors
Joanna Byrne, Maria Elia

Production Controllers
Erika Pepe, Rita Sinha

Jacket Designer
Mark Cavanagh

Illustrators
John Cox, Andrew Mackay

Picture Editor
Neil Fletcher

Picture Researchers
Laura Barwick, Will Jones

Managing Art Editor
Michelle Baxter

Managing Editor
Sarah Larter

Publishing Manager
Liz Wheeler

Art Directors
Phil Ormerod, Bryn Walls

Publisher
Jonathan Metcalf

DK INDIA

Editorial Manager
Glenda Fernandes

Project Designer
Mahua Mandal

Senior Designer
Mini Dhawan

Editors
Megha Gupta, Rukmini Kumar, Garima Sharma, Dipali Singh

Picture Researcher
Sakshi Saluja

DTP Manager
Balwant Singh

Senior DTP Designer
Harish Aggarwal

DTP Designers
Shanker Prasad, Arjinder Singh, Jaypal Singh, Bimlesh Tiwary, Anita Yadav, Tanveer Abbas Zaidi

AMERICAN MUSEUM OF NATURAL HISTORY

Editor-in-chief
François Vuilleumier, Ph.D.

Project Coordinators
Alex Navissi, Caitlin Roxby, Molly Leff

DEDICATION

F.V. dedicates this book to the memory of John Bull, John Farrand, and Stuart Keith, top birders, field guide authors, AMNH colleagues, first-rate ornithologists, and friends.

Material first published in *Birds of North America* 2009. This edition first published in the United States in 2011 by DK Publishing
345 Hudson Street
New York, NY 10014

16 17 18 10 9 8 7 6 5 4 3

003—ND115—Feb/2011

A catalog record for this book is available from the Library of Congress.

ISBN 978-0-7566-5868-7

DK books are available at special discounts when purchased in bulk for sales promotions, premiums, fund-raising, or educational use. For details, contact: DK Publishing Special Markets, 345 Hudson Street, New York, New York 10014 or SpecialSales@dk.com.

Printed and bound in China by L.Rex Printing Co. Ltd.

Discover more at
www.dk.com

CONTRIBUTORS

David Bird, Ph.D.
Nicholas L. Block
Peter Capainolo
Matthew Cormons
Malcolm Coulter, Ph.D.
Joseph DiCostanzo
Shawneen Finnegan
Neil Fletcher
Ted Floyd
Jeff Groth, Ph.D.
Paul Hess
Brian Hiller
Rob Hume
Thomas Brodie Johnson
Kevin T. Karlson
Stephen Kress, Ph.D.
William Moskoff, Ph.D.
Bill Pranty
Michael L. P. Retter
Noah Strycker
Paul Sweet
Rodger Titman, Ph.D.
Elissa Wolfson

Map Editor
Paul Lehman

Project Coordinator
Joseph DiCostanzo

CONTENTS

PREFACE

THRUSHES
Back in the early 1900s, the great wildlife artist Louis Agassiz Fuertes already painted birds in the style of modern field guides, as shown in this plate from Chapman's *Handbook of the Birds of Eastern North America.*

WITH ITS EASTERN AND WESTERN volumes, *Birds of North America* attempts to fill a gap in the North American bird book market. No other work offers, for every North American bird species, the same combination of stunning iconography, including beautiful photographs and precise distribution maps; scientifically accurate and readable accounts of salient characteristics; data on identification, behavior, habitat, voice, social structure, nest construction, breeding season, food, and conservation status; diagrams of flight patterns; statistics of size, wingspan, weight, clutch size, number of broods per year, and lifespan; and geographic information about breeding, wintering, and migration. Furthermore, no other bird book introduces, in such an up-to-date and lavishly illustrated manner, general material about birds: their evolution, classification, anatomy, flight, migration, navigation, courtship, mating, nests, and eggs. Scientific jargon has been avoided, but a glossary identifies concepts that benefit from an explanation. With their user-friendly format, these eastern and western guides to *Birds of North America* should permit readers either to enjoy studying one species account at a time, or browse to make cross comparisons.

Many field guides exist, as well as treatises on groups like gulls, hummingbirds, or sparrows; other books are dictionary-like, or focus on species of conservation concern. However, no bird book today can be called a "handbook," a concise reference work that can be conveniently carried around. I hope that these books will be useful in this role to all persons interested in birds, whether young or older, enthusiastic birder or beginner.

Historically, *Birds of North America* can be viewed as a successor to Frank M. Chapman's epochal *Handbook of the Birds of Eastern North America*, published in 1895. During his 54 years at the American Museum of Natural History in New York City, Chapman, dean of American ornithologists, blazed a trail that contributed substantially to what American ornithology, bird conservation, and birding have become. The facts that the new book has the imprint of the American Museum of Natural History, and that I, as its Editor-in-Chief, have worked there for 31 years as Curator of Ornithology and as Chairman of its Department of Ornithology, are not coincidental.

In his Handbook, Chapman treated all birds found in Eastern North America. The description of each species was followed by data on distribution, nest, and eggs, and a readable, often even brilliant text about habitat, behavior, and voice. The illustrations included plates by two pioneer American wildlife artists, Louis Agassiz Fuertes and Francis Lee Jaques, whose style inspired all those who followed them. Some of these

EASTERN AND WESTERN REGIONS

In a pioneering essay from 1908, Frank Chapman realized, on the basis of his own fieldwork, that the 100th Meridian corresponded to a rather clear-cut division of North American bird faunas into an Eastern and a Western region. Of course there are exceptions and the 100th Meridian line is not something that the birds themselves recognize. The invisible barrier is located in a transitional zone between habitats that represent, respectively, Eastern versus Western landscape types or biomes. Some, but not all, modern field guides use the 100th Meridian as a division between East and West.

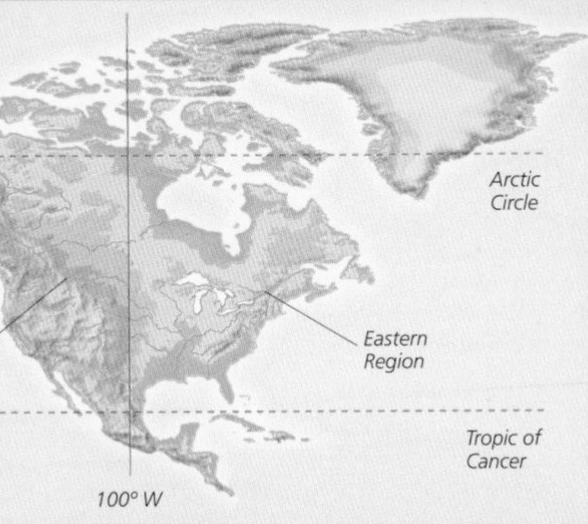

plates were, already then, executed in field guide fashion. Anybody who examines Chapman's *Handbook* today is struck by how modern it is. "Museum man" and "birder," Chapman was also a gifted educator and a good writer: a rare combination. Museum research gave him the taxonomic background, and fieldwork throughout North America sharpened his birding skills. As Editor-in-Chief of *Birds of North America*, working in the department Chapman created, enjoying the same extraordinary collection and library resources, and traveling as widely as he did, I have endeavored to make this new book a work of which he would have been proud. Don't leave home without it—and bring along binoculars and a pencil to jot down notes.

François Vuilleumier (signature)

François Vuilleumier
American Museum of Natural History,
New York City
February 2011

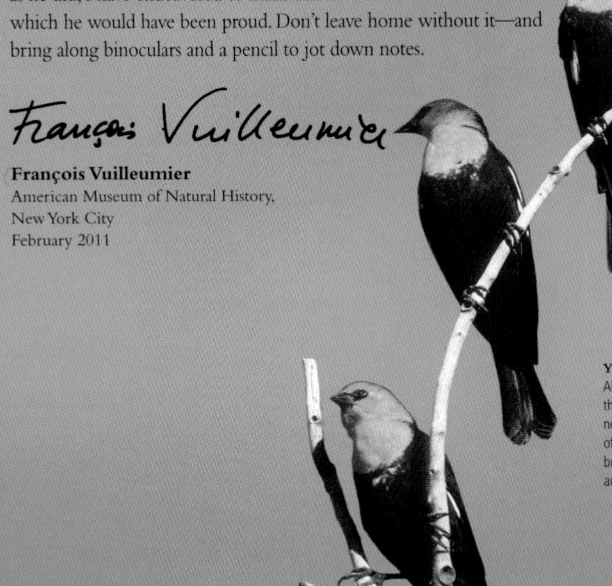

YELLOW GARLAND
Abundant in Western marshes, the Yellow-headed Blackbird is not only conspicuous because of the yellow head of males, but also because of their loud and strange vocalizations.

HOW THIS BOOK WORKS

This guide covers over 600 Western North American bird species. The species are arranged into three sections: the first profiles common species, each being given full-page treatment; the second covers rarer birds in quarter-page entries; the third section consists of a list of rare visitors.

▽ COMMON SPECIES

The main section of the book features the 369 most commonly seen bird species in Western North America. Each entry is clear and detailed, following the same format.

▽ INTRODUCTION

The species are organized conventionally by order, family, and genus. Related birds appear together, preceded by a group introduction. The book follows the most up-to-date avian classification system, based on the latest scientific research.

Family **Icteridae**

ORIOLES & BLACKBIRDS

The icterids exemplify the wonderful diversity that exists among birds. Most icterids are common and widespread, occurring from coast to coast. They are present in nearly every habitat in North America, from the arid Southwest and Florida to the boreal forest zone in the north, though not in the tundra. The species reveal a tremendous variety in color, nesting, and social behavior—from solitary orioles to vast colonies of comparatively drab blackbirds. One group of icterids, the cowbirds, are obligatory brood parasites. They make no nest, but lay their eggs in the nests of other birds, mostly small songbirds.

ORIOLES

Orioles are common seasonal migrants to North America. They are generally recognized by their contrasting black and orange plumage, although some species tend more toward yellow or chestnut shades. Orioles construct intricate hanging nests which display an impressive combination of engineering and weaving. Most oriole species have a loud and melodious song and show tolerance of humans, a combination that makes them popular throughout their range. Bullock's Oriole is the only oriole species that is widespread and common in the West; other western species are restricted to the Southwest or southern Texas. The migratory habits of orioles are mixed: Bullock's Oriole migrates south in the fall, while Audubon's and Altamira's Orioles are sedentary in southern Texas.

NECTAR LOVER

COWBIRDS

Cowbirds are strictly parasitic birds, and have been known to lay their eggs in the nests of nearly 300 different bird species in North and South America. The males of all three North American cowbird species are readily identified by their thick bills and dark, iridescent plumage. The females and immatures are drab by comparison.

SUBTLE BRILLIANCE
Although its plumage is dark, the Common Grackle displays a beautiful iridescence.

BLACKBIRDS & GRACKLES

This group of birds is largely covered with dark feathers, and their long, pointed bills and tails give them a streamlined appearance. Not as brilliantly colored as some of the other icterids, these are among the most numerous birds on the continent. After the breeding season they gather in huge flocks, and form an impressive sight.

MEADOWLARKS

Meadowlarks occur in both South and North America. The North American species have yellow breasts, but the South American species sport bright red breasts. Only the Western Meadowlark breeds commonly in the West. It is difficult to tell apart from its eastern counterpart, except by its song, yellow chest with a black bib, and a sweet singing voice.

BIG VOICE
A Meadowlark's melodious voice is a defining feature in many rural landscapes.

GROUP NAME
The common name of the group the species belong to is at the top of each page.

COMMON NAME

IN FLIGHT
Illustrations show the bird in flight, from above and/or below—differences of season, age, or sex are not always visible.

DESCRIPTION
Conveys the main features and essential character of the species including:

VOICE
A description of the species' calls and songs, given phonetically where possible.

NESTING
The type of nest and its usual location; the number of eggs in a clutch; the number of broods in a year; the breeding season.

FEEDING
How, where, and what the species feeds on.

SIMILAR SPECIES
Similar-looking species are identified and key differences pointed out.

LENGTH, WINGSPAN, AND WEIGHT
Length is tip of tail to tip of bill; measurements and weights are averages or ranges.

SOCIAL
The social unit the species is usually found in.

LIFESPAN
The length of life, in years, obtained from either zoo birds or from banding and recovery records of wild birds. The actual average or maximum life expectancy of many bird species is still unknown.

STATUS
The conservation status of the species; (p) means the data available is only provisional.

ORIOLES AND BLACKBIRDS

Order **Passeriformes** | Family **Icteridae**

Bullock's Oriole

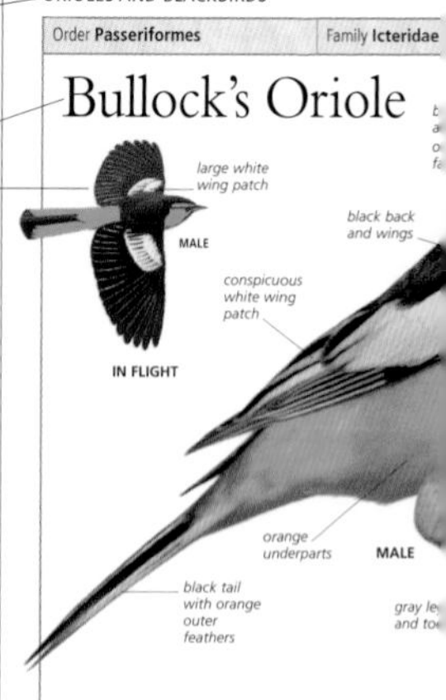

Bullock's Oriole is the western counterpart of th in both behavior and habitat. The two were co belong to a single species, the Northern Oriole (*I. g* because they interbreed where they overlap in the Recent studies, however, suggest that they are separ Unlike many other orioles, Bullock's is more resista parasites and removes cowbird eggs from its nest.
VOICE Varied string of one- and two-part notes of at the end; similar to, but less melodious, than the B
NESTING Hanging basket of woven plant strips loc branches; 4–5 eggs; 1 brood; March–June.
FEEDING Forages for insects, in particular grasshoppers and caterpillars, but also ants, beetles, and spiders; nectar and fruit when available.

SIMILAR SPECIES

HOODED ORIOLE see p.463 | BALTIMORE ORIOLE see p.463

Length **6½–7½in (16–19cm)**	Wingspan **10–12in**
Social **Pairs/Flocks**	Lifespan **Up to 8 y**

DATE SEEN	WHERE

374

HABITAT/BEHAVIOR
Photographs reveal the species in its habitat or show interesting behavior.

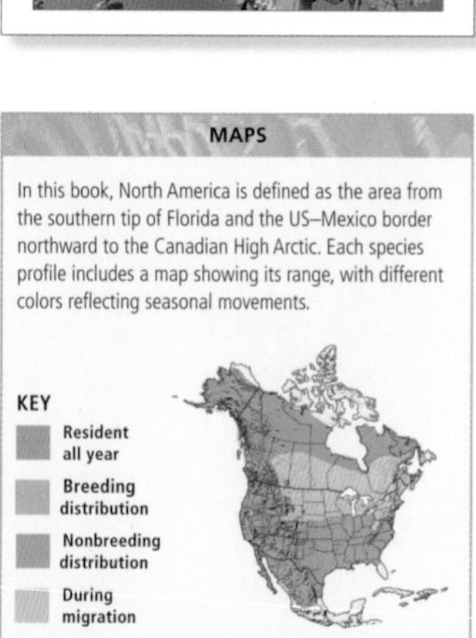

MAPS

In this book, North America is defined as the area from the southern tip of Florida and the US–Mexico border northward to the Canadian High Arctic. Each species profile includes a map showing its range, with different colors reflecting seasonal movements.

KEY
Resident all year
Breeding distribution
Nonbreeding distribution
During migration

SYMBOLS

♂ Male	Spring
♀ Female	Summer
Juvenile	Autumn
Immature	Winter

CLASSIFICATION
The top band of each entry provides the scientific names of order, family, and species (see glossary, pp. 472-473, for full definitions of these terms).

Species **Icterus bullockii**

FLIGHT: full, powerful wing beats, resulting n a "heavier" flight aspect than similar species.

slurred
song.

OCCURRENCE
Breeds commonly in riverine woodlands with willows and cottonwoods; also mixed hardwood forests, mesquite woodland, and groves of fruit trees. After breeding, Bullock's Orioles migrate southward and spend the winter from Mexico to Nicaragua.

THORNS
s Oriole
ch with long
t perturbed.

Weight	**1¹⁄₁₆–1⁹⁄₁₆oz (30–45g)**
Status	**Secure**

ES

RARE SPECIES

Family **Icteridae** | Species ***Icterus spurius***

Orchard Oriole
The way Orchard Orioles flit among leaves when foraging for insects recalls the behavior of wood-warblers. In addition, and unlike other orioles, it flutters its tail. A late arrival in spring, it is also an early species to leave in the fall. The foothills of the Rocky Mountains correspond approximately to its range border in the West.
OCCURRENCE Breeds in open forest and woodland edges with a mixture of evergreen and deciduous trees; also found in parks and gardens. Winters in Mexico, Central America, and South America.
VOICE Fast, not very melodious, series of high warbling notes mixed with occasional shorter notes ending in slurred *shheere*.

deep orange shoulders
MALE

Length **7–8in (18–20cm)** | Wingspan **9in (23cm)**

Family **Icteridae** | Species ***Icterus cucullatus***

Hooded Oriole
Tall palm trees in suburban gardens and urban parks, especially in California, have become popular nesting sites for the Hooded Oriole. Increasing numbers of palm trees, combined with the offerings of nectar intended for hummingbirds have contributed to the expansion of its range from California to the Southwest. By contrast, its numbers in Texas have been shrinking, in part because of its susceptibility to brood parasitism by Brown-headed and Bronzed Cowbirds.
OCCURRENCE Breeds in open woodlands along water courses, especially those containing palm trees. Winters in Mexico.
VOICE A harsh *weeek* call; song a weakly whined and rapid series of whistles where notes often run together; imitates other birds.

long, curved bill
MALE (BREEDING)

Length **7–8in (18–20cm)** | Wingspan **9–11in (23–28cm)**

Family **Icteridae** | Species ***Icterus galbula***

Baltimore Oriole
The brilliantly colored Baltimore Oriole, the eastern counterpart of the Bullock's Oriole, ranges westward in Canada to Alberta and, locally, eastern British Colombia. At the edge of their respective distributions, in the Great Plains, Baltimore and Bullock's Orioles interbreed. Ornithologists have, at times, considered them to be a single species.
OCCURRENCE A variety of woodlands, also parks and gardens. Most winter in Mexico, Colombia, and Venezuela.
VOICE Loud, clear, melodious song comprising several short notes in series, often of varying lengths.

straight, blue-gray bill
MALE

Length **8–10in (20–26cm)** | Wingspan **10–12in (26–30cm)**

Family **Icteridae** | Species ***Molothrus aeneus***

Bronzed Cowbird
The range of this species has been expanding in the US ever since it was first recorded in the early 1900s. This could be the result of human clearing of native habitats and replacing them with agricultural crops. A brood parasite, it has been recorded to lay its eggs in the nests of more than 80 bird species, and their young have fledged from over 30 of these. The females may work cooperatively to identify and parasitize the nests of other birds.
OCCURRENCE Inhabits open fields, pastures, scattered scrub, and suburban parks. In the US occurs from California to Texas, from Mexico to Panama and Colombia.
VOICE High and metallic with short notes, can be described as *gug-gub-bub-tzee-pss-tzee*.

bright red eye
MALE

Length **8in (20cm)** | Wingspan **13–14in (33–**

◁ RARE SPECIES
Over 200 less common birds are presented on pp. 418–469. Arranged in the same group order used in the main section, these entries consist of one photograph of the species accompanied by a description of the bird. Information on geographical distribution, occurrence, and voice is also given.

COLOR BAND
The information bands at the top and bottom of each entry are color-coded for each family.

PHOTOGRAPHS
These illustrate the species in different views and plumage variations. Significant differences relating to age, sex, and season (breeding/nonbreeding) are shown and the images labeled accordingly; if there is no variation, the images have no label. Unless stated otherwise, the bird shown is an adult.

FLIGHT PATTERNS
This feature illustrates and briefly describes the way the species flies. See panel below.

VAGRANTS ▷
Very rare and accidental visitors are listed at the back of the book with a brief indication of the species' status.

VAGRANTS & ACCIDENTALS

VAGRANTS & ACCIDENTALS
THE LIST THAT FOLLOWS INCLUDES species that occur rarely in western North America (defined in this book as Canada and the continental United States *west* of the 100th Meridian). These species can reach North America from Eurasia, Central or South America, Africa, and even Oceania, and Antarctica. The US and Canada can receive birds that drift off course, during migration, from eastern Asia across the Pacific Ocean, or from Europe across the Atlantic. Western Alaska has a high concentration of "vagrants" because the southwesternmost tip of the state forms a series of islands, the Aleutians, that reach almost all the way across the Bering Sea to the Russian Far East.

The occurrence of "vagrant" species is classified by the American Birding Association, depending on their relative frequency, and this terminology is followed in the "status" column for each species. **Rare** species are reported every year in small numbers. **Casual** visitors have been reported at least a dozen times. **Accidental** species have been recorded no more than five times. However, because of climatological, biological, and other factors, the status of "vagrant" species is constantly changing.

COMMON NAME	SCIENTIFIC NAME	FAMILY NAME	STATUS
Waterfowl			
Eurasian Wigeon	*Anas penelope*	Anatidae	Rare visitor from Eurasia to West Coast
Garganey	*Anas querquedula*	Anatidae	Rare visitor from Eurasia to the Pribilofs; casual in California
Whooper Swan	*Cygnus cygnus*	Anatidae	Rare visitor from Eurasia to Aleutians, south to California
Tufted Duck	*Aythya fuligula*	Anatidae	Rare visitor from Eurasia to Alaska; casual along the West Coast
Smew	*Mergellus albellus*	Anatidae	Rare visitor from Eurasia to Alaska; casual to California
American Black Duck	*Anas rubripes*	Anatidae	Introduced to British Columbia and Washington state
Petrels, Shearwaters, and Storm-Petrels			
Cook's Petrel	*Pterodroma cookii*	Procellariidae	Regular visitor from New Zealand off the coast of California
Flesh-footed Shearwater	*Puffinus carneipes*	Procellariidae	Rare visitor from New Zealand and Australia to California
Wedge-rumped Storm-Petrel	*Oceanodroma tethys*	Hydrobatidae	Rare visitor to California coast; breeds on Galapagos and islands off Peru
Ibises and Herons			
Wood Stork	*Mycteria americana*	Ciconiidae	Accidental visitor from Mexico to California
Glossy Ibis	*Plegadis falcinellus*	Threskiornithidae	Casual visitor from the East or Central America to California
Yellow-crowned Night Heron	*Nyctanassa violacea*	Ardeidae	Casual visitor from Mexico to California
Reddish Egret	*Egretta rufescens*	Ardeidae	Rare visitor from Mexico to California
Tricolored Heron	*Egretta tricolor*	Ardeidae	Rare visitor from Mexico to southern California
Little Blue Heron	*Egretta caerulea*	Ardeidae	Rare visitor from Mexico to West Coast from California to British Columbia
Pelicans and Relatives			
Brown Booby	*Sula leucogaster*	Sulidae	Rare visitor to southern California
Eagles			
Steller's Sea Eagle	*Haliaeetus pelagicus*	Accipitridae	Casual visitor from eastern Asia to Alaska
Plovers and Sandpipers			
Common Ringed Plover	*Charadrius hiaticula*	Charadriidae	Casual visitor from Eurasia to the Aleutian and Pribilof Islands
Lesser Sand Plover/ Mongolian Plover	*Charadrius mongolus*	Charadriidae	Rare visitor from Asia to West Alaska and Pacific Coast
Wood Sandpiper	*Tringa glareola*	Scolopacidae	Rare visitor from Eurasia to Alaska and south to California
American Woodcock	*Scolopax minor*	Scolopacidae	Casual from the East to the West and Southwest
Black-tailed Godwit	*Limosa limosa*	Scolopacidae	Casual visitor from Eurasia to the Aleutian and Pribilof Islands
Common Sandpiper	*Actitis hypoleucos*	Scolopacidae	Casual visitor from Eurasia to western Alaska and the Aleutian Islands
Gray-tailed Tattler	*Heteroscelus brevipes*	Scolopacidae	Rare visitor from Asia to Alaska, southward to California

470

MAPS
See panel, left. The occurrence caption describes the bird's preferred habitats and range within North America.

FLIGHT PATTERNS

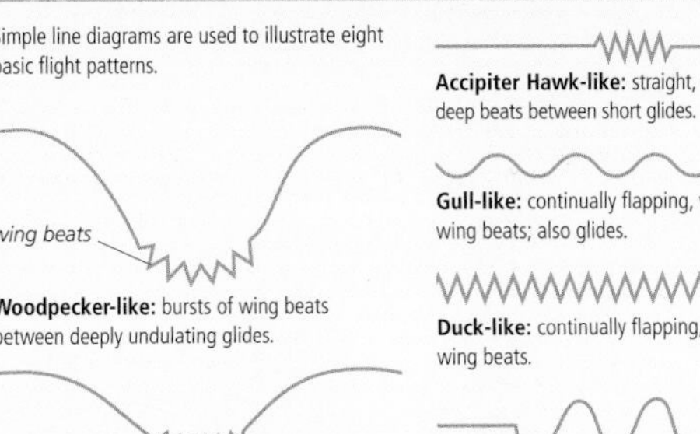

Simple line diagrams are used to illustrate eight basic flight patterns.

Woodpecker-like: bursts of wing beats between deeply undulating glides.

Finch-like: light, bouncy action with flurries of wing beats between deep, undulating glides.

Grouse-like: bursts of wing beats between short, straight glides.

Accipiter Hawk-like: straight, with several quick, deep beats between short glides.

Gull-like: continually flapping, with slow, steady wing beats; also glides.

Duck-like: continually flapping, with fast wing beats.

Buteo-like: deep, slow wing beats between soaring glides.

Swallow-like: swooping, with bursts of wing beats between glides.

EVOLUTION

ORNITHOLOGISTS AGREE THAT BIRDS evolved from dinosaurs about 150 million years ago, but there is still debate about the dinosaur group from which they descended. Around 10,000 species of birds exist today, living in many different kinds of habitats across the world, from desert to Arctic tundra. To reconstruct how avian evolution occurred, from *Archaeopteryx* on up to the present, scientists use many clues, especially fossil birds, and now DNA.

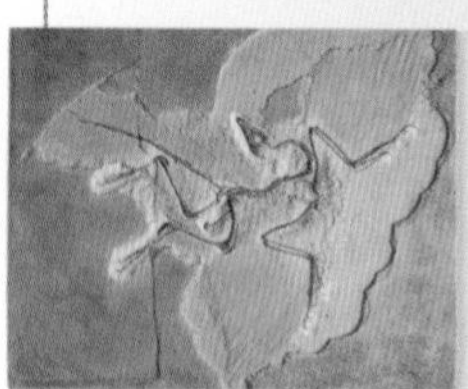

MISSING LINK?
Archaeopteryx, shown here, is a 145-million-year-old fossil. It had dinosaur-like teeth, but bird-like feathers.

SPECIATION

What are species and how do they evolve? Species are biological entities. When two species of a genus overlap they rarely interbreed and produce hybrids. The Northern Flicker has an eastern (yellow-shafted) and a western (red-shafted) form; after the discovery that these two forms interbreed in the Great Plains, the flickers, which were formerly "split" into two species, are now considered one. In other cases, a previously single species, such as the Sage Grouse, has been divided. Such examples illustrate how species evolve, first by geographic separation, followed in time by overlap. This process can take from tens of thousands to millions of years.

BIRD GENEALOGY

The diagram below is called a phylogeny, and shows how selected groups of birds are related to each other. The timescale at the top of the diagram is derived from both fossil and DNA evidence, which allows ornithologists to estimate when different lineages of birds diverged. The names of groups shown in bold are those living in North America.

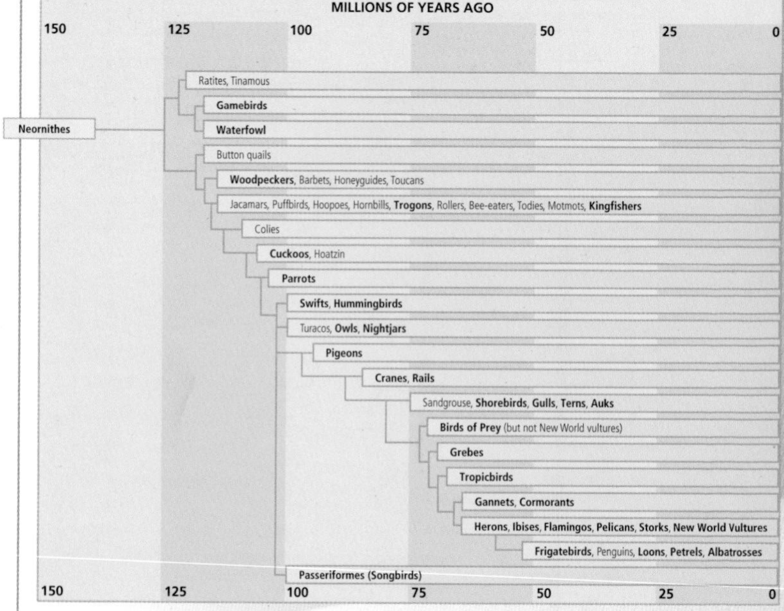

MILLIONS OF YEARS AGO

150 125 100 75 50 25 0

Neornithes

- Ratites, Tinamous
- **Gamebirds**
- **Waterfowl**
- Button quails
- **Woodpeckers**, Barbets, Honeyguides, Toucans
- Jacamars, Puffbirds, Hoopoes, Hornbills, **Trogons**, Rollers, Bee-eaters, Todies, Motmots, **Kingfishers**
- Colies
- **Cuckoos**, Hoatzin
- **Parrots**
- **Swifts, Hummingbirds**
- Turacos, **Owls, Nightjars**
- **Pigeons**
- **Cranes, Rails**
- Sandgrouse, **Shorebirds, Gulls, Terns, Auks**
- **Birds of Prey** (but not New World vultures)
- **Grebes**
- **Tropicbirds**
- **Gannets, Cormorants**
- **Herons, Ibises, Flamingos, Pelicans, Storks, New World Vultures**
- **Frigatebirds**, Penguins, **Loons, Petrels, Albatrosses**
- **Passeriformes (Songbirds)**

150 125 100 75 50 25 0

BLENDING IN
This magnificent species is diurnal, unlike most other owls, which are nocturnal. The Snowy Owl breeds in the Arctic tundra, and if the ground is covered with snow, it blends in perfectly.

CONVERGENCE

The evolutionary process during which birds of two distantly related groups develop similarities is called convergence. Carrion-eating birds of prey are one example. Old World vultures belong to the hawk family (Accipitridae), while New World vultures are more closely related to storks. However, both groups are characterized by hooked bills, bare heads, and weak talons. Convergence can involve anatomy and behavior, as in the vultures, or other traits, including habitat preference.

CAPE LONGCLAW

WESTERN MEADOWLARK

PARALLEL EVOLUTION
The African longclaws (family Motacillidae) and North American meadowlarks (family Icteridae) show convergence in plumage color and pattern. Both groups live in grasslands.

EXTINCTION

During the last 150 years, North America has lost the Passenger Pigeon, the Great Auk, the Carolina Parakeet, the Labrador Duck, and the Eskimo Curlew. Relentless hunting and habitat destruction are the main factors that have led to extinction. Some species that seemed doomed have had a reprieve. Thanks to a breeding and release program, the majestic California Condor soars once again over the Grand Canyon.

OVERHUNTING
The Passenger Pigeon was eradicated as a result of over hunting.

CLASSIFYING BIRDS

All past and present animal life is named and categorized into groups. Classifications reflect the genealogical relationships among groups, based on traits such as color, bones, or DNA. Birds make up the class "Aves," which includes "orders;" each "order" is made up of one or more "families." "Genus" is a subdivision of "family," and contains one or more "species." A species is a unique group of similar organisms that interbreed and produce fertile offspring. Some species have distinct populations, which are known as subspecies.

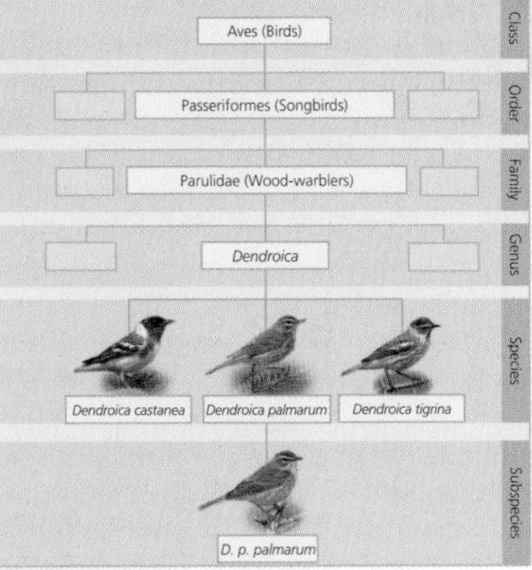

ANATOMY AND FLIGHT

In spite of their external diversity, birds are remarkably similar internally. To allow flight, birds have a skeleton that is both rigid and light. Rigidity is achieved by the fusion of some bones, especially the lower vertebrae, while lightness is maintained by having hollow limb bones. These are connected to air sacs, which, in turn, are connected to the bird's lungs.

SKELETON
Avian skeletal features include the furcula (wishbone), the keeled sternum (breastbone), and the fused tail vertebrae.

"hand"
"forearm"
neck vertebrae
bill
fused tail vertebrae
furcula
keeled sternum

FLIGHT ADAPTATIONS

For birds to be able to fly, they need light and rigid bones, a lightweight skull, and hollow wing and leg bones. In addition, pouch-like air sacs are connected to hollow bones, which reduce a bird's weight. The air sacs also function as a cooling system, which birds need because they have a high metabolic rate. The breast muscles, which are crucial for flight, attach to the keeled sternum (breastbone). Wing and tail feathers help support birds when airborne. Feathers wear out, and are regularly replaced during molt.

secondaries
tail feathers
uppertail coverts
rump
tertials
scapulars
primaries

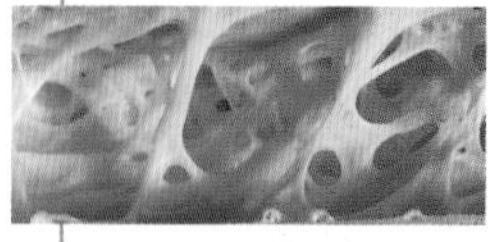

BIRD BONE STRUCTURE
Most bird bones, except those of penguins and other flightless birds, are hollow, which reduces their weight. A honeycomb of internal struts makes the bones remarkably strong.

LEGS, FEET, AND TOES

When you look at a bird's leg, you do not see its thigh, which is inside the body cavity, but the leg from the knee down. When we talk about a bird's feet we really mean its toes. The shin is a fused tibia and fibula. This fused bone plus the heel are known as the "tarso-metatarsus." The four examples below illustrate some toe arrangements.

UNDERPARTS
Underwing coverts have a regular pattern of overlapping rows. Short feathers cover the head, breast, belly, and flanks. In most birds, the toes are unfeathered.

WALKING
Ground-foraging birds usually have a long hind claw.

CLIMBING
Most climbers have two toes forward and two backward.

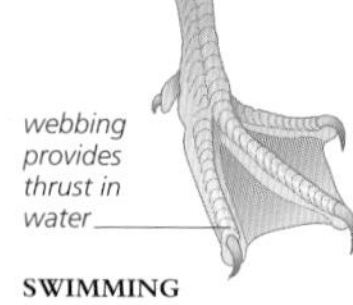

SWIMMING
Waterbirds have webbing between their toes.

used to grasp prey

HUNTING
Birds of prey have powerful toes and strong, sharp claws.

FEATHERS

All birds, by definition, have feathers. These remarkable structures, which are modified scales, serve two main functions: insulation and flight. Special muscles allow birds to raise their feathers or to flatten them against the body. In cold weather, fluffed-out feathers keep an insulating layer of air between the skin and the outside. This insulating capacity is why humans often find wearing "down" jackets so effective against the cold. The first feathers that chicks have after hatching are down feathers. The rigidity of the flight feathers helps create a supporting surface that birds use to generate thrust and lift.

TYPES OF FEATHERS
Birds have three main kinds of feathers: down, contour, and flight feathers. The rigid axis of all feathers is called the "rachis."

DOWN FEATHER · CONTOUR FEATHER · FLIGHT FEATHER

WING FUNCTIONS

Flapping, soaring, gliding, and hovering are among the ways birds use their wings. They also exhibit colors or patterns as part of territorial and courtship displays. Several birds, such as herons, open their wings like an umbrella when foraging in water for fish. An important aspect of wings is their relationship to a bird's weight. The ratio of a bird's wing area to its weight is called wing loading, which may be affected also by wing shape. An eagle has a large wing area to weight ratio, which means it has lower wing loading, whereas a swallow has a small wing area to weight ratio, and therefore high wing loading. This means that the slow, soaring eagle is capable of much more energy-efficient flight than the fast, agile swallow.

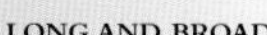

LONG AND BROAD
The broad, long, rectangular wings of an eagle allow it to soar. The outstretched alulae (bastard wings) give it extra lift.

POINTED
Broad at their base and tapering toward a point, and bent at the wrist, a swallow's wings enable fast flight and sharp turns.

SHORT AND ROUND
Short, broad, and round wings permit warblers to move easily in dense vegetation.

primary coverts
secondary coverts
coverts
neck
nape
crown
chin
throat
mantle
alula (bastard wing)

UPPERPARTS
The wing feathers from the "hand" of the bird are the primaries, and those on the "forearm" are the secondaries. Each set has its accompanying row of coverts. The tertials are adjacent to the secondaries.

WING AERODYNAMICS

The supporting surface of a bird's wing enables it to take off and stay aloft. Propulsion and lift are linked in birds—which use their wings for both—unlike in airplanes in which these two functions are separate. Large and heavy birds, like swans, flap their wings energetically to create propulsion, and need a long, watery runway before they can fly off. The California Condor can take off from a cliff with little or no wing flapping, but the Black and Turkey Vultures hop up from carrion, then flap vigorously, and finally use air flowing across their wings to soar. This diagram shows how airflow affects lift.

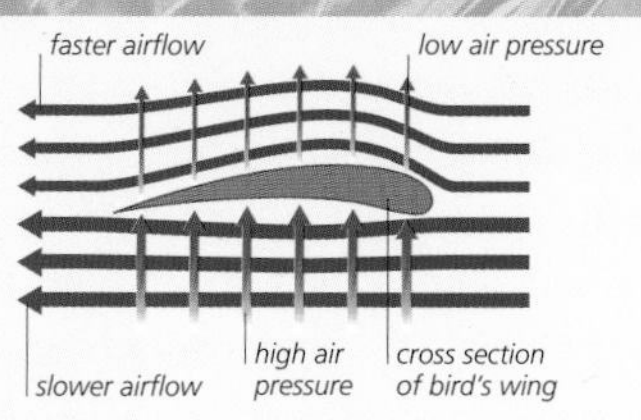

MIGRATION

UNTIL RECENTLY, THE MECHANICS, or the "how" of migration, was poorly understood. Today, however, ornithologists know that birds use a variety of cues including visual and magnetic, whether they migrate by day or by night. Birds do not leave northern breeding areas because of the winter cold, but because day-length is getting shorter and food scarcer.

NIGHT MIGRANTS
During migration, ornithologists can point a telescope on the moon and count the birds that cross its surface.

REFUELING
Red Knots stop on their journey from Tierra del Fuego to the Arctic to eat horseshoe crab eggs.

INSTINCTIVE MOVE

Even though many birds use visual cues and landmarks during their migration, for example, birds of prey flying along the Appalachians, "instinctive" behavior must control much of how and where they move. Instinct is a loose term that is hard to define, but ornithologists generally understand it as a genetically programmed activity. They assume that natural selection has molded a behavior as complex as migration by acting on birds' DNA; this hypothesis is reasonable, but hard to prove. Nevertheless, it would seem to be the only explanation why many juvenile shorebirds leave their breeding grounds after their parents, and yet find their way to their final destination.

NAVIGATION

One of the most puzzling aspects of migration is understanding how birds make their way from their summer breeding grounds to their winter destination. Ornithologists have devised experiments to determine the different components. Some of these components are innate, others learned. For example, if visual landmarks are hidden by fog, a faint sun can give birds a directional clue; if heavy clouds hide the sun, then the birds' magnetic compass may be used to ascertain their direction.

FINDING THE WAY
Birds coordinate information their brains receive from the sun, moon, stars, landmarks, and magnetite, or iron oxide, and use it as a compass.

OVERLAND FLIERS
Sandhill Cranes migrate over hills and mountains, from their Arctic tundra breeding grounds to the marshes of the Platte River in the midwestern US.

GLOBETROTTERS

Some bird species in North America are year-round residents, although a few individuals of these species move away from where they hatched at some time in the year. However, a large number of North American species are migratory. A few species breed in Alaska, but winter on remote southwest Pacific islands. Others breed in the Canadian Arctic Archipelago, fly over land and the Pacific Ocean, and spend the winter at sea off the coast of Peru. Many songbirds fly from the Gulf Coast to northern South America. The most amazing globetrotters, such as the Red Knot, fly all the way to Tierra del Fuego, making only a few stops along the way after their short breeding season in the Arctic tundra. The return journeys of some of these travelers are not over the same route—instead, their entire trip is elliptical in shape.

EPIC JOURNEY
The Arctic Tern is a notorious long-distance migrant, breeding in Arctic and Subarctic regions, and wintering in the pack ice of Antarctica before returning north, a round-trip distance of at least 25,000 miles (40,000km).

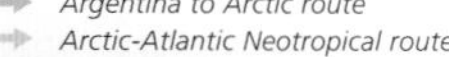

NEOTROPICAL MIGRANT
Many wood-warblers, such as this Blackpoll Warbler, breed in boreal forests, before migrating to their wintering grounds in the Caribbean, or Central or South America.

MIGRATION ROUTES
The map above shows the range of migration routes that some North American species take to and from their breeding grounds.

V-FORMATION
Geese and other large waterbirds fly in a V-formation. The leader falls back and is replaced by another individual, saving energy for all the birds.

PARTIAL MIGRANT

The American Robin is a good example of a partial migrant, a species in which the birds of some populations are resident, whereas others migrate out of their breeding range. Most Canadian populations of the American Robin fly south, US populations are largely resident, and quite a few birds from either population spend the winter in the Southwest, Florida, or Mexico.

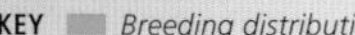

KEY
Breeding distribution
Resident all year
Nonbreeding distribution

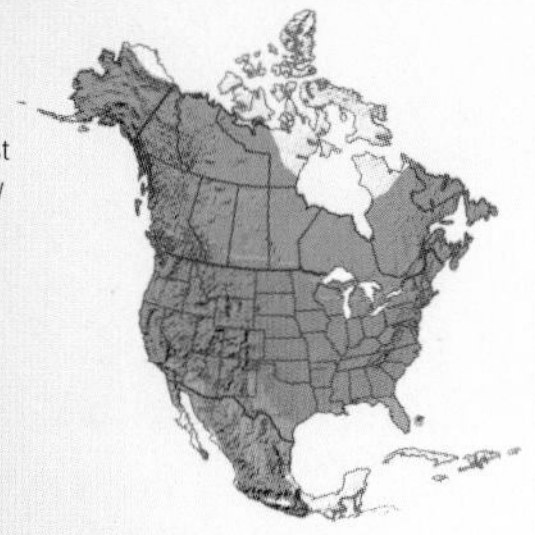

COURTSHIP AND MATING

WHETHER MONOGAMOUS OR NOT, males and females need to mate for their species to perpetuate itself. With most species, the male plays the dominant role of advertising a territory to potential mates using vocal or visual displays. Females then select a male, and if the two respond positively to each other, a period of courtship follows, ending in mating. The next steps are nest building, egg laying, and rearing the young.

DANCING CRANES
During courtship, Sandhill Cranes perform spectacular dances, the two birds of a pair leaping into the air with wings opened and legs splayed.

DISPLAYS

Mutual attraction between the sexes starts with some sort of display, usually performed by the male. These displays can take a number of forms, from flashing dazzling breeding plumage, conducting elaborate dancing rituals, performing complex songs, offering food or nesting material, or actually building a nest. Some birds, such as grebes, have fascinatingly intricate ceremonies, in which both male and female simultaneously perform the same water-dance. Because they are usually very ritualized, displays help ornithologists understand relationships among birds.

WELCOME HOME
Northern Gannets greet their mates throughout the breeding season by rubbing bills together and opening their wings.

LADIES' CHOICE
On a lek (communal display area), male Sage-Grouse inflate chest pouches while females flock around them and select a mate.

COURTSHIP FEEDING

In some species, males offer food to their mate to maintain the pair-bond. For example, male terns routinely bring small fish to their mates in a nesting colony, spreading their wings and tail until the females accept the fish.

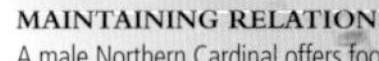

MAINTAINING RELATIONS
A male Northern Cardinal offers food to the female, which is a way of reinforcing their pair bond.

BREEDING

After mating, a nest is made, often by the female, where she lays from one to a dozen eggs. Not all birds make nests, however. Nightjars, for example, lay their eggs directly on the ground. In many species, incubation doesn't start until the female has laid all the eggs. Incubation, usually done by the female, varies from about 12 days to about 45 days. Songbirds breeding from the temperate zone northward to the Arctic show a range in clutch size with more eggs produced in the North than in the South. The breeding process can fail at any stage, for example, a predator can eat the eggs or the chicks. Some birds will nest again after such a failure, but others give up breeding for the season.

MATING TERNS
Mating is usually brief, and typically takes place on a perch or on the ground, but some species,like swifts, mate in the air. This male Black Tern balances himself by opening his wings.

MUTUAL PREENING
Many species of albatrosses, like these Black-footed Albatrosses from the Pacific, preen each other, with one bird softly nibbling the feathers on the other's head.

POLYGAMY
This Winter Wren collects nesting material for one of the several nests he will build.

MONOGAMOUS BONDS
Some birds, such as Snow Geese, remain paired for life after establishing a bond.

SINGLE FATHER

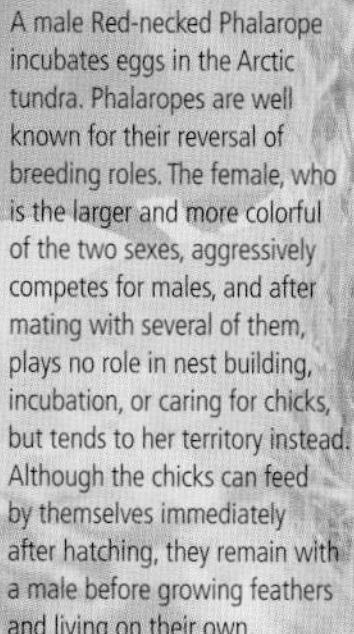

A male Red-necked Phalarope incubates eggs in the Arctic tundra. Phalaropes are well known for their reversal of breeding roles. The female, who is the larger and more colorful of the two sexes, aggressively competes for males, and after mating with several of them, plays no role in nest building, incubation, or caring for chicks, but tends to her territory instead. Although the chicks can feed by themselves immediately after hatching, they remain with a male before growing feathers and living on their own.

NESTS AND EGGS

MOST BIRD SPECIES BUILD THEIR OWN NEST, which is a necessary container for their eggs. Exceptions include some species of cuckoos and cowbirds, that lay their eggs in other species' nests. Nest-building is often done by the female alone, but in some species the male may help or even build it himself. Eggs are incubated either by females only, or by males and females, depending on the species. Eggs, consisting of 60 percent water, contain a fatty yolk for nourishment of the embryo, as well as sugars and proteins. Eggshells are hard enough to sustain the weight of incubating parents, yet soft enough for a chick to break its way out. Hatching is an energy-draining process, and can last for several hours.

NEST TYPES

In addition to the four types shown below, nests range from a simple scrape in the ground with a few added pebbles to an elaborate woven basket-like structure. Plant matter forms basic nest material. This includes twigs, grass stems, bark, lichens, mosses, plant down, and rootlets. Some birds add mud to their nest for strength. Others incorporate animal hair or feathers to improve its softness and insulation. Female eider ducks line their nest with down feathers plucked from their belly. Some birds include bits of plastic or threads in their nests. Several species of flycatchers add shed snakeskins to their nests. Many birds make their nest or lay their eggs deep inside the empty burrows of other animals. Burrowing Owls nest in prairie dog burrows, where they coexist with the rodents.

UNTIDY NEST
Huge stick nests, built on top of dead trees, are the hallmark of Ospreys. They also readily use custom-made nesting platforms erected by humans specifically for them.

EGG CUP
A clutch of three blue robin's eggs rest in a cup lined with grass stems and strengthened with mud. Robins build their nests either in shrubs or trees.

NATURAL CAVITY
This Northern Saw-whet Owl is nesting at the bottom of a cavity, in a tree that has probably been excavated by a woodpecker.

NEST BOX
Cavity-nesting bluebirds have been affected by habitat loss, and compete with other birds for nest sites, which may include human-made structures.

COMPLEX WEAVE
New World orioles weave intricate nests from dried grass stems and other plant material, and hang them from the tip of branches, often high up in trees.

EGG SHAPES

There are six basic egg shapes among birds, as illustrated to the right. The most common egg shapes are longitudinal or elliptical. Murres lay pear-shaped eggs, an adaptation for nesting on the narrow ledges of sea cliffs; if an egg rolls, it does so in a tight circle and remains on the ledge. Spherical eggs with irregular red blotches are characteristic of birds of prey. Pigeons and doves lay white oval eggs, usually two per clutch. The eggs of many songbirds, including sparrows and buntings, are conical and have a variety of dark markings on a pale background.

NEAT ARRANGEMENT
Many shorebirds, such as plovers and sandpipers, lay four conical eggs with the narrow ends pointed in toward each other.

COLOR AND SHAPE
Birds' eggs vary widely in terms of shape, colors, and markings. The American Robin's egg on the left is a beautiful blue.

PEAR SHAPED

LONGITUDINAL

ELLIPTICAL

OVAL

CONICAL

SPHERICAL

HATCHING CONDITION

After a period of incubation, which varies from species to species, chicks break the eggshell, some of them using an egg tooth, a special bill feature that falls off after hatching. After a long and exhausting struggle, the chick eventually tumbles out of the shell fragments. The transition from the watery medium inside the egg to the air outside is a tremendous physiological switch. Once free of their shell, the hatchlings recover from the exertion and either beg food from their parents or feed on their own.

FAST FEEDER
Coots, gallinules, and rails hatch with a complete covering of down, and can feed by themselves immediately after birth.

FOOD DELIVERY
Tern chicks, although able to move around, cannot catch the fish they need to survive, and must rely on their parents to provide food until they can fly.

PARENTAL GUIDANCE
Birds of prey, such as these Snowy Owl owlets, need their parents to care for them longer than some other bird species, and do not leave the nest until their feathers are sufficiently developed for their first flight.

BROOD PARASITISM

Neither cowbirds in the New World nor cuckoos in the Old World make a nest. Female cowbirds deposit up to 20 eggs in the nests of several other species. If the foster parents accept the foreign egg, they will feed the chick of the parasite until it fledges. In the picture below, a tiny wood-warbler feeds its adopted chick, a huge cowbird hatchling that has overgrown the nest. Whereas some host species readily incubate the foreign egg, others reject it or abandon the nest.

IDENTIFICATION

SOME SPECIES ARE EASY TO IDENTIFY, but in many other cases, species identification is tricky. In North America, a notoriously difficult group in terms of identification is the wood-warblers, especially in the fall, when most species have similar greenish or yellowish plumage.

BLUEBIRD VARIATIONS
Species of the genus *Sialia*, such as the Mountain Bluebird above, and the Eastern Bluebird below, are easy to identify.

GEOGRAPHIC RANGE

Each bird species in North America lives in a particular area that is called its geographic range. Some species have a restricted range; for example, Kirtland's Warbler occurs only in Michigan. Other species, such as the Red-tailed Hawk, range from coast to coast and from northern Canada to Mexico. Species with a broad range usually breed in a variety of vegetation types, while species with narrow ranges often have a specialized habitat; Kirtland's Warblers' is jack pine woodland.

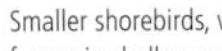

SIZE AND WEIGHT

From hummingbird to Tundra Swan and from extra-light (1/16oz) to heavy (15 lb), such is the range of sizes and weights found among the bird species of North America. Size can be measured in several ways, for example the length of a bird from bill-tip to tail-tip, or its wingspan. Size can also be estimated for a given bird in relationship with another that is familiar. For example, the less familiar Bicknell's Thrush can be compared with the well-known American Robin.

SIZE MATTERS
Smaller shorebirds, with shorter legs and bills, forage in shallow water, but larger ones have longer legs and bills and can feed in deeper water.

SEMIPALMATED PLOVER

LESSER YELLOWLEGS

HUDSONIAN GODWIT

LONG-BILLED CURLEW

GENERAL SHAPE

Just as birds come in all sizes, their body shapes vary, but size and shape are not necessarily correlated. In the dense reed beds in which it lives, the American Bittern's long and thin body blends in with stems. The round-bodied Sedge Wren hops in shrubby vegetation or near the ground where slimness is not an advantage. In dense forest canopy, the slender and long-tailed Yellow-billed Cuckoo can maneuver easily. Mourning Doves inhabit rather open habitats and their plumpness is irrelevant when it comes to their living space. The relative shape and length of wings and tail are often, but not always, an important component of how a particular bird species behaves.

AMERICAN BITTERN

YELLOW-BILLED CUCKOO

MOURNING DOVE

SEDGE WREN

BILL SHAPE

These images show a range of bill shapes and sizes relative to the bird's head size. In general, bill form, including length or thickness, corresponds to the kinds of food a birds consumes. With its pointed bill, the Mountain Chickadee picks tiny insects from crevices in tree bark. At another extreme, dowitchers probe mud with their long thin bills, feeling for worms. The avocet swishes its bill back and forth in briny water in search of shrimp.

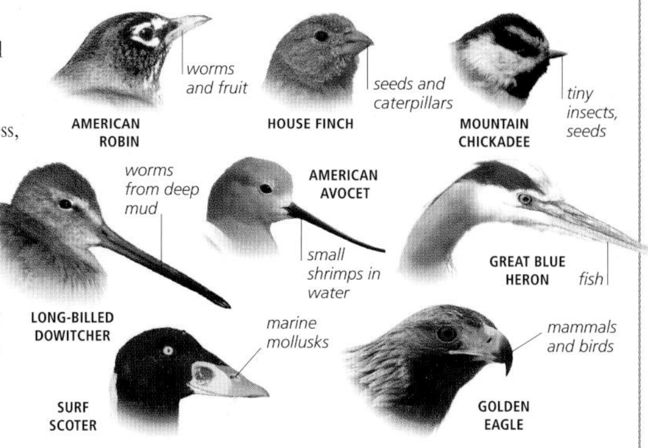

WING SHAPE

Birds' wing shapes are correlated with their flight style. The long, round-tipped wings of the Red-tailed Hawk are perfect for soaring, while the tiny wings of hummingbirds are exactly what is needed to hover in front of flowers and then to back away after a meal of nectar. When flushed, quails flutter with their round wings and quickly drop down.

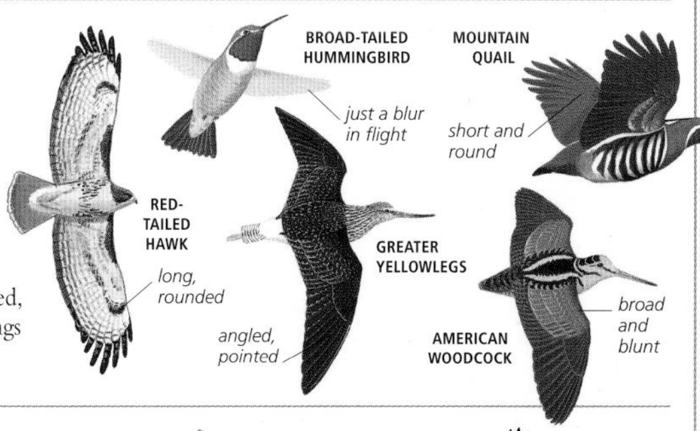

TAIL SHAPE

It is not clear why some songbirds, like the American Goldfinch, have a notched tail while other similar sized birds do not. Tail shapes vary as much as wing shapes, but are not so easily linked to a function or to the habitat in which a given species lives. Irrespective of shape, tails are needed for balance. In some birds, tail shape, color, and pattern are used in courtship displays or in defensive displays when threatened.

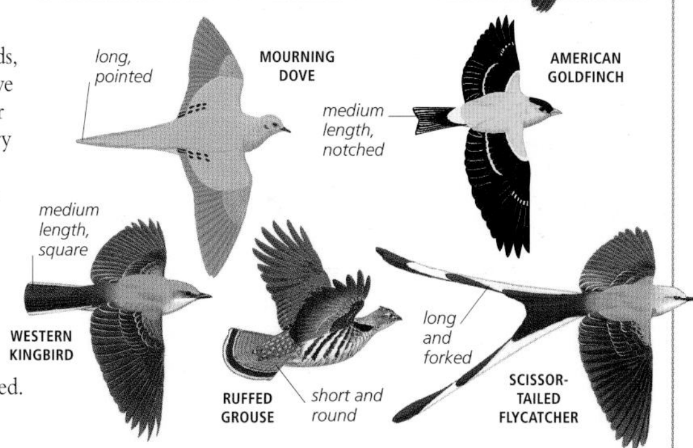

COLORS AND MARKINGS

Melanin and carotenoid pigments determine color. Gray and brown birds have melanin (under hormonal influence), yellow and red ones, carotenoid (derived from food). Flamingos are pink because they eat carotenoid-rich crustaceans. Diversity in color and markings also results from scattering of white light by feathers (producing blue colors) and optical interference (iridescence) due to the structural properties of some feathers (as in hummingbirds). Bare patches of skin are often used in displays.

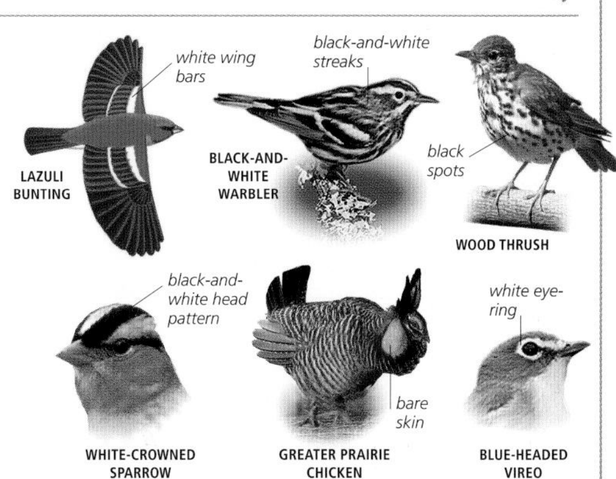

SPECIES GUIDE

GAMEBIRDS

THIS DIVERSE AND ADAPTABLE group of birds thrives in habitats ranging from hot desert to frozen tundra. Gamebirds spend most of their time on the ground, springing loudly into the air when alarmed.

QUAILS

Among the most terrestrial of all gamebirds, quails are renowned for their great sociability, often forming large family groups, or "coveys," of up to 100 birds. The five species found in western North America each live in a specific habitat or at a particular elevation, but the single species found in the East, the Northern Bobwhite, ranges over a variety of habitats.

DRESSED TO THRILL
With its striking plumage, Gambel's Quail is one of the best-known desert birds in southwestern North America.

GROUSE

The most numerous and widespread of gamebirds, the 12 different species of grouse can be divided into three groups based on their preferred habitats. Forest grouse include the Sooty Grouse and Dusky Grouse in the West, as well as the Spruce Grouse and Ruffed Grouse in the North. Prairie grouse, including the Sharp-tailed Grouse, are found throughout the middle of the continent. All three tundra and mountaintop grouse or ptarmigan are found in the extreme North and the Rockies. Grouse often possess patterns that match their surroundings, providing camouflage from both animal and human predators.

GRASSLAND GROUSE
The aptly named Sharp-tailed Grouse is locally common in western prairies. It searches for grasshoppers in the summer.

PHEASANTS & PARTRIDGES

These Eurasian gamebirds were introduced into North America in the 19th and 20th centuries to provide additional targets for recreational hunters. While some introductions failed, species such as the colorful Ring-necked Pheasant adapted well and now thrive in established populations.

SNOW BIRD
The Rock Ptarmigan's white winter plumage camouflages it against the snow, and help hide it from predators.

Order **Galliformes**	Family **Odontophoridae**	Species ***Callipepla californica***

California Quail

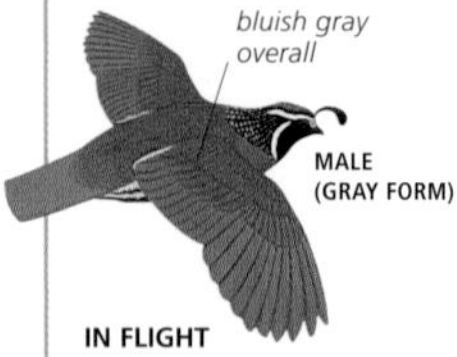
bluish gray overall
MALE (GRAY FORM)
IN FLIGHT

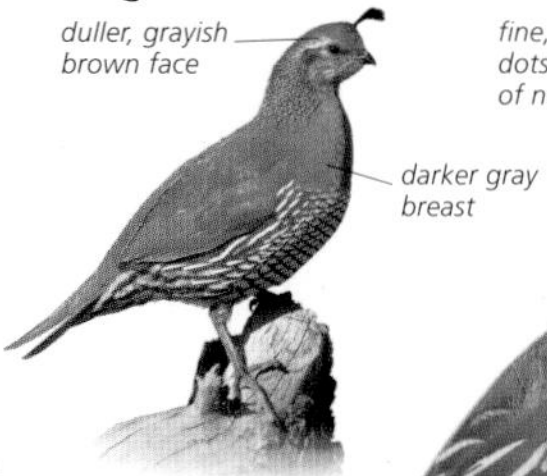
duller, grayish brown face
darker gray breast
FEMALE (GRAY FORM)

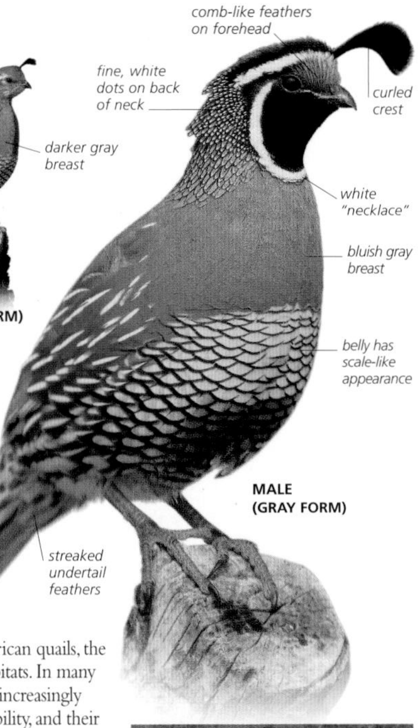
comb-like feathers on forehead
fine, white dots on back of neck
curled crest
white "necklace"
bluish gray breast
belly has scale-like appearance
MALE (GRAY FORM)
streaked undertail feathers

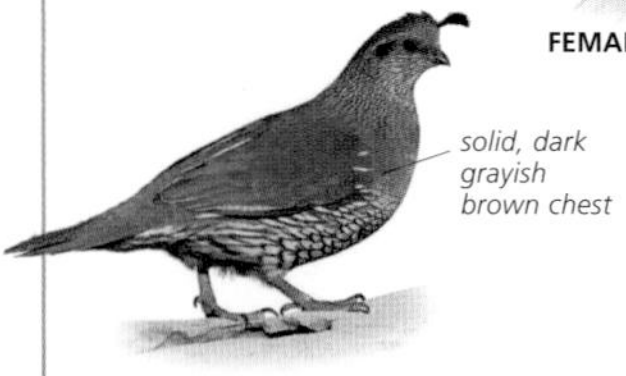
solid, dark grayish brown chest
FEMALE (BROWN FORM)

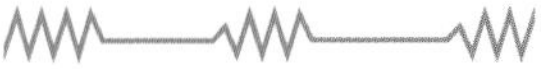

FLIGHT: loud, whirring takeoff and short bursts of rapid wing beats.

The most widespread of the western North American quails, the California Quail thrives in a wide variety of habitats. In many parts of their range, these dapper birds are becoming increasingly common in parks and suburban habitats. This adaptability, and their popularity among hunters, has led to the California Quail being introduced throughout the western US and southern British Columbia, as well as Hawaii, New Zealand, Australia, Chile, and other areas outside North America.

VOICE Separated covey call 3-syllable *chi-CA-go*; males use extended *cow* followed by *way way*, also low *kurrr*.

NESTING Shallow depression lined with grasses and hidden by vegetation; 10–12 eggs; 1 brood; May–August.

FEEDING Feeds primarily on green leaves and other plant matter; takes insects when available.

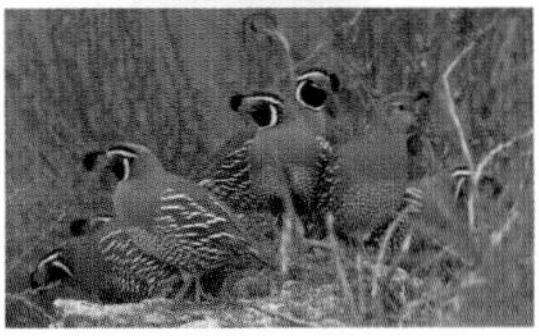

BIRDS OF A FEATHER
These gregarious quails are regularly found in flocks of up to 50 individuals.

SIMILAR SPECIES

MOUNTAIN QUAIL
see p.419
long, straight plumes
"zebra stripes" on underparts
GAMBEL'S QUAIL
see p.25
no scaling on belly

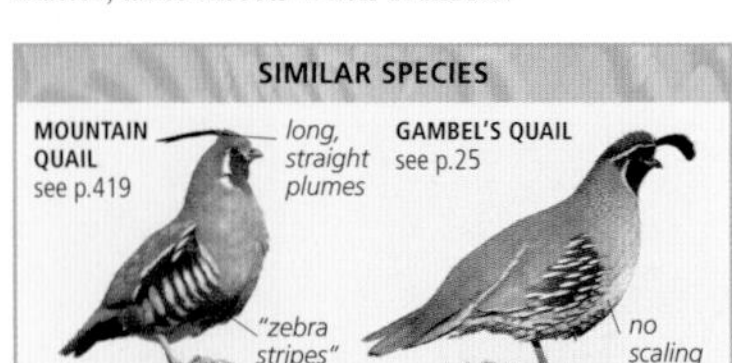

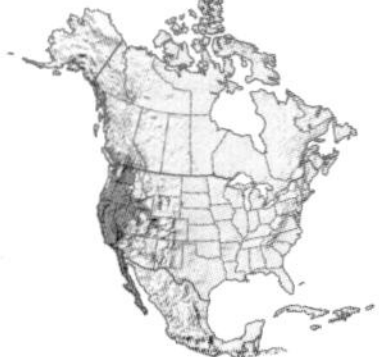

OCCURRENCE
Native range at mid- to low elevations along the mountain ranges and valleys from Baja California northward to central Oregon; prefers mixture of patchy oak scrub combined with agriculture and fallow fields. Permanent resident.

Length **9–11in (24–28cm)**	Wingspan **12–14in (30–35cm)**	Weight **6–7oz (175–200g)**
Social **Flocks**	Lifespan **Up to 6 years**	Status **Secure (p)**

DATE SEEN	WHERE	NOTES

Order **Galliformes**	Family **Odontophoridae**	Species ***Callipepla gambelii***

Gambel's Quail

rust-colored crown

short, broad wings

MALE

finely marked neck

black face

black, drooping plume

grayish back

brown and white streaks

IN FLIGHT

plain, grayish head

grayish brown face

pale belly

pale undertail

black spot on belly

FEMALE

MALE

Gambel's Quail is a highly social bird of the low-elevation deserts and valley floors of the Southwest, particularly Arizona and northern Mexico, where it it often known as the Desert or Arizona Quail. While tolerant of hot, dry conditions, its breeding success depends entirely on local rainfall, which produces the green plants that make up most of its diet. Gambel's Quail is a popular game bird throughout its range, readily identified by its drooping black "topknot," or plume, in addition to its distinctive calls.

VOICE Most common call: *chi-CA-go-go*; males attract mates with *kaa* or *kaaow;* alarmed birds utter *chip-chip-chip.*

NESTING Small depression defined by twigs and lined with grass and leaves, usually within cover; 10–12 eggs; 1 brood; March–June.

FEEDING Feeds mainly on seeds, green leaves, and grasses, also berries, cactus fruit; insects eaten by young and breeding birds.

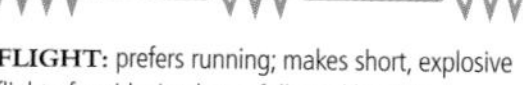

FLIGHT: prefers running; makes short, explosive flight of rapid wing beats followed by glide.

SHOWING OFF ITS CHEST
This Gambel's Quail shows its distinctive blue, white, and blackish underparts.

SIMILAR SPECIES

MOUNTAIN QUAIL
see p.419
long, thin, straight plume
chestnut-brown face
broadly striped flanks

CALIFORNIA QUAIL ♂
see p.24
buff forehead
scaly lower belly; no black spot

OCCURRENCE
Strongly associated with scrub/shrub river edge or gulley vegetation, including mesquite, various grasses, and a variety of cactus species, especially where these species border agricultural properties.

Length **9½–11in (24–28cm)**	Wingspan **12½–14in (32–35cm)**	Weight **6oz (175g)**
Social **Flocks**	Lifespan **Up to 4 years**	Status **Secure**

DATE SEEN	WHERE	NOTES

Order **Galliformes**	Family **Phasianidae**	Species ***Meleagris gallopavo***

Wild Turkey

MALE (EAST)

IN FLIGHT

black-and-white barred wings

rusty tail with black band

humped back

no feathers on head

long legs

IMMATURE

dark overall

iridescent bronze-and-purplish body

FEMALE

tail fanned in display

unfeathered blue-and-red head

dark body, with bronze iridescence

MALE (WEST)

hair-like "beard" on breast

Once proposed by Benjamin Franklin as the national emblem of the US, the Wild Turkey—the largest gamebird in North America—was eliminated from most of its original range by the early 1900s due to over-hunting and habitat destruction. Since then, habitat restoration and the subsequent reintroduction of Wild Turkeys has been very successful.

VOICE Well-known gobble, given by males especially during courtship; female makes various yelps, clucks, and purrs, based on mood and threat level.

NESTING Scrape on ground lined with grass; placed against or under protective cover; 10–15 eggs; 1 brood; March–June.

FEEDING Omnivorous, it scratches in leaf litter on forest floor for acorns and other food, mostly vegetation; also takes plants and insects from agricultural fields.

FLIGHT: after running, leaps into the air with loud, rapid wing beats, then glides.

COLLECTIVE DISPLAY
Once the population expands into new areas, numerous males will be seen displaying together.

OCCURRENCE
Found in mixed mature woodlands, fields with agricultural crops; also in various grasslands, close to swamps, but adaptable and increasingly common in suburban and urban habitats. Quite widespread, but patchily distributed across North America.

Length **2¾–4ft (0.9–1.2m)**	Wingspan **4–5ft (1.2–1.5m)**	Weight **10–24lb (4.5–11kg)**
Social **Flocks**	Lifespan **Up to 9 years**	Status **Secure**

DATE SEEN	WHERE	NOTES

Order **Galliformes**	Family **Phasianidae**	Species ***Bonasa umbellus***

Ruffed Grouse

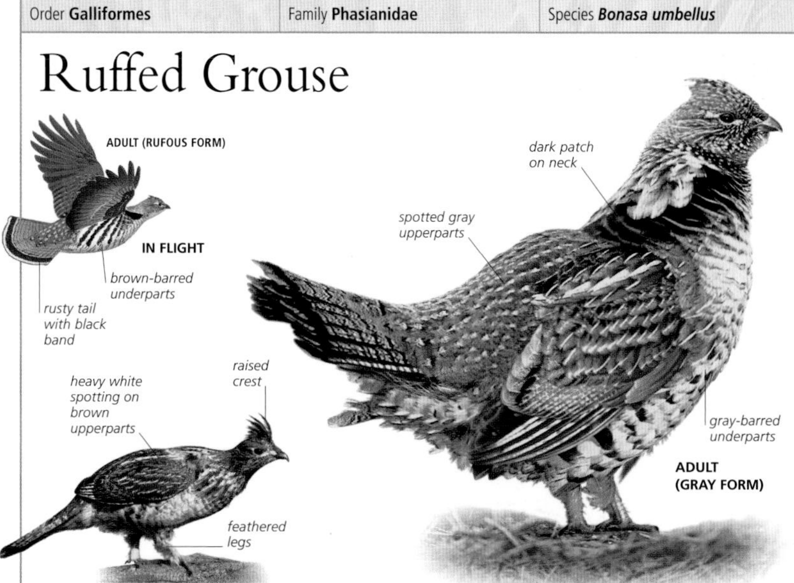

The Ruffed Grouse is perhaps the most widespread gamebird in North America. There are two color forms, rufous and gray, both allowing the birds to remain camouflaged and undetected on the forest floor, until they eventually burst into the air in an explosion of whirring wings. The male is well known for his extraordinary wing beating or "drumming" display, which he performs year-round, but most frequently in the spring.

VOICE Hissing notes, and soft *purrt, purrt, purrt* when alarmed, by both sexes; males "drumming" display when heard from distance resembles small engine starting, *thump…thump…thump...thump… thump...thuthuthuth.*

NESTING Shallow, leaf-lined bowl set against a tree trunk, rock or fallen log in forest; 6–14 eggs; 1 brood; March–June.

FEEDING Forages on ground for leaves, buds, and fruit; occasionally insects.

FLIGHT: an explosive takeoff, usually at close range, glides for a short distance before landing.

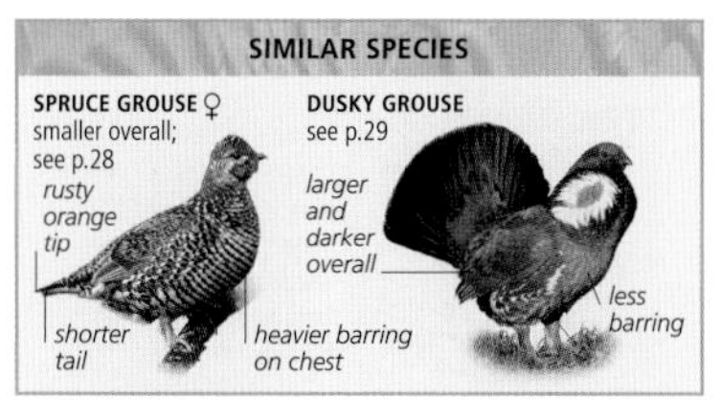

WARM RED
The rufous form of the Ruffed Grouse is more common in wetter parts of the continent.

OCCURRENCE
Found in young, mixed forests throughout the northern US and much of Canada except tundra. Southern edge of range extends along higher elevations of the Appalachians and middle levels of the Rocky Mountains, if suitable habitat is available.

Length **17–20in (43–51cm)**	Wingspan **20–23in (51–58cm)**	Weight **20–22oz (575–625g)**
Social **Solitary/Small flocks**	Lifespan **Up to 10 years**	Status **Secure**

DATE SEEN	WHERE	NOTES

Order **Galliformes**	Family **Phasianidae**	Species ***Canachites canadensis***

Spruce Grouse

Perhaps because of the remoteness of their habitat and lack of human contact, Spruce Grouse are not afraid of humans. This lack of wariness when approached has earned them the name "fool hens." Their specialized diet of pine needles causes the intestinal tract to expand in order to accommodate a large volume of food to compensate for its low nutritional value. There are two subspecies (*C. c. canadensis* and *C c. franklinii*), both of which have red and gray forms; Franklin's is found in the Northwest.

VOICE Mostly silent; males clap their wings during courtship display; females often utter long cackle at dawn and dusk.

NESTING Lined with moss, leaves, feathers; often at base of tree; naturally low area in forest floor 4–6 eggs; 1 brood; May–July.

FEEDING Feeds mostly on pine but also spruce needles; will eat insects, leaves, fruits, and seeds when available.

FLIGHT: generally avoids flying; when disturbed, bursts into flight on whirring wings.

RUFOUS BAND
The male "taiga" subspecies displays the thin rufous band on the tip of his tail.

SIMILAR SPECIES

RUFFED GROUSE see p.27
spotted gray upperparts
gray-barred underparts

DUSKY GROUSE see p.29
much larger
longer, charcoal-gray tail
grayer overall

OCCURRENCE
Present year-round in forests dominated by conifers, including Jack, Lodgepole, Spruce, Red Spruce, Black Spruce, Balsam Fir, Subalpine Fir, Hemlock, and Cedar. Found from western Alaska to the Atlantic Coast.

Length **14–17in (36–43cm)**	Wingspan **21–23in (53–58cm)**	Weight **16oz (450g)**
Social **Solitary**	Lifespan **Up to 10 years**	Status **Secure**

DATE SEEN	WHERE	NOTES

Order **Galliformes**	Family **Phasianidae**	Species ***Dendragapus obscurus***

Dusky Grouse

Once considered a single species, the Blue Grouse, the Dusky Grouse, and the Sooty Grouse are now considered distinct species. Male Dusky Grouse can be identified by their courtship displays, which are primarily ground-based and quieter than those of the Sooty Grouse, and by their reddish purple air sacs. The Dusky Grouse also has a plain tail, lacking the gray tip of the Sooty, and its chicks are more gray than brown.

VOICE A series of five soft hoots; also a hiss, growl, and cluck; females emit a whinnying cry.

NESTING Shallow scrape, usually lined with dead grass, leaves, or other plants, located under shrubs, against rocks or logs; 7–10 eggs; 1 brood; March–May.

FEEDING Feeds on leaves, flowers, fruit, also some insects; evergreen needles, buds, and cones in season.

FLIGHT: loud, short-distance flight with rapid wing beats before gliding to the ground.

FREEZING FOR SAFETY
This female Dusky Grouse stands still as a statue, relying on camouflage, not flight, for protection.

SIMILAR SPECIES

SPRUCE GROUSE ♀ see p.28
shorter tail; smaller

SOOTY GROUSE see p.30
darker overall; yellow air sacs

OCCURRENCE
Found in the northern and central Rocky Mountains in Canada and US in high or mid-altitude open forests and shrublands. Typically uses older, denser, mixed, or evergreen forests at higher elevations in winter, more open-country, lighter forests at lower elevations in summer.

Length **16–20in (41–51cm)**	Wingspan **25–28in (64–71cm)**	Weight **2½–2¾lb (1.1–1.3kg)**
Social **Solitary/Winter flocks**	Lifespan **Up to 14 years**	Status **Localized**

DATE SEEN	WHERE	NOTES

Order **Galliformes**	Family **Phasianidae**	Species ***Dendragapus fuliginosus***

Sooty Grouse

FLIGHT: rapid takeoff when pursued; short initial burst followed by flap-and-glide sequence.

The Sooty Grouse and the Dusky Grouse were recently classified as two separate species. Although primarily distinguished by its restriction to coastal mountain ranges, plumage and behavioral displays help differentiate the male Sooty Grouse from the Dusky Grouse. During courtship displays, which are most often performed in trees, the male Sooty Grouse shows rough-looking, yellow air sacs. Females and chicks have a browner overall appearance to their plumage than those of the Dusky Grouse.

VOICE Loud 6-syllable hooting; also growl, hiss, cluck, *purrr.*

NESTING Shallow depression lined with dead vegetation, usually under small pine trees; 5–8 eggs; 1 brood; March–May.

FEEDING Feeds primarily on evergreen needles, especially Douglas Fir; will take leaves, grasses, fruit, and insects when seasonally available.

CAUTIOUS PEEK
Female Sooty Grouse disturbed on the ground peer up through grasses to check for danger.

SIMILAR SPECIES

SPRUCE GROUSE ♀
see p.28
shorter tail; smaller

DUSKY GROUSE
see p.29
dull-red wattle; browner overall; dark-red air sacs during display

OCCURRENCE
Found west of the Rocky Mountains in Canada and the US, from sea level to the timberline. Breeds at lower elevations in open areas with grassland, forest clearings, and shrubs, and moves up into thicker evergreen forests at higher elevations in winter.

Length **16–20in (41–51cm)**	Wingspan **25–28in (64–71cm)**	Weight **2½–2¾lb (1.1–1.3g)**
Social **Solitary/Winter flocks**	Lifespan **Up to 14 years**	Status **Secure**

DATE SEEN	WHERE	NOTES

Order **Galliformes**	Family **Phasianidae**	Species ***Tympanuchus phasianellus***

Sharp-tailed Grouse

ADULT
mottled wings
IN FLIGHT
pale, wedge-shaped tail, with protruding central feathers

long central tail feather
tan eyebrow
naked pink skin
heavily mottled brown, white, and black upperparts
white undertail feathers
MALE
brown wings with white dots
white underside, with dark brown arrowheads along flanks

FLIGHT: flushes from hiding with rapid wing beats, then switches to glide-flap-glide.

The most widespread of the three species in its genus, the Sharp-tailed Grouse is able to adapt to the greatest variety of habitats. It is not migratory, but undertakes seasonal movements between grassland summer habitats and woodland winter habitats. These birds are popular with hunters and are legal quarry in most of their range. Elements of this grouse's spectacular courtship display have been incorporated into the culture and dance of Native American people, including foot stomping and tail feather rattling.

VOICE Male calls a variety of unusual clucks, cooing, barks, and gobbles during courtship; females cluck with different intonations.

NESTING Shallow depression lined with plant matter close at hand as well as some feathers from female, usually near overhead cover; 10–12 eggs; 1 brood; March–May.

FEEDING Forages primarily for seeds, leaves, buds, and fruit; also takes insects and flowers when available.

PRAIRIE DANCER
The courtship dance of the Sharp-tailed Grouse heralds the arrival of spring to the grasslands.

SIMILAR SPECIES

GREATER PRAIRIE CHICKEN see p.420
shorter, square tail
more heavily barred
naked orange skin

RING-NECKED PHEASANT ♀ see p.37
light brown
longer tail
scalloped pattern on underparts

OCCURRENCE
Has a northern and western distribution in North America, from Alaska (isolated population) southward to northern prairie states. Prefers a mixture of fallow and active agricultural fields combined with brushy forest edges and woodlots along river beds.

Length **15–19in (38–48cm)**	Wingspan **23–26in (58–66cm)**	Weight **26–34oz (750–950g)**
Social **Flocks**	Lifespan **Up to 7 years**	Status **Declining (p)**

DATE SEEN	WHERE	NOTES

Order **Galliformes**	Family **Phasainidae**	Species ***Lagopus leucura***

White-tailed Ptarmigan

The smallest and most southern of the three North American ptarmigan, the White-tailed Ptarmigan's native range is still largely intact. In the winter, its completely white plumage—unique among gamebird species—blends in perfectly with its icy mountain home. Its plumage is one of several adaptations to the inhospitable environment it inhabits. The feathers on its feet increase the surface area in contact with the ground, and so help to prevent the bird from sinking into the snow.

VOICE Males emit various cackling clucks, *cuk-cuk-cuuuk* during display; females cluck, purr, and growl softly.

NESTING Scrape in ground lined with plants and feathers; 4–8 eggs; 1 brood; May–June.

FEEDING Feeds heavily on willows, eating mostly leaves, buds, and twigs; insects when nesting.

FLIGHT: rarely flies unless pursued; flush on explosive wing beats, then flap-and-glide sequence.

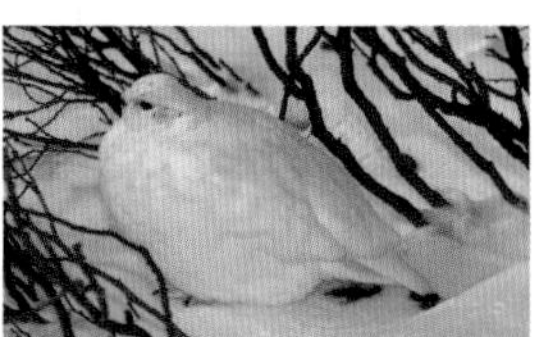

WHITE ON WHITE
Immobile on white snow, the male blends in superbly with the wintry surroundings.

SIMILAR SPECIES

ROCK PTARMIGAN ☼ see p.33
grayer summer plumage
larger overall

WILLOW PTARMIGAN ☼ see p.34
red comb
reddish brown summer plumage
white underparts
larger overall

OCCURRENCE
Has a more restricted distribution than Rock and Willow Ptarmigan, occurring from Alaska south to Idaho and Montana; small isolated populations exist in Colorado and New Mexico. Strongly associated with willow stands above tree-line; also meadows and evergreen stand mixtures.

Length **12in (30–31cm)**	Wingspan **20–22in (51–56cm)**	Weight **12–16oz (350–450g)**
Social **Large flocks**	Lifespan **Up to 15 years**	Status **Secure**

DATE SEEN	WHERE	NOTES

Order **Galliformes** | Family **Phasianidae** | Species ***Lagopus muta***

Rock Ptarmigan

MALE (WINTER)
black tail
all-white wings

mostly gray upperparts
gray wing patch
MALE (SUMMER)
IN FLIGHT

small bill
white plumage
FEMALE (WINTER)

brown-and-black barring
white wings
mottled belly
FEMALE (SUMMER)

black line between eye and bill
MALE (WINTER)

small, round head
red comb
small, delicate bill
"salt-and-pepper" barring on gray upperparts
white belly
feathered feet and toes
MALE (SUMMER)

FLIGHT: bursts into flight with rapid wing beats, followed by gliding and shallow flapping.

The Rock Ptarmigan is the most northern of the three ptarmigan species found in North America. Although some birds make a short migration to more southern wintering grounds, many remain on their breeding grounds year-round. This species is well known for its distinctive seasonal variation in plumage, which helps to camouflage it against its surroundings. Ptarmigan are a common food of the Inuit, who inhabit the same Arctic habitat.

VOICE Quiet; male call a raspy *krrrh*, also growls and clucks.

NESTING Small scrape or natural depression, lined with plant matter, often away from cover; 8–10 eggs; 1 brood; April–June.

FEEDING Feeds on buds, seeds, flowers, and leaves, especially birch and willow; eats insects in summer.

IN BETWEEN PLUMAGE
Various transitional plumage patterns can be seen on the Rock Ptarmigan in spring and fall.

SIMILAR SPECIES

WHITE-TAILED PTARMIGAN ☼
all-white tail in winter; see p.32
smaller overall
lighter brown upperparts

WILLOW PTARMIGAN ☼
see p.34
larger overall

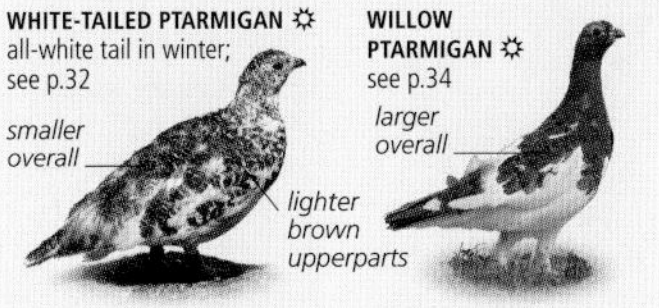

OCCURRENCE
Local in dry, rocky tundra and shrubby ridge tops; will use edges of open meadows and dense evergreen stands along fairly high-elevation rivers and streams during winter. Occurs throughout the Northern Hemisphere in Arctic tundra from Iceland to Kamchatka in the Russian Far East.

Length **12½–15½in (32–40cm)**	Wingspan **19½–23½in (50–60cm)**	Weight **16–23oz (450–650g)**
Social **Winter flocks**	Lifespan **Up to 8 years**	Status **Secure**

DATE SEEN	WHERE	NOTES

Order **Galliformes**	Family **Phasianidae**	Species ***Lagopus lagopus***

Willow Ptarmigan

FLIGHT: strong, rapid wing beats before gliding; prefers to walk.

The most common and widespread of the three ptarmigan species, the Willow Ptarmigan is the State Bird of Alaska. The Willow Ptarmigan is an unusual gamebird species, as male and female remain bonded throughout the chick-rearing process, in which the male is an active participant. The "Red Grouse" of British moors is a subspecies (*L. l. scotica*) of the Willow Ptarmigan.

VOICE Variety of purrs, clucks, hissing, meowing noises; *Kow-Kow-Kow* call given before flushing, possibly alerting others.

NESTING Shallow bowl scraped in soil, lined with plant matter, protected by overhead cover; 8–10 eggs; 1 brood; March–May.

FEEDING Mostly eats buds, stems, and seeds, but also flowers, insects, and leaves when available.

PERFECT BLEND-IN
Its reddish brown upperparts camouflage this summer ptarmigan in the shrubby areas it inhabits.

SIMILAR SPECIES

OCCURRENCE
Prefers tundra, in Arctic, sub-Arctic and subalpine regions. Thrives in willow thickets along low, moist river corridors; also in the low woodlands of the sub-Arctic tundra.

Length **14–17½in (35–44cm)**	Wingspan **22–24in (56–61cm)**	Weight **15–28oz (425–800g)**
Social **Winter flocks**	Lifespan **Up to 9 years**	Status **Secure**

DATE SEEN	WHERE	NOTES

Order **Galliformes**	Family **Phasianidae**	Species ***Alectoris chukar***

Chukar

A native of Eurasia, from eastern Europe to China, the Chukar was brought to North America in the early 1890s. In the mid-20th century, nearly a million birds were released in more than 40 US states and six Canadian provinces, after the Chukar became popular as a game bird. While most introductions failed, the species did succeed in some areas, especially on steep mountain slopes in the West. Chukars form large communal groups, or crèches, of up to 100 young birds, with 10–12 adults overseeing them.

VOICE When flushed, a thin whistled *peee*, then a series of squeals *pittoo-pittoo-pittoo*; *chukka-chuka-chuka-chuka* reunites flushed or dispersed covey.

NESTING Shallow scrape lined with nearby dead vegetation, well-concealed among shrubs and rocks on hillside; 7–12 eggs; 1 brood; March–May.

FEEDING Eats mainly seeds from various grasses and green succulent plants; berries; also eats insects.

FLIGHT: explosive takeoff from cover, usually heading downslope when flushed.

SIMILAR SPECIES

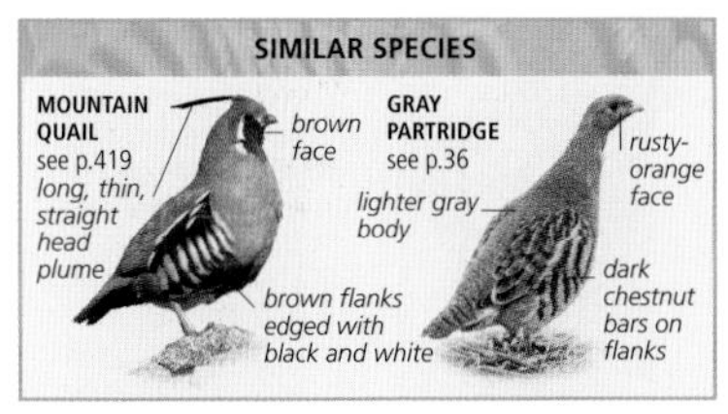

MAKING AN EFFORT
Perched on a rock, this Chukar calls loudly, stretching its neck to increase vocal capacity.

OCCURRENCE
Introduced to the West, released for shooting in the East; found on wide open areas and steep slopes at high elevation, up to 8,200ft (2,500m), with a mix of deep, brushy canyons and hillsides of loose rocks and boulders, sparse bush, low woody shrubs, grasses and aromatic herbs.

Length **13½–15in (34–38cm)**	Wingspan **19–22in (48–56cm)**	Weight **18–23oz (500–650g)**
Social **Family groups**	Lifespan **Up to 3 years**	Status **Secure**

DATE SEEN	WHERE	NOTES

Order **Galliformes**	Family **Phasianidae**	Species ***Perdix perdix***

Gray Partridge

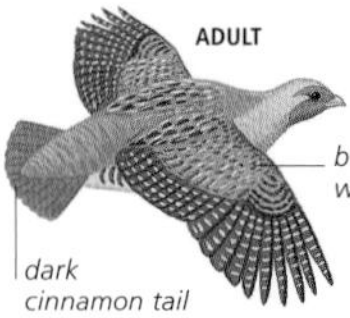

rusty head

ADULT

brown, rounded wings

dark cinnamon tail

IN FLIGHT

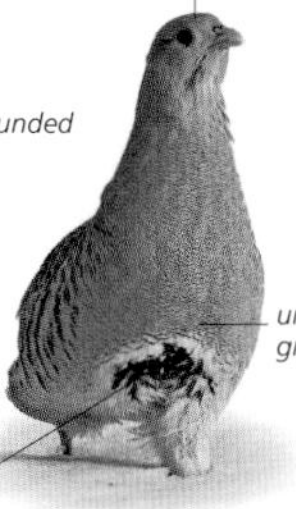

underparts gray overall

horseshoe-shaped belly patch

ADULT

cinnamon face

gray neck and chest with fine black barring

gray back with fine barring

ADULT

chestnut barred gray flanks

FLIGHT: erupts from cover on loud, rapid wing beats; levels off, flaps and glides; flies low.

A member of the pheasant family, the Gray Partridge is native to Eurasia. Introduced to North America in the late 18th century, it became a resident after repeated re-introductions. Hunters call it the Hungarian Partridge or "Hun" for short. This species has benefited from the mixture of agricultural and fallow fields, that resulted from long-term conservation programs, and its population is stable or expanding in the west. The isolated eastern populations, however, are declining due to changes in land use. This species is popular with hunters in both North America and Europe.

VOICE Short *kuk-kuk-kuk*, quickly and in a series when alarmed; *prruk-prruk* between adults and young when threatened.

NESTING Shallow depression in soil lined with vegetation, usually in hedgerows; 14–18 eggs; 1 brood; March–May.

FEEDING Eats mostly seeds and row crops such as corn and wheat; succulent green leaves in spring; insects when breeding.

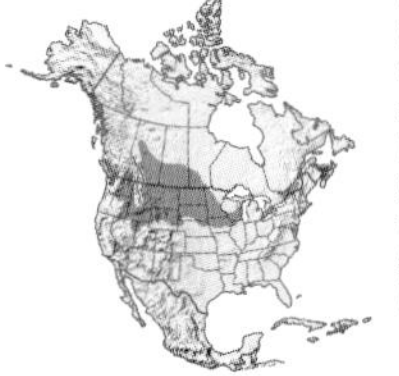

NOISY TAKEOFF
When the Gray Partridge takes flight its wings make a loud, whirring sound.

SIMILAR SPECIES

NORTHERN BOBWHITE ♀ see p.419
white streaks on rusty red body
buffy throat and face

CHUKAR see p.35
white face edged in black
red bill
black barring on white flanks

OCCURRENCE
Primarily agricultural fields of crops including corn, wheat, and oats, as well as associated hedgerows and fallow grasslands. Most birds are nonmigratory, but there is some movement by eastern birds after breeding.

Length **11–13in (28–33cm)**	Wingspan **17–20in (43–51cm)**	Weight **12–18oz (350–500g)**
Social **Family groups**	Lifespan **Up to 4 years**	Status **Secure**

DATE SEEN	WHERE	NOTES

Order **Galliformes**	Family **Phasianidae**	Species ***Phasianus colchicus***

Ring-necked Pheasant

FLIGHT: bursts vertically from cover on loud rapid wing beats; levels off, flaps, then glides.

A native of Asia, the variable-looking Ring-necked Pheasant was originally introduced in North America for recreational hunting purposes, and is now widely distributed across North America. Birds released after being bred in captivity are used to supplement natural reproduction for hunting purposes. In the wild, several females may lay eggs in the same nest—a phenomenon called "egg-dumping." There is a less common dark form, which can be distinguished principally because it lacks the distinctive white band around the neck.

VOICE Male emits a loud, raucous, explosive double note, *Karrk-KORK*, followed by loud wing-flapping; both sexes cackle when flushed.

NESTING Shallow bowl composed of grasses, usually on ground in tall grass or among low shrubs; 7–15 eggs; 1 brood; March–June.

FEEDING Feeds on corn and other grain, seeds, fruit, row crops, grass, leaves and shoots; eats insects when available.

SIMILAR SPECIES

GREATER SAGE GROUSE larger; see p.420

long, dark tail; pale breast; dark belly

SHARP-TAILED GROUSE slightly smaller; see p.31

shorter tail; darker brown overall

FLUSHED OUT
The Ring-necked Pheasant is a powerful flier when alarmed or flushed out of its cover.

OCCURRENCE
Widespread across southern Canada and the US; prefers mixture of active agricultural crops (especially corn fields), fallow fields, and hedgerows; also cattail marshes and wooded river bottoms. The Ring-necked Pheasant is native to Asia from the Caucasus east to China.

Length **19½–28in (50–70cm)**	Wingspan **30–34in (76–86cm)**	Weight **1¼–6½lb (0.5–3kg)**
Social **Solitary/Flocks**	Lifespan **Up to 4 years**	Status **Secure**

DATE SEEN	WHERE	NOTES

WATERFOWL

RECENT SCIENTIFIC studies indicate that waterfowl are closely related to gamebirds. Most species of waterfowl molt all their flight feathers at once after breeding, making them flightless for several weeks until they grow new ones.

GEESE

Ornithologists group geese and swans together into the subfamily Anserinae. Intermediate in body size and neck length between swans and ducks, geese are more terrestrial than either, and are often seen grazing on dry land. Like swans, geese pair for life. They are highly social, and most species are migratory, flying south for the winter in large flocks.

SWANS

Swans are essentially large, long-necked geese. Their heavier weight makes them ungainly on land, and they tend to be more aquatic than their smaller relatives. On water, however, they are extremely graceful. When feeding, a swan stretches its long neck to reach water plants at the bottom, submerging up to half its body as it does so. The Trumpeter Swan is North America's largest native waterfowl, growing up to 5ft (1.5m) long, and weighing up to 25lb (12kg).

DUCKS

Classified in their own subfamily, called the Anatinae, ducks are more varied than swans or geese, with many more species. They are loosely grouped by their feeding habits. Dabblers, or puddle ducks, such as the Mallard, teals, and wigeons, eat plants and animal matter, such as snails. They feed by upending on the surface of shallow water. By contrast, diving ducks, a group that includes scaups, scoters, eiders, mergansers, and the Ruddy Duck, dive deep underwater for their food.

INSTANT TAKEOFF
Puddle ducks like the Mallard can shoot straight out of the water and into the air.

GAGGLING GEESE
Gregarious Snow Geese form large, noisy flocks during migration and on winter feeding grounds.

Order **Anseriformes**	Family **Anatidae**	Species ***Anser albifrons***

Greater White-fronted Goose

The Greater White-fronted Goose is the most widespread goose in the Northern Hemisphere. It is easily distinguished by its black-barred belly and the patch of white at the base of its bill. There are five subspecies, two of which are commonly seen in North America. The "tundra" (*A. a. frontalis*) makes up the largest population, breeding in extreme northwestern Canada and Alaska. The "tule" (*A. a. gambeli*), while the larger, occurs in smaller numbers, and is restricted in range to north-central Canada.

VOICE Laugh-like *klow-yo* or *klew-yo-yo;* very musical in a flock.
NESTING Bowl-shaped nest made of plant material, lined with down, constructed near water; 3–7 eggs; 1 brood; May–August.
FEEDING Eats sedges, grasses, berries, and plants on both land and water in summer; feeds on grasses, seeds, and grains in winter.

FLIGHT: strong, direct flight; flies alone, in multiple lines, or in a V-formation.

FLIGHT FORMATIONS
This heavy-bodied, powerful flier can often be seen in tightly packed flocks.

SIMILAR SPECIES

CANADA GOOSE
see p.42
black head, neck, and bill
white chin strap

HEAVY GRAZER
Grass is the major component of this goose's diet.

OCCURRENCE
Different habitats are utilized for breeding and wintering. Nesting areas include tundra ponds and lakes, dry rocky fields, and grassy slopes in Alaska and northern Canada. In winter, coastal marshes, inland wetlands, agricultural fields, and refuges are used along Pacific Coast and Mexico.

Length **25–32in (64–81cm)**	Wingspan **4¼–5¼ft (1.3–1.6m)**	Weight **4–6½lb (1.8–3kg)**
Social **Flocks**	Lifespan **Up to 22 years**	Status **Secure**

DATE SEEN	WHERE	NOTES

Order **Anseriformes**	Family **Anatidae**	Species ***Anser caerulescens***

Snow Goose

FLIGHT: direct, strong flight with moderate wing beats in either V-shaped or bunched flocks.

The abundant Snow Goose has two subspecies. The "greater" *(A. c. atlanticus)* is slightly larger and is found breeding farther east. The smaller "lesser" *(A. c. caerulescens)* breeds farther west. Snow Geese have two color forms—white and "blue" (actually dark grayish brown with a white head), and there are also intermediate birds.

VOICE Basic a call nasal *whouk*, *kowk*, or *kow-luk*, also higher-pitched *heenk*; feeding call a series of *hu-hu-hur*.

NESTING Scrapes on hummock, lined with plant material and down; 2–6 eggs; 1 brood; May–July.

FEEDING Grazes on aquatic and terrestrial vegetation, including stems, seeds, leaves, tubers, and roots; also grain and young leaves in agricultural fields in winter.

TOUCHING DOWN
Snow Geese are well known for migrating in flocks that number in the tens of thousands.

SIMILAR SPECIES

GREATER WHITE-FRONTED GOOSE see p.39
orange legs

ROSS'S GOOSE see p.41
shorter bill
much smaller overall

OCCURRENCE
Breeding colonies in High Arctic from Wrangel Island in the West to Greenland in the East; a population of "lesser" Snow Geese breeds near Hudson Bay. Winters along interior valleys westward to coastal lowlands and central plateau of Mexico; Atlantic populations winter in coastal marshes.

Length **27–33in (69–83cm)**	Wingspan **4¼–5½ft (1.3–1.7m)**	Weight **3¾–6½lb (1.7–3kg)**
Social **Flocks**	Lifespan **Up to 27 years**	Status **Secure**

DATE SEEN	WHERE	NOTES

Order **Anseriformes**	Family **Anatidae**	Species ***Anser rossii***

Ross's Goose

ADULT (WHITE)
black wing tips
IN FLIGHT

light gray crown
dusky line through eye
gray wash on upperparts
IMMATURE (WHITE FORM)

round head
short, triangular bill
short, deeply furrowed neck
clean white upperparts
reddish pink legs
ADULT (WHITE FORM)

mostly dark brown upperparts
white rump and tail
ADULT (BLUE FORM)

FLIGHT: strong and direct, with rapid wing beats.

This diminutive white goose is not much bigger than a Mallard, and half the weight of a Snow Goose; like its larger relative, it also has a "blue" form. About 95 percent of Ross's Geese nest at a single sanctuary in Arctic Canada, the rest breed along Hudson Bay and at several island locations. Hunting reduced the population to just 6,000 in the early 1950s, but the species has rebounded substantially, becoming more common along the East Coast as numbers increase.

VOICE Call a *keek keek keeek*, higher-pitched than Snow Goose; also a harsh, low *kork* or *kowk*; quiet when feeding.

NESTING Plant materials placed on ground, usually in colonies with Lesser Snow Geese; 3–5 eggs; 1 brood; June–August.

FEEDING Grazes on grasses, sedges, and small grains.

TRAVELING IN FAMILIES
Groups migrate thousands of miles together, for example from northern Canada to central California.

SIMILAR SPECIES

SNOW GOOSE white form; see p.40 *larger bill* *longer neck* *pink legs*

SNOW GOOSE blue form; see p.40 *longer neck* *black patch on bill*

OCCURRENCE
Breeding grounds are amid tundra in scattered, high Arctic locations. Main wintering areas in California. On the wintering grounds, it feeds in agricultural fields, and also grasslands. Roosts overnight in several types of wetlands.

Length **22½–25in (57–64cm)**	Wingspan **3¼ft (1.1m)**	Weight **1¾–4½lb (0.85–2kg)**
Social **Flocks**	Lifespan **Up to 21 years**	Status **Localized**

DATE SEEN	WHERE	NOTES

Order **Anseriformes**	Family **Anatidae**	Species ***Branta canadensis***

Canada Goose

plain grayish brown wings with darker flight feathers
ADULT
IN FLIGHT
white U-shaped patch on rump

black head
very long neck
grayish brown upperparts and sides
broad white chin strap
paler upper breast
white undertail feathers
ADULT

smaller, white chin strap
dark brown overall
ADULT

The Canada Goose is the most common, widespread, and familiar goose in North America. Given its vast range, it is not surprising that the Canada Goose should have much geographic variation. Twelve subspecies have been recognized. With the exception of the Cackling Goose, which has recently been separated, it is difficult to confuse it, with its distinctive white chin strap, black head and neck, and grayish brown body, with any other species of goose. It is a monogamous species, and once pairs are formed, they stay together for life.

VOICE Male call *honk* or *bark*; females have higher pitched *hrink*.

NESTING Scrape lined with available plant matter and down, near water; 1–2 broods; 2–12 eggs; May–August.

FEEDING Grazes on grasses, sedges, leaves, seeds, agricultural crops, and berries; also insects.

FLIGHT: strong and direct with fairly slow, deep wing beats; often flies in V-formation.

TRICK OF THE LIGHT
A low sun can play tricks—these birds are actually pale grayish underneath.

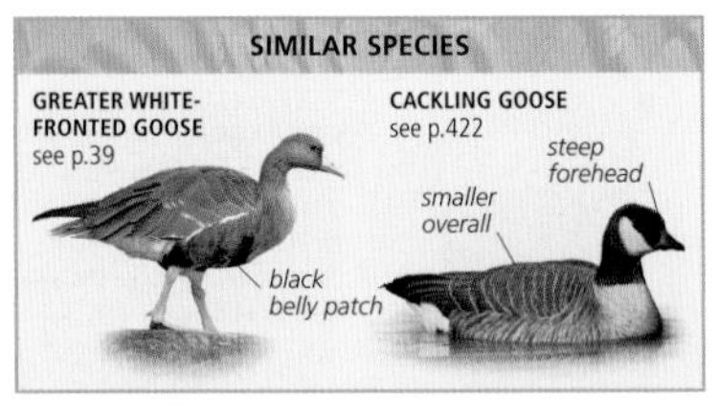

OCCURRENCE
Variety of inland breeding habitats near water, including grassy urban areas, marshes, prairie, parkland, coastal temperate forest, northern coniferous forest, and Arctic tundra. Winters in agricultural fields, mudflats, saltwater marshes, lakes, and rivers.

Length **2¼–3½ft (0.7–1.1m)**	Wingspan **4¼–5½ft (1.3–1.7m)**	Weight **6½–9¾lb (3–4.4kg)**
Social **Flocks**	Lifespan **Up to 25 years**	Status **Secure**

DATE SEEN	WHERE	NOTES

Order **Anseriformes**	Family **Anatidae**	Species ***Branta bernicla***

Brant

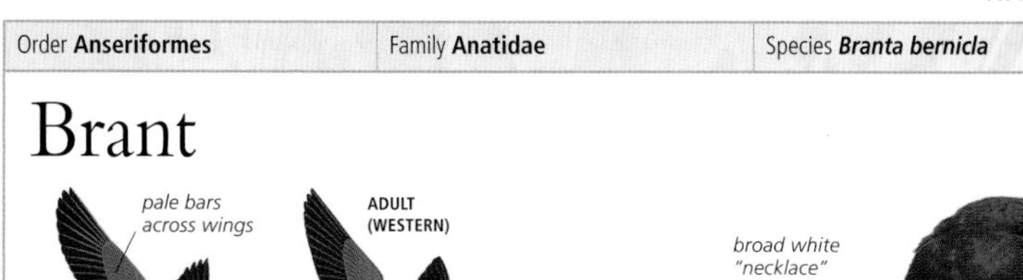

A small-billed, dark, stocky sea goose, the Brant winters on both the east and west coasts of North America. There are two subspecies in the US (three overall)—the pale-bellied "Atlantic" Brant (*B. b. hrota*), found in the east, and the darker "black" Brant (*B. b. nigricans*), in the west. In addition, there is an intermediate gray-bellied form that winters in the Puget Sound region along the Washington State coast. Unlike other North American geese, the Brant feeds mainly on eelgrass in winter.

VOICE Nasal *cruk*, harsh-sounding in tone; rolling series of *cut cut cut cronk*, with an upward inflection at end.

NESTING Scrape lined with grass, plant matter, and down on islands or gravel spits; 3–5 eggs; 1 brood; May–July.

FEEDING Eats grass and sedges when nesting; eelgrass in winter; also green algae, salt marsh plants, and mollusks.

FLIGHT: rapid and strong; low, irregular flight formations.

GRASSY MEAL
In winter, Brants forage almost exclusively on eelgrass between the high and low tide marks.

SIMILAR SPECIES

SNOW GOOSE (BLUE FORM) see p.40
pale wing feathers
darker underparts

CANADA GOOSE see p.42
broad, white chin strap
browner coloration

OCCURRENCE
Breeds in colonies in northern Canada and Alaska, and winters along both Pacific and Atlantic coasts. The western breeding population of the Brant ("black") winters from the Aleutian Islands to northern Mexico, while the pale-bellied form ("Atlantic") is restricted in range to the East Coast.

Length **22–26in (56–66cm)**	Wingspan **3½–4ft (1.1–1.2m)**	Weight **2½–4lb (1–1.8kg)**
Social **Flocks**	Lifespan **Up to 25 years**	Status **Secure**

DATE SEEN	WHERE	NOTES

Order **Anseriformes**	Family **Anatidae**	Species ***Cygnus columbianus***

Tundra Swan

Nesting in the Arctic tundra, this well-named species is North America's most widespread and smallest swan. Two populations exist, with one wintering in the West, and the other along the East Coast. The Tundra Swan can be confused with the Trumpeter Swan, but their different calls immediately distinguish the two species. When they are silent, weight and bill structure are the best way to tell them apart. In Eurasia, this species is known as Bewick's Swan and possesses a larger yellow patch at the base of its bill.

VOICE Clear, high-pitched yodelling *whoo-hooo* calls mixed with garbles, yelping, and barking sounds.

NESTING Mound-shaped nest made of plant matter near water; 3–6 eggs; 1 brood; May–September.

FEEDING Eats aquatic vegetation, insects, mollusks; also grain.

FLIGHT: flight pattern like that of other swans but with slightly faster wing beats.

WINTER FLOCKS
Its size, white plumage, and flocking habits make the Tundra Swan a conspicuous species.

SIMILAR SPECIES

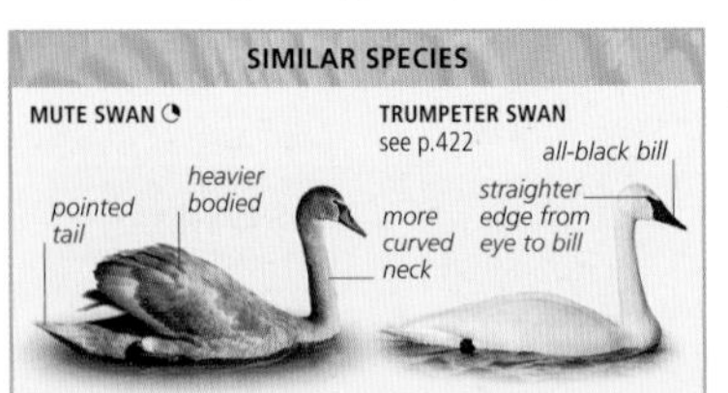

OCCURRENCE
Nests around lakes and pools in northern tundra from the Aleutians to the Yukon, and east to northwest Québec. Winters in southern British Columbia, western US, and mid-Atlantic states, mostly New Jersey to south Carolina. Winter habitat includes shallow coastal bays, ponds, and lakes.

Length **4–5ft (1.2–1.5m)**	Wingspan **6¼–7¼ft (1.9–2.2m)**	Weight **12–18lb (5.5–8kg)**
Social **Flocks**	Lifespan **Up to 21 years**	Status **Secure**

DATE SEEN	WHERE	NOTES

Order **Anseriformes**	Family **Anatidae**	Species ***Aix sponsa***

Wood Duck

The male Wood Duck is perhaps the most striking of all North American ducks. With its bright plumage, red eye and bill, and its long sleek crest that gives its head a helmet-shaped profile, the male is unmistakable. It is related to the Mandarin Duck of Asia. The Wood Duck is very dependent on mature swampy forestland. It is typically found on swamps, shallow lakes, ponds, and park settings that are surrounded by trees. Although it adapts to human activity, it is quite shy. When swimming, the Wood Duck can be seen jerking its head front to back. Of all waterfowl, this is the only species that regularly raises two broods each season.

VOICE Male gives a wheezy upslurred whistle *zweeet*; female's call a double-note, rising *oh-eek oh-eek*.

NESTING Nests in natural tree cavities or nest boxes in close proximity to water; 10–13 eggs; 2 broods; April–August.

FEEDING Forages for seeds, tree fruits, and small acorns; also spiders, insects, and crustaceans.

FLIGHT: rapid flight with deep wing beats; flies with head up; leaps straight off the water.

PLAIN BELLY
Wings raised, a male reveals one of the only plain areas of its plumage—its pale belly and underwing.

SIMILAR SPECIES

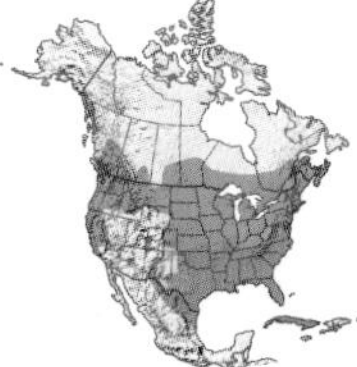

OCCURRENCE
Usually found throughout the year, along rivers, streams, and creeks, in swamps, and marshy areas. Has a preference for permanent bodies of water. If good aquatic feeding areas are unavailable, the Wood Duck feeds in open areas, including agricultural fields.

Length **18½–21½in (47–54cm)**	Wingspan **26–29in (66–73cm)**	Weight **16–30oz (450–850g)**
Social **Small flocks**	Lifespan **Up to 18 years**	Status **Secure**

DATE SEEN	WHERE	NOTES

Order **Anseriformes**	Family **Anatidae**	Species ***Anas strepera***

Gadwall

Although the Gadwall's appearance is somewhat somber, many birders consider this duck one of North America's most elegant species because of the subtlety of its plumage. Despite being common and widespread, Gadwalls are often overlooked because of their retiring behavior and relatively quiet vocalizations. This dabbling duck is slightly smaller and more delicate than the Mallard, yet female Gadwalls are often mistaken for female Mallards. Gadwalls associate with other species, especially in winter.

VOICE Low, raspy *meep* or *reb* given in quick succession; female *quack* similar to that of female Mallard, but higher-pitched and more nasal; high-pitched *peep*, or *pe-peep*; both sexes give *tickety-tickety-tickety* chatter while feeding.

NESTING Bowl nest made of plant material in a scrape; 8–12 eggs; 1 brood; April–August.

FEEDING Dabbles on the surface or below for seeds, aquatic vegetation, and invertebrates, including mollusks and insects.

FLIGHT: direct flight with fast wing beats; leaps straight off the water.

BROOD ON THE MOVE
Females lead their ducklings from their nest to a brood-rearing habitat that provides cover and ample food for the ducklings to forage.

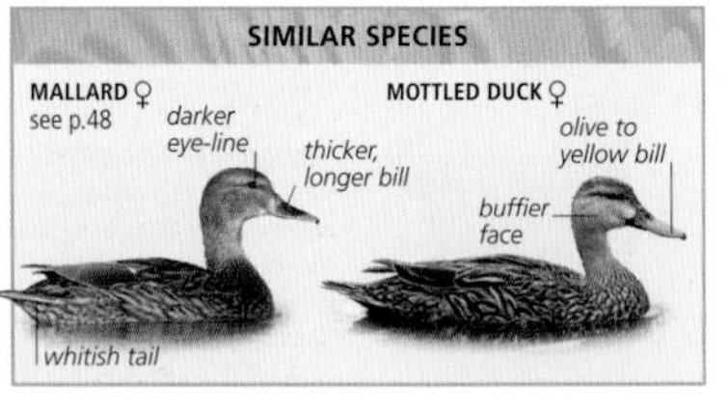

OCCURRENCE
From the western prairie pothole country of Canada and the northern US, the Gadwall's range has expanded as it has adapted to man-made bodies of water, such as reservoirs and ponds. In winter, mostly found on lakes, marshes, and along rivers.

Length **18–22½in (46–57cm)**	Wingspan **33in (84cm)**	Weight **18–45oz (500–1,250g)**
Social **Winter flocks**	Lifespan **Up to 19 years**	Status **Secure**

DATE SEEN	WHERE	NOTES

Order **Anseriformes**	Family **Anatidae**	Species ***Anas americana***

American Wigeon

Often found in mixed flocks with other ducks, the American Wigeon is a common and widespread, medium-sized dabbling duck. This bird is an opportunist that loiters around other diving ducks and coots, feeding on the vegetation they dislodge. It is more social during migration and in the nonbreeding season than when breeding.

VOICE Slow and fast whistles; male's most common call a slow, high-pitched, wheezy, 3-syllable *whew-whew-whew*, with middle note loudest; also, a faster *whee* whistle.

NESTING Depression lined with plant material and down, usually in tall grass away from water; 5–10 eggs; 1 brood; May–August.

FEEDING Grazes on grass, clover, algae, and, in agricultural fields; feeds on many seeds, insects, mollusks, and crustaceans during the breeding season.

FLIGHT: rapid, fairly deep wing beats; leaps almost vertically off the water.

COMING IN FOR LANDING
This male's cream-colored forehead is clearly visible, as is the sharp contrast between the white belly, and the pinkish breast and flanks.

FLAPPING WINGS
This bird has a white patch on its underwing, while the Eurasian Wigeon has a gray patch.

SIMILAR SPECIES

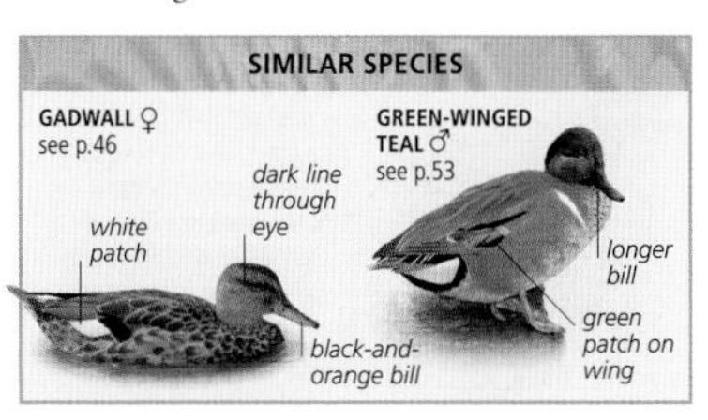

OCCURRENCE
The northernmost breeder of the dabbling ducks, occurs from Alaska to the Maritimes. Prefers pothole and grassland habitats; found almost anywhere near water in winter. Winters south to northern South America and the Caribbean, in freshwater and coastal bay habitats.

Length **17½–23in (45–58cm)**	Wingspan **33in (84cm)**	Weight **1⅛–3lb (0.5–1.3kg)**
Social **Flocks**	Lifespan **Up to 21 years**	Status **Secure**

DATE SEEN	WHERE	NOTES

Order **Anseriformes**	Family **Anatidae**	Species ***Anas platyrhynchos***

Mallard

The Mallard is perhaps the most familiar of all ducks, and occurs in the wild all across the Northern Hemisphere. It is the ancestor of most domestic ducks, and hybrids between the wild and domestic forms are frequently seen in city lakes and ponds, often with patches of white on the breast. Mating is generally a violent affair, but outside the breeding season the wild species is strongly migratory and gregarious, sometimes forming large flocks that may join with other species.

VOICE Male's call a quiet raspy *raab*; during courtship a high-pitched whistle; female call a *quack* or repeated in series.

NESTING Scrape lined with plant matter, usually near water, often on floating vegetation; 6–15 eggs; 1 brood; February–September.

FEEDING Feeds omnivorously on insects, crustaceans, mollusks, and earthworms when breeding; otherwise largely vegetarian; takes seeds, acorns, agricultural crops, aquatic vegetation, and bread.

FLIGHT: fast, shallow, and regular; often flies in groups.

STICKING TOGETHER
The mother leads her ducklings to water soon after they hatch. She looks after them until they can fend for themselves.

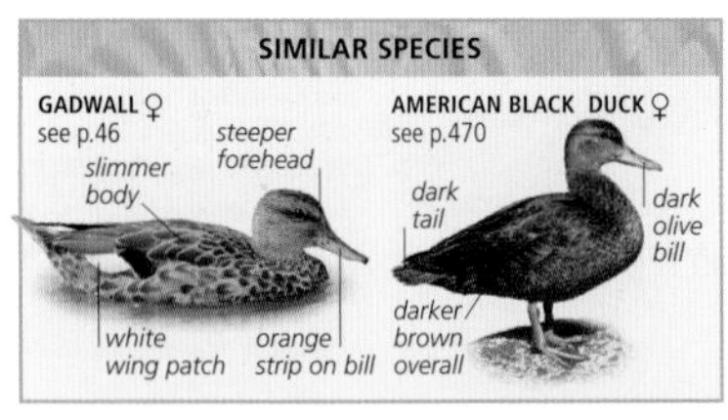

OCCURRENCE
Occurs throughout the region, choosing shallow water in natural wetlands, such as marshes, prairie potholes, ponds, and ditches; can also be found in man-made habitats such as city parks and reservoirs, preferring more open habitats in winter.

Length **19½–26in (50–65cm)**	Wingspan **32–37in (82–95cm)**	Weight **1⅞–3lb (0.9–1.4kg)**
Social **Flocks**	Lifespan **Up to 29 years**	Status **Secure**

DATE SEEN	WHERE	NOTES

Order **Anseriformes**	Family **Anatidae**	Species ***Anas discors***

Blue-winged Teal

This small dabbling duck is a common and widespread North American breeding species. With a bold white crescent between bill and eye on its otherwise slate-gray head and neck, the male Blue-winged Teal is quite distinctive. The Blue-winged and Cinnamon Teals, together with the Northern Shoveler, constitute the three "blue-winged" ducks; this is a feature that is conspicuous when the birds are flying. The Cinnamon and the Blue-winged Teals are almost identical genetically and interbreed to form hybrids. The Blue-winged Teal winters mostly south of the US and migrates back north in spring.

VOICE Male a high-pitched, raspy *peew* or low-pitched *paay* during courtship; female a loud single *quack*.

NESTING Bowl-shaped depression lined with grasses, close to water's edge, in meadows; 6–14 eggs; 1 brood; April–September.

FEEDING Eats seeds of a variety of plants; feeds heavily on insect larvae, crustaceans, and snails, when breeding.

FLIGHT: fast, twisting flight; flies in compact, small groups.

OUTSTRETCHED WING
Wing stretch behavior shows the white feathers between the blue forewing and green speculum.

SIMILAR SPECIES

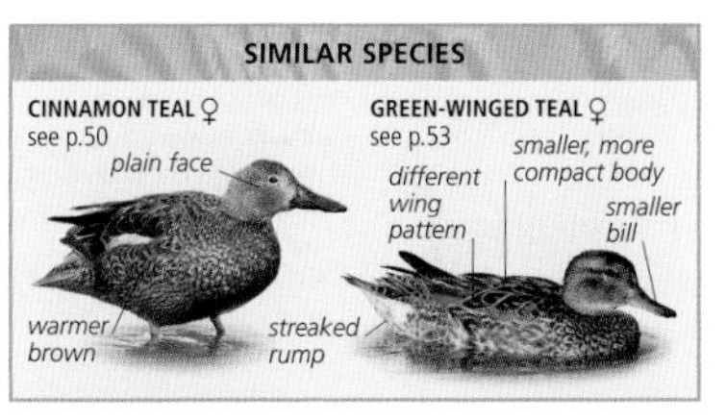

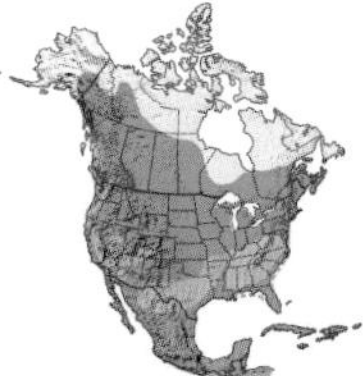

OCCURRENCE
Nests across North America, with highest numbers in the prairie and parkland regions of the midcontinent. Prefers shallow ponds or marshes during nesting; freshwater to brackish water and (less so) saltwater marshes during migration. In winter, prefers saline environments, including mangroves.

Length **14½–16in (37–41cm)**	Wingspan **23½–25in (60–64cm)**	Weight **11–18oz (300–500g)**
Social **Flocks**	Lifespan **Up to 17 years**	Status **Secure**

DATE SEEN	WHERE	NOTES

Order **Anseriformes**	Family **Anatidae**	Species ***Anas cyanoptera***

Cinnamon Teal

True to his English name, the male Cinnamon Teal is unmistakable in its rusty brown color adorned with blazing red eyes. A small duck, the Cinnamon Teal is the only North American dabbling duck that does not breed in the Great Plains and prairies of the midcontinent. It winters mostly in the coastal marshes and interior wetlands of Mexico. Common in the West, it is even seen in tiny roadside pools. Closely related to the Blue-winged Teal, the Cinnamon Teal shares with it its wing pattern. The latin name *cyanoptera* means "blue-winged."

VOICE Male a snuffled *chuk chuk chuk*; female a loud single *quack* and soft *gack gack gack ga*.

NESTING Shallow depression lined with grass near water; 4–16 eggs; 1 brood; March–September.

FEEDING Feeds on seeds of many plant species; adds aquatic insects, crustaceans, and snails, when breeding; omnivorous.

FLIGHT: rapid wing beats; very agile, making sharp turns.

FLOCKING TOGETHER
The cinnamon-colored males and tan females are often found together in flocks.

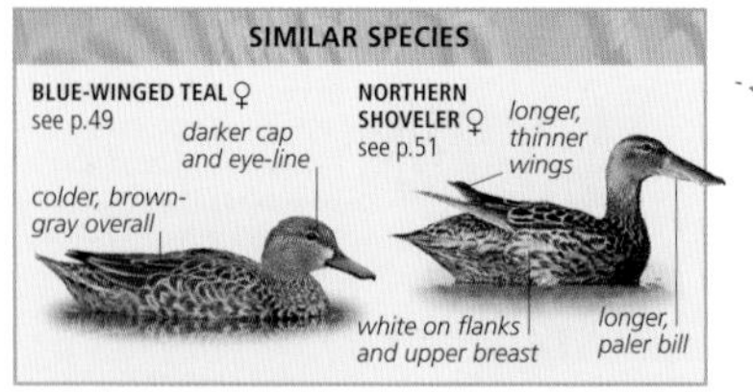

OCCURRENCE
Found in freshwater and brackish habitats of various sizes, such as marshes, reservoirs, flooded fields, ponds, ditches, and stock ponds. In the southern part of its wintering range, can also be found in tidal estuaries, salt marshes, and mangrove forests. Widespread in Central and South America.

Length **14–17in (36–43cm)**	Wingspan **22in (56cm)**	Weight **10–17oz (275–475g)**
Social **Winter flocks**	Lifespan **Up to 12 years**	Status **Secure**

DATE SEEN	WHERE	NOTES

Order **Anseriformes**	Family **Anatidae**	Species ***Anas clypeata***

Northern Shoveler

The Northern Shoveler is a common, medium-sized, dabbling duck found in North America and Eurasia. It is monogamous—pairs remain together longer than any other dabbler species. Its distinctive long bill is highly specialized; it is wider at the tip and contains thin, comb-like structures (called "lamellae") along the sides, used to filter food items from the water. Shovelers often form tight feeding groups, swimming close together as they sieve the water for prey.

VOICE Male call a nasal, muffled *thuk thuk...thuk thuk*; also a loud, nasal *paaaay*; female call a variety of *quacks*, singly or in a series of 4–5 descending notes.

NESTING Scrape lined with plant matter and down, in short plants, near water; 6–19 eggs; 1 brood; May–August.

FEEDING Forages for seeds; filters small crustaceans and mollusks out of the water.

FLIGHT: strong direct flight; male's wings make a rattling noise when taking off.

UPSIDE DOWN FEEDER
This male upends to feed below the water's surface, revealing his orange legs.

FILTER FEEDING
Their bills open, these ducks sieve small invertebrates from the water.

SIMILAR SPECIES

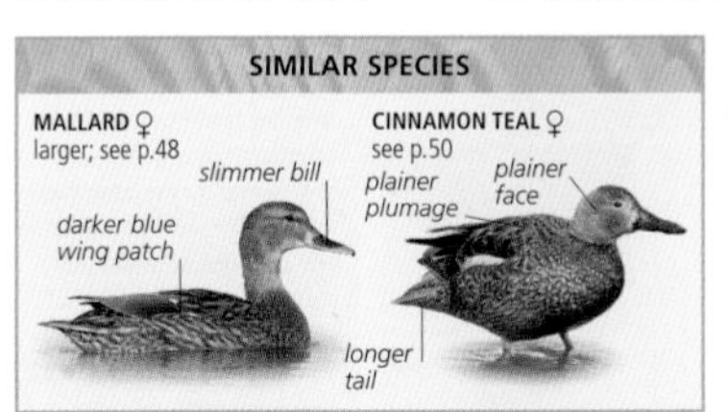

OCCURRENCE
Widespread across North America, south of the tundra. Breeds in a variety of wetlands, in edges of shallow pools with nearby tall and short grasslands. Occurs in fresh- and salt marshes, ponds, and other shallow bodies of water in winter; does not feed on land.

Length **17½–20in (44–51cm)**	Wingspan **27–33in (69–84cm)**	Weight **14–29oz (400–825g)**
Social **Flocks**	Lifespan **Up to 18 years**	Status **Secure**

DATE SEEN	WHERE	NOTES

Order **Anseriformes**	Family **Anatidae**	Species ***Anas acuta***

Northern Pintail

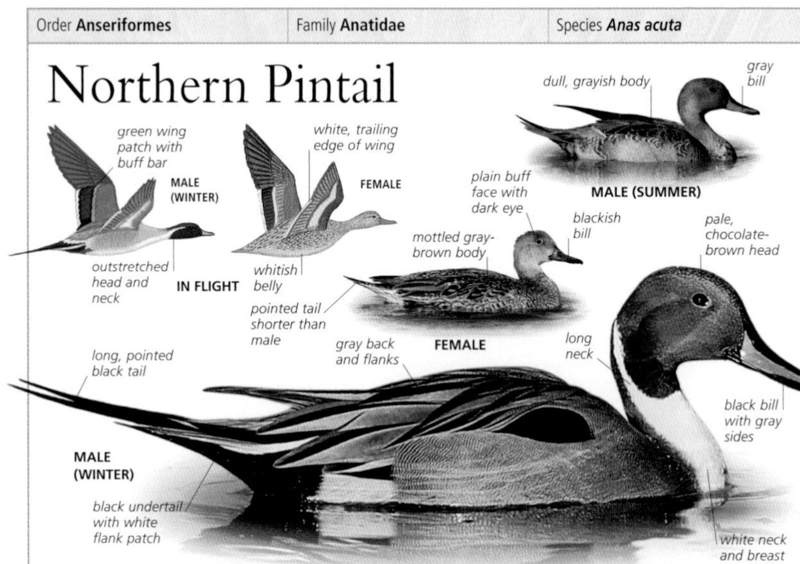

An elegant, long-necked dabbler, the Northern Pintail has extremely distinctive marking and a very long tail—in fact, the longest tail to be found on any freshwater duck. One of the earliest breeders in the year, these ducks begin nesting soon after the ice thaws. Northern Pintails were once one of the most abundant prairie breeding ducks. However, in recent decades, droughts, combined with the reduction of habitat on both their wintering and breeding grounds, have resulted in a significant decline in their population.

VOICE Male call a high-pitched rolling *prrreep prrreep;* lower-pitched wheezy *wheeeee*, which gets louder then drops off; female call a quiet, harsh *quack* or *kuk* singularly or as short series; also a loud *gaak*, often repeated.

NESTING Scrape lined with plant materials and down, usually in short grass, brush, or even in the open; 3–12 eggs; 1 brood; April–August.

FEEDING Feeds on grains, rice, seeds, aquatic weeds, insect larvae, crustaceans, and snails.

FLIGHT: fast, direct flight; can be very acrobatic in the air.

FEEDING TIME
Even when tipping up to feed, these pintails can be identified by their long, black, pointed tails.

OCCURRENCE
Widely distributed in North America; breeding in open country in shallow wetlands or meadows in mountainous forest regions. Found in tidal wetlands and saltwater habitats in migration and winter; dry harvested and flooded agricultural fields in autumn and winter.

Length **20–30in (51–76cm)**	Wingspan **35in (89cm)**	Weight **18–44oz (500–1,250g)**
Social **Flocks**	Lifespan **Up to 21 years**	Status **Declining**

DATE SEEN	WHERE	NOTES

Order **Anseriformes**	Family **Anatidae**	Species ***Anas crecca***

Green-winged Teal

MALE

green-and-black patch on hindwing

short neck

gray flanks

IN FLIGHT

dark green ear patch

rufous head

small, narrow, black bill

black-spotted breast

white vertical bar

finely detailed pattern

yellowish buff undertail feathers

MALE

horizontal, white line on sides

lacks white vertical bar

***A. c. crecca* (EURASIAN; RARE)**

darker face

steeper forehead

FEMALE

shoulder feathers with narrow pale edges

weaker face pattern

JUVENILE

The Green-winged Teal, the smallest North American dabbling duck, is slightly smaller than the Blue-winged and Cinnamon Teals, and lacks their blue wing patch. Its population is increasing, apparently because it breeds in more pristine habitats, and farther north, than the prairie ducks. The species has three subspecies, *A. c. crecca* (Eurasia), *A. c. carolinensis* (North America), and *A. c. nimia* (Aleutian Islands). *Carolinensis* males have a conspicuous vertical white bar, whereas Eurasian *crecca* males do not.

VOICE Male call a high-pitched, slightly rolling *crick crick*, similar to cricket; female a call quiet *quack*.

NESTING Shallow scrape on ground lined with nearby vegetation, often placed in dense vegetation near water; 6–9 eggs; 1 brood; April–September.

FEEDING Eats seeds, aquatic insects, crustaceans, and mollusks year-round; also feeds in grain fields in winter.

FLIGHT: fast flight; often flying in twisting, tight groups reminiscent of shorebird flocks.

SINGLE PARENT
The female duck is deserted by her partner during incubation, so she must provide all parental care.

SIMILAR SPECIES

BLUE-WINGED TEAL ♀ larger overall; see p.49

whitish spot at base of bill

different wing pattern

CINNAMON TEAL ♀ larger overall; see p.50

longer bill

rich brown overall

yellowish legs

OCCURRENCE
Breeds from central US northward to Canada and Alaska; around ponds in forests and deciduous woodlands. Prefers shallow vegetated wetlands. In winter and migration, inland and coastal marshes, sloughs, and agricultural fields. Winters south of the Caribbean and in southern Mexico.

Length **12–15½in (31–39cm)**	Wingspan **20½–23in (52–59cm)**	Weight **7–16oz (200–450g)**
Social **Flocks**	Lifespan **Up to 20 years**	Status **Secure**

DATE SEEN	WHERE	NOTES

Order **Anseriformes**	Family **Anatidae**	Species ***Aythya valisineria***

Canvasback

A large, elegant, long-billed diving duck, the Canvasback is a bird of prairie pothole country. Its specialized diet of aquatic plants has resulted in a smaller population than other ducks. With legs set toward the rear, it is an accomplished swimmer and diver, and is rarely seen on land. Weather conditions and brood parasitism by Redheads determine how successful the Canvasback's nesting is from year to year.

VOICE Mostly silent except during courtship when males make soft *cooing* noises; females emit a grating *krrrrr krrrrrr krrrrr*; females give loud *quack* when taking off; during winter, both sexes make soft wheezing series of *rrrr rrrr rrrr* sounds.

NESTING Platform over water built of woven vegetation; occasionally on shore; 8–11 eggs; 1 brood; April–September.

FEEDING Mainly eats aquatic tubers, buds, root stalks, and shoots, particularly those of wild celery; also eats snails when preferred plants are unavailable.

FLIGHT: direct strong flight; one of the fastest ducks; forms V-shaped flocks.

DEEP WATER
Canvasbacks prefer deeper-bodied waters that support the aquatic vegetation they eat.

OCCURRENCE
Found in potholes, marshes, and ponds in prairie parkland, tundra; northerly forests preferred where their favorite foods grow. Winters in large numbers in large bays and lakes, and deltas, with smaller numbers scattered across North America and Mexico.

Length **19–22in (48–56cm)**	Wingspan **31–35in (79–89cm)**	Weight **1¾–3½lb (0.8–1.6kg)**
Social **Flocks**	Lifespan **Up to 22 years**	Status **Secure**

DATE SEEN	WHERE	NOTES

Order **Anseriformes**	Family **Anatidae**	Species ***Aythya americana***

Redhead

The Redhead, a medium-sized diving duck belonging to the Pochard group, is native only to North America. Only when seen up close is it apparent that the male's seemingly gray upperparts and flanks are actually white, with dense, black, wavy markings. The Redhead often feeds at night and forages mostly around dusk and dawn, drifting during the day. It parasitizes other duck nests more than any other duck species, particularly those of the Canvasback and even other Redheads.

VOICE Male courtship call a wheezy rising then falling *whee ough*, also *meow*; female call a low, raspy *kurr kurr kurr.*

NESTING Weaves solid nest over water in dense vegetation such as cattails, lined with down; 7–14 eggs; 1 brood; May–September.

FEEDING Omnivore; feeds on aquatic plants, seeds, tubers, algae, insects, spiders, fish eggs, snails, and insect larvae; diet is variable depending on location.

FLIGHT: direct flight; runs on water prior to takeoff.

MALE DISPLAY
This male is performing a spectacular courtship display called a head throw, while remaining otherwise completely still on the water.

EASY IDENTIFICATION
The long blue bill with a whitish band and black tip is clearly visible in males.

SIMILAR SPECIES

OCCURRENCE
Breeds in shallow wetlands across the Great Basin and Prairie Pothole region, very densely in certain marsh habitats. The bulk of the population winters in coastal lagoons along the Atlantic Coast and the Gulf of Mexico.

Length **17–21in (43–53cm)**	Wingspan **30–31in (75–79cm)**	Weight **1⅜–3¼lbs (0.6–1.5kg)**
Social **Flocks**	Lifespan **Up to 21 years**	Status **Secure**

DATE SEEN	WHERE	NOTES

Order **Anseriformes**	Family **Anatidae**	Species ***Aythya collaris***

Ring-necked Duck

A resident of freshwater ponds and lakes, the Ring-necked Duck is a fairly common medium-sized diving duck. A more descriptive and suitable name might have been Ring-billed Duck as the bold white band on the bill tip is easy to see whereas the thin chestnut ring around the neck can be very difficult to observe. The tall, pointed head is quite distinctive, peaking at the rear of the crown. When it sits on the water, this bird typically holds its head high.

VOICE Male normally silent; female makes low *kerp kerp* call.

NESTING Floating nest built in dense aquatic vegetation, often in marshes; 6–14 eggs; 1 brood; May–August.

FEEDING Feeds in water at all times, either by diving, tipping up, or dabbling for aquatic plant tubers and seeds; also eats aquatic invertebrates such as clams and snails.

FLIGHT: strong flier with deep, rapid wing beats; flight somewhat erratic.

UNIQUE BILL
A white outline around the base of the bill and the white band on the bill are unique markings.

FLAPPING WINGS
Bold white wing linings are apparent when the Ring-necked Duck flaps its wings.

OCCURRENCE
Breeds across Canada, south of the Arctic zone, in shallow freshwater marshes and bogs; sporadically in the western US. Winters in freshwater and brackish habitats such as swamps, lakes, estuaries, reservoirs, and flooded fields. Migrants are found in the Midwest near stands of wild rice.

Length **15–18in (38–46cm)**	Wingspan **24–25in (62–63cm)**	Weight **1⅛–2lbs (500–900g)**
Social **Flocks**	Lifespan **Up to 20 years**	Status **Secure**

DATE SEEN	WHERE	NOTES

Order **Anseriformes**	Family **Anatidae**	Species ***Aythya affinis***

Lesser Scaup

The Lesser Scaup, far more numerous than its somewhat larger relative (their size and weight ranges overlap), is also the most abundant diving duck in North America. The two species are very similar in appearance and are best identified by shape. Identification must be done cautiously as head shape changes with position. For example, the crown feathers are flattened just before diving in both species; thus, scaups are best identified when they are not moving.

VOICE Males mostly silent except during courtship when they make a wheezy *wheeow wheeow wheeow* sound; females give repetitive series of grating *garrrf garrrf garrrf* notes.

NESTING Nest built in tall vegetation or under shrubs, sometimes far from water, also on islands and mats of floating vegetation; 8–11 eggs; 1 brood; May–September.

FEEDING Feeds mainly on leeches, crustaceans, mollusks, aquatic insects, and aquatic plants and seeds.

FLIGHT: rapid, direct flight; can jump off water more easily than other diving ducks.

PREENING SCAUP
Ducks are meticulous preeners, and the Lesser Scaup is no exception.

SIMILAR SPECIES

RING-NECKED DUCK ♀ see p.56
prominent white eye-ring
solid dark back

GREATER SCAUP ♀ see p.422
more tawny brown upperparts
more white around bill

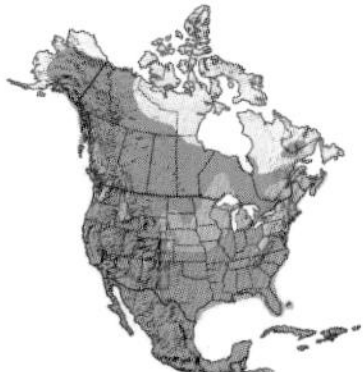

OCCURRENCE
Breeds inland from Alaska to eastern Canada in open northern forests and forested tundra. Winters in the Caribbean, southern US, and south to northern South America. Majority winter along coasts; others winter inland on lakes and reservoirs.

Length **15½–17½in (39–45cm)**	Wingspan **27–31in (68–78cm)**	Weight **1–2¾lb (0.45–1.2kg)**
Social **Flocks**	Lifespan **Up to 18 years**	Status **Secure**

DATE SEEN	WHERE	NOTES

Order **Anseriformes**	Family **Anatidae**	Species ***Histrionicus histrionicus***

Harlequin Duck

This small, hardy duck is a superbly skilful swimmer, diving to forage on the bottom of turbulent streams for its favorite insect prey. Despite the male's unmistakable plumage at close range, it looks very dark from a distance. With head and long tail held high, in winter it can be found among crashing waves, alongside larger and bigger-billed Surf and White-winged Scoters, who feed in the same habitat.

VOICE Male a high-pitched squeak earning it the nickname "sea mice"; female's call a raspy *ekekekekekek*.

NESTING Nests near water under vegetation or base of tree; also tree cavities; 3–9 eggs; 1 brood; April–September.

FEEDING Dives for insects and their larvae, and fish roe when breeding; in winter, eats mollusks, crustaceans, crabs, snails, fish roe, and barnacles.

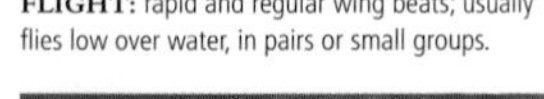

FLIGHT: rapid and regular wing beats; usually flies low over water, in pairs or small groups.

MALE GROUPS
After the breeding season, many males may gather and forage together.

PAIR IN FLIGHT
Note the crisp white markings on the slate-blue male in flight.

SIMILAR SPECIES

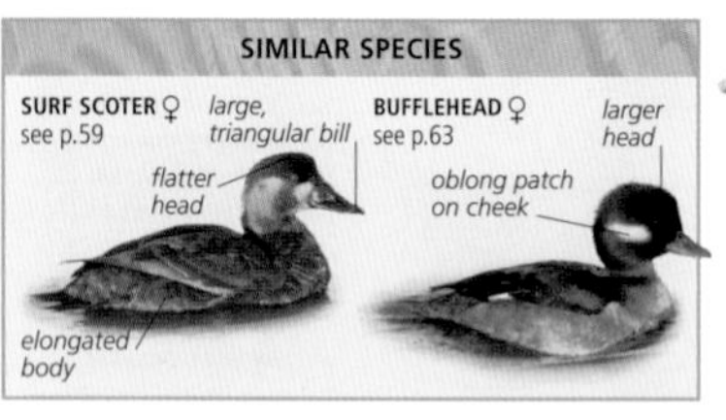

OCCURRENCE
Breeds near rushing coastal and mountain streams. During winter, found in small groups or mixed in with other sea ducks close to the shore, particularly along shallow rocky shorelines, jetties, rocky beaches, and headlands. Western populations are widespread, unlike Eastern ones. Also breeds in Iceland.

Length **13–21½in (33–54cm)**	Wingspan **22–26in (56–66cm)**	Weight **18–26oz (500–750g)**
Social **Small flocks**	Lifespan **Unknown**	Status **Secure**

DATE SEEN	WHERE	NOTES

Order **Anseriformes**	Family **Anatidae**	Species ***Melanitta perspicillata***

Surf Scoter

Surf Scoters, one of three species of scoters living in North America, migrate up and down both coasts, often with the other species. They take their name from the way they dive for mollusks on the sea floor, in shallow coastal waters, through heavy surf. Groups often dive and resurface in unison. Black and Surf Scoters can be difficult to tell apart as both have all-black wings. The underside of the Surf Scoter's wings are uniform black, whereas the Black Scoter has gray flight feathers, which contrast with the black underwing feathers.

VOICE Normally silent; courting male's variety of calls includes liquid gurgled *puk-puk*, bubbled whistles, and low croaks; female call a harsh *crahh,* reminiscent of a crow.

NESTING Ground nest lined with down and vegetation on brushy tundra, often under low branches of a conifer tree; 5–10 eggs; 1 brood; May–September.

FEEDING Dives for mollusks and other aquatic invertebrates.

FLIGHT: strong wing beats; flies in bunched up groups; male's wings hum or whistle in flight.

DISTINGUISHING FEATURES
The white forehead and bright orange bill, in addition to the red-orange legs and toes, identify male Surf Scoters.

SIMILAR SPECIES

GREATER SCAUP ♀ see p.422
no white patches on cheek; thinner bill

WHITE-WINGED SCOTER ♀ see p.60
long, sloping forehead; longer bill

OCCURRENCE
Nests on lake islands in forested regions of interior Alaska and northern Canada. Nonbreeders in summer and adults in winter are strictly coastal, with numbers decreasing from north to south along the Pacific coast. In the East, most overwinter in the mid-Atlantic coast region.

Length **19–23½in (48–60cm)**	Wingspan **30in (77cm)**	Weight **1¾–2¾lb (0.8–1.2kg)**
Social **Flocks/Pairs**	Lifespan **Unknown**	Status **Secure**

DATE SEEN	WHERE	NOTES

Order **Anseriformes**	Family **Anatidae**	Species ***Melanitta fusca***

White-winged Scoter

The White-winged Scoter is the largest of the three scoters. When visible, the white wing patch makes identification easy. Females are quite similar to immature male and female Surf Scoters and can be identified by head shape, extent of bill feathering, and shape of white areas on the face. When diving, this scoter leaps forward and up, arching its neck, and opens its wings when entering the water. Underwater, White-winged Scoters open their wings to propel and stabilize themselves.

VOICE Mostly silent; courting males emit a whistling note; female call a growly *karr*.

NESTING Depression lined with twigs and down in dense thickets, often far from water; 8–9 eggs; 1 brood; June–September.

FEEDING Dives for mollusks and crustaceans; sometimes eats fish and aquatic plants.

FLIGHT: direct with rapid wing beats; flies low over the water in small groups.

WHITE FLASH IN FLIGHT
Scoters often migrate or feed in mixed flocks. The white wing patches are striking in flight.

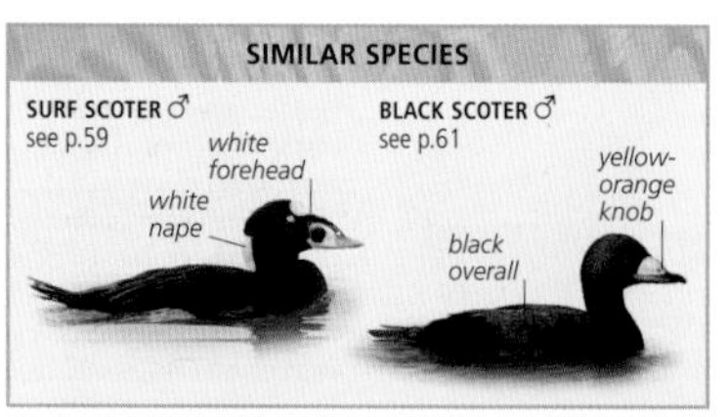

OCCURRENCE
Majority breed in dense colonies in interior Alaska and western Canada on large freshwater or brackish lakes or ponds, sometimes on saltwater lakes. Winters along both coasts, large bays, inlets, and estuaries. Rarely winters inland, except on the Great Lakes.

Length **19–23in (48–58cm)**	Wingspan **31in (80cm)**	Weight **2¾–4¾lb (0.9–1.9kg)**
Social **Flocks/Colonies**	Lifespan **Up to 18 years**	Status **Secure**

DATE SEEN	WHERE	NOTES

Order **Anseriformes**	Family **Anatidae**	Species ***Melanitta nigra***

Black Scoter

Black Scoters, the most vocal of the scoters, are medium-sized sea ducks that winter along both coasts of North America. Riding high on the waves, they form dense flocks, often segregated by gender. While swimming, the Black Scoter sometimes flaps its wings and while doing so drops its neck low down, unlike the other two scoters. This scoter breeds in two widely separated sub-Arctic breeding areas and is one of the least studied ducks in North America. The Eurasian subspecies, known as the Common Scoter, has much less orange on its bill with a smaller knob at the base.

VOICE Male call a high-whistled *peeew*; female a low raspy *kraaa*.

NESTING Depression lined with grass and down, often in tall grass on tundra; 5–10 eggs; 1 brood; May–September.

FEEDING Dives in saltwater for mollusks, crustaceans, and plant matter; feeds on aquatic insects and freshwater mussels.

FLIGHT: strong wing beats; male's wings make whistling sound during takeoff.

YELLOW BILL
Male Black Scoters are distinctive with their black plumage and yellow bill-knob.

OCCURRENCE
Breeding habitat is somewhat varied, but is generally close to fairly shallow, small lakes. Winters along both coasts. Populations wintering farther north prefer water over cobbles, gravel, or offshore ledges, whereas in southern locations, sandier habitats are chosen.

Length **17–21in (43–53cm)**	Wingspan **31–35in (79–90cm)**	Weight **1¾–2¾lb (0.8–1.2kg)**
Social **Flocks**	Lifespan **Unknown**	Status **Declining**

DATE SEEN	WHERE	NOTES

Order **Anseriformes**	Family **Anatidae**	Species ***Clangula hyemalis***

Long-tailed Duck

The Long-tailed Duck, which used to be called the Oldsquaw, is a small, compact sea duck. The male has two extremely long tail feathers, which are often held up in the air like a pennant. The male's loud calls are quite musical, and, when heard from a flock, have a chorus-like quality, hence the name *Clangula*, which is Latin for "loud." The Long-tailed Duck is capable of diving for a prolonged period of time, and can reach depths of 200ft (60m), making it one of the deepest diving ducks. Its three-part molt is more complex than that of other ducks.

VOICE Male call a *ang-ang-eeeooo* with yodelling quality; female barking *urk* or *uk* alarm call.

NESTING Shallow depression in ground lined with plant matter; 6–9 eggs; 1 brood; May–September.

FEEDING Dives to bottom of freshwater or saltwater habitats for mollusks, crustaceans, insects, fish, and roe.

FLIGHT: flies low over the water, somewhat erratically, with fast, fluttering wing beats.

UNMISTAKABLE MALE
In winter, dark wings, a white body with black breast-band, and a long tail make this male unmistakable.

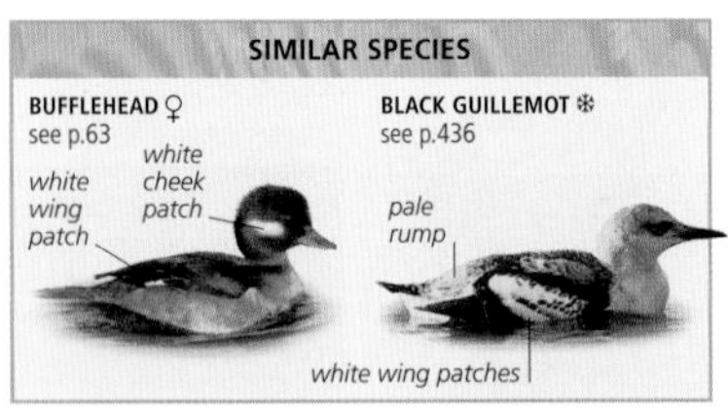

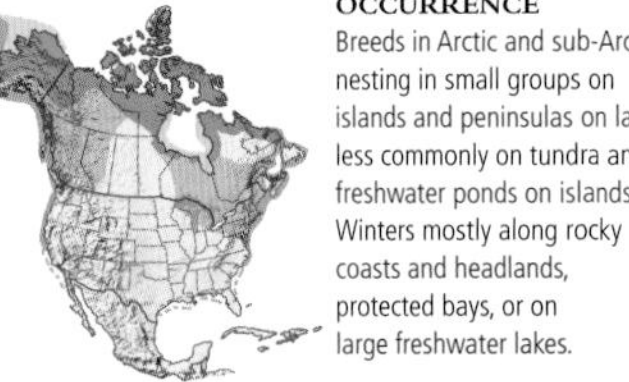

OCCURRENCE
Breeds in Arctic and sub-Arctic, nesting in small groups on islands and peninsulas on lakes, less commonly on tundra and freshwater ponds on islands. Winters mostly along rocky coasts and headlands, protected bays, or on large freshwater lakes.

Length **14–23in (35–58cm)**	Wingspan **28in (72cm)**	Weight **18–39oz (500–1,100g)**
Social **Flocks**	Lifespan **Up to 22 years**	Status **Secure**

DATE SEEN	WHERE	NOTES

Order **Anseriformes**	Family **Anatidae**	Species ***Bucephala albeola***

Bufflehead

The smallest diving duck in North America, the Bufflehead is a close relative of the Common and Barrow's Goldeneyes. Males make a bold statement with their striking head pattern. In flight, males resemble the larger Common Goldeneye, yet the large white area on their head makes them easy to distinguish. The Common Goldeneye's wings create a whirring sound in flight whereas the Bufflehead's do not. The northern limit of the Bufflehead's breeding range corresponds to that of the Northern Flicker, as the ducks usually nest in abandoned Flicker cavities.

VOICE Male a low growl or squeal; chattering during breeding; female mostly silent except during courtship or calling to chicks.

NESTING Cavity nester, no nesting material added, near water; 7–9 eggs; 1 brood; April–September.

FEEDING Dives for aquatic invertebrates: usually insects in freshwater, mollusks and crustaceans in saltwater; also eats seeds.

FLIGHT: very rapid wing beats; no flight sound, unlike Goldeneyes.

IMMEDIATE TAKE OFF
Unlike other diving ducks, the small, compact Bufflehead can take off almost vertically.

SIMILAR SPECIES

HOODED MERGANSER ♂ see p.66
smaller, with white cheek patch

RUDDY DUCK ♂❄ see p.69
dark cap
longer bill
larger size

OCCURRENCE
Breeds in forest from Alaska to eastern Canada, in woodlands near small lakes and permanent ponds, where young are raised. Winters largely along the Pacific and Atlantic Coasts with lower densities scattered across the continent, south to northern Mexico, and in Bermuda.

Length **12½–15½in (32–39cm)**	Wingspan **21½–24in (54–61cm)**	Weight **10–18oz (275–500g)**
Social **Flocks**	Lifespan **Up to 15 years**	Status **Secure**

DATE SEEN	WHERE	NOTES

Order **Anseriformes**	Family **Anatidae**	Species ***Bucephala clangula***

Common Goldeneye

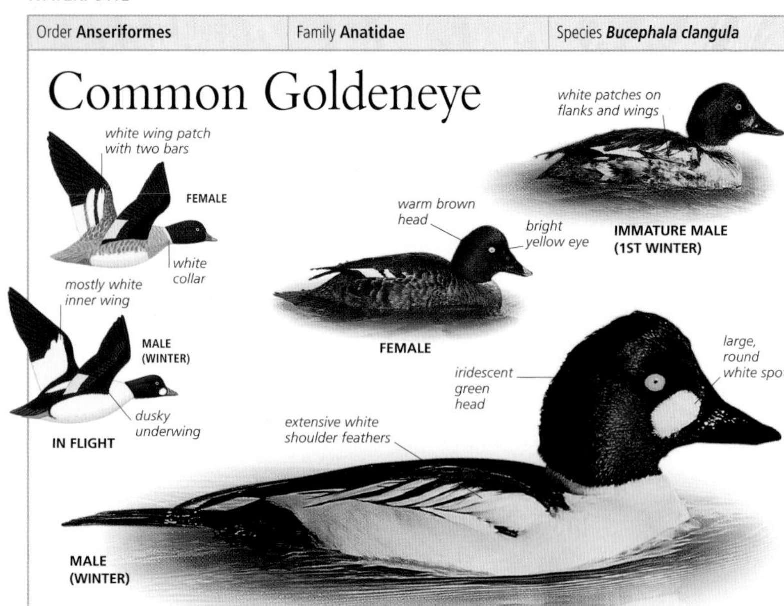

Common Goldeneyes closely resemble Barrow's Goldeneyes. Found in North America and Eurasia, this is a medium-sized, compact diving duck. It is aggressive and very competitive with members of its own species, as well as other cavity-nesting ducks. It regularly lays eggs in the nests of other species—a behavior that is almost parasitic. Before diving, the Common Goldeneye flattens its feathers in preparation for underwater foraging. The female's head shape changes according to her posture.

VOICE Courting males make a faint *peent* call; females a harsh *gack* or repeated *cuk* calls.

NESTING Cavity nester in holes made by other birds, including Pileated Woodpeckers, in broken branches or hollow trees; also commonly uses nest boxes; 4–13 eggs; 1 brood; April–September.

FEEDING Dives during breeding season for insects; in winter, mollusks and crustaceans; sometimes eats fish and plant matter.

FLIGHT: rapid with fast wing beats; male's wings make a tinkling sound in flight.

MALE TAKING OFF
Quite a long takeoff, involving energetically running on the water, leaves a trail of spray.

SIMILAR SPECIES

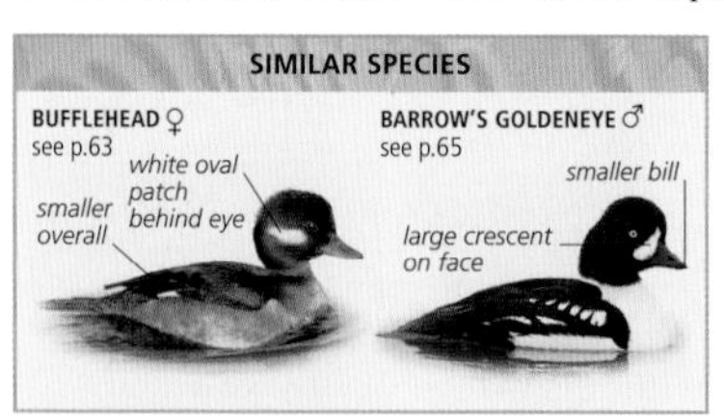

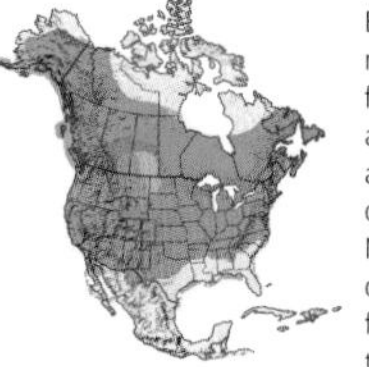

OCCURRENCE
Breeds along wetlands, lakes, and rivers with clear water in northern forests, where large trees provide appropriate nest cavities. Winters across continent, with highest densities located from north New England to the mid-Atlantic on coastal bays and in the West from coastal southeast Alaska to British Columbia.

Length **15½–20in (40–51cm)**	Wingspan **30–33in (77–83cm)**	Weight **19–44oz (550–1,300g)**
Social **Flocks**	Lifespan **Up to 15 years**	Status **Secure**

DATE SEEN	WHERE	NOTES

Order **Anseriformes**	Family **Anatidae**	Species ***Bucephala islandica***

Barrow's Goldeneye

Barrow's Goldeneye is a slightly larger, darker version of the Common Goldeneye. Although the female can be identified by her different head structure, her bill color varies seasonally and geographically. Eastern Barrow's have blacker bills with less yellow, and western populations have entirely yellow bills, which darken in summer. During the breeding season, the majority of Barrow's Goldeneyes are found in mountainous regions of northwestern North America.

VOICE Males normally silent; courting males grunt *ka-KAA*; females *cuc* call, slightly higher pitched than Common Goldeneye.

NESTING Tree cavity in holes formed by Pileated Woodpeckers, often broken limbs or hollow trees; also uses nest boxes; 6–12 eggs; 1 brood; April–September.

FEEDING Dives in summer for insects, some fish, and roe; in winter, mainly mollusks and crustaceans; some plant matter.

FLIGHT: rapid flight with fast, deep wing beats; flies near water surface on short flights.

COURTING DISPLAY
A male thrusts his head back and gives a guttural call. His feet then kick back, driving him forward.

SIMILAR SPECIES

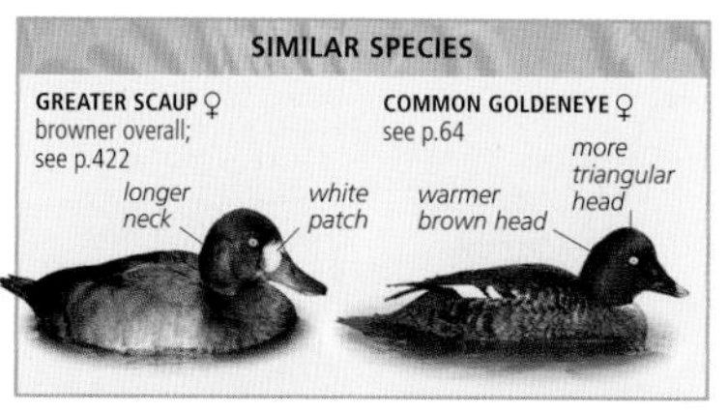

OCCURRENCE
Winters along the Pacific Coast between southeast Alaska and Washington, with small populations in eastern Canada. Smaller numbers found inland from the lower Colorado River to Yellowstone National Park. Eastern population is localized in winter with the highest count in St. Lawrence estuary.

Length **17–19in (43–48cm)**	Wingspan **28–30in (71–76cm)**	Weight **17–46oz (475–1,300g)**
Social **Flocks**	Lifespan **Up to 18 years**	Status **Secure**

DATE SEEN	WHERE	NOTES

Order **Anseriformes**	Family **Anatidae**	Species ***Lophodytes cucullatus***

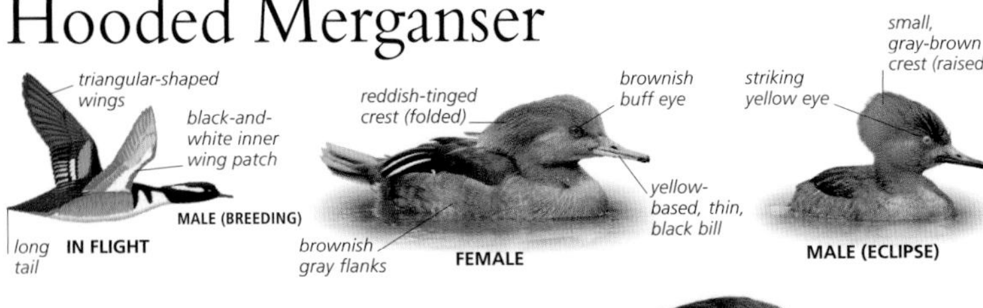

This dapper, miniature fish-eater is the smallest of the three mergansers. Both male and female Hooded Mergansers have crests that they can raise or flatten. When the male raises his crest, the thin horizontal white stripe turns into a gorgeous white fan, surrounded by black. Although easily identified when swimming, the Hooded Merganser and the Wood Duck can be confused when seen in flight since they both are fairly small with bushy heads and long tails.

VOICE Normally silent; during courtship, males produce a low, growly, descending *pah-hwaaaaa*, reminiscent of a frog; females give a soft *rrrep*.

NESTING Cavity nester; nest lined with down feathers in a tree or box close to or over water; 6–15 eggs; 1 brood; February–June.

FEEDING Dives for fish, aquatic insects, and crayfish, preferably in clear and shallow fresh waters, but also in brackish waters.

FLIGHT: low, fast, and direct; shallow wing beats; quiet whirring noise produced by wings.

FANHEAD SPECTACULAR
The male's magnificent black-and-white fan of a crest is like a beacon in the late afternoon light.

SIMILAR SPECIES

WOOD DUCK ♀ see p.45
bold, white eye-ring
blue wing patch

RED-BREASTED MERGANSER ♀ see p.68
rustier head with ragged crest
steel gray-and-white plumage

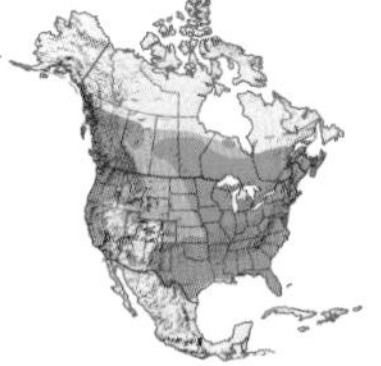

OCCURRENCE
Prefers forested small ponds, marshes, or slow-moving streams during the breeding season. During winter, occurs in shallow water in both fresh- and saltwater bays, estuaries, rivers, streams, ponds, freshwater marshes, and flooded sloughs.

Length **15½–19½in (40–49cm)**	Wingspan **23½–26in (60–66cm)**	Weight **16–31oz (450–875g)**
Social **Small flocks**	Lifespan **Unknown**	Status **Secure**

DATE SEEN	WHERE	NOTES

Order **Anseriformes**	Family **Anatidae**	Species ***Mergus merganser***

Common Merganser

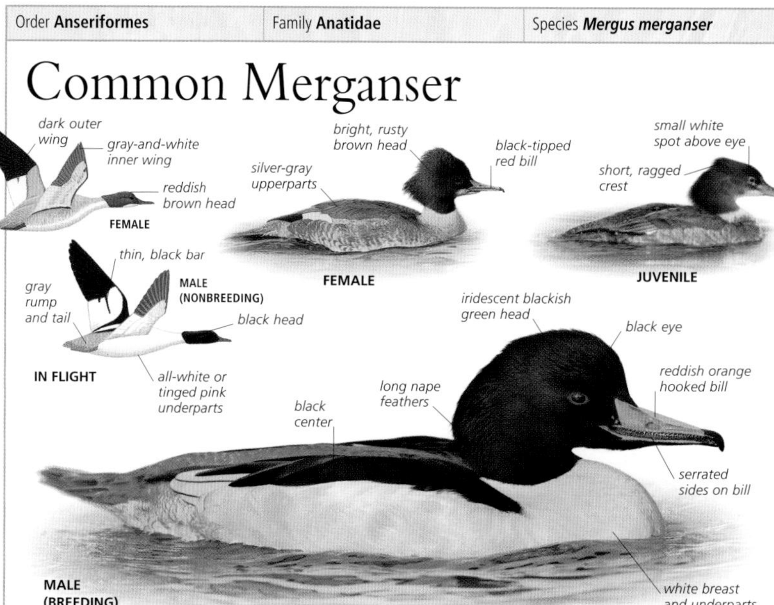

The largest of the three merganser species in North America, the Common Merganser is called a Goosander in the UK. This large fish-eater is common and widespread, particularly in the northern portion of its range. It is often found in big flocks on lakes or smaller groups along rivers. It spends most of its time on the water, using its serrated bill to catch fish underwater.

VOICE Mostly silent, except when alarmed or during courtship; females give a low-pitched harsh *karr* or *gruk*, the latter also given in series; during courtship, males emit a high-pitched, bell-like note and other twangy notes; alarm call a hoarse *grrr* or *wak*.

NESTING Cavity nester sometimes high in trees; uses nest boxes, nests on ground; 6–17 eggs; 1 brood; April–September.

FEEDING Eats mostly fish (especially fond of trout and salmon, but also carp and catfish), aquatic invertebrates, frogs, small mammals, birds, and plants.

FLIGHT: fast with shallow wing beats; often flying low over the water.

FEEDING ON THE MOVE
This female Common Merganser is trying to swallow, head-first, a rather large fish.

SIMILAR SPECIES

COMMON GOLDENEYE ♂ see p.64
white patch; black-and-white pattern

RED-BREASTED MERGANSER ♀ see p.68
smaller, more lightly built; thinner bill

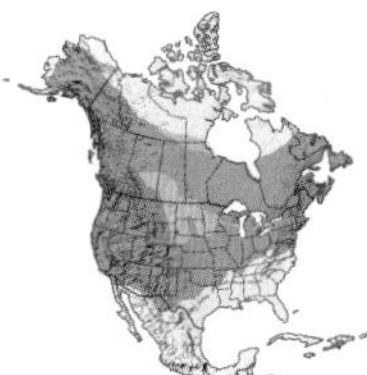

OCCURRENCE
Breeds in the northern forests from Alaska to Newfoundland; winters south to north central Mexico. It winters farther north than most other waterfowl as long as water remains open. Prefers fresh- to saltwater locations.

Length **21½–28in (54–71cm)**	Wingspan **34in (86cm)**	Weight **1¾–4¾lb (0.8–2.1kg)**
Social **Flocks**	Lifespan **Up to 13 years**	Status **Secure**

DATE SEEN	WHERE	NOTES

Order **Anseriformes**	Family **Anatidae**	Species ***Mergus serrator***

Red-breasted Merganser

The Red-breasted Merganser, like the other saw-billed mergansers, is an elegant fish-eating duck. Both sexes are easily recognized by their long, sparse, somewhat ragged-looking double crest. Red-breasted Mergansers are smaller than Common Mergansers, but much larger than the Hooded. The Red-breasted Merganser, unlike the other two mergansers, nests on the ground, in loose colonies, often among gulls and terns, and is protected by its neighbors.

VOICE During courtship males make a raucous *yeow-yeow* call; females emit a raspy *krrr-krrr.*

NESTING Shallow depression on ground lined with down and plant material, near water; 5–11 eggs; 1 brood; May–July.

FEEDING Dives for small fish such as herring and minnows; also salmon eggs; at times flocks coordinate and drive fish together.

FLIGHT: fast flying duck with very rapid, regular, and shallow flapping.

KEEPING CLOSE
Red-breasted Mergansers are gregarious at all times of year, often feeding in loose flocks.

SIMILAR SPECIES

OCCURRENCE
Most northern range of all the mergansers, nests across Arctic and sub-Arctic regions, tundra and northerly forests, along coasts, inland lakes, river banks, marsh edges, and coastal islands. Winters farther south than other mergansers, mostly in protected bays, estuaries, or on the Great Lakes.

Length **20–25in (51–64cm)**	Wingspan **26–29in (66–74cm)**	Weight **1¾–2¾lb (0.8–1.3kg)**
Social **Flocks/Colonies**	Lifespan **Up to 9 years**	Status **Secure**

DATE SEEN	WHERE	NOTES

Order **Anseriformes**	Family **Anatidae**	Species ***Oxyura jamaicensis***

Ruddy Duck

Small and stiff-tailed, the Ruddy Duck is comical in both its appearance and behavior. Both sexes often hold their tail in a cocked position, especially when sleeping. During courtship displays, the male points its long tail skyward while rapidly thumping its electric blue bill against its chest, ending the performance with an odd, bubbling sound. In another display, males make a popping sound by slapping their feet on the water's surface. Large feet, on legs set far back on its body, make the Ruddy Duck an excellent swimmer and diver; however, on land it is perhaps one of the most awkward of diving ducks. Females are known to push themselves along instead of walking.

VOICE Females give a nasal *raanh* and high pitched *eeek*; males vocally silent, but make popping noises with feet.

NESTING Platform, bowl-shaped nest built over water in thick emergent vegetation, rarely on land; 6–10 eggs; 1 brood; May–September.

FEEDING Dives for aquatic insects, larvae, crustaceans, and other invertebrates, particularly when breeding; during winter, also eats plants.

FLIGHT: rapid and direct, with fast wing beats; not very agile in flight, which seems labored.

HEAVY HEAD
A female "sitting" on the water streamlines her body before she dives, making her head look large.

SIMILAR SPECIES

OCCURRENCE
Breeds in the prairie pothole region in wetland habitats; marshes, ponds, reservoirs, and other open shallow water with emergent vegetation and open areas. Majority winter on freshwater habitats from ponds to large lakes; smaller numbers found on brackish coastal marshes, bays, and estuaries.

Length **14–17in (35–43cm)**	Wingspan **22–24in (56–62cm)**	Weight **11–30oz (300–850g)**
Social **Flocks**	Lifespan **Up to 13 years**	Status **Secure**

DATE SEEN	WHERE	NOTES

LOONS

WORLDWIDE THERE ARE ONLY five species of loon, comprising a single genus (*Gavia*), a single family (the Gaviidae), and a single order (the Gaviiformes). The five species are limited to the Northern Hemisphere, where they are found in both northern North America and northern Eurasia. One feature of loons is that their legs are positioned so far to the rear of their body that loons must shuffle on their bellies when they go from water to land. Not surprisingly, therefore, loons are almost entirely aquatic birds. In summer they are found on rivers, lakes, and ponds, where they nest close to the water's edge. After breeding, they occur along coasts, often after flying hundreds of miles away from their freshwater breeding grounds. Excellent swimmers and divers, loons are unusual among birds in that their bones are less hollow than those of other groups. Consequently, loons can expel air from their lungs and compress their body feathers until they slowly sink beneath the surface. They can remain submerged like this for several minutes. A loon's wings are relatively small in proportion to its body weight. This means that they have to run a long way across the surface of the water, flapping energetically, before they can become airborne. Once in the air they keep on flapping and can fly at up to 60mph (95kmh).

LOON RANGER
The Common Loon has a wider range than any other in North America, as its name suggests.

FLIGHT SHAPE
The humped back and drooping neck of this Red-throated Loon are typical of loons in flight.

PROVIDING FOR THE FUTURE
A Red-throated Loon gives a fish to its chick to gulp down headfirst and whole.

Order **Gaviiformes**	Family **Gaviidae**	Species ***Gavia stellata***

Red-throated Loon

Even when seen from a distance, this elegant loon is almost unmistakable, with a pale, slim body, upward tilted head, and a thin, upturned bill. Unlike other Loons, the Red-throated Loon can leap straight into the air from both land and water, although most of the time it needs a "runway." The Red-throated Loon has an elaborate breeding ritual—side by side, a pair of birds races upright across the surface of water. Downy chicks climb onto the parents back only when very young.

VOICE High gull-like or even cat-like wail and low goose-like growl; vocal on breeding grounds, otherwise silent.

NESTING Scrape with mud and vegetation added during incubation, placed at water's edge in coastal and lake bays, shallow ponds, often at high altitudes; 2 eggs; 1 brood; April–July.

FEEDING Mainly eats fish; also spiders, crustaceans, and mollusks; flies long distances from shallow ponds when food is scarce.

FLIGHT: very direct; fast, with constant wing beats; head held lower than other loons.

TAKING OFF
While this bird is using the water's surface to takeoff, it can leap directly into flight from water and land.

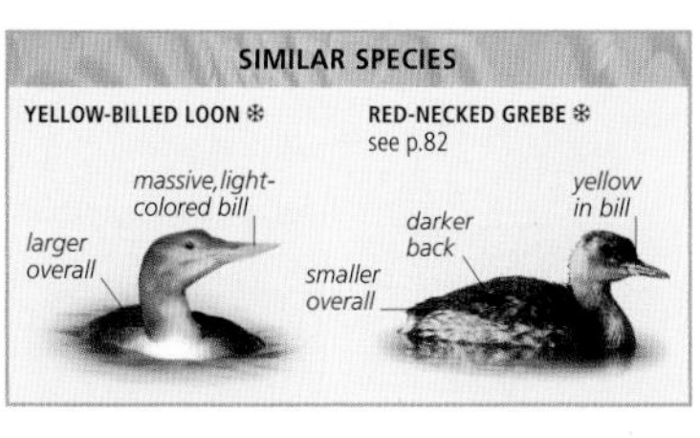

OCCURRENCE
Lives in open areas within northern boreal forest, muskeg, and tundra; in Canadian Arctic Archipelago, sometimes in areas almost devoid of vegetation. Winters on the Great Lakes, and both coasts southwards to Florida and northern Mexico.

Length **24–27in (61–69cm)**	Wingspan **3½ft (1.1m)**	Weight **3¼lb (1.5kg)**
Social **Solitary/Loose flocks**	Lifespan **Up to 23 years**	Status **Declining**

DATE SEEN	WHERE	NOTES

Order **Gaviiformes**	Family **Gaviidae**	Species ***Gavia pacifica***

Pacific Loon

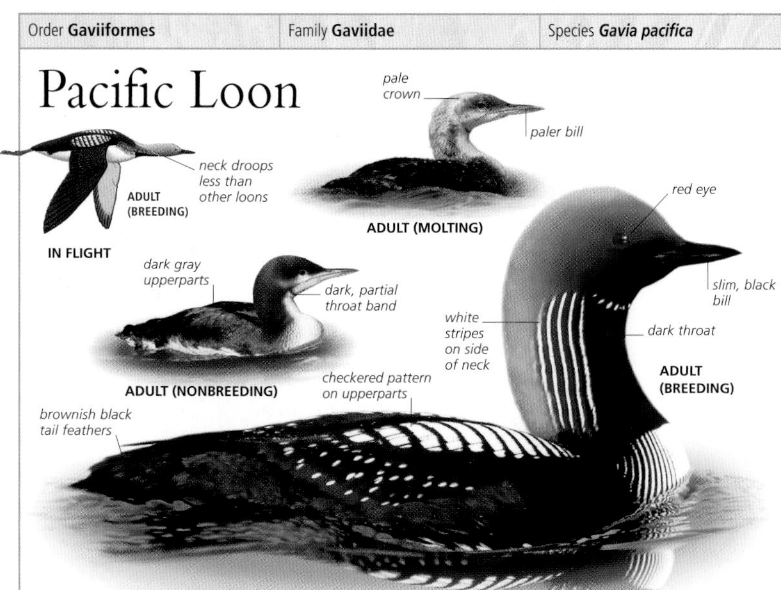

Although the Pacific Loon's breeding range is about a third of that of the Common Loon, it is believed to be the most abundant loon species in North America. It shares its habitat in northern Alaska with the nearly identical, but slightly larger and darker Arctic Loon. It is a conspicuous migrant along the Pacific Coast in spring, but disappears to its remote breeding grounds in summer. The Pacific Loon is an expert diver and swimmer, capable of remaining underwater for sustained periods of time, usually in pursuit of fish. However, on its terrestrial nesting site, its chicks are vulnerable to a number of mammalian predators.

VOICE Deep barking *kowk*; high-pitched wail, croaks, and growls when breeding; makes a yelping noise when diving.

NESTING Simple scrape in flat area close to water, vegetation and mud added during incubation; 1–2 eggs; June–July.

FEEDING Eats fish, aquatic insects, and mollusks in breeding lake or nearby waters; may dip or dive, depending on the depth.

FLIGHT: swift and direct with constant wing beats; humped back, but head in line with body.

LEVEL GROUND
As loons cannot takeoff from land, nest sites need to be on flat land close to the water.

SIMILAR SPECIES

ARCTIC LOON ☼ — darker nape; bolder black-and-white stripes on neck

ARCTIC LOON ❄ — heavier bill; brownish neck and head

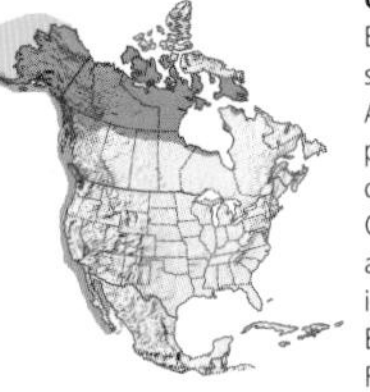

OCCURRENCE
Breeds across Arctic and sub-Arctic North America, from Alaska and northern Canadian provinces to Hudson Bay and on some of the islands of the Canadian Arctic; tundra lakes and muskeg. Small numbers in Great Lakes and along East coast from Québec to Florida. Vagrant elsewhere.

Length **23–29in (58–74cm)**	Wingspan **2¾–4¼ft (0.9–1.3m)**	Weight **2½–5½lb (1–2.5kg)**
Social **Flocks**	Lifespan **Up to 25 years**	Status **Secure**

DATE SEEN	WHERE	NOTES

Order **Gaviiformes**	Family **Gaviidae**	Species ***Gavia immer***

Common Loon

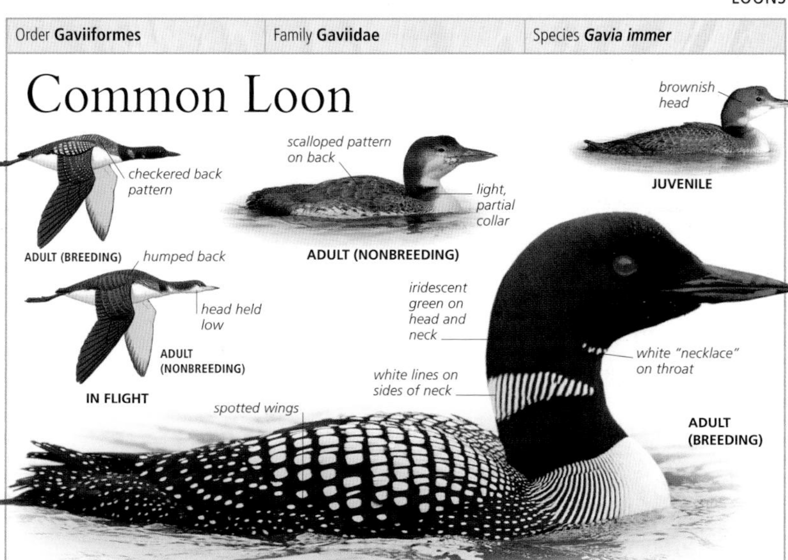

The Common Loon has the largest range of all loons in North America and is the only species to nest in a few of the northern states. It is slightly smaller than the Yellow-billed Loon but larger than the other three loons. It can remain underwater for well over 10 minutes, although it usually stays submerged for 40 seconds to 2 minutes while fishing, or a few more minutes if it is being pursued. Evidence shows that, occasionally, it interbreeds with its closest relative, the Yellow-billed Loon, in addition to the Arctic and Pacific Loons.

VOICE Most recognized call a 3–10 note falsetto yodel, rising, then fading; other calls similar in quality.

NESTING Simple scrape in large mound of vegetation, a few feet from open water; 2 eggs; 1 brood; April–June.

FEEDING Feeds primarily on fish underwater; also eats crustaceans, mollusks, amphibians, leeches, insects, and aquatic plants.

FLIGHT: fast, direct, with constant wing beats; head and neck held just above belly.

COZY RIDE
Downy Common Loon chicks climb up the backs of male and female adults for a safe ride.

BATHING RITUAL
Common Loons often shake their wings after bathing.

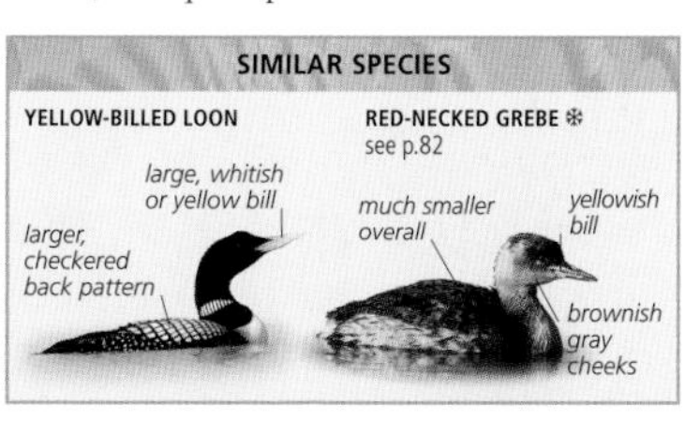

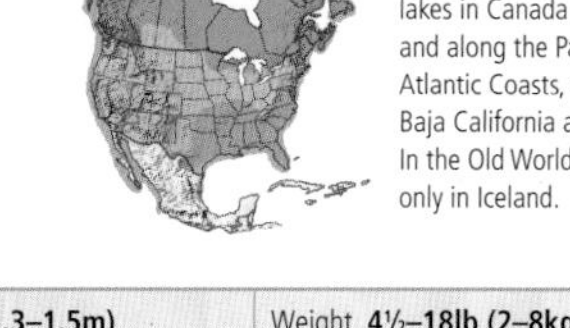

OCCURRENCE
Breeds across North America, Canada, and south to northern US. Winters on large ice-free lakes in Canada and the US, and along the Pacific and Atlantic Coasts, south to Baja California and Florida. In the Old World breeds only in Iceland.

Length **26–36in (66–91cm)**	Wingspan **4¼–5ft (1.3–1.5m)**	Weight **4½–18lb (2–8kg)**
Social **Family groups**	Lifespan **Up to 30 years**	Status **Vulnerable**

DATE SEEN	WHERE	NOTES

TUBENOSES

THE NAME "TUBENOSES" IS GIVEN to several families of seabirds with tubular nostrils, which help get rid of excess salt and may enhance their sense of smell. Tubenoses are all members of the order Procellariiformes.

FLAP AND GLIDE
Shearwaters alternate stiff-winged flapping with bouts of gliding over the ocean's surface, or in strong winds, glide in wide arcs, high over the waves.

ALBATROSSES

The long, narrow wings of albatrosses (family Diomedeidae) are perfectly suited for tackling the strong, constant winds that prevail on the southern oceans that form their main habitat. While they are expert gliders, albatrosses cannot take off from the ground without sufficient wing to give them lift.

SHEARWATERS

Shearwaters and gadfly petrels (family Procellariidae) are smaller than albatrosses. Like their larger relatives they are excellent gliders, but their lighter weight and proportionately shorter wings mean that they use more powered flight than albatrosses. They range over all the world's oceans. With its numerous islands, the Pacific Ocean is home to a greater variety of shearwaters than the Atlantic. During and after storms are the best times to look for these birds from the shore, because this is when they drift away from the deep sea due to wind and waves.

STORM-PETRELS

The smallest tubenoses in North American waters, the storm-petrels (family Hydrobatidae) are also the most agile fliers. They often patter or "dance" as they fly just above the surface of the ocean in search of small fish, squid, and crustaceans. Storm-petrels spend most of their lives flying over the open sea, only visiting land in the breeding season, when they form colonies. The apparent fragility and small size of storm-petrels is belied by their ability to live as far away from land as their larger relatives, the albatrosses and shearwaters. Storm-petrels are nocturnal at their breeding colonies and nest under the ground, in burrows, or under rocks, two traits that reduce the chance of predation.

HOOKED BILL
All tubenoses have hooked bills in addition to their tubular nostrils.

STRONG PAIR BOND
After elaborate courtship displays, albatrosses generally pair for life. The rituals are simpler in later years.

Order **Procellariiformes**	Family **Procellariidae**	Species ***Fulmarus glacialis***

Northern Fulmar

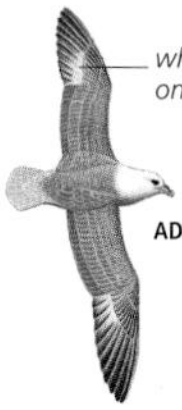

white patch on wing

ADULT

IN FLIGHT

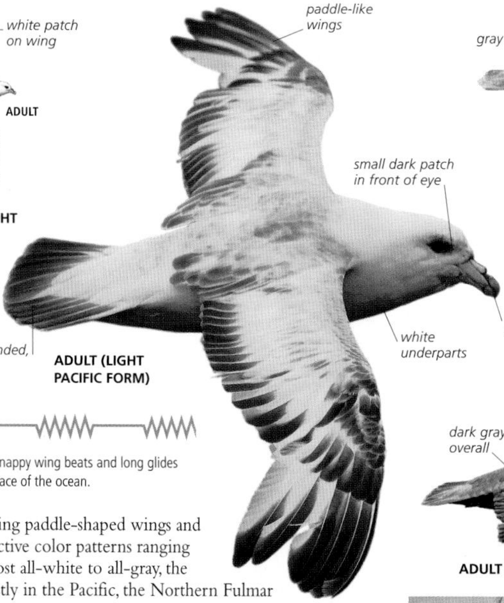

paddle-like wings

small dark patch in front of eye

thick, yellow bill

white underparts

short, rounded, gray tail

ADULT (LIGHT PACIFIC FORM)

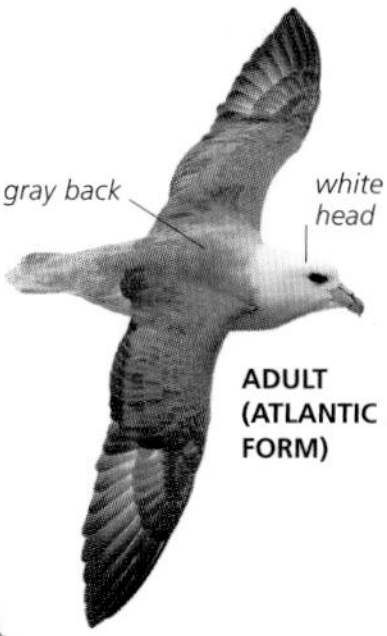

gray back

white head

ADULT (ATLANTIC FORM)

dark gray overall

ADULT (DARK PACIFIC FORM)

FLIGHT: snappy wing beats and long glides near the surface of the ocean.

Possessing paddle-shaped wings and distinctive color patterns ranging from almost all-white to all-gray, the latter mostly in the Pacific, the Northern Fulmar is among the most common seabirds in places like the Bering Sea. It breeds at high latitudes, then disperses south to offshore waters along both coasts of the continent. It can regularly be seen in large mixed flocks containing albatrosses, shearwaters, and small petrels. Fulmars often follow boats, eager to pounce on the offal thrown overboard by fishermen.

VOICE Mostly silent at sea; occasionally utters cackles and grunts.

NESTING Scrape in rock or soil on edge of cliff; 1 egg; 1 brood; May–October.

FEEDING Picks fish and offal from the surface of the ocean; also dives underwater to catch fish.

FEEDING FRENZY
Large numbers of Northern Fulmars compete for the offal discarded by fishing trawlers.

SIMILAR SPECIES

SOOTY SHEARWATER
see p.76
more slender wings
dark bill
dark overall

GREATER SHEARWATER
more slender wings
dark cap
white collar

OCCURRENCE
Breeds on remote, high, coastal cliffs in Alaska and northern Canada; winters at sea in offshore Pacific and Atlantic waters, farther north than most other seabirds. Breeds in Europe, northward to Greenland, Svalbard; also parts of Russia.

Length **17½–19½in (45–50cm)**	Wingspan **3¼–3½ft (1–1.1m)**	Weight **16–35oz (0.45–1kg)**
Social **Flocks**	Lifespan **Up to 50 years**	Status **Secure**

DATE SEEN	WHERE	NOTES

Order **Procellariiformes**	Family **Procellariidae**	Species ***Puffinus griseus***

Sooty Shearwater

FLIGHT: rapid, stiff wing beats, interspersed with glides; arcs up highly in strong winds.

Sooty Shearwaters are extremely long-distance migrants, with both Atlantic and Pacific populations undergoing lengthy circular migrations. Pacific birds in particular travel as far as 300 miles (480km) per day and an extraordinary 45,000 miles (72,500km) or more per year. Huge flocks of this species are often seen off the coast of California. It is fairly easy to identify off the East Coast of the US, as it is the only all-dark shearwater found there.

VOICE Silent at sea; occasionally gives varied, agitated vocalizations when feeding, very loud calls at breeding colonies.

NESTING In burrow or rocky crevice; 1 egg; 1 brood; October–May.

FEEDING Dives and picks at surface for small schooling fish and mollusks such as squid.

HUGE FLOCKS
Sooty Shearwaters are often found in "rafts" numbering many thousands of birds.

TUBENOSE
Shearwaters are tubenoses, so-called for the salt-excreting tubes on their bills.

SIMILAR SPECIES

SHORT-TAILED SHEARWATER see p.77
dark upperparts; dark cap; shorter bill; pale throat

GREATER SHEARWATER
white tail band; white collar

OCCURRENCE
Sooty Shearwaters breed on islands in the southern ocean and nearby waters, some colonies number thousands of pairs. Postbreeding movements take them north into the Pacific and Atlantic Ocean, on 8-shaped migrations.

Length **18in (46cm)**	Wingspan **3ft 3in (1m)**	Weight **27oz (775g)**
Social **Flocks**	Lifespan **Unknown**	Status **Secure**

DATE SEEN	WHERE	NOTES

Order **Procellariiformes**	Family **Procellariidae**	Species ***Puffinus tenuirostris***

Short-tailed Shearwater

Short-tailed Shearwaters are abundant off the Alaskan coast in the summer, where they have been seen in gigantic groups numbering perhaps in the millions. The total world population may be about 50 million. The Short-tailed Shearwater spends most of its life at sea, and its migration route follows a huge figure 8 around the North Pacific. Field identification is difficult, as they look very similar to Sooty Shearwaters. However, the Short-tailed Shearwater has some distinguishing features. It is more compact overall, with a rounder crown, shorter bill, a dark head contrasting with a paler throat and breast, and more uniform underwings, that may include a pale part extending onto the outer wing feathers.

VOICE Silent at sea; varied, agitated vocalizations when feeding.

NESTING Burrow dug in peat; 1 egg; 1 brood; September–April.

FEEDING Dives and picks at surface for small schooling fish, squid, octopus, and crustaceans.

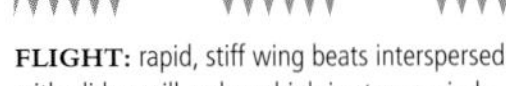

FLIGHT: rapid, stiff wing beats interspersed with glides; will arch up high in strong winds.

DARK BIRD
A rounded head, short bill, pale throat, and dark underwings identify this bird.

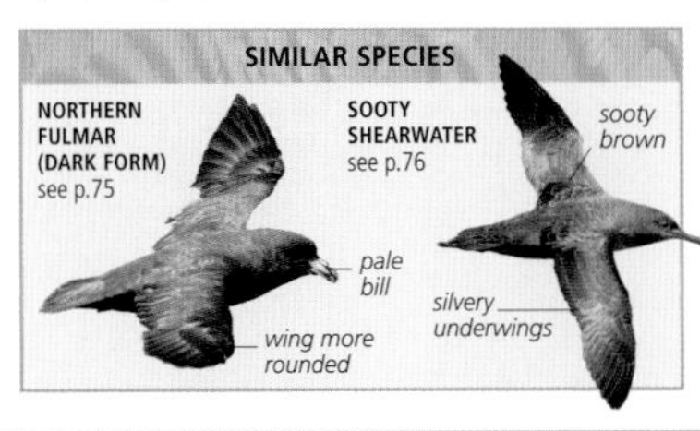

OCCURRENCE
Breeds on islands off eastern Australia from New South Wales to Tasmania; migrates north to spend its winter (US summer) in the Gulf of Alaska and the Bering Sea, where it is common; during spring migration (US fall and early winter) it passes along the West Coast of North America.

Length **17in (43cm)**	Wingspan **3ft 3in (1m)**	Weight **19oz (550g)**
Social **Large flocks**	Lifespan **Unknown**	Status **Secure**

DATE SEEN	WHERE	NOTES

Order **Procellariiformes**	Family **Hydrobatidae**	Species ***Oceanodroma leucorhoa***

Leach's Storm-Petrel

long, angled wings

ADULT

IN FLIGHT

white rump with thin, dark line down center

ADULT

brown bar across blackish wings

dark sooty black underwings

dark smudge beside eye

forked tail

dark sooty brown underparts

ADULT

FLIGHT: buoyant, deep wing beats low over ocean's surface, interrupted by twists and turns.

Leach's Storm-Petrel is widespread in both the Atlantic and Pacific Oceans, unlike most other storm-petrels. It breeds in colonies on islands off the coasts, coming to land at night and feeding offshore during the day, often many miles from the colony. This wide-ranging storm-petrel has both geographical and individual variation; most populations show a white rump, but others have a dark rump that is the same color as the rest of the body. Leach's Storm-Petrel can be distinguished from the similar Band-rumped Storm-Petrel by its notched tail and swooping flight.

VOICE At nesting sites, often from burrows, calls are long series of soft purring and chattering sounds.

NESTING Underground burrow on island free of predators such as rats; 1 egg; 1 brood; May–November.

FEEDING Gleans small crustaceans and small fish from the water's surface while in flight.

BALANCING ACT
Leach's Storm-Petrels will occasionally balance themselves with their toes while foraging.

SIMILAR SPECIES

BAND-RUMPED STORM-PETREL
white of rump extends toward belly

BLACK STORM-PETREL see p.424
dark rump

OCCURRENCE
Breeds on islands in the Pacific Ocean from Alaska and the Aleutian Islands south to California; in the Atlantic Ocean, from Newfoundland to Maine. After breeding, it wanders widely on both oceans, keeping well out of sight of land.

Length **7–8½in (18–22cm)**	Wingspan **17½–19in (45–48cm)**	Weight **1⁹⁄₁₆–1¾oz (45–50g)**
Social **Colonies**	Lifespan **Up to 36 years**	Status **Secure**

DATE SEEN	WHERE	NOTES

Order **Procellariiformes**	Family **Hydrobatidae**	Species ***Oceanodroma furcata***

Fork-tailed Storm-Petrel

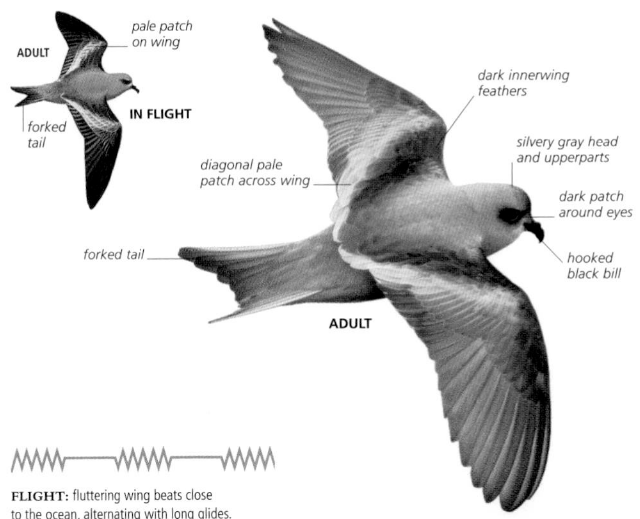

FLIGHT: fluttering wing beats close to the ocean, alternating with long glides.

The Fork-tailed Storm-Petrel is one of the most distinctive of all storm-petrels in North American waters, with its ghostly silvery gray plumage, and forked tail. It is the most northerly breeding storm-petrel in the North Pacific, nesting all the way north to the Aleutian Islands. It incubates its eggs at lower temperatures than other petrels do, and its chicks can be left alone between feeding for a longer time—apparently an adaptation to northern conditions. Its chicks can also lower their body temperature, thereby conserving energy.

VOICE Silent at sea; various purring sounds at colonies.

NESTING Underground burrow on offshore island; 1 egg; 1 brood; March–November.

FEEDING Plucks shrimps, squids, and small fish from the surface of the ocean.

AERIAL SURVEY
Flying low over the ocean, the Fork-tailed Storm-Petrel looks out for fish below.

SIMILAR SPECIES

LEACH'S STORM-PETREL see p.78
dark brown overall
white rump patch

ASHY STORM-PETREL see p.424
slightly smaller
brown overall

OCCURRENCE
Breeds in colonies on offshore rocky islands from California northward to Alaska, mostly to the Aleutian Islands, and south to islands off British Columbia; also Washington and Oregon. Post-breeding dispersal takes birds to the Bering Sea and to offshore waters of California.

Length **8in (20cm)**	Wingspan **18in (46cm)**	Weight **2oz (55g)**
Social **Colonies**	Lifespan **At least 14 years**	Status **Secure**

DATE SEEN	WHERE	NOTES

GREBES

GREBES RESEMBLE LOONS and share many of their aquatic habits, but anatomical and molecular features show that they are actually unrelated. They are placed in a different order: the Podicipediformes. Grebes have streamlined bodies, which offer little resistance when diving and swimming. Underwater their primary means of propulsion is the sideways motion of their lobed toes. The legs are placed far back on a grebe's body, which greatly aids the bird when it swims above or below the surface. Grebes have short tails, and their trailing legs and toes serve as rudders when they fly. The position of the legs makes it impossible, however, for grebes to stand upright for long or easily walk on land. This means that grebes are tied to water even when breeding; and their nests are usually partially floating platforms, built on beds of water plants. Grebes' toes have broad lobes that splay when the bird thrusts forward through the water with its feet. Grebes dive to catch fish with a short, forward arching spring. Unusually among birds, they swallow feathers, apparently to trap fish bones and protect their stomachs, then periodically disgorge them. Like loons, grebes can control their buoyancy by exhaling air and compressing their plumage so that they sink quietly below the surface. They are strong fliers and migratory.

PIED BILL
The black-and-white bill pattern clearly distinguishes this bird as the Pied-billed Grebe.

A FINE DISPLAY
This Horned Grebe reveals the colorful plumes on its head as part of its elaborate courtship display.

SIDE BY SIDE
This pair of Western Grebes is displaying their elaborate courtship behavior.

Order **Podicipediformes**	Family **Podicipedidae**	Species ***Podilymbus podiceps***

Pied-billed Grebe

The widest ranging of the North American grebes, the Pied-billed Grebe is tolerant of highly populated areas and is often seen breeding on lakes and ponds across North America. It is a powerful swimmer and can remain submerged for 16–30 seconds when it dives. In contrast to some of the elaborate displays from other grebe species, its courtship ritual is more vocal than visual and a pair usually duet-call in the mating season. Migration, conducted at night, is delayed until its breeding area ices up and food becomes scarce. The Pied-billed Grebe is capable of sustained flights of over 2,000 miles (3,200km).

VOICE Various grunts and wails; in spring, call a cuckoo-like repeated gobble *kup-kup-Kaow-Kaow-kaow*, gradually speeding up.

NESTING Floating nest of partially decayed plants and clipped leaves, attached to emergent vegetation in marshes and quiet waters; 4–7 eggs; 2 broods; April–October.

FEEDING Dives to catch a variety of crustaceans, fish, amphibians, insects, and other invertebrates; also picks prey from emergent vegetation, or catches them mid-air.

FLIGHT: strong, direct flight with rapid wing beats, but rarely seen.

BACK OFF
When alarmed, a Pied-billed Grebe may flap its wings in a defensive display.

SIMILAR SPECIES

OCCURRENCE
Breeds on a variety of water bodies, including coastal brackish ponds, seasonal ponds, marshes, and even sewage ponds. Winters in the breeding area if food and open water are available, otherwise chooses still waters resembling its breeding habitat.

Length **12–15in (31–38cm)**	Wingspan **18–24in (46–62cm)**	Weight **13–17oz (375–475g)**
Social **Family groups**	Lifespan **At least 3 years**	Status **Vulnerable**

DATE SEEN	WHERE	NOTES

Order **Podicipediformes**	Family **Podicipedidae**	Species ***Podiceps grisegena***

Red-necked Grebe

The Red-necked Grebe is smaller than Western and Clark's Grebes, but larger than the other North American grebes. It migrates over short to medium distances and spends the winter along both coasts, where large flocks may be seen during the day. It runs along the water's surface to become airborne, although it rarely flies. This grebe doesn't come ashore often; it stands erect, but walks awkwardly, and prefers to sink to its breast and shuffle along.

VOICE Nasal, gull-like call on breeding grounds, evolves into bray, ends with whinny; also honks, rattles, hisses, purrs, and ticks.

NESTING Compact, buoyant mound of decayed and fresh vegetation in sheltered, shallow marshes and lakes, or artificial wetlands; 4–5 eggs; 1 brood; May–July.

FEEDING An opportunistic hunter, eats fish, crustaceans, aquatic insects, worms, mollusks, salamanders, and tadpoles.

FLIGHT: fast, direct, wing beats, with head and outstretched neck mostly level with line of body.

COURTSHIP DISPLAY
This courting pair face each other, with outstretched necks and raised neck feathers.

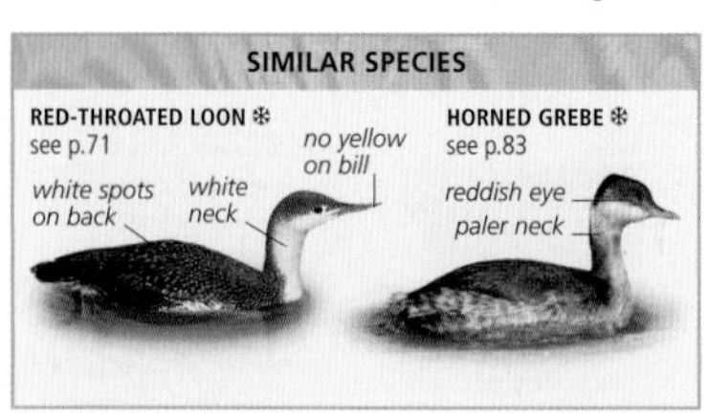

OCCURRENCE
Breeds from northern prairies and forests, almost to the tree line in the northwest; limited to suitable interior bodies of water such as large marshes and small lakes. Winters primarily in estuaries, inlets, bays, and offshore shallows along Atlantic and Pacific Coasts; can also be found on the Great Lakes.

Length **16½–22in (42–56cm)**	Wingspan **24–35in (61–88cm)**	Weight **1¾–3½lb (0.8–1.6kg)**
Social **Pairs/Loose flocks**	Lifespan **Up to 6 years**	Status **Vulnerable**

DATE SEEN	WHERE	NOTES

Order **Podicipediformes**	Family **Podicipedidae**	Species ***Podiceps auritus***

Horned Grebe

The timing of the Horned Grebe's migration depends largely on the weather—this species may not leave until its breeding grounds get iced over, nor does it arrive before the ice melts. Its breeding behavior is well documented since it is approachable on nesting grounds and has an elaborate breeding ritual. This grebe's so-called "horns" are in fact yellowish feather patches located behind its eyes, which it can raise at will.

VOICE At least 10 calls, but descending *aaanrrh* call most common in winter, ends in trill; muted conversational calls when birds are in groups.

NESTING Floating, soggy nest, hidden in vegetation, in small ponds and lake inlets; 3–9 eggs; 1 brood; May–July.

FEEDING Dives in open water or forages among plants, mainly for small crustaceans and insects, but also leeches, mollusks, amphibians, fish, and some vegetation.

FLIGHT: strong, rapid wing beats; runs on water to become airborne; rarely takes off from land.

HITCHING A RIDE
In common with other grebes, Horned Grebe chicks often ride on the back of a swimming parent.

SIMILAR SPECIES

OCCURRENCE
Breeds in small freshwater, even slightly brackish, ponds and marshes, including man-made ponds. Prefers areas with open water and patches of sedges, cattails, and other wetland vegetation. Winters on saltwater close to shore; also on large bodies of freshwater.

Length **12–15in (30–38cm)**	Wingspan **18–24in (46–62cm)**	Weight **11–20oz (300–575g)**
Social **Pairs/Loose flocks/Colonies**	Lifespan **Up to 5 years**	Status **Declining**

DATE SEEN	WHERE	NOTES

Order **Podicipediformes**	Family **Podicipedidae**	Species ***Podiceps nigricollis***

Eared Grebe

The most abundant grebe in North America, the Eared Grebe is quite remarkable in terms of physiology. After breeding, it undergoes a complex and drastic reorganization of body-fat stores, along with changes in muscle, heart, and digestive organ mass to prepare it for fall migration. All of this increases the bird's energy reserves and body mass, but renders it flightless. It may have the longest periods of flightlessness of any flying bird—up to 10 months.

VOICE Various trills during courtship, including squeaky, rising *poo-eep*; sharp *chirp* when alarmed; usually silent at other times.

NESTING Sodden nest of decayed bottom plants anchored in thinly spaced reeds or submerged vegetation in shallow water of marshes, ponds, and lakes; 1 brood; 1–8 eggs; May–July.

FEEDING Forages underwater for small crustaceans and aquatic insects; also small fish and mollusks; consumes worms in winter.

FLIGHT: flies with neck outstretched, held at a low angle; rarely flies except during migration.

SALTY WATER
The Eared Grebe prefers salty water at all times except when breeding.

SIMILAR SPECIES

RED-NECKED GREBE ❄ see p.82 — browner cap; thicker bill

HORNED GREBE ❄ see p.83 — white tip on bill; more distinct white cheek

OCCURRENCE
Breeds in marshes, shallow lakes, and ponds. After breeding, many birds seek saline waters, such as Mono Lake, or lakes in Utah where their favorite foods thrive—brine shrimp and alkali flies. Winters in coastal bays of Pacific coast and is a vagrant on Atlantic coast. Also breeds in Eurasia.

Length **12–14in (30–35cm)**	Wingspan **22½–24in (57–62cm)**	Weight **7–26oz (200–725g)**
Social **Flocks**	Lifespan **Up to 12 years**	Status **Secure**

DATE SEEN	WHERE	NOTES

Order **Podicipediformes**	Family **Podicepedidae**	Species ***Aechmophorus occidentalis***

Western Grebe

Western and Clark's Grebes are strictly North American species. They share much of their breeding habitat and elaborate mating rituals, and were, until 1985, classified as different color forms of a single species. Interbreeding is uncommon, perhaps because of slight differences in calls, bill colors, and facial patterns. Although hybrids are rare, they appear to be fertile, and produce chicks of their own. Female Western Grebes are smaller than males and have smaller, thinner, slightly upturned bills. The Western Grebe dives more frequently than Clark's, and remains submerged for about 30 seconds.

VOICE Nine calls, each with a specific purpose, such as alarm, begging, and mating calls; advertising call a harsh, rolling two-noted *krrrikk krrreek*.

NESTING Floating pile of available plants, attached to thick growth of submerged vegetation; occasionally constructed on land; 2–3 eggs; 1 brood; May–July.

FEEDING Mainly catches a wide variety of freshwater or saltwater fish; also crustaceans, worms, occasionally insects.

FLIGHT: fast and direct with rapid wing beats; neck extended with feet stretched out behind.

SELF-DEFENSE
The posture of this Western Grebe shows it is ready to defend itself when threatened.

SIMILAR SPECIES

HIGHLY SOCIAL
Western Grebes, much like Clark's Grebes, are highly gregarious in all seasons.

OCCURRENCE
Western North America, breeds from southern Canada to Mexico, in freshwater lakes and marshes with open water and emergent vegetation; rarely on tidewater marshes; also man-made marshes and artificial habitats. Winters along Pacific Coast, in bays and estuaries in the southwest US and Mexico.

Length **21½–30in (55–75cm)**	Wingspan **30–39in (76–100cm)**	Weight **1¾–4lb (0.8–1.8kg)**
Social **Flocks**	Lifespan **At least 15 years**	Status **Declining**

DATE SEEN	WHERE	NOTES

Order **Podicipediformes**	Family **Podicipedidae**	Species ***Aechmophorus clarkii***

Clark's Grebe

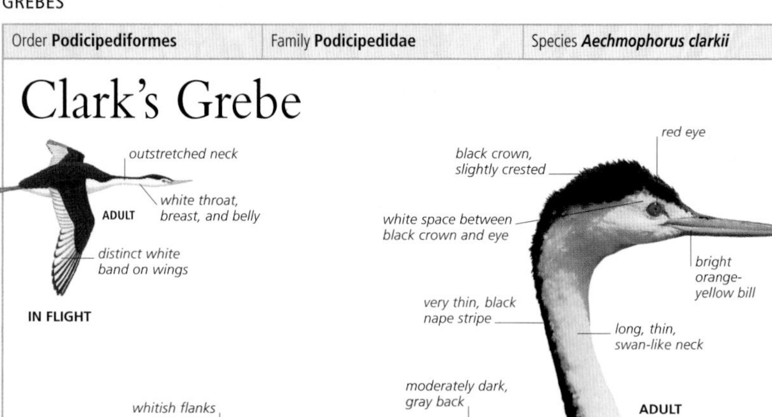

Clark's and Western grebes are closely related and very difficult to distinguish. They rarely fly except when migrating at night. Both species seldom come to land, where their movement is awkward because their legs and toes are located so far back, although they have been reported to run upright rapidly. Their flight muscles suffer wastage after their arrival on the breeding grounds, which also inhibits their ability to travel, but during the incubation period adults may feed several miles from the colony by following continuous water trails.

VOICE Variety of different calls, including a harsh, reedy, grating, 2-syllable, single, rising *kree-eekt* advertising call.

NESTING Floating pile of available plants, attached to thick growth of submerged vegetation; occasionally constructed on land; 2–3 eggs; 1 brood; May–July.

FEEDING Mainly catches saltwater or freshwater fish; also crustaceans.

FLIGHT: swift and direct with quick wing beats; neck extended with feet trailing.

HOW TO SWALLOW?
It is not unusual for grebes to catch large fish; they crush the head first before swallowing.

FORAGING IN DEEP WATER
Clark's Grebe has a distinctive white S-shaped neck and black crown.

SIMILAR SPECIES

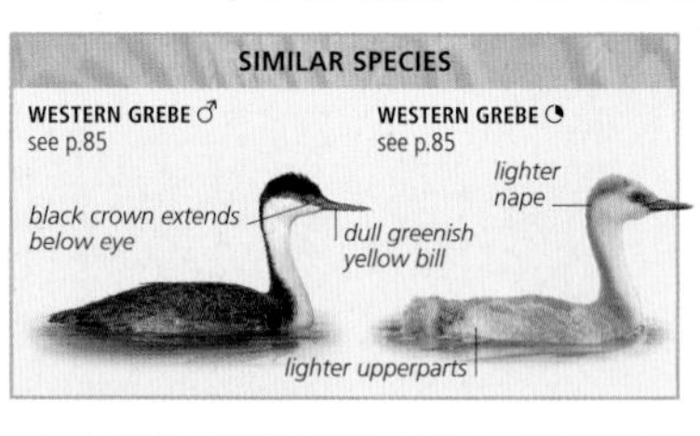

OCCURRENCE
Breeds in freshwater lakes and marshes with open water bordered by emergent vegetation; rarely tidewater marshes; has been nesting in man-made Lake Havasu marshes since 1960s. Winters along Pacific Coast, and in bays and estuaries in the southwest US and Mexico.

Length **21½–30in (55–75cm)**	Wingspan **32in (82cm)**	Weight **1½–3¾lb (0.7–1.7kg)**
Social **Flocks**	Lifespan **At least 15 years**	Status **Declining**

DATE SEEN	WHERE	NOTES

STORKS, IBISES, & HERONS

THESE ARE LARGE water and wetland birds that have long legs and look rather similar, but have different habits. They eat fish and other aquatic prey as well as plants. Most breed in colonies.

IBISES

Birds of the marshlands or of dry land, ibises (Threskiornithidae) are characterized by rounded bodies, long legs, short tails, rounded wings, and small, often bare, heads on curved necks that merge into long, curved bills. Their medium-length legs and strong feet allow an easy, long-striding walk. Gregarious birds, ibises fly in long lines or in "V" formation. They feed mostly on insects, worms, small mollusks, and crustaceans, probing for prey in the water and wet mud.

EYE-CATCHING IBIS
The White-faced Ibis has a distinctive white patch around its eye in the breeding season.

BITTERNS, HERONS, & EGRETS

These are mostly waterside birds (Ardeidae), with long slender toes, broad wings, short tails, forward-facing eyes, and dagger-shaped bills. Bitterns and night-herons have smooth, dense feathers on their nape, while egrets' long, slender necks are tightly feathered, with a "kink" that allows them to make lightning-fast stabs for prey. Bitterns, herons, and egrets fly with their legs trailing and their necks coiled into their shoulders. Some make obvious, bulky treetop nests and feed in the open, but others, especially bitterns, nest and feed secretively. In fact, often the only clue to a bittern's presence in dense reedbeds is the booming call it makes to keep in touch with its mate.

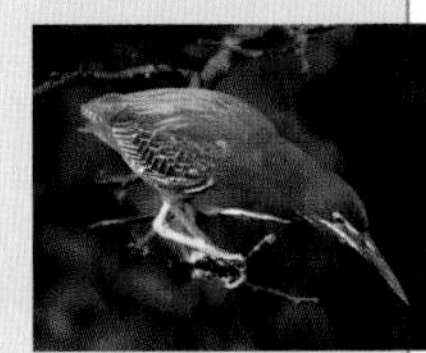

EVER ALERT
The Green Heron stalks fish by watching and waiting patiently until prey is near.

DANCING ON AIR
The Great Egret's courtship display often involves spreading its wings and leaping in a kind of aerial dance.

Order **Ciconiiformes**	Family **Threskiornithidae**	Species ***Plegadis chihi***

White-faced Ibis

dark, bronze-green overall
trailing legs
ADULT (BREEDING)
IN FLIGHT

dark legs
greenish, iridescent wings
dark face
ADULT (NONBREEDING)

bronze metallic gloss
white face
dark chestnut chest and neck
pink to red, naked skin between eye and long, curved bill
reddish legs and feet
ADULT (BREEDING)

dull, non-iridescent plumage
paler face and neck
JUVENILE

The White-faced Ibis is not only the most widespread member of its family in North America but also the only ibis found commonly in its range. Very similar to the closely related Glossy Ibis, it is separable in winter only by its reddish eye and the absence of a thin blue line around the face, though the two are only likely to be seen together in the Louisiana area.

VOICE Generally silent; soft calls at the nest, including feeding calls, vocalizations after mating, and greeting calls to mates and chicks; outside breeding, a raucous *khah* or *krah*.

NESTING Flat or columnar nest lined with plant matter, such as cattail, or bulrush in low trees or shrubs over shallow water, or on ground on small islands; 2–5 eggs; 1 brood; May–July.

FEEDING Captures prey below soil by probing with bill; eats aquatic prey such as crayfish, small fish, and frogs.

FLIGHT: strong and direct, with rapid wing beats, alternating with glides; soars on thermals.

LARGE FLOCKS
The White-faced Ibis is social, feeding and traveling in flocks, which can be large.

SIMILAR SPECIES

GLOSSY IBIS see p.470
less white on face
darker legs

BLACK-CROWNED NIGHT-HERON ◔ see p.90
thick, straight bill
brown, streaked body

OCCURRENCE
Found in freshwater wetlands, especially in flooded fields, but also in marshes and lake edges with cattails and bulrushes. Although birds may disperse farther east after breeding, they are, for the most part, restricted to the western part of the United States, and in Central and South America.

Length **23in (59cm)**	Wingspan **36in (92cm)**	Weight **22oz (625g)**
Social **Flocks/Colonies**	Lifespan **Up to 14 years**	Status **Secure**

DATE SEEN	WHERE	NOTES

Order **Ciconiiformes**	Family **Ardeidae**	Species ***Botaurus lentiginosus***

American Bittern

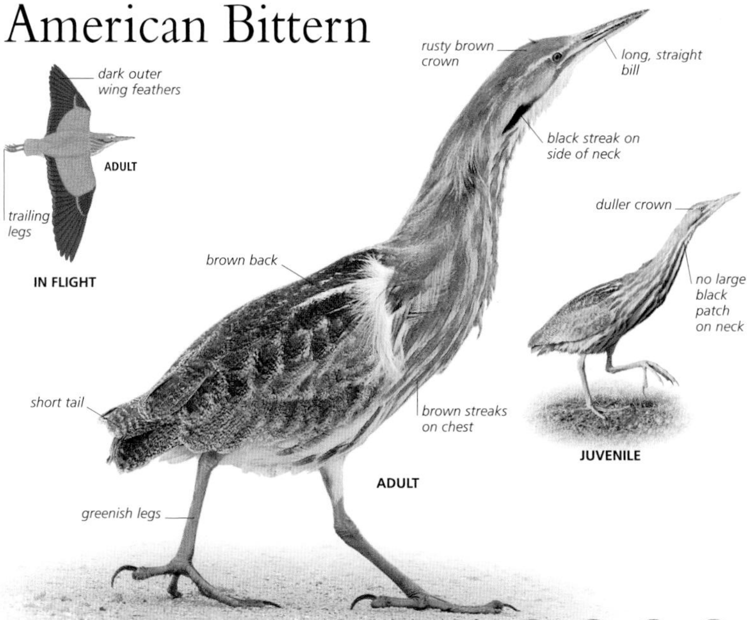

The American Bittern's camouflaged plumage and secretive behavior help it to blend into the thick vegetation of its freshwater wetland habitat. It is heard much more often than it is seen; its call is unmistakable and has given rise to many evocative colloquial names, such as "thunder pumper."

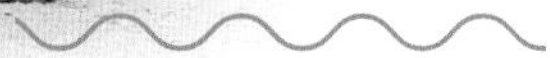

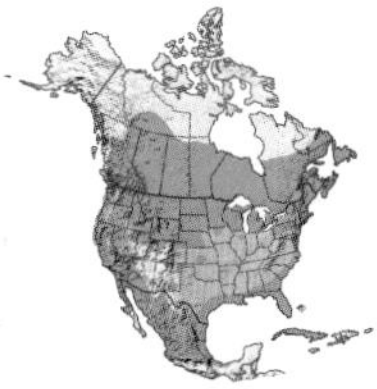

FLIGHT: steady, deep, slightly stiff wing beats; usually flies relatively low and direct.

VOICE Deep, resonant *pump-er-unk, pump-er-unk*; calls mainly at dawn, dusk, and nighttime, but also during the day in the early mating season.
NESTING Platform or mound constructed of available marsh vegetation, usually over shallow water; 2–7 eggs; 1 brood; April–August.
FEEDING Stands still or moves slowly, then strikes downward with bill to catch prey; eats fish, insects, crustaceans, snakes, amphibians, and small mammals.

OCCURRENCE
Breeds in heavily vegetated freshwater wetlands across the northern US and southern Canada; also occasionally in estuarine wetlands; winters in southern and coastal wetlands where temperatures stay above freezing; can appear in any wetland habitat during migration.

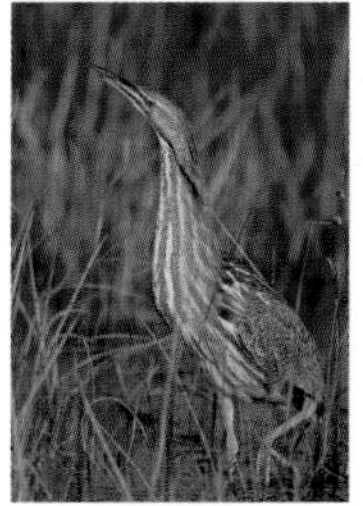

LOOKING UP
Bitterns are secretive birds, but can occasionally be found walking slowly through reeds.

SIMILAR SPECIES

LEAST BITTERN
see p.425

BLACK-CROWNED NIGHT-HERON ◔
see p.90

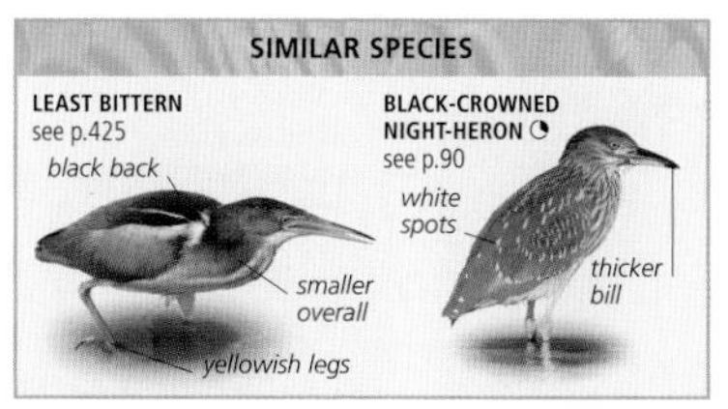

Length **23½–31in (60–80cm)**	Wingspan **3½–4¼ft (1.1–1.3m)**	Weight **13–20oz (375–575g)**
Social **Solitary**	Lifespan **At least 8 years**	Status **Declining**

DATE SEEN	WHERE	NOTES

Order **Ciconiiformes**	Family **Ardeidae**	Species ***Nycticorax nycticorax***

Black-crowned Night-Heron

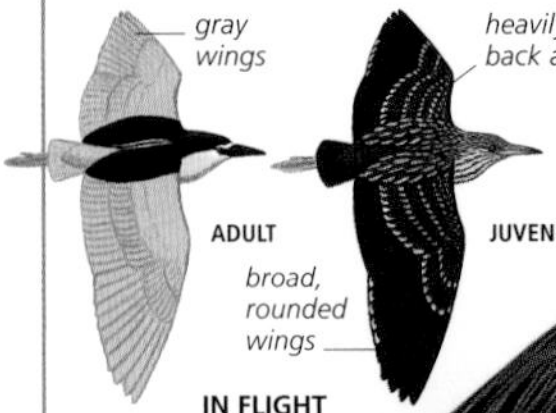

gray wings
ADULT
heavily speckled back and wings
JUVENILE
broad, rounded wings
IN FLIGHT

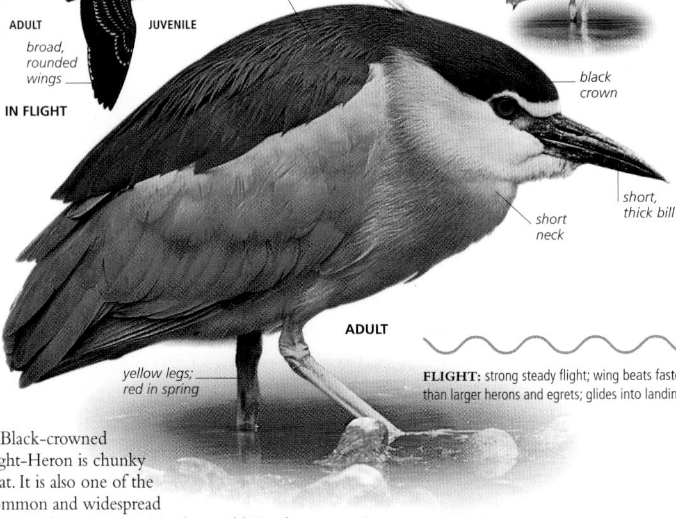

long, white head plumes
black back
black crown
short, thick bill
short neck
yellow legs; red in spring
ADULT

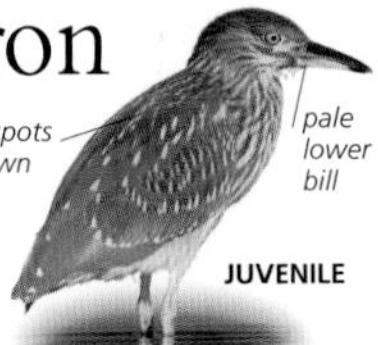

white spots on brown back
pale lower bill
JUVENILE

FLIGHT: strong steady flight; wing beats faster than larger herons and egrets; glides into landing.

The Black-crowned Night-Heron is chunky and squat. It is also one of the most common and widespread herons in North America and in the world. But because, as its name suggests, it is mainly active at twilight and at night, many people have never seen one. However, its distinctive barking call can be heard at night—even at the center of large cities.

VOICE Loud, distinctive *quark* or *wok*, often given in flight and around colonies.

NESTING Large stick nests built usually 20–40ft (6–12m) up in trees; 3–5 eggs; 1 brood; November–August.

FEEDING Feeds primarily on aquatic animals, such as fish, crustaceans, insects, and mollusks; also eggs and chicks of colonial birds, such as egrets, ibises, and terns.

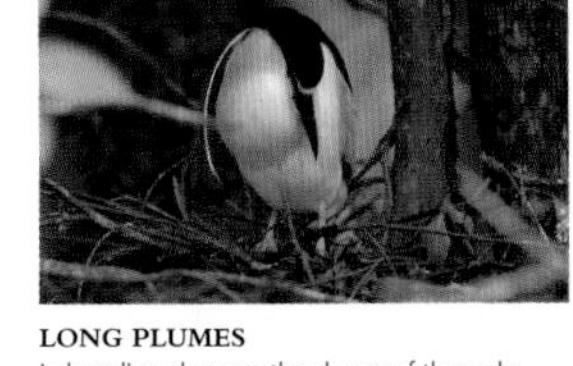

LONG PLUMES
In breeding plumage, the plumes of the male of this species are longer than the female's.

SIMILAR SPECIES

YELLOW-CROWNED NIGHT-HERON see p.470

GREEN HERON smaller overall; see p.91

gray neck
black-and-white head
rufous neck
thinner bill

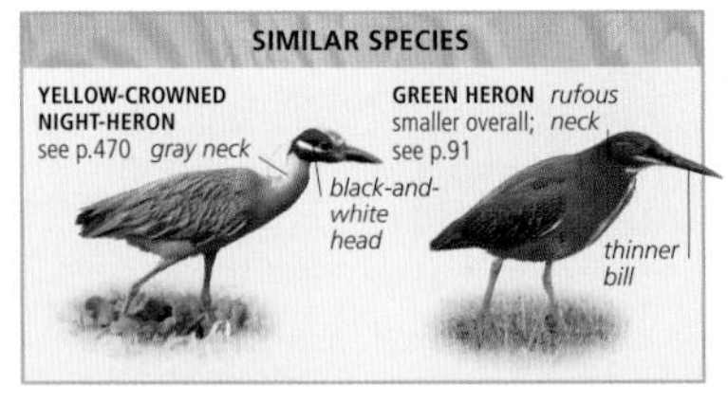

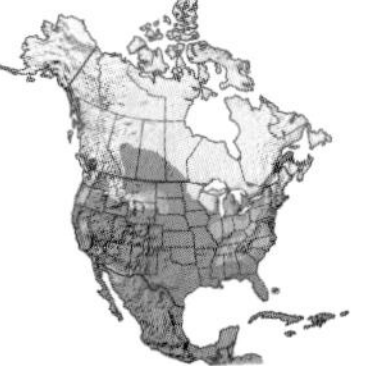

OCCURRENCE
Widespread; can be found wherever there are waterbodies, such as lakes, ponds, streams; generally absent from higher elevations. Colonies often on islands or in marshes; colony sites may be used for decades. In winter, found in areas where water remains open.

Length **23–26in (58–65cm)**	Wingspan **3½–4ft (1.1–1.2m)**	Weight **1½–2½lb (0.7–1kg)**
Social **Colonies**	Lifespan **Up to 21 years**	Status **Secure**

DATE SEEN	WHERE	NOTES

Order **Ciconiiformes**	Family **Ardeidae**	Species ***Butorides virescens***

Green Heron

ADULT (BREEDING)

greenish back

IN FLIGHT

short, rufous neck

greenish black cap

white chin

thin, straight, black bill

cream streak extends from throat to belly

yellowish legs and feet

ADULT (NONBREEDING)

white speckles on wings

paler bill

JUVENILE

long back plumes

glossy orange legs

ADULT (BREEDING)

A small, solitary, and secretive bird of dense thicketed wetlands, the Green Heron can be difficult to observe. This dark, crested heron is most often seen flying away from a perceived threat, emitting a loud squawk. While the Green Heron of North and Central America has now been recognized as a separate species, it was earlier grouped with the Green-backed Heron (*B. striatus*), which is found in the tropics and subtropics throughout the world.

VOICE Squawking *keow* when flying from disturbance.

NESTING Nest of twigs often in bushes or trees, often over water but also on land; 1–2 broods; 3–5 eggs; March–July.

FEEDING Stands quietly on the shore or in shallow water and strikes quickly; mainly fish, but also frogs, insects, and spiders.

FLIGHT: direct, a bit plodding, and usually over short distances.

READY TO STRIKE
Green Herons usually catch their prey by lunging forward and downward with their whole body.

SIMILAR SPECIES

BLACK-CROWNED NIGHT-HERON see p.90
larger overall
thicker bill

YELLOW-CROWNED NIGHT-HERON see p.470
larger overall

OCCURRENCE
An inhabitant of swampy thickets, but occasionally dry land close to water across much of North America, but missing in the plains, the Rocky Mountains, and the western deserts that do not provide appropriate wetlands. Winters in coastal wetlands.

Length **14½–15½in (37–39cm)**	Wingspan **25–27in (63–68cm)**	Weight **7–9oz (200–250g)**
Social **Solitary/Pairs/Small flocks**	Lifespan **Up to 10 years**	Status **Secure**

DATE SEEN	WHERE	NOTES

Order **Ciconiiformes**	Family **Ardeidae**	Species ***Bubulcus ibis***

Cattle Egret

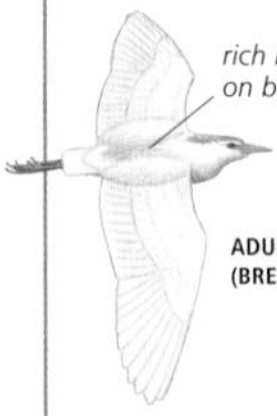

rich buff on back

ADULT (BREEDING)

IN FLIGHT

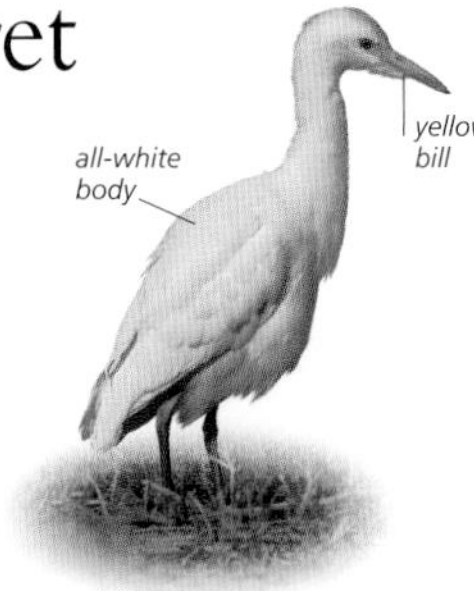

all-white body

yellow bill

ADULT (NONBREEDING)

rich buff crown

yellow bill, reddish in spring

short neck

white body and wings

rich buff on breast in spring

ADULT (BREEDING)

yellow legs and feet

looks all-white in flight at long range

dark legs and feet

ADULT (BREEDING)

FLIGHT: flies with regular wing beats; neck crooked and legs extended.

Unlike most other herons, the Cattle Egret is a grassland species that rarely wades in water, and is most likely to be seen in association with livestock, feeding on the insects disturbed by their feet. It is thought to have originated in the shortgrass prairies of Africa and is now found worldwide. It was first seen in Florida in 1941, but expanded rapidly and has now bred in over 40 US states.

VOICE Generally silent; vocal at the nest: *rick-rack* common.

NESTING Nest of branches or plants placed in trees over ground; also in trees or shrubs over water; 2–5 eggs; 1 brood; March–October.

FEEDING Eats in groups, consumes insects, spiders as well as larger animals such as frogs; insects stirred up in grasslands by cattle.

VOCAL BREEDERS
This bird almost never calls away from a breeding colony, but is vocal near its nests.

SIMILAR SPECIES

GREAT EGRET see p.94
long bill
much larger
black legs and toes

SNOWY EGRET see p.95
black bill
yellow toes

OCCURRENCE
Since the 1940s, it has expanded to many habitats in much of North America, primarily in grasslands and prairies, but also wetland areas. In tropical regions, the Cattle Egrets flock around the cattle feeding in shallow wetlands.

Length **20in (51cm)**	Wingspan **31in (78cm)**	Weight **13oz (375g)**
Social **Colonies**	Lifespan **Up to 17 years**	Status **Secure**

DATE SEEN	WHERE	NOTES

Order **Ciconiiformes**	Family **Ardeidae**	Species ***Ardea herodias***

Great Blue Heron

dark wing tips
ADULT
crooked neck
IN FLIGHT

dark tail
brownish body
JUVENILE

white face
dark bill
gray neck
blue-gray body
shaggy plumes
dark legs
MALE

yellowish bill
large, white bird
light legs
GREAT WHITE HERON (FLORIDA KEYS)

light-colored head, often all white
light bill
overall similar to Great Blue
WÜRDEMANN'S HERON (SOUTHERN FLORIDA)

FLIGHT: deep-flapping, regular wing beats.

This is one of the three largest herons in the world—the Great Blue in North America, the Gray in Eurasia, and the Cocoi in South America—all of which are all interrelated, but classified separately. The Great Blue Heron is a common inhabitant of a variety of North American waterbodies, from marshes to swamps, as well as along sea coasts. Its majestic, deliberate flight is a highly wonderful sight to behold.

VOICE Mostly silent; gives a loud, barking squawk or *crank* in breeding colonies or when disturbed.

NESTING Nest of twigs and branches; usually in colonies, but also singly; in trees, often over water, but also over ground; 2–4 eggs; 1–2 broods; February–August.

FEEDING Catches prey with quick jab of bill; primarily fish.

LOFTY ABODE
Great Blue Herons nest in small colonies in trees, and often roost in them.

SIMILAR SPECIES

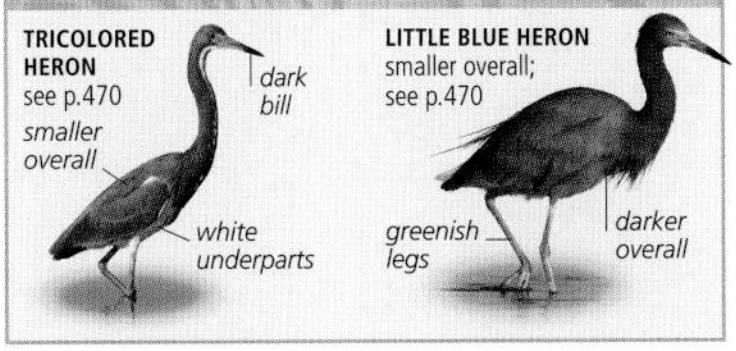

TRICOLORED HERON
see p.470
smaller overall
dark bill
white underparts

LITTLE BLUE HERON
smaller overall; see p.470
greenish legs
darker overall

OCCURRENCE
Across southern Canada and the US in wetlands, such as marshes, lake edges, and along rivers and swamps; also in marine habitats, especially tidal grass flats. The Great White Heron is common in mangroves in the Florida Keys; also West Indies and Yucatán.

Length **2¾–4¼ft (0.9–1.3m)**	Wingspan **5¼–6½ft (1.6–2m)**	Weight **4¾–5½lb (2.1–2.5kg)**
Social **Solitary/Flocks**	Lifespan **Up to 20 years**	Status **Secure**

DATE SEEN	WHERE	NOTES

Order **Ciconiiformes**	Family **Ardeidae**	Species ***Ardea alba***

Great Egret

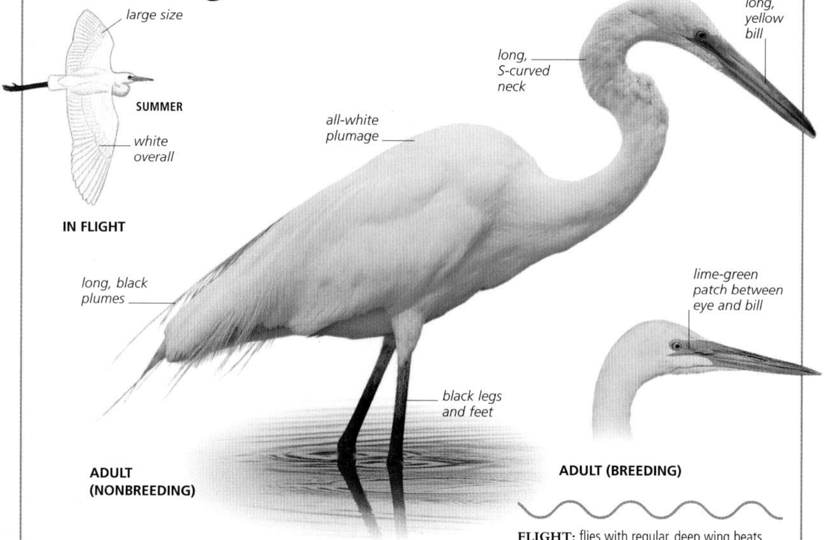

large size
SUMMER
white overall
IN FLIGHT

long, yellow bill
long, S-curved neck
all-white plumage
long, black plumes
black legs and feet
ADULT (NONBREEDING)

lime-green patch between eye and bill
ADULT (BREEDING)

FLIGHT: flies with regular, deep wing beats.

This large white heron is found on every continent except Antarctica. When feeding, the Great Egret would apparently rather forage alone than in flocks—it maintains space around itself, and will defend a territory of 10ft (3m) in diameter from other wading birds. This territory "moves" with the bird as it feeds. In years of scarce food supplies, a chick may kill a sibling, permitting the survival of at least one bird.

VOICE Largely vocal during courtship and breeding; otherwise, *kraak* or *cuk-cuk-cuk* when disturbed or in a combative encounter.

NESTING Nest of twigs in trees, over land or water; 2–4 eggs; 1 brood; March–July.

FEEDING Catches prey with quick thrust of bill; feeds on aquatic prey, primarily fish, also crustaceans.

TREE PERCHES
Great Egrets nest in trees and regularly perch in them when not feeding.

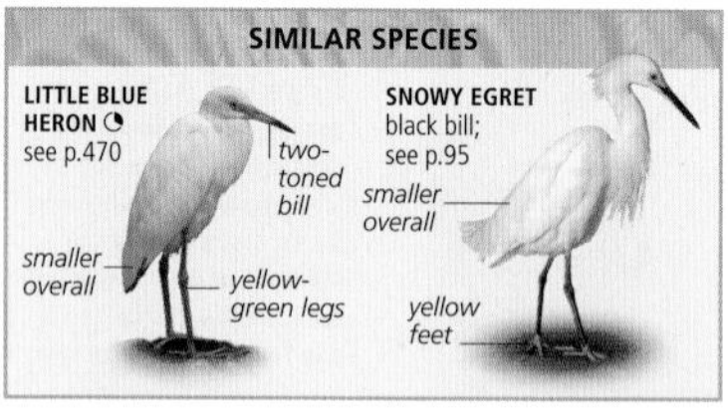

SIMILAR SPECIES

LITTLE BLUE HERON ◔ see p.470
two-toned bill
smaller overall
yellow-green legs

SNOWY EGRET black bill; see p.95
smaller overall
yellow feet

OCCURRENCE
Breeds in trees over water or on islands; forages in almost all types of freshwater and marine wetlands from marshes and ponds to rivers. Migratory over much of its North American range; more southerly populations resident. Distance migrated depends on severity of winter.

Length **3¼ft (1m)**	Wingspan **6ft (1.8m)**	Weight **1¾–3¼ft (0.8–1.5kg)**
Social **Solitary**	Lifespan **Up to 25 years**	Status **Secure**

DATE SEEN	WHERE	NOTES

Order **Ciconiiformes**	Family **Ardeidae**	Species ***Egretta thula***

Snowy Egret

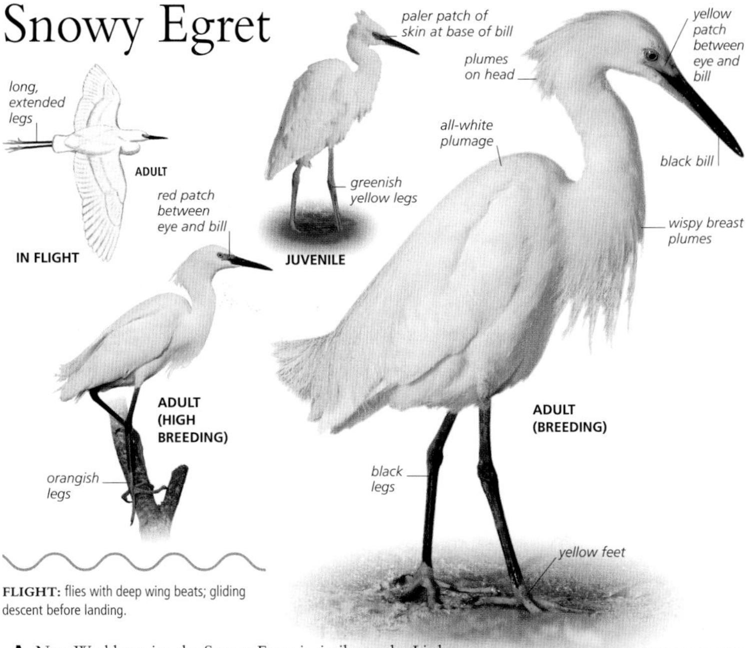

long, extended legs
ADULT
IN FLIGHT
paler patch of skin at base of bill
greenish yellow legs
JUVENILE
red patch between eye and bill
ADULT (HIGH BREEDING)
orangish legs
plumes on head
yellow patch between eye and bill
all-white plumage
black bill
wispy breast plumes
ADULT (BREEDING)
black legs
yellow feet

FLIGHT: flies with deep wing beats; gliding descent before landing.

A New World species, the Snowy Egret is similar to the Little Egret. It is very adaptable in estuarine and freshwater habitats. When foraging, it uses a wide variety of behaviors, including wing-flicking, foot-stirring, and foot-probing to get its prey moving, making it easier to capture.

VOICE High-pitched *Aargaarg* when flushed; low-pitched *Arg* and *Raah* aggressive calls; *Aarg* call during attacks and pursuits.

NESTING Small sticks, branches, and rushes over water or on land; also on ground, in shrubs, mangroves, and other trees; 3–5 eggs; 1 brood; March–August.

FEEDING Feeds on aquatic prey, from invertebrates, such as insects, shrimp, and prawns, to small fish, amphibians, and snakes.

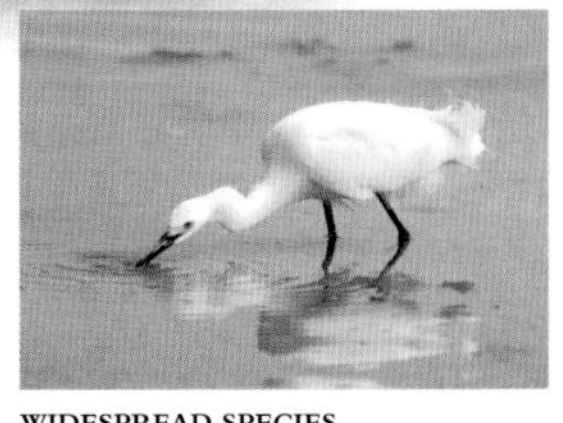

WIDESPREAD SPECIES
Snowy Egrets feed in a wide variety of wetland habitats, using different foraging techniques.

SIMILAR SPECIES

GREAT EGRET
see p.94

LITTLE BLUE HERON ◔
see p.470

yellow bill
black legs and feet
black legs and feet

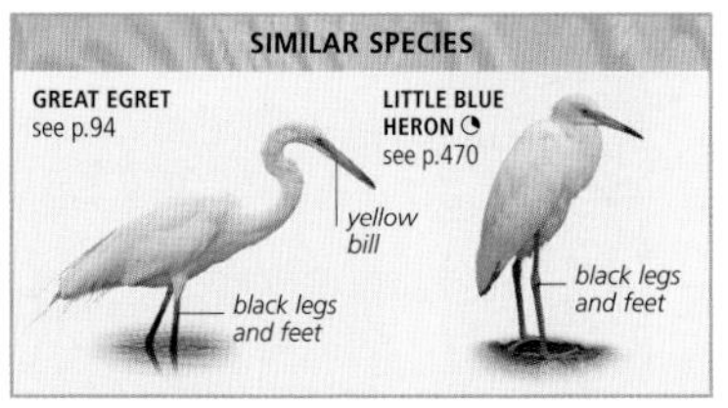

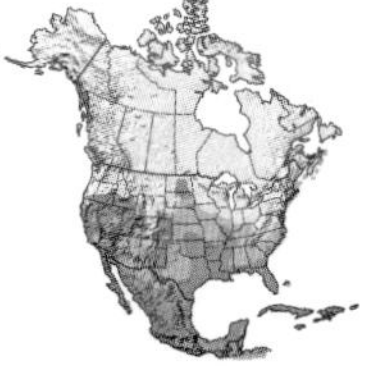

OCCURRENCE
Found in a wide variety of wetlands throughout North America: from mangroves in Florida to marshlands in New England and the western US. Highly adaptable and widely found. Sites of breeding colonies may change from year to year within a set range.

Length **24in (62cm)**	Wingspan **3½ft (1.1m)**	Weight **12oz (350g)**
Social **Solitary**	Lifespan **Up to 22 years**	Status **Secure**

DATE SEEN	WHERE	NOTES

PELICANS & RELATIVES

PELICANS AND THEIR relatives belong to an order of large to huge fish-eating birds, Pelecaniformes, with four toes connected by leathery webs, and with fleshy, elastic pouches beneath their bills.

WING SPREADING
For this Neotropic Cormorant grooming includes spreading its wings to dry them in the sun.

PELICANS

The pelican family includes seven large species, two of which—the American White Pelican and the Brown Pelican—breed in North America. All pelicans are buoyant swimmers and excellent fliers, capable of great lift on their long, broad wings with wing feathers spread. Flocks can be seen soaring to great heights on migration and when flying to feeding grounds. Pelicans feed by sweeping with open bills for fish, often cooperatively, or by plunging from a height to scoop up fish and water in their large, flexible bill pouches.

CORMORANTS

With 36 species worldwide, these are medium to large waterbirds, some marine, others freshwater, with broad, long wings, rounded tails, short, strong legs and hook-tipped bills often tilted upward when swimming. In flight, the neck is extended and noticeably kinked. When hunting for fish, cormorants dive from the surface of the water, rolling smoothly under or with a forward leap, and then swim underwater with closed wings, using their webbed toes for propulsion. Most are dark birds, apart from distinctive facial patterns on areas of bare skin which become more colorful in early spring. Most cormorants nest on cliff ledges, others use both cliffs and trees. There is one flightless and highly endangered cormorant species in the Galápagos Islands.

WATER BIRD
Webbed feet help Brown Pelicans negotiate water with ease, while strong wings allow easy takeoffs.

Order **Pelecaniformes**	Family **Pelecanidae**	Species ***Pelecanus erythrorhynchos***

American White Pelican

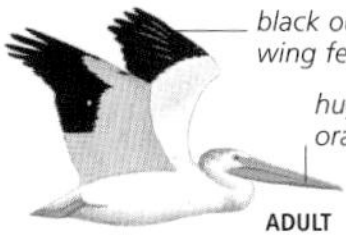

black outer wing feathers
huge, orange bill
ADULT
IN FLIGHT

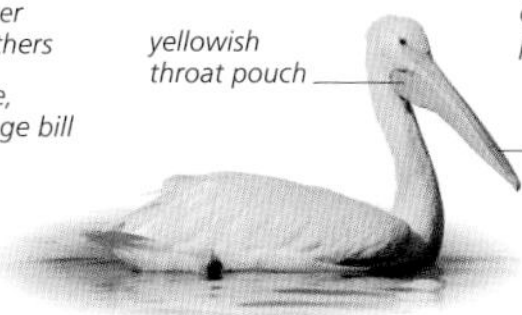

yellowish throat pouch
orange throat pouch
duller yellow bill
ADULT (WINTER)

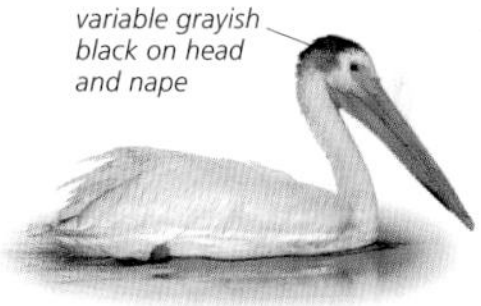

variable grayish black on head and nape
ADULT (POSTBREEDING)

white head
orange-yellow straight bill
ridge on bill
all-white plumage
bright orange feet
ADULT (BREEDING)

FLIGHT: once in flight, alternates strong but shallow beats with glides; soars in flocks.

This enormous, unmistakable white bird, with its distinctive, oversized bill, is a highly social inhabitant of large lakes and marshes in western North America. It is a colonial bird, with most of the world's population being concentrated in a handful of large colonies in isolated wetland complexes in deserts and prairies. The American White Pelican forms foraging flocks, which beat their wings in coordinated movements to drive fish into shallow water, where they can be caught more easily.

VOICE Usually silent except around nesting colonies; around the nest, young and adults exchange various grunts and hisses.

NESTING Depression in the ground, both sexes incubate; 1–2 eggs; 1 brood; April–August.

FEEDING Mainly gulps down small fish, occasionally eats small amphibians, and crayfish.

LARGE COLONIES
The White Pelican is highly social and is usually seen feeding or roosting in large groups.

SIMILAR SPECIES

WOOD STORK see p.470
bare head
curved bill
long thin legs

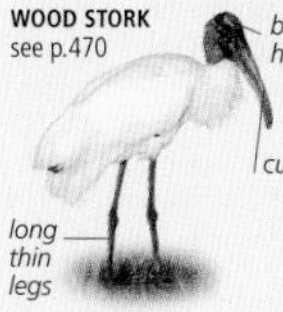

BROWN PELICAN see p.98
gray bill
dark underparts

OCCURRENCE
Breeds on islands in freshwater lakes in south-central Canada, intermontane areas of the western US, and in coastal northeastern Mexico; an early spring migrant, often returning to breeding grounds in early March. Winters in coastal regions from California and Texas to Mexico and Central America.

Length **4¼–5½ft (1.3–1.7m)**	Wingspan **7¾–9½ft (2.4–2.9m)**	Weight **12–20lb (5.5–9kg)**
Social **Colonies**	Lifespan **Up to 26 years**	Status **Vulnerable**

DATE SEEN	WHERE	NOTES

Order **Pelecaniformes**	Family **Pelecanidae**	Species ***Pelecanus occidentalis***

Brown Pelican

ADULT
IN FLIGHT
bulky and dark

head mainly white
ADULT (NONBREEDING)

extensive white on wings
ADULT (BREEDING)

long neck
ADULT (POSTBREEDING)

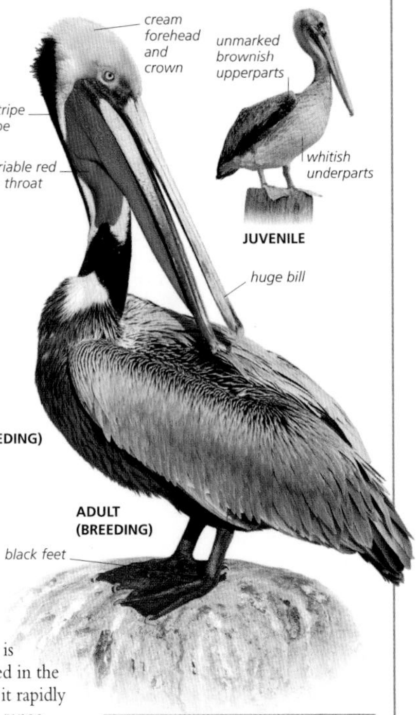

cream forehead and crown
dark stripe on nape
variable red on throat
huge bill
black feet
ADULT (BREEDING)

unmarked brownish upperparts
whitish underparts
JUVENILE

FLIGHT: flies low over surface of the water; alternates glides with wing beats.

This huge and conspicuous inhabitant of warm coastal regions is an ungainly species on land but is amazingly graceful in flight. Sadly, numbers plummeted in the 1960s when DDT was used widely as a pesticide, but it rapidly recovered in recent decades, and is now expanding its range northward along both coasts. The color of its throat varies according to geographic location and time of year.

VOICE Silent most of the time; vocal at nest colonies; adults and juveniles communicate with grunts and hisses; courting birds give a strange, deliberate *heart-hark*, repeated slowly.

NESTING Pile of debris, usually on ground; 2–3 eggs; 1 brood; February–August.

FEEDING Adults plunge headfirst into water to scoop up fish near the surface; does not herd fish, like the American White Pelican.

RESTING TOGETHER
Brown Pelicans are social most of the year, and can often be seen roosting in groups.

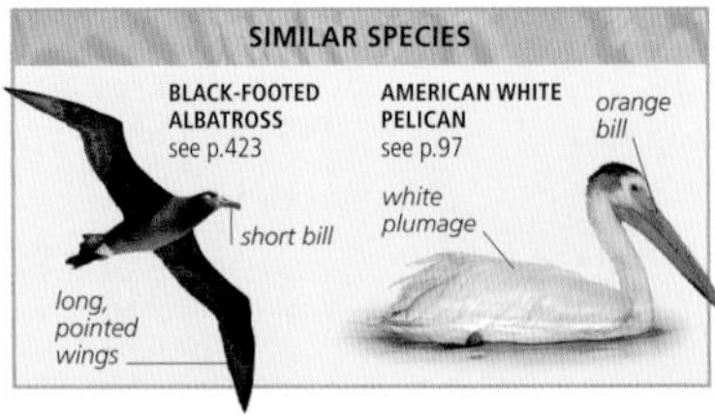

SIMILAR SPECIES

BLACK-FOOTED ALBATROSS see p.423
short bill
long, pointed wings

AMERICAN WHITE PELICAN see p.97
orange bill
white plumage

OCCURRENCE
Found in and around warm coastal waters, flying above the water's surface over the cresting waves; small numbers breed in the interior US; individuals and small flocks can be found around docks and marinas.

Length **4–4¼ft (1.2–1.3m)**	Wingspan **6½–7ft (2–2.1m)**	Weight **4–8¾lb (1.8–4kg)**
Social **Colonies**	Lifespan **Up to 10 years**	Status **Secure**

DATE SEEN	WHERE	NOTES

Order **Pelecaniformes**	Family **Phalacrocoracidae**	Species ***Phalacrocorax penicillatus***

Brandt's Cormorant

black overall
ADULT (BREEDING)
IN FLIGHT
outstretched neck
no facial whiskers
lacks blue chin
relatively short tail
ADULT (NONBREEDING)
rounded head
long dark bill
white facial "whiskers"
blue chin
pale brownish throat patch
black upperparts with oily sheen
black underparts
ADULT (BREEDING)

FLIGHT: constant, rapid wing beats low over water in V-shaped flocks; glides while landing.

Brandt's Cormorant is the only cormorant with a blue chin, edged with a pale brownish patch. Unlike the Double-crested Cormorant, Brandt's fly with their necks straight. This species is found only along the Pacific Coast of North America. During the breeding season, it depends heavily on food from the nutrient-rich upwellings of the California Current. Named after a German who was the director of the zoological museum in St. Petersburg, Russia, this species is at risk from commercial fishing, pollution, and recreational disturbance.

VOICE Emits croaks, growls, gargles and coughing sounds.

NESTING Circular, drum-shaped nest of grass, moss, weeds, seaweed, sticks, and rubbish, on gentle slopes of islands or ledges on cliffs; 1–6 eggs; 1 brood; April–August.

FEEDING Dives and chases after surface- and bottom-dwelling fish; grasps fish in bill, crushes it, and swallows it head-first.

DRYING OUT
Like all cormorants, this species stretches its wings to drain its soggy feathers after diving for fish.

SIMILAR SPECIES

DOUBLE-CRESTED CORMORANT see p.100
lighter colored overall
large yellow or orange throat pouch

PELAGIC CORMORANT see p.101
slender neck
very thin bill

OCCURRENCE
Breeding colonies are found on offshore or near-shore islands or on mainland promontories on the Pacific coast of North America occasionally found in inshore lagoons; winters in sheltered inlets and other protected waters or on open ocean within 1 mile (1.6km) of land.

Length **28–31in (70–79cm)**	Wingspan **3½ft (1.1m)**	Weight **3–6lb (1.4–2.7kg)**
Social **Flocks/Colonies**	Lifespan **Up to 18 years**	Status **Secure**

DATE SEEN	WHERE	NOTES

Order **Pelecaniformes**	Family **Phalacrocoracidae**	Species ***Phalacrocorax auritus***

Double-crested Cormorant

FLIGHT: regular wing beats, occasional glides; over water, flies close to the surface; often soars.

This species is the most widespread of the North American cormorants. It often flies high over land in V-shaped flocks, but is mostly seen swimming in the water with its head and neck visible, or resting on trees and rocks, sometimes with its wings spread. While fishing, it dives from the surface of the water and chases fish underwater, using its webbed toes for propulsion.

VOICE Deep grunt-like calls while nesting, roosting, and fishing; *t-t-t-t* call before taking off and *urg-urg-urg* before landing; prolonged *arr-r-r-r-r-t-t* while mating, and *eh-hr* as threat.

NESTING Nests of twigs and sticks, seaweed, and trash, lined with grass; built on ground, cliffs, or in trees usually in colonies; 3-5 eggs; 1 brood; April–August.

FEEDING Pursues slow-moving or schooling fish; feeds on insects, crustaceans, amphibians, and, rarely, on voles and snakes.

DRYING OFF
Like all cormorants, the Double-crested usually perches with wings spread, to dry its feathers.

SIMILAR SPECIES

BRANDT'S CORMORANT see p.99
throat pouch paler and less visible

NEOTROPIC CORMORANT see p.425
shorter body
longer tail

OCCURRENCE
Breeds in a wide range of aquatic habitats, including ponds, artificial and natural lakes, slow-moving rivers, estuaries, lagoons, and seashores; winters on coastlines and sandbars in coastal inlets; roosts near catfish farms in some areas.

Length **28–35in (70–90cm)**	Wingspan **3½–4ft (1.1–1.2m)**	Weight **2¾–5½lb (1.2–2.5kg)**
Social **Flocks**	Lifespan **Up to 18 years**	Status **Secure**

DATE SEEN	WHERE	NOTES

Order **Pelecaniformes**	Family **Phalacrocoracidae**	Species ***Phalacrocorax pelagicus***

Pelagic Cormorant

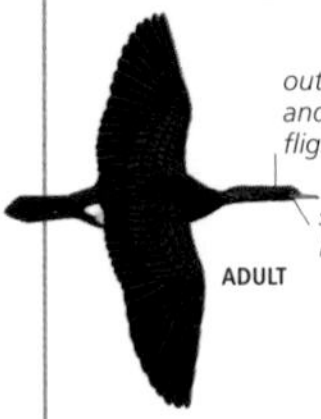

FLIGHT: rapid with regular, steady wing beats; glides before landing.

The Pelagic Cormorant is the smallest cormorant species in North America. Although a marine bird, its English (and scientific) name, *pelagicus*, meaning "oceanic," is misleading because this bird mostly inhabits inshore waters. This bird is most visible at its roosting sites, where it spends much of its time drying its feathers. The Pelagic Cormorant has not been well studied because it is more solitary than the other cormorant species in North America. Like all cormorants it is threatened by the disturbance of its nesting colonies, oil spills, entanglement in fishing nets, and pollution.

VOICE Female 2-note call *igh-ugh*, similar to ticking grandfather clock; male call note *purring* or *arr-arr-arr;* both utter croaks, hisses, and low groans.

NESTING Saucer-shaped nest of grass, seaweed, sticks, feathers, and marine debris, cemented to cliff face with guano; 3–5 eggs; 1 brood; May–October.

FEEDING Dives from water's surface for any medium-sized fish, and also invertebrates, such as shrimps, worms, and hermit crabs.

SITTING LOW
Pelagic Cormorants sit low in the water with only their head, neck, and back visible.

SIMILAR SPECIES

OCCURRENCE
Found in rocky habitat on outer coast, shallow bays, inlets, estuaries, harbors, and lagoons; nesting colonies found on steep cliffs on forested and grassy islands, and on rocky promontories along the shoreline; also seen on built structures such as wharf pilings, bridges, and harbor buoys.

Length **20–30in (51–76cm)**	Wingspan **3¼–4ft (1–1.2m)**	Weight **2¾–5¼lb (1.3–2.4kg)**
Social **Solitary/Pairs**	Lifespan **Up to 17 years**	Status **Secure**

DATE SEEN	WHERE	NOTES

BIRDS OF PREY

THE DEFINING FEATURES of birds of prey, or raptors, are strong feet with sharp talons for catching and holding prey, and a powerful, hooked bill for tearing the catch to pieces. Vultures eat carrion, not live prey.

VULTURES

Of the seven New World species of vulture, three occur in North America: the Black Vulture, the Turkey Vulture, which has an acute sense of smell that enables it to detect carrion hidden from sight beneath the forest canopy, and the rare California Condor, the continent's largest soaring land bird. All three can stay in the air for hours on end, using the lift provided by updrafts to minimize the energy spent on wing flapping.

WEAK TOOL
In spite of its sharp beak, the Turkey Vulture cannot always break the skin of carcasses.

FALCONS

Ranging in size from the diminutive American Merlin, with northern breeding habitats, to the large, powerful Gyrfalcon, which nests in the Arctic, this group also includes the Kestrel, the Prairie Falcon, and perhaps the best-known raptor of all—the fast-diving Peregrine Falcon. Falcon prey ranges from insects to large mammals and birds.

EAGLES AND HAWKS

This group covers a wide range of raptors of varying sizes, from the iconic Bald Eagle and the majestic Golden Eagle to smaller birds, such as the Northern Harrier, and various hawks and kites. These birds use a wide range of hunting methods. For example, forest-dwelling hawks rely on speed and stealth to pounce on small birds among the trees in a sudden, short dash. By contrast, the Osprey hovers over water until it sees a fish below, then dives steeply, pulling up at the last moment to pluck its prey clean out of the water with its talons.

DOUBLE SHOT
When there are lots of fish running in a tight school, the Osprey has the strength and skill to catch two with one dive.

Order **Falconiformes**	Family **Cathartidae**	Species ***Cathartes aura***

Turkey Vulture

long wings
silvery gray flight feathers
ADULT
IN FLIGHT
blackish back feathers, edged brown
brownish gray head
JUVENILE
naked skin
small, red head
brownish back
long tail
SUB-ADULT
black underparts
pink legs

FLIGHT: seldom flaps; mostly soars with wings held in a V-shape, gently tipping from side to side.

The most widely distributed vulture in North America, the Turkey Vulture is found in most of the US and has expanded its range into southern Canada. It possesses a better sense of smell than the Black Vulture, which often follows it and displaces it from carcasses. The Turkey Vulture's habit of defecating down its legs, which it shares with the Wood Stork, may serve to cool it or to kill bacteria with its ammonia content.

VOICE Silent, but will hiss at intruders; also grunts.

NESTING Dark recesses, such as under large rocks or stumps, on rocky ledges in caves, and crevices, in mammal burrows and hollow logs, and abandoned buildings; 1–3 eggs; 1 brood; March–August.

FEEDING Feeds on a wide range of wild and domestic carrion, mostly mammals, also birds, reptiles, amphibians, and fish; occasionally takes live prey such as nestlings or trapped birds.

SOAKING UP THE SUN
Turkey Vultures often spread their wings to sun themselves and increase their body temperature.

SIMILAR SPECIES

BLACK VULTURE
see p.426

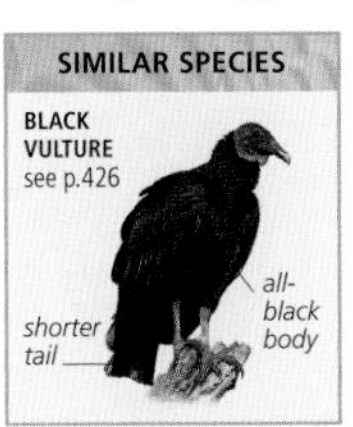

OCCURRENCE
Generally forages and migrates over mixed farmland and forest; prefers to nest in forested or partly forested hillsides offering hidden ground protected from disturbance; roosts in large trees such as cottonwoods, on rocky outcrops, and on power line transmission towers; some winter in urban areas and near landfills.

Length **25–32in (64–81cm)**	Wingspan **5½–6ft (1.7–1.8m)**	Weight **4½lb (2kg)**
Social **Flocks**	Lifespan **At least 17 years**	Status **Secure**

DATE SEEN	WHERE	NOTES

Order **Falconiformes**	Family **Falconidae**	Species ***Falco sparverius***

American Kestrel

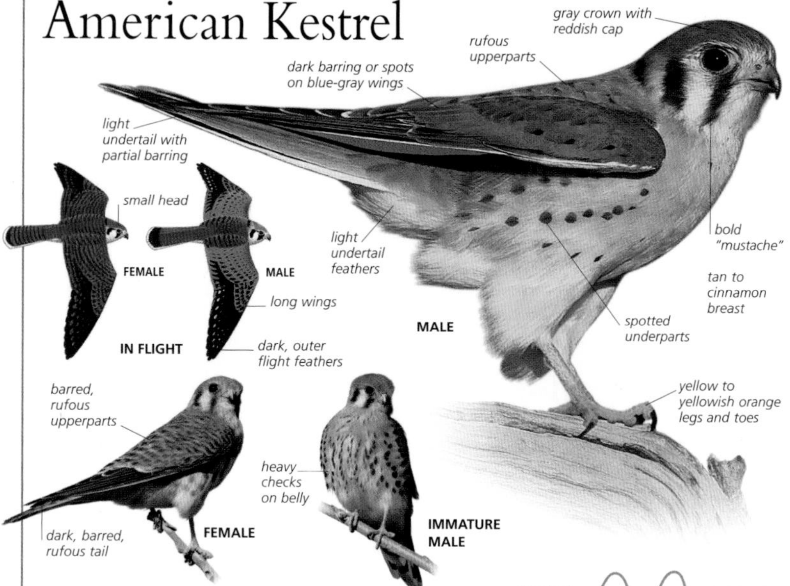
gray crown with reddish cap
rufous upperparts
dark barring or spots on blue-gray wings
light undertail with partial barring
small head
FEMALE
MALE
long wings
IN FLIGHT
dark, outer flight feathers
light undertail feathers
MALE
bold "mustache"
tan to cinnamon breast
spotted underparts
yellow to yellowish orange legs and toes
barred, rufous upperparts
heavy checks on belly
dark, barred, rufous tail
FEMALE
IMMATURE MALE

The smallest of the North American falcons, the American Kestrel features long pointed wings, a "tooth and notch" bill structure, and the dark brown eyes typical of falcons, though kestrels have shorter toes than other falcons. This may be due to the fact that kestrels often dive into long grass to capture insects and small mammals, which would be more difficult with long, thin toes. Male and female American Kestrels show differences in plumage, and also in size.

VOICE Common call a high-pitched *killy-killy-killy*.

NESTING Natural cavities, crevices, holes in dead trees, woodpeckers' holes, crevices in barns, man-made nest boxes if constructed and located properly; 4–5 eggs; 1 brood; April–June.

FEEDING Plunges for grasshoppers and crickets in spring and summer; small birds and mice in fall and winter; lizards and snakes.

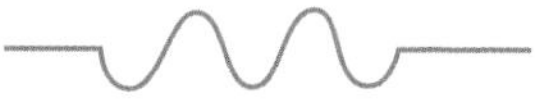

FLIGHT: delicate and almost moth-like; may hover in one place for long, searching for prey.

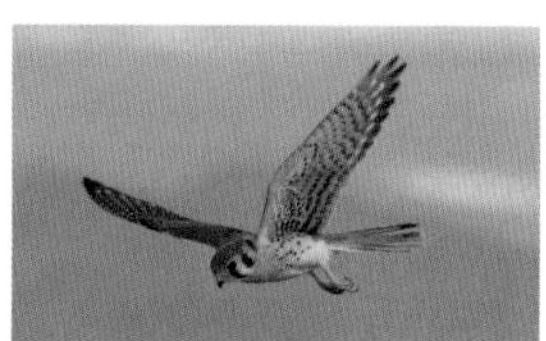

HIGH FLIER
A male American Kestrel hovers over a field, its sharp eyes scanning the ground for insects and rodents.

SIMILAR SPECIES
MERLIN
see p.105
no distinct stripes on head
SHARP-SHINNED HAWK
see p.112
brownish upperparts
darker belly
longer toes

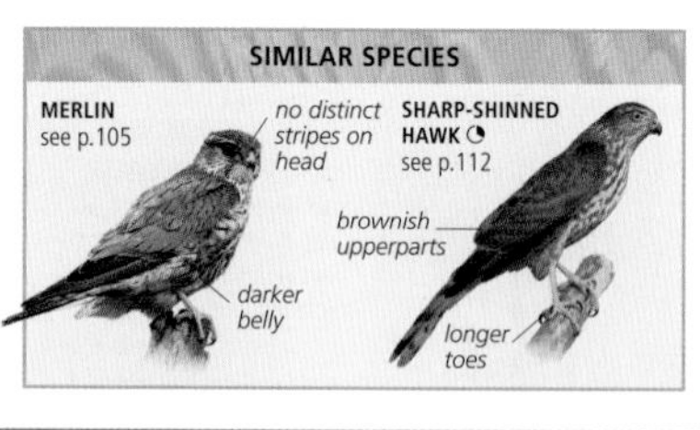

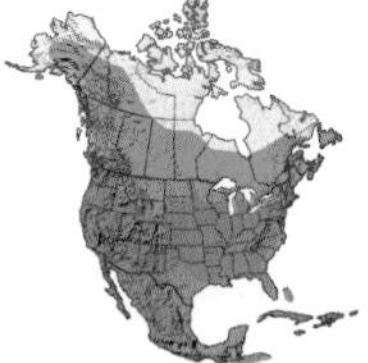

OCCURRENCE
From near the northern tree line in Alaska and Canada south, east, and west throughout most of North America. Also occurs in Central and South America. Habitat ranges from semi-open tree groves to grasslands, cultivated and fallow farmland, and open desert.

Length **9in (23cm)**	Wingspan **22in (56cm)**	Weight **3½–4oz (100–125g)**
Social **Family groups**	Lifespan **10–15 years**	Status **Vulnerable**

DATE SEEN	WHERE	NOTES

Order **Falconiformes**	Family **Falconidae**	Species ***Falco columbarius***

Merlin

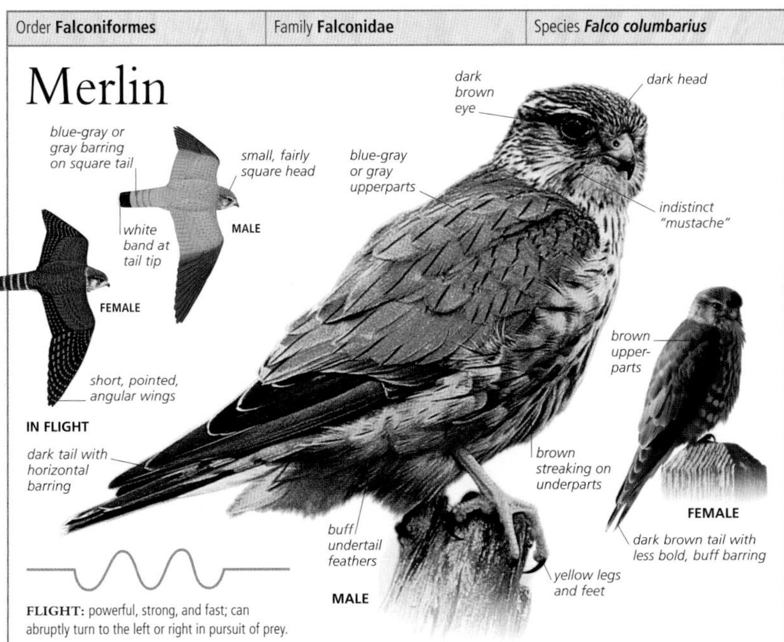

FLIGHT: powerful, strong, and fast; can abruptly turn to the left or right in pursuit of prey.

Merlins are small, fast-flying falcons that were formerly known as "pigeon hawks," because their shape and flight are similar to those strong fliers. Merlins can overtake and capture a wide variety of prey. They can turn on a dime, and use their long, thin toes, typical of falcons, to pluck birds from the air after launching a direct attack. Males are smaller than females, and different in color. Both males and females show geographical color variations.

VOICE Male call a high-pitched *ki-ki-ki-ki*; female call a low-pitched *kek-ek-ek-ek-ek*.

NESTING Small scrapes on ground in open country, or abandoned nests of other species, such as crows, in forested areas; 4–6 eggs; 1 brood; April–June.

FEEDING Catches small birds in midair, and occasionally birds as large as doves; also feeds on small mammals, including bats.

ABOUT TO ROUSE
An adult female Merlin sits on a moss-covered rock, about to "rouse," or fluff out and shake her feathers.

SIMILAR SPECIES

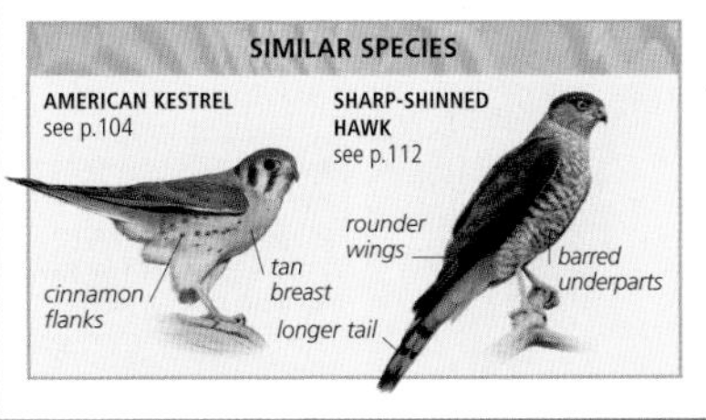

OCCURRENCE
Breeds from northern California east to Newfoundland, and south to Louisiana, Texas, and Mexico. Merlins can be seen hunting along coastlines, over marshlands and open fields, and in desert areas. Eastern birds migrate to southern areas.

Length **10in (25cm)**	Wingspan **24in (61cm)**	Weight **5–7oz (150–200g)**
Social **Pairs/Family groups**	Lifespan **10–15 years**	Status **Secure**

DATE SEEN	WHERE	NOTES

Order **Falconiformes**	Family **Falconidae**	Species ***Falco mexicanus***

Prairie Falcon

Prairie Falcons are light-colored, buoyant residents of the arid regions of North America. They blend in well with their surroundings (cliff faces and dry grass), where they are invisible to their prey. Prairie Falcons chase their prey close to the ground and do not often dive or "stoop" on prey from a great height. Ground squirrels are important prey items in some areas, and breeding is often linked with the squirrels' emergence. The sexes are very similar in coloration, though juveniles have a streaked rather than spotted breast. The underwing pattern with almost black feathers in the "wingpits" is distinctive; no other North American falcon shows this mark.

VOICE Repeated shrill *kik-kik-kik-kik-kik*.

NESTING Slight, shallow scrapes, almost always located on high cliff ledges or bluffs; 3–6 eggs; 1 brood; March–July.

FEEDING Feeds on small to medium-sized birds and small mammals, such as ground squirrels.

FLIGHT: fast flight; capable of soaring and diving; usually chases prey low above the ground.

STRIKING MUSTACHE
An inquisitive Prairie Falcon stares at the camera. The white cheek is obvious from this angle.

OCCURRENCE
Interior North America, from central British Columbia east to western North Dakota and south to southern California, and Mexico, Arizona, northern Texas. Found in open plains, prairies, and grasslands, dotted with buttes or cliffs. A partial migrant, it moves east of its breeding range in winter.

Length **16in (41cm)**	Wingspan **3¼ (1m)**	Weight **22–30oz (625–850g)**
Social **Solitary/Pairs**	Lifespan **10–20 years**	Status **Localized**

DATE SEEN	WHERE	NOTES

Order **Falconiformes**	Family **Falconidae**	Species ***Falco peregrinus***

Peregrine Falcon

long, pointed wings
short tail
ADULT
IN FLIGHT
streaked underparts
brown upperparts
JUVENILE
light yellow or bluish gray legs and toes
barred underwings
barred undertail feathers
prominent dark "mustache"
ADULT
dark "hood" on head
yellow eye-ring
bluish gray upperparts
dark spots on light buff breast
light underparts with horizontal barring
ADULT
yellow toes and legs

FLIGHT: powerful and direct; faster, deeper wing beats during pursuit; also soars.

Peregrine Falcons are distributed worldwide and are long-distance travelers—"Peregrine" means "wanderer." It has been shown to dive from great heights at speeds of up to 200mph (320kmph)—a technique known as "stooping." Like all true falcons, this species has a pointed "tooth" on its upper beak and a "notch" on the lower one, and it instinctively bites the neck of captured prey to kill it. From the 1950s–1980s, its breeding ability was reduced by the insecticide DDT, which resulted in thin eggshells that could easily be crushed by the parent. Peregrines were then bred in captivity, and later released into the wild. Their status is now secure.

VOICE Sharp *hek-hek-hek* when alarmed.

NESTING Shallow scrape on cliff or building (nest sites are used year after year); 2–5 eggs; 1 brood; March–June.

FEEDING Dives on prey—birds of various sizes in flight; now feeds on pigeons in cities.

PARENTAL CARE
An adult Peregrine gently feeds a hatchling bits of meat; the remaining egg is likely to hatch soon.

SIMILAR SPECIES

GYRFALCON see p.426
larger and stockier
longer tail
less defined "hood"

PRAIRIE FALCON see p.106
lighter head color
light sandy brown upperparts

OCCURRENCE
A variety of habitats across northern North America, ranging from open valleys to cities with tall buildings. Peregrines prefer to inhabit cliffs along sea coasts, in addition to inland mountain ranges, but also occur in open country such as scrubland and salt marshes.

Length **16in (41cm)**	Wingspan **3¼–3½ft (1–1.1m)**	Weight **22–35oz (620–1,000g)**
Social **Solitary/Pairs**	Lifespan **15–20 years**	Status **Secure**

DATE SEEN	WHERE	NOTES

Order **Falconiformes**	Family **Accipitridae**	Species ***Pandion haliaetus***

Osprey

wing tips at slight backward angle

dark band running across wing

wings bowed while soaring

barred tail

ADULT

ADULT

black eye stripe

finely barred underwings

IN FLIGHT

dark brown upperparts

crest on head

black mask on face

black bill

speckled chest

white underparts

pale gray legs and feet

ADULT

FLIGHT: stiff wing beats interspersed with glides; occasionally soars on migration.

Sometimes referred to as the "fish hawk" or "fish eagle," the Osprey is the only bird of prey in North America that feeds almost exclusively on live fish. Sharp spicules (tiny, spike-like growths) on the pads of its feet, its reversible outer toes, and an ability to lock its talons in place enable it to hold onto slippery fish. Some populations declined between the 1950s and 1980s due to the use of dangerous pesticides. However, the ban on use of these chemicals, along with availability of artificial nest sites and a tolerance of nearby human activity has allowed the Osprey to return to its former numbers. It is Nova Scotia's official bird.

VOICE Slow, whistled notes, falling in pitch: *tiooop, tioooop, tiooop*; also screams by displaying male.

NESTING Twig nest on tree, cliff, rock pinnacles, boulders, ground; 1–4 eggs; 1 brood; March–August.

FEEDING Dives to catch fish up to top 3ft (90cm) of water.

IMPROVING AERODYNAMICS
Once caught, a fish is held with its head pointing forward reducing drag as the bird flies.

SIMILAR SPECIES

BALD EAGLE (2ND YEAR)
see p.110

no crook in wings during flight

paler tail

GOLDEN EAGLE
see p.120

dark brown head

brown, feathered legs

OCCURRENCE
Breeds in a wide variety of habitats: northern forests, near shallow reservoirs, along freshwater rivers and large lakes, estuaries and salt marshes, coastal deserts and desert saltflat lagoons. Migrates through and winters in similar habitats.

Length **21–23in (53–58cm)**	Wingspan **5–6ft (1.5–1.8m)**	Weight **3–4½lb (1.4–2kg)**
Social **Solitary/Pairs**	Lifespan **Up to 25 years**	Status **Secure**

DATE SEEN	WHERE	NOTES

Order **Falconiformes**	Family **Accipitridae**	Species ***Elanus leucurus***

White-tailed Kite

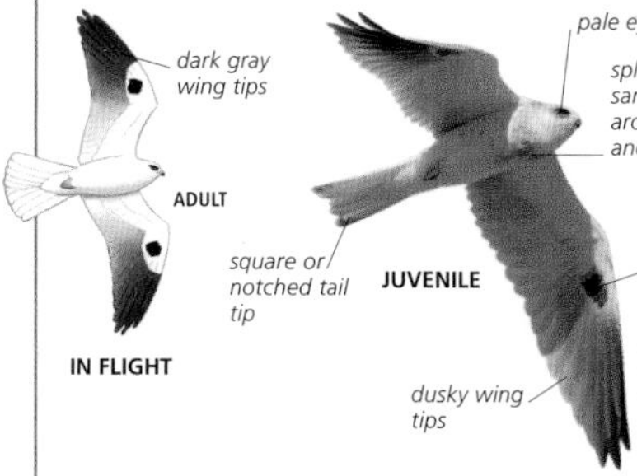

dark gray wing tips

ADULT

IN FLIGHT

pale eye

splashes of sandy rufous around neck and breast

square or notched tail tip

JUVENILE

dark wrist mark

dusky wing tips

white head and neck

orange eye

thin, black bill

gray upperparts, black triangle on shoulder

dusky gray wing tips

whitish underside

ADULT

white-sided tail

FLIGHT: fast, shallow wing beats interspersed with glides; hovers with tail down.

Formerly known as the Black-shouldered Kite, the White-tailed Kite almost disappeared from North America due to hunting and egg-collecting, but its numbers have rebounded in California. It is also found in Oregon, Washington, Florida, southern Texas, and from Mexico to Central and South America. These birds can be easily identified by their falcon-like shape, gray-and-white plumage, and hovering behavior when hunting for rodents in open grasslands. When not breeding, White-tailed Kites roost communally in groups of about 100. The species is largely sedentary, but dispersal takes place after breeding, especially of young birds.

VOICE Whistle-like *kewt* and an *eee-grack* call.

NESTING Twig nest lined with grass or hay; 4 eggs; 1–2 broods; February–August.

FEEDING Captures rodents such as voles and field mice; also birds, lizards, and insects from a hovering position.

A HIGH PERCH IS BEST
The White-tailed Kite like to perch as high up in trees as possible.

SIMILAR SPECIES

MISSISSIPPI KITE see p.427

darker body

deep red eyes

NORTHERN HARRIER ♂ see p.111

dark grayish wings

marked underparts

OCCURRENCE
Limited range in the US, breeds and winters in a restricted range; found in open grassland areas, and over large agricultural fields, as well as in rough wetlands with low, reedy, or brushy growth, open oak woodland and light savanna woods. Especially fond of damp, riverside areas.

Length **13–15in (33–38cm)**	Wingspan **3ft 3in–3½ft (1–1.1m)**	Weight **11–12oz (300–350g)**
Social **Colonies**	Lifespan **Up to 6 years**	Status **Secure**

DATE SEEN	WHERE	NOTES

Order **Falconiformes**	Family **Accipitridae**	Species ***Haliaeetus leucocephalus***

Bald Eagle

JUVENILE *dark head* *white tail*

ADULT *white head* *brown body*

IN FLIGHT

white belly and underwings mottled brown *dark brown eyes*

IMMATURE (2ND YEAR)

dark brown overall *dark bill starting to turn yellow at base*

IMMATURE (1ST YEAR)

dark eyestripe on whitish face

IMMATURE (3RD YEAR)

pure white head with yellow eyes *yellow, hooked bill* *dark chocolate-brown overall* *long, wedge-shaped, white tail* *yellow legs and toes*

ADULT

FLIGHT: slow, powerful wing beats; soars and glides on broad, wide wings held at a right angle.

The Bald Eagle was selected by an act of Congress in 1782 as the national emblem of the US. With its white head and tail, this large bird of prey, although an opportunist, prefers to scavenge on carrion and steal prey from other birds, including Ospreys. It was nearing extinction because the use of DDT led to reproductive failure. Declared endangered in 1967, the bird's population has since rebounded.

VOICE Suprisingly high-pitched voice, 3–4 notes followed by a rapidly descending series.

NESTING Huge stick nest, usually in tallest tree; 1–3 eggs; 1 brood; March–September.

FEEDING Favors carrion, especially fish, also eats birds, mammals, reptiles; steals fish from Osprey.

SIMILAR SPECIES

FERRUGINOUS HAWK dark head; see p.118 *whitish underparts*

GOLDEN EAGLE ◔ white in flight feathers; see p.120 *feathered legs*

SUBSTANTIAL ABODE
Bald eagles make the largest stick nest of all raptors; it can weigh up to two tons.

OCCURRENCE
Widespread across Canada and much of the US. Breeds in forested areas near water; also shoreline areas ranging from undeveloped to relatively well-developed with marked human activity; winters along major river systems and in coastal areas and occasionally even in arid regions of southwest US.

Length **28–38in (71–96cm)**	Wingspan **6½ft (2m)**	Weight **6½–14lb (3–6.5kg)**
Social **Solitary/Pairs**	Lifespan **Up to 28 years**	Status **Secure**

DATE SEEN	WHERE	NOTES

Order **Falconiformes**	Family **Accipitridae**	Species ***Circus cyaneus***

Northern Harrier

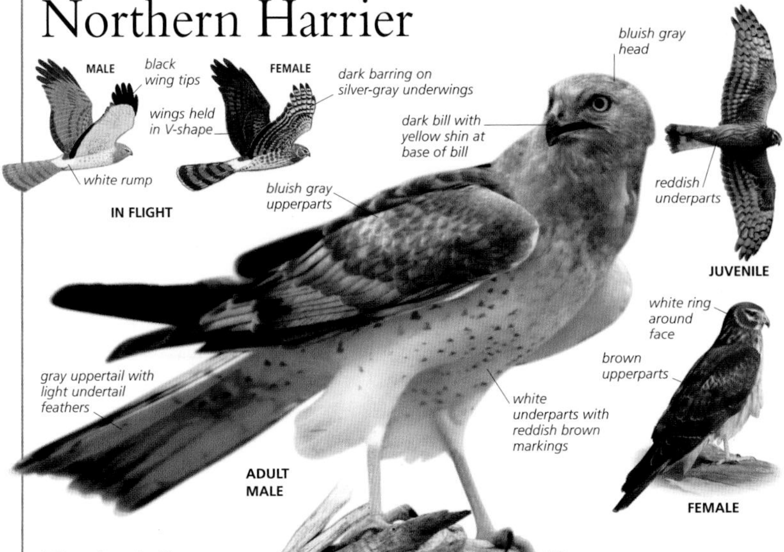

MALE
black wing tips
wings held in V-shape
white rump
FEMALE
dark barring on silver-gray underwings
IN FLIGHT

bluish gray head
dark bill with yellow shin at base of bill
bluish gray upperparts
gray uppertail with light undertail feathers
white underparts with reddish brown markings
ADULT MALE

reddish underparts
JUVENILE

white ring around face
brown upperparts
FEMALE

Found nearly all over North America, the Northern Harrier is most often seen flying buoyantly low in search of food. A white rump, V-shaped wings, and tilting flight make this species easily identifiable. The blue-gray males are quite different to the dark-brown females. The bird's most recognizable characteristic is its owl-like face, which contains stiff feathers to help channel in sounds from prey. Northern Harriers are highly migratory throughout their range.

VOICE Call given by both sexes in rapid succession at nest: *kek* becomes more high-pitched when intruders are spotted.

NESTING Platform of sticks on ground in open, wet field; 4–6 eggs; 1 brood; April–September.

FEEDING Mostly hunts rodents, such as mice and muskrats; also birds, frogs, reptiles; occasionally takes larger prey such as rabbits.

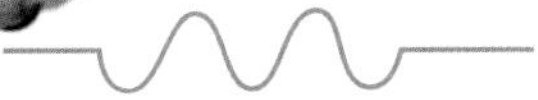

FLIGHT: low and slow with lazy flaps, alternating with buoyant, brusquely tilting glides.

WATERY DWELLING
To avoid predators, Northern Harriers prefer to raise their young on wet sites in tall, dense vegetation.

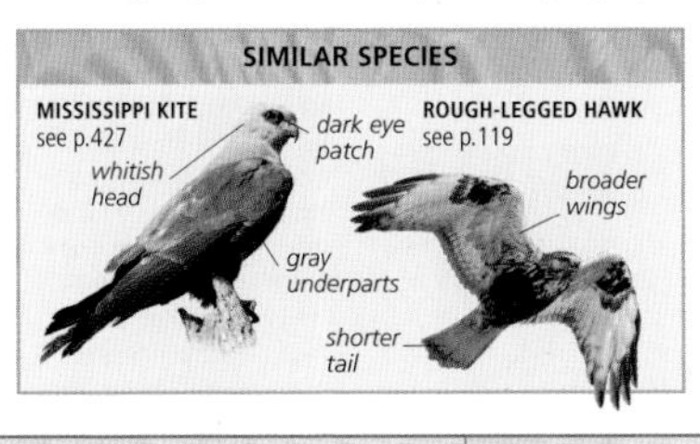

OCCURRENCE
Breeds in a variety of open wetlands: marshes, meadows, pastures, fallow fields across most of North America; winters in open habitats like deserts, coastal sand dunes, cropland, grasslands, marshy, and riverine areas.

Length **18–20in (46–51cm)**	Wingspan **3½–4ft (1.1m–1.2m)**	Weight **11–26oz (300–750g)**
Social **Solitary/Pairs/Colonies**	Lifespan **Up to 16 years**	Status **Secure**

DATE SEEN	WHERE	NOTES

Order **Falconiformes**	Family **Accipitridae**	Species ***Accipiter striatus***

Sharp-shinned Hawk

This small and swift hawk is quite adept at capturing birds, occasionally even taking species larger than itself. The Sharp-shinned Hawk's short, rounded wings and long tail allow it to make abrupt turns and lightning-fast dashes in thick woods and dense shrubby terrain. With needle-like talons, long, spindle-thin legs, and long toes, this hawk is well adapted to snatching birds in flight. The prey is plucked before being consumed or fed to the nestlings.

VOICE High-pitched, repeated *kiu kiu kiu* call; sometimes makes squealing sound when disturbed at nest.

NESTING Sturdy nest of sticks lined with twigs or pieces of bark; sometimes an old crow or squirrel nest; 3–4 eggs; 1 brood; March–June.

FEEDING Catches small birds, such as sparrows and wood-warblers, on the wing, or takes them unaware while perched.

FLIGHT: rapid, direct, and strong; nimble enough to maneuver in dense forest; soars during migration.

HUNTING BIRDS
A Sharp-shinned Hawk pauses on the ground with a freshly captured sparrow in its talons.

OCCURRENCE
Deep coniferous forests and mixed hardwood–conifer woodlands across North America from the tree limit in northern Canada to the Gulf states. During fall migration sometimes seen in flocks of hundreds of individuals. Winters in Central America from Guatemala to Panama.

Length **11in (28cm)**	Wingspan **23in (58cm)**	Weight **3½–6oz (100–175g)**
Social **Solitary/Flocks**	Lifespan **At least 10 years**	Status **Secure**

DATE SEEN	WHERE	NOTES

Order **Falconiformes**	Family **Accipitridae**	Species ***Accipiter cooperii***

Cooper's Hawk

FLIGHT: fast with rapid wing beats interspersed with glides; sometimes soars.

A secretive and inconspicuous bird, Cooper's Hawk was named by Charles Bonaparte, nephew of French Emperor Napoleon Bonaparte, for William C. Cooper, a noted New York naturalist. It is a typical woodland hawk, capable of quickly maneuvering through dense vegetation. Although it prefers to stay close to cover, it will venture out in search of food. Should a human approach the nest of a Cooper's Hawk, the brooding adult will quietly glide down and away from the nest tree rather than attack the intruder.

VOICE Most common call a staccato *ca-ca-ca-ca*; other vocalizations include as many as 40 different calls.

NESTING Medium-sized, stick nest, usually in a large deciduous tree; 4–5 eggs; 1 brood; April–May.

FEEDING Catches birds, such as robins and blackbirds; larger females can capture grouse; also eats chipmunks, small squirrels, and even bats.

DENSE BARRING
This hawk has characteristic fine, reddish brown, horizontal barring on its undersides.

OCCURRENCE
Breeds in woodlands across northern North America, southern Canada, and the northern US, south to Florida, Texas, and northwestern Mexico. Likes mature deciduous forests with leaf cover, and also roosts in conifers. Winters in southwestern US and Mexico.

Length **15½–17½in (40–45cm)**	Wingspan **28–34in (70–86cm)**	Weight **13–19oz (375–525g)**
Social **Solitary/Pairs**	Lifespan **At least 10 years**	Status **Secure**

DATE SEEN	WHERE	NOTES

Order **Falconiformes**	Family **Accipitridae**	Species ***Accipiter gentilis***

Northern Goshawk

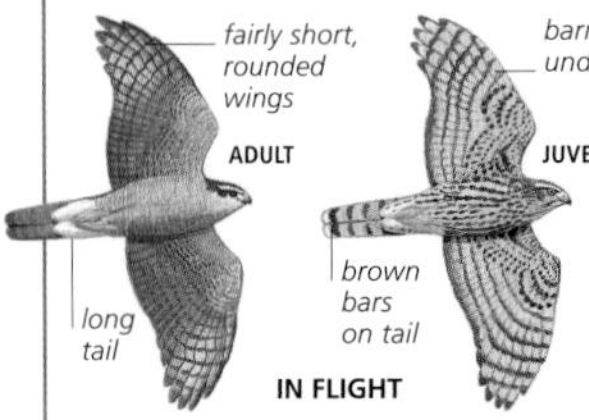
fairly short, rounded wings
ADULT
barred underwings
JUVENILE
long tail
brown bars on tail
IN FLIGHT

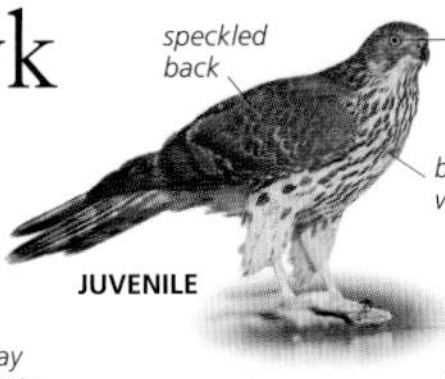
speckled back
light yellow iris
buff underparts with vertical streaks
JUVENILE

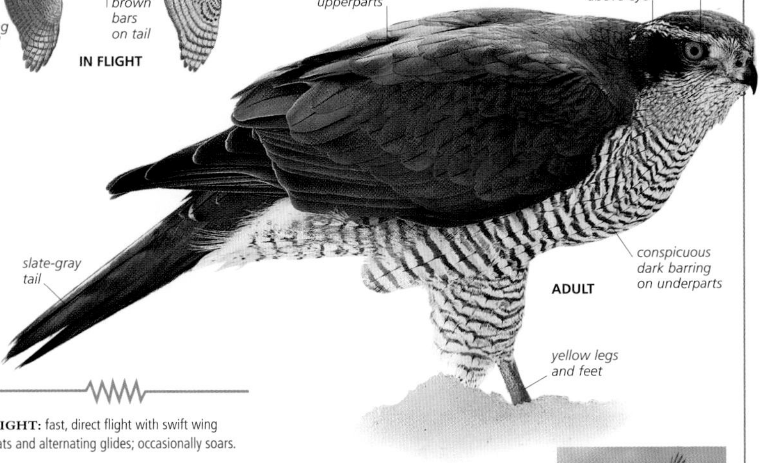
yellow to orange eye
conspicuous white stripe above eye
slate-gray upperparts
slate-gray tail
conspicuous dark barring on underparts
ADULT
yellow legs and feet

FLIGHT: fast, direct flight with swift wing beats and alternating glides; occasionally soars.

The powerful and agile Northern Goshawk is secretive by nature and not easily observed, even in regions where it is common. It has few natural enemies, but will defend its territories, nests, and young fiercely, by repeatedly diving and screaming at intruders that get too close. Spring hikers and turkey-hunters occasionally discover Northern Goshawks by wandering into their territory and being driven off by the angry occupants.

VOICE Loud, high-pitched *gek-gek-gek* when agitated.

NESTING Large stick structures lined with bark and plant matter in the mid- to lower region of tree; 1–3 eggs; 1 brood; May–June.

FEEDING Sits and waits on perch before diving rapidly; preys on birds as large as grouse and pheasants; also mammals, including hares and squirrels.

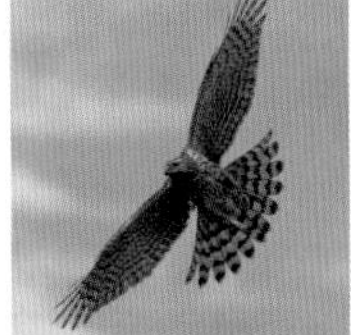

OCCASIONAL SOARER
A juvenile Northern Goshawk takes advantage of a thermal, soaring over its territory.

SIMILAR SPECIES

GYRFALCON (GRAY FORM) see p.426

longer, pointed wings
no streaks on underparts

COOPER'S HAWK see p.113

brownish upperparts
streaked underparts

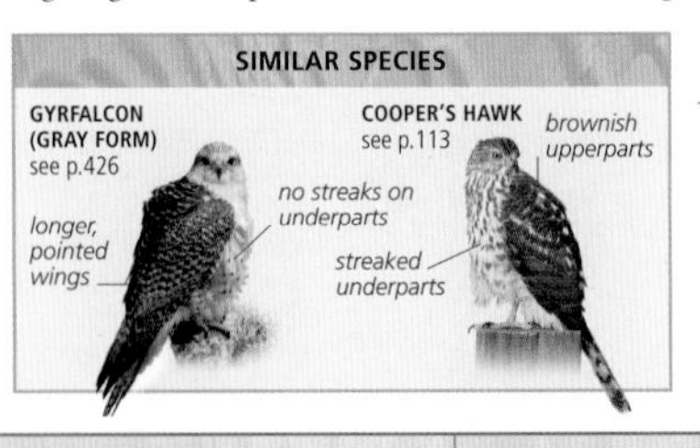

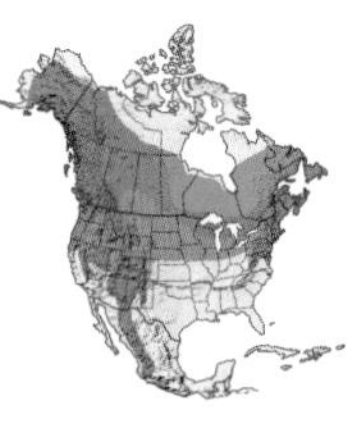

OCCURRENCE
Breeds in deep deciduous, coniferous, and mixed woodlands in northern North America, from the tundra–taiga border south to California, northern Mexico, and Pennsylvania in the eastern US, absent from east central US. The Northern Goshawk is widespread in northern Eurasia.

Length **21in (53cm)**	Wingspan **3½ft (1.1m)**	Weight **2–3lb (0.9–1.4kg)**
Social **Solitary/Pairs**	Lifespan **Up to 20 years**	Status **Secure**

DATE SEEN	WHERE	NOTES

Order **Falconiformes**	Family **Accipitridae**	Species ***Buteo lineatus***

Red-shouldered Hawk

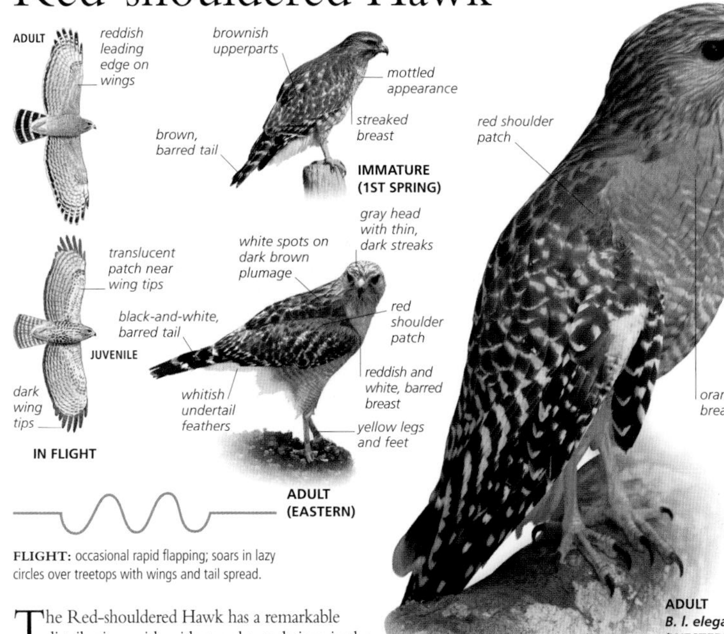

FLIGHT: occasional rapid flapping; soars in lazy circles over treetops with wings and tail spread.

The Red-shouldered Hawk has a remarkable distribution, with widespread populations in the East, Northeast, and Midwest, then in the West, from Oregon to Baja California, despite a geographical gap of 1,000 miles (1,600km) between the two regions. Eastern birds are divided into four subspecies; western populations belong to the subspecies *B. l. elegans.* The red shoulder patches are not always evident, but the striped tail and translucent "windows" in the wings are easily identifiable.

VOICE Call a whistled *kee-aah*, accented on first syllable, descending on second.

NESTING Platform of sticks, dried leaves, bark, moss, and lichens in trees not far from water; 3–4 eggs; 1 brood; March–July.

FEEDING Catches mice, chipmunks, and voles; also snakes, toads, frogs, crayfish, and small birds.

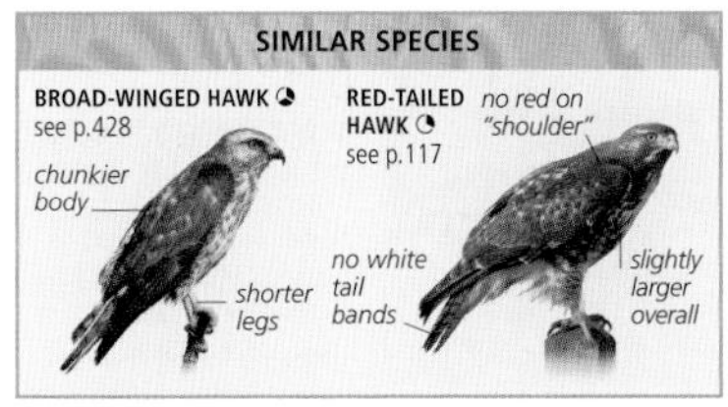

CHESTNUT WING
When seen from below, the reddish forewing of this adult hawk is clearly visible.

OCCURRENCE
Eastern populations breed in woodlands and forest, deciduous or mixed, whereas those in the West occur in oak woodlands and eucalyptus groves. In Florida, this species also lives in mangroves. Northeastern birds migrate to Mexico.

Length **17–24in (43–61cm)**	Wingspan **3–3½ft (0.9–1.1m)**	Weight **17–27oz (475–775g)**
Social **Solitary/Flocks**	Lifespan **Up to 18 years**	Status **Declining (p)**

DATE SEEN	WHERE	NOTES

Order **Falconiformes**	Family **Accipitridae**	Species ***Buteo swainsoni***

Swainson's Hawk

long pointed wings
dark wing tips
ADULT (LIGHT FORM)
JUVENILE (LIGHT FORM)
dark chest
IN FLIGHT

reddish breast and belly
ADULT (INTERMEDIATE FORM)

whitish head
spotted underparts
JUVENILE (LIGHT FORM)

dark brown head and breast
spotted underparts
ADULT (DARK FORM)

white face and chin
slender shape overall
pale reddish upper chest
white underbelly
longish tail
wing tips reach end of tail when perched
ADULT (LIGHT FORM)

FLIGHT: soaring, buoyant flight with deep wing beats; will often hover and hang motionless.

Swainson's Hawk is perhaps most famous for its spectacular 6,000-mile (9,650km) fall migration from the Canadian prairies to the lower regions of South America, when thousands can be observed soaring in the air at any one time. While migrating, this hawk averages 125 miles (200km) a day. There are three color forms: light, dark, and an intermediate form between the two.

VOICE Alarm call a shrill, plaintive scream *kreeeee* given by both sexes; high-pitched *keeeoooo* fading at the end.

NESTING Bulky, flimsy pile of sticks or various debris, in solitary tree or on utility poles; 1–4 eggs; 1 brood; April–July.

FEEDING Eats ground squirrels, pocket gophers, mice, voles, bats, rabbits; also snakes, lizards, songbirds.

ON THE LOOKOUT
This slim, elegant species will perch before diving for its prey.

OCCURRENCE
Breeds in scattered trees along streams; found in areas of open woodland, sparse shrubland, grasslands, and agricultural land; winters in native Argentinian grassland, and in harvested fields where grasshoppers are found abundantly.

SIMILAR SPECIES

HARRIS'S HAWK see p.427
chestnut thighs and wing patches
long legs
white on tail

RED-TAILED HAWK see p.117
bulkier overall
shorter wings
red tail

Length **19–22in (48–56cm)**	Wingspan **4½ft (1.4m)**	Weight **1½–3lb (0.7–1.4kg)**
Social **Solitary/Pairs/Flocks**	Lifespan **Up to 19 years**	Status **Declining (p)**

DATE SEEN	WHERE	NOTES

Order **Falconiformes**	Family **Accipitridae**	Species ***Buteo jamaicensis***

Red-tailed Hawk

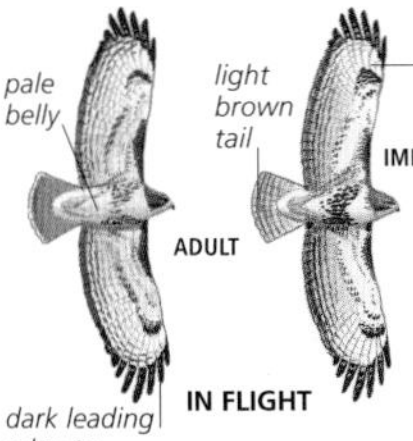

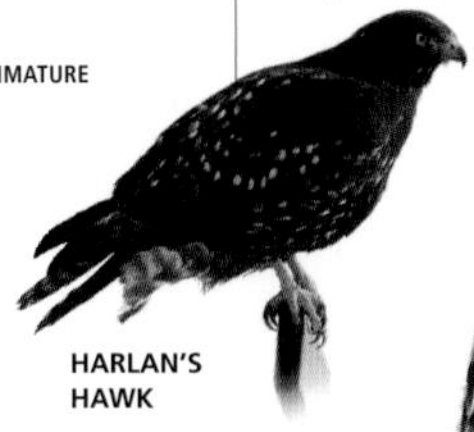

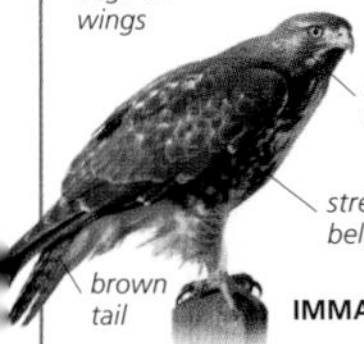

pale belly
light brown tail
pale outer wing feathers
IMMATURE
ADULT
dark leading edge to wings
IN FLIGHT
very dark plumage with white spots
HARLAN'S HAWK
brown overall
streaked belly band
brown tail
IMMATURE
brownish eye
reddish brown streaking on head
white spots on back
ADULT (LIGHT FORM)
yellowish legs and toes
distinctive rufous tail

FLIGHT: soaring flight punctuated with lazy, slow wing flaps; hangs motionless in the wind.

Of all North American hawks, the Red-tailed Hawk is the most widely distributed and commonly seen. As many as 15 subspecies have been described to date, varying in coloration, tail markings, and size. The very dark Harlan's Hawk, which breeds in Alaska and northwestern Canada, was at one time considered a subspecies, but genetic studies have since confirmed it as a separate species. While it occasionally stoops on prey, the Red-tailed Hawk usually adopts a sit-and-wait approach.

VOICE Call *kee-eee-arrr* that rises then descends over a period of 2–3 seconds.

NESTING Large platform of sticks, twigs on top of tall tree, cliff, building, ledge, or billboard; 2 eggs; 1 brood; February–September.

FEEDING Captures small mammals, such as voles, mice, rats; birds including pheasant, quail; small reptiles; carrion also eaten.

FLYING HIGH
A Red-tailed Hawk soaring over an open field is a common sight; this bird is an immature.

SIMILAR SPECIES

FERRUGINOUS HAWK (LIGHT FORM) see p.118
larger bill
larger overall
mostly white underparts

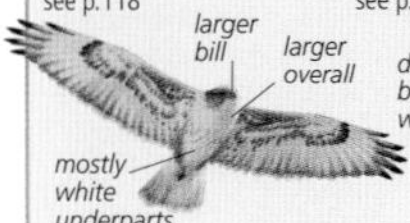

ROUGH-LEGGED HAWK (DARK FORM) see p.119
dark band on white tail

OCCURRENCE
Breeds, forages in open areas in wide range of habitats and altitudes: scrub desert, grasslands, agricultural fields and pastures, coniferous and deciduous woodland, and tropical rainforest. Prefers areas with tall perch sites; can be found in suburban woodlots.

Length **18–26in (46–65cm)**	Wingspan **3½–4¼ft (1.1–1.3m)**	Weight **1½–3¼lb (0.7–1.5kg)**
Social **Solitary/Pairs**	Lifespan **Up to 21 years**	Status **Secure**

DATE SEEN	WHERE	NOTES

Order **Falconiformes**	Family **Accipitridae**	Species ***Buteo regalis***

Ferruginous Hawk

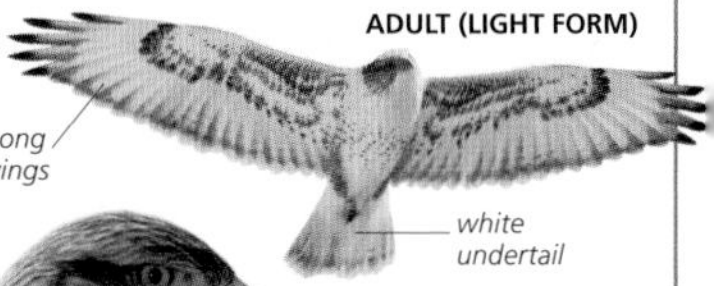

ADULT (LIGHT FORM)
relatively long pointed wings
white undertail

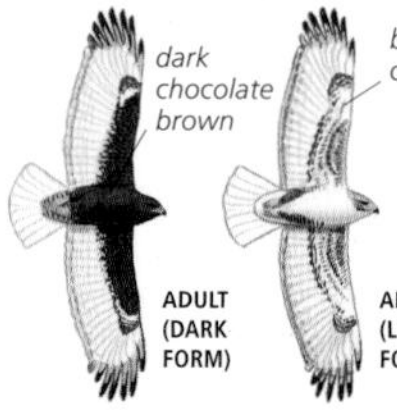

dark chocolate brown
brown and white contrast on wings
ADULT (DARK FORM)
ADULT (LIGHT FORM)
IN FLIGHT

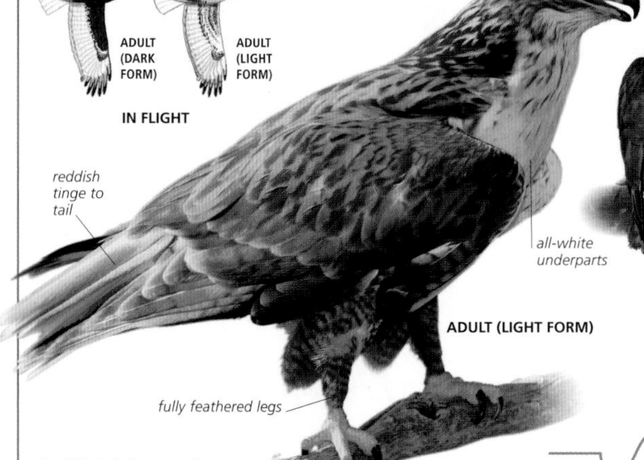

large bill
reddish tinge to tail
all-white underparts
ADULT (LIGHT FORM)
fully feathered legs

dark brown overall
JUVENILE (DARK FORM)
dark spots on belly
JUVENILE (LIGHT FORM)

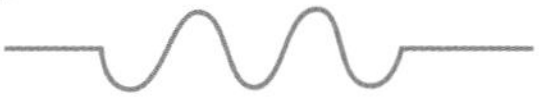

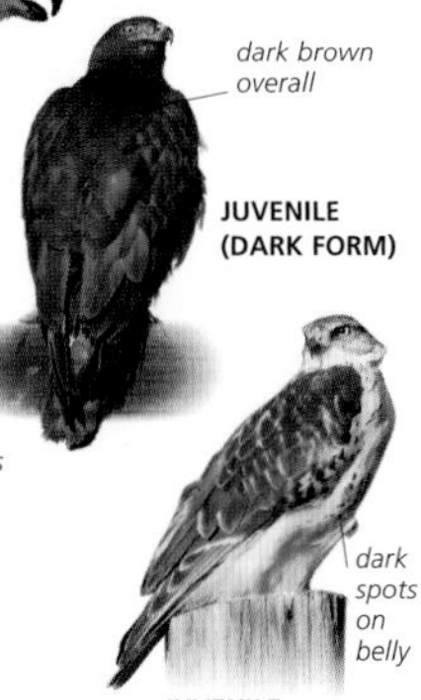

FLIGHT: slow, deep wing beats alternating with lazy glides; soars high with thermals.

This inhabitant of open country is the largest North American hawk. Its Latin name *regalis* means kingly, and its English name refers to its rusty coloring. It is a versatile nester: it builds its stick nests on cliffs or nearly level ground, trees, and man-made structures like farm buildings. Regrettably, its preference for prairie dogs, which are declining because of habitat loss, shooting, and pesticide use, threatens Ferruginous Hawk populations.

VOICE Screaming *Kree-aa* or *kaah, kaah* during courtship; quieter, lower-pitched, longer alarm call.

NESTING Large stick nest of old sagebrush stems, sticks, and various debris, lined with bark strips; 2–4 eggs; March–August.

FEEDING Hunts mainly rabbits, hares, ground squirrels, and prairie dogs; rarely fledgling birds, amphibians, and reptiles.

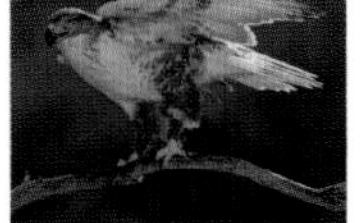

PERCHED HUNTER
The Ferruginous Hawk usually hunts from a perch such as a rock or a branch.

SIMILAR SPECIES

RED-TAILED HAWK, (LIGHT FORM)
see p.117
smaller bill
dark rufous tail
smaller overall
ROUGH-LEGGED HAWK
see p.119
smaller bill
white tail with dark band

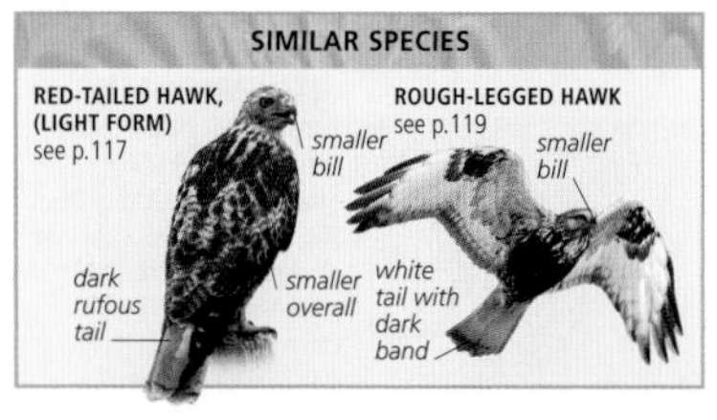

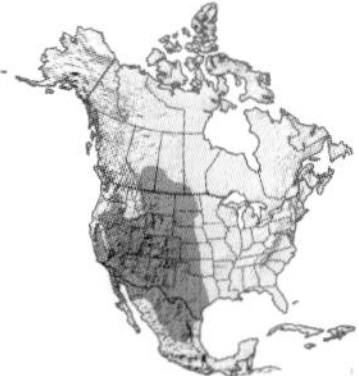

OCCURRENCE
In western North America, breeds in low-elevation grasslands interrupted by cliffs or isolated trees for nesting; winters across southwestern US and Mexico in open terrain ranging from grassland to desert.

Length **22–27in (56–69cm)**	Wingspan **4¼–4½ft (1.3–1.4m)**	Weight **2½–4½lb (1–2kg)**
Social **Solitary/Pairs**	Lifespan **Up to 20 years**	Status **Secure**

DATE SEEN	WHERE	NOTES

Order **Falconiformes**	Family **Accipitridae**	Species ***Buteo lagopus***

Rough-legged Hawk

dark wing tips

ADULT

dark tail band

IN FLIGHT

bold black patch

FEMALE

black trailing edge

one line before tail tip

pale forehead

short, broad head

MALE

JUVENILE

black belly

barred underparts

thin bands near tail tip

white tail with faint black band at tip

plain gray brown or frosty feather edges

MALE

FLIGHT: strong wing beats; usually soars on thermals; frequently hovers in one spot.

The Rough-legged Hawk is known for its extensive variation in plumage—some individuals are almost completely black, whereas others are much paler, very nearly cream or white. The year to year fluctuation in numbers of breeding pairs in a given region strongly suggest that this species is nomadic, moving about as a response to the availability of its rodent prey.

VOICE Wintering birds silent; breeding birds utter loud, cat-like mewing or thin whistles, slurred downward when alarmed.

NESTING Bulky mass of sticks, lined with grasses, sedges, feathers and fur from prey, constructed on cliff ledge; 2–6 eggs; 1 brood; April–August.

FEEDING Hovers in one spot over fields in search of prey; lemmings and voles in spring and summer; mice and shrews in winters; variety of birds, ground squirrels, and rabbits year-round.

ABUNDANT FOOD SUPPLY
When small mammals are abundant, these hawks produce large broods on cliff ledges in the tundra.

SIMILAR SPECIES

NORTHERN HARRIER ◔ see p.111
reddish underparts
longer wings

FERRUGINOUS HAWK see p.118
reddish upperparts
white underparts

OCCURRENCE
Breeds in rough, open country with low crags and cliffs, in high subarctic and Arctic regions; found on the edge of extensive forest or forest clearings, and in treeless tundra, uplands, and alpine habitats. Winters in open areas with fields, marshes, and rough grasslands.

Length **19–20in (48–51cm)**	Wingspan **4¼–4½ft (1.3–1.4m)**	Weight **1½–3lb (0.7–1.4kg)**
Social **Solitary**	Lifespan **Up to 18 years**	Status **Secure**

DATE SEEN	WHERE	NOTES

Order **Falconiformes**	Family **Accipitridae**	Species ***Aquila chrysaetos***

Golden Eagle

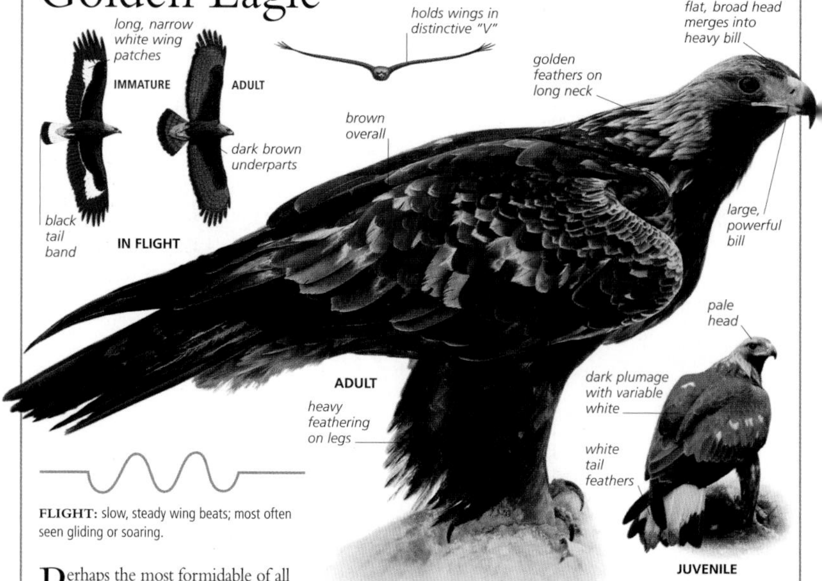

long, narrow white wing patches
IMMATURE
ADULT
black tail band
dark brown underparts
IN FLIGHT
holds wings in distinctive "V"
brown overall
golden feathers on long neck
flat, broad head merges into heavy bill
large, powerful bill
ADULT
heavy feathering on legs
pale head
dark plumage with variable white
white tail feathers
JUVENILE

FLIGHT: slow, steady wing beats; most often seen gliding or soaring.

Perhaps the most formidable of all North American birds of prey, the Golden Eagle is found mostly in the western part of the continent. It defends large territories ranging from 8–12 square miles (20–30 square kilometers), containing up to 14 nests. Although its appears sluggish, it is amazingly swift and agile, and employs a variety of hunting techniques to catch specific prey. Shot and poisoned by ranchers and trappers, it is unfortunately also faced with dwindling habitat and food sources due to human development.

VOICE Mostly silent, but breeding adults yelp and mew.

NESTING Large pile of sticks and vegetation on cliffs, in trees, and on man-made structures; 1–3 eggs; 1 brood; April–August.

FEEDING Eats mammals, such as hares, rabbits, ground squirrels, prairie dogs, marmots, foxes, and coyotes; also birds.

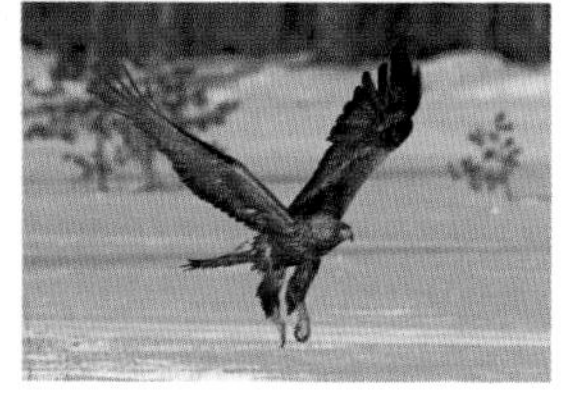

POWER AND STRENGTH
The Golden Eagle symbolizes all birds of prey, with its sharp talons, hooked bill, and large size.

SIMILAR SPECIES

BALD EAGLE ◕ see p.110

white head and neck
some pale wing feathers

FERRUGINOUS HAWK ◔ **(DARK FORM)** see p.118

no golden tinge
smaller overall

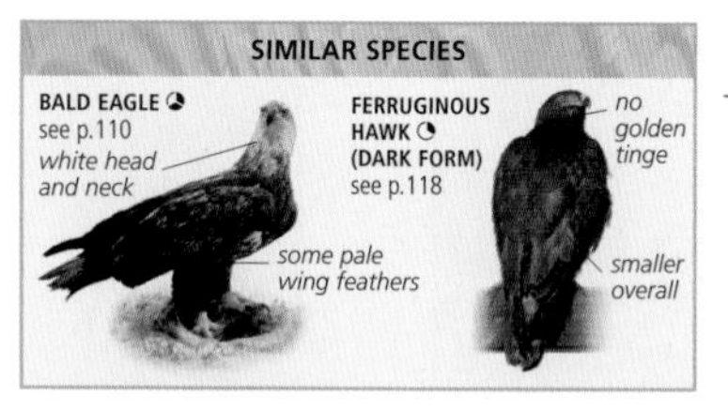

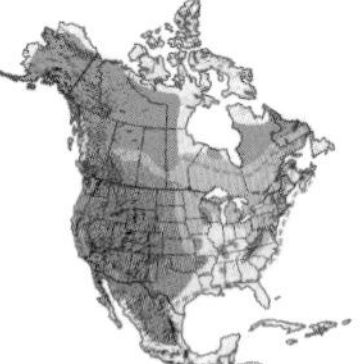

OCCURRENCE
In North America occurs mostly in grasslands, wetlands, and rocky areas; breeds south to Mexico, in open and semi-open habitats from sea level to 12,000ft (3,500m) including tundra, shrublands, grasslands, coniferous forests, farmland, areas close to streams or rivers; winters in open habitat.

Length **28–33in (70–84cm)**	Wingspan **6–7¼ft (1.8–2.2m)**	Weight **6½–13lb (3–6kg)**
Social **Solitary/Pairs**	Lifespan **Up to 39 years**	Status **Declining (p)**

DATE SEEN	WHERE	NOTES

RAILS & RELATIVES

THE RALLIDAE, OR RAIL family, is a diverse group of small to medium-sized marsh birds. In the US and Canada, rallids, as they are known collectively, are represented by three rails, three crakes, two gallinules, and a coot. Rails and crakes inhabit dense marshland and are secretive, solitary, and inconspicuous, whereas coots and gallinules are seen on open water. Rallids are chicken-like birds with stubby tails and short, rounded wings. Rails have drab, camouflage coloring, and are long-legged, long-billed, and narrow-bodied. Crakes are smaller but similar, with shorter necks and stout, stubby bills. Both rails and crakes walk and run on the ground in marsh vegetation, but can swim well. Colorful gallinules include the Common Moorhen and the Purple Gallinule. Rallids look like weak flyers, but many migrate great distances at night. None has a specialized diet; their food includes insects, small crabs, slugs, snails, and plant matter. Rallids nest in pairs, the birds keep in close contact by calling loudly and clearly.

THIN AS A RAIL
This marsh-dwelling Clapper Rail has a narrow body that enables it to slip easily through reedbeds.

FLAT LANDING
Purple Gallinules can land safely on lily pads, because their large toes spread their weight.

CRANES

CRANES ARE LARGE wading birds, superficially similar to storks and to the larger herons and egrets. However, several anatomical differences place them in a different family (Gruidae), within a different order (Gruiformes). The two North American crane species have much lighter bills than storks. Typically, too, long inner wing feathers form a "bustle" on a standing crane, giving it a different profile than a heron. Additionally, cranes fly with their necks straight out, rather than in the tight S-curve regularly seen in similar-sized herons. The Whooping Crane is the tallest bird in North America, standing nearly 5ft (1.5m) high.

CRANE RALLY
Large numbers of Sandhill Cranes gather on feeding grounds in winter. Groups arrive in V-formation.

Order **Gruiformes**	Family **Rallidae**	Species ***Coturnicops noveboracensis***

Yellow Rail

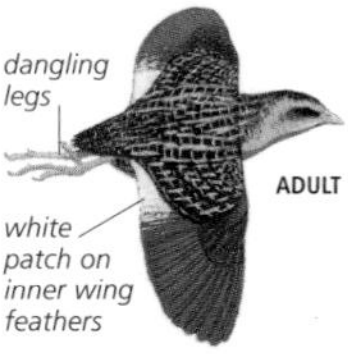
dangling legs
ADULT
white patch on inner wing feathers
IN FLIGHT

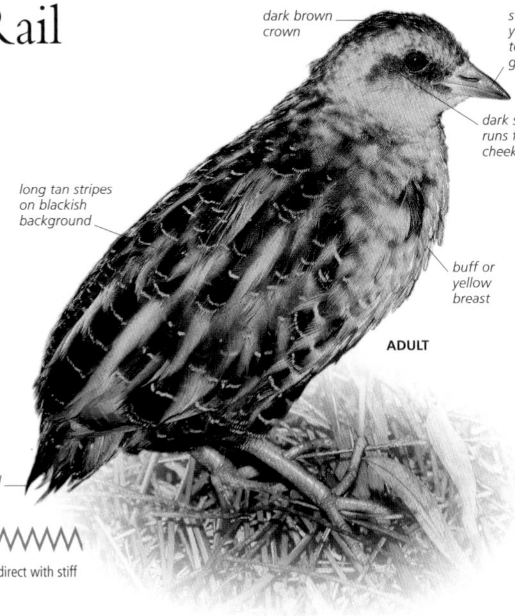
dark brown crown
stubby yellow to olive-gray bill
dark stripe runs from cheek to bill
long tan stripes on blackish background
buff or yellow breast
ADULT
short tail

FLIGHT: low, weak, short, and direct with stiff wing beats; dangling legs.

Although widespread, the diminutive, secretive, nocturnal Yellow Rail is extremely difficult to observe in its dense, damp, grassy habitat, and is detected mainly by its voice. The Yellow Rail, whose Latin name of *noveboracensis* means "New Yorker," has a small head, almost no neck, a stubby bill, a plump, almost tail-less body, and short legs. The bill of the male turns yellow in the breeding season; for the rest of the year, it is olive-gray like the female's. Although the Yellow Rail tends to dart for cover when disturbed, when it does fly, it reveals a distinctive white patch on its inner wing.

VOICE Two clicking calls followed by three more given by males, usually at night, reminiscent of two pebbles being struck together; also descending cackles, quiet croaking, and soft clucking.

NESTING Small cup of grasses and sedges, on the ground or in a plant tuft above water, concealed by overhanging vegetation; 8–10 eggs; 1 brood; May–June.

FEEDING Plucks seeds, aquatic insects, various small crustaceans, and mollusks (primarily small freshwater snails) from vegetation or ground; forages on the marsh surface or in shallow water, hidden by grass.

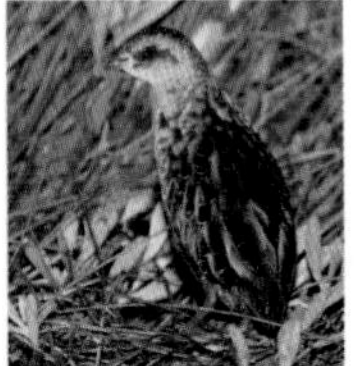

CURIOUS LISTENER
Imitating the "tick" calls of the Yellow Rail is often an effective way to lure it out into the open.

SIMILAR SPECIES

SORA see p.124

black streaks on brown upperparts
gray underparts

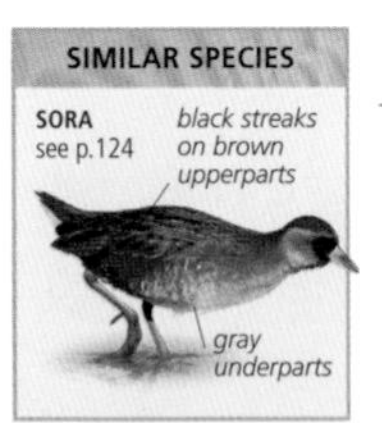

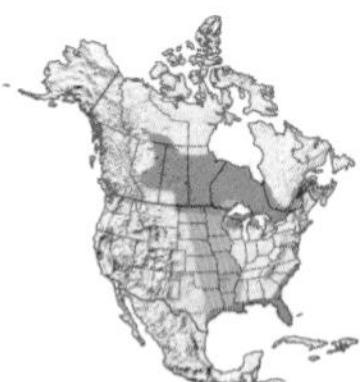

OCCURRENCE
Breeds in brackish and freshwater marshes and wet sedge meadows in Canada and the north central US; there is an isolated breeding population in Oregon. Winters predominantly in coastal marshes along the eastern seaboard.

Length **7¼in (18.5cm)**	Wingspan **11in (28cm)**	Weight **1¾oz (50g)**
Social **Pairs**	Lifespan **Unknown**	Status **Secure**

DATE SEEN	WHERE	NOTES

Order **Gruiformes**	Family **Rallidae**	Species ***Rallus limicola***

Virginia Rail

A smaller version of the King Rail, this freshwater marsh dweller is similar to its other relatives, more often heard than seen. Distributed in a wide range, the Virginia Rail spends most of its time in thick, reedy vegetation, which it pushes using its "rail thin" body and flexible vertebrae. Although it spends most of its life walking, it can swim and even dive to escape danger. The Virginia Rail is a partial migrant that leaves its northern breeding grounds in winter.

VOICE Series of pig-like grunting *oinks* that start loud and sharp, becoming steadily softer; also emits a series of double notes *ka-dik ka-dik*.

NESTING Substantial cup of plant material, concealed by bent-over stems; 5–12 eggs; 1–2 broods; April–July.

FEEDING Actively stalks prey or may wait and dive into water; primarily eats snails, insects, and spiders, but may also eat seeds.

FLIGHT: weak and struggling with outstretched neck and legs trailing behind.

HARD TO SPOT
The secretive Virginia Rail is difficult to spot in its reedy habitat.

SIMILAR SPECIES

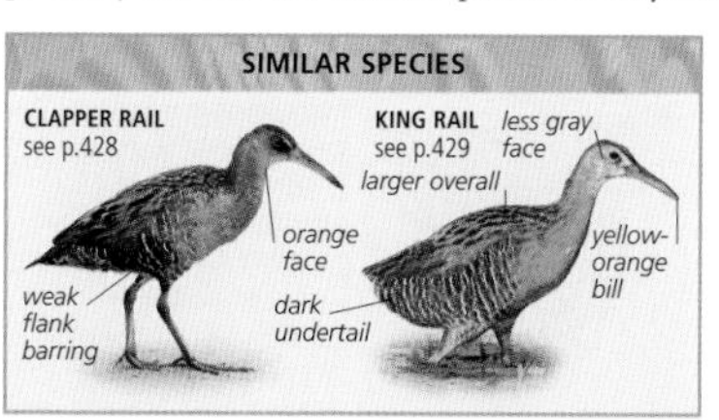

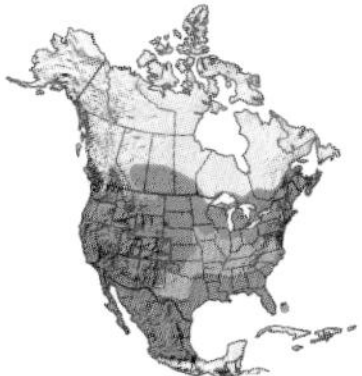

OCCURRENCE
Breeds in freshwater habitats across North America, and is found throughout the year along the West Coast of the US. Other western populations move to central Mexico for the winter.

Length **9½in (24cm)**	Wingspan **13in (33cm)**	Weight **3oz (85g)**
Social **Pairs**	Lifespan **Unknown**	Status **Secure**

DATE SEEN	WHERE	NOTES

Order **Gruiformes**	Family **Rallidae**	Species ***Porzana carolina***

Sora

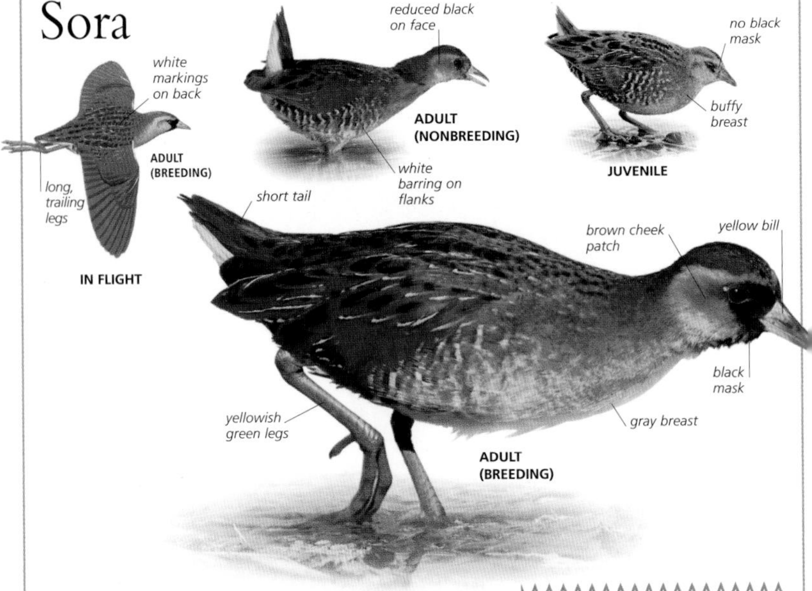

white markings on back
long, trailing legs
ADULT (BREEDING)
IN FLIGHT

reduced black on face
ADULT (NONBREEDING)
white barring on flanks

no black mask
buffy breast
JUVENILE

short tail
brown cheek patch
yellow bill
black mask
yellowish green legs
gray breast
ADULT (BREEDING)

Despite being the most widely distributed rail in North America, the Sora is rarely seen. It breeds in freshwater marshes and migrates hundreds of miles south in winter regardless of its weak and hesitant flight. It swims well, with a characteristic head-bobbing action. The Sora can be spotted walking at the edge of emergent vegetation—its yellow bill and black mask distinguish it from other rails.

VOICE Call a long, high, and loud, descending, horse-like whinny *ko-wee-hee-hee-hee-hee*; has an upslurred whistle.

NESTING Loosely woven basket of marsh vegetation suspended above water or positioned in clumps of vegetation on the water's surface; 8–11 eggs; 1 brood; May–June.

FEEDING Rakes vegetation with feet or pulls with bill in search of seeds of wetland plants, insects, spiders, and snails.

FLIGHT: appears weak, yet strenuous; wing beats hurried and constant.

CHICKEN-LIKE WALK
A rare sight, the Sora walks chicken-like through a marsh, its body in a low crouch.

OCCURRENCE
Breeds in freshwater marshes with emergent vegetation across most of temperate North America; rarely in salt marshes along the Atlantic Coast. Winters in freshwater, saltwater, and brackish marshes with spartina grass from the southern US to northern South America.

Length **8½in (22cm)**	Wingspan **14in (36cm)**	Weight **2⅝oz (75g)**
Social **Solitary**	Lifespan **Unknown**	Status **Secure**

DATE SEEN	WHERE	NOTES

Order **Gruiformes**	Family **Rallidae**	Species ***Gallinula chloropus***

Common Moorhen

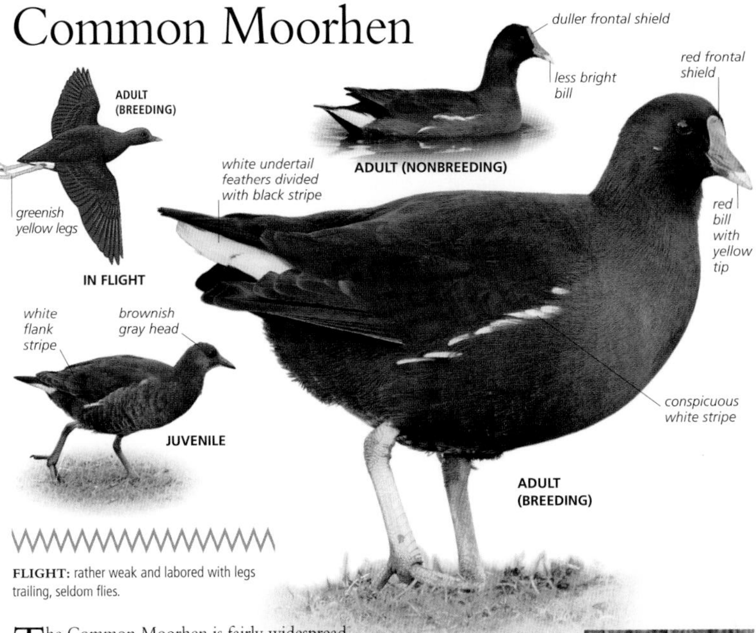

ADULT (BREEDING)

greenish yellow legs

IN FLIGHT

duller frontal shield

less bright bill

ADULT (NONBREEDING)

white undertail feathers divided with black stripe

red frontal shield

red bill with yellow tip

white flank stripe

brownish gray head

JUVENILE

conspicuous white stripe

ADULT (BREEDING)

FLIGHT: rather weak and labored with legs trailing, seldom flies.

The Common Moorhen is fairly widespread in the eastern US, although its distribution is more patchy in the western states. It has similarities in behavior and habitat to both the true rails and coots. Equally at home on land and water, its long toes allow it to walk easily over floating vegetation and soft mud. When walking or swimming, the Common Moorhen nervously jerks its short tail, revealing its white undertail feathers, and bobs its head.

VOICE A variety of hen-like clucks and cackles, including an explosive *krrooo*.

NESTING Bulky platform of aquatic vegetation with growing plants pulled over to conceal it, or close to water; 5–11 eggs, 1–3 broods; May–August, maybe year round in Florida.

FEEDING Forages mainly on aquatic and terrestrial plants and aquatic vegetation; also eats snails, spiders, and insects.

DUAL HABITAT
A walker and a swimmer, the Moorhen is equally at home on land and in water.

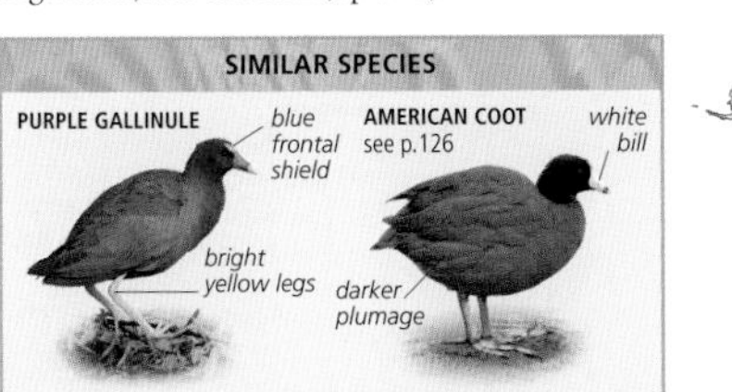

OCCURRENCE
Breeds in freshwater habitats in the eastern US and Canada; more localized in the West. Winters in warmer areas with open water, such as southern California and Mexico. Also found in Central and South America.

Length **14in (36cm)**	Wingspan **21in (53cm)**	Weight **11oz (325g)**
Social **Pairs**	Lifespan **Up to 10 years**	Status **Secure**

DATE SEEN	WHERE	NOTES

Order **Gruiformes**	Family **Rallidae**	Species ***Fulica americana***

American Coot

This duck-like species is the most abundant and widely distributed of North American rails. Its lobed toes make it well adapted to swimming and diving, but are somewhat of an impediment on land. Its flight is clumsy; it becomes airborne with difficulty, running along the water surface before taking off. American Coots form large flocks on open water in winter, often associating with ducks—an unusual trait for a member of the rail family.

VOICE Various raucous clucks, grunts, and croaks and an explosive *keek*.

NESTING Bulky cup of plant material placed in aquatic vegetation on or near water; 5–15 eggs; 1–2 broods; April–July.

FEEDING Forages on or by diving under shallow water and on land; primarily herbivorous, but also eats snails, insects, spiders, tadpoles, fish, and even carrion.

FLIGHT: low and labored; runs for quite a long distance to takeoff.

SWIMMING AWAY
The red-headed, baldish looking American Coot chicks leave the nest a day after hatching.

SIMILAR SPECIES

PURPLE GALLINULE — red bill with yellow tip; bright yellow legs

COMMON MOORHEN see p.125 — gray head; white flank stripe

OCCURRENCE
Breeds in open water habitats west of the Appalachians and in Florida. Moves from the northern parts of its range in winter to the southeastern US, where open water persists; also migrates to western and southern Mexico.

Length **15½in (40cm)**	Wingspan **24in (61cm)**	Weight **16oz (450g)**
Social **Flocks**	Lifespan **Up to 22 years**	Status **Secure**

DATE SEEN	WHERE	NOTES

Order **Gruiformes**	Family **Gruidae**	Species ***Grus canadensis***

Sandhill Crane

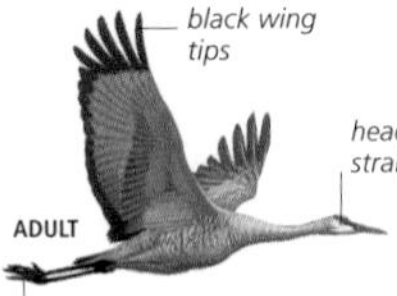

black wing tips

head held straight

ADULT

trailing legs

IN FLIGHT

brownish head

body with pale brown smudges

JUVENILE

red crown

long black bill

pale cheek

long neck

ADULT

rusty body

shaggy feathers

long, black legs

"IRON-STAINED" PLUMAGE

FLIGHT: alternates slow, steady flapping with periods of gliding; flocks in single file.

These large, slender, and long-necked birds are famous for their elaborate courtship dances, far-carrying vocalizations, and remarkable migrations. Their bodies are sometimes stained with a rusty color, supposedly because they probe into mud which contains iron; when a bird preens, this is transferred from its bill to its plumage. Sandhill Cranes are broadly grouped into "Lesser" and "Greater" populations that differ in the geographical location of their breeding grounds and migration routes.

VOICE Call loud, wooden, hollow bugling, audible at great distances; noisy in flight and courtship.

NESTING Mound of sticks and grasses placed on ground; 1 egg; 1 brood; April–September.

FEEDING Eats shoots, grain; also aquatic mollusks and insects.

MEMORABLE IMAGE

Its long neck, large wings, and distinctive red crown make it unmistakable.

SIMILAR SPECIES

GREAT BLUE HERON ◔ see p.93

dark crown

paler legs

WHOOPING CRANE see p.429

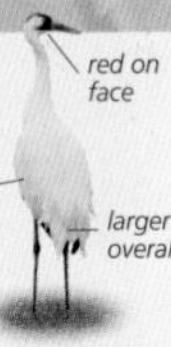

red on face

all-white plumage

larger overall

OCCURRENCE

Breeds in muskeg, tundra, and forest clearings across northwestern North America, east to Québec and the Great Lakes; large wintering and migratory flocks often densely packed, roosting in or near marshes. Winters south to northern Mexico.

Length **2¾–4ft (0.8–1.2m)**	Wingspan **6–7½ft (1.8–2.3m)**	Weight **7¾–11lb (3.5–5kg)**
Social **Flocks**	Lifespan **Up to 25 years**	Status **Secure**

DATE SEEN	WHERE	NOTES

Families **Haematopodidae, Recurvirostridae, Charadriidae, Scolopacidae, Laridae, Sternidae, Alcidae**

SHOREBIRDS, GULLS, & AUKS

THE DIVERSE SHOREBIRD, gull, and auk families together form the order Charadriiformes. They are small to medium-sized, mostly migratory birds, associated with aquatic habitats. Over 100 species are found in North America.

TYPICAL GULL
Most large gulls, such as this Western Gull, have white heads and underparts with long dark wings and a bright sturdy bill.

SHOREBIRDS

The various species popularly known as shorebirds belong to several different families. In North America there are the oystercatchers (Haematopodidae), the avocets and stilts (Recurvirostridae), the plovers (Charadriidae), the sandpipers (Scolopacidae), and the phalaropes (the subfamily Phalaropodinae, of Scolopacidae). They have long legs in proportion to their bodies, and a variety of bills, ranging from short to long, thin, thick, straight, down-curved, and up-curved.

GULLS

The over 20 species of North American gulls in the family Laridae all share similar stout body shapes, sturdy bills, and webbed toes. Nearly all are scavengers. Closely associated with coastal areas, few gulls venture far out to sea. Some species are seen around fishing ports and harbors, or inland, especially in urban areas and garbage dumps.

TERNS

Terns are specialized long-billed predators that dive for fish. More slender and elegant than gulls, nearly all are immediately recognizable when breeding, with their black caps and long, pointed bills. The related Black Skimmer also catches fish but has a different bill.

AUKS, MURRES, & PUFFINS

Denizens of the northern oceans, these birds only come to land to breed. Most nest in colonies on sheer cliffs overlooking the ocean, but puffins excavate burrows in the ground, and some murrelets nest away from predators high up in treetops far inland.

COLOR-CHANGE BILL
The bright colors of a breeding Tufted Puffin's bill fade to more muted tones in winter, after the breeding season.

ON THE MOVE
Dunlins and other sandpipers gather in large, highly coordinated flocks on migration.

Order **Charadriiformes**	Family **Haematopodidae**	Species ***Haematopus bachmani***

Black Oystercatcher

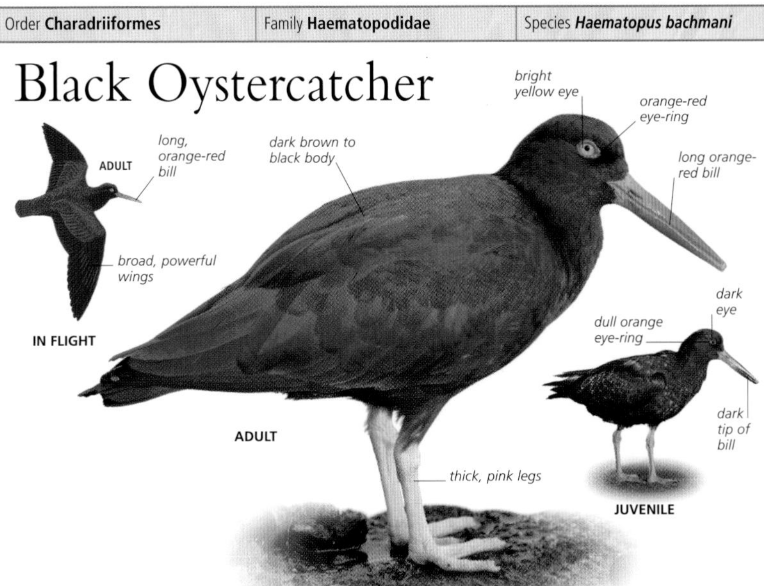

This large, striking oystercatcher shares the typical round-bodied, hunch-backed, and squat-necked shape of other oystercatchers, as well as their typically thick legs and bill. But it is instantly recognizable because of its all-dark plumage, making the pale eyes and colorful bill all the more conspicuous. It is restricted to rocky coasts, where it feeds in pairs or family groups, using well-defined territories in summer. In winter, the birds gather in larger flocks where they are numerous, sometimes in hundreds, where mussels and barnacles are abundant. These are noisy, demonstrative birds, and always entertaining to watch.

VOICE Flight call a loud, whistled *wheeu*, with emphasis on first part of call; alarm call sharper *wheep*; courtship and posturing calls a series of whistles based on flight call, accelerating into descending piping calls.

NESTING Simple scrape just above high-tide line, often lined with broken shells and pebbles; 2–3 eggs; 1 brood; May–June.

FEEDING Feeds on slightly submerged shellfish beds; diet includes mollusks, particularly mussels and limpets; also eats a variety of crustaceans, such as crabs and barnacles; oysters are rarely consumed.

FLIGHT: strong, powerful flight with shallow wing beats.

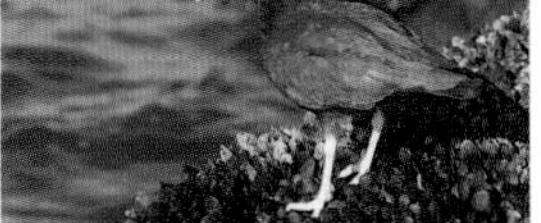

BARNACLE LOVER
The Black Oystercatcher can be spotted walking on top of exposed barnacle beds at low tide.

SIMILAR SPECIES

see p.429

OCCURRENCE
Feeds in the area between the high and low tide marks on rocky shores of western North America, from Alaska southward to Baja California. Breeds just above high-tide line on rocky headlands or sand, shell, and gravel beaches. In winter, also found on rocky jetties in southern part of range.

Length **16½–18½in (42–47cm)**	Wingspan **30–34in (77–86cm)**	Weight **18–25oz (500–700g)**
Social **Pairs/Flocks**	Lifespan **10–15 years**	Status **Secure**

DATE SEEN	WHERE	NOTES

Order **Charadriiformes**	Family **Recurvirostridae**	Species ***Himantopus himantopus***

Black-necked Stilt

ADULT

long, angular, black wings

no white spot above red eye

long, slender neck

IN FLIGHT

scaly appearance

less contrasting head pattern than adult

shorter, stubbier bill

JUVENILE

white spot above red eye

black mask encircles eye

black upperparts

long, needle-like black bill

slender, tapered body

white underparts

MALE

long, bright pink legs

brownish wash to back

duller legs than male

FEMALE

This tall, slender, elegant, and black-and-white shorebird is a familiar sight at ponds and lagoons in the western and southern US. Even among the shorebirds, it is remarkably long-legged, at times almost grotesquely so: in flight, it often crosses its trailing feet as if for extra control and support. Breeding takes place in small colonies, with several pairs sharing the same site. In winter, these tall birds are often seen in small flocks of about 25 individuals. These groups feed quietly in sheltered areas, but they aggressively drive visitors away with their raucous calls, dog-like yips, and noisy communal protests. The increased use of pesticides and loss of wetland habitat could cause a decline in its numbers in the future. The US populations belong to the subspecies *mexicanus*.

VOICE Flight and alarm call a loud, continuous poodle-like *yip-yip-yip*, given in a long series when alarmed.

NESTING Simple scrape lined with grass in soft soil; 4 eggs; 1 brood; April–May.

FEEDING Walks slowly in shallow water, picking food off surface; diet includes tadpoles, shrimp, snails, flies, worms, clams, small fish, and frogs.

FLIGHT: direct, but somewhat awkward due to long, trailing legs; deep wing beats.

FRIENDLY BUNCH
Black-necked Stilts are gregarious by nature, and often roost together in shallow water.

OCCURRENCE
Breeds around marshes, shallow grassy ponds, lake margins, and man-made waterbodies, such as reservoirs; uses similar habitats during migration and winter, as well as shallow lagoons, flooded fields, and mangrove swamps. Southern birds migrate locally only.

Length **14–15½in (35–39cm)**	Wingspan **29–32in (73–81cm)**	Weight **4–8oz (125–225g)**
Social **Small flocks**	Lifespan **Up to 19 years**	Status **Secure**

DATE SEEN	WHERE	NOTES

Order **Charadriiformes**	Family **Recurvirostridae**	Species ***Recurvirostra americana***

American Avocet

FLIGHT: fast, direct, and graceful; very long legs extend beyond tail.

With its long, thin, and upturned bill, this graceful, long-legged shorebird is unmistakable when foraging. When it takes off, its striking plumage pattern is clearly visible. It is the only one of the four avocet species in the world that changes plumage when breeding. Breeding birds have a cinnamon head and neck, and bold, patterns on their black-and-white wings and upperparts. The American Avocet forms large flocks during migration and in winter.

VOICE Flight call a variable melodic *kleet*, loud and repetitive, given when alarmed and by foraging birds.

NESTING Simple scrape in shallow depression; 4 eggs; 1 brood; May–June.

FEEDING Uses specialized bill to probe, scythe, or jab a variety of aquatic invertebrates, small fish, and seeds; walks steadily in belly-deep water to chase its prey.

FORAGING FLOCK
These birds walk through shallow water in flocks searching mainly for insects and crustaceans.

TRICKY BALANCE
During mating, the male supports himself with raised wings as the female extends her neck forward.

OCCURRENCE
Breeds in temporary wetlands, in dry to arid regions. In winter and migration, found in shallow water habitats, including ponds, reservoirs, fresh- and saltwater marshes, tidal mudflats, and lagoons. Each year, a flock of about 10,000 birds winters at Bolivar Flats, Texas. Regular East Coast visitor.

Length **17–18½in (43–47cm)**	Wingspan **29–32in (74–81cm)**	Weight **10–12oz (275–350g)**
Social **Large flocks**	Lifespan **Up to 9 years**	Status **Secure**

DATE SEEN	WHERE	NOTES

Order **Charadriiformes**	Family **Charadriidae**	Species ***Pluvialis dominica***

American Golden Plover

ADULT (BREEDING)
dark tail
black-and-white face
ADULT (NON-BREEDING)
gray underwing
diffused streaks on breast
IN FLIGHT
brownish upperparts
dark cap
small, thin bill
uniformly dusky underparts
ADULT (NONBREEDING)
crisply checkered upperparts
slim, tapered body
neatly mottled breast
JUVENILE
white stripe from forehead to nape
tan-and-black spangled upperparts
black underparts
black legs
ADULT (BREEDING)

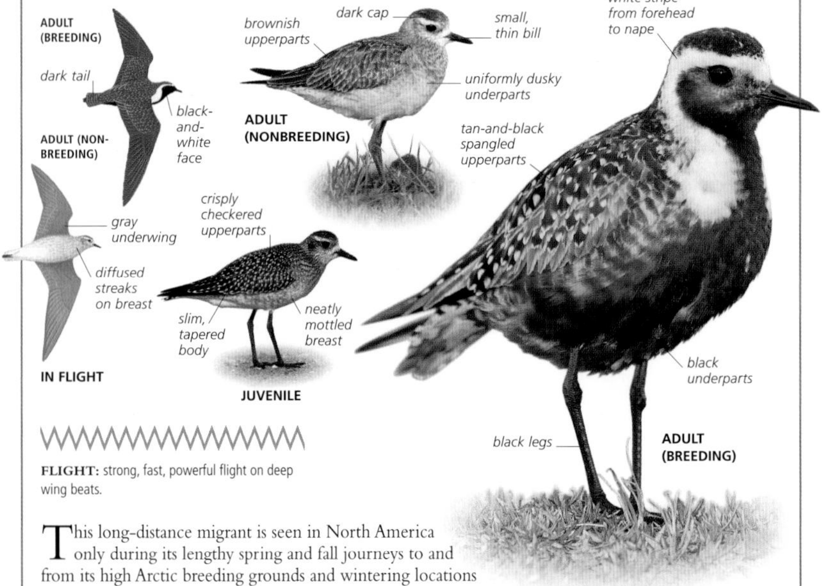

FLIGHT: strong, fast, powerful flight on deep wing beats.

This long-distance migrant is seen in North America only during its lengthy spring and fall journeys to and from its high Arctic breeding grounds and wintering locations in southern South America. An elegant, slender, yet large plover, it prefers inland grassy habitats and plowed fields to coastal mudflats. The American Golden Plover's annual migration route includes a feeding stop at Labrador, then a 1,550–1,860 miles (2,500–3,000km) flight over the Atlantic Ocean to South America.

VOICE Flight call a whistled two-note *queE-dle*, or *klee-u*, with second note shorter and lower pitched; male flight song a strong, melodious whistled *kid-eek*, or *kid-EEp*.

NESTING Shallow depression lined with lichens in dry, open tundra; 4 eggs; 1 brood; May–July.

FEEDING Forages in run, pause, and pluck sequence on insects, mollusks, crustaceans, and worms; also berries and seeds.

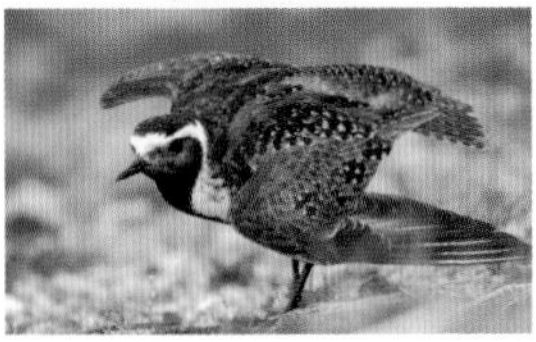

DISTRACTION TECHNIQUE
This breeding American Golden Plover is feigning an injury to its wing to draw predators away from its eggs or chicks in its nest.

SIMILAR SPECIES

PACIFIC GOLDEN PLOVER ❄
see p.429
larger bill
longer legs
PACIFIC GOLDEN PLOVER ◔
see p.429
checkered gold-and-black upperparts
pale golden wash

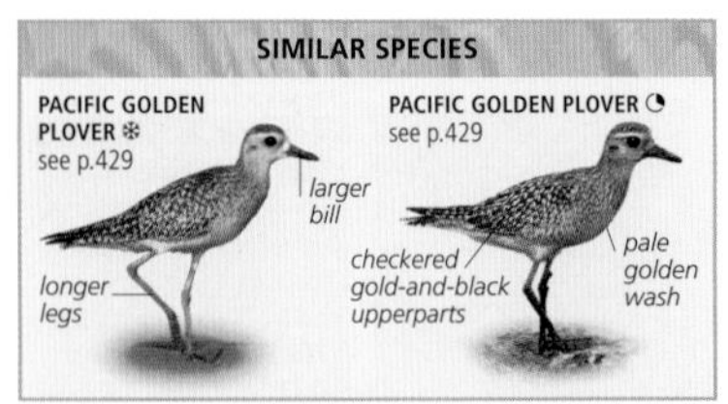

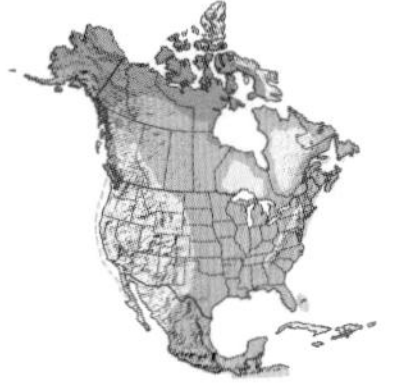

OCCURRENCE
Breeds in Arctic tundra habitats. In migration, it occurs in prairies, tilled farmlands, golf courses, pastures, airports; also mudflats, shorelines, and beaches. In spring, seen in Texas and Great Plains; in fall, uncommon in northeast Maritimes and New England; scarce along the Pacific Coast.

Length **9½–11in (24–28cm)**	Wingspan **23–28in (59–72cm)**	Weight **4–7oz (125–200g)**
Social **Solitary/Small flocks**	Lifespan **Unknown**	Status **Secure**

DATE SEEN	WHERE	NOTES

Order **Charadriiformes**	Family **Charadriidae**	Species ***Pluvialis squatarola***

Black-bellied Plover

white rump
black outer wing feathers
white wing stripe
MALE (BREEDING)
white-edged, dark-centered feathers
checkered upperparts
markedly streaked breast
JUVENILE
ADULT (NONBREEDING)
diffused streaks to upper breast
whitish underparts
whitish crown
checkered, black-and-white upperparts
black cheeks
ADULT (NONBREEDING)
black underwing patch
IN FLIGHT
darker crown
black belly
duller plumage than male
MALE (BREEDING)
FEMALE (MOLTING TO BREEDING PLUMAGE)

FLIGHT: straight and fast; powerful wing beats.

The Black-bellied Plover is the largest and most common of the three North American *Pluvialis* plovers. Its preference for open feeding habitats, its bulky structure, and very upright stance make it a fairly conspicuous species. The Black-bellied Plover's black underwing patches, visible in flight, are present in both its breeding and nonbreeding plumages and distinguish it from the other *Pluvialis* plovers.

VOICE Typical call a 3-syllabled, clear, plaintive, whistled *whEE-er-eee*, with middle note lower; flight song of male during breeding softer, with accent on second syllable.

NESTING Shallow depression lined with mosses and lichens in moist to dry lowland tundra; 1–5 eggs; 1 brood; May–July.

FEEDING Forages mainly along coasts in typical plover style: run, pause, and pluck; eats insects, worms, bivalves, and crustaceans.

CASUAL WADING
The Black-bellied Plover wades in shallow water but does most of its foraging in mudflats.

SIMILAR SPECIES

AMERICAN GOLDEN PLOVER ❄ see p.132
dark cap
dingy, brownish upperparts

MOUNTAIN PLOVER ❄ see p.430
sandy brown upperparts
white underparts

OCCURRENCE
Breeds in High Arctic habitats from western Russia across the Bering Sea to Alaska, and east to Baffin Island; winters primarily in coastal areas from southern Canada and US, south to southern South America. Found inland during migration. Migrates south all the way to South America.

Length **10½–12in (27–30cm)**	Wingspan **29–32in (73–81cm)**	Weight **5–9oz (150–250g)**
Social **Flocks**	Lifespan **Up to 12 years**	Status **Secure**

DATE SEEN	WHERE	NOTES

Order **Charadriiformes**	Family **Charadriidae**	Species ***Charadrius semipalmatus***

Semipalmated Plover

pointed wings
black tail band
ADULT (BREEDING)
IN FLIGHT

scalloped feather edges
pale base of bill
brownish breastband
JUVENILE

white eyestripe
brownish crown
brownish upperparts
black bill with orange base
diffused brownish collar
white underparts
yellowish legs
ADULT (NONBREEDING)

yellow eye-ring
black forecrown
black breastband
orange legs
ADULT (BREEDING)

Similar in appearance to the Eurasian Common Ringed Plover, the Semipalmated Plover is a small shorebird with a tapered shape. It is a familiar sight in a wide variety of habitats during migration and in winter, when these birds gather in loose flocks. A casual walk down a sandy beach between fall and spring might awaken up to 100 Semipalmated Plovers, sleeping in slight depressions in the sand, though flocks of up to 1,000 birds may also be encountered.

VOICE Flight call a whistled, abrupt double note, *chu-WEEp*, with soft emphasis on second syllable; courtship display song is a version of flight call followed by rough *r-r-r-r-r-r-r*, ending with a slurred, descending *yelp*.

NESTING Simple scrape on bare or slightly vegetated ground in Arctic tundra; 3–4 eggs; 1 brood; May–June.

FEEDING Forages in typical plover style: run, pause, and pluck; eats aquatic mollusks, crustaceans, flies, beetles, and spiders.

FLIGHT: straight, fast; with fluttering wing beats.

BY SIGHT AND FEEL
Semipalmated Plovers locate prey by sight or through the sensitive soles of their toes.

SIMILAR SPECIES

WILSON'S PLOVER see p.430
heavier, dark bill
pinkish legs

RINGED PLOVER
wider breastband

OCCURRENCE
Breeding habitat is Arctic or sub-Arctic tundra, well-drained gravel, shale, or other sparsely vegetated ground. During migration, mudflats, saltwater marshes, lake edges, tidal areas, and flooded fields. During winter, coastal or near coastal habitats.

Length **6¾–7½in (17–19cm)**	Wingspan **17–20½in (43–52cm)**	Weight **1¹⁄₁₆–2½oz (30–70g)**
Social **Solitary/Flocks**	Lifespan **Up to 6 years**	Status **Secure**

DATE SEEN	WHERE	NOTES

Order **Charadriiformes**	Family **Charadriidae**	Species ***Charadrius vociferus***

Killdeer

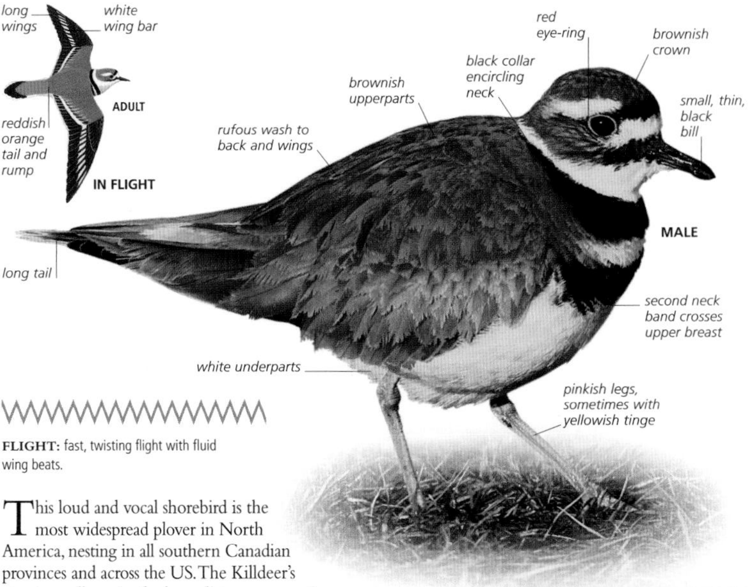

long wings
white wing bar
ADULT
reddish orange tail and rump
IN FLIGHT
red eye-ring
brownish crown
black collar encircling neck
brownish upperparts
small, thin, black bill
rufous wash to back and wings
MALE
long tail
second neck band crosses upper breast
white underparts
pinkish legs, sometimes with yellowish tinge

FLIGHT: fast, twisting flight with fluid wing beats.

This loud and vocal shorebird is the most widespread plover in North America, nesting in all southern Canadian provinces and across the US. The Killdeer's piercing call carries for long distances, sometimes causing other birds to fly away in fear of imminent danger. These birds often nest near human habitation, allowing a close observation of their vigilant parental nature with young chicks.

VOICE Flight call a rising, drawn out *deeee*; alarm call a loud, penetrating *dee-ee*, given repetitively; agitated birds also give series of *dee* notes, followed by rising trill.

NESTING Scrape on ground, sometimes in slight depression; 4 eggs; 1 brood (north), 2–3 broods (south); March–July.

FEEDING Forages in typical plover style: run, pause, and pick; eats a variety of invertebrates such as worms, snails, grasshoppers, and beetles; also small vertebrates and seeds.

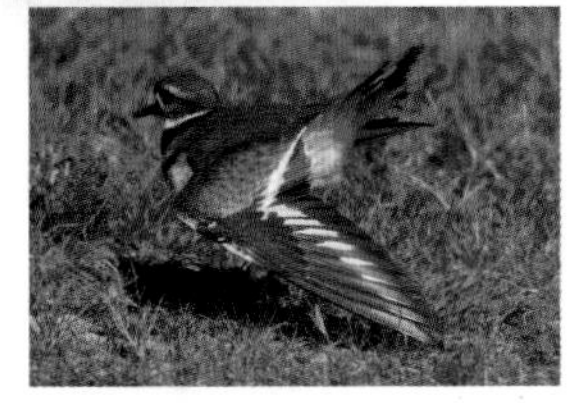

CLEVER MANEUVER
The Killdeer lures intruders away from its nest with a "broken wing" display.

SIMILAR SPECIES

SEMIPALMATED PLOVER ❄
see p.134
single dark neckband
orange-yellow legs
smaller overall
WILSON'S PLOVER
see p.430
single, black collar
pinkish legs
short tail

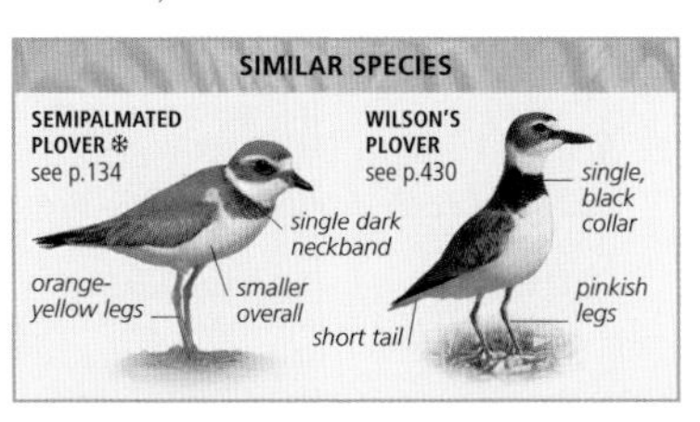

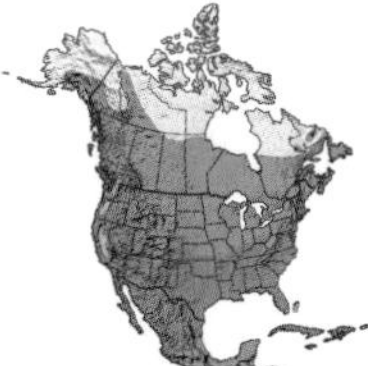

OCCURRENCE
Widespread across Canada and the US, the Killdeer occurs in a wide variety of habitats. These include shorelines, mudflats, lake and river edges, sparsely grassy fields and pastures, golf courses, roadsides, parking lots, flat rooftops, driveways, and other terrestrial habitats.

Length **9–10in (23–26cm)**	Wingspan **23–25in (58–63cm)**	Weight **2¼–3⅛ oz (65–90g)**
Social **Small flocks**	Lifespan **Up to 10 years**	Status **Secure**

DATE SEEN	WHERE	NOTES

Order **Charadriiformes**	Family **Charadriidae**	Species ***Charadrius melodus***

Piping Plover

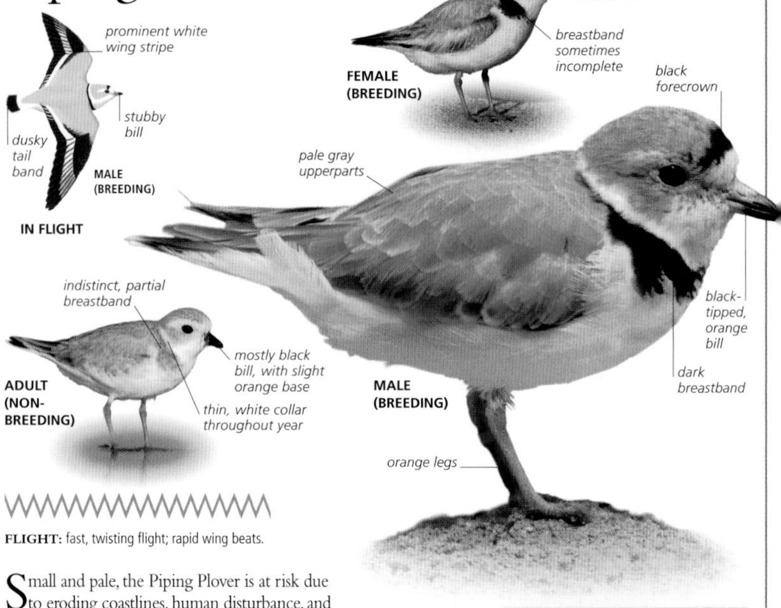
less pronounced black markings than male
breastband sometimes incomplete
FEMALE (BREEDING)
prominent white wing stripe
stubby bill
dusky tail band
MALE (BREEDING)
IN FLIGHT
black forecrown
pale gray upperparts
indistinct, partial breastband
mostly black bill, with slight orange base
ADULT (NON-BREEDING)
thin, white collar throughout year
MALE (BREEDING)
black-tipped, orange bill
dark breastband
orange legs

FLIGHT: fast, twisting flight; rapid wing beats.

Small and pale, the Piping Plover is at risk due to eroding coastlines, human disturbance, and predation by foxes, raccoons, and cats. With its pale gray back, it is well camouflaged along beaches or in dunes, but conservation measures, such as fencing off nesting beaches and control of predators, are necessary to restore populations. Two subspecies of the Piping Plover are recognized; one nests on the Atlantic Coast, and the other inland.

VOICE Clear, whistled *peep* call in flight; quiet *peep-lo* during courtship and contact; high-pitched *pipe-pipe-pipe* song.

NESTING Shallow scrape in sand, gravel, dunes, or salt flats; 4 eggs; 1 brood; April–May.

FEEDING Typical run, pause, and pluck plover feeding style; diet includes marine worms, insects, and mollusks.

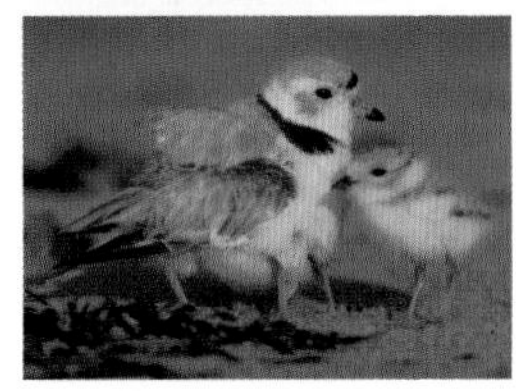

VULNERABLE NESTS
The fragile nature of their preferred nesting sites has led to this species becoming endangered.

SIMILAR SPECIES

SEMIPALMATED PLOVER ❄
see p.134
dark, brown upperparts
SNOWY PLOVER ❄
see p.137
black bill
narrow, white collar
darker legs

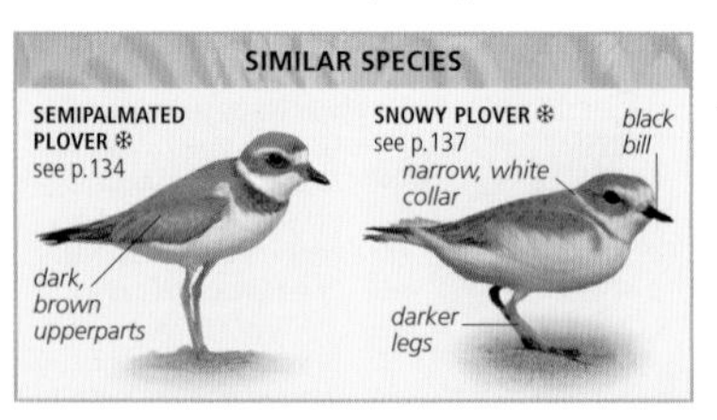

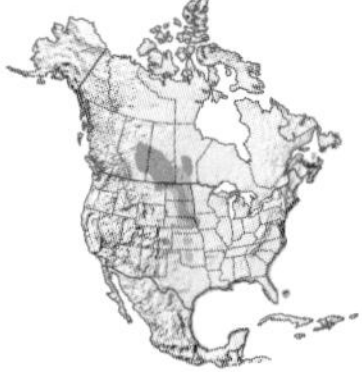

OCCURRENCE
Found along beaches, in saline sandflats, and adjacent mudflats; during winter, found exclusively along the Atlantic and Gulf Coasts, sandflats, and mudflats. Inland subspecies nests on sand or gravel beaches adjacent to large lakes, rivers, and saline lakes.

Length **6½–7in (17–18cm)**	Wingspan **18–18½in (45–47cm)**	Weight **1⅝–2⅜oz (45–65g)**
Social **Small flocks**	Lifespan **Up to 11 years**	Status **Vulnerable**

DATE SEEN	WHERE	NOTES

Order **Charadriiformes**	Family **Charadriidae**	Species ***Charadrius alexandrinus***

Snowy Plover

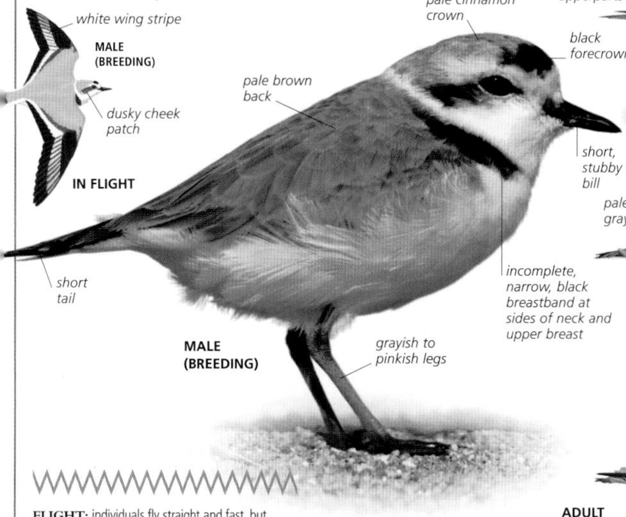
white wing stripe
MALE (BREEDING)
dusky cheek patch
IN FLIGHT
pale cinnamon crown
pale brown back
black forecrown
short, stubby bill
short tail
incomplete, narrow, black breastband at sides of neck and upper breast
grayish to pinkish legs
MALE (BREEDING)

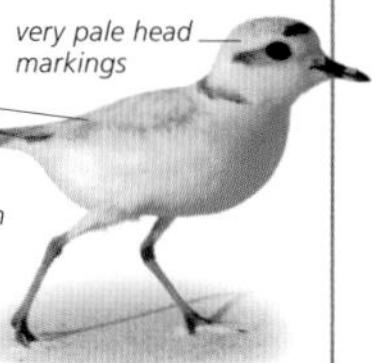
very pale head markings
very pale upperparts
GULF COAST FEMALE (BREEDING)

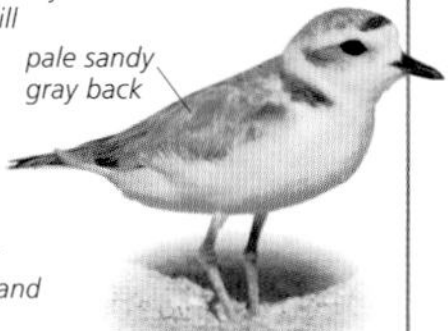
pale sandy gray back
GULF COAST MALE (BREEDING)

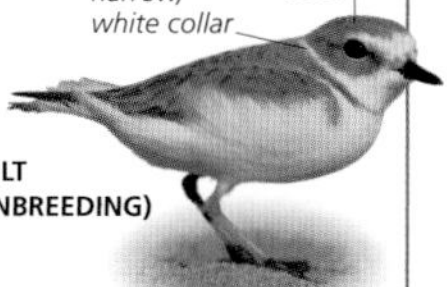
blocky head
narrow, white collar
ADULT (NONBREEDING)

FLIGHT: individuals fly straight and fast, but flocks wheel and bank in synchrony when alarmed.

The smallest and palest of all North American plovers, the Snowy Plover's cryptic coloration blends in so well with its beach and dune habitat that it often remains unnoticed. This bird often runs faster and covers longer distances than other beach plovers, sprinting along the sand for extended spurts, like sanderlings. Nests are frequently destroyed by weather, disturbance, or predators, but the birds readily construct new nests, even up to six times in the face of regular losses. Nevertheless, habitat destruction has resulted in shrinking populations, and the species is designated as threatened along the Pacific Coast.

VOICE Repeated *tow-heet*; *purrt* and single *churr*, typically silent when not breeding, tinkling *ti* at roosts or before flight.

NESTING Shallow scrape in sand; 2–3 eggs; 2–3 broods; March–June.

FEEDING Feeds in run, pause, and pluck style on terrestrial and aquatic invertebrates, such as snails and clams.

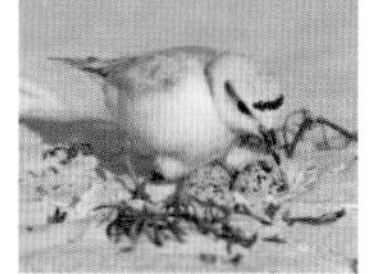

TRULY SNOWY
The Snowy Plover breeds in sandy areas that are as pale as snow.

SIMILAR SPECIES

SEMIPALMATED PLOVER ◔
see p.134

brown breastband

PIPING PLOVER ♂
see p.136

plumper overall
orange legs

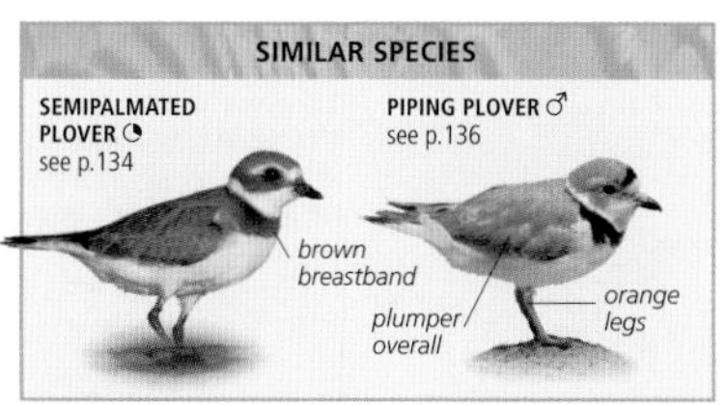

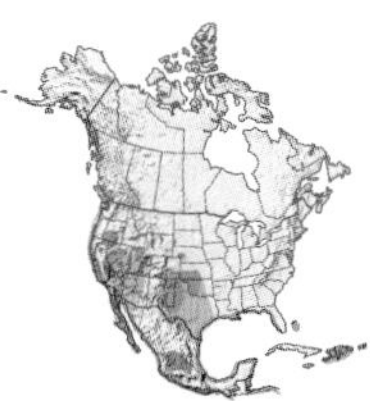

OCCURRENCE
Breeds on open beach and dune habitats on the Pacific and Gulf Coasts, and inland on brackish lakes in the Great Basin and southern Great Plains region. Coastal birds are only partially migratory, but most inland birds winter at the coast.

Length **6–6½in (15–17cm)**	Wingspan **16–18in (41–46cm)**	Weight **1¼–2⅛oz (35–60g)**
Social **Large flocks**	Lifespan **Up to 4 years**	Status **Declining**

DATE SEEN	WHERE	NOTES

Order **Charadriiformes**	Family **Scolopacidae**	Species ***Gallinago gallinago***

Wilson's Snipe

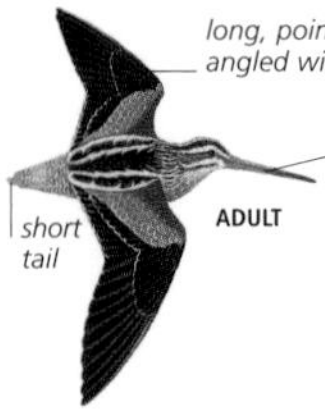

long, pointed, angled wings
long bill
short tail
ADULT

IN FLIGHT

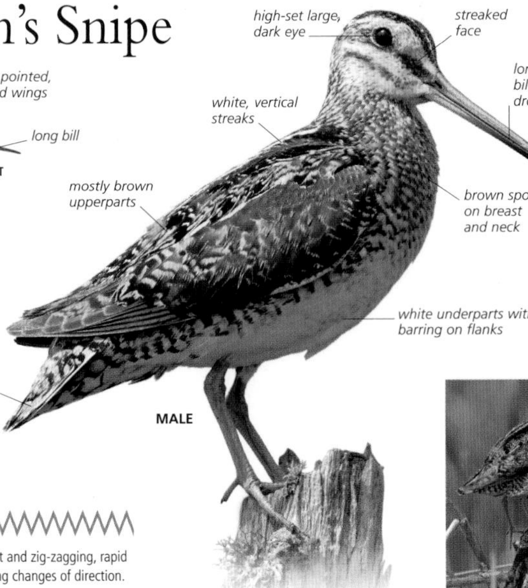

high-set large, dark eye
streaked face
long, tapered bill, slightly drooping at tip
white, vertical streaks
mostly brown upperparts
brown spots on breast and neck
white underparts with barring on flanks
short russet tail

MALE

FLIGHT: extremely fast and zig-zagging, rapid wing beats; erratic-looking changes of direction.

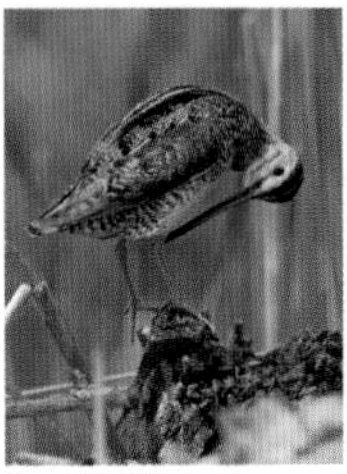

RUSSET TAIL
Wilson's Snipe's russet-colored tail is usually hard to see, but it is evident on this preening bird.

Also known as the Common Snipe, this secretive and well-camouflaged member of the sandpiper family has an unsettled taxonomic history. On its breeding grounds Wilson's Snipe produces rather eerie sounds during its aerial, mainly nocturnal, display flights. The birds fly up silently from the ground, then, from about 330ft (100m) up, they descend quickly, with their tail feathers spread, producing a unique, loud and vibrating sound through modified feathers. The North American populations belong to subspecies *delicata*.

VOICE Alarm and overhead flight call raspy *kraitsch*; perched and low flying breeding birds give repetitive, monotonous *kup-kup-kup-kup* in alarm or aggression; distinctive whistling sound during territorial displays.

NESTING Elaborate woven nest lined with fine grass on ground, sedge, or moss; 4 eggs; 1 brood; May–June.

FEEDING Forages in mud or shallow water; probes deep into subsoil; diet includes mostly insect larvae, but also crustaceans, earthworms, and mollusks.

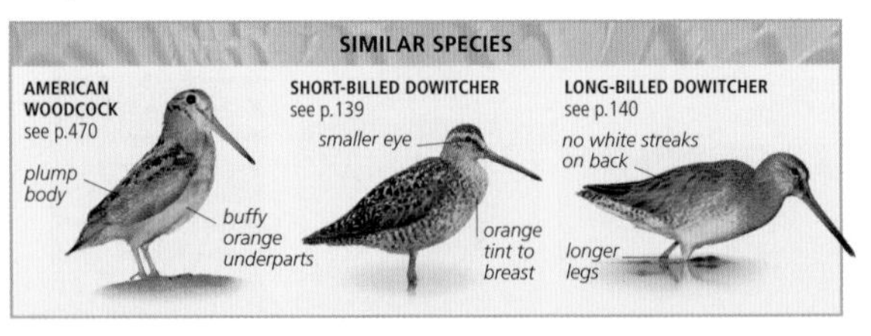

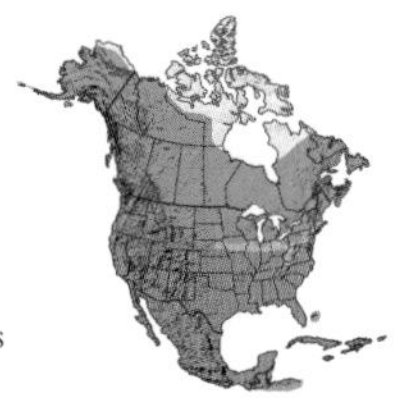

OCCURRENCE
Widespread from Alaska to Québec and Labrador south of the tundra zone; breeds in a variety of wetlands, including marshes, bogs, and open areas with rich soil. Winters further south, where it prefers damp areas with vegetative cover, such as marshes, wet fields, and other bodies of water.

SIMILAR SPECIES

AMERICAN WOODCOCK
see p.470

plump body
buffy orange underparts

SHORT-BILLED DOWITCHER
see p.139

smaller eye
orange tint to breast

LONG-BILLED DOWITCHER
see p.140

no white streaks on back
longer legs

Length **10–11in (25–28cm)**	Wingspan **17–19in (43–48cm)**	Weight **2⅞–5oz (80–150g)**
Social **Solitary**	Lifespan **Up to 10 years**	Status **Secure**

DATE SEEN	WHERE	NOTES

Order **Charadriiformes**	Family **Scolopacidae**	Species ***Limnodromus griseus***

Short-billed Dowitcher

white slash from rump to mid-back
ADULT (BREEDING)
long, pointed wings
IN FLIGHT
orange-fringed feathers
flanks less heavily streaked
JUVENILE
dark-centered upperpart feathers
ADULT
L. g. griseus
orange wash to face, neck, breast, and underparts
long, stout bill
variable spotting on upper breast
greenish yellow legs
streaked flanks
slightly larger bill
ADULT
L. g. hendersoni
plain gray upperparts
white belly
ADULT (NONBREEDING)

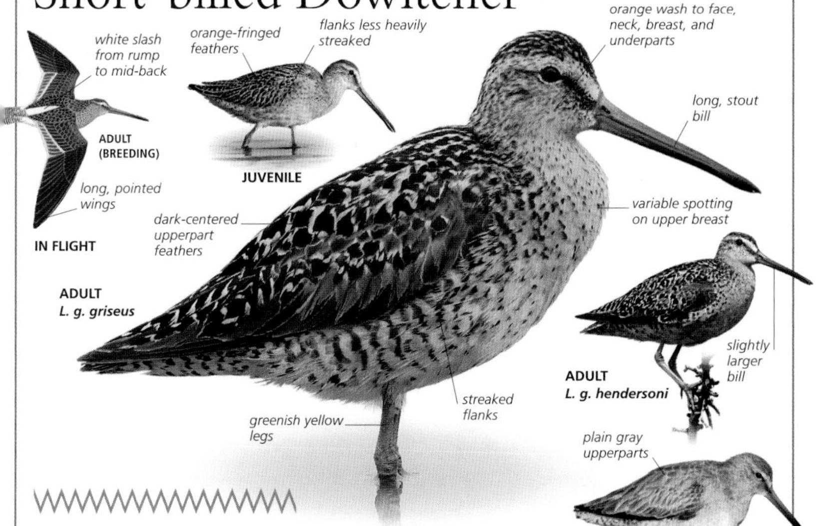

FLIGHT: swift, powerful with quick wing beats.

The Short-billed Dowitcher is a common visitor along the Atlantic, Gulf, and Pacific Coasts. Its remote and bug-infested breeding areas in northern bogs have hindered the study of its breeding behavior until recent years. There are three subspecies (*L. g. griseus*, *L. g. hendersoni*, and *L. g. caurinus*), which differ in plumage, size, and respective breeding areas. Recent knowledge about shape and structure has helped ornithologists distinguish the Short-billed from the Long-billed Dowitcher.

VOICE Flight call low, plaintive *tu-tu-tu*, 3–4 notes; flight song *tu-tu*, *tu-tu*, *toodle-ee*, *tu-tu*, ending with low *anh-anh-anh*.

NESTING Simple depression, typically in sedge hummock; 4 eggs; 1 brood; May–June.

FEEDING Probes in "sewing machine" feeding style with water up to belly for aquatic mollusks, crustaceans, and insects.

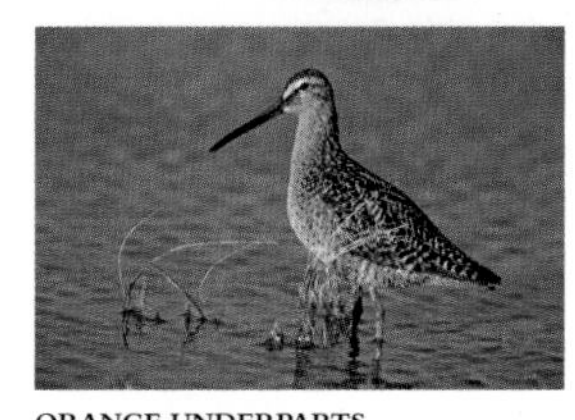

ORANGE UNDERPARTS
In complete breeding plumage, the Short-billed Dowitcher is orange, even in late afternoon light.

SIMILAR SPECIES

WILSON'S SNIPE ♂
see p.138
shorter legs
LONG-BILLED DOWITCHER
see p.140
slightly thicker neck
slightly longer legs

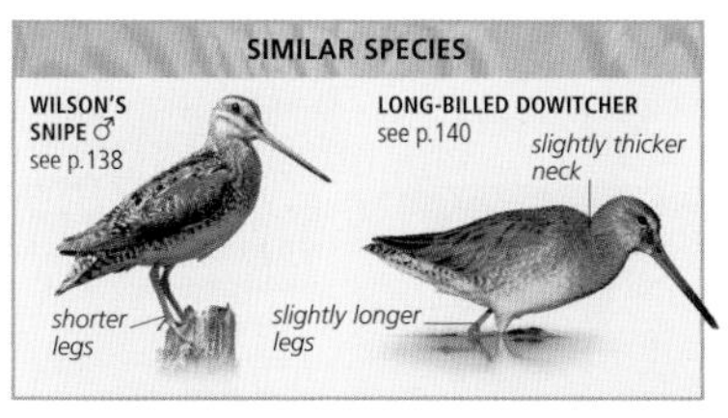

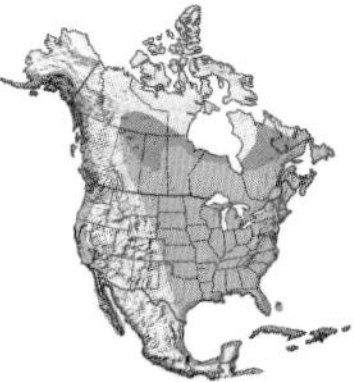

OCCURRENCE
Breeds mostly in sedge meadows or bogs with interspersed spruce and tamaracks between subarctic tundra and boreal forest. Migrates south to Central and South America, preferring coastal mudflats, salt marshes or adjacent freshwater pools.

Length **9–10in (23–25cm)**	Wingspan **18–20in (46–51cm)**	Weight **2½–5½oz (70–155g)**
Social **Pairs/Flocks**	Lifespan **Up to 20 years**	Status **Secure (p)**

DATE SEEN	WHERE	NOTES

Order **Charadriiformes**	Family **Scolopacidae**	Species ***Limnodromus scolopaceus***

Long-billed Dowitcher

It was not until 1950 that, after museum and field studies, scientists recognized two separate species of dowitcher in North America. The Long-billed Dowitcher is usually slightly larger, longer-legged, and heavier in the chest and neck than the Short-billed Dowitcher. The breeding ranges of the two species are separate, but their migration and en route stop-over areas overlap. The Long-billed Dowitcher is usually found in freshwater wetlands, and in the fall most of its population occurs west of the Mississippi River.

VOICE Flight and alarm call sharp, whistled *keek*, given singly or in series when agitated; song buzzy *pipipipipipi-chi-drrr.*

NESTING Deep sedge or grass-lined depression in sedge or grass; 4 eggs; 1 brood; May–June.

FEEDING Probes wet ground with "sewing-machine" motion for spiders, snails, worms, insects, and seeds.

FLIGHT: swift, direct flier with fast, powerful wing beats.

TOUCHY FEELY
Sensitive touch-receptors at the tip of the bird's bill enable it to feel in the mud for food.

OCCURRENCE
Breeds in wet, grassy meadows or coastal sedge tundra near freshwater pools. Migrates to Mexico and Central America, south to Panama, where found in freshwater habitats, including ponds, flooded fields, lake shores, also sheltered lagoons, salt marsh pools, and tidal mudflats.

Length **9½–10in (24–26cm)**	Wingspan **18–20½in (46–52cm)**	Weight **3–4oz (85–125g)**
Social **Pairs/Flocks**	Lifespan **Unknown**	Status **Secure**

DATE SEEN	WHERE	NOTES

Order **Charadriiformes**	Family **Scolopacidae**	Species ***Limosa fedoa***

Marbled Godwit

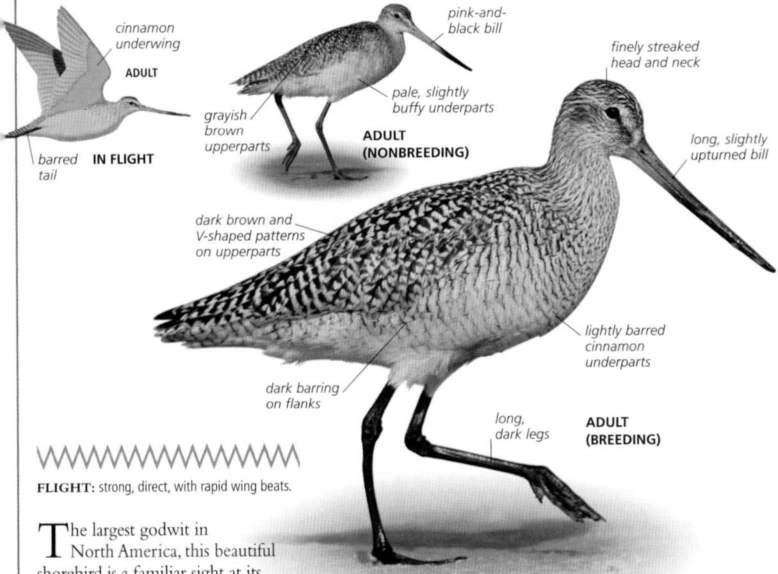

cinnamon underwing
ADULT
barred tail
IN FLIGHT

pink-and-black bill
grayish brown upperparts
pale, slightly buffy underparts
ADULT (NONBREEDING)

finely streaked head and neck
long, slightly upturned bill
dark brown and V-shaped patterns on upperparts
lightly barred cinnamon underparts
dark barring on flanks
long, dark legs
ADULT (BREEDING)

FLIGHT: strong, direct, with rapid wing beats.

The largest godwit in North America, this beautiful shorebird is a familiar sight at its coastal wintering areas. Its distinctive brown-and-cinnamon plumage and the fact that it chooses open habitats, such as mudflats and floodplains, to feed and roost, make the Marbled Godwit a conspicuous species. A monogamous bird, the Marbled Godwit is also long-lived—the oldest bird recorded was 29 years old.

VOICE Call a nasal *ah-ahk*, and single *ahk*; breeding call, *goddWhit, wik-wik*; other calls include *rack-a, karatica, ratica, ratica.*

NESTING Depression in short grass in Alaska; also nests on vegetation in water; 4 eggs; 1 brood; May–July.

FEEDING Probes mudflats, beaches, short grass for insects, especially grasshoppers; also crustaceans, mollusks, and small fish.

EASILY RECOGNIZED
Its large size and buffy to cinnamon color make this godwit a very distinctive shorebird.

SIMILAR SPECIES

HUDSONIAN GODWIT white rump; see p.430 black barring overall

BLACK-TAILED GODWIT see p.470 smaller overall; deep orange neck and breast

OCCURRENCE
Breeds in the grassy marshes of the Great Plains. During migration and in winter, prefers sandy beaches and coastal mudflats with adjoining meadows or savannas in California and the Gulf of Mexico. Also seen on inland wetlands and along lake shores.

Length **16½–19in (42–48cm)**	Wingspan **28–32in (70–81cm)**	Weight **10–16oz (275–450g)**
Social **Winter flocks**	Lifespan **Up to 29 years**	Status **Secure**

DATE SEEN	WHERE	NOTES

Order **Charadriiformes**	Family **Scolopacidae**	Species ***Numenius phaeopus***

Whimbrel

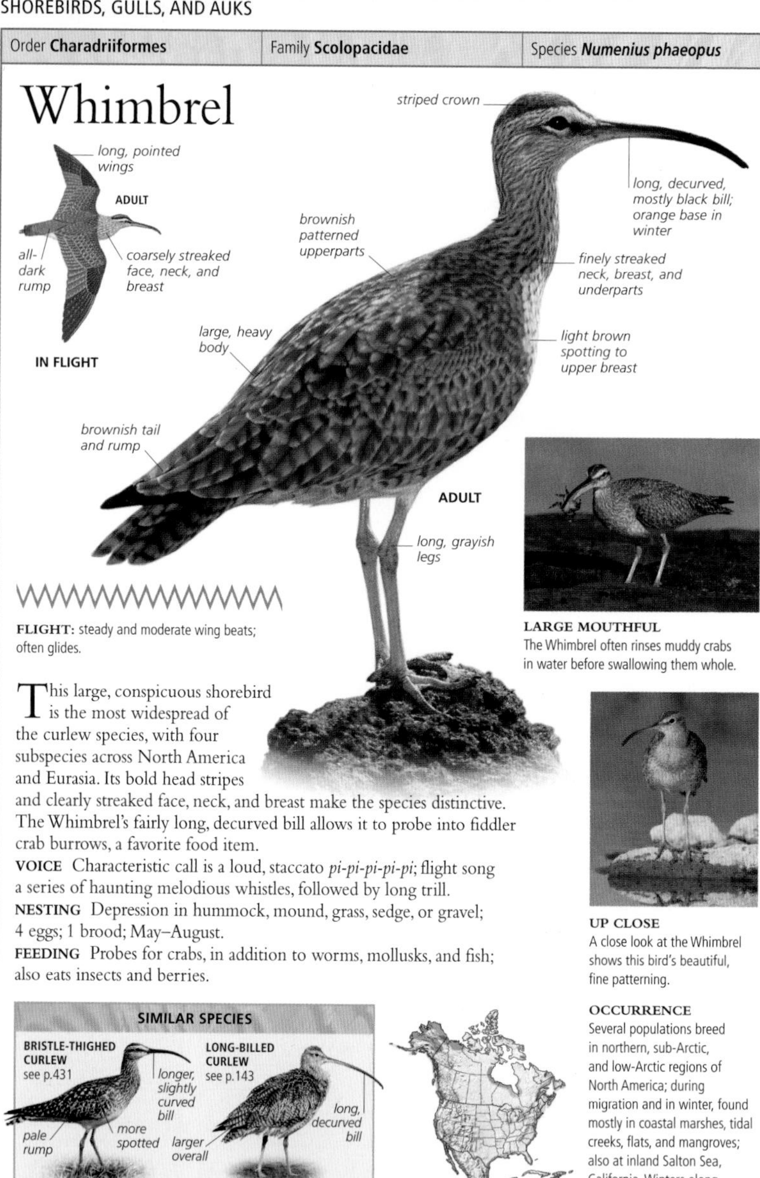

FLIGHT: steady and moderate wing beats; often glides.

LARGE MOUTHFUL
The Whimbrel often rinses muddy crabs in water before swallowing them whole.

This large, conspicuous shorebird is the most widespread of the curlew species, with four subspecies across North America and Eurasia. Its bold head stripes and clearly streaked face, neck, and breast make the species distinctive. The Whimbrel's fairly long, decurved bill allows it to probe into fiddler crab burrows, a favorite food item.

VOICE Characteristic call is a loud, staccato *pi-pi-pi-pi-pi*; flight song a series of haunting melodious whistles, followed by long trill.

NESTING Depression in hummock, mound, grass, sedge, or gravel; 4 eggs; 1 brood; May–August.

FEEDING Probes for crabs, in addition to worms, mollusks, and fish; also eats insects and berries.

UP CLOSE
A close look at the Whimbrel shows this bird's beautiful, fine patterning.

SIMILAR SPECIES

BRISTLE-THIGHED CURLEW see p.431
longer, slightly curved bill
pale rump
more spotted

LONG-BILLED CURLEW see p.143
long, decurved bill
larger overall

OCCURRENCE
Several populations breed in northern, sub-Arctic, and low-Arctic regions of North America; during migration and in winter, found mostly in coastal marshes, tidal creeks, flats, and mangroves; also at inland Salton Sea, California. Winters along rocky coasts in South America.

Length **15½–16½in (39–42cm)**	Wingspan **30–35in (76–89cm)**	Weight **11–18oz (300–500g)**
Social **Flocks**	Lifespan **Up to 19 years**	Status **Secure**

DATE SEEN	WHERE	NOTES

Order **Charadriiformes**	Family **Scolopacidae**	Species ***Numenius americanus***

Long-billed Curlew

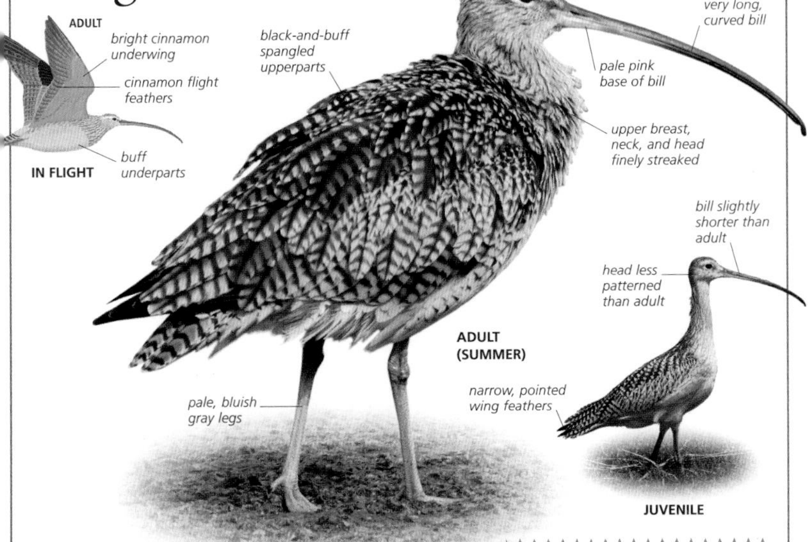

ADULT
bright cinnamon underwing
cinnamon flight feathers
buff underparts
IN FLIGHT
black-and-buff spangled upperparts
very long, curved bill
pale pink base of bill
upper breast, neck, and head finely streaked
bill slightly shorter than adult
head less patterned than adult
ADULT (SUMMER)
narrow, pointed wing feathers
pale, bluish gray legs
JUVENILE

The Long-billed Curlew has the southernmost breeding range and northernmost wintering range of the four North American curlews. It is also one of nine species of birds that are endemic to the grasslands of the Great Plains. Its large size and tame behavior on its wintering grounds in North America add to its mystique. The curvature of its bill is adapted to probe for food in soft mud and sand.

VOICE Flight call a 2-note *cur-LUoo*, often accompanied by rapid *qui-pi-pi-pi-pi*; flight song consists of haunting whistles, trills *werr-EEEer.*

NESTING Shallow depression in sparsely vegetated prairie habitat; 4 eggs; 1 brood; April–May.

FEEDING Picks insects on the surface or probes in soft mud for insects, crustaceans, mollusks, and worms; also eats fish.

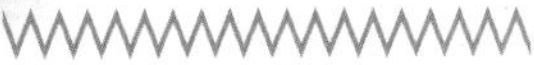

FLIGHT: graceful and strong series of flaps alternating with a glide.

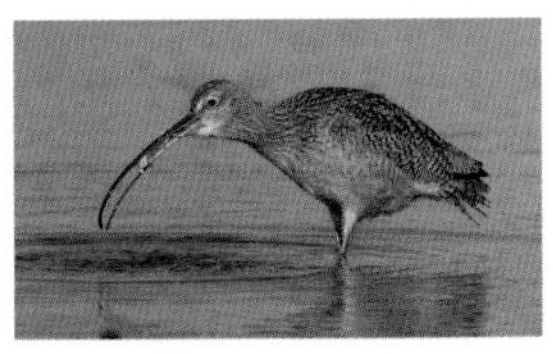

APTLY NAMED
The Long-billed Curlew is the longest billed shorebird in North America.

SIMILAR SPECIES
MARBLED GODWIT
see p.141
straight bill
more rounded body shape
darker, grayish legs
WHIMBREL
smaller;
see p.142
streaks on face, neck, and breast
brownish upperparts

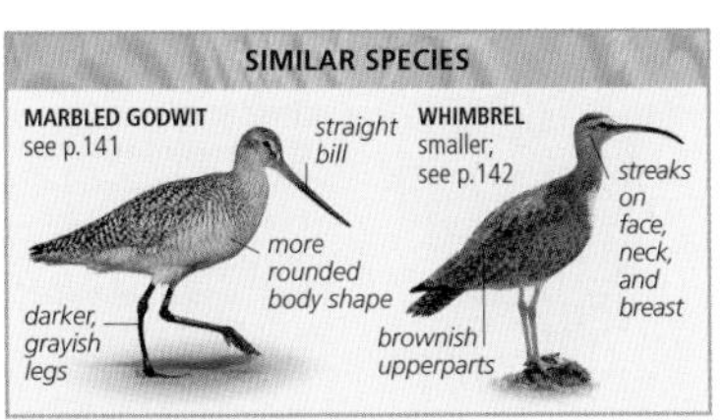

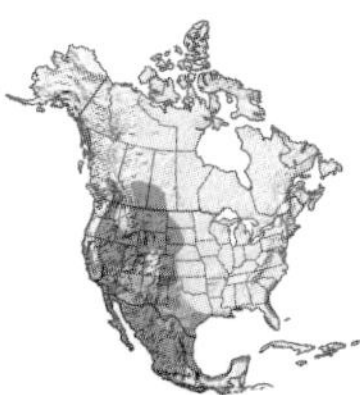

OCCURRENCE
Breeds in prairies, short grass and mixed-grass habitats of the Great Basin and Great Plains. Winters in wet pastures, marshes, beaches, and tidal mudflats primarily of California, Texas, and Mexico, with some stragglers occurring in Florida. Generally not a "shorebird" found along shores.

Length **20–26in (51–65cm)**	Wingspan **30–39in (75–100cm)**	Weight **16–28oz (450–800g)**
Social **Solitary/Winter flocks**	Lifespan **At least 8 years**	Status **Vulnerable**

DATE SEEN	WHERE	NOTES

Order **Charadriiformes**	Family **Scolopacidae**	Species ***Tringa melanoleuca***

Greater Yellowlegs

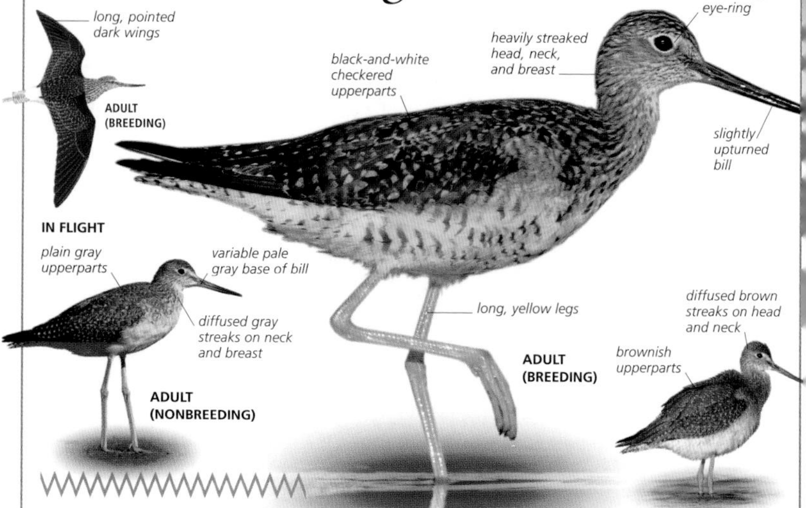

long, pointed dark wings

ADULT (BREEDING)

IN FLIGHT

bold white eye-ring

heavily streaked head, neck, and breast

black-and-white checkered upperparts

slightly upturned bill

plain gray upperparts

variable pale gray base of bill

diffused gray streaks on neck and breast

ADULT (NONBREEDING)

long, yellow legs

ADULT (BREEDING)

diffused brown streaks on head and neck

brownish upperparts

JUVENILE

FLIGHT: direct, strong, and swift; legs trail behind tail.

This fairly large shorebird often runs frantically in many directions while pursuing small prey. It is one of the first northbound spring shorebird migrants, and one of the first to return south in late June or early July. Its plumage, a mixture of brown, black, and white checkered upperparts, and streaked underparts, is more streaked during the breeding season.

VOICE Call a loud, penetrating *tew-tew-tew*; agitated birds make repetitive *keu* notes; song a continuous *too-whee.*

NESTING Simple scrape in moss or peat, usually close to water; 4 eggs; 1 brood; May–June.

FEEDING Picks water surface and mud for small aquatic and terrestrial crustaceans and worms; also eats small fish, frogs, seeds, and berries.

EFFECTIVE METHOD
The Greater Yellowlegs often catches its prey by sweeping its bill sideways through water.

SIMILAR SPECIES

LESSER YELLOWLEGS see p.145

thinner, more pointed bill

less angular body contours

WILLET see p.148

heavier, thicker bill

lacks checkered upperparts

OCCURRENCE
Breeds in openings in northerly forests with bogs and wet meadows, a habitat called muskegs. In migration and winter, uses a wide variety of shallow water habitats, including freshwater and saltwater marshes, reservoirs, and tidal mudflats.

Length **11½–13in (29–33cm)**	Wingspan **28–29in (70–74cm)**	Weight **4–8oz (125–225g)**
Social **Solitary/Flocks**	Lifespan **Unknown**	Status **Secure**

DATE SEEN	WHERE	NOTES

Order **Charadriiformes**	Family **Scolopacidae**	Species ***Tringa flavipes***

Lesser Yellowlegs

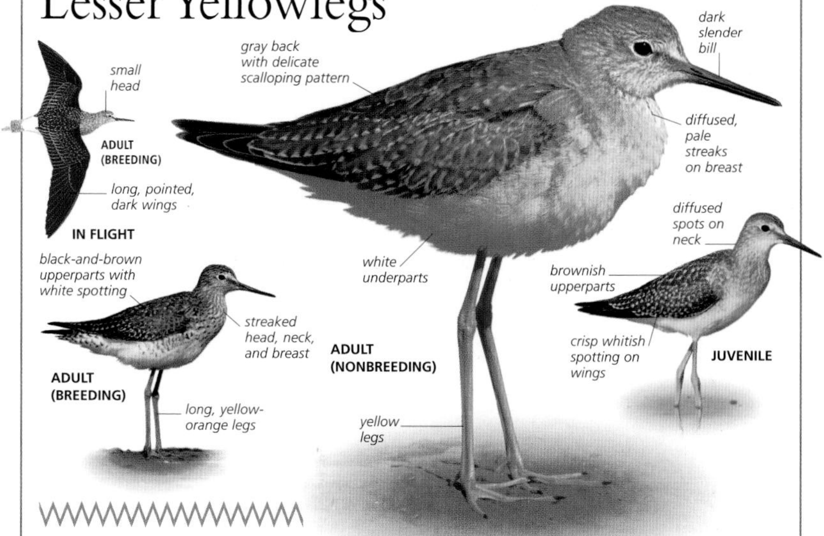

small head
ADULT (BREEDING)
long, pointed, dark wings
IN FLIGHT
black-and-brown upperparts with white spotting
streaked head, neck, and breast
ADULT (BREEDING)
long, yellow-orange legs
gray back with delicate scalloping pattern
white underparts
ADULT (NONBREEDING)
yellow legs
dark slender bill
diffused, pale streaks on breast
diffused spots on neck
brownish upperparts
crisp whitish spotting on wings
JUVENILE

FLIGHT: straight and fast; with gliding and sideways banking; legs trail behind body.

With its smaller head, thinner bill, and smoother body shape, the Lesser Yellowlegs has a more elegant profile than the Greater Yellowlegs. It prefers smaller, freshwater, or brackish pools to open saltwater habitats, and it walks quickly and methodically while feeding. Although this species is a solitary feeder, it is often seen in small to large loose flocks in migration and winter.

VOICE Low, whistled *tu*, or *tu-tu* call; series of *tu* or *cuw* notes when agitated; display song a *pill-e-wee, pill-e-wee, pill-e-wee.*

NESTING Depression in ground or moss, lined with grass and leaves; 4 eggs; 1 brood; May–June.

FEEDING Eats a wide variety of aquatic and terrestrial insects, mollusks, and crustaceans, especially flies and beetles; also seeds.

READY TO FLY
This Lesser Yellowlegs raises its wings before takeoff.

SIMILAR SPECIES

GREATER YELLOWLEGS see p.144
larger and heavier
longer, thicker bill

SOLITARY SANDPIPER see p.146
shorter, greenish yellow legs
more defined breast streaks

OCCURRENCE
Breeds in northerly forest with clearings, and where forest meets tundra. In migration and in winter, uses wide variety of shallow wetlands, including flooded pastures and agricultural fields, swamps, lake and river shores, tidal creeks, and brackish mudflats. Winters from Mexico to Argentina.

Length **9–10in (23–25cm)**	Wingspan **23–25in (58–64cm)**	Weight **2–3⅜oz (55–95g)**
Social **Flocks**	Lifespan **Unknown**	Status **Secure**

DATE SEEN	WHERE	NOTES

Order **Charadriiformes**	Family **Scolopacidae**	Species ***Tringa solitaria***

Solitary Sandpiper

long, pointed wings

ADULT (BREEDING)

dark flight feathers

IN FLIGHT

brown-and-white checkered upperparts

brownish streaked crown and head

JUVENILE

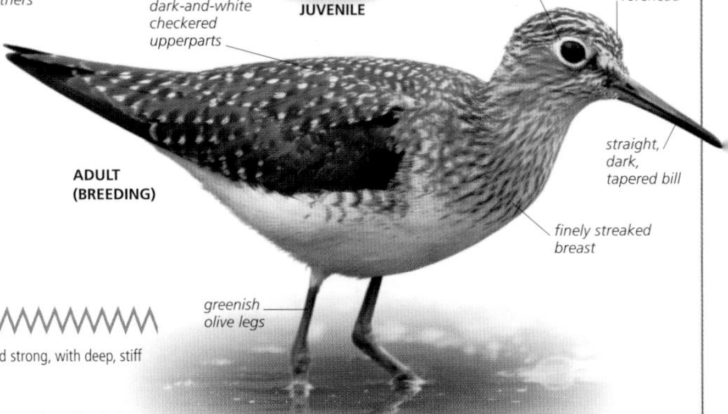

conspicuous white eye-ring

roundish forehead

dark-and-white checkered upperparts

ADULT (BREEDING)

straight, dark, tapered bill

finely streaked breast

greenish olive legs

FLIGHT: graceful and strong, with deep, stiff wing beats.

Alexander Wilson described this species in 1813, naming it, quite appropriately, "Solitary." This sandpiper seldom associates with other shorebirds as it moves nervously along margins of wetlands. When feeding, the Solitary Sandpiper constantly bobs its head like the Spotted Sandpiper. When disturbed, the Solitary Sandpiper often flies directly upward, and when landing, it keeps its wings upright briefly, flashing the white underneath, before carefully folding them to its body.

VOICE Flight and alarm call a high-pitched *weet-weet-weet* or *pit*; display song a *pit-pit-pit-pit*; *kik-kik-kik*.

NESTING Abandoned nests in trees (a unique behavior for a North American shorebird); 4 eggs; 1 brood; May–June.

FEEDING Eats insects, small crustaceans, snails, and small frogs.

LONE RANGER
This sandpiper is indeed solitary and is found in quiet, sheltered habitats and along river shores.

SIMILAR SPECIES

LESSER YELLOWLEGS see p.145
slimmer body
yellow-orange legs

SPOTTED SANDPIPER see p.147
bulkier body
shorter bill
shorter legs

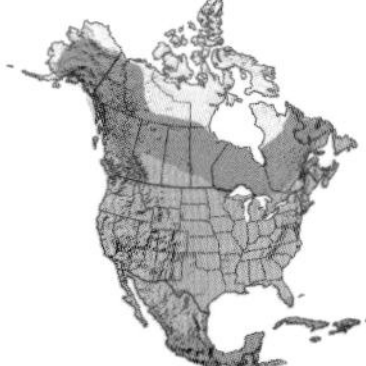

OCCURRENCE
Breeds primarily in bogs in northern forests; in winter and during migration, occurs in sheltered pools or muddy areas near forests. Winters from Mexico down to South America, sometimes in tiny pools at high altitude in the Andes; also riverbanks, streams, rain pools, and ditches.

Length **7½–9in (19–23cm)**	Wingspan **22–23in (56–59cm)**	Weight **1 1/16–2¼oz (30–65g)**
Social **Solitary/Small flocks**	Lifespan **Unknown**	Status **Secure**

DATE SEEN	WHERE	NOTES

Order **Charadriiformes**	Family **Scolopacidae**	Species ***Actitis macularia***

Spotted Sandpiper

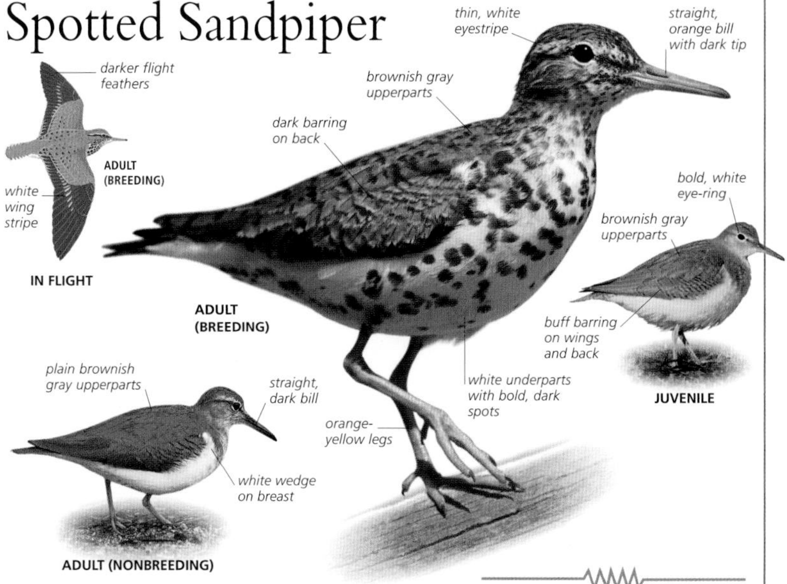

darker flight feathers
ADULT (BREEDING)
white wing stripe
IN FLIGHT
thin, white eyestripe
straight, orange bill with dark tip
brownish gray upperparts
dark barring on back
ADULT (BREEDING)
bold, white eye-ring
brownish gray upperparts
buff barring on wings and back
JUVENILE
white underparts with bold, dark spots
orange-yellow legs
plain brownish gray upperparts
straight, dark bill
white wedge on breast
ADULT (NONBREEDING)

One of only two species of the genus *Actitis*, from the Latin meaning "a coastal inhabitant," this small, short-legged sandpiper is the most widespread shorebird in North America. It is characterized by its quick walking pace, its habit of constantly teetering and bobbing its tail, and its unique style of flying low over water with stiff wing beats. These birds have an unusual mating behavior, in which the females take on an aggressive role, defending territories and mating with three or more males per season.

VOICE Call a clear, ringing note *tee-tee-tee-tee*; flight song a monotonous *cree-cree-cree*.

NESTING Nest cup shaded by or scrape built under herbaceous vegetation; 3 eggs; 1–3 broods; May–June.

FEEDING Eats many items, including adult and larval insects, mollusks, small crabs, and worms.

FLIGHT: mostly shallow, rapidly, stiffly fluttering wing beats, usually low above water.

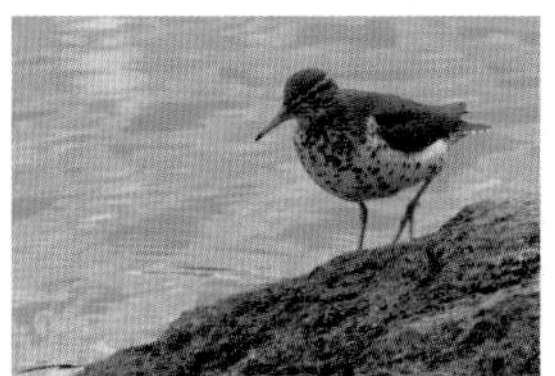

BEHAVIORAL QUIRKS
This sandpiper "teeters," raising and lowering its tail while walking along the water's edge.

SIMILAR SPECIES

SOLITARY SANDPIPER ◔ see p.146

COMMON SANDPIPER see p.470

more slender body
longer legs
streaked breast
longer tail
more grayish green legs

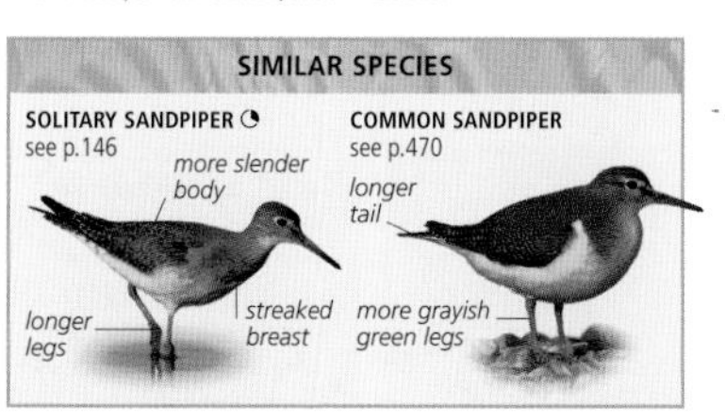

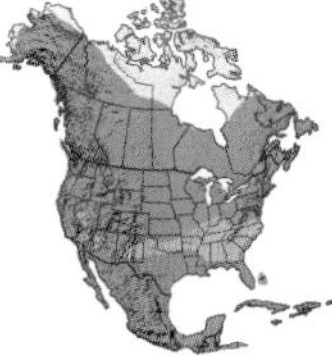

OCCURRENCE
Breeds across North America in a wide variety of grassy, brushy, forested habitats near water, but not high Arctic tundra. During migration and in winter found in habitats near freshwater, including lake shores, rivers, streams, beaches, sewage ponds, ditches, seawalls, sometimes estuaries.

Length **7¼–8in (18.5–20cm)**	Wingspan **15–16in (38–41cm)**	Weight **1 9/16–1¾oz (45–50g)**
Social **Small flocks**	Lifespan **Up to 12 years**	Status **Secure**

DATE SEEN	WHERE	NOTES

Order **Charadriiformes**	Family **Scolopacidae**	Species ***Catoptrophorus semipalmatus***

Willet

bold black-and-white wing pattern
ADULT (WESTERN WINTER)
unpatterned, pale underparts
IN FLIGHT

crisp, thin, buff fringes
grayish upperparts
white stripe above eye
dark patch between eye and bill
JUVENILE
C. s. inornatus
(WESTERN)

long, grayish, straight bill
plain gray upperparts

brownish upperparts with dense, dark feathers
straight, thick bill with pinkish base
pale underparts
ADULT
C. s. inornatus
(WESTERN; WINTER)

strong, dark barring on underside
ADULT
C. s. semipalmatus
(EASTERN; BREEDING)

FLIGHT: strong, fast, and direct on powerful wing beats.

The two distinct subspecies of the Willet, Eastern (*C. s. semipalmatus*) and Western (*C. s. inornatus*), differ in breeding habit, plumage coloration, vocalizations, and migratory habits. The Eastern Willet leaves North America from September to March; whereas the Western Willet winters along southern North American shorelines south to South America.

VOICE Flight call a loud *kyah-yah*; alarm call a sharp, repeated *kleep*; song an urgent, rapid *pill-will-willet*.

NESTING Depression in vegetated dunes, wetlands, prairies, or salt marshes; 4 eggs; 1 brood; April–June.

FEEDING Picks, probes, or swishes for crustaceans, such as fiddler and mole, crab, aquatic insects, marine worms, small mollusks, and fish.

EXPOSED PERCH
Willets display on exposed perches at breeding grounds.

SIMILAR SPECIES

GREATER YELLOWLEGS see p.144
longer neck
yellowish orange legs

WANDERING TATTLER 1ST see p.431
stockier body
yellowish legs

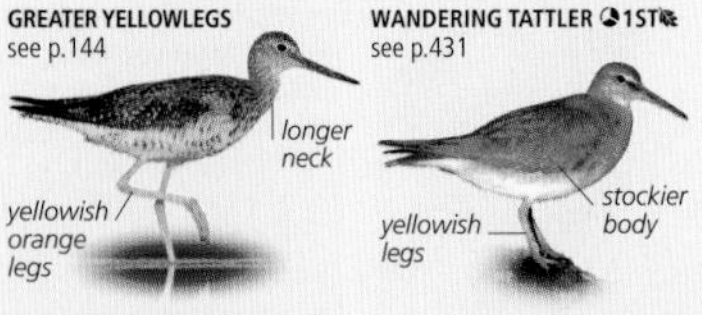

OCCURRENCE
Eastern subspecies breeds in coastal saltwater habitats: salt marshes, barrier islands, beaches, mangroves; winters in similar habitats. Western subspecies breeds near sparsely vegetated prairie wetlands or adjacent semi-arid grasslands; winters in coastal regions.

Length **12½–16½in (32–42cm)**	Wingspan **21½–28½in (54–72cm)**	Weight **7–12oz (200–350g)**
Social **Flocks**	Lifespan **Up to 10 years**	Status **Secure**

DATE SEEN	WHERE	NOTES

Order **Charadriiformes**	Family **Scolopacidae**	Species ***Arenaria interpres***

Ruddy Turnstone

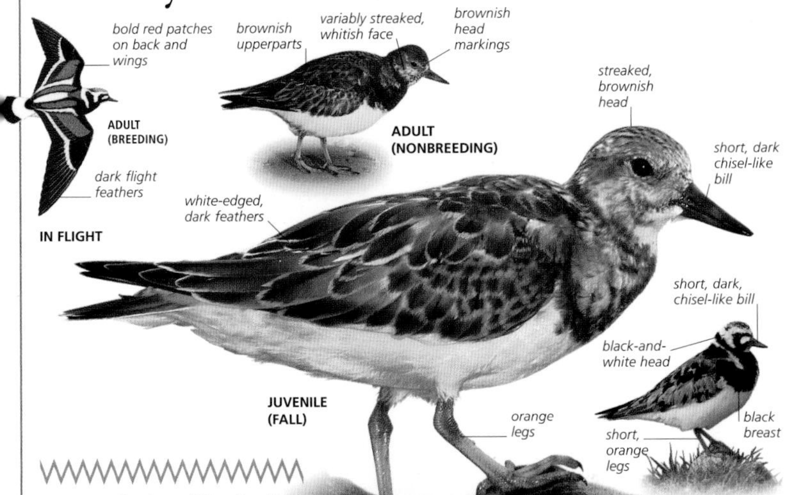
bold red patches on back and wings
ADULT (BREEDING)
dark flight feathers
IN FLIGHT
brownish upperparts
variably streaked, whitish face
brownish head markings
ADULT (NONBREEDING)
streaked, brownish head
short, dark chisel-like bill
white-edged, dark feathers
short, dark, chisel-like bill
black-and-white head
JUVENILE (FALL)
orange legs
black breast
short, orange legs
ADULT (BREEDING)

FLIGHT: swift and strong flight, with quick wing beats.

This tame, medium-sized, and stocky sandpiper with a chisel-shaped bill is a common visitor along the shorelines of North and South America. On its high-Arctic breeding grounds, it is bold and aggressive and is able to drive off predators as large as the Glaucous Gull and Parasitic Jaeger. The Ruddy Turnstone was given its name because of its reddish back color and because of its habit of flipping and overturning items like mollusk shells and pebbles, or digging in the sand and looking for small crustaceans and other marine invertebrates. Two subspecies live in Arctic North America: *A. i. interpres* in northeastern Canada and *A. i. morinellas* elsewhere in Canada and Alaska.

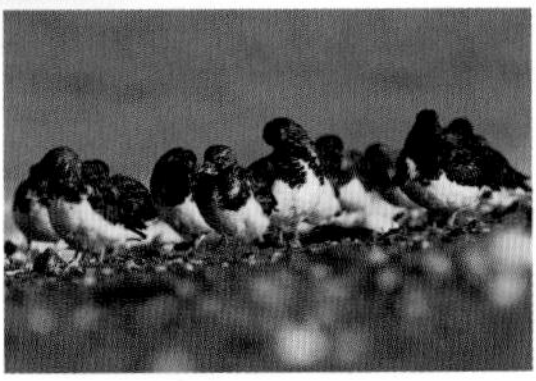

WINTER GATHERINGS
Ruddy Turnstones often congregate in large winter flocks on rocky shorelines.

VOICE Rapid chatter on breeding ground: *TIT-wooo TIT-woooRITtititititit*; flight call a low, rapid *kut-a-kut*.

NESTING Simple scrape lined with lichens and grasses in dry, open areas; 4 eggs; 1 brood; June.

FEEDING Forages along shoreline for crustaceans, insects, including beetles, spiders; also eats plants.

SIMILAR SPECIES

BLACK TURNSTONE
see p.150

darker overall
duller legs
no rust color in plumage

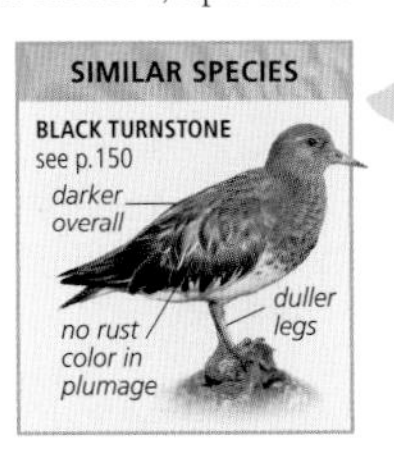

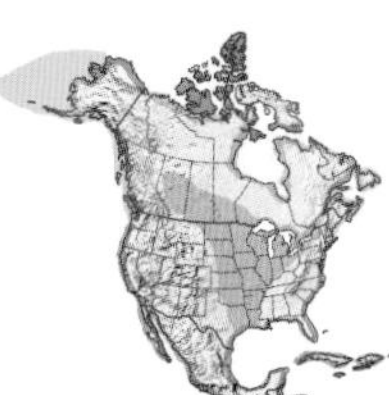

OCCURRENCE
Breeds in High Arctic: wide-open, barren, and grassy habitats and rocky coasts, usually near water. In winter, on sandy or gravel beaches and rocky shorelines, from northern California to South America, and from northern Massachusetts south along Atlantic and Gulf Coasts.

Length **8–10½in (20–27cm)**	Wingspan **20–22½in (51–57cm)**	Weight **3½–7oz (100–200g)**
Social **Flocks**	Lifespan **Up to 7 years**	Status **Secure**

DATE SEEN	WHERE	NOTES

Order **Charadriiformes**	Family **Scolopacidae**	Species ***Arenaria melanocephala***

Black Turnstone

The Black Turnstone is found along the entire North American Pacific coastline in winter, from Kodiak Island, Alaska, to the Gulf of California. Highly dependent on rocky shorelines, the zebra-like but cryptic plumage of this species blends in well, and it becomes almost invisible when it forages or roosts on dark, rocky surfaces. Although the Black Turnstone flips stones and beach litter in search of food, it uses its chisel-like bill to pry loose or crack tougher prey, particularly mussels and barnacles. On its breeding grounds, this species is a vocal and aggressive defender of the nesting community, even physically attacking predators such as jaegars.

VOICE Flight call a *breerp*, often continued as rapid chattering; variety of trills, purrs, and a *tu-whit* call.

NESTING Hollow depression in tundra; 4 eggs; 1 brood; May–June.

FEEDING Eats invertebrates such as mussels, barnacles, limpets, snails, and crabs, also seeds, small bird eggs, and carrion.

FLIGHT: swift and direct, with strong, shallow wing beats.

CRACKING IT
Black Turnstones use their chisel-shaped bills to break open barnacles on rocks.

SIMILAR SPECIES

RUDDY TURNSTONE see p.149

OCCURRENCE
Breeds in tundra of western Alaska; also inland along rivers and lakes. It is strictly coastal during migration and winter where it is found in the tidal zone of rocky shorelines, on sand and gravel beaches, mudflats, and rocky jetties of the West Coast, south to Baja California.

Length **8½–10½in (22–27cm)**	Wingspan **20–22½in (51–57cm)**	Weight **3⅛–6oz (90–175g)**
Social **Flocks**	Lifespan **At least 4 years**	Status **Secure**

DATE SEEN	WHERE	NOTES

Order **Charadriiformes**	Family **Scolopacidae**	Species ***Aphriza virgata***

Surfbird

white wing stripe

black tail band

ADULT (NONBREEDING)

IN FLIGHT

sooty gray streaks on head and neck

white eye-ring

plain, sooty upperparts

stubby, short bill with yellow base

rust-and-black upperparts

dark V-shaped marks on belly

gray breast

ADULT (BREEDING)

diffused streaking on head and breast

uniformly gray upperparts

pale-fringed feathers

scattered gray marks on belly

ADULT (MOLTING)

short, stocky yellow legs

ADULT (NONBREEDING)

The chunky, stubby-billed Surfbird has a dual lifestyle—it breeds in the high mountain tundra of Alaska and then migrates to the rocky Pacific coasts of both North and South America. Some individuals migrate as far as southern Chile, a round trip of about 19,000 miles (30,500km) each year. This remarkable wintering range is among the largest of all North American shorebirds. The extent of the rust color on the upperparts of breeding Surfbirds is variable.

VOICE Flight call a soft *whiff-if-if*; feeding flocks soft, chattering *whiks*; display call *kree, kree…ki-drr ki-drr*, and *quoy quoy quoy*.

NESTING Shallow lined depression on vegetated or bare ground; 4 eggs; 1 brood; May–June.

FEEDING Eats mainly insects, especially beetles; also aquatic mollusks and crustaceans, such as mussels and barnacles.

FLIGHT: swift and direct, with strong, powerful wing beats.

COASTAL PROXIMITY
Except when breeding, Surfbirds spend their lives along rocky intertidal shores.

SIMILAR SPECIES

PURPLE SANDPIPER ❄

purplish gray upperparts

longer bill

ROCK SANDPIPER
see p.431

darker feathers on back

longer, slightly curved bill

short, yellow-orange legs

OCCURRENCE
Breeds in low to high-elevation steep, rocky slopes of ridges and mountains; the rest of the year it spends exclusively on rocky Pacific coastlines, typically within 6½ft (2m) of the high-tide line (the narrowest range of all North American shorebirds).

Length **9½–10½in (24–27cm)**	Wingspan **25–27in (63–68cm)**	Weight **4–8oz (125–225g)**
Social **Small flocks**	Lifespan **Unknown**	Status **Secure**

DATE SEEN	WHERE	NOTES

Order **Charadriiformes**	Family **Scolopacidae**	Species ***Calidris canutus***

Red Knot

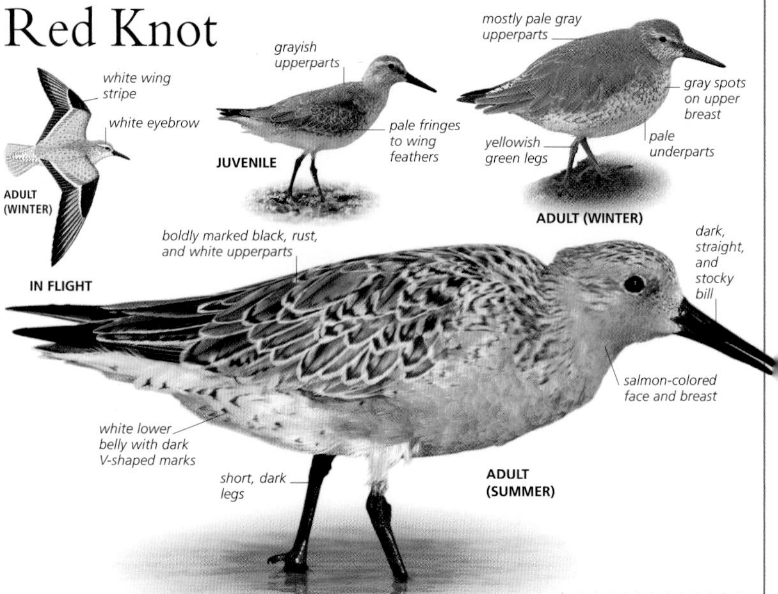
white wing stripe
white eyebrow
ADULT (WINTER)
IN FLIGHT
grayish upperparts
pale fringes to wing feathers
JUVENILE
mostly pale gray upperparts
gray spots on upper breast
yellowish green legs
pale underparts
ADULT (WINTER)
boldly marked black, rust, and white upperparts
dark, straight, and stocky bill
salmon-colored face and breast
white lower belly with dark V-shaped marks
short, dark legs
ADULT (SUMMER)

A substantial, plump sandpiper, the Red Knot is the largest North American shorebird in the genus *Calidris*. There are two North American subspecies—*C. c. rufa* and *C. c. roselaari*. Noted for its extraordinary long-distance migration, *C. c. rufa* flies about 9,300 miles (15,000km) between its high-Arctic breeding grounds and wintering area in South America, especially in Tierra del Fuego, at the tip of South America. Recent declines have occurred in this population, attributed to over-harvesting of horseshoe crab eggs—its critical food source. With the population of *C. c. rufa* having declined from over 100,000 birds in the mid-1980s to below 15,000 today, the Red Knot is now listed as endangered in New Jersey, and faces possible extinction.

VOICE Flight call a soft *kuEEt* or *kuup*; display song *eerie por-meeee por-meeee*, followed by *por-por por-por*.

NESTING Simple scrape in grassy or barren tundra, often lined; 4 eggs; 1 brood; June.

FEEDING Probes mud or sand for insects, plant material, small mollusks, crustaceans, especially small snails, worms, and other invertebrates.

FLIGHT: powerful, swift, direct flight with rapid wing beats.

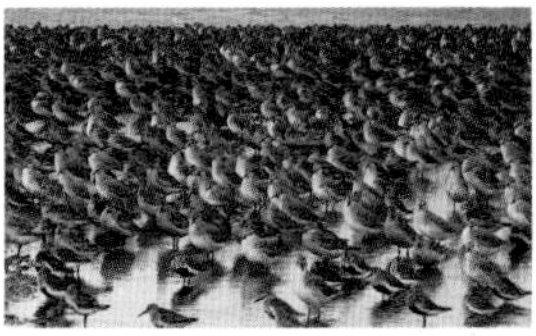

STAGING AREAS
Red Knots form dense flocks during migration and on their wintering grounds.

SIMILAR SPECIES

BLACK-BELLIED PLOVER
see p.133

large, dark eye
longer, dark legs

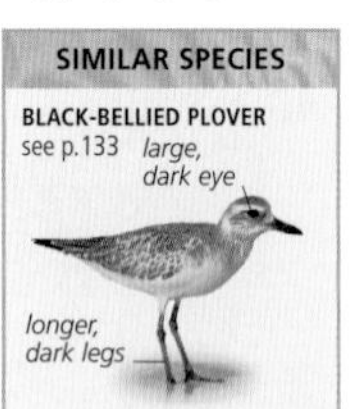

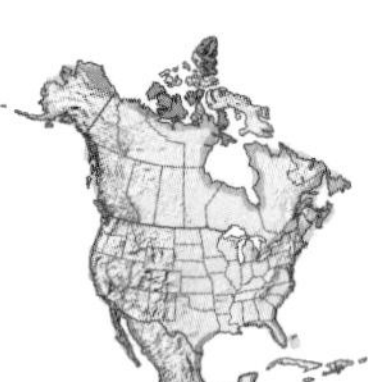

OCCURRENCE
Breeds in flat, barren tundra in high-Arctic islands and peninsulas. Mostly coastal during migration and winter, preferring sandbars, beaches, and tidal flats, where it congregates in huge flocks.

Length **9–10in (23–25cm)**	Wingspan **23–24in (58–61cm)**	Weight **3⅜–8oz (95–225g)**
Social **Large flocks**	Lifespan **Unknown**	Status **Declining**

DATE SEEN	WHERE	NOTES

Order **Charadriiformes**	Family **Scolopacidae**	Species ***Calidris alba***

Sanderling

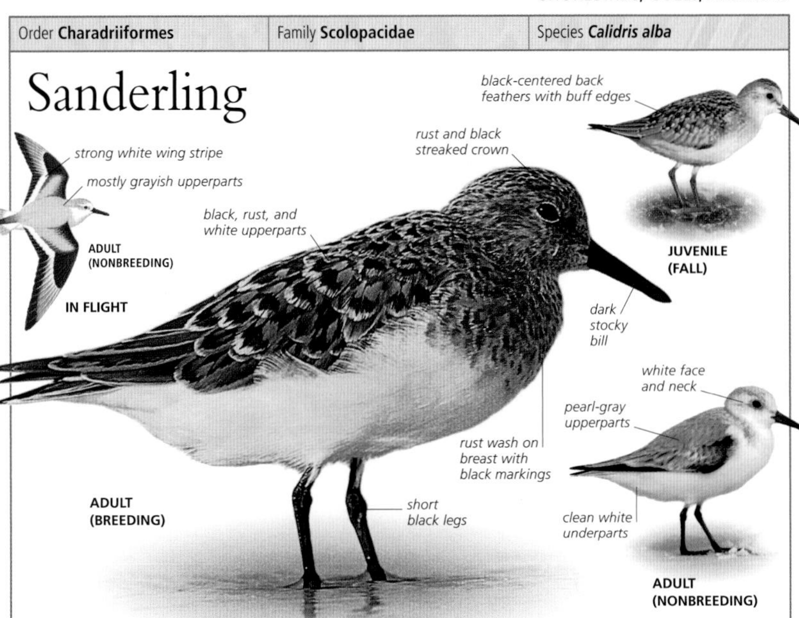

The Sanderling is probably the best-known shorebird in the world. It breeds in some of the most remote, high-Arctic habitats, from Greenland to Siberia, but occupies just about every temperate and tropical shoreline in the Americas when not breeding. Indeed, its wintering range spans both American coasts, from Canada to Argentina. Feeding in flocks, it is a common sight in winter on sandy beaches. In many places, though, the bird is declining rapidly, with pollution of the sea and shore, and the disturbance caused by people using beaches for various recreational purposes, the main causes.

VOICE Flight call squeaky *pweet*, threat call *sew-sew-sew*; display song harsh, buzzy notes and chattering *cher-cher-cher*.

NESTING Small, shallow depression on dry, stony ground; 4 eggs; 1–3 broods; June–July.

FEEDING Probes along the surf-line in sand for insects, small crustaceans, small mollusks, and worms.

FLIGHT: rapid, free-form; birds in flocks twisting and turning as if they were one.

CHASING THE WAVES
The sanderling scampers after retreating waves to pick up any small creatures stranded by the sea.

SIMILAR SPECIES

OCCURRENCE
Breeds in barren high-Arctic coastal tundra of northernmost Canada, including the islands, north to Ellesmere Island. During winter months and on migration, found along all North American coastlines, but especially sandy beaches; inland migrants found along lake and river edges.

Length **7½–8in (19–20cm)**	Wingspan **16–18in (41–46cm)**	Weight **1⁷⁄₁₆–3½oz (40–100g)**
Social **Small flocks**	Lifespan **Up to 10 years**	Status **Declining**

DATE SEEN	WHERE	NOTES

Order **Charadriiformes**	Family **Scolopacidae**	Species ***Calidris pusilla***

Semipalmated Sandpiper

This is the most abundant of the so-called "peep" *Calidiris* sandpipers, especially in the eastern US. Flocks of up to 300,000 birds gather on migration staging areas. As a species, though, it can be hard to identify, due to plumage variation between juveniles and breeding adults, and a bill that varies markedly in size and shape from west to east. Semipalmated sandpipers from northeasterly breeding grounds may fly nonstop to their South American wintering grounds in the fall.

VOICE Flight call *chrrk* or higher, sharper *chit*; display song monotonous, droning trill, often repeated for minutes at a time.

NESTING Shallow, lined scrape in short grass habitat; 4 eggs; 1 brood; May–June.

FEEDING Probes mud for aquatic and terrestrial invertebrates such as mollusks, worms, and spiders.

FLIGHT: fast and direct on narrow, pointed, wings; flies in large flocks in winter.

SLEEPING TOGETHER
Semipalmated Sandpipers form large feeding or resting flocks on migration and in winter.

OCCURRENCE
Breeds in Arctic and sub-Arctic tundra habitats near water; in Alaska, on outer coastal plain. Migrants occur in shallow fresh- or saltwater and open muddy areas with little vegetation, such as intertidal flats or lake shores. Winters in Central and South America, south to Brazil and Peru.

SIMILAR SPECIES

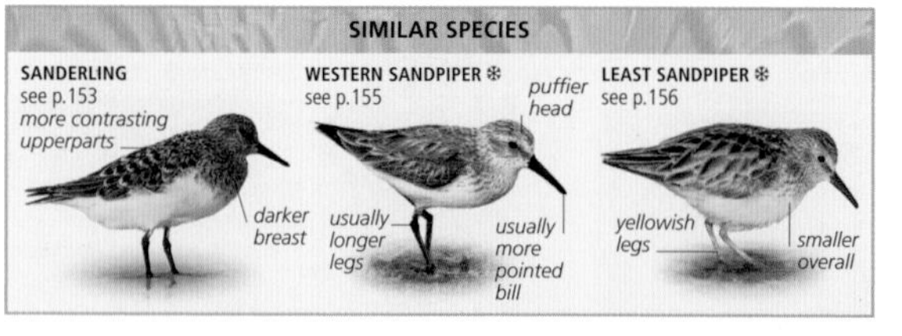

Length **5¼–6in (13.5–15cm)**	Wingspan **13½–15in (34–38cm)**	Weight **½–1 7/16oz (14–40g)**
Social **Large flocks**	Lifespan **Up to 12 years**	Status **Secure**

DATE SEEN	WHERE	NOTES

Order **Charadriiformes**	Family **Scolopacidae**	Species ***Calidris mauri***

Western Sandpiper

Despite its restricted breeding range in western Alaska, the Western Sandpiper is one of the most common shorebirds in the Western Hemisphere. During its spring migration spectacularly large flocks are seen at several Pacific coast locations. At the Copper River Delta in Alaska, for instance, over four million Western Sandpipers stop on their way to their tundra breeding grounds to fatten up and refuel for the last hop northward. Many of these migrate over relatively short distances to winter along US coastlines, so the timing of their molt in fall is earlier than that of the similar Semipalmated Sandpiper, which migrates later in winter.

VOICE Flight call loud *chir-eep*; flushed birds make *sirp* call, or *chir-ir-ip*; song *tweer, tweer, tweer*, followed by descending trill.

NESTING Shallow depression on drained Arctic and sub-Arctic tundra; 4 eggs; 1 brood; May–June.

FEEDING Probes mud for insect larvae, crustaceans, and worms.

FLIGHT: direct, rapid flight on narrow, pointed wings; in large flocks.

FORAGING FOR FOOD
The Western Sandpiper feels for hidden prey with the touch-sensitive tip of its bill.

SIMILAR SPECIES

SEMIPALMATED SANDPIPER see p.154
smaller, more rounded head
slightly shorter legs
smaller, more blunt-tipped bill

DUNLIN see p.160
longer, downcurved bill
dusky head and neck

OCCURRENCE
Breeds in wet sedge, grassy habitats with well-drained microhabitats; in migration and in winter, prefers shallow freshwater or saltwater habitats with open muddy or sandy areas and little vegetation, such as intertidal mudflats and lake shores. Winters along both coasts.

Length **5½–6½in (14–16cm)**	Wingspan **14–15in (35–38cm)**	Weight **11/16–1¼oz (19–35g)**
Social **Flocks**	Lifespan **Up to 9 years**	Status **Secure**

DATE SEEN	WHERE	NOTES

Order **Charadriiformes**	Family **Scolopacidae**	Species ***Calidris minutilla***

Least Sandpiper

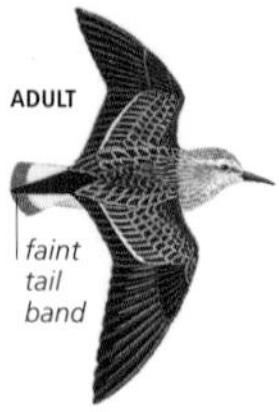
ADULT
faint tail band
IN FLIGHT

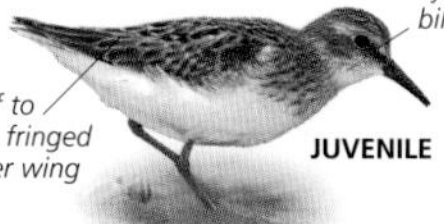
dark patch between eye and bill
buff to rust fringed inner wing
JUVENILE

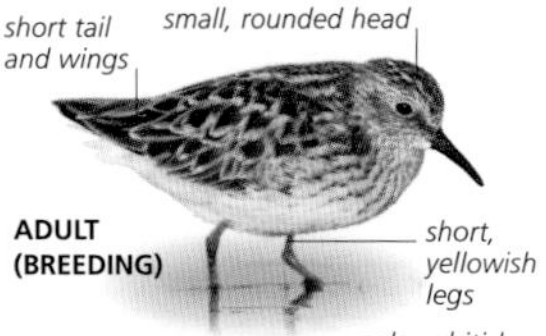
short tail and wings
small, rounded head
ADULT (BREEDING)
short, yellowish legs

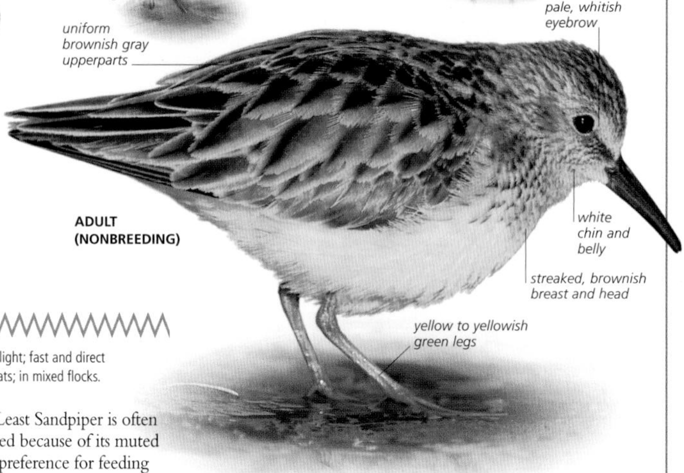
pale, whitish eyebrow
uniform brownish gray upperparts
ADULT (NONBREEDING)
white chin and belly
streaked, brownish breast and head
yellow to yellowish green legs

FLIGHT: level flight; fast and direct on quick wing beats; in mixed flocks.

The little Least Sandpiper is often overlooked because of its muted plumage and preference for feeding unobtrusively near vegetative cover. With its brown or brownish gray plumage, the Least Sandpiper virtually disappears in the landscape when feeding crouched down on wet margins of water bodies. The bird is often found in small to medium flocks, members of which typically are nervous when foraging, and frequently burst into flight, only to alight a short way off.

VOICE Its flight call, *kreeeep*, rises in pitch, often repeated two-syllable *kree-eep*; display call trilled *b-reeee, b-reeee, b-reeee.*

NESTING Depression in open, sub-Arctic habitat near water; 4 eggs; 1 brood; May–June.

FEEDING Forages for variety of small terrestrial and aquatic prey, especially sand fleas, mollusks, and flies.

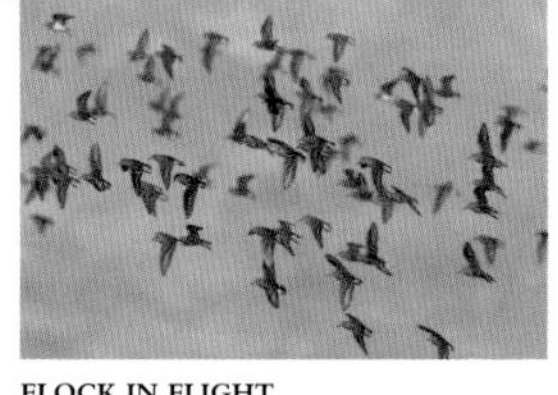

FLOCK IN FLIGHT
The narrow pointed wings of the Least Sandpiper allow it to fly fast and level.

SIMILAR SPECIES

SEMIPALMATED SANDPIPER ☼
see p.154
grayer overall
whiter throat
larger overall
PECTORAL SANDPIPER
see p.159
larger overall
heavier bill

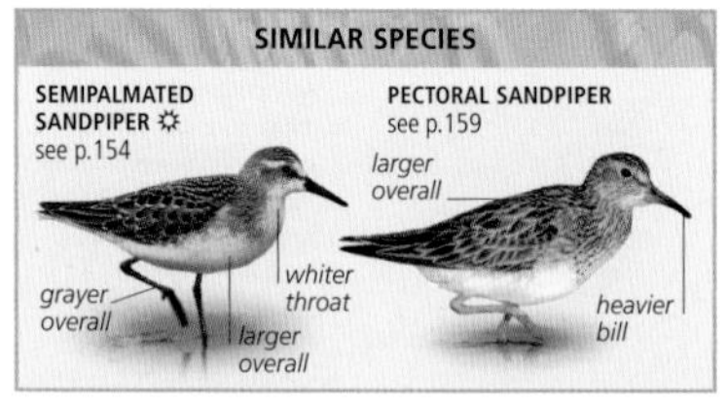

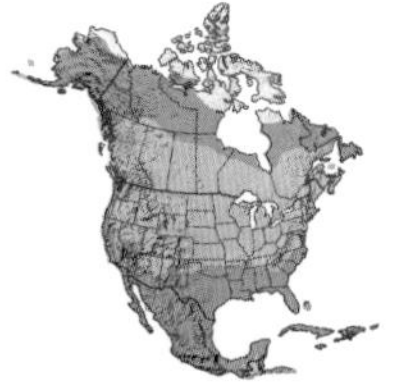

OCCURRENCE
Breeds in wet low-Arctic areas from Alaska and the Yukon to Québec and Newfoundland. During migration and in winter, uses muddy areas such as lake shores, riverbanks, flooded fields, and tidal flats. Winters from southern North America south to Peru and Brazil.

Length **4¾in (12cm)**	Wingspan **13–14in (33–35cm)**	Weight **5/16–1oz (9–27g)**
Social **Flocks**	Lifespan **Up to 16 years**	Status **Secure**

DATE SEEN	WHERE	NOTES

Order **Charadriiformes**	Family **Scolopacidae**	Species ***Calidris fuscicollis***

White-rumped Sandpiper

The White-rumped Sandpiper undertakes one of the longest migrations of any bird in the Western Hemisphere. From its high-Arctic breeding grounds in Alaska and Canada, it migrates in several long jumps to extreme southern South America—about 9,000–12,000 miles (14,500–19,300km), twice a year. Almost the entire population migrates through the central US in spring, with several stopovers, which are critical to the success of its journey. While associating with other shorebird species during migration and winter, it can be overlooked in the crowd. Its insect-like call and white rump aid identification.

VOICE Call a very high-pitched, insect-like *tzeet*; flight song an insect-like, high-pitched, rattling buzz, interspersed with grunts.

NESTING Shallow depression in usually wet but well-vegetated tundra; 4 eggs; 1 brood; June.

FEEDING Picks and probes for insects, spiders, earthworms, and marine worms; also some plant matter.

FLIGHT: fast, strong, and direct flight with deep wing beats.

WING POWER
Long narrow wings enable this species to migrate to and from the Arctic and Tierra del Fuego.

SIMILAR SPECIES

SEMIPALMATED SANDPIPER see p.154
slightly rufous crown
more distinct streaks on breast

BAIRD'S SANDPIPER see p.158
no white rump

OCCURRENCE
Breeds in wet but well-vegetated tundra, usually near ponds, lakes, or streams. In migration and winter, grassy areas: flooded fields, grassy lake margins, rivers, ponds, grassy margins of tidal mudflats, and roadside ditches. On wintering grounds, often associates with Baird's Sandpiper.

Length **6–6¾in (15–17cm)**	Wingspan **16–18in (41–46cm)**	Weight **⅞–1¾oz (25–50g)**
Social **Flocks**	Lifespan **Unknown**	Status **Secure**

DATE SEEN	WHERE	NOTES

Order **Charadriiformes**	Family **Scolopacidae**	Species ***Calidris bairdii***

Baird's Sandpiper

FLIGHT: strong and direct, with deep, quick wing beats.

Baird's Sandpiper is less well known than the other North American *Calidris* sandpipers. It was described in 1861, later than its relatives, by the famous North American ornithologist Elliott Cowes, a former surgeon in the US Army, in honor of Spencer Fullerton Baird. Both men were founding members of the AOU (the American Ornithologists' Union). From its high Arctic, tundra habitat, Baird's Sandpiper moves across North America and the western US, into South America, and all the way to Tierra del Fuego, a remarkable biannual journey of 6,000–9,000 miles (9,700–14,500km).

VOICE Flight call a low, dry *preep*; song on Arctic breeding ground: *brraay, brray, brray*, followed by *hee-aaw, hee-aaw, hee-aaw*.

NESTING Shallow depression in coastal or upland tundra; 4 eggs; 1 brood; June.

FEEDING Picks and probes for insects and larvae; also spiders and pond crustaceans.

FEEDING IN FLOCKS
Flocks of this sandpiper rush about in search of food in shallow water and muddy areas.

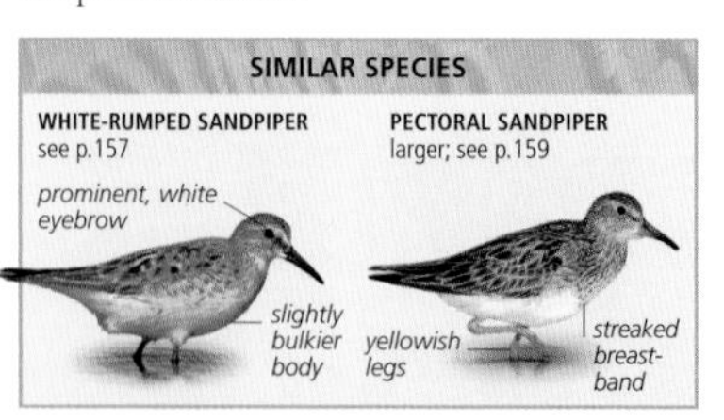

OCCURRENCE
Breeds in tundra habitats of high Arctic Alaska and Canada. During migration and winter, inland freshwater habitats: lake and river margins, wet pastures, rice fields; also tidal flats at coastal locations. In winter, common in the high Andes of South America, and sometimes all the way to Tierra del Fuego.

Length **5¾–7¼in (14.5–18.5cm)**	Wingspan **16–18½in (41–47cm)**	Weight **1$\frac{1}{16}$–2oz (30–55g)**
Social **Flocks**	Lifespan **Unknown**	Status **Secure**

DATE SEEN	WHERE	NOTES

Order **Charadriiformes**	Family **Scolopacidae**	Species ***Calidris melanotos***

Pectoral Sandpiper

long, graceful, pointed wings
ADULT
darker flight feathers
IN FLIGHT
rust-edged, dark centered feathers
rust crown and cheeks with black streaks
JUVENILE
streaked crown and face
curved bill with orange base
brownish upperparts, with buff fringes
medium length, stocky bill
ADULT
heavily streaked breast
white belly
yellowish legs

This medium-sized sandpiper is a true champion of long-distance migration. From their breeding grounds in the high Arctic to their wintering grounds on the pampas of southern South America, some birds travel up to 30,000 miles (48,000km) each year. The Pectoral Sandpiper is a promiscuous breeder, with males keeping harems of females in guarded territories. Males mate with as many females as they can attract with a display that includes a deep, booming call, and flights, but take no part in nest duties. Males migrate earlier than females, both sexes prefer wet, grassy habitats during migration and in winter.

VOICE Flight call low, trilled *chrrk*; display song deep, hollow, hooting: *whoop, whoop, whoop*.

NESTING Shallow depression on ridges in moist to wet sedge tundra; 4 eggs; 1 brood; June.

FEEDING Probes or jabs mud for larvae, and forages for insects and spiders on tundra.

FLIGHT: fast and direct, with rapid, powerful wing beats; flocks zig-zag when flushed.

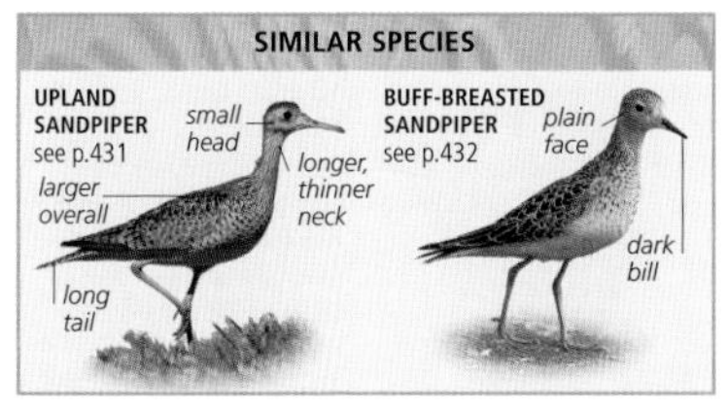

LONG JOURNEYS
This species migrates long distances to arrive in southern South American for the winter.

OCCURRENCE
In North America, breeds in northern Alaska, northern Yukon, Northern Territories, and some islands of the Canadian Arctic Archipelago, in wet, grassy tundra, especially near coasts. On migration and in winter favors wet pastures, the grassy margins of ponds and lakes, and salt marshes.

Length **7½–9in (19–23cm)**	Wingspan **16½–19½in (42–49cm)**	Weight **1¾–4oz (50–125g)**
Social **Migrant flocks**	Lifespan **Up to 4½ years**	Status **Secure**

DATE SEEN	WHERE	NOTES

Order **Charadriiformes**	Family **Scolopacidae**	Species ***Calidris alpina***

Dunlin

JUVENILE
white sided rump
thin white wing bar
IN FLIGHT

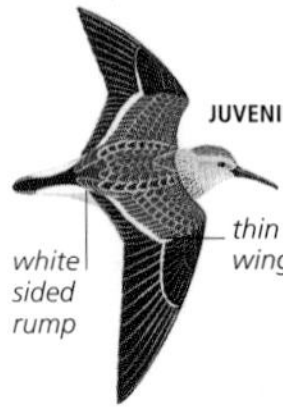

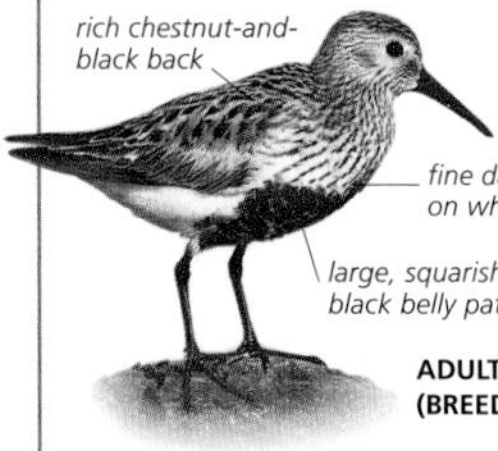

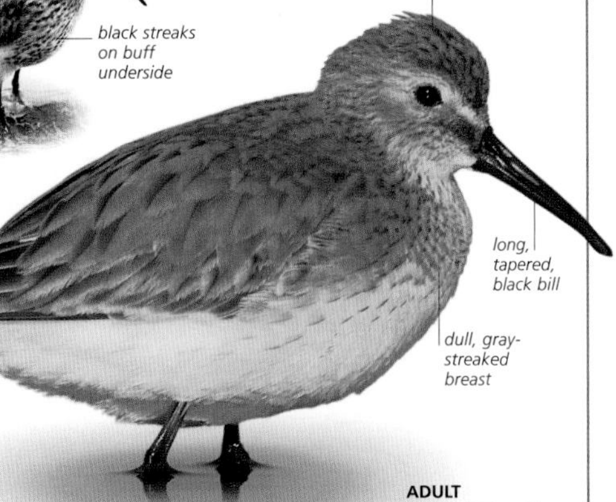

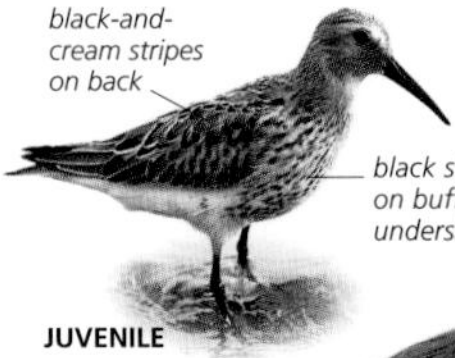

black-and-cream stripes on back
black streaks on buff underside
JUVENILE

dull gray-brown head and back
long, tapered, black bill
dull, gray-streaked breast
ADULT (NONBREEDING)

rich chestnut-and-black back
fine dark streaks on whitish breast
large, squarish, black belly patch
ADULT (BREEDING)

FLIGHT: swift and direct flight, with rapid wing beats.

The Dunlin is one of the most abundant and widespread of North America's shorebirds, but of the ten recognized subspecies, only three breed in North America: *C. a. arcticola*, *C. a. pacifica*, and *C. a. hudsonia*. The Dunlin is unmistakable in its striking, red-backed, black-bellied breeding plumage. In winter it sports much drabber colors, but more than makes up for this by gathering in spectacular flocks of many thousands of birds on its favorite coastal mudflats.

VOICE Call accented trill, *drurr-drurr*, that rises slightly, then descends; flight call *jeeezp*; song *wrraah-wrraah*.

NESTING Simple cup lined with grasses, leaves, and lichens in moist to wet tundra; 4 eggs; 1 brood; June–July.

FEEDING Probes for marine, freshwater, terrestrial invertebrates: clams, worms, insect larvae, crustaceans; also plants and small fish.

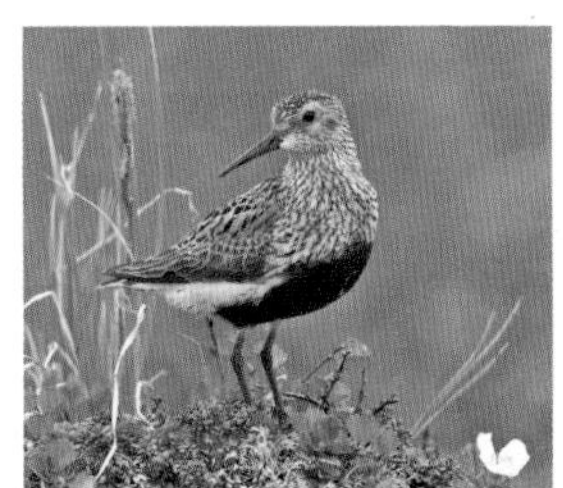

OLD RED BACK
The Dunlin was once known as the Red-backed Sandpiper due to its distinct breeding plumage.

SIMILAR SPECIES

STILT SANDPIPER ❄
see p.161

longer, thinner neck
yellowish green legs

CURLEW SANDPIPER ❄
see p.471

less streaking on chest
longer legs

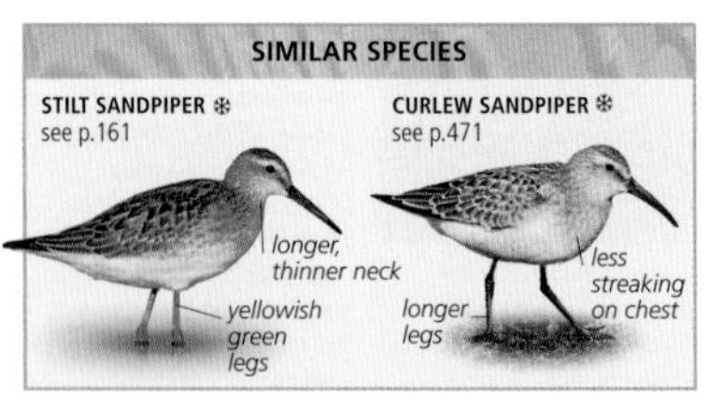

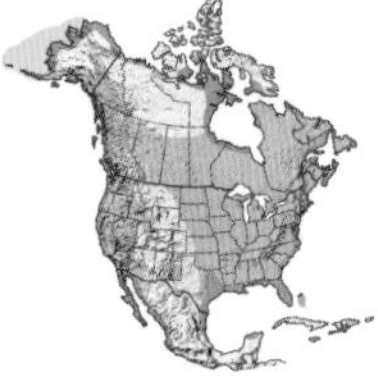

OCCURRENCE
Breeds in Arctic and sub-Arctic moist, wet tundra, often near ponds, with drier islands for nest sites. In migration and winter, prefers coastal areas with extensive mudflats and sandy beaches; also feeds in flooded fields and seasonal inland wetlands.

Length **6½–8½in (16–22cm)**	Wingspan **12½–17½in (32–44cm)**	Weight **1⁹⁄₁₆–2¼oz (45–65g)**
Social **Large flocks**	Lifespan **Up to 24 years**	Status **Declining**

DATE SEEN	WHERE	NOTES

Order **Charadriiformes**	Family **Scolopacidae**	Species ***Calidris himantopus***

Stilt Sandpiper

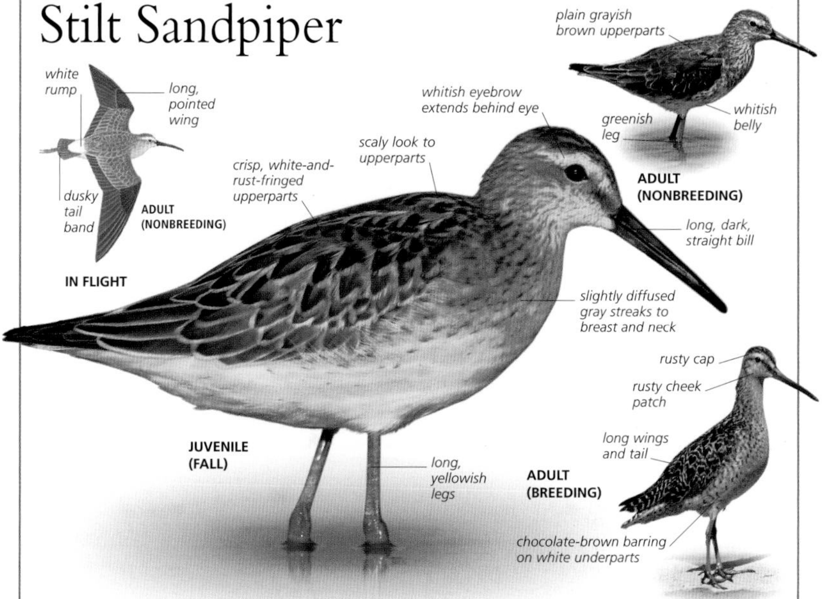

white rump
long, pointed wing
dusky tail band
ADULT (NONBREEDING)
IN FLIGHT
plain grayish brown upperparts
greenish leg
whitish belly
ADULT (NONBREEDING)
whitish eyebrow extends behind eye
scaly look to upperparts
crisp, white-and-rust-fringed upperparts
long, dark, straight bill
slightly diffused gray streaks to breast and neck
JUVENILE (FALL)
long, yellowish legs
rusty cap
rusty cheek patch
long wings and tail
ADULT (BREEDING)
chocolate-brown barring on white underparts

The slender Stilt Sandpiper is uncommon and unique to North America, where it breeds in several small areas of northern tundra. It favors shallow, freshwater habitats, where it feeds in a distinctive style, walking slowly through belly-deep water with its neck outstretched and bill pointed downward. It either picks at the surface, or submerges itself, keeping its tail raised up all the while. During migration it forms dense, rapidly moving flocks that sometimes include other sandpiper species.

VOICE Flight or alarm call low, muffled *chuf*; also *krrit* and sharp *kew-it*; display call *xxree-xxree-xxree-xxree-ee-haw, ee-haw*.

NESTING Shallow depression on raised knolls or ridges in tundra; 4 eggs; 1 brood; June.

FEEDING Eats mostly adult and larval insects; also some snails, mollusks, and seeds.

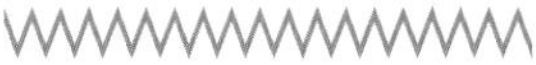

FLIGHT: fast and direct, with rapid beats of its long wings.

SIMILAR SPECIES
DUNLIN ❄
see p.160
shorter neck
shorter, black legs
CURLEW SANDPIPER ❄
see p.471
black legs
curved bill

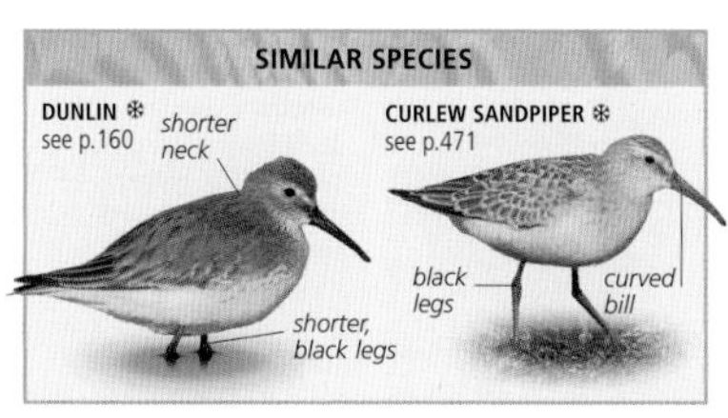

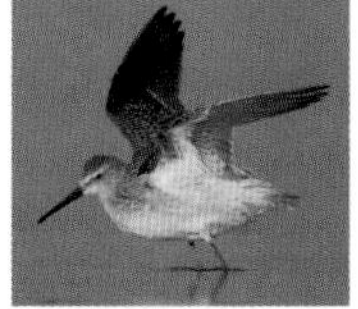

PALE BELOW
Wading through shallow water, this Stilt Sandpiper displays its whitish underparts.

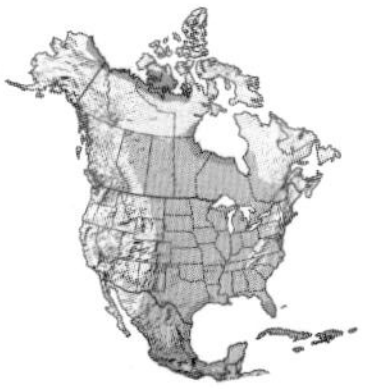

OCCURRENCE
Breeds in moist to wet coastal tundra on well-drained, raised knolls or ridges in Alaska, Yukon, and northwestern territories and Hudson Bay. During migration and in winter, prefers freshwater habitats, such as flooded fields, marsh pools, reservoirs, and sheltered lagoons to tidal mudflats.

Length **8–9in (20–23cm)**	Wingspan **17–18½in (43–47cm)**	Weight **1¾–2⅛oz (50–60g)**
Social **Pairs/Flocks**	Lifespan **At least 3 years**	Status **Secure**

DATE SEEN	WHERE	NOTES

Order **Charadriiformes**	Family **Scolopacidae**	Species ***Phalaropus tricolor***

Wilson's Phalarope

A truly American phalarope, Wilson's is the largest of the three phalarope species. Unlike its two relatives, it does not breed in the Arctic, but in the shallow wetlands of western North America, and winters mainly in continental habitats of Bolivia and Argentina instead of in the ocean. This species can be found employing the feeding technique of spinning in shallow water to churn up adult and larval insects, or running in various directions on muddy wetland edges with its head held low to the ground while chasing and picking up insects. This bird is quite tolerant of humans on its breeding grounds, but this attitude changes immediately before migration, as it has gained weight and its movement is sluggish.

VOICE Flight call a low, nasal *werpf*; also higher, repetitive *emf, emf, emf, emf*, or *luk, luk, luk*.

NESTING Simple scrape lined with grass; 4 eggs; 1 brood; May–June.

FEEDING Eats brine shrimp, various insects, and insect larvae.

FLIGHT: fast and direct with quick wing beats.

ODD ONE OUT

Unlike its two essentially oceanic relatives, Wilson's Phalarope is also found in freshwater habitats.

SIMILAR SPECIES

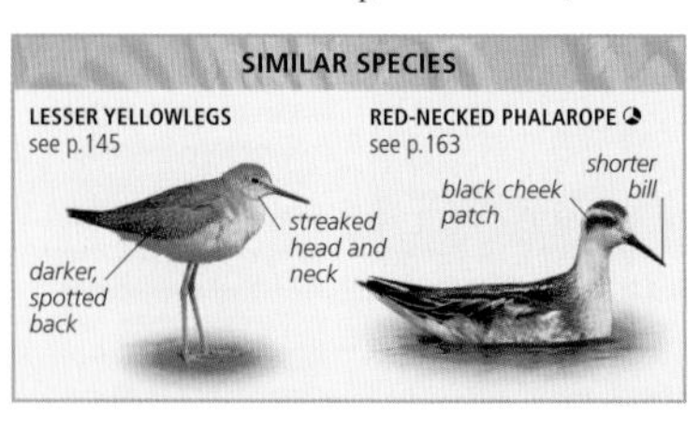

OCCURRENCE

Breeds in shallow, grassy wetlands of interior North America; during migration and winter, occurs in salty lakes and saline ponds as well as inland waterbodies. In winter, tens of thousands can be seen in the middle of Titicaca Lake in Bolivia.

Length **8½–9½in (22–24cm)**	Wingspan **15½–17in (39–43cm)**	Weight **1¼–3oz (35–85g)**
Social **Large flocks**	Lifespan **Up to 10 years**	Status **Secure**

DATE SEEN	WHERE	NOTES

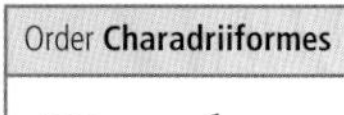

Order **Charadriiformes**	Family **Scolopacidae**	Species ***Phalaropus lobatus***

Red-necked Phalarope

This aquatic sandpiper spends much of its life in deep ocean waters feeding on tiny plankton; each year, after nine months at sea, it comes to nest in the Arctic. Its Latin name *lobatus* reflects the morphology of its feet, which are webbed (lobed). Both the Red-necked Phalarope and the Red Phalarope are oceanic birds that are found in large flocks or "rafts" far from shore. However, both species are occasionally found swimming inland, in freshwater habitats. Like the other two phalaropes, the Red-necked has a fascinating and unusual reversal of typical sex roles. The female is more brightly colored and slightly larger than the male; she will also pursue the male, compete savagely for him, and will migrate shortly after laying her eggs.

VOICE Flight call a hard, squeaky *pwit* or *kit*; on breeding grounds, vocalizations include variations of flight call notes.

NESTING Depression in wet sedge or grass; 3–4 eggs; 1–2 broods; May–June.

FEEDING Eats plankton; also insects, brine shrimp, and mollusks.

FLIGHT: fast and direct, with rapid wing beats.

SINGLE FATHER
Male phalaropes perform all nesting and rearing duties after the female lays the eggs.

SIMILAR SPECIES

WILSON'S PHALAROPE ◔ see p.162
paler face
larger overall

RED PHALAROPE ◔ see p.432
slightly thicker bill
larger head and thicker neck

OCCURRENCE
Breeds in wet tundra, on raised ridges, or hummocks, but during migration and in winter, occurs far out at sea and away from shores, although sometimes found in freshwater habitats.

Length **7–7½in (18–19cm)**	Wingspan **12½–16in (32–41cm)**	Weight **1 1/16–1 9/16oz (30–45g)**
Social **Flocks**	Lifespan **Unknown**	Status **Secure**

DATE SEEN	WHERE	NOTES

Order **Charadriiformes**	Family **Laridae**	Species ***Larus heermanni***

Heermann's Gull

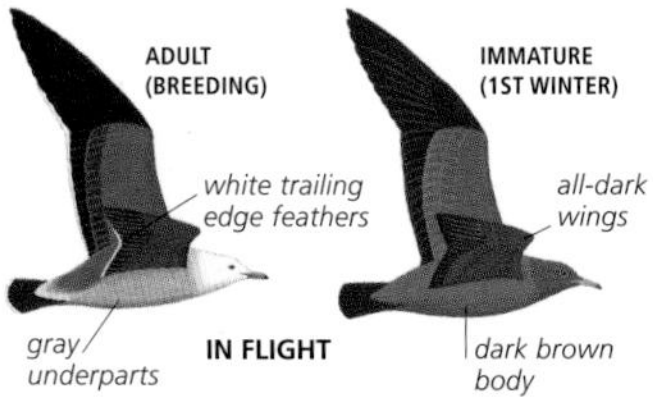

ADULT (BREEDING)
white trailing edge feathers
gray underparts
IMMATURE (1ST WINTER)
all-dark wings
dark brown body
IN FLIGHT

pale base to bill
chocolate-brown body
IMMATURE (1ST WINTER)

red eye-ring
white head
gray body
red bill with black tip
black legs
ADULT (BREEDING)

duller bill
mottled head
ADULT (NONBREEDING)

FLIGHT: flight strong, direct, and a bit heavy.

In North America, the breeding Heermann's Gull is the only gull with a dark gray body and white head. These features, along with its bright red bill, make this gull unmistakable. In nonbreeding plumage, the head is mottled dark and the bill is black-tipped. Juveniles are generally dark brown, with pale patches at the base of their bills. These gulls have black legs in all plumages, unlike any other North American gull, except the Black-legged Kittiwake.

VOICE Nasal *caw* or *cow-awk* call; not very vocal away from breeding grounds.

NESTING Depression lined with dead grass or twigs in sand, small rocks, or grass; usually nests with terns; 1–3 eggs; 1 brood; March–July.

FEEDING Feeds on fish, crustaceans, mollusks, squid, and lizards; in breeding colonies, takes eggs of terns and gulls; also scavenges.

WHITE EDGES
The white trailing edge of the wing and the white tip of the tail are obvious in flight.

OCCURRENCE
A truly western North American gull, it nests on islands off Baja California; over 90 percent of the world's population nests on Isla Raza; occasionally in California; after breeding spreads north along coast to British Columbia, uncommon north of Monterey; rare inland and accidental elsewhere.

Length **18–21in (46–53cm)**	Wingspan **4¼ft (1.3m)**	Weight **13–23oz (375–650g)**
Social **Colonies**	Lifespan **Up to 13 years**	Status **Secure**

DATE SEEN	WHERE	NOTES

Order **Charadriiformes**	Family **Laridae**	Species ***Larus canus***

Mew Gull

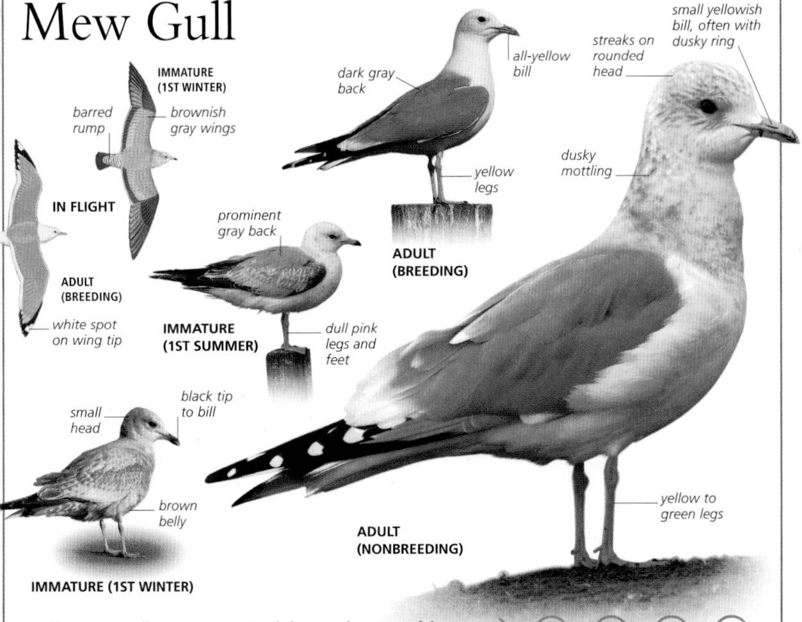
IMMATURE (1ST WINTER)
barred rump
brownish gray wings
IN FLIGHT
ADULT (BREEDING)
white spot on wing tip
dark gray back
all-yellow bill
yellow legs
ADULT (BREEDING)
prominent gray back
IMMATURE (1ST SUMMER)
dull pink legs and feet
small head
black tip to bill
brown belly
IMMATURE (1ST WINTER)
small yellowish bill, often with dusky ring
streaks on rounded head
dusky mottling
yellow to green legs
ADULT (NONBREEDING)

The Mew Gull was given its English name because of the sound of its call. Its small bill and rounded head give it a rather dove-like profile. It can be confused with the widespread Ring-billed Gull, which it resembles in all plumages. Some taxonomists split the Mew Gull into four species—the European "Common Gull" (*L. c. canus*), the northeastern Asian species (*L. c. heinei*), the "Kamchatka Gull" (*L. c. kamtschatschensis*), and the North American "Short-billed Gull" (*L. c. brachyrhynchus*).

VOICE Shrill mewing calls; higher pitched than other gulls.

NESTING Platform of mainly dry vegetation in trees or on ground; 1–5 eggs; 1 brood; May–August.

FEEDING Eats aquatic crustaceans and mollusks, insects, fish, bird eggs, chicks; scavenges trash and steals food from other birds.

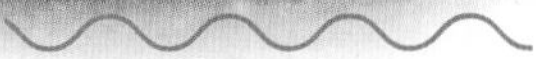

FLIGHT: wing beats faster than larger, similar-looking gulls.

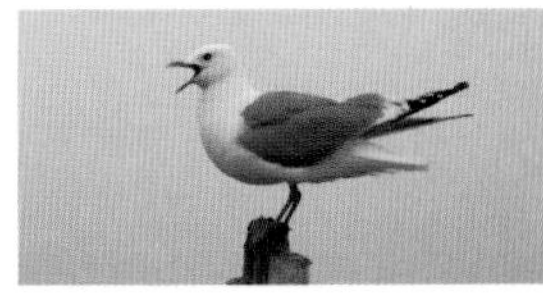

PLAIN YELLOW BILL
Although back color and bill size vary in different forms, all adult Mew Gulls have plain yellowish bills.

SIMILAR SPECIES

RING-BILLED GULL
see p.166
paler back
dark mark on bill
smaller white spots in wing tips
RING-BILLED GULL
see p.166
flatter head
paler back
larger bill

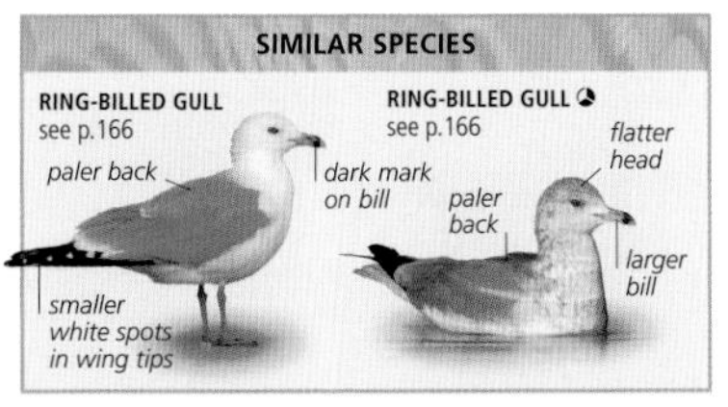

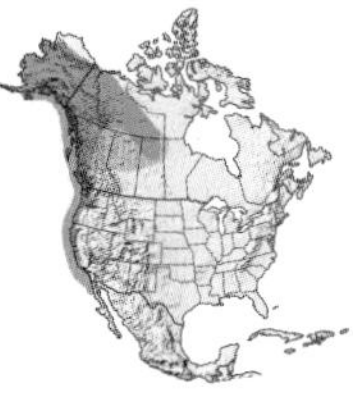

OCCURRENCE
Breeds in Alaska, except extreme north and northwest Canada, south along coast to British Columbia; winters along the Pacific Coast south to Baja California and inland on major river systems. Casual to accidental across the continent to Atlantic Coast.

Length **15–16in (38–41cm)**	Wingspan **3ft 3in–4ft (1–1.2m)**	Weight **13–18oz (375–500g)**
Social **Pairs/Colonies**	Lifespan **Up to 24 years**	Status **Secure**

DATE SEEN	WHERE	NOTES

Order **Charadriiformes**	Family **Laridae**	Species ***Larus delawarensis***

Ring-billed Gull

white wing spots
ADULT (BREEDING)
IN FLIGHT

dark eye · *mottled gray back* · *black-tipped, pink bill* · *white neck*
IMMATURE (1ST WINTER)

heavily mottled back · *mottled underparts* · *pink legs*
JUVENILE

fine streaks on head · *gray back* · *olive-yellow legs*
ADULT (NONBREEDING)

pale gray back
IMMATURE (2ND WINTER)

black band on yellow bill · *pale eye, with red eye-ring* · *pale gray back* · *white markings on outer wing feathers* · *white underparts* · *yellowish or greenish legs*
ADULT (BREEDING)

FLIGHT: quick, deep wing beats; strong, direct flight, soaring on thermals.

One of the most common birds in North America, the medium-sized Ring-billed Gull is distinguished by the black band on its yellow bill. From the mid-19th to the early 20th century, population numbers crashed due to hunting and habitat loss. Protection allowed the species to make a spectacular comeback, and in the 1990s, there were an estimated 3–4 million birds. It can often be seen scavenging in parking lots at malls.

VOICE Call a slightly nasal and whiny *kee-ow* or *meee-ow*; series of 4–6 *kyaw* notes, higher pitched than Herring Gull.

NESTING Shallow cup of plant matter on ground in open areas, usually near low vegetation; 1–5 eggs; 1 brood; April–August.

FEEDING Picks food while walking; also dips and plunges in water; eats small fish, insects, grain, small rodents; also scavenges.

BLACK WING MARKING
The sharply demarcated black wing tips are prominent from both above and below.

SIMILAR SPECIES

MEW GULL
see p.165
round head · *darker mantle* · *small bill*

MEW GULL 1ST
see p.165
round head · *less distinct streaks* · *small bill*

OCCURRENCE
Breeds in freshwater habitats in the interior of the continent. In winter, switches to mostly saltwater areas and along both the East and West Coasts; also along major river systems and reservoirs. Found year-round near the southern Great Lakes.

Length **17–21½in (43–54cm)**	Wingspan **4–5ft (1.2–1.5m)**	Weight **11–25oz (300–700g)**
Social **Colonies**	Lifespan **Up to 32 years**	Status **Secure**

DATE SEEN	WHERE	NOTES

Order **Charadriiformes**	Family **Laridae**	Species ***Larus californicus***

California Gull

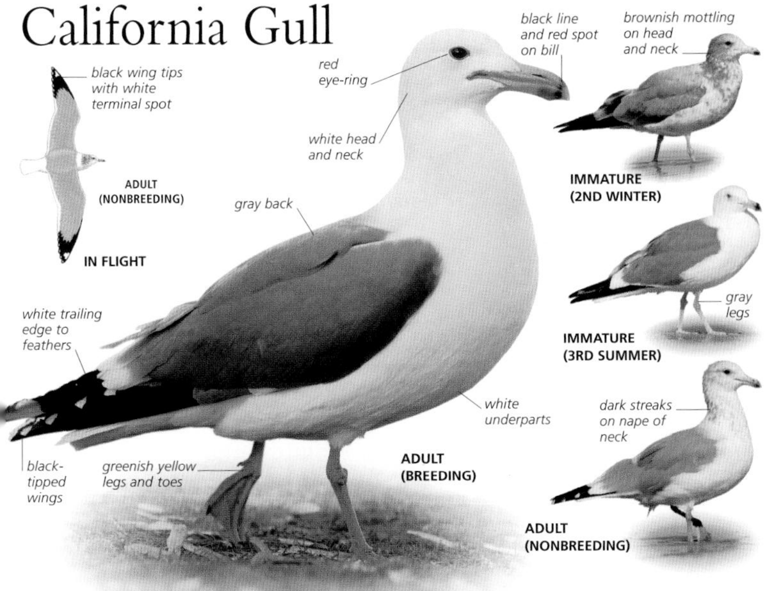

black wing tips with white terminal spot
ADULT (NONBREEDING)
IN FLIGHT
red eye-ring
white head and neck
gray back
white trailing edge to feathers
black-tipped wings
greenish yellow legs and toes
white underparts
ADULT (BREEDING)
black line and red spot on bill
brownish mottling on head and neck
IMMATURE (2ND WINTER)
gray legs
IMMATURE (3RD SUMMER)
dark streaks on nape of neck
ADULT (NONBREEDING)

Slightly smaller than the Herring Gull, the medium-sized California Gull has a darker back and longer wings. In breeding plumage, it can also be distinguished by the black and red coloration on its bill and its greenish yellow legs. In winter and on young birds, dark streaks are prominent on the nape of the neck. A common interior gull, it is honored by a large, gilded statue in Salt Lake City that commemorates the birds' rescue of the settlers' crops from a plague of grasshoppers in 1848.

VOICE Call a repeated *kee-yah, kee-yah, kee-yah.*

NESTING Shallow scrape, lined with feathers, bones, and vegetation, usually on islands; 2–3 eggs; 1 brood; May–July.

FEEDING Forages around lakes for insects, mollusks; hovers over cherry trees dislodging fruits with its wings.

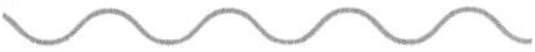

FLIGHT: strong and direct, but somewhat stiff, with deep wing beats.

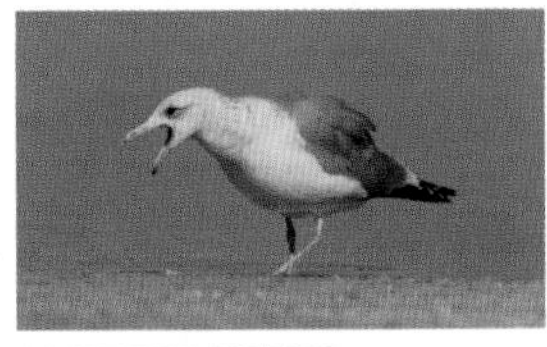

AGGRESSIVE POSTURE
This California Gull is displaying signs of aggression—possibly against another bird.

SIMILAR SPECIES

HERRING GULL ☼
see p.172
paler back
pink legs
larger body
HERRING GULL ❄
see p.172
heavy streaking on head
paler back

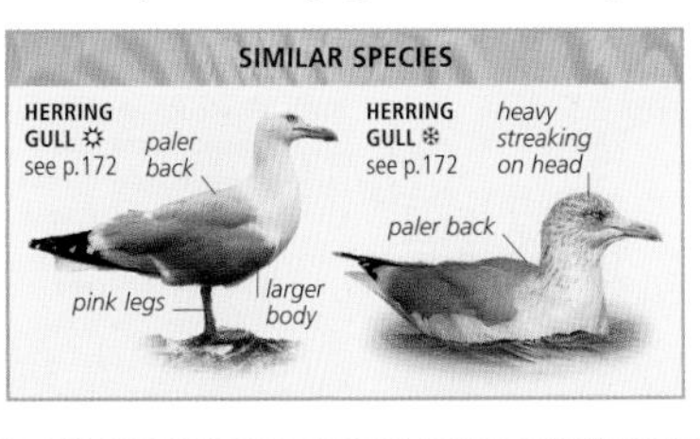

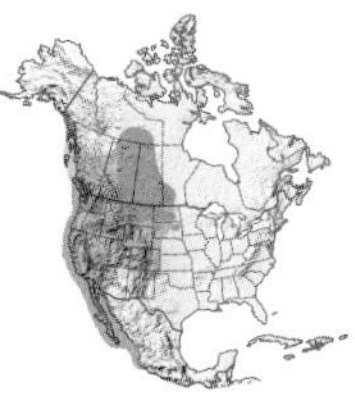

OCCURRENCE
Breeds at scattered locations across interior western Canada and the US. Some of the largest colonies are on the highly saline Mono Lake and the Great Salt Lake; winters along the Pacific Coast from British Columbia to Mexico; strays increasingly reported in the East.

Length **17½–20in (45–51cm)**	Wingspan **4–4½ft (1.2–1.4m)**	Weight **18–35oz (0.5–1kg)**
Social **Colonies**	Lifespan **Up to 30 years**	Status **Secure**

DATE SEEN	WHERE	NOTES

Order **Charadriiformes**	Family **Laridae**	Species ***Larus glaucescens***

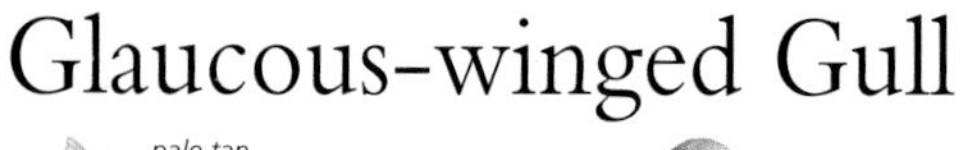

Glaucous-winged Gull

The Glaucous-winged Gull, the most common large gull on the north Pacific coast, is found around towns and cities, even nesting on the roofs of shorefront buildings. This species commonly interbreeds with Western Gulls in the southern part of its range, and with Herring and Glaucous Gulls in the north, producing intermediate birds that are more difficult to identify.

VOICE Call a slow, deep *aah-aah-aah*; many types of calls heard around colonies; voice lower pitched than Herring Gull.

NESTING Scrape surrounded by ring of torn up grass or other vegetation; forms colonies usually on small, low islands; 2–3 eggs; 1 brood; May–August.

FEEDING Snatches fish, aquatic mollusks, and crustaceans while walking, swimming, or diving; also scavenges carrion and trash.

FLIGHT: strong and graceful; shallow wing beats; also soars.

PALE WINGS
The Glaucous-winged Gull is named for its delicate, pale, bluish gray wings.

OCCURRENCE
Breeds along coast of northwest Oregon northward to the Bering Sea coast of Alaska; winters within its breeding range and southward, to Gulf of California; primarily a coastal and offshore gull (farther offshore in winter); it is very rare inland and accidental to central US.

Length **23–24in (58–62cm)**	Wingspan **4½–5ft (1.4–1.5m)**	Weight **2–2¾lb (0.9–1.3kg)**
Social **Colonies**	Lifespan **Up to 32 years**	Status **Secure**

DATE SEEN	WHERE	NOTES

Order **Charadriiformes**	Family **Laridae**	Species ***Larus occidentalis***

Western Gull

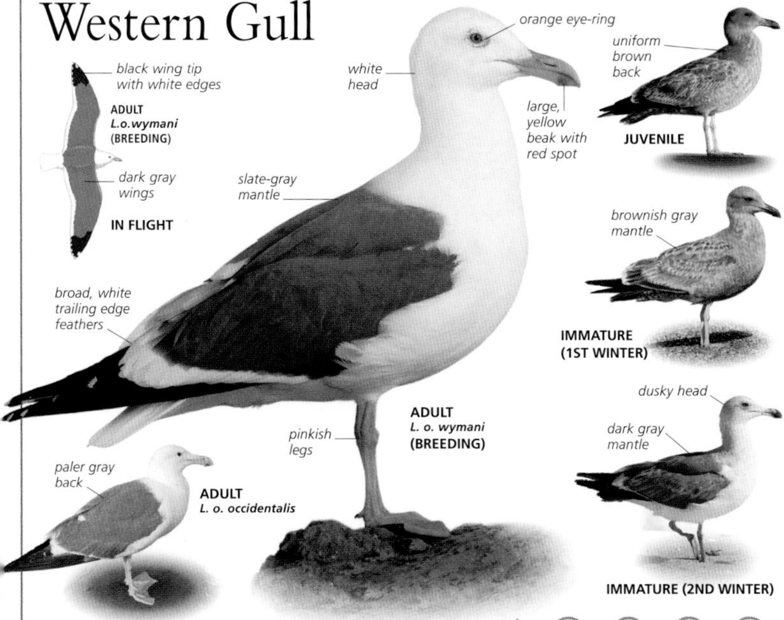

black wing tip with white edges
ADULT *L.o.wymani* (BREEDING)
dark gray wings
IN FLIGHT

white head
orange eye-ring
large, yellow beak with red spot
slate-gray mantle
broad, white trailing edge feathers
pinkish legs
ADULT *L. o. wymani* (BREEDING)

paler gray back
ADULT *L. o. occidentalis*

uniform brown back
JUVENILE

brownish gray mantle
IMMATURE (1ST WINTER)

dusky head
dark gray mantle
IMMATURE (2ND WINTER)

The Western Gull is the only dark-backed gull found regularly within its normal range and habitat. However, identification is complicated due to two subspecies: the paler *occidentalis* in the north, and the darker *wymani* in the south. Western Gulls interbreed with Glaucous-winged Gulls, producing confusing hybrids. The total population of these gulls is small, and the small number of nesting colonies makes conservation a concern.

VOICE Shrill, repeated *heyaa...heyaa...heyaa* similar to Herring Gull, but lower in pitch, harsher; very vocal at breeding sites.

NESTING Scrape filled with vegetation, usually next to bush or rock; 3–4 eggs; 1 brood; April–August.

FEEDING Eats crabs, squid, insects, fish, bird eggs, and chicks; also eats sea lion pups; scavenges.

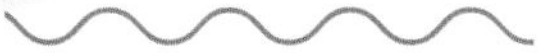

FLIGHT: strong, slow with heavy wing beats; also commonly soars.

DARK UNDERWINGS
The undersides of the outer wing feathers are much darker in this bird than in similar species.

OCCURRENCE
Nests on offshore islands along West Coast; about one-third of the total population breeds on Southeast Farallon Island, west of San Francisco; nonbreeders and wintering birds occur along the coast and in major bays and estuaries southward to Baja California; very rare inland or far offshore.

Length **22–26in (56–66cm)**	Wingspan **4¼–4½ft (1.3–1.4m)**	Weight **1¾–2¾lb (0.8–1.2kg)**
Social **Colonies**	Lifespan **Up to 28 years**	Status **Secure**

DATE SEEN	WHERE	NOTES

Order **Charadriiformes**	Family **Laridae**	Species ***Larus hyperboreus***

Glaucous Gull

FLIGHT: heavy, slow, and powerful; often glides and soars.

The Glaucous Gull is the largest of the "white-winged" gulls. Its large, pale shape is immediately apparent in a group of gulls as it appears like a large white spectre among its smaller, darker cousins. In the southern part of its US winter range, pale immatures are encountered more frequently than adults. In the Arctic, successful pairs of Glaucous Gulls maintain the bonds with their mates for years, often returning to the same nest site year after year.

VOICE Similar to that of the Herring Gull, but slightly harsher and deeper; hoarse, nasal *ku-ku-ku*.

NESTING Shallow cup lined with vegetation on ground, at edge of tundra pools, on cliffs and ledges and islands; 1–3 eggs; 1 brood; May–July.

FEEDING Eats fish, crustaceans, mollusks; also eggs and chicks of waterfowl, small seabirds, and small mammals.

NORTHERN VISITOR
This large gull is an uncommon visitor over most of North America during the winter months.

SIMILAR SPECIES

OCCURRENCE
Breeds along the high-Arctic coast, rarely inland; winters along northern Atlantic and Pacific coasts and the Great Lakes; frequently seen at Niagara Falls. Strays, usually immatures, can occur inland anywhere where concentrations of gulls are found, such as trash dumps.

Length **26–30in (65–75cm)**	Wingspan **5–6ft (1.5–1.8m)**	Weight **2¾–6lb (1.2–2.7kg)**
Social **Colonies**	Lifespan **Up to 21 years**	Status **Secure**

DATE SEEN	WHERE	NOTES

Order **Charadriiformes**	Family **Laridae**	Species ***Larus thayeri***

Thayer's Gull

The classification of Thayer's Gull as a species is still slightly puzzling. After it was described in 1915, it was classified as a subspecies of the Herring Gull, but in the 1970s, it was considered a full species. Although it is still usually treated as a separate species, many authorities now consider the Thayer's Gull to be a subspecies of the Iceland Gull. When standing with the Herring and Iceland Gulls, this bird is difficult to identify. Positive identification is complicated further by the existence of hybrid gulls of various parentages.

VOICE Mewing squeals, like herring gulls' familiar *kee-yow*; calls more on breeding grounds than on wintering grounds.

NESTING On cliff ledges; 2–3 eggs; 1 brood; May–August.

FEEDING Picks fish, mollusks, and crustaceans from the water's surface; swallows food while in flight.

FLIGHT: steady and direct, but wing beat varies greatly with wind conditions.

TWO-TONED WINGS
Immature birds have two-toned wings, with a prominent pale patch on the outer flight feathers.

OCCURRENCE
Nests on cliff ledges of fiords facing the Canadian high Arctic. Winter movements not fully understood; occurs mainly along the Pacific Coast, but is also found across the interior and along the East Coast.

Length **22½–25in (57–64cm)**	Wingspan **4¼–5ft (1.3–1.5m)**	Weight **25–39oz (700–1,100g)**
Social **Colonies**	Lifespan **Unknown**	Status **Secure (p)**

DATE SEEN	WHERE	NOTES

Order **Charadriiformes**	Family **Laridae**	Species ***Larus argentatus***

Herring Gull

white spots near wing tips
ADULT (BREEDING)
gray wings
light head
barred gray-brown overall
IMMATURE (2ND WINTER)
mottled brown back
barred brown body
IMMATURE (1ST WINTER)
large, yellow bill with red spot
white head and neck
gray back
streaked head
ADULT (NONBREEDING)
IN FLIGHT
black outer wing feathers
white underparts
pink legs
ADULT (BREEDING)
streaked head and neck
ADULT (NONBREEDING)

The Herring Gull is the archetypal, large "white-headed" gull to which nearly all other gulls are compared. When people mention "seagulls" they usually refer to the Herring Gull, but this term is misleading because the Herring Gull, like most other gulls, does not commonly go far out to sea—it is a bird of near-shore waters, coasts, lakes, rivers, and inland waterways. Now very common, the Herring Gull was nearly wiped out in the late 19th and early 20th century by plumage hunters and egg collectors.

VOICE Typical call a high-pitched, shrill, repeated *heyaa... heyaa...heyaa...heyaa*; vocal throughout the year.

NESTING Shallow bowl on ground lined with feathers, vegetation, detritus; 2–4 eggs; 1 brood; April–August.

FEEDING Eats fish, crustaceans, mollusks, worms; eggs and chicks of other seabirds; scavenges carrion, garbage; steals from other birds.

FLIGHT: steady, regular, slow wing beats; also commonly soars and glides.

MASTER SCAVENGER
A common sight near any water body, the Herring Gull is an expert scavenger of carrion and trash.

SIMILAR SPECIES

RING-BILLED GULL
see p.166
smaller overall
black ring on bill
yellow-green legs

CALIFORNIA GULL
see p.167
black-and-red spot on bill
greenish legs

OCCURRENCE
Found throughout North America along coasts and inland on lakes, rivers, and reservoirs; also frequents garbage dumps. Breeds in northeastern US and across Canada. Migrates southward across much of the continent to winter in coastal areas and along lakes and major rivers.

Length **22–26in (56–66cm)**	Wingspan **4–5ft (1.2–1.5m)**	Weight **28–42oz (800–1,200g)**
Social **Colonies**	Lifespan **At least 35 years**	Status **Secure**

DATE SEEN	WHERE	NOTES

Order **Charadriiformes**	Family **Laridae**	Species ***Larus philadelphia***

Bonaparte's Gull

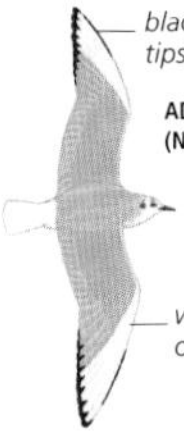

black wing tips
ADULT (NONBREEDING)
white flash on outer wings
IN FLIGHT

blackish "ear" spot
white head
gray neck
ADULT (NONBREEDING)

gray back
brown patches on wing
IMMATURE (1ST WINTER)

black hood
short bill
gray back and wings
white wedge on wing
orange-red legs
white underparts with rosy glow when breeding
ADULT (BREEDING)

Lighter and more delicate than the other North American gulls, Bonaparte's Gull is commonly distinguished in winter by the blackish smudge behind each eye and the large, white wing patch. It is one of America's most abundant gulls. In 1989, for example, more than 120,000 were estimated to have occured in one harbor near Cleveland, Ohio. This species was named after the French ornithologist Charles Lucien Bonaparte (nephew of Napoleon), who lived in New Jersey in the 1820s.

FLIGHT: graceful, light, and agile; rapid wing beats; can be mistaken for a tern in flight.

VOICE Harsh *keek, keek*; can be vocal in feeding flocks, *kew, kew, kew.*
NESTING Stick nest of twigs, branches, tree bark, lined with mosses or lichens; usually in conifers 5–20ft (1.5–6m) above ground; also in rushes over water; 1–4 eggs; 1 brood; May–July.
FEEDING Catches insects in flight on breeding grounds; picks crustaceans, mollusks, and small fish from water's surface; also plunge-dives.

TERN-LIKE GULL
Bonaparte's Gulls are very social and, flying in flocks, these pale, delicate birds look like terns.

WHITE UNDERWINGS
In all plumages, Bonaparte's Gulls have white underwings, unlike other similar small gulls.

SIMILAR SPECIES

BLACK-HEADED GULL
dark outer wing feathers
red bill
larger overall

LITTLE GULL
smaller overall
uniform gray upperwing

OCCURRENCE
During breeding season, found in northern forest zone, in lakes, ponds, or bogs; on migration, may be found anywhere where there is water: ponds, lakes, sewage pools, or rivers. Winters on Great Lakes and along the coast; often found in large numbers at coastal inlets.

Length **11–12in (28–30cm)**	Wingspan **35in–3ft 3in (90–100cm)**	Weight **6–8oz (175–225g)**
Social **Flocks**	Lifespan **Up to 18 years**	Status **Secure**

DATE SEEN	WHERE	NOTES

Order **Charadriiformes**	Family **Laridae**	Species ***Larus pipixcan***

Franklin's Gull

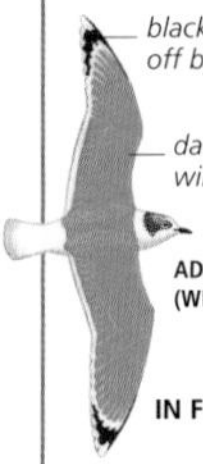
black wing tips set-off by white band
dark gray wings
ADULT (WINTER)
IN FLIGHT

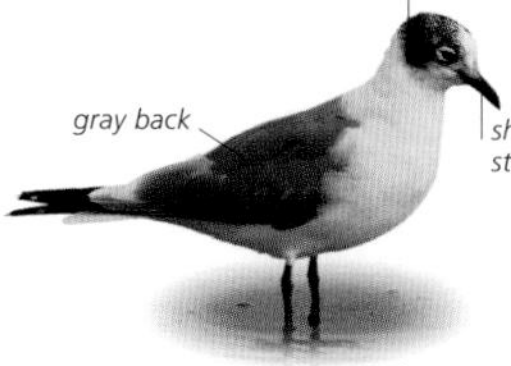
dark back of head
gray back
short, straight bill
ADULT (WINTER)

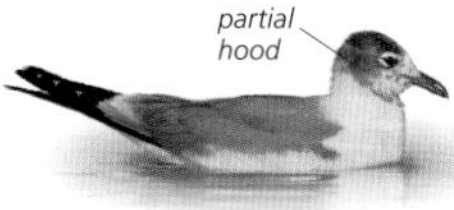
partial hood
IMMATURE (1ST SUMMER)

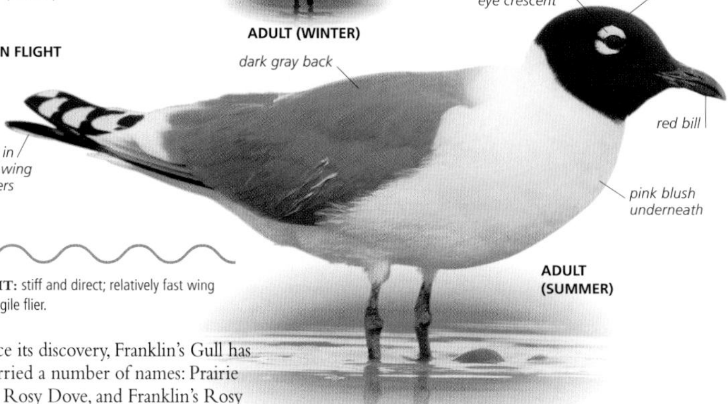
broken white eye crescent
black head
dark gray back
red bill
white in outer wing feathers
pink blush underneath
ADULT (SUMMER)

FLIGHT: stiff and direct; relatively fast wing beats; agile flier.

Since its discovery, Franklin's Gull has carried a number of names: Prairie Dove, Rosy Dove, and Franklin's Rosy Gull—"Dove" alluding to its dainty appearance and "rosy" to the pink blush of its undersides. Its official name honors British Arctic explorer, John Franklin, on whose first expedition, the bird was discovered in 1823. Unlike other gulls, this species has two complete molts each year. As a result, its plumage usually looks fresh and it rarely has the scruffy look of some other gulls.

VOICE Nasal *weeh-a, weeh-a*; shrill *kuk kuk kuk kuk*; extremely vocal around breeding colonies.

NESTING Floating mass of bulrushes or other plants; material added as nest sinks; 2–4 eggs; 1 brood; April–July.

FEEDING Feeds mainly on earthworms and insects during breeding and some seeds, taken while walking or flying; opportunistic feeder during migration and winter.

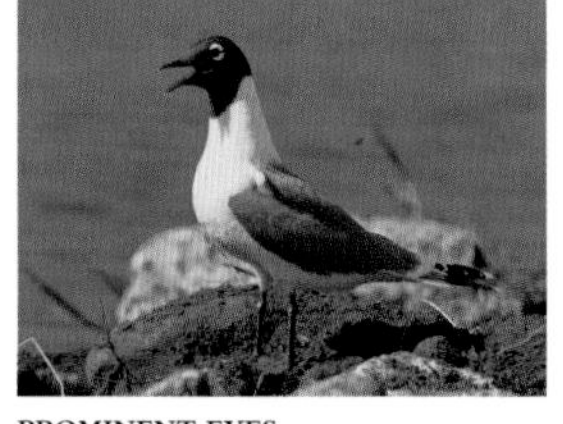

PROMINENT EYES
In all plumages, Franklin's Gull has much more prominent white eye-crescents than similar species.

SIMILAR SPECIES

LAUGHING GULL
see p.471
longer, drooped bill
longer legs
LAUGHING GULL ◔ ❄
see p.471
smaller eye-crescents
longer, drooped bill
longer legs

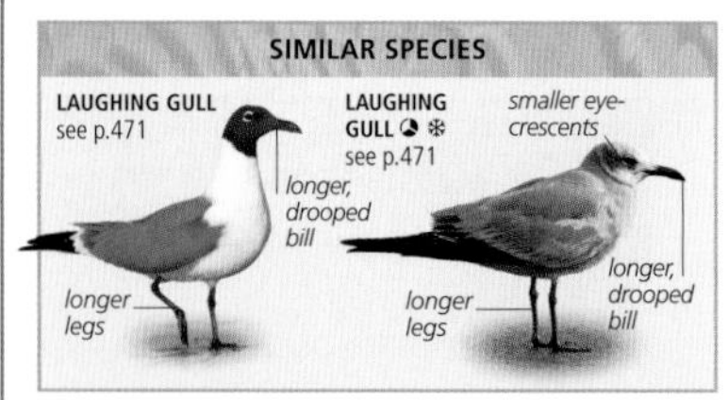

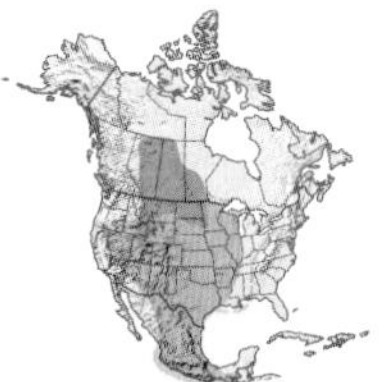

OCCURRENCE
In summer, a bird of the high prairies; always nests over water. On migration often found in agricultural areas; large numbers frequent plowed fields or follow plows. Winters mainly along the Pacific Coast of South America.

Length **12½–14in (32–36cm)**	Wingspan **33in–3ft 1in (85–95cm)**	Weight **8–11oz (225–325g)**
Social **Colonial**	Lifespan **At least 10 years**	Status **Secure**

DATE SEEN	WHERE	NOTES

Order **Charadriiformes**	Family **Laridae**	Species ***Rissa tridactyla***

Black-legged Kittiwake

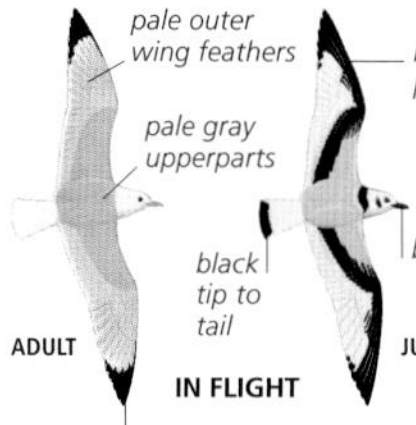
pale outer wing feathers
pale gray upperparts
black "M" pattern in wings
black tip to tail
black bill
ADULT
IN FLIGHT
JUVENILE
black wing tip

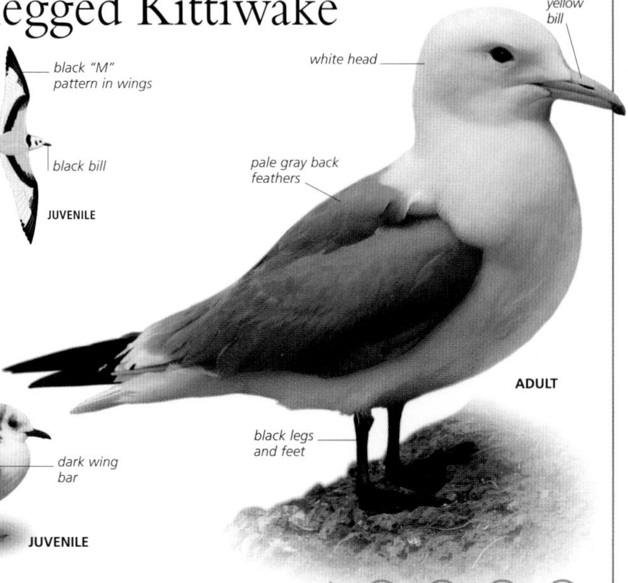
greenish yellow bill
white head
pale gray back feathers
ADULT
black legs and feet

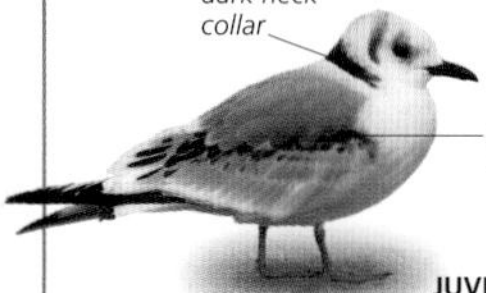
dark neck collar
dark wing bar
JUVENILE

A kittiwake nesting colony is an impressive sight, with sometimes thousands of birds lined up along steep cliff ledges overlooking the sea. The ledges are often so narrow that the birds' tails stick out over the edge. Kittiwakes have sharper claws than other gulls, probably to give them a better grip on their ledges. In the late 20th century, the Black-legged Kittiwake population expanded greatly in the Canadian maritime provinces, with numbers doubling in the Gulf of St. Lawrence.

VOICE Repeated, nasal *kit-ti-wake, kit-ti-wake* call; vocal near nesting cliffs; usually silent in winter.

NESTING Mound of mud and vegetation on narrow cliff ledge; 1–3 eggs; 1 brood; April–August.

FEEDING Snatches small marine fish and invertebrates from the surface, or dives just below the water's surface; feeds in flocks.

FLIGHT: very stiff-winged; rapid, shallow wing beats; overall more buoyant than most gulls.

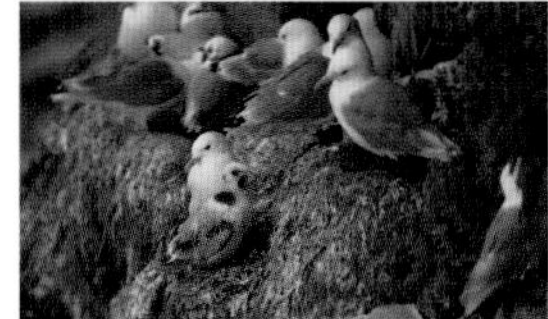

LIVING ON THE EDGE
Young and adult kittiwakes pack together tightly on their precariously narrow cliff ledges.

SIMILAR SPECIES

RING-BILLED GULL
see p.166

RED-LEGGED KITTIWAKE
see p.433

heavier, dark-marked bill
white spots in outer wing feathers
darker shoulder feathers
red legs
gray underwings

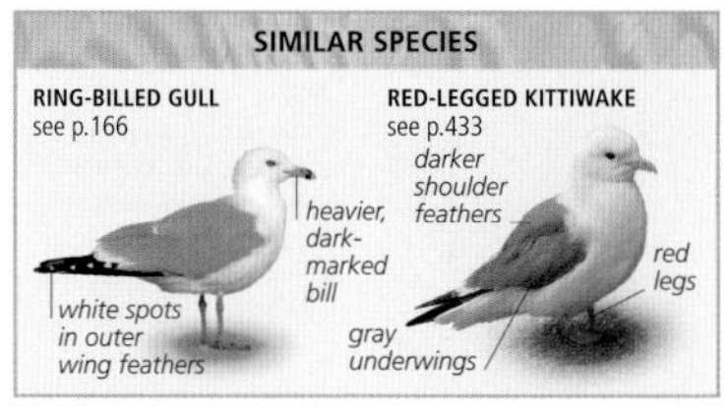

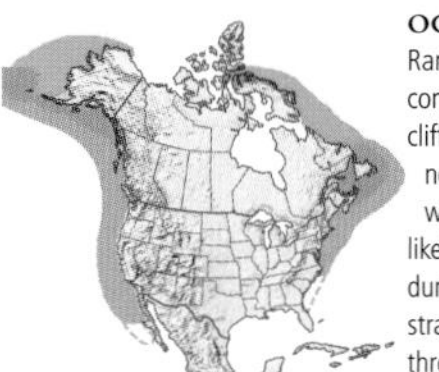

OCCURRENCE
Rarely seen far from the ocean; common in summer around sea cliffs, with ledges suitable for nesting, and nearby offshore waters; winters at sea; most likely to be seen from land during and after storms; strays have appeared throughout the interior.

Length **15–16in (38–41cm)**	Wingspan **3ft 1in–4ft (0.95m–1.2m)**	Weight **11–18oz (300–500g)**
Social **Colonies**	Lifespan **Up to 26 years**	Status **Secure**

DATE SEEN	WHERE	NOTES

Order **Charadriiformes**	Family **Laridae**	Species ***Sterna caspia***

Caspian Tern

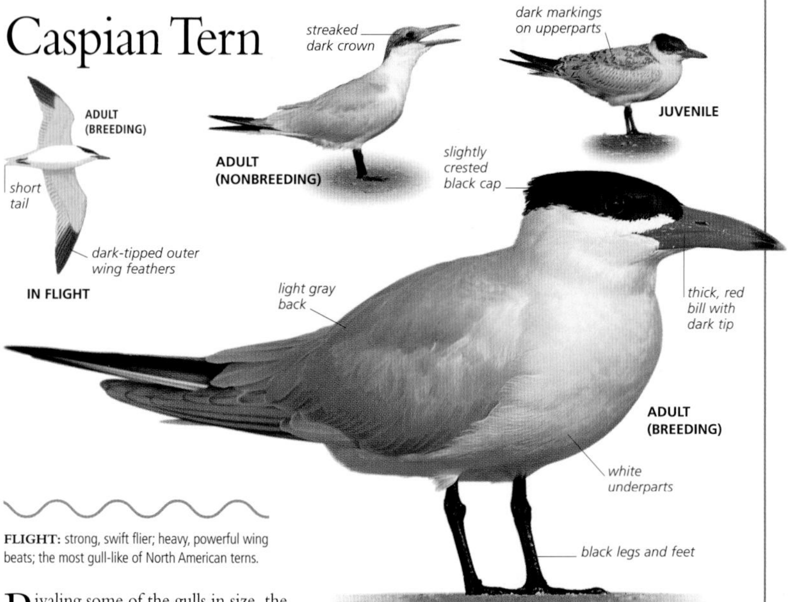
ADULT (BREEDING)
short tail
dark-tipped outer wing feathers
IN FLIGHT
streaked dark crown
ADULT (NONBREEDING)
dark markings on upperparts
JUVENILE
slightly crested black cap
thick, red bill with dark tip
light gray back
ADULT (BREEDING)
white underparts
black legs and feet

FLIGHT: strong, swift flier; heavy, powerful wing beats; the most gull-like of North American terns.

Rivaling some of the gulls in size, the Caspian Tern is the world's largest tern. Unlike other "black-capped" terns, it never has a completely white forehead, even in winter. In nonbreeding plumage the cap is very heavily streaked. The Caspian Tern is known for its predatory habits, stealing prey from other seabirds, as well as snatching eggs from, and hunting the chicks of, other gulls and terns. It is aggressive in defending its nesting territory, giving hoarse alarm calls and rhythmically opening and closing its beak in a threatening display to intruders.

VOICE Hoarse, deep *kraaa, kraaa*; also barks at intruders; male's wings vibrate loudly in courtship flight.

NESTING Shallow scrape on ground; 2–3 eggs; 1 brood; May–August.

FEEDING Plunges into water to snatch fish, barnacles, and snails.

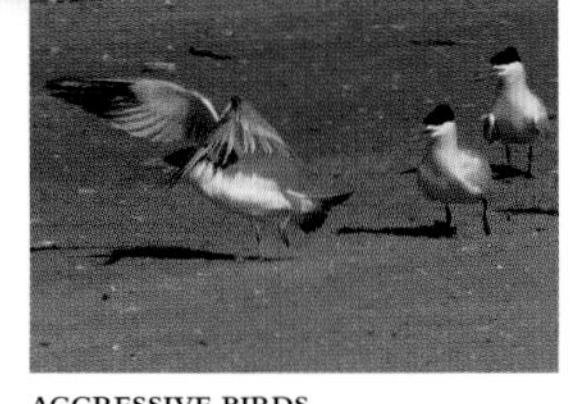

AGGRESSIVE BIRDS
The Caspian Tern is one of the most aggressive terns, though actual physical contact is rare.

SIMILAR SPECIES
ELEGANT TERN
see p.433
smaller overall
thin, orange-yellow bill
ROYAL TERN
see p.434
thinner, orange bill
slender build

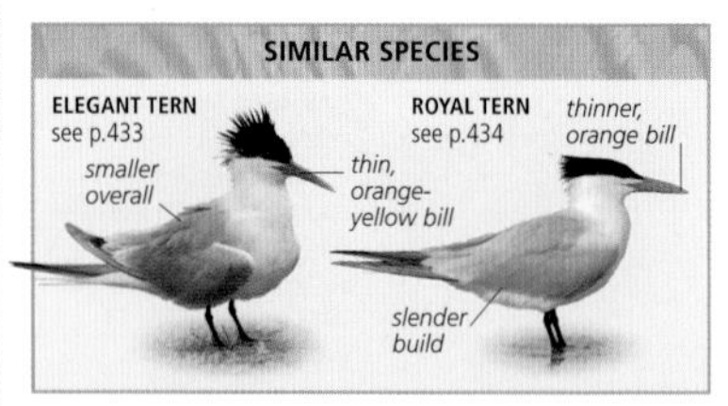

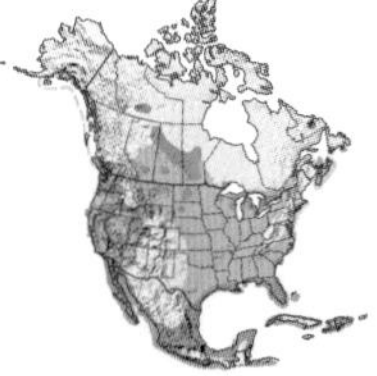

OCCURRENCE
Found in a variety of aquatic habitats, freshwater and marine; rare offshore; breeds on interior lakes, salt marsh, and on coastal barrier islands; winters on and near the coast. May be seen on marshes and wetlands during migration.

Length **18½–21½in (47–54cm)**	Wingspan **4¼–5ft (1.3–1.5m)**	Weight **19–27oz (525–775g)**
Social **Colonies/Pairs**	Lifespan **Up to 30 years**	Status **Declining**

DATE SEEN	WHERE	NOTES

Order **Charadriiformes**	Family **Laridae**	Species ***Sterna hirundo***

Common Tern

FLIGHT: graceful, steady and strong; wing beats relatively deep.

One of North America's most widespread terns, the Common Tern was nearly wiped out in the late 19th century by hunters seeking its feathers. The 1918 Migratory Bird Treaty helped protect it, and numbers increased, but populations have declined again in recent decades due to human disturbance, habitat loss, and pollution.

VOICE Common call loud *keee-aarr* descending at end; emits *kek-kek-kek-kek* call when attacking intruders; vocal in colonies; also calls elsewhere.

NESTING Shallow scrape on bare sand, often gravel or similar surface, dry vegetation and debris used during incubation; 2–3 eggs; 1 brood; May–August.

FEEDING Plunges for prey, snatches from water's surface, catches insects in flight; mainly eats fish but also crustaceans, squid, and insects.

SIMILAR SPECIES

ARCTIC TERN ☼ see p.434

FORSTER'S TERN see p.178

FEEDING FLOCK
A flock of Common Terns focus on a school of fish, diving to catch them. Fishermen watch for such flocks to locate fish.

OCCURRENCE
Found almost anywhere with water during migration. Winters in Central and South America. One population breeds along the barrier beaches and coasts northwards from the Carolinas; a second population occurs around lakes and wetland in the northern interior.

Length **12–14in (31–35cm)**	Wingspan **30–31in (75–80cm)**	Weight **3⅜–5oz (95–150g)**
Social **Colonies**	Lifespan **Up to 26 years**	Status **Declining**

DATE SEEN	WHERE	NOTES

Order **Charadriiformes**	Family **Laridae**	Species ***Sterna forsteri***

Forster's Tern

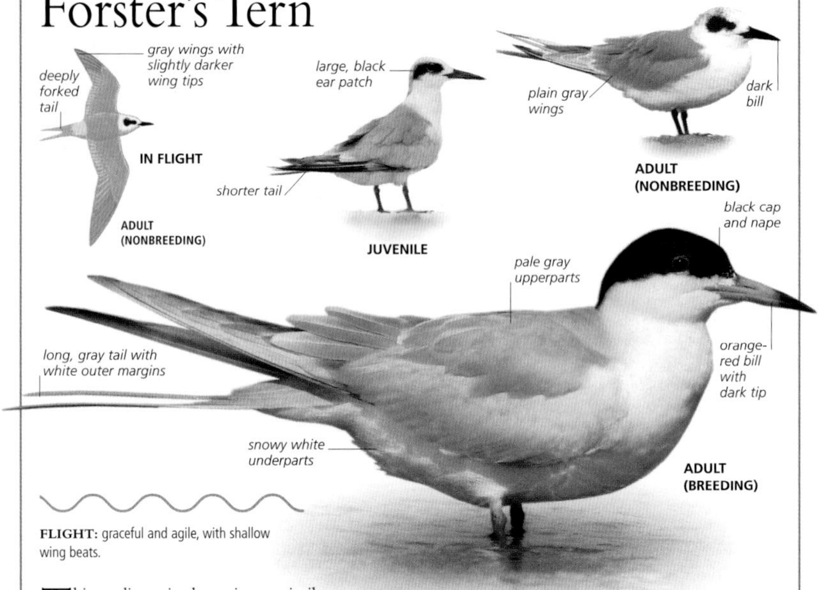

gray wings with slightly darker wing tips
deeply forked tail
IN FLIGHT
ADULT (NONBREEDING)
large, black ear patch
shorter tail
JUVENILE
plain gray wings
dark bill
ADULT (NONBREEDING)
black cap and nape
pale gray upperparts
orange-red bill with dark tip
long, gray tail with white outer margins
snowy white underparts
ADULT (BREEDING)

FLIGHT: graceful and agile, with shallow wing beats.

This medium-sized tern is very similar in appearance to the Common Tern. The features that differentiate it from the Common Tern are its lighter outer wing feathers and longer tail. Early naturalists could not tell the two species apart until 1834 when English botanist Thomas Nuttall made the distinction. He named this tern after Johann Reinhold Forster, a naturalist who accompanied the English explorer Captain Cook on his epic second voyage (1772-75).

VOICE Harsh, descending *kyerr*; more nasal than Common Tern.

NESTING Shallow scrape in mud or sand, but occasionally nests on top of muskrat lodge or on old grebe nest; sometimes constructs raft of floating vegetation; 2–3 eggs; 1 brood; May–August.

FEEDING Catches fish and crustaceans with shallow plunge-diving, often only head submerges; also catches insects in flight.

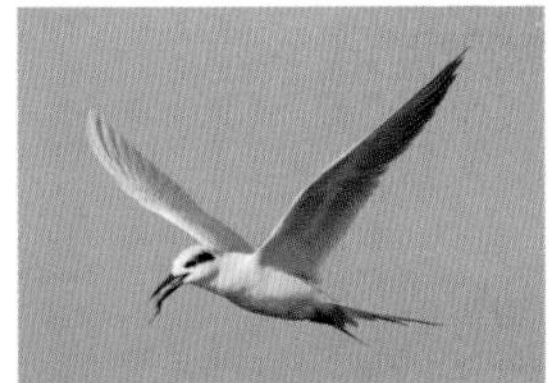

BLACK EARS
With its black ear patch, Foster's Tern is more distinctive in nonbreeding than breeding plumage.

SIMILAR SPECIES

COMMON TERN
see p.177
ARCTIC TERN
see p.434
shorter red bill
redder bill
shorter neck
shorter tail
shorter legs

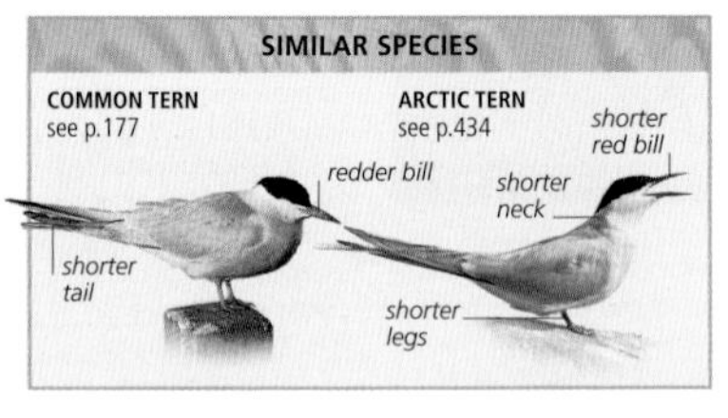

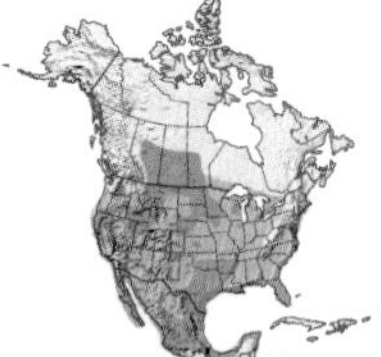

OCCURRENCE
Breeds in northeastern Mexico, in freshwater and saltwater marshes with large stretches of open water. Winters on both coasts and across southern US states, unlike the Common Tern, which primarily winters in South America.

Length **13–14in (33–36cm)**	Wingspan **29–32in (73–82cm)**	Weight **4–7oz (125–190g)**
Social **Colonies**	Lifespan **Up to 16 years**	Status **Secure**

DATE SEEN	WHERE	NOTES

Order **Charadriiformes**	Family **Laridae**	Species ***Chlidonias niger***

Black Tern

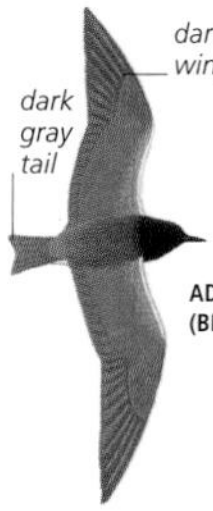

dark gray wings

dark gray tail

ADULT (BREEDING)

IN FLIGHT

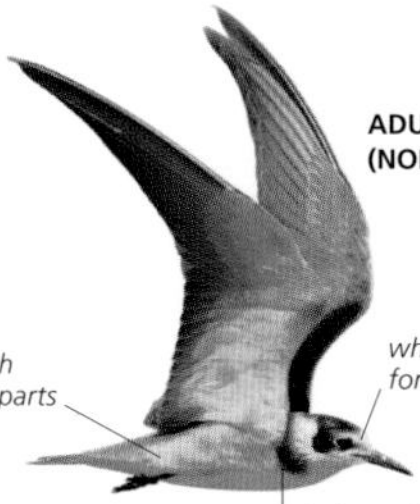

ADULT (NONBREEDING)

whitish underparts

white forehead

dark smudge on sides

black head

black bill

gray upperparts

black breast

ADULT (BREEDING)

white rump

black legs and toes

FLIGHT: very agile, but somewhat erratic-looking, bouncy flight; strong, deep wing beats.

The Black Tern is a small, elegant, marsh-dwelling tern that undergoes a remarkable change in appearance from summer to winter—more so than any other regularly occurring North American tern. The Black Tern's breeding plumage can cause the bird to be confused with the closely related White-winged Tern, which is an accidental visitor to North America. The Black Tern's nonbreeding plumage is much paler than its breeding plumage—the head turns white with irregular black streaks, and the neck, breast, and belly become whitish gray.

VOICE Call nasal and harsh *krik*, *kip*, or *kik*; most vocal during breeding, but calls throughout the year.

NESTING Shallow cup on top of floating mass of vegetation, sometimes on top of muskrat lodges; usually 3 eggs; 1 brood; May–August.

FEEDING Picks prey off water's surface or vegetation; rarely plunge dives; in summer, feeds on mainly insects, caught from the air or ground, also freshwater fish; in winter, eats mainly small sea fish.

FLOATING NEST

A floating nest is a dry place to lay eggs and raise chicks in a watery environment.

SIMILAR SPECIES

OCCURRENCE

Freshwater marshes in summer, but nonbreeding plumaged birds—probably young—occasionally seen along the coast. During migration, can be found almost anywhere near water. Winters in the marine coastal waters of Central and South America.

Length **9–10in (23–26cm)**	Wingspan **25–35in (63–88cm)**	Weight **1¾–2½oz (50–70g)**
Social **Colonies**	Lifespan **Up to 9 years**	Status **Vulnerable**

DATE SEEN	WHERE	NOTES

Order **Charadriiformes**	Family **Stercorariidae**	Species ***Stercorarius pomarinus***

Pomarine Jaeger

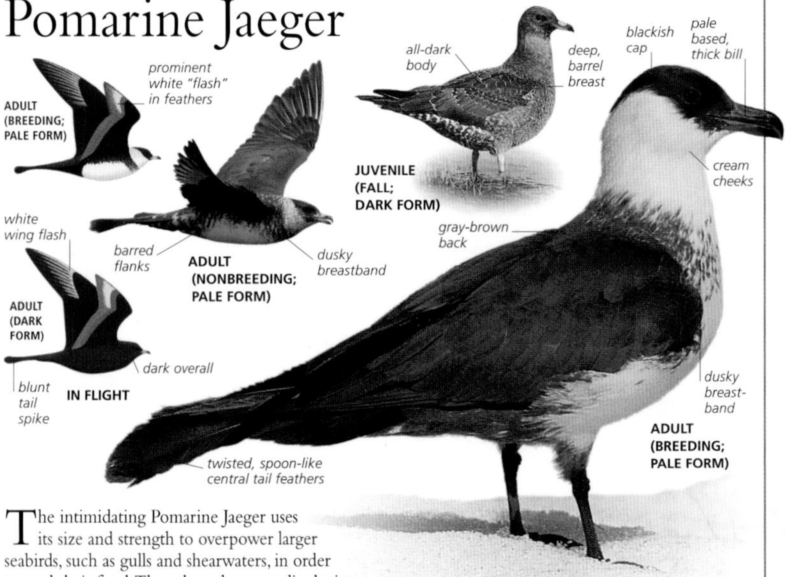

ADULT (BREEDING; PALE FORM) — prominent white "flash" in feathers

ADULT (NONBREEDING; PALE FORM) — barred flanks; dusky breastband

ADULT (DARK FORM) — white wing flash; dark overall; blunt tail spike

IN FLIGHT

JUVENILE (FALL; DARK FORM) — all-dark body; deep, barrel breast

ADULT (BREEDING; PALE FORM) — blackish cap; pale based, thick bill; cream cheeks; gray-brown back; dusky breast-band; twisted, spoon-like central tail feathers

The intimidating Pomarine Jaeger uses its size and strength to overpower larger seabirds, such as gulls and shearwaters, in order to steal their food. Thought to be nomadic during the breeding season, it only nests opportunistically, when populations of lemmings are at their peak to provide food for its young. Although larger and more powerful than the Parasitic Jaeger, the Pomarine Jaeger is not as acrobatic in the air and is readily driven away from breeding territories by the more dynamic Parasitic Jaeger. Interestingly, research suggests that the Pomarine Jaeger is actually more closely related to the large skuas—such as the Great and South Polar Skuas—than to other jaegers.

VOICE Nasal *cow-cow-cow* and various sharp, low whistles.

NESTING Shallow unlined depression on a rise or hummock in open tundra; 2 eggs; 1 brood; June–August.

FEEDING Hunts lemmings and other rodents; eats fish or scavenges refuse from fishing boats during nonbreeding season; often steals fish from other seabirds, such as gulls.

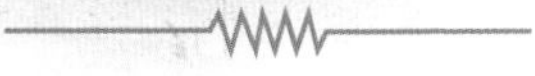

FLIGHT: powerful, deep, quick wing beats, with glides; rapid twists and turns in pursuit of prey.

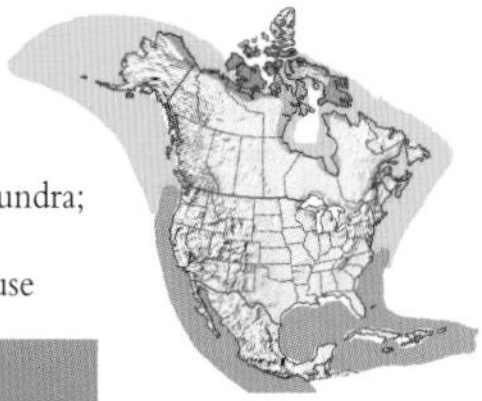

SIMILAR SPECIES

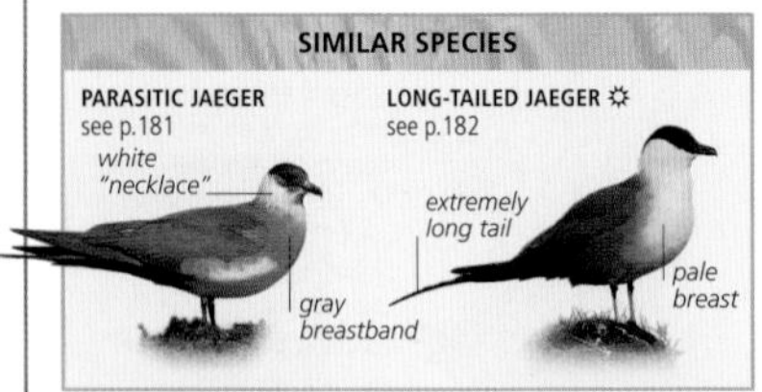

OBVIOUS FEATURE
The twisted, spoon-like central tail feathers are clearly visible when the Pomarine Jaeger flies.

OCCURRENCE
Breeds on open tundra in the Canadian Arctic. Migrates north in spring and south in fall, along coasts and also far offshore. Most often seen when brought close to land by gales. Storm-driven birds very occasionally found inland. More commonly seen on West Coast than East Coast; winters far out at sea.

Length **17–20in (43–51cm)**	Wingspan **4ft (1.2m)**	Weight **23–26oz (650–750g)**
Social **Solitary**	Lifespan **Unknown**	Status **Secure**

DATE SEEN	WHERE	NOTES

Order **Charadriiformes**	Family **Stercorariidae**	Species ***Stercorarius parasiticus***

Parasitic Jaeger

white wing patch
barring on wings
IN FLIGHT
ADULT (PALE FORM)
ADULT (DARK FORM)
pale cheek patch
mostly dark brown overall
ADULT (DARK FORM)
dark cap
pale cheek
dark upperparts
long, pointed, central feathers
ADULT (INTERMEDIATE FORM)
dark legs and toes
white belly
wide gray breastband

FLIGHT: swift wing beats interspersed with fast glides,interrupted by twisting and climbing.

A true avian pirate of the high seas, the Parasitic Jaeger routinely seeks food by chasing, bullying, and forcing other seabirds to drop or regurgitate fish or other food they have caught. Unlike most jaegers, the Parasitic Jaeger is adaptable in its feeding habits so that it can forage and raise its young under a wide range of environmental conditions. Breeding on the Arctic tundra, it migrates to offshore areas during the nonbreeding season.

VOICE Variety of terrier-like yelps and soft squeals, often during interactions with other jaegers or predators, usually around nesting territories.

NESTING Shallow unlined depression on a rise or hummock in open tundra; 2 eggs; 1 brood; May–August.

FEEDING Steals fish and other aquatic prey from gulls and terns; catches small birds, eats eggs, or hunts small rodents on breeding grounds.

PARASITIC PIRATE
This Parasitic Jaeger is harrying a gull by pecking at it, to make it disgorge its hard-won meal.

SIMILAR SPECIES

POMARINE JAEGER see p.180
two long, central, twisted tail feathers
heavy hooked bill

LONG-TAILED JAEGER see p.182
black cap
longer pointed tail

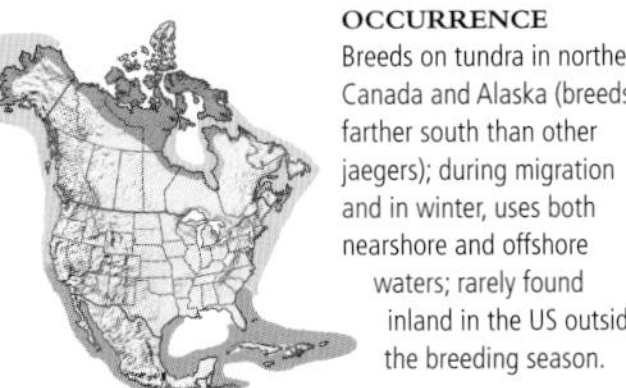

OCCURRENCE
Breeds on tundra in northern Canada and Alaska (breeds farther south than other jaegers); during migration and in winter, uses both nearshore and offshore waters; rarely found inland in the US outside the breeding season.

Length **16–18½in (41–47cm)**	Wingspan **3ft 3in–3½ ft (1–1.1m)**	Weight **13–18oz (375–500g)**
Social **Solitary/Small flocks**	Lifespan **Up to 18 years**	Status **Secure**

DATE SEEN	WHERE	NOTES

Order **Charadriiformes**	Family **Stercorariidae**	Species ***Stercorarius longicaudus***

Long-tailed Jaeger

FLIGHT: direct, swift glides with rapid wing beats; more buoyant and light than other jaegers.

This elegant and striking species is a surprisingly fierce Arctic and marine predator. Though the Long-tailed Jaeger occasionally steals food from small gulls and terns, it is much less proficient at such piracy than its larger relatives, and usually hunts for its own food. Indeed, the Long-tailed Jaeger is so dependent on there being an abundance of lemmings in the Arctic that in years when lemming numbers dip low, the bird may not even attempt to nest, because there would not be enough lemmings with which to feed its chicks.

VOICE Calls include a chorus of *kreek*, a loud *kreer* warning call, whistles, and high-pitched, sharp clicks.

NESTING Shallow, unlined depression on a rise or hummock in open tundra; 2 eggs; 1 brood; May–August.

FEEDING Hunts lemmings on tundra breeding grounds; takes fish, beetles, and mayflies from water surface; occasionally steals small fish from terns.

DEFENSIVE MOVES
This species protects its territory with angry calls, aggressive swoops, and distraction displays.

SIMILAR SPECIES

POMARINE JAEGER see p.180
long twisted feathers; hooked bill

PARASITIC JAEGER see p.181
thin bill; shorter tail

OCCURRENCE
Breeds on tundra in northern Canada and Alaska—generally the most northern breeding jaeger; on migration and in winter uses mostly offshore waters; very rarely seen inland in winter.

Length **19–21in (48–53cm)**	Wingspan **3½ft (1.1m)**	Weight **10–11oz (275–300g)**
Social **Solitary/Flocks**	Lifespan **Up to 8 years**	Status **Secure**

DATE SEEN	WHERE	NOTES

Order **Charadriiformes**	Family **Alcidae**	Species ***Uria aalge***

Common Murre

black wing
ADULT (BREEDING)
slender head and bill
IN FLIGHT

white eye-ring
white line extending backwards from eye
dark brown upperparts and breast
ADULT (WHITE BRIDLED FORM)

curved, black line droops behind eye
white face and throat
ADULT (NONBREEDING)

black head
long, straight, black bill
white underparts
black back
grayish legs and toes
ADULT (BREEDING)

FLIGHT: fairly quick with rapid wing beats; close to water's surface.

Abundant, penguin-like birds of the cooler northern oceans, Common Murres are often seen standing upright on cliffs. They are strong fliers and adept divers, to a depth of 500ft (150m). Their large nesting colonies, on rocky sea cliff ledges, are so densely packed that incubating adults may touch each other on both sides. Common Murre eggs are pointed at one end—when pushed, they roll around in a circle, reducing the risk of rolling off the nesting ledge. It has been suggested that unique egg markings may help adults recognize their own eggs.

VOICE Low-pitched, descending call given from cliffs or water, reminiscent of trumpeting elephant.

NESTING Directly on bare rock near shore, on wide cliff ledge, or large crevice; 1 egg; 1 brood; May-July.

FEEDING Pursues small schooling fish, such as herring, sand lance, and haddock; also crustaceans, marine worms, and squid.

BREEDING COLONY
Crowded together, Common Murres are not territorial but will defend a personal space.

SIMILAR SPECIES

THICK-BILLED MURRE see p.435
thick, pale line between eye and bill

RAZORBILL ☼
bill with white bar near tip

OCCURRENCE
Breeds close to rocky shorelines, nesting on coastal cliff ledges or flat rocks on top of sea stacks on both East and West coasts. Found farther offshore during nonbreeding season, spending extended periods on the open ocean and in large bays. Winters at sea.

Length **17½in (44cm)**	Wingspan **26in (65cm)**	Weight **35oz (1,000g)**
Social **Colonies**	Lifespan **At least 40 years**	Status **Localized**

DATE SEEN	WHERE	NOTES

Order **Charadriiformes**	Family **Alcidae**	Species ***Cepphus columba***

Pigeon Guillemot

The Pigeon Guillemot, a North Pacific seabird, is found along rocky shores in small colonies or isolated pairs. This auk nests in burrows or under rocks, often on small islands that provide protection from land-bound predators. The male excavates a burrow, or chooses an abandoned burrow or crevice, to build a nest. During the breeding season, the bird's striking red-orange legs and mouth lining are used in courtship displays to attract a mate.

VOICE Excited, squeaky whistles, and twitters; nesting birds give a weak whistle *peeeee*.

NESTING Shallow scrape in burrow or crevice; 2 eggs; 1 brood; May–August.

FEEDING Feeds near shore; dives to seabed, then uses bill to forage for small rock eels, sculpin, crabs, shrimp, marine worms, and mollusks; carries food for chicks in beak.

FLIGHT: flies close to water surface with very rapid, fluttering wing beats.

PREDATOR BECOMES PREY
Predatory gulls can kill adult Pigeon Guillemots and sometimes eat their chicks and eggs.

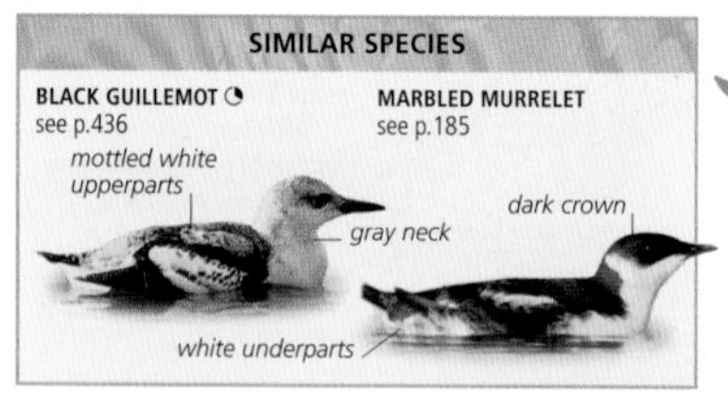

OCCURRENCE
Breeds on rocky islands, coastlines, and cliffs where it is less accessible to predators. At sea, it generally remains close to rocky coasts, except in the Bering Sea, where it is found further out along the edges of the pack ice. In winter, some populations are forced south by sea ice.

Length **13½in (34cm)**	Wingspan **23in (58cm)**	Weight **18oz (500g)**
Social **Colonies**	Lifespan **Up to 14 years**	Status **Localized**

DATE SEEN	WHERE	NOTES

Order **Charadriiformes**	Family **Alcidae**	Species ***Brachyramphus marmoratus***

Marbled Murrelet

ADULT (NONBREEDING)
white patches on side of rump
dark overall
ADULT (BREEDING)
IN FLIGHT
dark face patch
white collar
ADULT (NONBREEDING)
dark brown head
spotted chin, throat, and chest
ADULT (BREEDING)
dark tail
speckled upperparts
dark brown back
mottled underparts

The breeding habits of the Marbled Murrelet, a bird of both sea and forest, remained a mystery until 1974, when the first nest was discovered high in a Douglas Fir in a California park. Unlike most auks and their relatives, which have black and white breeding plumage, the Marbled Murrelet's breeding plumage is brown, to camouflage the bird on its nest in the branches of trees or, in places, on the ground. Ornithologists are eager to learn more about this secretive seabird, even as its numbers decline due to clear-cutting of old-growth conifer forests, where it nests, entanglement of the bird in fishing gear, and oil pollution out at sea, where it feeds.

VOICE Flight call series of high-pitched, squealing, slightly descending *kleeer* notes.

NESTING In northern part of its range, on island mountainsides; in the south, on tree limbs in old-growth forests; 1 egg; 1 brood; April–September.

FEEDING Short dives to catch small fish and crustaceans in shallow offshore waters, "flying" underwater; feeds at night, in pairs.

FLIGHT: straight, fast, and low over water, with extremely rapid wing beats.

RUNNING ON WATER
The Marbled Murrelet flaps its wings energetically and runs across the surface to become airborne.

SIMILAR SPECIES

KITTLITZ'S MURRELET
see p.436

OCCURRENCE
Relies on marine and forested habitats for both feeding and breeding, on Pacific coasts from Alaska to California; at sea, usually found near coast, in relatively shallow waters. In the breeding season, travels back and forth between the sea and inland breeding grounds.

Length **10in (26cm)**	Wingspan **16in (41cm)**	Weight **8oz (225g)**
Social **Pairs/Small groups**	Lifespan **Unknown**	Status **Vulnerable**

DATE SEEN	WHERE	NOTES

Order **Charadriiformes**	Family **Alcidae**	Species ***Synthliboramphus antiquus***

Ancient Murrelet

Of the five murrelets that occur regularly in North America, this little species is the most numerous. Like its close relatives, Xantus's Murrelet and Craveri's Murrelet, the Ancient Murrelet usually raises two chicks, and takes them out to sea when they are just a few days old, usually under the cover of darkness. The Ancient Murrelet can also leap straight out of the sea and into flight. White eyebrow-like plumes on the head, combined with a shawl-like gray back, give the bird its supposedly "ancient" appearance.

VOICE Short, high-pitched trills and rattles given by nesting birds while perched in trees.

NESTING Burrow in soft soil, often among forest tree roots; 2 eggs; 1 brood; June–August.

FEEDING Dives for prey in groups, often at the same time, driving schools of small fish to the surface; Euphansiid shrimps, which are about 1in (2.5cm) long, are its primary diet.

FLIGHT: flies fast, low, and straight with rapid wing beats; capable of quick takeoff from water.

GROUP FEEDER
The Ancient Murrelet flies low to the water in flocks on the lookout for food.

SIMILAR SPECIES

XANTUS'S MURRELET see p.436

CRAVERI'S MURRELET see p.436

OCCURRENCE
Lives in the north Pacific, and Bering Sea. Concentrates where food is abundant—most often in straits, sounds, and coastal waters—where it often feeds quite close to shore. Nests on coastal islands, mainly on forest floors but also where there is proper cover and sufficient peaty soil to dig burrows.

Length **10in (26cm)**	Wingspan **17in (43cm)**	Weight **7oz (200g)**
Social **Colonies**	Lifespan **At least 4 years**	Status **Localized**

DATE SEEN	WHERE	NOTES

Order **Charadriiformes**	Family **Alcidae**	Species ***Ptychoramphus aleuticus***

Cassin's Auklet

This secretive little seabird usually nests in an underground burrow, which can take a breeding pair many weeks to scratch out. Parent birds fish by day, returning to the nest in the safety of darkness to avoid gulls and other predators. Nestlings encourage regurgitation by nibbling at a white spot at the base of the parent's lower mandible. Uniquely for a member of the alcid family, Cassin's Auklet has been known to raise more than one brood in a season.

VOICE Hoarse, rhythmic night calls in colonies; squeals and peeps when in burrow; silent at sea.

NESTING On offshore islands, in crevices or burrows; 1 egg; 1–2 broods; March–September.

FEEDING Dives and swims underwater using wings to pursue small crustaceans, fish, and squid.

FLIGHT: low over the surface of the sea, with rapid wing beats.

RUNNING ON WATER
After a long run and some energetic wing beating, Cassin's Auklet eventually takes off from the water.

SIMILAR SPECIES

MARBLED MURRELET (BREEDING) see p.185
paler head
reddish brown upperparts

KITTLITZ'S MURRELET (BREEDING)
lacks white stripe on underwing; see p.436
mottled brown-and-white feathers

OCCURRENCE
Pacific distribution; breeds on cliffs, grassy plains, or slopes on coastal islands. During the nonbreeding season, northern birds found in deep waters beyond the continental shelf, where upwelling currents bring food from the depths. Southern birds remain near their colonies year-round.

Length **9in (23cm)**	Wingspan **15in (38cm)**	Weight **6oz (175g)**
Social **Colonies**	Lifespan **At least 6 years**	Status **Localized**

DATE SEEN	WHERE	NOTES

Order **Charadriiformes**	Family **Alcidae**	Species ***Cerorhinca monocerata***

Rhinoceros Auklet

This robust bird is closely related to puffins, and is the only auk with a prominent "horn" on top of its bill; it is this structure that gives the bird its common name. The Rhinoceros Auklet forages closer to shore than its puffin relatives, and usually returns to its nesting colonies at night. This trusting seabird often allows boats to approach very closely. It became locally extinct, but re-established its population on California's Farallon Islands in the 1970s when non-native rabbits that were competing for nesting burrows were removed. When fishing, it carries its catch in its beak, rather than in a throat pouch like other auks.

VOICE Adults give series of low, mooing calls, as well as short barks and groans.

NESTING Cup of moss or twigs on islands, under vegetation, in crevice or long, soil burrow; 1 egg; 1 brood; April–September.

FEEDING Forages underwater during breeding season, looks for small schooling fish for nestlings; also eats crustaceans; powerful diver and swimmer.

FLIGHT: swift, direct with quick wing beats; takeoff appears labored.

SUBMARINE-LIKE
Its body nearly submerged and its head looking behind, this Rhinoceros Auklet is ready to dive.

SIMILAR SPECIES

PARAKEET AUKLET ♂
see p.437

OCCURRENCE
Throughout temperate North Pacific waters, generally south of puffin habitat. Typically lives far out at sea, but may feed near shore where currents concentrate food; usually forages and returns to nesting colonies by night.

Length **15in (38cm)**	Wingspan **22in (56cm)**	Weight **16oz (450g)**
Social **Colonies**	Lifespan **Unknown**	Status **Localized**

DATE SEEN	WHERE	NOTES

Order **Charadriiformes**	Family **Alcidae**	Species ***Fratercula cirrhata***

Tufted Puffin

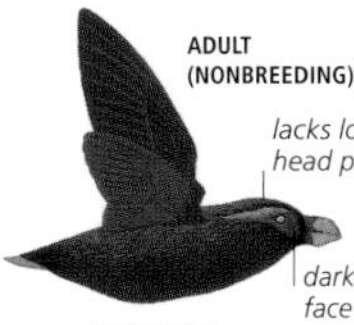

ADULT (NONBREEDING)

lacks long golden head plumes

dark face

IN FLIGHT

no plumes

yellow bill

ADULT (POSTBREEDING)

large, rounded head

white face

long golden plumes on back of head and nape

orange bill

stocky black body

rounded wings

dark underparts

ADULT (BREEDING)

orange legs and toes

FLIGHT: just above the ocean with strong, rapid wing beats.

Tufted Puffins, found along the northern Pacific coast, may be spotted hopping over rocky ledges, sitting alone on the sea, paddling along the surface before taking off, or flying only a couple of feet above the water. Like other puffin species, they partially open their wings underwater as they pursue prey, keeping their tail and feet spread to aid propulsion and steering. This bird's name arises from the curly golden plumes of feathers that adorn its head during the breeding season. It is the largest of the three puffin species, and can be distinguished from the Horned Puffin by its dark underparts, and from the Atlantic Puffin by its distribution.

VOICE Low, moaning growl given from burrow.

NESTING Chamber, lined with grass or feathers, at end of tunnel, under rocks, or in burrow; 1 egg; 1 brood; May–August.

FEEDING Dives deep to capture small fish, especially sand lance, juvenile pollock, and capelin; adults consume prey underwater, or take it ashore to feed their chicks.

TUFTED PAIR
These distinctive and popular birds breed in colonies and usually mate for life.

SIMILAR SPECIES

RHINOCEROS AUKLET
see p.188

darker face

smaller bill

RHINOCEROS AUKLET
see p.188

no white on face

slimmer build

OCCURRENCE
Breeds on rocky islands, and coastal cliffs of the North Pacific, especially treeless offshore islands with sea cliffs or grassy slopes; elevation may help them take flight. Found over unusually wide geographic and climatic range. Winters at sea, usually over deep waters of the central North Pacific.

Length **15in (38cm)**	Wingspan **25in (64cm)**	Weight **27oz (775g)**
Social **Colonies**	Lifespan **Up to 30 years**	Status **Localized**

DATE SEEN	WHERE	NOTES

PIGEONS & DOVES

THE LARGER SPECIES WITHIN the family Columbidae are known as pigeons, and the smaller ones as doves, although there is no actual scientific basis for this distinction. All Columbidae are fairly heavy, plump birds with relatively small heads and short necks. They have slender bills with the nostrils positioned in a fleshy mound at the base. Among other things, members of this family have strong wing muscles, making them powerful and agile fliers. When alarmed, they burst into flight, with their wings emitting a distinctive clapping or swishing sound. Pigeons and doves secrete a nutritious "crop-milk" to feed their young. Despite human activity having severely affected members of this family in the past (the leading cause of the Passenger Pigeon's extinction in the 19th century is thought to be overhunting), the introduced Rock Pigeon has adapted and proliferated worldwide, as has the recently introduced Eurasian Collared-Dove, albeit on a smaller scale. The introduced Spotted Dove has not shown a similar tendency for explosive expansion, however, and remains limited to southern California and the islands of Hawaii. Among the species native to North America, only the elegant Mourning Dove is as widespread as the various species of introduced birds.

NATIVE PIGEON
A native species, the Band-tailed Pigeon is sadly declining through much of its range.

DOVE IN THE SUN
The Mourning Dove sunbathes each side of its body in turn, its wings and tail outspread.

Order **Columbiformes**	Family **Columbidae**	Species ***Columba livia***

Rock Pigeon

black wing bars
white underwings
white rump
ADULT
IN FLIGHT

no wing bars
variably colored body
ADULT (FERAL)

iridescence on neck
short bill
gray back
two black wing bars
dark-tipped tail
ADULT (ANCESTRAL FORM)

The Rock Pigeon was introduced to the Atlantic coast of North America by 17th century colonists. Now feral, this species is found all over the continent, especially around farms, cities, and towns. This medium-sized pigeon comes in a wide variety of plumage colors and patterns, including bluish gray, checkered, rusty-red, and nearly all-white. Its wings usually have two dark bars on them—unique among North American pigeons. The variability of the Rock Pigeon influenced Charles Darwin as he developed his theory of natural selection.

VOICE Soft, gurgling *coo, roo-c'too-coo,* for courtship and threat.

NESTING Twig nest on flat, sheltered surface, such as caves, rocky outcrops, and buildings; 2 eggs; several broods; year-round.

FEEDING Eats seeds, fruit, and rarely, insects; human foods such as popcorn, bread, peanuts; various farm crops in rural areas.

FLIGHT: strong, direct; can reach speeds up to around 60mph (95kph).

CITY PIGEONS
Most Rock Pigeons in North America descend from domesticated forms and exhibit many colors.

OCCURRENCE
Across southern Canada and North America; nests in human structures of all sorts; resident. Original habitat in the Old World was (and still is) sea cliffs and inland canyons; found wild in some places, such as dry regions of North Africa, but feral in much of the world.

Length **11–14in (28–36cm)**	Wingspan **20–26in (51–67cm)**	Weight **9–14oz (250–400g)**
Social **Solitary/Flocks**	Lifespan **Up to 6 years**	Status **Secure**

DATE SEEN	WHERE	NOTES

Order **Columbiformes**	Family **Columbidae**	Species ***Columba fasciata***

Band-tailed Pigeon

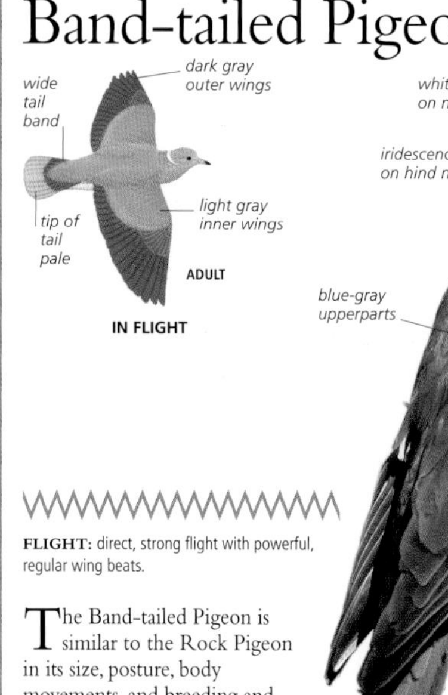

FLIGHT: direct, strong flight with powerful, regular wing beats.

The Band-tailed Pigeon is similar to the Rock Pigeon in its size, posture, body movements, and breeding and feeding behavior. However, in North America the Band-tailed Pigeon's distribution is limited to the dry, mountain forests of several southwestern states, and the wet coastal forests of the West Coast, from the southeastern tip of Alaska south to Baja California. The distinguishing features of the Band-tailed Pigeon are its yellow bill and legs, a white band just above the iridescent green patch on the back of its neck—and its eponymous banded tail.

VOICE Often silent, but emits series of two-noted, low-frequency *whooos* punctuated with a pause.

NESTING Flat, saucer-shaped, rather flimsy platform of twigs, needles, and moss in a variety of trees; 1 egg; 1 brood; April–October.

FEEDING Forages on the ground for grain, seeds, fruit, acorns, and pine nuts; hangs upside down by its toes from the branches of shrubs and trees to eat dangling nuts and flowers that are otherwise out of reach.

LARGE PIGEON
This is North America's largest pigeon, bigger than the Rock Pigeon by about 10 percent.

UNIFORMITY
Unlike Rock Pigeons, Band-tailed Pigeons in flocks have very uniform plumage.

SIMILAR SPECIES

OCCURRENCE
Breeds and winters in temperate conifer rain forests along the Pacific coast, and in mountain conifer and mixed-species forests in the interior. Lives in urban and rural areas where there are evergreen trees and access to grains, fruit, and feeders. Some populations are resident, others migratory.

Length **13–16in (33–41cm)**	Wingspan **26in (66cm)**	Weight **12–13oz (350–375g)**
Social **Flocks**	Lifespan **Up to 18 years**	Status **Declining**

DATE SEEN	WHERE	NOTES

Order **Columbiformes**	Family **Columbidae**	Species ***Zenaida macroura***

Mourning Dove

One of the most familiar, abundant, and widespread of North American birds, the Mourning Dove is a long-tailed, plump, medium-sized dove with a small head. It has a grayish tan body with a pale, rosy breast and black spots on folded wings. While coveted by hunters—as many as 70 million are shot annually—the Mourning Dove is also well known to those who live on farms and in suburbia. Found all across North America, the species is divided into four subspecies—two of which occur in North America—the larger grayish brown *Z. m. carolinensis*, east of the Mississippi River, and the smaller, paler *Z. m. marginella* in the west.

VOICE Mellow, owl-like call: *hoO-Oo-oo, hoo-hoo-hoo.*

NESTING Flat, flimsy twig platform, mostly in trees, sometimes on the ground; 2 eggs; 2 broods; February–October.

FEEDING Forages mainly for seeds on the ground; obtains food quickly and digests it later at roost.

FLIGHT: swift, direct flight, with fairly quick wing beats; twists and turns sometimes.

SIMILAR SPECIES

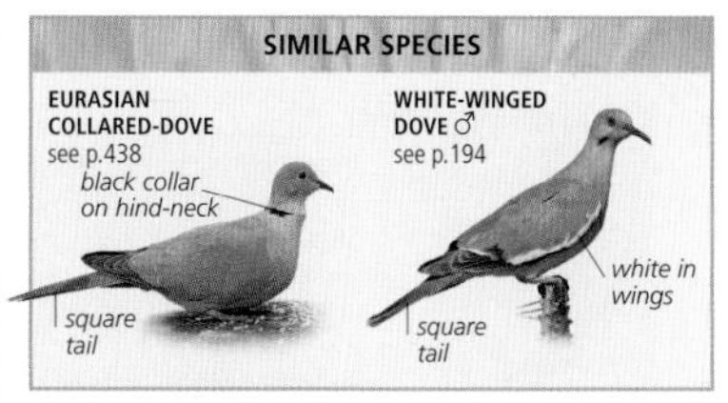

FAMILIAR SIGHT The Mourning Dove is North America's most widespread member of this family.

OCCURRENCE Breeds in a wide variety of habitats but shuns extensive forests; human-altered vegetation favored for feeding, including farmland and suburbia. Winters in small to medium sheltered woodland while feeding in grain fields; winters in southern Mexico and Central America.

Length **9–13½in (23–34cm)**	Wingspan **14½–17½in (37–45cm)**	Weight **3–6oz (85–175g)**
Social **Pairs/Winter flocks**	Lifespan **Up to 19 years**	Status **Secure**

DATE SEEN	WHERE	NOTES

Order **Columbiformes**	Family **Columbidae**	Species ***Zenaida asiatica***

White-winged Dove

FLIGHT: swift, direct flight with quick, regular wing beats; maximum height about 200ft (60m).

As one of the larger gray-colored dove species in North America, the White-winged Dove is best identified in flight by the conspicuous white bands on its wings. When perched, the bright blue skin around its orange eyes and its longish, square tail with a white tip can be seen. This species has been expanding its population northwards in recent decades, though not as quickly as the Eurasian Collared-Dove. Increased farmland habitat and ornamental trees, both favorite roosting places, are the most likely cause. In common with many other doves, the nest is a somewhat flimsy structure, and eggs or nestlings frequently fall to their end if the nest is disturbed, or when there are high winds.

VOICE Distinctive, drawn-out cooing: *who-cooks-for-you*; also makes five-note variation from the nest: *la-coo-kla-coo-kla*.

NESTING Frail platform of twigs, moss, and grasses, on a sturdy branch in dense-canopied trees; 2 eggs; 2 broods; March–September.

FEEDING Forages for seeds, wild nuts, and fruit on the ground and in elevated locations; prefers corn, sorghum, wheat, and sunflower.

DESERT DWELLER
The White-winged Dove is much more at home in semi-arid and desert areas than the Mourning Dove.

OCCURRENCE
Breeds and winters in dense, thorny woodlands dominated by mesquite and Texas Ebony; deserts with cactus, palo verde, and other scrub plants; riverine woodlands, orchards, and residential areas. Formerly only abundant in the US in the Rio Grande Valley, it has now expanded north to Oklahoma.

Length **11½in (29cm)**	Wingspan **19in (48cm)**	Weight **5oz (150g)**
Social **Solitary/Flocks**	Lifespan **Up to 21 years**	Status **Localized**

DATE SEEN	WHERE	NOTES

CUCKOOS & RELATIVES

CUCKOOS ARE NOTORIOUS for laying eggs in other birds' nests, but of the three species in North America, one never does this, and two seldom do so. Their close relatives on the continent are the Greater Roadrunner, and two species of Ani.

CUCKOOS

Generally shy and reclusive, the Black-billed Cuckoo, Yellow-billed Cuckoo, and Mangrove Cuckoo all favor dense, forested habitats. All three species usually build a nest and raise their own offspring. The Black-billed Cuckoo and the Yellow-billed Cuckoo occasionally lay their eggs in other birds' nests, including each other's, and even the nests of their own species. In flight, cuckoos are often mistaken for small birds of prey. They sometimes pounce on lizards, frogs, and other small animals—even small birds—but mostly they glean insects from the foliage of trees. Much remains to be learned about these birds.

WEATHER BIRD
Folklore has it that the Yellow-billed Cuckoo, or "Raincrow," calls mostly on cloudy days.

GREATER ROADRUNNER

The Greater Roadrunner is a ground-based member of the Cuckoo family, and an inhabitant of the arid Southwest. It is capable of running at over 15mph (25kph), and is one of the few species of birds that actively hunts rattlesnakes, doing so in pairs. The Greater Roadrunner has been seen pulling small birds out of mist nets set by scientists for research purposes. It does not fly often, and rarely above a few yards.

ANIS

In North America both the Groove-billed Ani and the Smooth-billed Ani are at the northern edge of their range, being much more widespread in open country in tropical and subtropical regions farther south. Anis are typically weak, short-distance fliers, but, like the Greater Roadrunner, they are sturdy on their feet and often run and hop after their insect prey. They breed communally, several pairs of birds laying their eggs in one nest, then all help to raise the young.

STRONG STOMACH
The Black-billed Cuckoo can safely eat caterpillars that are poisonous to other birds.

PERCHED TO KILL
After catching a lizard, the Greater Roadrunner bashes it repeatedly against a rock before gulping it down.

Order **Cuculiformes**	Family **Cuculidae**	Species ***Coccyzus erythropthalmus***

Black-billed Cuckoo

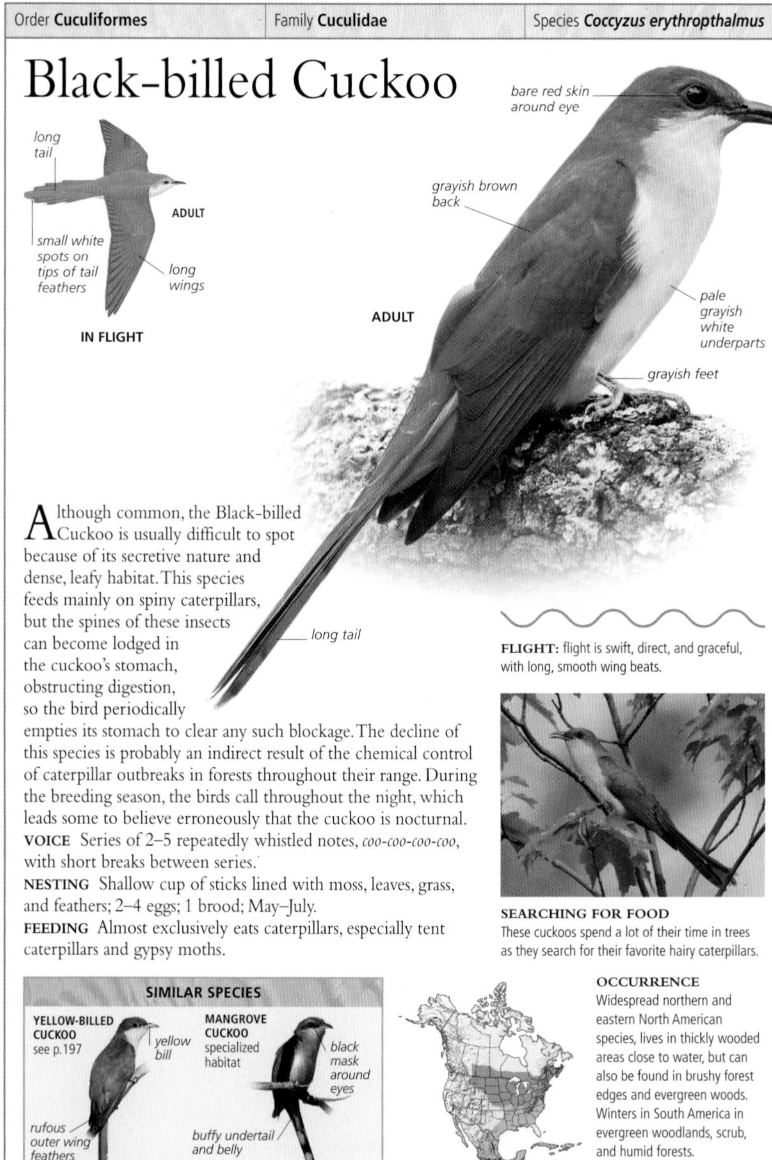

Although common, the Black-billed Cuckoo is usually difficult to spot because of its secretive nature and dense, leafy habitat. This species feeds mainly on spiny caterpillars, but the spines of these insects can become lodged in the cuckoo's stomach, obstructing digestion, so the bird periodically empties its stomach to clear any such blockage. The decline of this species is probably an indirect result of the chemical control of caterpillar outbreaks in forests throughout their range. During the breeding season, the birds call throughout the night, which leads some to believe erroneously that the cuckoo is nocturnal.

VOICE Series of 2–5 repeatedly whistled notes, *coo-coo-coo-coo*, with short breaks between series.

NESTING Shallow cup of sticks lined with moss, leaves, grass, and feathers; 2–4 eggs; 1 brood; May–July.

FEEDING Almost exclusively eats caterpillars, especially tent caterpillars and gypsy moths.

FLIGHT: flight is swift, direct, and graceful, with long, smooth wing beats.

SEARCHING FOR FOOD
These cuckoos spend a lot of their time in trees as they search for their favorite hairy caterpillars.

SIMILAR SPECIES

YELLOW-BILLED CUCKOO see p.197
yellow bill
rufous outer wing feathers

MANGROVE CUCKOO specialized habitat
black mask around eyes
buffy undertail and belly

OCCURRENCE
Widespread northern and eastern North American species, lives in thickly wooded areas close to water, but can also be found in brushy forest edges and evergreen woods. Winters in South America in evergreen woodlands, scrub, and humid forests.

Length **11–12in (28–31cm)**	Wingspan **16–19in (41–48cm)**	Weight **1 9/16–2oz (45–55g)**
Social **Solitary**	Lifespan **Up to 5 years**	Status **Secure (p)**

DATE SEEN	WHERE	NOTES

Order **Cuculiformes**	Family **Cuculidae**	Species ***Coccyzus americanus***

Yellow-billed Cuckoo

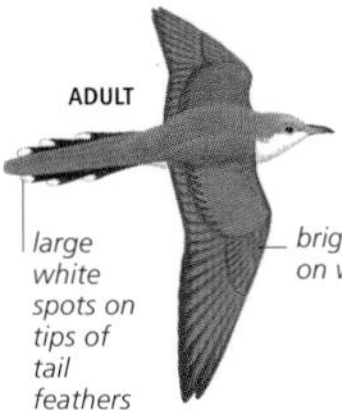
ADULT
large white spots on tips of tail feathers
bright rufous on wings
IN FLIGHT

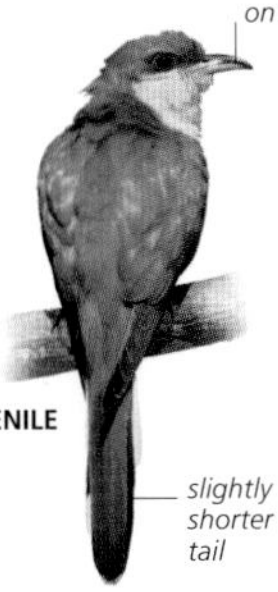
more black on bill
JUVENILE
slightly shorter tail

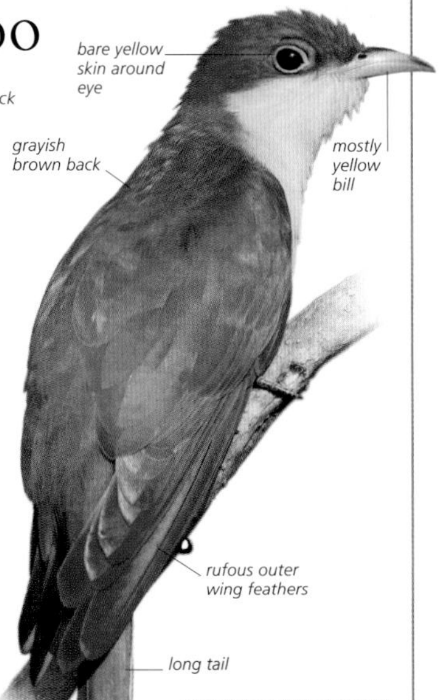
bare yellow skin around eye
grayish brown back
mostly yellow bill
ADULT
rufous outer wing feathers
long tail

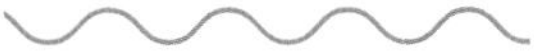

FLIGHT: flight is swift using long strokes to maintain level pattern.

The Yellow-billed Cuckoo is a shy, slow-moving bird, with a reputation for fairly odd behaviors, including its habit of calling more often on cloudy days. This tendency has earned it the nickname "rain crow" in some areas. In addition to raising young in its own nest, females often lay eggs in the nests of more than a dozen other species, especially during years with abundant food. The host species may be chosen on the basis of how closely the color of its eggs matches those of the cuckoo's. This brood parasitism is the rule in the Yellow-billed Cuckoo, which is an Old World species, and occurs in North America as a widespread vagrant.

VOICE Call a series of 10–12 low notes that slow down as it progresses, *ca ca ca ca coo coo coo cowl cowl cowl.*

NESTING Flimsy oval-shaped platform of small sticks and branches, often lined with leaves and strips of plants; 2–4 eggs; 1–2 broods; May–August.

FEEDING Mostly consumes insects such as grasshoppers, crickets, katydids, and caterpillars of several moth species; also eats seeds.

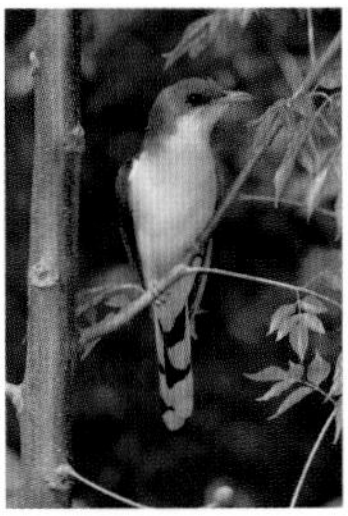

RARE SIGHT
Given the habitat they prefer and their skittish nature, a clear view of a Yellow-billed Cuckoo is rare.

SIMILAR SPECIES
BLACK-BILLED CUCKOO
see p.196
all-black bill
no rufous on wings
MANGROVE CUCKOO
black mask around eyes
buffy undertail and belly

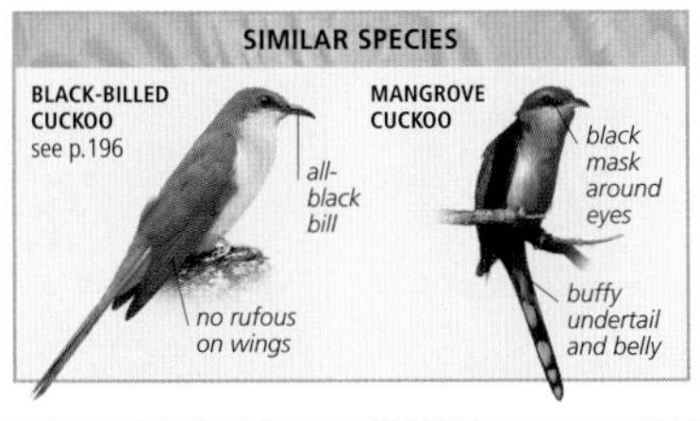

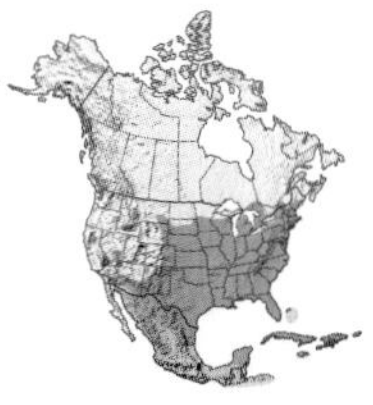

OCCURRENCE
Has a wide range in the US. Found primarily in open forests with a mix of openings and thick understory cover, especially those near water. Winters in similar habitats in Central and South America.

Length **10–12in (26–30cm)**	Wingspan **17–20in (43–51cm)**	Weight **2–2¼oz (55–65g)**
Social **Small winter flocks**	Lifespan **Up to 4 years**	Status **Secure (p)**

DATE SEEN	WHERE	NOTES

Order **Cuculiformes**	Family **Cuculidae**	Species ***Geococcyx californianus***

Greater Roadrunner

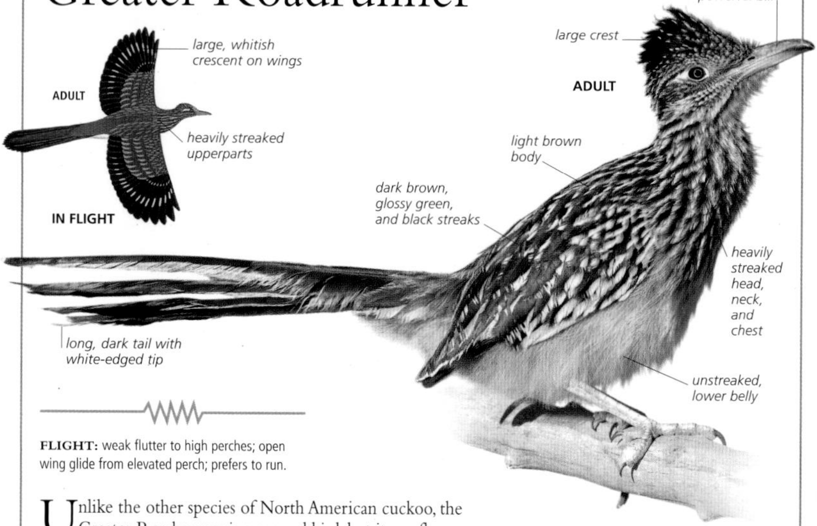
large, whitish crescent on wings
ADULT
heavily streaked upperparts
IN FLIGHT
long, thick, powerful bill
large crest
ADULT
light brown body
dark brown, glossy green, and black streaks
heavily streaked head, neck, and chest
long, dark tail with white-edged tip
unstreaked, lower belly

FLIGHT: weak flutter to high perches; open wing glide from elevated perch; prefers to run.

Unlike the other species of North American cuckoo, the Greater Roadrunner is a ground bird, but it can fly, despite preferring to run. Its speed enables it to overcome and chase prey on foot, especially lizards and small birds. Its generalized feeding habits allow this bird to take advantage of whatever food resources it comes across. This may be one of the main reasons roadrunners are expanding their range.

VOICE Cooing *coo-coo-coo-cooo-cooooo* series of 4–5 descending notes.

NESTING Shallow, loosely organized cup of twigs and branches, lined with grass, animal hair, and feathers; 3–5 eggs; 2 broods; April–September.

FEEDING Eats a wide variety of insects, small reptiles such as lizards, birds, and mammals; also eggs and carrion.

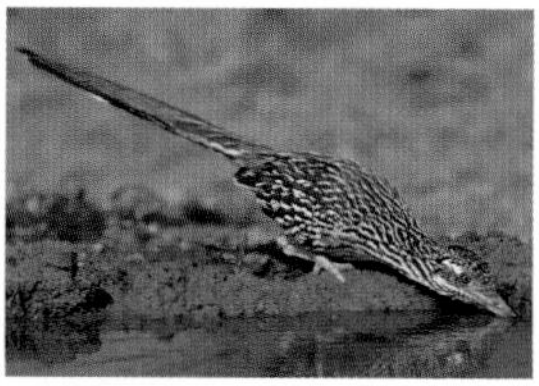

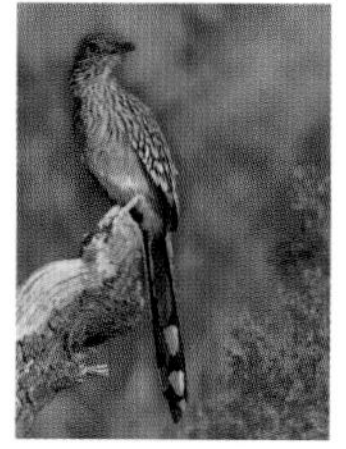

DRINKING
Roadrunners obtain much of their moisture from the food they eat, but will take full advantage of water whenever it is available.

LOFTY ABODE
This species nests off the ground, and can occasionally be seen occupying elevated perches.

SIMILAR SPECIES

PLAIN CHACHALACA

darker, solid color
unstreaked upperparts

RING-NECKED PHEASANT ♀
see p.37

no crest
lighter brown overall
plump body
larger overall

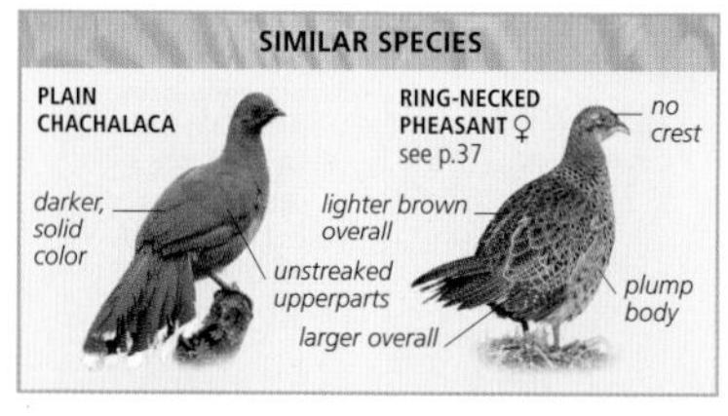

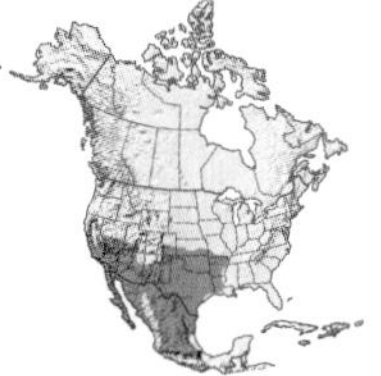

OCCURRENCE
Widespread across southeastern US, from California to Louisiana, and north to Utah, Colorado, Kansas, and Arkansas; lives at low elevations in open brushy areas mixed with thorn scrub such as mesquite; also pinyon-juniper shrubbery, and deserts and chaparral. Resident.

Length **21in (53cm)**	Wingspan **23in (58cm)**	Weight **11oz (300g)**
Social **Solitary/Pairs**	Lifespan **Up to 6 years**	Status **Secure**

DATE SEEN	WHERE	NOTES

OWLS

OWLS HAVE FASCINATED humans throughout history, partly because of their nocturnal habits and eerie cries. They are placed in the order Strigiformes, and two families are represented in North America: the Barn Owl is classified in Tytonidae, other North American owl species are in the Strigidae. Most owls are active primarily at night and have developed adaptations for living in low-light environments. Their large eyes are sensitive enough to see in the dark, and face forward to maximize binocular vision. Since the eyes are fixed in their sockets, a flexible neck helps owls turn their heads almost 180° toward a direction of interest. Ears are offset on each side of the head to help identify the source of a sound; "ear tufts" on some species, however, are for visual effect and unrelated to hearing. Many owls have serrations on the forward edges of their flight feathers to cushion airflow, so their flight is silent while stalking prey. All North American owls are predatory to some degree and they inhabit most areas of the continent. The Burrowing Owl is unique in that it hunts during the day and nests underground.

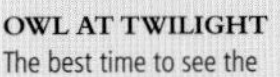

OWL AT TWILIGHT
The best time to see the nocturnal Barn Owl is often at dawn or dusk.

BIG HORNS
The "ear" tufts of the Great Horned Owl are taller than those of other "tufted" owls.

SNOW SWOOP
The Great Gray Owl can hunt by sound alone, allowing it to locate and capture prey hidden even beneath a thick snow cover.

Order **Strigiformes**	Family **Tytonidae**	Species ***Tyto alba***

Barn Owl

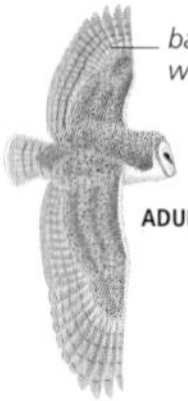
barring on wings and tail
ADULT
IN FLIGHT

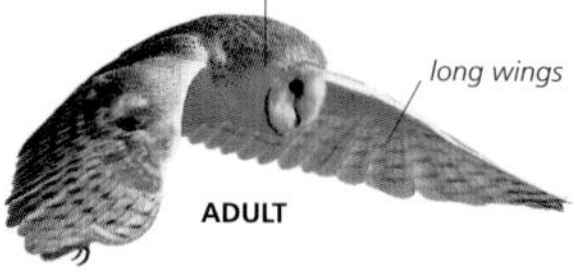
head lacks "ear" tufts
long wings
ADULT

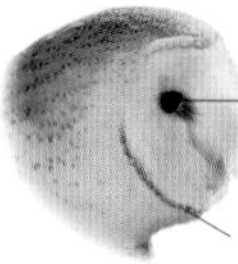
dark eyes
ruff surrounds facial disk
ADULT

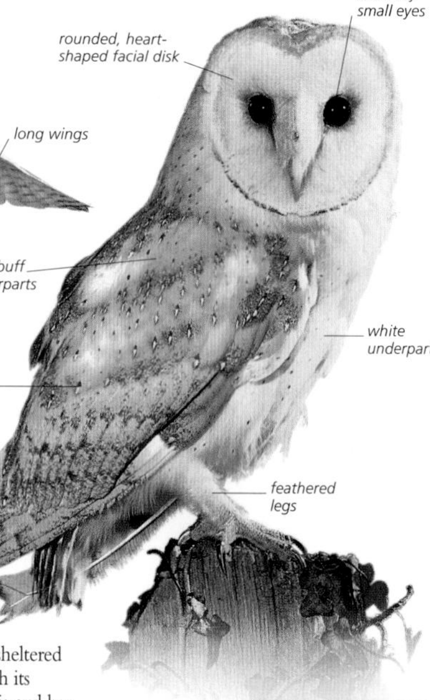
relatively small eyes
rounded, heart-shaped facial disk
pale buff upperparts
white underparts
gray and black spots
feathered legs

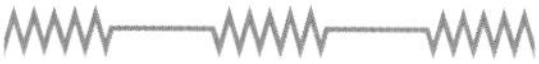

FLIGHT: irregular bursts of flapping, interspersed with short glides, banking, doubling back, fluttering.

Aptly named, the Barn Owl inhabits old sheds, sheltered rafters, and empty buildings in rural fields. With its affinity for human settlement, and 32 subspecies, this owl has an extensive range covering every continent except Antarctica. Although widespread, the Barn Owl is secretive. Primarily nocturnal, it can fly undetected until its screeching call pierces the air. The Barn Owl is endangered in several Midwestern states as a result of modern farming practices, which have decimated prey populations and reduced the number of barns for nesting.

VOICE Typical call loud, raspy, screeching shriek, *shkreee,* often given in flight; also clicking sounds associated with courtship.

NESTING Unlined cavity in tree, cave, building, hay bale, or nest box; 5–7 eggs; 1–2 broods; March–September.

FEEDING Hunts on the wing for small rodents such as mice; research reveals it can detect the slightest rustle made by prey even in total darkness.

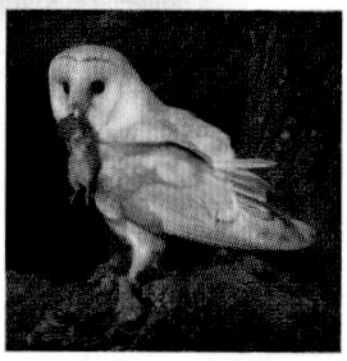

NOCTURNAL HUNTER
The Barn Owl hunts at night for small rodents, but may be seen before sunset feeding its young.

SIMILAR SPECIES

SNOWY OWL
see p.203

SHORT-EARED OWL
see p.213

black markings on female and juvenile
dark barring on underparts
dark patches on outer wing

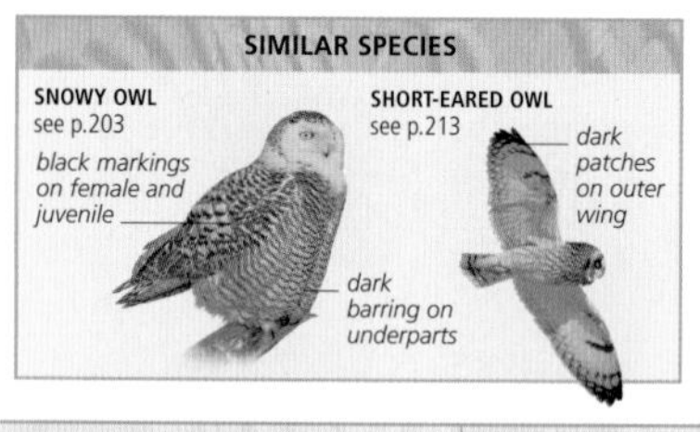

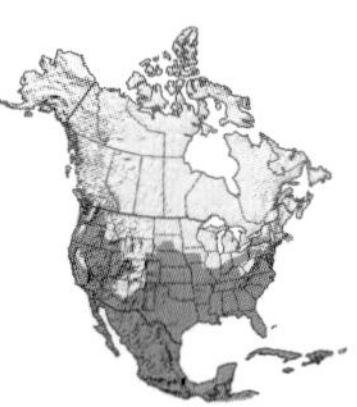

OCCURRENCE
In North America breeds from northwestern and northeastern US south to Mexico. Resident in all except very north of range. Prefers open habitats, such as desert, grassland, and fields, wherever prey and suitable nest sites are available. Generally not found in mountain or heavily forested areas.

Length **12½–15½in (32–40cm)**	Wingspan **3ft 3in (100cm)**	Weight **14–25oz (400–700g)**
Social **Solitary**	Lifespan **Up to 8 years**	Status **Declining**

DATE SEEN	WHERE	NOTES

Order **Strigiformes**	Family **Strigidae**	Species ***Otus flammeolus***

Flammulated Owl

FLIGHT: straight flight with steady wing beats; often hovers while foraging.

The tiny Flammulated Owl nests in dry mountain pine forests from British Columbia to Mexico, moving south to Central America for the winter months. Its dark, watery-looking eyes distinguish it from other species of small North American owls. Entirely nocturnal, it is heard more often than seen. When the Flammulated Owl is visible, its trademark reddish brown plumage blends quite well with the color of pine tree bark. This species appears to breed in loose colonies, although this may reflect patchiness in habitat quality. Like some other owls, it has a "red" and "gray" form.

VOICE Series of soft low-frequency toots, often difficult to locate, can continue for hours; barks and screams when disturbed at nest site.

NESTING Cavity in tree, woodpecker hole, nest box; 3–4 eggs; 1–2 broods; May–August.

FEEDING Hunts from stationary perch, from which it flies to capture insects—mostly moths and beetles—from branches, foliage, or ground.

BLENDING IN
If this owl peeks out of a tree-hole, its plumage blends in remarkably well with the bark.

SIMILAR SPECIES

WESTERN SCREECH-OWL see p.202
yellow eyes

NORTHERN SAW-WHET OWL see p.211
yellow eyes
different streaking

OCCURRENCE
Breeds in semiarid mountain forests, especially Ponderosa and Yellow Pine, open wooded areas at middle elevations with scattered clearings, older trees, and groves of saplings. Winters in habitat similar to breeding season, primarily in southern Mexico, Guatemala, and El Salvador.

Length **6–6¾in (15–17cm)**	Wingspan **16in (41cm)**	Weight **1 9/16–2¼oz (45–65g)**
Social **Solitary**	Lifespan **Up to 8 years**	Status **Secure**

DATE SEEN	WHERE	NOTES

Order **Strigiformes**	Family **Strigidae**	Species ***Otus kennicottii***

Western Screech-Owl

The Western Screech-Owl is tolerant of human presence, and lives in a wide variety of wooded areas, including suburban habitats. Because of its nocturnal habits, the Western Screech-Owl is heard more often than it is seen; its "bouncing ball" call, sometimes repeated for hours, is a familiar sound in much of western North America. This species exhibits significant differences in plumage color and size (six subspecies in North America), depending on its geographical location.

VOICE Series of toots accelerating and descending in pitch; also occasional trills, barks, chirps; female higher-pitched.

NESTING Hole in a tree, nest box, woodpecker cavity; 2–5 eggs; 1 brood; March–July.

FEEDING Sits quietly under canopy waiting to spot small prey below, then pounces; eats small birds and mammals, insects, crayfish, and worms.

FLIGHT: straight, steady flight, seldom over long distances; rarely hovers or glides.

GOOD CAMOUFLAGE This roosting Western Screech-Owl blends in with the bark color of a tree.

OCCURRENCE
Breeds from British Columbia southward to Baja California and continental Mexico. Favors riverside and mixed deciduous woodlands, but uses many types of woodlands, parks, and gardens in residential areas; most common at lower elevations. Nonmigratory.

Length **7½–10in (19–25cm)**	Wingspan **21–22in (53–56cm)**	Weight **3½–11oz (100–300g)**
Social **Family groups**	Lifespan **Up to 13 years**	Status **Secure**

DATE SEEN	WHERE	NOTES

Order **Strigiformes**	Family **Strigidae**	Species ***Nyctea scandiaca***

Snowy Owl

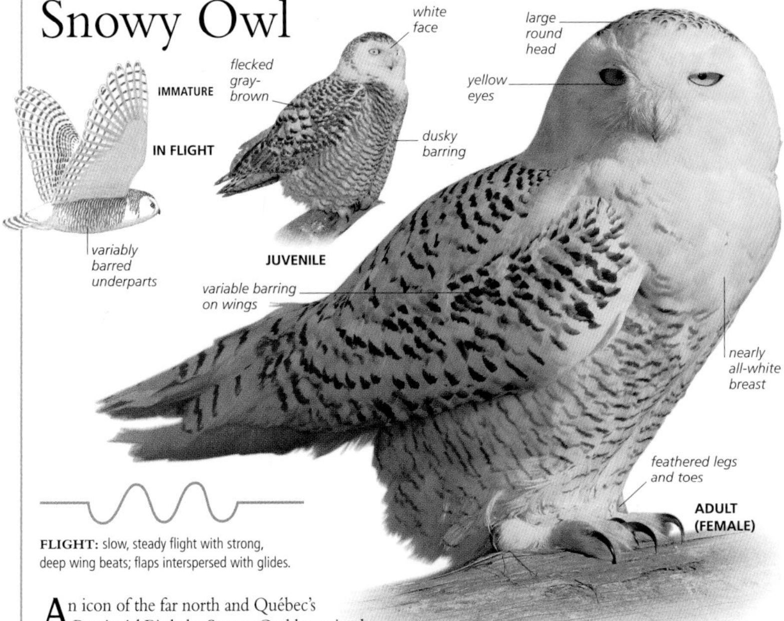
IMMATURE
IN FLIGHT
variably barred underparts
flecked gray-brown
white face
dusky barring
JUVENILE
large round head
yellow eyes
variable barring on wings
nearly all-white breast
feathered legs and toes
ADULT (FEMALE)

FLIGHT: slow, steady flight with strong, deep wing beats; flaps interspersed with glides.

An icon of the far north and Québec's Provincial Bird, the Snowy Owl has gained celebrity status for its occasional winter forays into northern US states. This is a bird of the open tundra, where it hunts from headlands or hummocks and nests on the ground. In such a harsh environment, the Snowy Owl largely depends on lemmings for prey. It is fiercely territorial, and will valiantly defend its young in the nest even against larger animals, such as the Arctic Fox.

VOICE Deep hoots, doubled or given in a short series, usually by male; also rattles, whistles, and hisses.

NESTING Scrape in ground vegetation or dirt, with no lining; 3–12 eggs; 1 brood; May–September.

FEEDING Mostly hunts lemmings, but takes whatever other small mammals, birds, and occasionally fish it can find.

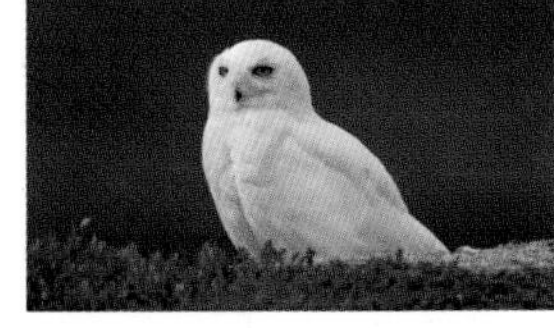

SNOWY MALE
Some adult males show no barring at all and have pure white plumage.

SIMILAR SPECIES

BARN OWL
see p.200
black eyes
golden brown
SHORT-EARED OWL
see p.213
mottled brown markings
larger overall

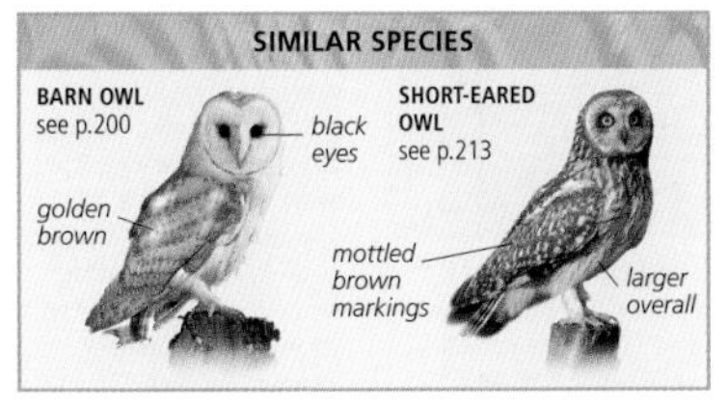

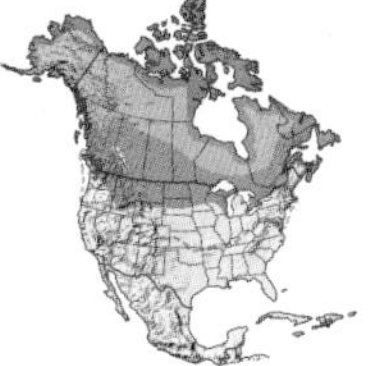

OCCURRENCE
Breeds in the tundra of Eurasia and northern North America, north to Ellesmere Island; North American birds winter south to the Great Plains. In some years, many North American birds winter south of their normal range, including in dunes, marshes, and airfields, as far south as Idaho and New Jersey.

Length **20–27in (51–68cm)**	Wingspan **4¼–5¼ft 1.3–1.6m)**	Weight **3½–6½lb (1.6–2.9kg)**
Social **Solitary**	Lifespan **Up to 9 years**	Status **Vulnerable**

DATE SEEN	WHERE	NOTES

Order **Strigiformes**	Family **Strigidae**	Species ***Bubo virginianus***

Great Horned Owl

yellow eye

large "ears"

rusty facial disk

ADULT

heavy barring of underparts

barring on undertail

FLIGHT: fairly slow with heavy wing beats alternating with short glides; swoops when hunting.

The Great Horned Owl is perhaps the archetypal owl. Large and adaptable, it is resident from Alaska to Tierra del Fuego. With such a big range, geographical variation occurs; at least 13 subspecies have been described. The southernmost populations—*B. v. magellanicus*, from Peru to Patagonia—are often considered a distinct species. The Great Horned Owl's deep hoots are easily recognized, and can often be heard in movie soundtracks. The bird is the top predator in its food chain, often killing and eating other owls, and even skunks. An early breeder, it starts hooting in the middle of winter, and often lays its eggs in January.

VOICE Series of hoots *whoo-hoo-oo-o*; also screams, barks, and hisses; female higher-pitched.

NESTING Old stick nest, in tree, exposed cavity, cliff, human structure, or on the ground; 1–5 eggs; 1 brood; January–April.

FEEDING Hunts mammals, reptiles, amphibians, birds, and insects; mostly nocturnal.

RECYCLING
The Great Horned Owl breeds in old stick nests constructed by other large birds, like crows.

OCCURRENCE
In North America, found in nearly every type of habitat except Arctic tundra. Prefers fragmented landscapes: desert, swamp, prairie, woodland, and urban areas. Rare only in the Appalachian Mountains in the East and in the Sonoran and Mohave Deserts in the West.

Length **18–25in (46–63cm)**	Wingspan **3–5ft (0.9–1.6m)**	Weight **1⅞–5½lb (0.9–2.5kg)**
Social **Solitary**	Lifespan **Up to 28 years**	Status **Secure**

DATE SEEN	WHERE	NOTES

Order **Strigiformes**	Family **Strigidae**	Species ***Strix varia***

Barred Owl

rounded wings

ADULT

IN FLIGHT

large round head

dark eyes

conspicuously yellowish bill

barring on breast

streaking on belly

ADULT

brown upperparts

heavy white spotting

ADULT

barred tail

FLIGHT: glides silently among trees, interspersed with flaps; rarely hovers.

The Barred Owl is more adaptable and aggressive than its close relative the Spotted Owl. Recent range expansions have brought the two species into closer contact, which has resulted in the Barred Owl displacing the Spotted Owl, as well as occasional interbreeding. The Barred Owl is mostly nocturnal, but may also call or hunt during the day.

VOICE Series of hoots in rhythm: *who-cooks-for-you, who-cooks-for-you-all*; also pair duetting (at different pitches), cawing, cackling, and guttural sounds.

NESTING No nest; lays eggs in broken-off branches, cavities, old stick nests; 1–5 eggs; 1 brood; January–September.

FEEDING Perches quietly and waits to spot prey below, then pounces; eats small mammals, birds, amphibians, reptiles, insects, and spiders.

WOODED HABITATS
The Barred Owl is very much at home in dense woodlands, including conifer forests.

OCCURRENCE
Widespread, though not evenly so, in North America from British Columbia across to the Maritimes and much of the eastern US. Found in a variety of wooded habitats—from cypress swamps in the south to conifer rain forest in the Northwest—and in mixed hardwoods.

Length **17–19½in (43–50cm)**	Wingspan **3½ft (1.1m)**	Weight **17–37oz (475–1,050g)**
Social **Solitary**	Lifespan **Up to 18 years**	Status **Secure**

DATE SEEN	WHERE	NOTES

Order **Strigiformes**	Family **Strigidae**	Species ***Strix nebulosa***

Great Gray Owl

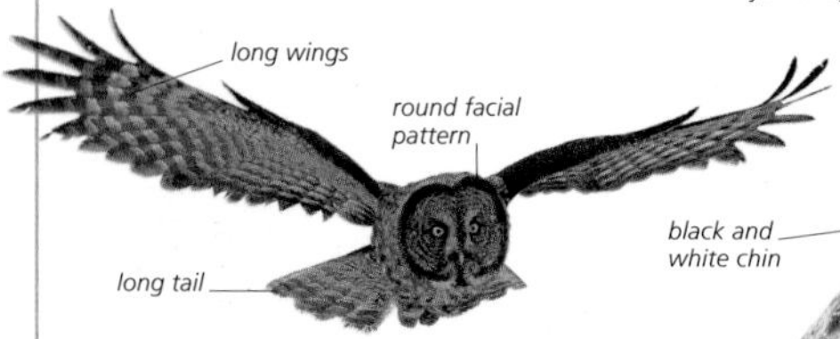

long wings
round facial pattern
long tail
ADULT
long wings
ADULT
IN FLIGHT
white crescents between small yellow eyes
gray and white facial disks
black and white chin
mottled gray upperparts
heavily streaked underparts
thickset body
ADULT

With a thick layer of feathers that insulate it against cold northern winters, the Great Gray Owl is North America's tallest owl, although it weighs less than the Great Horned Owl or Snowy Owl. Its excellent hearing makes it an efficient rodent hunter. Often able to detect prey by sound alone, it will often plunge through deep snow, or into a burrow, to snatch unseen prey. This bird is primarily nocturnal, but may also hunt by daylight, usually at dawn or dusk.

VOICE Slow series of deep hoots, evenly spaced; also variety of hisses and chattering noises around nest site.

NESTING Reuses old eagle or hawk nests, broken-off trees; 2–5 eggs; 1 brood; March–July.

FEEDING Eats rodents and other small mammals; waits to pounce from perch or hunts in flight.

FLIGHT: deep, methodical wing beats, interspersed with glides; hovers while hunting.

SIMILAR SPECIES

GREAT HORNED OWL see p.204
"ear" tufts
barring on belly

BARRED OWL see p.205
dark eyes
barring on breast

MAKESHIFT NEST
The Great Gray Owl often utilizes hollow snags as nesting sites, besides reusing deserted nests.

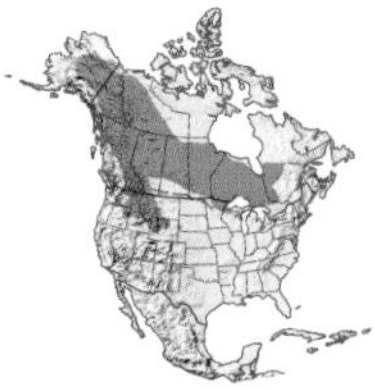

OCCURRENCE
In North America, resident across northern forests from Alaska to Québec, south to Montana and Wyoming. Also resident in Eurasia from Scandinavia to the Russian Far East. Found in taiga, and muskeg (peat bogs), in fir, spruce, and pine forests.

Length **24–33in (61–84cm)**	Wingspan **4½ft (1.4m)**	Weight **1½–3¾lb (0.7–1.7kg)**
Social **Solitary**	Lifespan **Up to 14 years**	Status **Secure**

DATE SEEN	WHERE	NOTES

Order **Strigiformes**	Family **Strigidae**	Species ***Surnia ulula***

Northern Hawk Owl

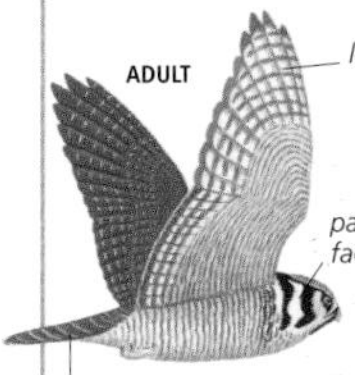

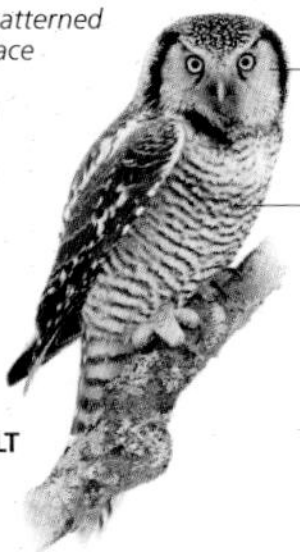

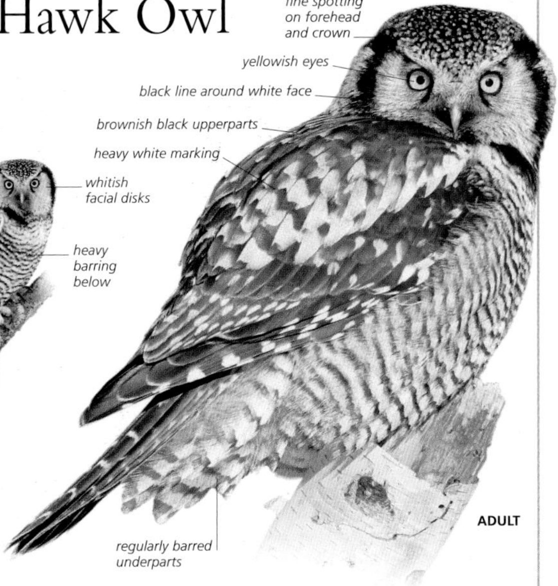

ADULT
long wings
patterned face
long tail
IN FLIGHT

whitish facial disks
heavy barring below
ADULT

fine spotting on forehead and crown
yellowish eyes
black line around white face
brownish black upperparts
heavy white marking
regularly barred underparts
ADULT

Whether swooping low through a bog or perching at the tip of a branch, the Northern Hawk Owl is as falcon-like as it is owl-like, being streamlined, a powerful flier, and an active daytime hunter. It is patchily distributed across the northern North American forests, far from most human settlements, so it is seldom seen—and is not well studied—on its breeding grounds. In winter the bird is somewhat nomadic and is occasionally seen south of its breeding range for a few days or weeks in southern Canada and the northern US.

VOICE Ascending, whistled, drawn-out trill; also chirps, screeches, and yelps.

NESTING Cavities, hollows, broken-off branches, old stick nests, nest boxes; 3–13 eggs; 1 brood; April–August.

FEEDING Swoops like a falcon, from an elevated perch, to pounce on prey; preys mainly on rodents in summer, and on grouse, ptarmigan, and other birds in summer.

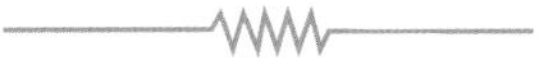

FLIGHT: powerful, deep wing beats; glides; highly maneuverable, occasionally soars.

OCCURRENCE
Breeds across the forests of northern Canada, from Alaska to Québec and Newfoundland, in sparse woodland or mixed conifer forest with swamps, bogs, burnt areas, or storm damage. In winter occasionally moves south to southern Canada, Great Lakes region and New England.

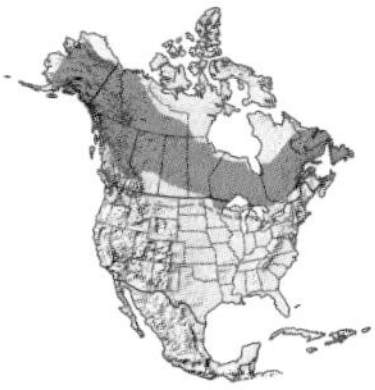

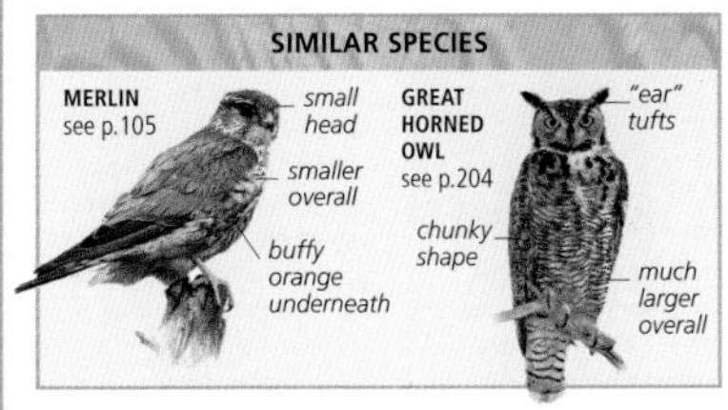

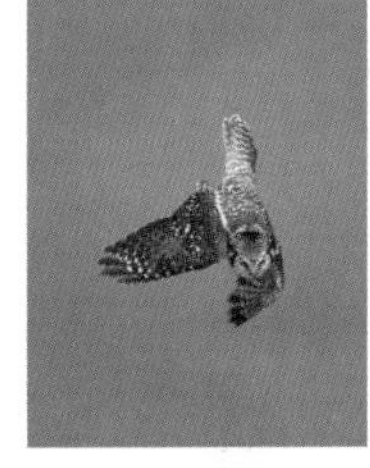

KEEN-EYED OWL
The Northern Hawk Owl hunts mainly by sight, swooping down on prey from a high perch.

SIMILAR SPECIES

MERLIN see p.105

small head
smaller overall
buffy orange underneath

GREAT HORNED OWL see p.204

"ear" tufts
chunky shape
much larger overall

Length **14–17½in (36–44cm)**	Wingspan **31in (80cm)**	Weight **11–12oz (300–350g)**
Social **Family groups**	Lifespan **Up to 10 years**	Status **Secure**

DATE SEEN	WHERE	NOTES

Order **Strigiformes**	Family **Strigidae**	Species ***Glaucidium gnoma***

Northern Pygmy-Owl

spotted crown
round head
yellow eye
yellowish bill
heavily streaked whitish underparts
ADULT
long tail, with brown and white barring

FLIGHT: undulating, rapid series of flaps, followed by glide with wings tucked.

In spite of its small size, the Northern Pygmy-Owl is a fierce hunter. It regularly preys on other birds, including relatively large ones such as Northern Bobwhites. When hunting, it gradually moves closer to its prey by making short, zigzagging flights from tree to tree before pouncing. It is often active during the day, most frequently around dawn and dusk, and in winter is often seen in gardens, swooping down on birds at feeders. The Northern Pygmy-Owl is one of two *Glaucidium* pygmy-owls in North America. Like the rare Ferruginous Pygmy-Owl (*G. brasilianum*), it has "false eyes"—a pair of black-feathered spots on the back of its head. These may act as a deterrent to potential attackers, especially when the owl is sleeping.

VOICE Hollow *poot, poot, poot* calls, 1–2 seconds apart, continuing in series for minutes or more; also excited trill.

NESTING Usually unlined cavity in tree; 2–7 eggs; 1 brood; April–July.

FEEDING Pounces from perch, pinning prey to the ground; eats, insects, reptiles, birds, and mammals.

DAYTIME HUNTER
Unlike most other species of owl, the Northern Pygmy-Owl is often active during the day.

OCCURRENCE
Breeds in western North American mountains from British Columbia to California, Arizona, and New Mexico, and from Mexico to Honduras; can be found in mixed spruce, fir, pine, hemlock, cedar, and oak woodlands; nests at higher elevations, and often winters lower down.

Length **6½–7in (16–18cm)**	Wingspan **15in (38cm)**	Weight **2⅛–2½oz (60–70g)**
Social **Family groups**	Lifespan **Unknown**	Status **Secure**

DATE SEEN	WHERE	NOTES

Order **Strigiformes**	Family **Strigidae**	Species ***Athene cunicularia***

Burrowing Owl

short, rounded wings
ADULT
brown ear feathers
IN FLIGHT
short tail

white streaking on forehead and crown
chest spotted with white
short tail
ADULT

yellow eyes
white contrasting with dark brown band below
brown upperparts with white spotting
white spots
brown streaks on lower belly
ADULT
short tail
long, feathered legs

FLIGHT: buoyant, often undulating; close to ground; sometimes hovers while hunting.

The Burrowing Owl is unique among North American owls in nesting underground. Usually it uses the abandoned burrows of prairie dogs, ground squirrels, armadillos, badgers, and other mammals. Where such burrows are scarce, however—in built-up areas of Florida, notably—it excavates its own burrow, digging out the soil with its bill and scraping it away with its feet. Usually it nests in loose colonies, too. Active by day or night, the Burrowing Owl hunts prey on foot or on the wing. Populations of the bird in southern areas of North America tend to stay there year-round, but those farther north move south to Mexico for the winter.

VOICE *Coo-cooo*, or *ha-haaa*, with accent on second syllable; also clucks, chatters, warbles, and screams.

NESTING Cavity lined with grass, feathers, sometimes animal dung, at end of burrow; 8–10 eggs; 1 brood; March–August.

FEEDING Walks, hops, runs, hovers, or flies from perch to capture mainly insects, and occasionally small mammals, birds, reptiles, and amphibians.

ON THE ALERT
A Burrowing Owl keeps watch from the entrance of its burrow, which can be 10ft (3m) long.

OCCURRENCE
Breeds in Florida, the western US, and southwestern Canada, in a wide range of open, well-drained habitats not prone to flooding, including pastures, plains, deserts, grasslands, and steppes, but also developed area, up to about 6,500ft (2,000m). Partial migrant.

Length **7½–10in (19–25cm)**	Wingspan **21½in (55cm)**	Weight **5oz (150g)**
Social **Loose colonies**	Lifespan **Up to 9 years**	Status **Declining**

DATE SEEN	WHERE	NOTES

Order **Strigiformes**	Family **Strigidae**	Species ***Aegolius funereus***

Boreal Owl

FLIGHT: quick, strong wing beats; adept at maneuvering; glides down to attack prey.

Unusual for owls, the female Boreal Owl is bigger than the male. Males will mate with two or three females in years when voles and other small rodents are abundant. The Boreal Owl roosts on an inconspicuous perch by day and hunts at night, detecting its prey by sound. In the US it is elusive and rarely seen, as it breeds at high elevations in isolated western mountain ranges. White spotting on the crown, a grayish bill, and a black facial disk distinguish the Boreal Owl from the Northern Saw-whet Owl.

VOICE Prolonged series of whistles, usually increasing in volume and intensity toward the end; also screeches and hisses; can be heard from afar.

NESTING Natural and woodpecker-built tree cavities, also nest boxes; 3–6 eggs; 1 brood; March–July.

FEEDING Mainly eats small mammals, occasionally birds and insects; pounces from elevated perch; sometimes stores prey.

DAYTIME ROOSTING
The Boreal Owl roosts in dense vegetation by day, even when the branches are laden with snow.

SIMILAR SPECIES

NORTHERN PYGMY-OWL see p.208
black streaks on belly
longer tail

NORTHERN SAW-WHET OWL see p.211
lacks dark frame to facial disk
dark bill

OCCURRENCE
Breeds in northern forests from Alaska to Newfoundland and Québec, south into the Rockies to Colorado and New Mexico. Largely sedentary, but irregular movements take place south of the breeding range, southward to New England and New York. In the Old World it is called Tengmalm's Owl.

Length **8½–11in (21–28cm)**	Wingspan **21½–24in (54–62cm)**	Weight **3⅜–8oz (90–225g)**
Social **Solitary**	Lifespan **Up to 11 years**	Status **Secure**

DATE SEEN	WHERE	NOTES

Order **Strigiformes**	Family **Strigidae**	Species ***Aegolius acadicus***

Northern Saw-whet Owl

FLIGHT: swift and direct; low to ground with quick wing beats; swoops up to perch.

One of the most secretive yet common and widespread owls in North America, the Northern Saw-whet Owl is much more often heard than seen. Strictly nocturnal, it is concealed as it sleeps by day in thick vegetation, usually in conifers. Although the same site may be used for months if it remains undisturbed, it is never an easy bird to locate and, like most owls, it is elusive, even though it sometimes roosts in large garden trees. When it is discovered, the Northern Saw-whet Owl "freezes," and relies on its camouflage rather than flying off. At night it watches intently from a perch, before swooping down to snatch its prey.

VOICE Series of rapid whistled notes, on constant pitch; can continue for minutes on end; also whines and squeaks.

NESTING Unlined cavity in tree, usually old woodpecker hole or nest box; 4–7 eggs; 1 brood; March–July.

FEEDING Hunts from elevated perch; eats small mammals, including mice and voles; also eats insects and small birds.

RARE SIGHT
Despite being abundant in its range, this shy species is seldom seen.

SIMILAR SPECIES

ELF OWL see p.440
gray back
darker face
smaller overall

BOREAL OWL see p.210
spotted crown
black facial border

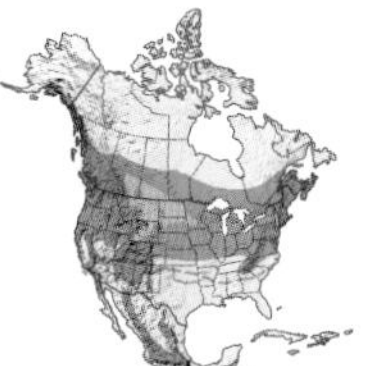

OCCURRENCE
Breeds from Alaska and British Columbia to Maritimes; in the West, south to Mexico; in the East, south to Appalachians; coniferous and mixed deciduous forests, swampy forests, wooded wetlands, bogs. Winters in southern to central states, in open woodlands, pine plantations, and shrubby areas.

Length **7–8½in (18–21cm)**	Wingspan **16½–19in (42–48cm)**	Weight **3½oz (100g)**
Social **Solitary**	Lifespan **Up to 10 years**	Status **Secure**

DATE SEEN	WHERE	NOTES

Order **Strigiformes**	Family **Strigidae**	Species ***Asio otus***

Long-eared Owl

tan patch on outer wing
dark wrist patch
gray tips
IN FLIGHT

long "ear" tufts
rusty face disks
slender body
finely streaked underparts
ADULT

conspicuous "ear" tufts
dark eye-ring
yellow eye
black bill
mottled upperwings
ADULT

FLIGHT: quick, deep wing beats and long glides; often hovers while hunting.

Although widely distributed across Eurasia and North America, the Long-eared Owl is seldom seen, being secretive and nocturnal. By day it roosts high up and out of sight in thick cover. Only at nightfall does it fly out to hunt on the wing over open areas, patrolling for small mammals. Its wing feathers, like those of many other owls, have sound-suppressing structures that allow it to fly almost silently.

VOICE Evenly spaced *hooo* notes, continuously repeated, about 3 seconds apart, typically 10–50 per series, sometimes more; barks when alarmed.

NESTING Old stick nests of ravens, crows, magpies, and hawks; 2–7 eggs; 1 brood; March–July.

FEEDING Preys mainly on mice and other small rodents, occasionally small birds.

OWL ON THE WING
In flight this bird's "ear" tufts are flattened back and not visible, but the face and underwing markings are clearly revealed.

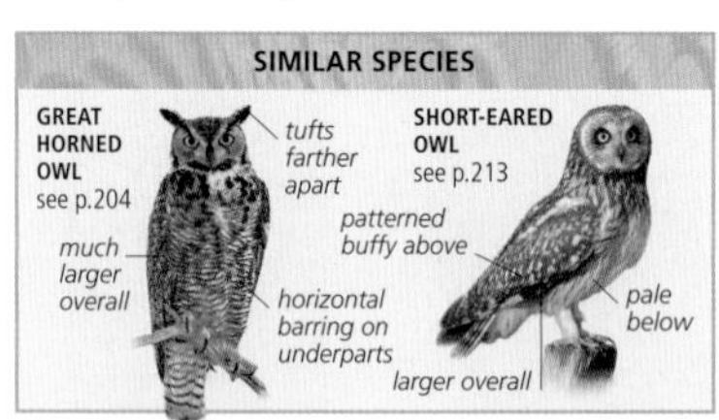

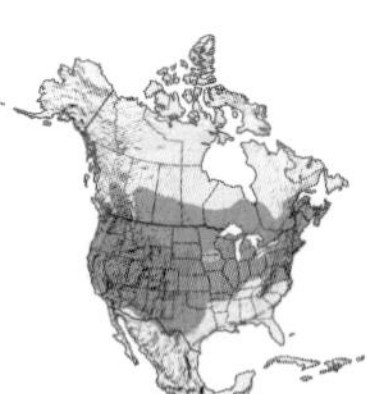

OCCURRENCE
Breeds in old nests, especially in dense stands of cottonwood, willow, juniper, and conifers near open areas suitable for hunting. Occasionally uses old nests in tree holes, cliffs, or on ground in dense vegetation; in winter, up to 100 birds in roosts. Northern birds move south for winter; some western birds resident.

Length **14–15½in (35–40cm)**	Wingspan **34–39in (86–98cm)**	Weight **8–15oz (225–425g)**
Social **Solitary/Winter flocks**	Lifespan **Up to 27 years**	Status **Secure**

DATE SEEN	WHERE	NOTES

Order **Strigiformes**	Family **Strigidae**	Species ***Asio flammeus***

Short-eared Owl

FLIGHT: light, slow, buoyant, harrier-like, maneuverable; often hovers, sometimes soars.

This owl is often seen on cloudy days or toward dusk, floating above and patrolling low, back and forth, over open fields, looking and listening for prey, sometimes with Northern Harriers. Although territorial in the breeding season, it may winter in communal roosts of up to 200 birds, occasionally alongside Long-eared Owls. About 10 subspecies are widely distributed across five continents and numerous islands, including the Greater Antilles, Galápagos, the Falklands and Hawaii. Unlike other North American owls, the Short-eared Owl builds its own nest.

VOICE Usually silent; male courtship call a rapid *hoo hoo hoo*, often given during display flights; about 16 notes in 3 seconds; also barking, *chee-oww*.

NESTING Scrape lined with grass and feathers on ground; 4–7 eggs; 1–2 broods; March–June.

FEEDING Eats small mammals and some birds.

SIMILAR SPECIES

NORTHERN HARRIER see p.111

LONG-EARED OWL see p.212

LOOKOUT POST
Perched on a branch, a Short-eared Owl keeps a wary eye on any intruder on its territory.

OCCURRENCE
Breeds in open areas, including prairie, grasslands, tundra, fields, and marshes across northern North America, from Alaska, the Yukon, and British Columbia to Québec, and Newfoundland, south to the western and central prairies, and east to New England. Partial migrant.

Length **13½–16in (34–41cm)**	Wingspan **2¾–3½ft (0.9–1.1m)**	Weight **11–13oz (325–375g)**
Social **Solitary/Winter flocks**	Lifespan **Up to 13 years**	Status **Vulnerable**

DATE SEEN	WHERE	NOTES

NIGHTJARS & NIGHTHAWKS

ALTHOUGH WIDESPREAD and common throughout North America, species of the family Caprimulgidae are heard more often than they are seen. The exceptions to this rule are the two species of Common Nighthawks that regularly forage for insects at dawn and dusk. All nighthawks are medium-sized birds that use their long wings and wide tails to make rapid and graceful turns to capture their insect prey in the air. They feed predominantly on large flying insects such as moths. Their wide, gaping mouths are surrounded by bristles that aid foraging efforts, and they have very small legs and toes. Both nightjars and nighthawks are similar in coloration and pattern, with a mottled mixture of various browns, grays, and blacks that provides impeccable camouflage when they hide during daylight hours. This ability to hide in plain sight is useful during the nesting season, when all nightjars lay their patterned eggs directly on the ground, without any nest material. The nature of the camouflage pattern of their feathers makes it difficult to distinguish between species when they rest in trees or on the ground. The most reliable means of telling species apart is their voice. If seen, the placement and nature of white markings, combined with the style of flight, are the best means of identification. Most members of the family migrate and move southward as insects become dormant in the North. Nightjars are also known as "Goatsuckers" because in ancient Greece it was believed that they sucked blood from goats.

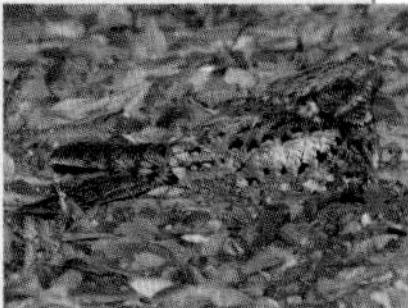

PART OF THE LITTER
Not many bird species match the leaf litter of the forest floor as well as nightjars, as this Chuck-will's-widow shows.

SITTING PRETTY
Unusually for birds, members of the nightjar family, such as this Common Nighthawk, often perch lengthwise on branches.

ELEGANT HUNTER
This Lesser Nighthawk male soars through the air, hunting for insects, which it catches on the wing.

Order **Caprimulgiformes**	Family **Caprimulgidae**	Species ***Chordeiles minor***

Common Nighthawk

FLIGHT: erratic flight with deep wing beats interrupted by banking glides.

Common Nighthawks are easy to spot as they swoop over parking lots, city streets, and athletics fields during the warm summer months. They are more active at dawn and dusk than at night, pursuing insect prey up to 250ft (80m) in the air. The species once took the name Booming Nighthawk, a reference to the remarkable flight display of the male birds, during which they dive rapidly towards the ground, causing their feathers to vibrate and produce a characteristic "booming" sound.

VOICE Nasal *peeent*; also soft clucking noises from both sexes.

NESTING Nests on ground on rocks, wood, leaves, or sand, also on gravel-covered rooftops in urban areas; 2 eggs; 1 brood; May–July.

FEEDING Catches airborne insects, especially moths, mayflies, and beetles, also ants; predominantly active at dusk and dawn.

A RARE SIGHT
Common Nighthawks are seen in flight more often than other caprimulgids, but it is a rare treat to see one resting on a perch.

SIMILAR SPECIES

LESSER NIGHTHAWK more buffy barring on underside of wings; see p.441

COMMON PAURAQUE longer, rounded tail with white patches

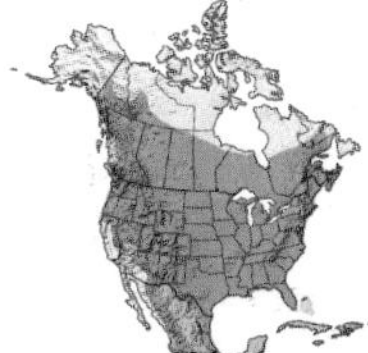

OCCURRENCE
Wide variety of open habitats, such as cleared forests, fields, grassland, beaches, and sand dunes; also common in urban areas, including cities. The most common and widespread North American nighthawk, this species also occurs in Central and South America.

Length **9–10in (23–26cm)**	Wingspan **22–24in (56–61cm)**	Weight **2⅞oz (80g)**
Social **Solitary/Flocks**	Lifespan **Up to 9 years**	Status **Declining**

DATE SEEN	WHERE	NOTES

Order **Caprimulgiformes**	Family **Caprimulgidae**	Species ***Phalaenoptilus nuttallii***

Common Poorwill

This nocturnal bird is the smallest North American nightjar, with much shorter wings than its relatives, and a stubbier tail, but a comparatively large head. In 1946, scientists discovered that it was able to go into a state of torpor, similar to mammalian hibernation. During "hibernation" its body temperature is about 64°F (18°C) instead of the usual 106°F (41°C), and it may remain in this state for several weeks during cold weather when food is unavailable. This may account for its colloquial name, "sleeping one," among the Hopi of the Southwest. Males and females are similar in appearance, but the male has whitish corners to its tail, while the female's are more buffy.

VOICE Call low *purr-WHEEOO* or *pooor-WEELLUP*, whistled at night when perched in the open.

NESTING Eggs laid on the ground among rocks, sometimes under shrubs; 2 eggs; 2 broods; May–August.

FEEDING Jumps up from the ground and flies briefly to capture night-flying insects, such as moths and beetles.

FLIGHT: brief, erratic; with slow and deep wing beats.

GRAVEL ROADS
The Common Poorwill uses gravel roads as a convenient place from which to jump at flying insects.

SIMILAR SPECIES

CHUCK-WILL'S-WIDOW see p.441
larger overall
browner upperparts

WHIP-POOR-WILL see p.441
larger bill
large white patches on tail

OCCURRENCE
Breeds from the western US southward into Mexico, in arid habitats with much bare ground and sparse vegetation, such as grasses, shrubs, and cacti. Winters in northern Mexico.

Length **7½–8½in (19–21cm)**	Wingspan **15½–19in (40–48cm)**	Weight **1¼–2oz (35–55g)**
Social **Solitary**	Lifespan **Up to 3 years**	Status **Secure**

DATE SEEN	WHERE	NOTES

Family **Apodidae**

SWIFTS

SWIFTS SPEND ALMOST all their daylight hours, as well as many night hours plying the skies. The most aerial birds in North America—if not the world—swifts eat, drink, court, mate, and even sleep on the wing. Unsurprisingly, swifts are some of the fastest and most acrobatic flyers of the bird world. Several species have been clocked at over 100mph (160kph). They feed on insects caught in zooming, zigzagging, and dashing pursuits. The family name, based on the Greek *apous*, which means "without feet," originates from the ancient belief that swifts had no feet and lived their entire lives in the air.

ACROBATIC FLOCKS
White-throated Swifts are usually seen in groups of a handful to hundreds of birds.

Family **Trochilidae**

HUMMINGBIRDS

FOUND ONLY IN the Americas, hummingbirds are sometimes referred to as the crown jewels of the bird world. The first sight of a glittering hummingbird can be a life-changing experience. The amount of iridescence in their plumage varies from almost none to what seems like every feather. Most North American male hummingbirds have a colorful throat patch called a gorget, but females tend to lack this shiny attribute. Because iridescent colors are structural and not pigment-based, a gorget can often appear blackish until seen at the correct angle toward the light. Hummingbirds are the only birds that can fly backward, an adaptation that allows them to move easily among and between flowers. Flying sideways, up, down, and hovering are also within hummingbirds' abilities, and all are achieved by their unique figure-eight, rapid wing strokes and reduced wing bone structure. Their long, thin bills give them access to nectar in tubular flowers. Of the 14 species of hummingbirds in the West, about six are restricted to southwestern states. A couple of western species are restricted to California's coastal habitats, and one, the Rufous Hummingbird, breeds all the way north to Alaska.

AGGRESSIVE MALES
This male Ruby-throated Hummingbird defends his territory from a perch. This species is rare in the West.

NECTAR FEEDERS
All North American hummingbirds, such as this Black-chinned, subsist on nectar from wildflowers.

Order **Apodiformes**	Family **Apodidae**	Species ***Chaetura vauxi***

Vaux's Swift

This acrobatic and fast-flying bird is North America's smallest swift; it is slightly shorter than its eastern counterpart, the Chimney Swift. Its western range, small size, rapid and fluttering flight, and distinctive shape help distinguish this species from others. Vaux's Swifts are typically found foraging in flocks over mature forest and can be easily spotted on cold, cloudy days, often mixed with other swifts. Very large flocks are also sighted seemingly "pouring" into communal roost sites at dusk. It is fairly reliant on mature forest, and areas where this habitat has diminished have seen a corresponding decline in populations of Vaux's Swift. They may wander more widely in search of food in poor weather, even over towns.

VOICE High, insect-like chips and twittering in flight, often ending in buzzy trill.

NESTING Shallow cup of twigs, needles, and saliva attached to inside of hollow tree, rarely on chimneys; 4–6 eggs; 1 brood; June–September.

FEEDING Catches a wide variety of flying insects on the wing, including flies, moths, bees, beetles, and many others.

FLIGHT: swift, erratic flight; shallow, fluttering wing beats; acrobatic and bat-like when feeding.

AERIAL ACROBAT
Vaux's Swifts rarely land, spending all day hawking insects and even mating in flight.

SIMILAR SPECIES

BLACK SWIFT see p.441
larger overall
blackish body
longer, notched tail

CHIMNEY SWIFT see p.442
longer tail and wings

OCCURRENCE
Occurs in North America from southeastern Alaska to California, where it breeds primarily in coniferous forests, nesting in large, hollow trunks; forages widely in many habitats. Resident population in Mexico, North American migrants move to Central America.

Length **4¾in (12cm)**	Wingspan **12in (30cm)**	Weight **½–⅞oz (15–25g)**
Social **Migrant flocks**	Lifespan **Up to 7 years**	Status **Declining**

DATE SEEN	WHERE	NOTES

Order **Apodiformes**	Family **Apodidae**	Species ***Aeronautes saxatalis***

White-throated Swift

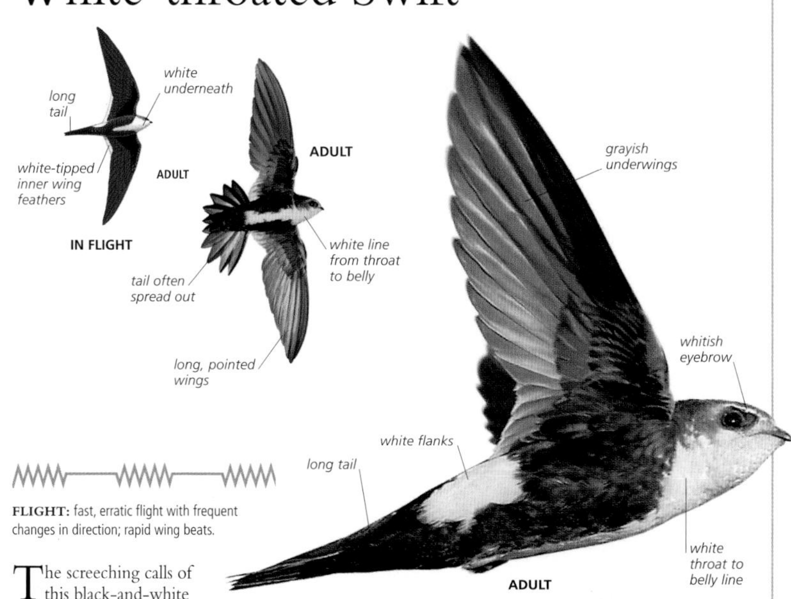

FLIGHT: fast, erratic flight with frequent changes in direction; rapid wing beats.

The screeching calls of this black-and-white swift are a familiar sound in canyon country. Often seen racing around the cliffs in which they nest, White-throated Swifts are distinguished from other North American swifts by their black-and-white plumage and longer tail. This is also the only swift that winters in North America in large numbers. This species has become increasingly common in urban areas, as it has adapted to nesting in human structures that resemble its natural nest sites, such as bridges and quarries. As with other swifts, huge flocks of White-throated Swifts can be seen rushing into communal roosts at dusk, particularly outside the breeding season.

VOICE Drawn-out, descending, shrill twitter, *tee-tee-tee-ter-ter-ter-trr-trr-trr*, commonly given by flocks; occasionally gives two-note call in flight or sharp single note.

NESTING Shallow cup of feathers and saliva in rock, wall, crevice, or human structure; 3–6 eggs; 1 brood; March–August.

FEEDING Forages on a variety of aerial insects.

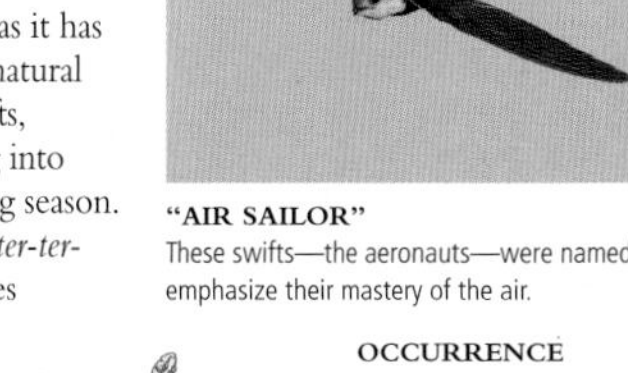

"AIR SAILOR"
These swifts—the aeronauts—were named to emphasize their mastery of the air.

SIMILAR SPECIES

VIOLET-GREEN SWALLOW ♂ slower flight and wing beats; see p.292

OCCURRENCE
Breeds in western North America, from British Columbia to California, eastward to the Dakotas, and south to New Mexico. Prefers hilly and mountainous areas; forages over a wide variety of habitats and winters in extreme southwestern North America, in communal roosts in canyons.

Length **6¾in (17cm)**	Wingspan **15in (38cm)**	Weight **1¹⁄₁₆–1⁹⁄₁₆oz (30–45g)**
Social **Flocks**	Lifespan **Unknown**	Status **Secure**

DATE SEEN	WHERE	NOTES

Order **Apodiformes**	Family **Trochilidae**	Species ***Archilochus alexandri***

Black-chinned Hummingbird

The Black-chinned Hummingbird is widespread across the western US, where it is found in a number of different environments. It readily accepts offerings of sugar water from birdfeeders. During courtship, the males perform a distinctive dive display comprising several broad arcs in addition to a short, back-and-forth "shuttle" display. The latter is accompanied by a droning noise produced by the bird's wings.

VOICE Call a soft, thick *chic*; fast, buzzy *tsi-tsi-tsi-tsi-tsi-tsi-tsi-tsi* is used to chase off other birds; song soft, warbling, very rarely heard.

NESTING Tiny cup of plant down, with leaves or lichen on the exterior, bound with spider's silk; usually built in a deciduous tree; 2 eggs; 1–2 broods; April–August.

FEEDING Drinks nectar from flowers; eats small insects and spiders, caught aerially or gleaned from foliage.

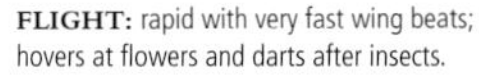

FLIGHT: rapid with very fast wing beats; hovers at flowers and darts after insects.

TAIL WAGGER
Black-chinned Hummingbirds regularly wag their tails from side to side while feeding.

OCCURRENCE
Widespread in a variety of habitats, particularly scrub and woodlands close to rivers and streams, and irrigated urban areas; also found in drier habitats; forages away from breeding habitat where nectar sources are found. Winters along the Pacific Coast of Mexico.

Length **3½in (9cm)**	Wingspan **4¾in (12cm)**	Weight **1/16–3/16oz (2–5g)**
Social **Solitary**	Lifespan **Up to 8 years**	Status **Secure**

DATE SEEN	WHERE	NOTES

Order **Apodiformes**	Family **Trochilidae**	Species ***Calypte anna***

Anna's Hummingbird

pale throat
MALE
square tail
IN FLIGHT
rose-red head, sides of neck, and throat
short, straight, black bill
iridescent green upperparts
green upperparts
slightly notched, dark green tail
grayish underparts
greenish sides and flanks
MALE
green crown and nape
reddish spots or flecks on throat
pale gray underparts
FEMALE
rounded, green tail
mottled rosy crown
IMMATURE (MALE)

The most common garden hummingbird along the Pacific Coast from British Columbia to Baja California, the iridescent rose-red helmet of a male Anna's Hummingbird is spectacular and distinctive. The females are rather drab by comparison. This adaptable hummingbird has expanded its range dramatically in the last century because of the availability of garden flowers and feeders. It previously bred only in areas of dense evergreen shrubs along the coast of southern California. The males perform an impressive diving display to court females.

VOICE Call a hard, sharp *tsit*, often doubled or given in series when perched; fast, buzzy chatter used to chase off other birds; song variable series of thin, high, buzzing, warbled notes.

NESTING Tiny cup of mostly plant down, with lichen on the exterior, bound with spider's silk, built in trees or shrubs; 2 eggs; 2 broods; December–July.

FEEDING Drinks nectar from flowers; eats small insects and spiders, caught aerially or gleaned from foliage.

FLIGHT: rapid flight with very fast wing beats; hovers at flowers and darts after insects.

VARIABLE THROAT
Mature female Anna's Hummingbirds often show small iridescent patches on their throats.

OCCURRENCE
Primary breeding habitat is dense coastal shrubbery and open woodland; also human areas. Habitat during migration and in winter largely dependent on available nectar sources; range expands northward and eastward during this time. Some birds winter in northwestern Mexico; vagrant in the East.

Length **4in (10cm)**	Wingspan **5in (13cm)**	Weight **3/32–7/32oz (3–6g)**
Social **Solitary**	Lifespan **Up to 8 years**	Status **Secure**

DATE SEEN	WHERE	NOTES

Order **Apodiformes**	Family **Trochilidae**	Species ***Selasphorus platycercus***

Broad-tailed Hummingbird

The trilling sound generated by the male Broad-tailed Hummingbird's wings in flight is commonly heard in the alpine meadows of the Rocky Mountains and is likely a substitute for song during displays. Birds may arrive on their breeding grounds before the snow melts or flowers bloom, and they survive on insects and tree sap. During courtship, males perform spectacular dives, with their wings trilling loudly during the descent. They also have a buzzing display, bobbing back and forth in front of females.

VOICE Call a sharp *chik*; also short, buzzy warning call, *tssrr*; chase call variable, squeaky twittering.

NESTING Tiny cup of plant down, with lichen and leaves on exterior, bound with spider's silk, and built in trees; 1–2 eggs; 1–2 broods; April–August.

FEEDING Sucks nectar from flowers; insects and arthropods caught in air or on foliage.

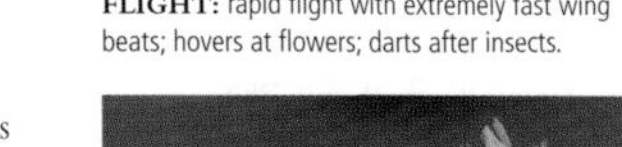

FLIGHT: rapid flight with extremely fast wing beats; hovers at flowers; darts after insects.

LOUD APPROACH
Whirring and trilling wings often announce the presence of a male Broad-tailed Hummingbird.

RESTING AFTER FEEDING
This male, perched on a twig, rests after an energy-draining bout of feeding.

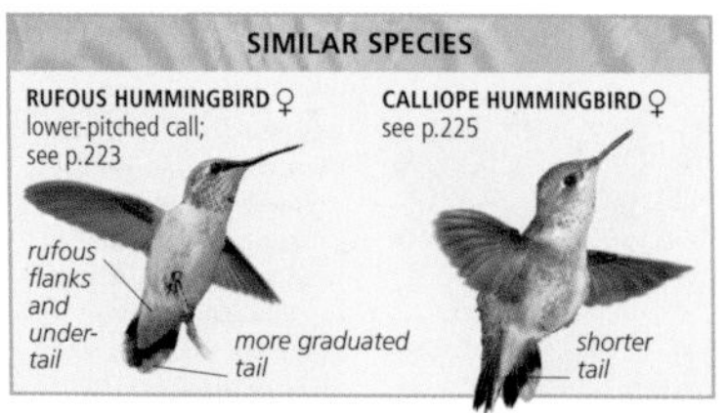

OCCURRENCE
Inhabits a variety of mid- to high-elevation forest types; early migrants arrive in March in southern states and most leave by September; some individuals winter along the Gulf Coast. Winters mostly in fairly arid habitats in northeastern Mexico. Also breeds in northern Mexico.

Length **4in (10cm)**	Wingspan **5in (13cm)**	Weight **$\frac{3}{32}$–$\frac{5}{32}$oz (3–4g)**
Social **Solitary**	Lifespan **Up to 12 years**	Status **Secure**

DATE SEEN	WHERE	NOTES

Order **Apodiformes**	Family **Trochilidae**	Species ***Selasphorus rufus***

Rufous Hummingbird

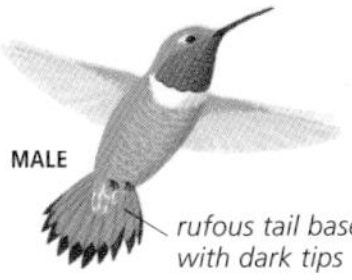

MALE
rufous tail base with dark tips
IN FLIGHT

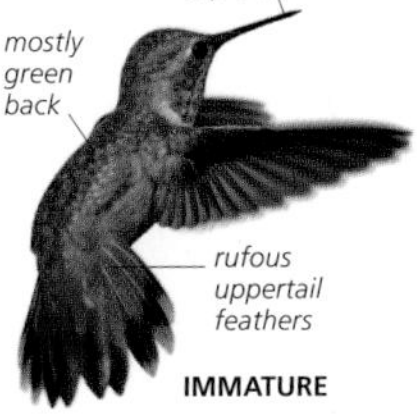

wrinkled top bill
mostly green back
rufous uppertail feathers
IMMATURE

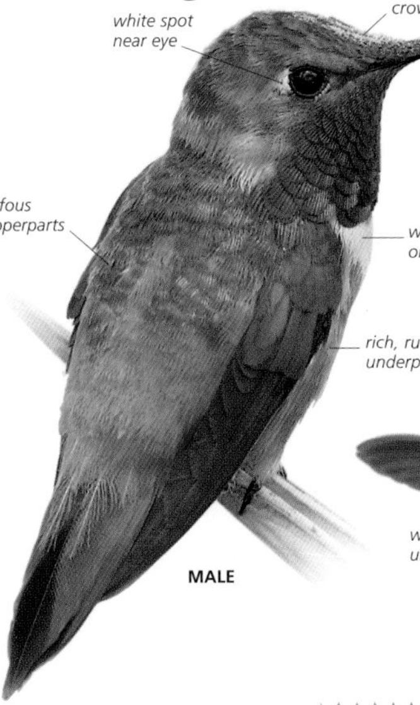

green to bronze-green crown
white spot near eye
straight, smooth bill
rufous upperparts
white patch on breast
rich, rufous underparts
MALE

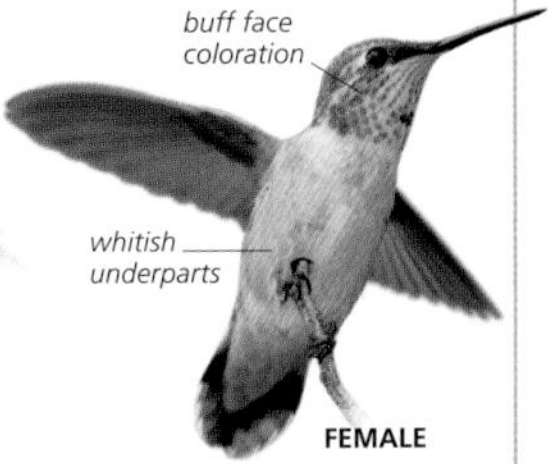

buff face coloration
whitish underparts
FEMALE

One of the most aggressive hummingbirds, the Rufous Hummingbird packs quite a punch, despite its small size; it often chases other hummingbirds away from nectar sources. This bird also breeds farther north than any other North American species of hummingbird and undertakes a lengthy migration. Males are recognizable by their overall fiery orange-rufous color, but females and immature birds are difficult to distinguish from Allen's Hummingbirds.

VOICE Call a hard *chuk*, sometimes in steady series or doubled; also short, buzzy warning call, *tssrr*; chase call a fast, raspy twitter, *tzzerr tichupy tichupy*.

NESTING Tiny cup of plant down, lichen, and other plant matter on exterior, bound with spider's silk, in shrubs or trees; 2 eggs; 1–2 broods; April–July.

FEEDING Drinks nectar from flowers and sap from trees; catches small insects and other arthropods in the air or gleans them off foliage.

FLIGHT: fast flight with extremely rapid wing beats; hovers at flowers; darts after insects.

SIMILAR SPECIES

BROAD-TAILED HUMMINGBIRD ♀ higher-pitched call; see p.222

ALLEN'S HUMMINGBIRD ♂ see p.224

dull pinkish flanks
broad tail

entirely green back

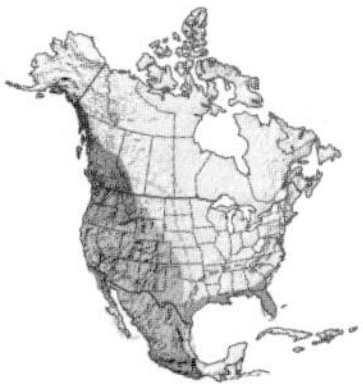

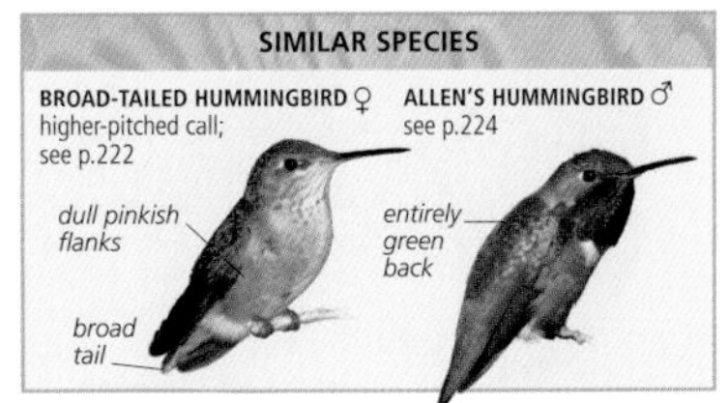

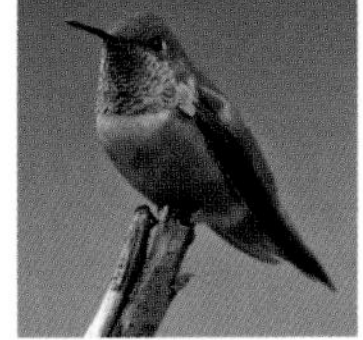

FIERY MALE
With temperaments matching their bold, flame-like color, males aggressively defend territories.

OCCURRENCE
Breeds in old-growth forest clearings, bushy country, as well as urban gardens; early migrants appear in March; most leave by August; it has become a regular winter inhabitant along the Gulf Coast and southern California; fall or winter vagrants are becoming more common in the East.

Length **3½in (9cm)**	Wingspan **5in (13cm)**	Weight **3/32–7/32oz (3–6g)**
Social **Solitary**	Lifespan **Up to 12 years**	Status **Secure**

DATE SEEN	WHERE	NOTES

Order **Apodiformes**	Family **Trochilidae**	Species ***Selasphorus sasin***

Allen's Hummingbird

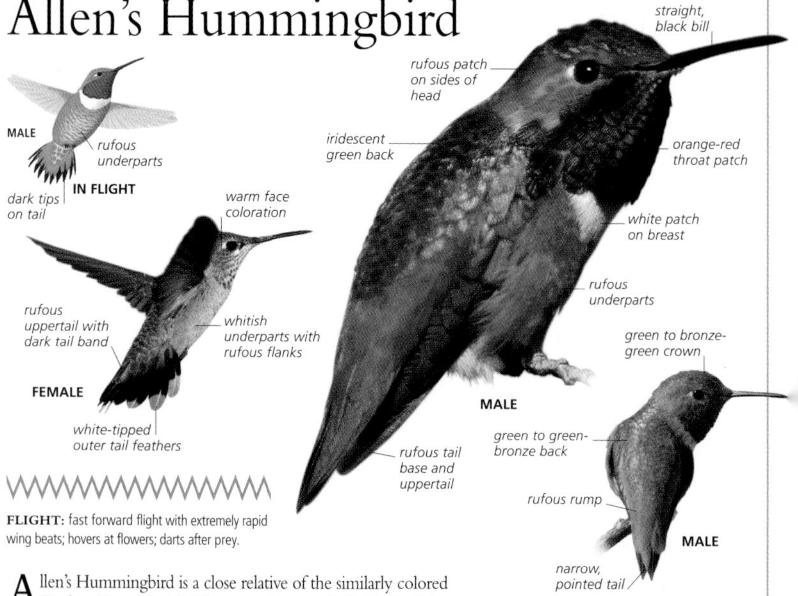

MALE
rufous underparts
dark tips on tail
IN FLIGHT
warm face coloration
rufous uppertail with dark tail band
whitish underparts with rufous flanks
FEMALE
white-tipped outer tail feathers
straight, black bill
rufous patch on sides of head
iridescent green back
orange-red throat patch
white patch on breast
rufous underparts
MALE
rufous tail base and uppertail
green to bronze-green crown
green to green-bronze back
rufous rump
MALE
narrow, pointed tail

FLIGHT: fast forward flight with extremely rapid wing beats; hovers at flowers; darts after prey.

Allen's Hummingbird is a close relative of the similarly colored Rufous Hummingbird. In some plumages, individuals of these two species are hard, or even impossible, to tell apart. The range of this species is limited to the Pacific Coast and the adjacent interior of the western US from Oregon to California. Male Allen's Hummingbirds perform a spectacular flight display near females, which includes dives and a pendulum-like side-to-side motion, during which they make odd, buzzy, almost metallic sounds.

VOICE Call a hard *chuk*, in steady series or doubled; short, buzzy warning call, *tssrr*; chase call a fast, raspy twitter, *tzzerr tichupy tichupy*.

NESTING Tiny cup of plant matter and lichen, lined with plant down, bound with spider's silk, built in shrubs or trees; 2 eggs; 2 broods; February–July.

FEEDING Drinks nectar from a variety of flowers; catches small insects and spiders aerially or picks them off foliage.

EARLY BREEDER
Males may arrive on the California coast and establish territories there as early as January.

SIMILAR SPECIES

RUFOUS HUMMINGBIRD ♂ see p.223
mostly rufous back

CALLIOPE HUMMINGBIRD ♀ softer call; see p.225
smaller overall
shorter tail
dull buffy flanks

OCCURRENCE
The subspecies *S. s. sasin* breeds in a narrow belt of fog-affected habitat along the US west coast January–August; the second subspecies (*S. s. sedentarius*) is resident in dense shrubs on the Channel Islands of southern California and parts of the mainland; very rare east to Gulf Coast.

Length **3½in (9cm)**	Wingspan **5in (13cm)**	Weight **1/16–5/32oz (2–4g)**
Social **Solitary**	Lifespan **Up to 5 years**	Status **Secure**

DATE SEEN	WHERE	NOTES

Order **Apodiformes**	Family **Trochilidae**	Species ***Stellula calliope***

Calliope Hummingbird

streaked, rose throat patch
MALE
short, square tail
IN FLIGHT
small, dark streaks on throat
bronzy green above
buffy flanks
FEMALE
short, straight bill
purple, beard-like throat patch
pale breast
iridescent greenish upperparts
MALE
short tail

FLIGHT: rapid with very fast wing beats; hovers at flowers and darts after insects.

The Calliope Hummingbird is North America's smallest bird. Despite its diminutive size, it is just as territorial as other hummingbird species; the females even attack squirrels trying to rob their nests. The streaky, purplish throat patch of the males is unique, but the plainer females can be confused with other hummingbird species when their small size is not evident in a direct comparison. The male courtship display includes a number of J-shaped dives, which are accompanied by a high *tzzt-zing* at the bottom, in addition to a buzzing hover display in front of a female.

VOICE Relatively silent for a hummingbird; call a soft, high *chip*, sometimes doubled or repeated; series of high buzzes and chips used to chase off other birds.

NESTING Tiny cup of plant material and lichen, bound with spider's silk and lined with plant down, usually under an overhanging conifer branch; 2 eggs; 1 brood; May–August.

FEEDING Catches small insects aerially or gleans insects and spiders from foliage; also drinks nectar.

ATTRACTED TO SAP
The Calliope Hummingbird commonly feeds on sap and the insects attracted to it.

MOUNTAIN GEM
Like other hummingbirds, this mountain dweller hovers to take nectar from flowers.

SIMILAR SPECIES

OCCURRENCE
Present in western mountains primarily March–September; breeds mostly in coniferous mountain forests, meadows, and thickets; spring migrants found in a variety of lower elevation habitats; fall migrants are found at higher elevations; very rare in winter along the Gulf Coast.

Length **3¼in (8cm)**	Wingspan **4¼in (10.5cm)**	Weight **1/16–5/32oz (2–4g)**
Social **Solitary**	Lifespan **Up to 12 years**	Status **Secure**

DATE SEEN	WHERE	NOTES

Family **Trogonidae**

TROGONS

TROGONS ARE WIDESPREAD birds of the tropical and subtropical forests of the world, but only one, the Elegant Trogon, regularly occurs north of Mexico. Like woodpeckers, parrots, and some other arboreal birds, they have four toes arranged in opposing pairs for grasping branches. Uniquely in trogons, the inner toe is reversed, instead of the outer toe as in other birds. Most species have long, square tails with distinctive black-and-white bands on the underside. Trogons have a slow, undulating flight pattern similar to that of woodpeckers, although they can easily outpace a predator if necessary. Trogons are also famously thin-skinned—to such an extent that their feathers are poorly anchored and easily fall out when they fly.

SIT AND WAIT
This Elegant Trogon spends most of its time sitting quietly while waiting for prey.

Family **Alcedinidae**

KINGFISHERS

KINGFISHERS ARE A PRIMARILY tropical family that apparently originated in Australasia. Three species are found in the US and Canada, but only one, the Belted Kingfisher, is widespread. Like most species of kingfishers, these birds are large-headed and large-billed but have comparatively short legs and toes. Although North American kingfishers lack the array of bright blues, greens, and reds associated with their tropical and European counterparts, they are striking birds, distinguished by chestnut-colored chest bands and white underparts. North American kingfisher species are primarily fish-eaters but also eat frogs and crayfish. After catching a fish, they routinely stun their prey by beating it against a perch, before turning the fish around so that it can be eaten head first. Smaller species such as the Green Kingfisher are shy and not often seen. North American and South American kingfishers are almost always found near water, including lakes, estuaries, rivers, and brooks. In other parts of the world, however, such as Australia, several species are terrestrial, and live in a variety of habitats ranging from savanna to woodland, often far from water.

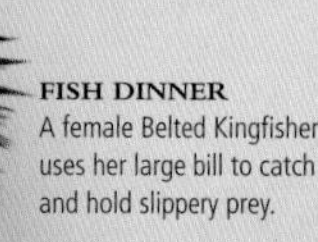

FISH DINNER
A female Belted Kingfisher uses her large bill to catch and hold slippery prey.

DAZZLING GEM
The tropical Green Kingfisher, which is only found in Texas, is a small and striking species.

Order **Coraciiformes**	Family **Alcedinidae**	Species ***Megaceryle alcyon***

Belted Kingfisher

Its stocky body, double-pointed crest, large head, and contrasting white collar distinguish the Belted Kingfisher from other species in its range. This kingfisher's loud and far-carrying rattles are heard more often than the bird is seen. Interestingly, it is one of the few birds in North America in which the female is more colorful than the male. The Belted Kingfisher can be found in a large variety of aquatic habitats, both coastal and inland, vigorously defending its territory, all year round.

VOICE Harsh mechanical rattle given in flight or from a perch; sometimes emits screams or trill-like warble during breeding.

NESTING Unlined chamber in subterranean burrow 3–6ft (1–2m) deep, excavated in earthen bank usually over water, but sometimes in ditches, sand, or gravel pits; 6–7 eggs; 1 brood; March–July.

FEEDING Plunge-dives from branches or wires to catch a wide variety of fish near the surface, including sticklebacks and trout; also takes crustaceans, such as crayfish.

FLIGHT: strongly flaps its wings and then glides after two or three beats; frequently hovers.

SIMILAR SPECIES

RINGED KINGFISHER ♂ see p.445

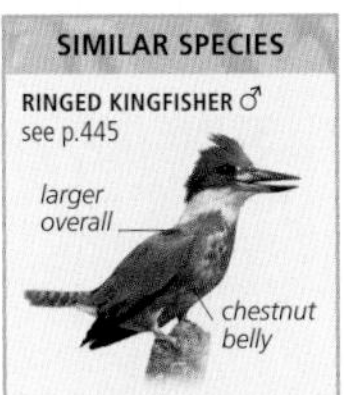

CATCH OF THE DAY
The female's chestnut belly band and flanks are clearly visible here as she perches with her catch.

OCCURRENCE
Breeds and winters around clear, open waters of streams, rivers, lakes, estuaries, and protected marine shorelines, where perches are available and prey is visible. Avoids water with emergent vegetation. Northern populations migrate south to Mexico, Central America, and the West Indies.

Length **11–14in (28–35cm)**	Wingspan **19–23in (48–58cm)**	Weight **5–6oz (150–175g)**
Social **Solitary**	Lifespan **Unknown**	Status **Secure**

DATE SEEN	WHERE	NOTES

WOODPECKERS

THE THREE GROUPS of closely related species that constitute the family Picidae are found throughout North America. They are a physically striking group adapted to living on tree trunks.

WOODPECKERS

Typical North American woodpecker species share a distinct set of characteristics and behaviors. They use pecking and drumming to construct nests and communicate. This is made possible by a very thick skull, adapted to withstand the shock of continually pecking wood. Woodpeckers nest in cavities in dead trees, and are vulnerable to the loss of their specialized habitats due to forest clearing.

SAPSUCKERS

Sapsuckers feed on tree sap as a primary source of nourishment for both adults and their young. They have tongues tipped with stiff hairs to allow sap to stick to them. The holes sapsuckers create in order to extract sap from trees attract insects, which make up the main protein source in the sapsucker diet. Because sapsuckers damage living trees, some orchard growers consider them to be pests.

BALANCING ACT
The Yellow-bellied Sapsucker rests its stiff tail against a tree to maintain its balance.

FLICKERS

Flickers are relatively large members of the family Picidae and spend more time feeding on the ground than other woodpeckers, consuming ants and other insects. They often forage in open areas around human habitation. Flickers are notable for their colorful underwing feathers and their distinctive white rumps.

RED ALERT
With its crimson head, the Red-headed Woodpecker is an instantly recognizable North American birds.

COMMON FLICKER
The Northern Flicker can be found across the entire North American continent. This male belongs to the western red-shafted form.

Order **Piciformes**	Family **Picidae**	Species ***Melanerpes lewis***

Lewis' Woodpecker

long, broad wings

ADULT

blackish green rump

very dark upperparts

IN FLIGHT

dull brown head

no gray collar

blackish brown upperparts

JUVENILE

blackish green head

broad silvery gray collar

black upperparts with glossy green sheen

black bill

dark red forehead and cheek

silvery and rosy red underparts

ADULT (SUMMER)

blackish green tail

FLIGHT: rather slow, deep wing beats; flight is level rather than undulating.

The iridescent dark green back and the salmon-red abdomen of Lewis' Woodpecker distinguishes it from any other bird in North America. Juveniles, however, have a brownish head and underparts and lack the gray collar, red face, and pink belly. Lewis' Woodpecker is also notably quieter than other woodpeckers, but it aggressively defends its food sources from other woodpeckers, especially in the winter. During flight, the bird accomplishes acrobatic maneuvers in pursuit of flying insects, sallying out from a perch in order to catch them. Alexander Wilson, the founder of North American ornithology, named this species in 1811, to honor Meriwether Lewis, because it was collected during the Lewis and Clark expedition.

VOICE *Churrs* sound; drumming not loud.
NESTING Cavity nester, usually in dead tree trunks, with preference for natural cavities and previously used nest holes; 6–7 eggs; 1 brood; May–August.
FEEDING Eats a variety of flying insects during breeding season; acorns, other nuts, and fruits, at other times.

FAVORITE HANGOUT
This bird is found in a variety of habitats, but is most common in Ponderosa pine forests.

LOVE NEST
Lewis' Woodpecker excavates cavities in dead trees for nesting purposes.

OCCURRENCE
Prefers open Ponderosa pine forests for breeding, especially old growth stands that have been modified by burning. Also found in riverine woodlands with cottonwood trees. Has a distinct fondness for open canopy. In winter, favors oak woodlands and nut and fruit orchards.

Length **10–11in (25–28cm)**	Wingspan **19–20in (48–51cm)**	Weight **3¼–5oz (90–150g)**
Social **Solitary**	Lifespan **Unknown**	Status **Localized**

DATE SEEN	WHERE	NOTES

Order **Piciformes**	Family **Picidae**	Species ***Melanerpes formicivorus***

Acorn Woodpecker

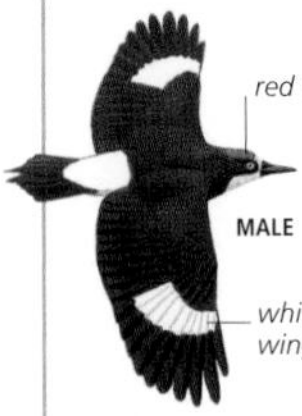

red crown
MALE
white wing patch
IN FLIGHT

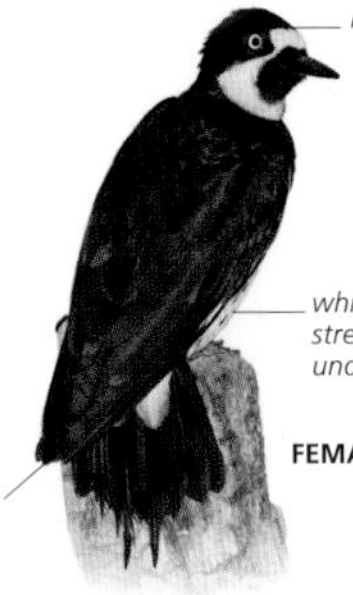

black crown
white, finely streaked underparts
black wing feathers
FEMALE

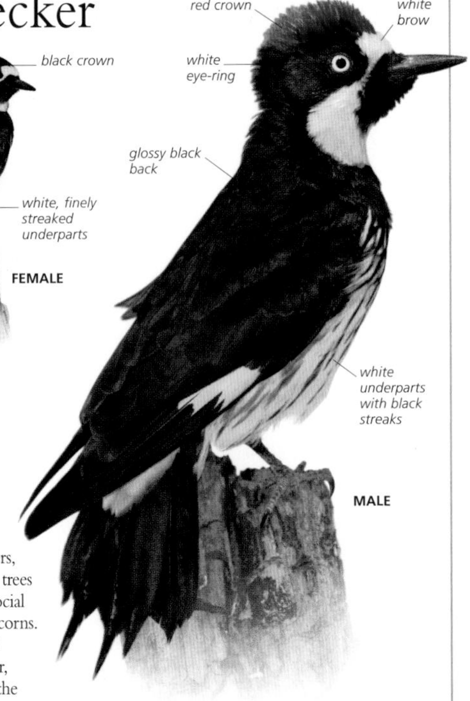

red crown
white brow
white eye-ring
glossy black back
white underparts with black streaks
MALE

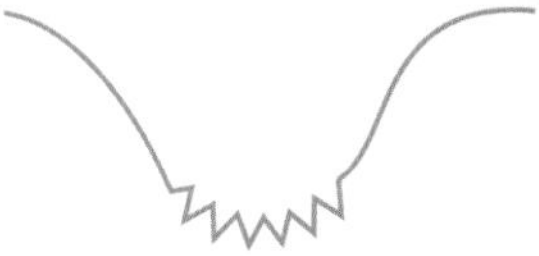

FLIGHT: typical woodpecker undulations with short periods of wing beats then closing of wings.

Unlike other North American woodpeckers, the Acorn Woodpecker stores its food in trees for its winter supply. A very loud and highly social species, family members cooperate to gather acorns. The birds prefer old forests because these tend to produce more acorns and the wood is softer, making it easier to excavate cavities and store the acorns. This makes the species highly dependent on oak trees. They adopt areas where there is more than one species of oak, so that if one species fails to produce, another might yield acorns.

VOICE Primary year-round call a loud *waka-waka-waka*, repeated often; drumming accelerates towards the end.

NESTING Cavities in trunks or limbs of dead trees; 4–6 eggs; April–June.

FEEDING Feeds mainly on acorns; fruits and insects also eaten.

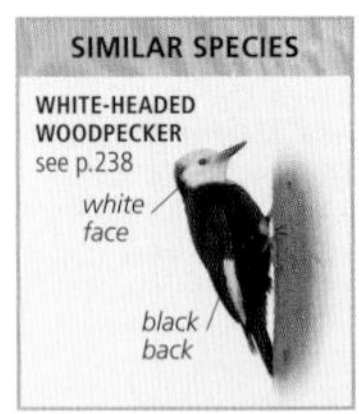

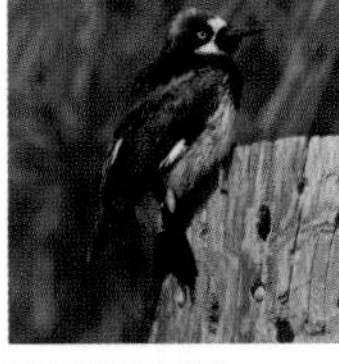

TREE CAVITIES
A nest site may contain several cavities for breeding, typically in a large tree.

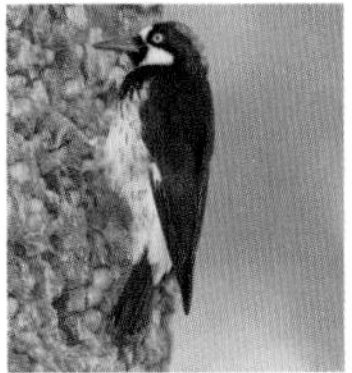

STORING FOOD
An obsessive acorn storer, it drills holes in oaks and accumulates large numbers of acorns.

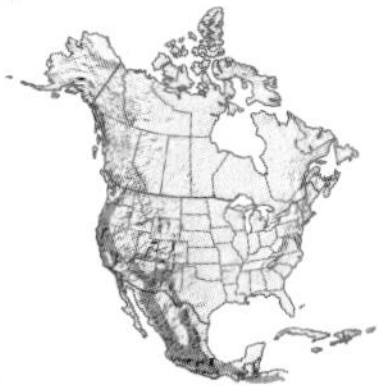

OCCURRENCE
This western US and Mexican species primarily uses oak and pine-oak woodlands as its breeding and wintering habitat. Also found in urban parks and suburban areas where oak trees are present. Will use areas with other kinds of trees as long as oak trees also occur in the vicinity.

SIMILAR SPECIES

WHITE-HEADED WOODPECKER
see p.238

white face
black back

Length **7–9in (17.5–23cm)**	Wingspan **14–17in (36–43cm)**	Weight **2¼–3oz (65–85g)**
Social **Family groups**	Lifespan **Up to 16 years**	Status **Secure**

DATE SEEN	WHERE	NOTES

Order **Piciformes**	Family **Picidae**	Species ***Sphyrapicus thyroideus***

Williamson's Sapsucker

white rump
black tail
FEMALE
IN FLIGHT
MALE
black wings with white patches
brown head
brown overall with barred plumage
FEMALE
dark back
white wing patch
JUVENILE MALE
dark bill
red throat
white head stripe
black back
barred flanks
MALE

The Williamson's Sapsucker is one of the four sapsucker species occurring in North America. Unlike other sapsuckers, the male and female plumages are so dissimilar that it is difficult to believe they belong to the same species. Williamson's Sapsucker has very specific habitat needs, partly because of its rather strict dependence on the sap and phloem, the innermost bark layer of trees. This secretive sapsucker can be located in the breeding season by its rather hesitant drumming, which occurs in an uneven series. With its white rump the female looks like a flicker in flight.

VOICE Primary call nasal *churr;* also a mewing call.

NESTING Excavates cavity in dead wood; 5–6 eggs; 1 brood; May–July.

FEEDING Mainly eats tree sap and ants during the breeding season; nonbreeding birds feed on the sap, phloem, and fruit of trees.

DRILLING FOR FOOD These birds drill holes in tree barks and then eat the sap and insects that emerge.

FLIGHT: undulating flight pattern, similar to other sapsuckers.

OCCURRENCE
A species of the Intermountain West, breeding in coniferous forest. Winters at lower elevations, where it mainly occupies pine-oak woodlands, in the southeastern US and in Mexico.

Length **9in (23cm)**	Wingspan **17in (43cm)**	Weight **1¾oz (50g)**
Social **Pairs**	Lifespan **Unknown**	Status **Declining**

DATE SEEN	WHERE	NOTES

Order **Piciformes**	Family **Picidae**	Species ***Sphyrapicus varius***

Yellow-bellied Sapsucker

The Yellow-bellied Sapsucker, with its red, black, and white coloring and soft yellow wash on its underparts, is a striking bird. Like its relatives, the Red-breasted Sapsucker and the Red-naped Sapsucker, it drills holes in trees to drink sap. It was only in 1983 that the sapsuckers were allocated to four separate species. This is one of the only two North American woodpeckers that are completely migratory, with females moving farther south than males. The other species is the Red-naped Sapsucker, its western relative.

VOICE Primary call a mewing *wheer-wheer-wheer.*

NESTING Cavities in dead trees; 5–6 eggs; 1 brood; May–June.

FEEDING Drinks sap; eats ants and other small insects; feeds on the inner bark of trees, also a variety of fruit.

FLIGHT: typical woodpecker, undulating flight pattern with intermittent flapping and gliding.

STRIKING SPECIES
The Yellow-bellied Sapsucker's white rump and black-and-white forked tail are clearly evident here.

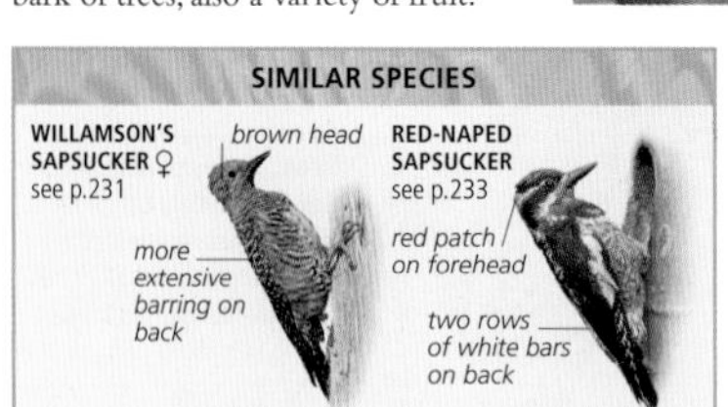

OCCURRENCE
Breeds in eastern Alaska, Canada, and south to the Appalachians. Prefers either deciduous forests or mixed deciduous-coniferous forests; preferably young forests. In winter, it is found in open wooded areas in southeastern states, Caribbean islands, and Central America.

Length **8–9in (20–23cm)**	Wingspan **16–18in (41–46cm)**	Weight **1¾ oz (50g)**
Social **Solitary/Pairs**	Lifespan **Up to 7 years**	Status **Secure**

DATE SEEN	WHERE	NOTES

Order **Piciformes**	Family **Picidae**	Species ***Sphyrapicus nuchalis***

Red-naped Sapsucker

The Red-naped Sapsucker is closely related to the Red-breasted Sapsucker and the Yellow-bellied Sapsucker. Indeed, where these three species overlap geographically, they occasionally interbreed, and birds with intermediate plumages can sometimes be seen. Like the other sapsuckers, this bird drills concentric rings in trees, and extends its specialized tongue into the wound to reach the sap.

VOICE Mewing *wheer-wheer-wheer*, virtually identical to that of the Red-breasted and Yellow-bellied sapsuckers.

NESTING Cavity nester; 4–5 eggs; 1 brood; May–August.

FEEDING Feeds on sap and seeds; fruit and other vegetable matter; also insects and spiders.

FLIGHT: typical woodpecker, undulating flight pattern, with intermittent flapping and gliding.

ASPEN DWELLER
The Red-naped Sapsucker excavates its nest cavities in live aspens.

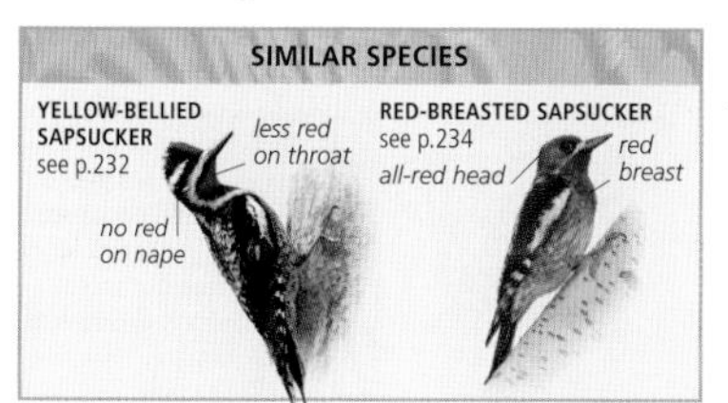

OCCURRENCE
Breeds in coniferous forest, intermixed with aspen, in the Rocky Mountains from western Canada south to California; also riverine woodlands. Winter habitats include forests, open woodlands, parks, and orchards in the Southwest. North American populations migrate south to Mexico.

Length **8–9in (20–23cm)**	Wingspan **17in (43cm)**	Weight **2⅛oz (60g)**
Social **Solitary/Migrant flocks**	Lifespan **Up to 3 years**	Status **Localized**

DATE SEEN	WHERE	NOTES

Order **Piciformes**	Family **Picidae**	Species ***Sphyrapicus ruber***

Red-breasted Sapsucker

white rump
yellowish spots on back
MALE (*S. r. ruber*)
IN FLIGHT
deep red head
ADULT (*S. r. ruber*)
duller head
heavy white markings on upperparts
ADULT (*S. r. daggetti*)
red head
thick bill
large white patch on wing
red breast
pale yellowish belly
black back with white feathers
ADULT (*S. r. daggetti*)

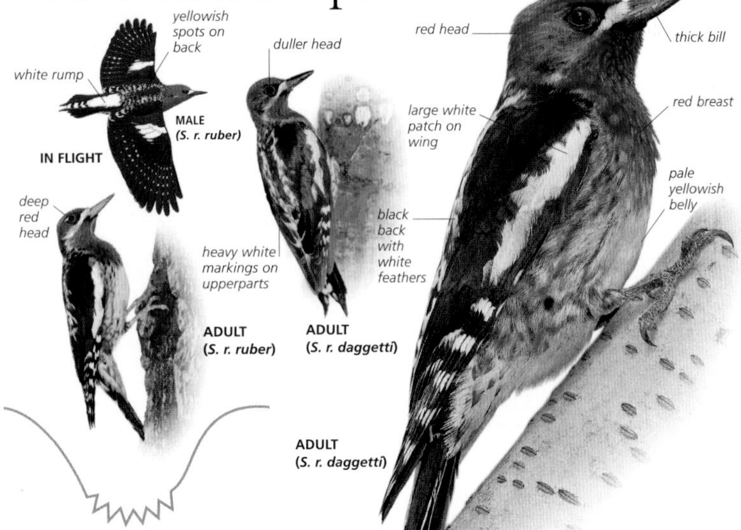

FLIGHT: undulating flight pattern with intermittent flapping and gliding.

Apart from its distinctive red head and breast, the Red-breasted Sapsucker resembles other sapsuckers—so much so that the interrelated Red-breasted, Red-naped, and Yellow-bellied Sapsuckers were once all considered to belong to the same species. Like its relatives, the Red-breasted Sapsucker drills holes in tree trunks to extract sap. Other birds and mammals, such as squirrels and bats, obtain food from these holes. The northern subspecies, *S. r. ruber,* occurs from Alaska to Oregon, and has a back lightly marked with gold spots and a more brightly colored head. Its southern counterpart, *S. r. daggetti*, has a back more heavily marked with white.

VOICE Call reminiscent of a mewing cat; normally does not vocalize outside the breeding season.

NESTING Excavates cavity in deciduous trees such as aspen and willow, but will also nest in conifers if deciduous trees are not available; 4–5 eggs; 1 brood; May–July.

FEEDING Mainly drills for sap from a number of plants; also eats the insects that have become trapped in the sap.

RED-HEADED DRILLER
Red-breasted Sapsuckers drill holes in trees to drink sap and eat the insects attracted to it.

OCCURRENCE
Breeds in a wide range of habitats, including coniferous forests, but may also select deciduous forests and habitats along rivers. Prefers areas with dead trees. A partial migrant, it winters within its breeding range, but also moves south, as far as northern Baja California.

SIMILAR SPECIES

RED-NAPED SAPSUCKER see p.233

Length **8–9in (20–23cm)**	Wingspan **15–16in (38–41cm)**	Weight **2oz (55g)**
Social **Solitary**	Lifespan **2–3 years**	Status **Localized**

DATE SEEN	WHERE	NOTES

Order **Piciformes**	Family **Picidae**	Species ***Picoides scalaris***

Ladder-backed Woodpecker

A bird of the southwestern US, the Ladder-backed Woodpecker has conspicuous, zebra-like black-and-white barring on its back, and a wide black-and-white striped facial pattern. The male, like many other North American woodpeckers, has a red crown. This nonmigratory species can be seen year-round in its range. The Ladder-backed Woodpecker occasionally hybridizes with its closest relative, the Nuttall's Woodpecker. Desert cacti are used both as a place to breed and as a food source.

VOICE Two main calls: short *peek* call, and rattle- or whinny-like call of many notes; call descends at end.

NESTING Excavates cavity in dead or dying wood; 4–5 eggs; 1 brood; May–July.

FEEDING Males forage lower and on the ground, probing for insects, sometimes around cactus roots; females forage higher, gleaning insects from bark; also feeds on fruits of cactus.

FLIGHT: undulating and swift.

SIMILAR SPECIES

NUTTALL'S WOODPECKER ♂ see p.446

TREE GRUB
This male Ladder-backed Woodpecker has just extracted a beetle larva from a tree trunk.

OCCURRENCE
Breeds in arid scrub, montane shrubbery, wooded canyons, and pine-oak woodlands. In southern Arizona, the bird is seen in grasslands, but in Colorado it is found in pinyon-juniper woodlands. Winters in same habitats as it is a nonmigratory species. Occurs south to Nicaragua.

Length **7¼in (18.5cm)**	Wingspan **11–12in (28–30cm)**	Weight **1¹⁄₁₆–1¼oz (30–35g)**
Social **Unknown**	Lifespan **Up to 4 years**	Status **Declining**

DATE SEEN	WHERE	NOTES

Order **Piciformes**	Family **Picidae**	Species ***Picoides pubescens***

Downy Woodpecker

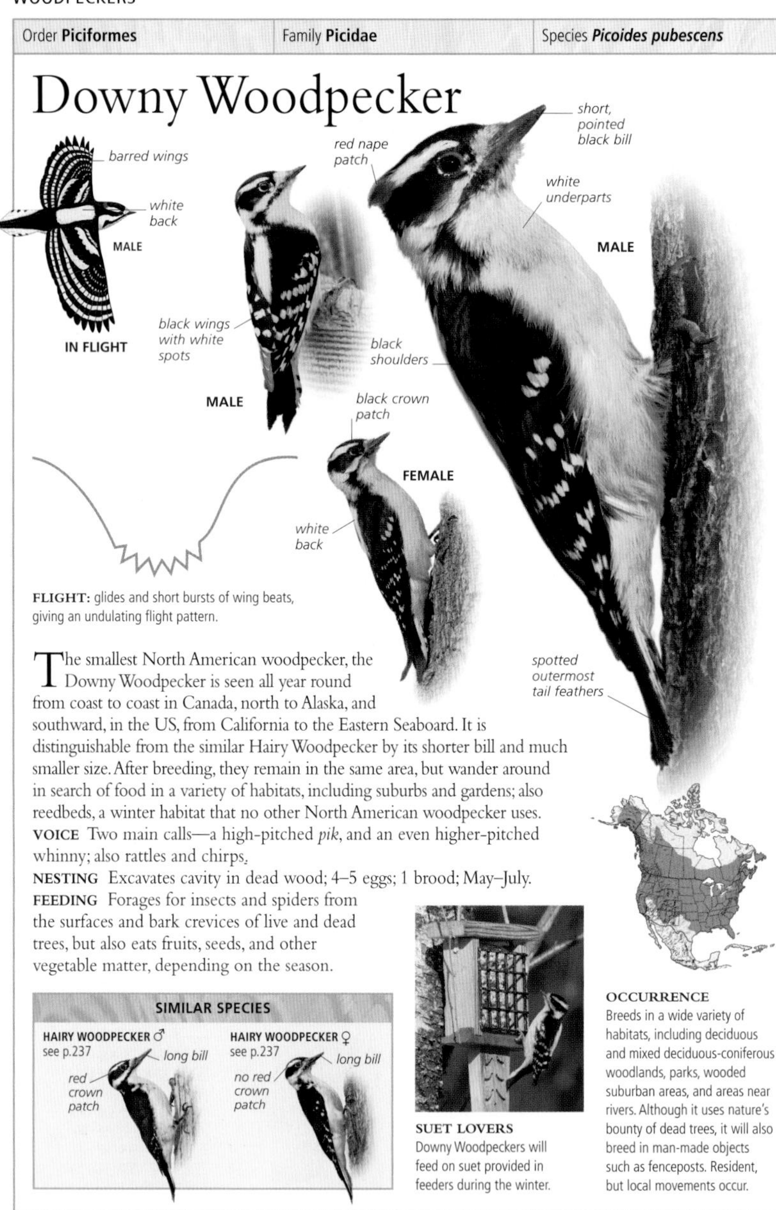

FLIGHT: glides and short bursts of wing beats, giving an undulating flight pattern.

The smallest North American woodpecker, the Downy Woodpecker is seen all year round from coast to coast in Canada, north to Alaska, and southward, in the US, from California to the Eastern Seaboard. It is distinguishable from the similar Hairy Woodpecker by its shorter bill and much smaller size. After breeding, they remain in the same area, but wander around in search of food in a variety of habitats, including suburbs and gardens; also reedbeds, a winter habitat that no other North American woodpecker uses.

VOICE Two main calls—a high-pitched *pik*, and an even higher-pitched whinny; also rattles and chirps.

NESTING Excavates cavity in dead wood; 4–5 eggs; 1 brood; May–July.

FEEDING Forages for insects and spiders from the surfaces and bark crevices of live and dead trees, but also eats fruits, seeds, and other vegetable matter, depending on the season.

SIMILAR SPECIES

HAIRY WOODPECKER ♂ see p.237 — long bill; red crown patch

HAIRY WOODPECKER ♀ see p.237 — long bill; no red crown patch

SUET LOVERS
Downy Woodpeckers will feed on suet provided in feeders during the winter.

OCCURRENCE
Breeds in a wide variety of habitats, including deciduous and mixed deciduous-coniferous woodlands, parks, wooded suburban areas, and areas near rivers. Although it uses nature's bounty of dead trees, it will also breed in man-made objects such as fenceposts. Resident, but local movements occur.

Length **6–7in (15–18cm)**	Wingspan **10–12in (25–30cm)**	Weight **$1^1/_{16}$oz (30g)**
Social **Solitary/Flocks**	Lifespan **Up to 11 years**	Status **Secure**

DATE SEEN	WHERE	NOTES

Order **Piciformes**	Family **Picidae**	Species ***Picoides villosus***

Hairy Woodpecker

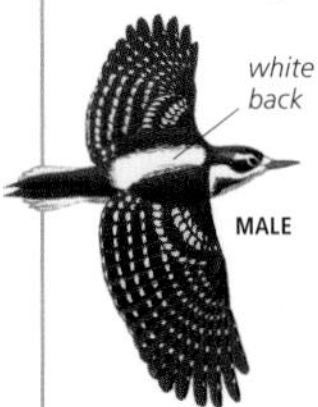

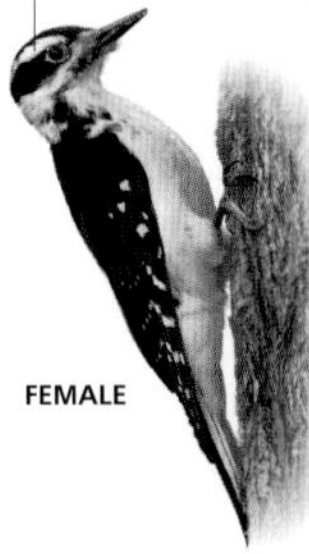

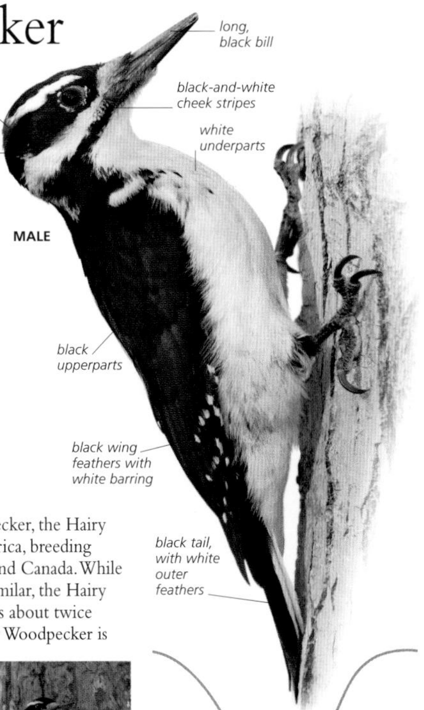

white back
MALE
IN FLIGHT
no red patch on back of head
FEMALE
red patch on back of head
black nape
MALE
long, black bill
black-and-white cheek stripes
white underparts
black upperparts
black wing feathers with white barring
black tail, with white outer feathers

Like its smaller relative, the Downy Woodpecker, the Hairy Woodpecker is widespread in North America, breeding and wintering from coast to coast in the US and Canada. While in many respects the two species look quite similar, the Hairy Woodpecker has a larger and thicker bill and is about twice as large as the Downy Woodpecker. The Hairy Woodpecker is a bird of forests, where it uses live tree trunks both as nesting sites and as places to forage.

VOICE Call a bold, grating, sharp *Peek,* similar to that of the Downy Woodpecker, but lower in pitch, and louder. Drumming a rather loud, even series of taps.

NESTING Excavates cavity in live trees; 4 eggs; 1 brood; May–July.

FEEDING Eats mainly insects and their larvae; also nuts and seeds.

FLIGHT: undulating; short glides alternating with wing beats.

HOME SWEET HOME
The Hairy Woodpecker is generally found in forests and prefers mature woodland areas, using both deciduous and coniferous trees.

SIMILAR SPECIES

DOWNY WOODPECKER ♂ see p.236
shorter bill
black markings on outer wing feathers

DOWNY WOODPECKER ♀ see p.236
shorter bill
black markings on outer wing feathers

OCCURRENCE
Breeds primarily in forests, both deciduous and coniferous, but also in more open woodlands, swamps, suburban parks, and wooded areas. Resident in North America all year round, though in the far north of its range it may move south for the winter.

Length **9–9½in (23–24cm)**	Wingspan **15–16in (38–41cm)**	Weight **2½oz (70g)**
Social **Solitary/Winter flocks**	Lifespan **At least 16 years**	Status **Secure**

DATE SEEN	WHERE	NOTES

Order **Piciformes**	Family **Picidae**	Species ***Picoides albolarvatus***

White-headed Woodpecker

With its white head, black body, and white wing patches, the White-headed Woodpecker of western North America is striking; its plumage pattern is unique among North American woodpeckers. While it is common in some areas of its geographically restricted range, its population is vulnerable, especially in the Northwest, because of forest fragmentation. Ponderosa pine seeds are basic to its diet, and poor pine crops may result in low breeding success. In winter, males and females tend to forage separately, and females feed lower in trees.

VOICE Most common call 2–3 note sharp *peek-it* or *pitit*.

NESTING Excavates nest in dead trees and snags; 4–5 eggs; 1 brood; May–July.

FEEDING Eats arthropods, including ants, beetles, and spiders; also berries, and seeds, particularly pine seeds.

FLIGHT: undulating flight pattern typical of woodpeckers.

SIMILAR SPECIES

ACORN WOODPECKER see p.230
white forehead patch
red crown

PARENTING CHORES
This bird is carrying food back to the nest to feed its young.

OCCURRENCE
A strictly western North American bird, occurs from British Columbia to California in mountain pine forests, especially with Ponderosa pines. Habitat specialist, but many birds move to lower elevations in winter, can be seen in deserts of Montana, Wyoming, and California.

Length **9–9½in (23–24cm)**	Wingspan **16–17in (41–43cm)**	Weight **2oz (55g)**
Social **Solitary**	Lifespan **Unknown**	Status **Localized**

DATE SEEN	WHERE	NOTES

Order **Piciformes**	Family **Picidae**	Species ***Picoides tridactylus dorsalis***

American Three-toed Woodpecker

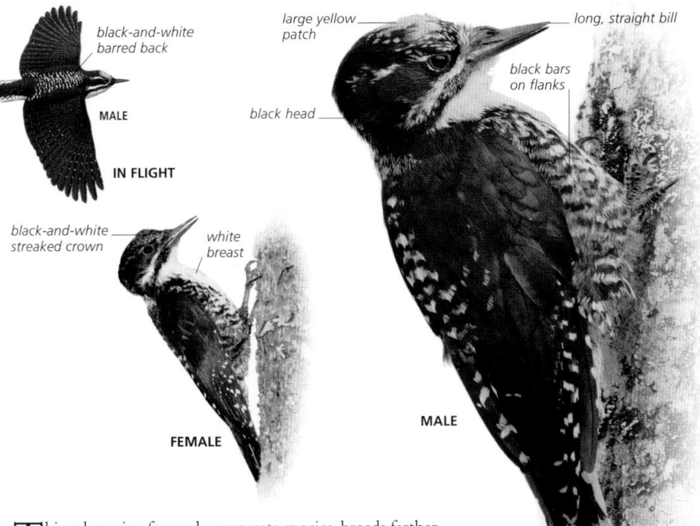

This subspecies, formerly a separate species, breeds farther north than any other North American woodpecker, including its close relative, the Black-backed Woodpecker. It resembles the Black-backed Woodpecker in terms of size and head markings, and because they are the only two North American woodpeckers with three toes on each foot. The population of this woodpecker is decreasing as a result of habitat loss. This bird and its relative require mature forests with old or dead trees.

VOICE Call notes *queep*, *quip*, or *pik*; generally quiet, likened to the Yellow-bellied Sapsucker.

NESTING Excavates cavity mainly in dead or dying wood, sometimes in live wood; 4 eggs; 1 brood; May–July.

FEEDING Flakes off bark and eats insects underneath, mainly the larvae of Bark Beetles.

FLIGHT: undulating flight with rapid wing beats typical of other woodpeckers.

COLOR VARIATION

The streaks on this species' back are highly variable; some populations have nearly all-white backs.

SIMILAR SPECIES

BLACK-BACKED WOODPECKER shorter call; see p.240

OCCURRENCE

Breeds in mature northern coniferous forests across Canada and through the Rockies. Since it is largely nonmigratory, this is also the winter habitat for most populations, although it is found in more open areas in winter.

Length **8–9in (20–23cm)**	Wingspan **15in (38cm)**	Weight **2¼–2½oz (65–70g)**
Social **Solitary/Pairs**	Lifespan **Unknown**	Status **Vulnerable**

DATE SEEN	WHERE	NOTES

Order **Piciformes**	Family **Picidae**	Species ***Picoides arcticus***

Black-backed Woodpecker

white spots on outer wings
black back
MALE
IN FLIGHT

black cap
FEMALE

long, black bill
yellow cap on black head
white stripe on head
white underparts
black back and wings
MALE

Formerly called the Black-backed Three-toed Woodpecker, this species has a black back and heavily barred flanks. Despite being widespread across the northern US, southern Canada, and southern Alaska, this bird is difficult to find. The Black-backed Woodpecker often occurs in areas of burned forest, eating wood-boring beetles that occur after outbreaks of fire. This diet is very specialized, and the species is greatly affected by forestry programs, which prevent the spread of fire. Although it overlaps geographically with the American Three-toed Woodpecker, the two are rarely found together in the same locality.

VOICE Main call a single *pik*.

NESTING Cavity excavated in tree; 3–4 eggs; 1 brood; May–July.

FEEDING Eats beetles, especially larvae of wood-boring beetles, by flaking off bark.

FLIGHT: typical undulating flight of woodpeckers.

FREQUENT MOVING
This bird excavates a new nest cavity each year, rarely returning in subsequent years.

SIMILAR SPECIES

AMERICAN THREE-TOED WOODPECKER
see p.239

OCCURRENCE
Inhabitant of northern and mountain coniferous forests that require fire for renewal. Breeding occurs soon after sites are burned as new colonies are attracted to the habitat. In Michigan's Upper Peninsula, the bird uses trees similar to those in its northern habitat.

Length **9–9½in (23–24cm)**	Wingspan **15–16in (38–41cm)**	Weight **2½oz (70g)**
Social **Pairs**	Lifespan **Unknown**	Status **Secure**

DATE SEEN	WHERE	NOTES

Order **Piciformes**	Family **Picidae**	Species ***Colaptes auratus***

Northern Flicker

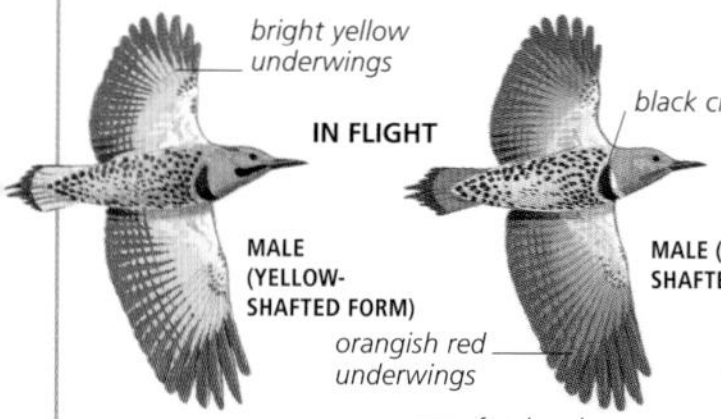

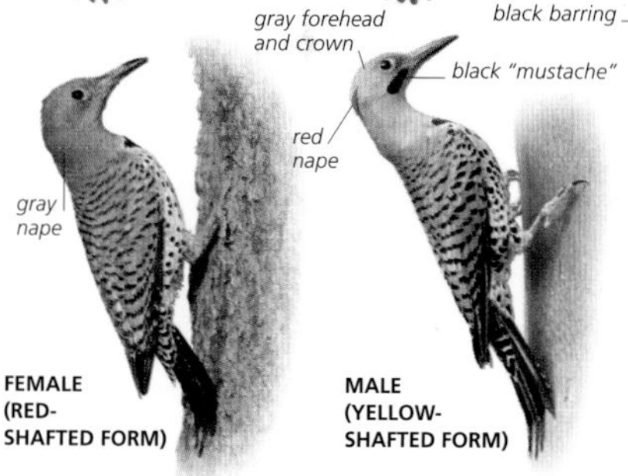

buffy forehead
gray nape
red "mustache"
bright yellow underwings
IN FLIGHT
black crescent
MALE (YELLOW-SHAFTED FORM)
MALE (RED-SHAFTED FORM)
orangish red underwings
brownish back with black barring
gray forehead and crown
black "mustache"
red nape
gray nape
FEMALE (RED-SHAFTED FORM)
MALE (YELLOW-SHAFTED FORM)
MALE (RED-SHAFTED FORM)

In contrast to other North American woodpeckers, the Northern Flicker is a ground forager. The two subspecies, the Yellow-shafted Flicker (*auratus*) in the East, and Red-shafted Flicker (*cafer*) in the West, interbreed in a wide area in the Great Plains. They can be distinguished when in flight, as the underwing feathers will either be a vivid yellow or a striking red, as their names indicate.

VOICE Two main calls; loud *kew-kew-kew*, each note ascending at the end; the other, softer call, described as *wicka-wicka-wicka*.

NESTING Cavity usually in dead wood, but sometimes in live wood; 6–8 eggs; 1 brood; May–June.

FEEDING Feeds mainly on ants in breeding season; also fruits in winter.

FLIGHT: rapid wing beats followed by glides; fewer undulations than most woodpeckers.

SHARING CHORES
The Northern Flicker nests in tree cavities, where parents take turns incubating eggs.

SIMILAR SPECIES

GILDED FLICKER
see p.446
cinnamon crown
paler brown back

FEET ON THE GROUND
Unlike other woodpeckers, flickers can be found foraging for ants on the ground.

OCCURRENCE
A common species found in woodland in every part of the US, the southern half of Canada, and north into Alaska. During breeding season, prefers open woodlands and forest edge; also suburbs. Little is known about this bird's winter habitat.

Length **12–13in (31–33cm)**	Wingspan **19–21in (48–53cm)**	Weight **4oz (125g)**
Social **Solitary**	Lifespan **9 years**	Status **Secure**

DATE SEEN	WHERE	NOTES
7/23/19	SU campus	

Order **Piciformes**	Family **Picidae**	Species ***Dryocopus pileatus***

Pileated Woodpecker

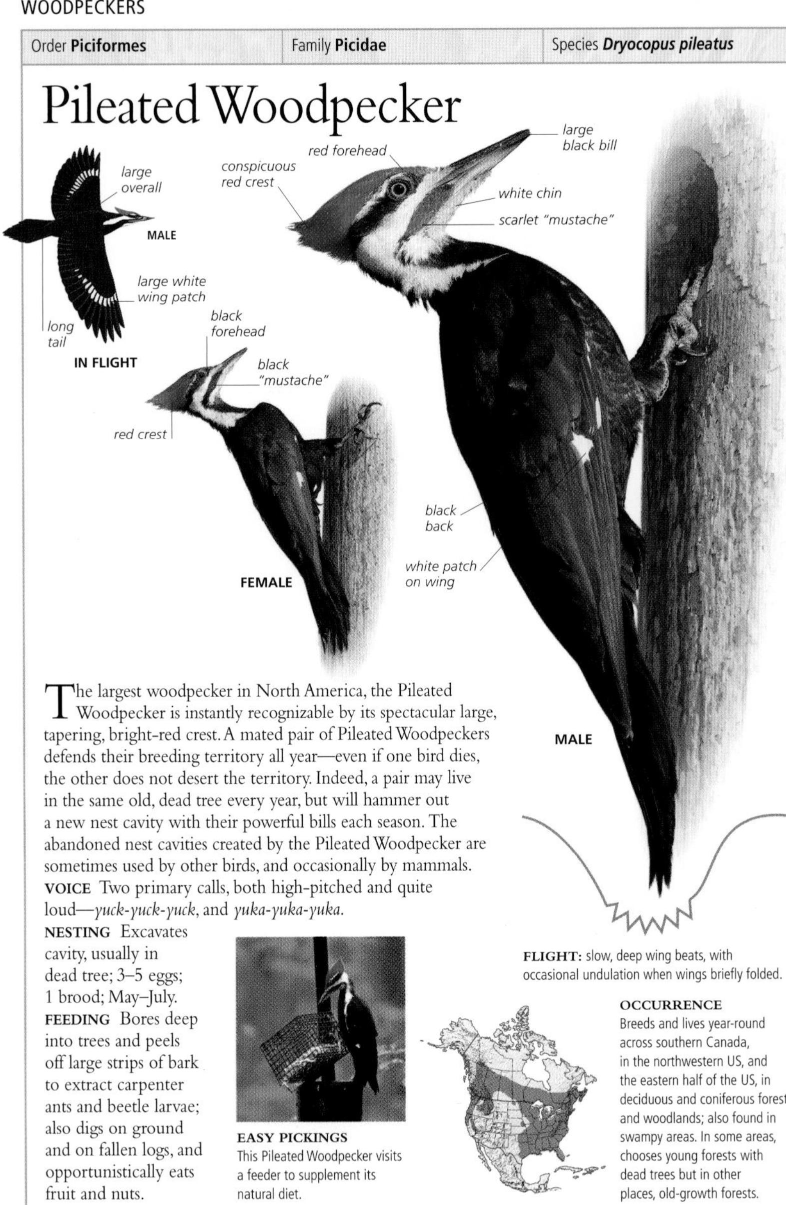

The largest woodpecker in North America, the Pileated Woodpecker is instantly recognizable by its spectacular large, tapering, bright-red crest. A mated pair of Pileated Woodpeckers defends their breeding territory all year—even if one bird dies, the other does not desert the territory. Indeed, a pair may live in the same old, dead tree every year, but will hammer out a new nest cavity with their powerful bills each season. The abandoned nest cavities created by the Pileated Woodpecker are sometimes used by other birds, and occasionally by mammals.

VOICE Two primary calls, both high-pitched and quite loud—*yuck-yuck-yuck*, and *yuka-yuka-yuka*.

NESTING Excavates cavity, usually in dead tree; 3–5 eggs; 1 brood; May–July.

FEEDING Bores deep into trees and peels off large strips of bark to extract carpenter ants and beetle larvae; also digs on ground and on fallen logs, and opportunistically eats fruit and nuts.

EASY PICKINGS
This Pileated Woodpecker visits a feeder to supplement its natural diet.

FLIGHT: slow, deep wing beats, with occasional undulation when wings briefly folded.

OCCURRENCE
Breeds and lives year-round across southern Canada, in the northwestern US, and the eastern half of the US, in deciduous and coniferous forest and woodlands; also found in swampy areas. In some areas, chooses young forests with dead trees but in other places, old-growth forests.

Length **16–18in (41–46cm)**	Wingspan **26–30in (66–76cm)**	Weight **10oz (275g)**
Social **Pairs**	Lifespan **Up to 9 years**	Status **Secure**

DATE SEEN	WHERE	NOTES

FLYCATCHERS

BIRDS POPULARLY KNOWN as "flycatchers" occur in many parts of the world, but songbirds in several different families have this name. With the exception of some Old World flycatchers that stray into Alaska, the North American species are members of a single family—the Tyrant Flycatchers (Tyrannidae). With about 400 species, this is the largest bird family in the New World. These birds are uniform in appearance, with only a hint of the diversity in the family that is found in Central and South America. Most are drab-colored, olive-green or gray birds, sometimes with yellow underparts. The Vermilion Flycatcher is a striking exception, as is the gray and salmon-pink Scissor-tailed Flycatcher, which also has elongated outer tail feathers. Members of the genus *Empidonax* include some of the most difficult birds to identify in North America; they are best distinguished by their songs. Typical flycatcher feeding behavior is to sit on a branch or exposed perch, then sally to catch flying insects. Tyrannid flycatchers are found across North America, except in Arctic regions. Many live in wooded habitats, though others prefer woodland edges and deserts. Nearly all flycatchers are long-distance migrants and spend the northern winter in Central and South America.

ERECT STANCE
A large headed look and erect posture are typical of this Eastern Phoebe. This species is rare in the West.

TYRANT BEHAVIOR
Such aggressive display by Couch's Kingbird reflects its English and generic names.

BIG MOUTHS
Young Dusky Flycatchers display the wide bills that help them catch flying insects as adults.

Order **Passeriformes**	Family **Tyrannidae**	Species ***Sayornis nigricans***

Black Phoebe

two pale wing bars
ADULT
rounded wings
IN FLIGHT
grayish brown head and chest
rusty wing bars
JUVENILE
black upperparts
black head
fairly short, black bill
sooty black breast and throat
white belly
ADULT
black legs and feet
black tail

North America's only black-and-white flycatcher, the distinctive Black Phoebe is found in the southwestern part of the continent, where it is a year-round resident. This area is the northernmost part of the bird's range, which extends southward to Argentina. This species is commonly found close to water, where it conducts most of its foraging. It has even been known to dive into ponds to capture minnows—an unusual foraging method for a flycatcher. In the breeding season the male shows his mate potential nest sites by hovering in front of a likely spot, with the female deciding where the nest will eventually be.

VOICE Simple *tsip* call; also *tweedle-deedle-eek* during courting or when chasing rivals; song a *tee-hee, tee-hoo* or *sisee, sitsew.*

NESTING Open cup of mud mixed with grass, cemented to wall, or under bridge, cliff, or eave; 2–5 eggs; 2–3 broods; March–June.

FEEDING Mainly catches flying insects, but will also pick insects from ground; occasionally dives for small fish; also eats berries.

FLIGHT: direct with steady wing beats; hovers while foraging; vertical zig-zag courting display.

PERCHED AND ALERT
The Black Phoebe perches in an upright position, with its tail dipping and fanning.

OCCURRENCE
In the US, breeds and winters in Oregon, California, Nevada, Utah, Arizona, New Mexico, and Texas, in areas close to water, such as coastal cliffs, banks of rivers, streams, lakes, and ponds. Also seen at fountains and cattle troughs. Forages in open areas over water or grassland.

Length **6in (15.5cm)**	Wingspan **11in (28cm)**	Weight **½–¹¹⁄₁₆oz (15–20g)**
Social **Solitary**	Lifespan **Up to 8 years**	Status **Secure**

DATE SEEN	WHERE	NOTES

Order **Passeriformes**	Family **Tyrannidae**	Species ***Sayornis saya***

Say's Phoebe

Say's Phoebe breeds farther north than any other flycatcher in its family. Although it is a bird of open country, it is not particularly shy around people, and from early spring to late fall is a common sight on ranches and farms. Its contrasting dark cap is conspicuous even at a distance as it perches on bushes, boulders, or power lines, often wagging its tail. Shortly after a pair is formed on the breeding grounds, the male will hover in front of potential nest sites, in a manner similar to the Black Phoebe. The pair bond among Say's Phoebes is relatively weak, though, and does not last through the summer.

VOICE Call a *pee-ee* or *pee-ur*; also a whistled *churr-eep*, which may be integrated with a chatter; primary song a *pit-see-eur* and *pit-eet*.

NESTING Shallow cup of twigs, moss, or stems on ledge or in rocky crevice; 3–7 eggs; 1–2 broods; April–July.

FEEDING Catches insects in flight, such as beetles, wasps, grasshoppers, and crickets; also eats berries.

FLIGHT: direct, with regular wing beats; chases may be erratic; hovers while foraging.

HOVERING MALE
Say's Phoebes characteristically hover in the breeding season.

SIMILAR SPECIES

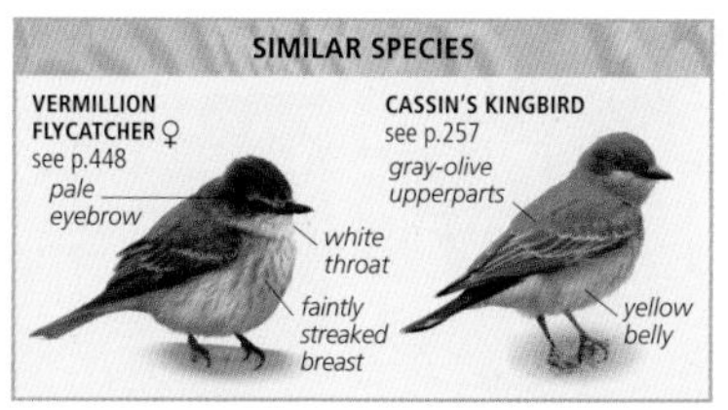

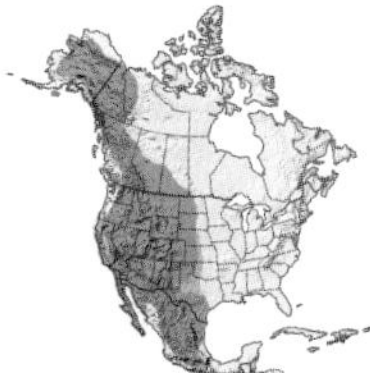

OCCURRENCE
Breeds in dry, open, or semi-open country, such as desert canyons, sagebrush ranch, and agricultural areas; generally avoids watercourses. Birds in the southwestern US are resident year-round, but those breeding farther north fly south for the winter.

Length **7in (17.5cm)**	Wingspan **13in (33cm)**	Weight **$^{11}/_{16}$oz (20g)**
Social **Solitary**	Lifespan **At least 3–4 years**	Status **Secure**

DATE SEEN	WHERE	NOTES

Order **Passeriformes**	Family **Tyrannidae**	Species ***Contopus cooperi***

Olive-sided Flycatcher

short tail

ADULT (SUMMER)

pointed wings

IN FLIGHT

large, dark head

lower base of bill often dull orange

brownish gray back

dull white throat

brownish olive flanks

white belly

ADULT (SUMMER)

FLIGHT: fast and direct, with deep, rapid wing beats; turns sharply to chase prey.

The Olive-sided Flycatcher is identified by its distinctive song, large size, and contrasting belly and flank colors, which make its underside appear like a vest with the buttons undone. Both members of a breeding pair are known to aggressively defend their territory. This flycatcher undertakes a long journey from northern parts of North America to winter in Panama and the Andes.

VOICE Call an evenly spaced *pip-pip-pip*; song a loud 3-note whistle: *quick-THREE-BEERS* or *whip-WEE-DEER*.

NESTING Open cup of twigs, rootlets, lichens; 2–5 eggs; 1 brood; May–August.

FEEDING Sits and waits for prey to fly past its perch before swooping after it; eats flying insects, such as bees, wasps, and flying ants.

BUILDING THE NEST
The female Olive-sided Flycatcher usually constructs the nest on her own.

EXPOSED PERCH
This species can often be found singing from an exposed twig emerging from the canopy.

SIMILAR SPECIES

OCCURRENCE
Breeds in mountainous, northern coniferous forests at edges or openings around ponds, bogs, meadows where standing dead trees occur. Also found in post-fire forests with abundant stumps. Winters in forest edges with tall trees and stumps.

Length **7–8in (18–20cm)**	Wingspan **13in (33cm)**	Weight **$1\frac{1}{16}$–$1\frac{1}{4}$oz (30–35g)**
Social **Solitary**	Lifespan **Up to 7 years**	Status **Declining**

DATE SEEN	WHERE	NOTES

Order **Passeriformes**	Family **Tyrannidae**	Species ***Contopus sordidulus***

Western Wood-pewee

slight crest
dark brown eye
dark gray back and head
ADULT

two pale wing bars
pale gray underparts
short legs
ADULT

pale throat
ADULT
pointed wings
IN FLIGHT

FLIGHT: flurries of rapid wing beats; returns to open perch with quivering wings.

This species is a widespread breeder in many forested habitats of western North America. Where its range overlaps that of the Eastern Wood-pewee, it shows no evidence of interbreeding. It vocalizes from high perches, principally during the breeding season, but also during winter and while on migration. The Western Wood-pewee forages aerially on insects in much the same way as swallows do. Adults are very aggressive toward laying parasitic intruders, however, they accept Brown-headed Cowbird eggs, though few fledge successfully from their nests. The Western Wood-pewee is a migrant that winters in the Andes from Colombia to Bolivia.

VOICE Calls burry *bzew* and infrequent *chip*; male's dawn song *pee-pip-pip* or *tswee-tee-teet*, given alternately with *pee-er.*

NESTING Shallow cup of woven grasses in fork of horizontal branch; 2–4 eggs; 1 brood; May–August.

FEEDING Sit-and-wait hunter; primarily eats flies, bees, wasps, ants, beetles, and moths; also forages for flying insects.

PERCHED AND ALERT
The crest is apparent in this alert bird probably on the look-out for prey.

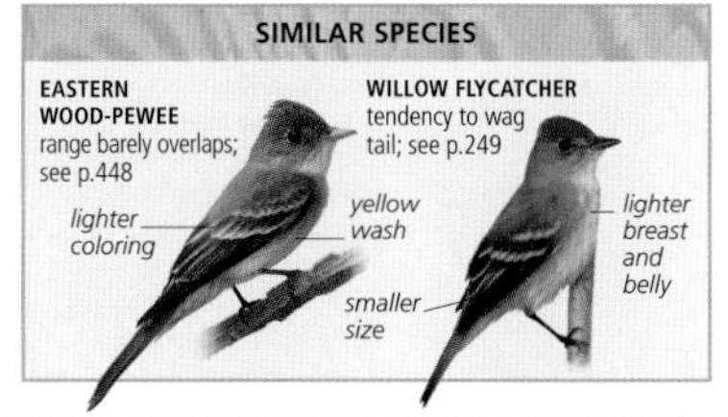

OCCURRENCE
Open woodlands, forest edges and beside rivers and other water bodies; also in dry forests. Absent from dense forests. Large-diameter trees, open understory, stumps, and woodland edges are important. Winters in mature tropical forests. Breeds in Mexico and Central America to Nicaragua.

Length **6¼in (16cm)**	Wingspan **10½in (27cm)**	Weight **⅜–½oz (11–14g)**
Social **Solitary**	Lifespan **Up to 6 years**	Status **Secure**

DATE SEEN	WHERE	NOTES

Order **Passeriformes**	Family **Tyrannidae**	Species ***Empidonax flaviventris***

Yellow-bellied Flycatcher

ADULT
bright wing bars
green back and head
rounded wings
IN FLIGHT

rounded crown
broad base of bill
yellowish belly
ADULT
square tail

big head
conspicuous yellow eye-ring
yellow-olive throat
white wing bars
ADULT

FLIGHT: short flights to forage; slightly undulating, longer flights.

The Yellow-bellied Flycatcher is characteristic of northern coniferous forests and *Sphagnum*-moss peatlands. It is not well known, because of the remote locations it inhabits and its secretive habitats. The Yellow-bellied Flycatcher is much more often heard than seen. It remains on its breeding grounds for only about two months, then migrates through the eastern US to winter quarters in southern Mexico and Central America to Panama, where it favors the shade of coffee plantations.

VOICE Call *chu-wee* and abrupt *brrrrt*; song abrupt *killink*, *che-lek*, or *che-bunk*, with variations.

NESTING Cup of moss, twigs, and needles on or near ground, often in a bog; 3–5 eggs; 1 brood; June–July.

FEEDING Catches insects in the air or gleans mosquitoes, midges, and flies from foliage; sometimes eats berries and seeds.

YELLOW BELLY
A frontal view clearly shows this species' field mark.

OCCURRENCE
Breeds from Alaska to Québec, Newfoundland, and the northeast US (New England) in boreal forests and bogs dominated by spruce trees. Winters in Mexico and Central America to Panama, in lowland forests, second-growth, and riverine habitats.

Length **5½in (14cm)**	Wingspan **8in (20cm)**	Weight **9/32–½oz (8–15g)**
Social **Solitary**	Lifespan **At least 4 years**	Status **Secure**

DATE SEEN	WHERE	NOTES

Order **Passeriformes**	Family **Tyrannidae**	Species ***Empidonax traillii***

Willow Flycatcher

FLIGHT: weak and fluttering; swoops and hovers when pursuing insects.

The Willow Flycatcher is only distinguished from the nearly identical Alder Flycatcher by its song. It is a strongly territorial bird, spreading its tail and flicking it upward during aggressive encounters. The Willow Flycatcher is, however, a frequent victim of brood parasitism by the Brown-headed Cowbird, which lays its eggs in the flycatcher's nest and removes the eggs that were already inside. Compounded by loss of suitable breeding habitat, this may be a major reason for the Willow Flycatcher's decline, especially in the case of the southwestern subspecies, *E. t. extimus*, which is now considered endangered.

VOICE Calls include soft, dry *whit* and several buzzy notes; song sharp *fitz-bew* with accent on the first syllable; also *creet*.

NESTING Rather loose and untidy cup in base of shrub near water; 3–4 eggs; 1 brood; May–August.

FEEDING Eats insects, mostly caught in flight; eats fruit in winter.

UNEVEN WORKLOAD
Although both parents feed their young, the female Willow Flycatcher does so the most.

SIMILAR SPECIES

ALDER FLYCATCHER different song; see p.250
bolder wing bars

LEAST FLYCATCHER see p.251
larger head
bold white eye-ring

OCCURRENCE
Breeds from southern Canada to eastern and southwestern US, mainly in willow thickets and other moist shrubby areas along watercourses. On winter grounds, it favors lighter woodland, shrubby clearings, and brush near water in coastal areas.

Length **5–6¾in (13–17cm)**	Wingspan **7½–9½in (19–24cm)**	Weight **3/8–9/16oz (11–16g)**
Social **Solitary**	Lifespan **Up to 11 years**	Status **Declining**

DATE SEEN	WHERE	NOTES

Order **Passeriformes**	Family **Tyrannidae**	Species ***Empidonax alnorum***

Alder Flycatcher

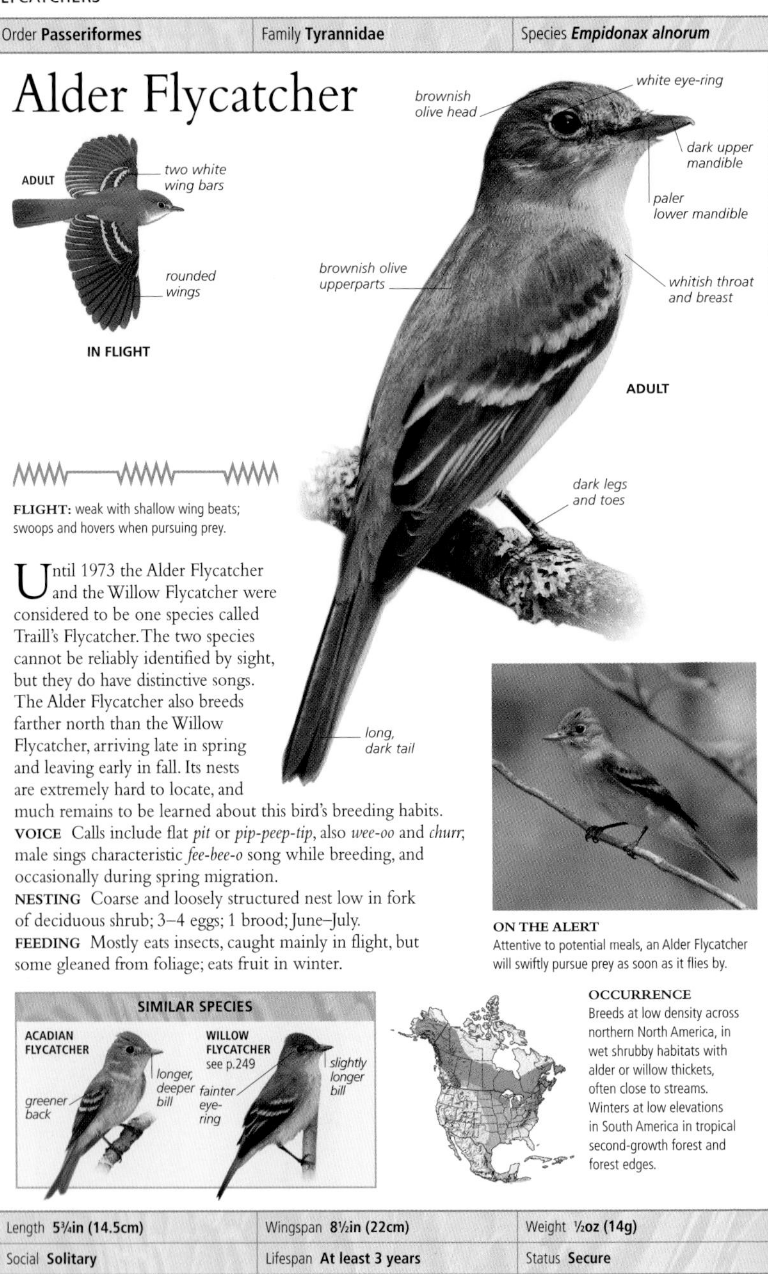

FLIGHT: weak with shallow wing beats; swoops and hovers when pursuing prey.

Until 1973 the Alder Flycatcher and the Willow Flycatcher were considered to be one species called Traill's Flycatcher. The two species cannot be reliably identified by sight, but they do have distinctive songs. The Alder Flycatcher also breeds farther north than the Willow Flycatcher, arriving late in spring and leaving early in fall. Its nests are extremely hard to locate, and much remains to be learned about this bird's breeding habits.

VOICE Calls include flat *pit* or *pip-peep-tip*, also *wee-oo* and *churr*; male sings characteristic *fee-bee-o* song while breeding, and occasionally during spring migration.

NESTING Coarse and loosely structured nest low in fork of deciduous shrub; 3–4 eggs; 1 brood; June–July.

FEEDING Mostly eats insects, caught mainly in flight, but some gleaned from foliage; eats fruit in winter.

ON THE ALERT
Attentive to potential meals, an Alder Flycatcher will swiftly pursue prey as soon as it flies by.

SIMILAR SPECIES

ACADIAN FLYCATCHER — longer, deeper bill; greener back

WILLOW FLYCATCHER see p.249 — slightly longer bill; fainter eye-ring

OCCURRENCE
Breeds at low density across northern North America, in wet shrubby habitats with alder or willow thickets, often close to streams. Winters at low elevations in South America in tropical second-growth forest and forest edges.

Length **5¾in (14.5cm)**	Wingspan **8½in (22cm)**	Weight **½oz (14g)**
Social **Solitary**	Lifespan **At least 3 years**	Status **Secure**

DATE SEEN	WHERE	NOTES

Order **Passeriformes**	Family **Tyrannidae**	Species ***Empidonax minimus***

Least Flycatcher

FLIGHT: direct, short forays with rapid wing beats to catch prey; sometimes hovers briefly.

The smallest eastern member of the *Empidonax* genus is a solitary bird and is very aggressive towards intruders encroaching upon its breeding territory, including other species of flycatcher. This combative behavior reduces the likelihood of acting as unwitting host parents to eggs laid by the Brown-headed Cowbird. The Least Flycatcher is very active, and frequently flicks its wings and tail upward. Common in the eastern US in mixed and deciduous woodland, especially at the edges, it spends a short time—up to only two months—on its northern breeding grounds before migrating south. Adults molt in winter, while young molt before and during fall migration.

VOICE Call soft, short *whit*; song frequent, persistent, characteristic *tchebeck*, sings during spring migration and breeding season.

NESTING Compact cup of tightly woven bark strips and plant fibers in fork of deciduous tree; 3–5 eggs; 1 brood; May–July.

FEEDING Feeds principally on insects, such as flies, midges, beetles, ants, butterflies, and larvae; occasionally eats berries and seeds.

YELLOW TINGE
The subtle yellow tinge to its underparts and white undertail feathers are evident here.

SIMILAR SPECIES

WILLOW FLYCATCHER see p.249
longer bill
larger body

ALDER FLYCATCHER see p.250
larger overall
wider tail

OCCURRENCE
Breeds in coniferous and mixed deciduous forests across North America, east of Rockies to East Coast; occasionally in conifer groves or wooded wetlands, often near openings or edges. Winters in Central America in varied habitat from second-growth evergreen woodland to arid scrub.

Length **5¼in (13.5cm)**	Wingspan **7¾in (19.5cm)**	Weight **9/32–7/16oz (8–13g)**
Social **Solitary**	Lifespan **Up to 6 years**	Status **Secure**

DATE SEEN	WHERE	NOTES

Order **Passeriformes**	Family **Tyrannidae**	Species ***Empidonax hammondii***

Hammond's Flycatcher

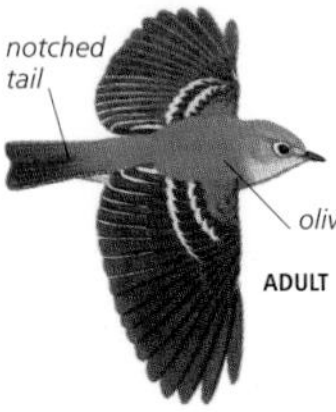

notched tail
olive back
ADULT
IN FLIGHT

gray head
small, dark bill
tear-shaped spot behind eye
grayish white throat and upper breast
olive breast and flanks
two white wing bars
ADULT
yellow tinge to lower belly
notched tail

FLIGHT: short, direct flights to pursue prey; occasionally hovers.

Hammond's Flycatcher is a small, gray migrant from Central and South America. It is generally silent on its wintering grounds, but starts performing its distinctive song shortly after arriving on its breeding grounds. In the breeding season, males are competitive and aggressive, and are known to lock together in mid-air to resolve their territorial squabbles. Since this species is dependent on mature old-growth forest, logging is thought to be adversely affecting its numbers.

VOICE Calls *peek* or *wheep*; song of 3 elements—dry, brisk *se-put*, low, burry *tsurrt*, or *greep*, and drawn-out *chu-lup*.

NESTING Compact open cup of plant fibers and fine grass saddled on large branch; 3–4 eggs; 1 brood; May–August.

FEEDING Sit-and-wait predator; pursues flying insects from perch.

DISTINCTIVE EYE-RING
Hammond's Flycatcher's white tear-shaped spot behind the eye is only visible in good lighting.

SIMILAR SPECIES

DUSKY FLYCATCHER distinctive "whit" call; see p.253
mouse gray overall
wider, longer bill

GRAY FLYCATCHER wags tail; see p.254
smaller body
paler overall

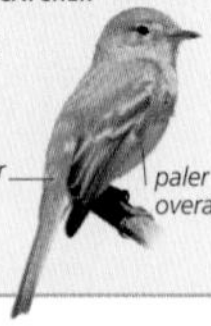

OCCURRENCE
Breeds in mature coniferous and mixed woodland from Alaska to California. Inhabits primarily dense firs or conifers, but also occurs in aspen and other broadleaf mixed forests. Winters in oak-pine forests and dry shrubbery in the highlands of Mexico and Central America.

Length **5–6in (12.5–15cm)**	Wingspan **9in (22cm)**	Weight **9/32–7/16oz (8–12g)**
Social **Solitary**	Lifespan **Up to 7 years**	Status **Secure**

DATE SEEN	WHERE	NOTES

Order **Passeriformes**	Family **Tyrannidae**	Species ***Empidonax oberholseri***

Dusky Flycatcher

inconspicuous eye-ring
dark gray upperparts
grayish olive above
wide wing bars
ADULT
notched or square tail
long tail

wing bars
ADULT
faint, white edge to tail
IN FLIGHT

rounded head
less defined markings than adult
JUVENILE
narrow tail

FLIGHT: flies out or hovers for prey; also drops to the ground.

The Dusky Flycatcher waits on a perch to locate a flying insect, flies out to catch it, and then returns to its position to consume it, often wiping its bill on the perch after completing its meal. It lives in mountainous areas of the western US and Canada, where it is vulnerable to storms that can severely impact a local breeding population by flattening the trees. The Dusky Flycatcher prefers shrubby habitats, and can benefit from forestry practices that open up dense stands of conifers.

VOICE Call a soft *whit*, vocal in early morning; song a 2-syllabled rising *prll-it*, rough, low-pitched *prrdrrt*, high, clear *pseet.*

NESTING Tight, open grass cup in upright fork of shrub or low tree; 3–5 eggs; 1 brood; May–August.

FEEDING Catches insects in flight; sometimes from bark, rarely from ground; also eats caterpillars, wasps, bees, moths, butterflies.

FEEDING TIME
This adult Dusky Flycatcher is feeding three hungry nestlings in an open cupped nest.

SIMILAR SPECIES

HAMMOND'S FLYCATCHER
see p.252
eye-ring expands behind eye
longer wings
shorter, thinner, darker bill

GRAY FLYCATCHER
see p.254
distinctive downward tail dip

OCCURRENCE
Breeds in west North America, through west US into Mexico, in open coniferous forest, mountain thickets, aspen groves, water-side thickets, open brush, and chaparral. Winters in the highlands of Mexico, south to Oaxaca, in oak scrub and pine-oak; also in open riverine woods, and semi-arid scrub.

Length **5–6in (13–15cm)**	Wingspan **8–9in (20–23cm)**	Weight **5/16–3/8oz (9–11g)**
Social **Solitary**	Lifespan **Up to 8 years**	Status **Secure**

DATE SEEN	WHERE	NOTES

Order **Passeriformes**	Family **Tyrannidae**	Species ***Empidonax wrightii***

Gray Flycatcher

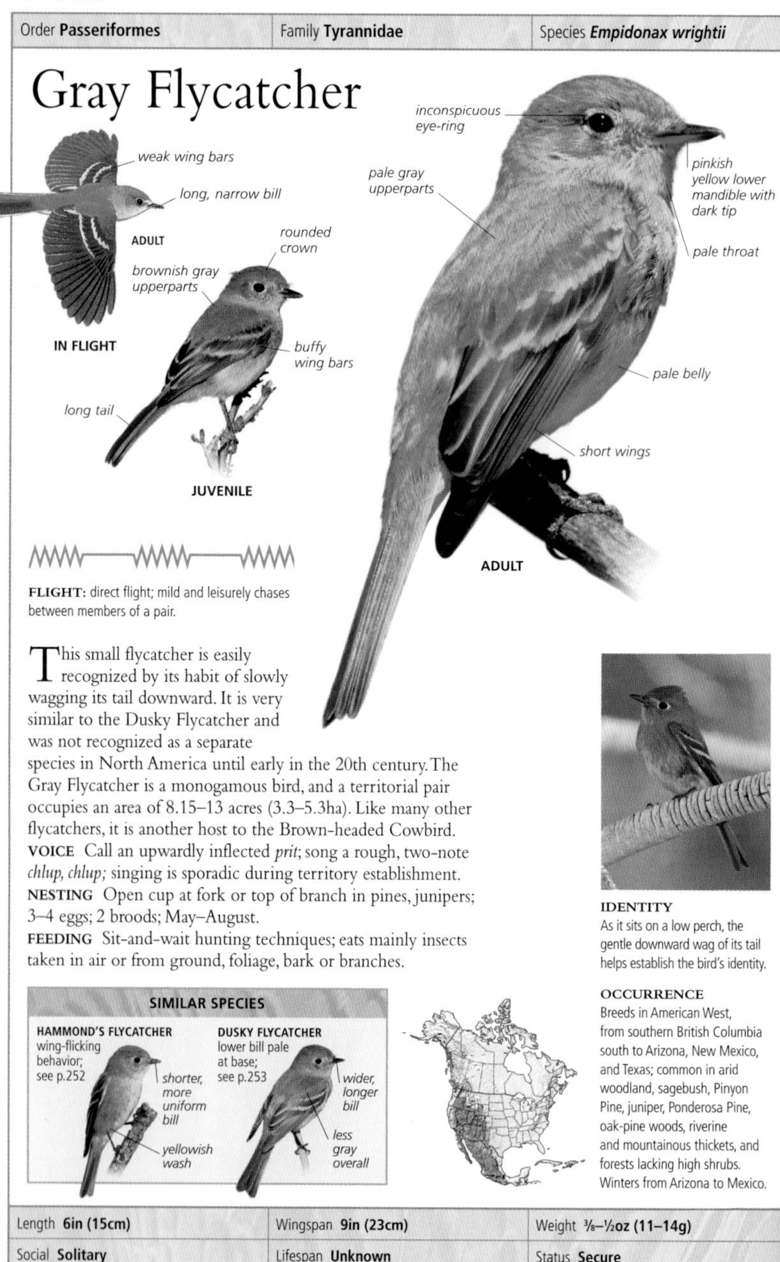

FLIGHT: direct flight; mild and leisurely chases between members of a pair.

This small flycatcher is easily recognized by its habit of slowly wagging its tail downward. It is very similar to the Dusky Flycatcher and was not recognized as a separate species in North America until early in the 20th century. The Gray Flycatcher is a monogamous bird, and a territorial pair occupies an area of 8.15–13 acres (3.3–5.3ha). Like many other flycatchers, it is another host to the Brown-headed Cowbird.

VOICE Call an upwardly inflected *prit*; song a rough, two-note *chlup, chlup;* singing is sporadic during territory establishment.

NESTING Open cup at fork or top of branch in pines, junipers; 3–4 eggs; 2 broods; May–August.

FEEDING Sit-and-wait hunting techniques; eats mainly insects taken in air or from ground, foliage, bark or branches.

IDENTITY
As it sits on a low perch, the gentle downward wag of its tail helps establish the bird's identity.

SIMILAR SPECIES

HAMMOND'S FLYCATCHER wing-flicking behavior; see p.252 shorter, more uniform bill; yellowish wash

DUSKY FLYCATCHER lower bill pale at base; see p.253 wider, longer bill; less gray overall

OCCURRENCE
Breeds in American West, from southern British Columbia south to Arizona, New Mexico, and Texas; common in arid woodland, sagebush, Pinyon Pine, juniper, Ponderosa Pine, oak-pine woods, riverine and mountainous thickets, and forests lacking high shrubs. Winters from Arizona to Mexico.

Length **6in (15cm)**	Wingspan **9in (23cm)**	Weight **⅜–½oz (11–14g)**
Social **Solitary**	Lifespan **Unknown**	Status **Secure**

DATE SEEN	WHERE	NOTES

Order **Passeriformes**	Family **Tyrannidae**	Species ***Empidonax difficilis***

Pacific-slope Flycatcher

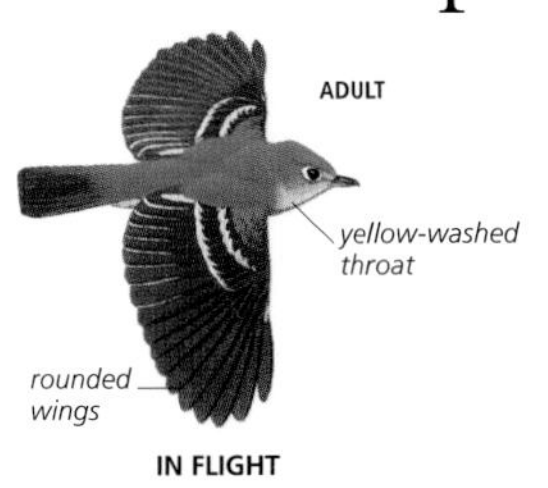

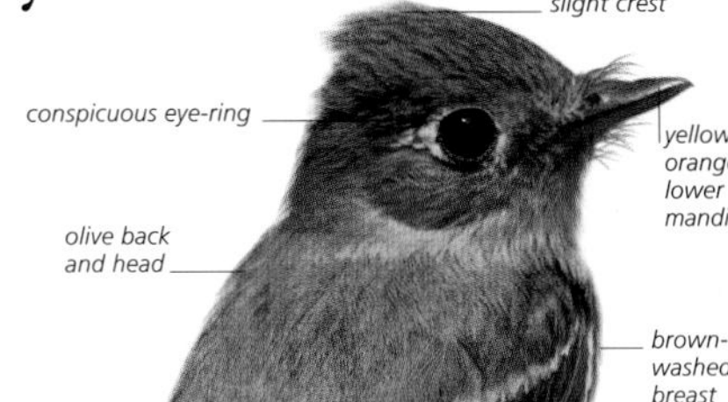

FLIGHT: sallies forth from a perch to hawk or glean insects.

The Pacific-slope Flycatcher is almost identical to the Cordilleran Flycatcher—both were formerly considered to be one species called the Western Flycatcher. Differences in song led researchers to find genetic and behavioral differences between the two species. A population of Pacific-slope Flycatchers found on the Channel Islands off California may also be a distinct species, larger than mainland forms. The Pacific-slope Flycatcher is a short-distance migrant that winters in Mexico. The female is active during nest-building and incubation, but the male provides food for nestlings.

VOICE Call *chrrip, seet, zeet*; song 3 squeaky, repeated syllables *ps-SEET, ptsick, seet*, or *TSEE-wee, pttuck, tseep*.

NESTING Open cup, often with shelter above, in fork of tree or shelf on bank or bridge; 2–4 eggs; 2 broods; April–July.

FEEDING Feeds on insects caught in air or gleaned from foliage: beetles, wasps, bees, flies, moths, caterpillars, spiders; rarely berries.

DISTINCT MARKINGS
The Pacific-slope Flycatcher has distinct buffy wing bars and a streaked breast and belly.

SIMILAR SPECIES

YELLOW-BELLIED FLYCATCHER see p.248
bolder wing bars
blacker wings
shorter tail

CORDILLERAN FLYCATCHER see p.256
yellowish underparts

OCCURRENCE
Breeds to west of mountains from northern British Columbia to southern California in humid coastal coniferous forest, Pine Oak forest, and dense second-growth forest. Resides in well-shaded woods, along stream bottoms, and steep-walled ravines.

Length **6–7in (15–17.5cm)**	Wingspan **8–9in (20–23cm)**	Weight **9/32–7/16oz (8–12g)**
Social **Solitary**	Lifespan **Up to 6 years**	Status **Declining**

DATE SEEN	WHERE	NOTES

Order **Passeriformes**	Family **Tyrannidae**	Species ***Empidonax occidentalis***

Cordilleran Flycatcher

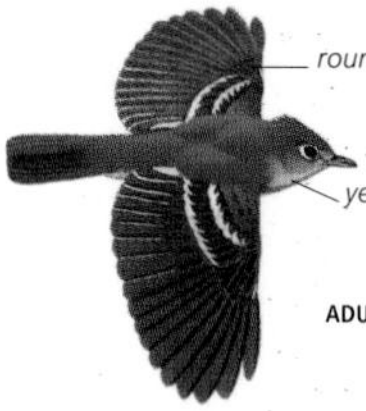

rounded wings

yellowish throat

ADULT

IN FLIGHT

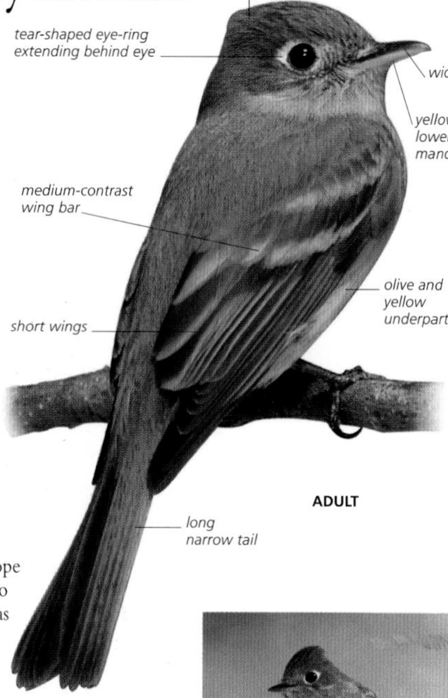

crest

tear-shaped eye-ring extending behind eye

wide bill

yellow-pink lower mandible

medium-contrast wing bar

olive and yellow underparts

short wings

ADULT

long narrow tail

FLIGHT: short feeding flights between perches to hawk insects.

The Cordilleran Flycatcher is nearly indistinguishable from the Pacific-slope Flycatcher; even their songs are difficult to differentiate. The Cordilleran, however, has slightly larger and darker upperparts and more olive and yellow underparts than its Pacific-slope relative. Often nesting in man-made structures, this bird is found east of the Rocky Mountains, from central British Columbia south to the Arizona border. The sexes look alike and are monogamous, behaving territorially during the breeding season. Most molting occurs when the birds are wintering.

VOICE Call *seet*, vocalizes principally on breeding grounds, with occasional calls at other times; song *ps-SEET, ptsick, seet*.

NESTING Cup on rocky outcrop, in natural cavity or root mass; 2–5 eggs; 2 broods; April–July.

FEEDING Feeds on insects; waits on perch to fly out for hunt.

CRESTED

The Cordilleran Flycatcher shows a more marked crest than the Pacific-slope species..

SIMILAR SPECIES

YELLOW-BELLIED FLYCATCHER see p.248

greener back

darker wing feathers

PACIFIC-SLOPE FLYCATCHER see p.255

smaller overall

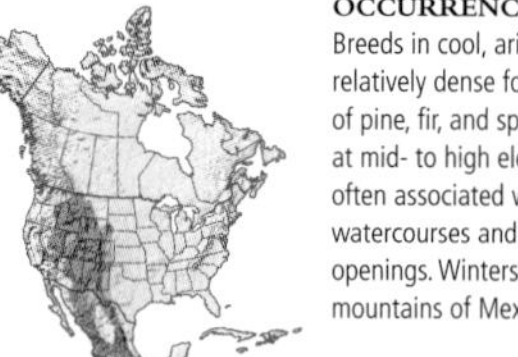

OCCURRENCE

Breeds in cool, arid, relatively dense forests of pine, fir, and spruce, at mid- to high elevation, often associated with watercourses and openings. Winters in the mountains of Mexico.

Length **6–7in (15–17.5cm)**	Wingspan **9in (23cm)**	Weight **3/8–7/16oz (11–13g)**
Social **Solitary**	Lifespan **Unknown**	Status **Secure**

DATE SEEN	WHERE	NOTES

Order **Passeriformes**	Family **Tyrannidae**	Species ***Tyrannus vociferans***

Cassin's Kingbird

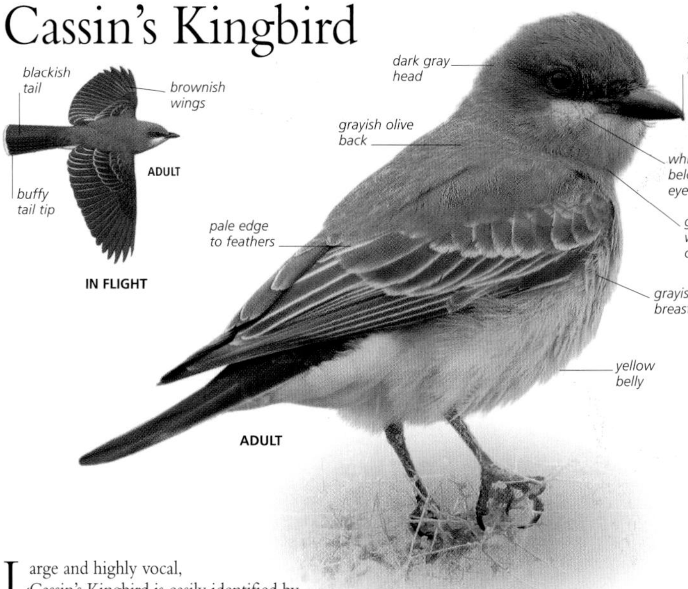
blackish tail
brownish wings
ADULT
buffy tail tip

IN FLIGHT

dark gray head
small bill, hooked at tip
grayish olive back
white below eye
grayish white chin
pale edge to feathers
grayish breast
yellow belly

ADULT

Large and highly vocal, Cassin's Kingbird is easily identified by its preference for territorial behavior and open perches, from where it swoops on insect prey. Courting birds impress each other in a display in which they hover in unison over a favorite perch. Cassin's Kingbird overlaps in range with the Western Kingbird, although there appears to be minimal competition between the two species. However, the nesting success of Cassin's Kingbird's is lower in areas where both birds occur.

VOICE Calls *ch-tuur* and low, nasal *chi-beer* or *chi-queer;* dawn song 1–2 rasping sounds followed by a prolonged *keecyur.*

NESTING Large, bulky open cup of twigs and rootlets; on branch high in deciduous tree; 3–5 eggs; 1 brood; April–August.

FEEDING Mainly insectivorous; feeds on beetles, bees, wasps, ants, flies, aphids, and grasshoppers; also eats fruit.

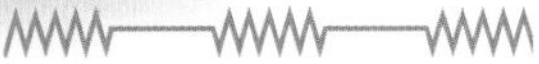

FLIGHT: direct, strong; males engage in "tumble flight"—fly up, stall, twist, pitch, tumble down.

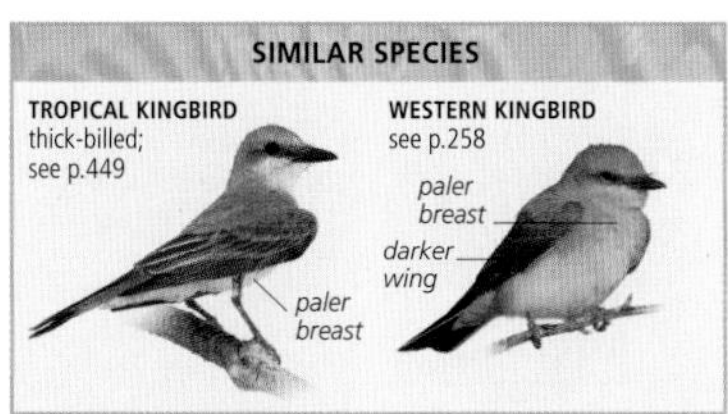

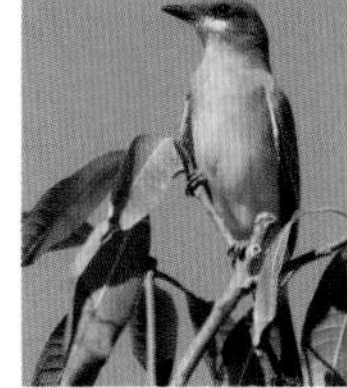

HIGH ALERT
This gray-breasted Cassin's Kingbird is perched and alert in mature riverine woodland.

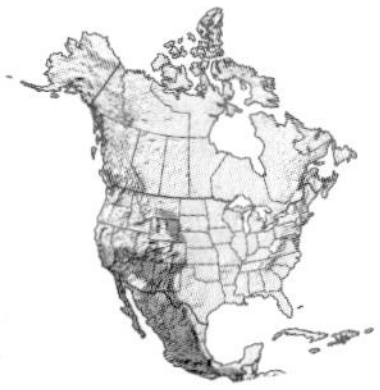

OCCURRENCE
Breeds in Wyoming, Montana, South Dakota, Oklahoma, Texas, Arizona, California, and New Mexico in waterside woodland, Pinyon pine, juniper forests, grassland, desert scrub, rural, and suburban habitats. US population winters south to Mexico and Guatemala, overlapping with resident population.

SIMILAR SPECIES

TROPICAL KINGBIRD
thick-billed; see p.449

paler breast

WESTERN KINGBIRD
see p.258

paler breast
darker wing

Length **8–9in (20–23cm)**	Wingspan **16in (41cm)**	Weight **1⁹⁄₁₆oz (45g)**
Social **Solitary**	Lifespan **Unknown**	Status **Secure**

DATE SEEN	WHERE	NOTES

Order **Passeriformes**	Family **Tyrannidae**	Species ***Tyrannus verticalis***

Western Kingbird

A conspicuous summer breeder in the US, the Western Kingbird occurs in open habitats in much of western North America. The white outer edges on its outer tail feathers distinguish it from other kingbirds. Its population has expanded eastward over the last 100 years. A large, loosely defined territory is defended against other kingbirds when breeding begins in spring; a smaller core area is defended as the season progresses.

VOICE Calls include *whit*, *pwee-t*, and chatter; song, regularly repeated sharp *kip* notes and high-pitched notes.

NESTING Open, bulky cup of grass, rootlets, and twigs in tree, shrub, utility pole; 2–7 eggs; 1 brood; April–July.

FEEDING Feeds on a wide variety of insects; also berries and fruit.

FLIGHT: agile, fast, direct, flapping flight; flies to catch insects; hovers to pick bugs on vegetation.

FENCE POST
A favorite place for the Western Kingbird to perch, and look around, is on fenceposts.

QUENCHING THIRST
A juvenile Western Kingbird drinks at the edge of a shallow pools of water.

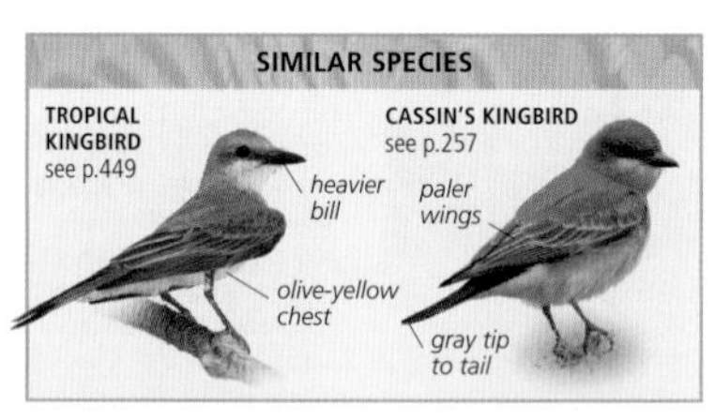

OCCURRENCE
Widespread in southern Canada and the western US, in open habitats, such as grasslands, savannah, desert shrub, pastures, and cropland, near elevated perches; particularly near water. Winters in similar habitats and in tropical forest and shrubbery from Mexico to Costa Rica.

Length **8–9in (20–23cm)**	Wingspan **15–16in (38–41cm)**	Weight **1¼–1 9/16 oz (35–45g)**
Social **Solitary**	Lifespan **Up to 6 years**	Status **Secure**

DATE SEEN	WHERE	NOTES

Order **Passeriformes**	Family **Tyrannidae**	Species ***Tyrannus tyrannus***

Eastern Kingbird

ADULT

white-tipped tail

white throat

IN FLIGHT

dark crown and cheeks, almost black

dark eyes

faint gray "necklace"

white throat and underparts

pale edges to wing feathers

ADULT

white belly

black legs and toes

white undertail feathers

relatively short, thick bill

slate-gray back

ADULT

black tail with white tip

The Eastern Kingbird is a tame and widely distributed bird. It is a highly territorial species and is known for its aggressive behavior toward potential predators, particularly crows and hawks, which it pursues relentlessly. It is able to identify and remove the eggs of the Brown-headed Cowbird when they are laid in its nest. The Eastern Kingbird is generally monogamous and pairs will return to the same territory in subsequent years. This species winters in tropical South America, where it forages for fruit in the treetops of evergreen forests.

VOICE Principal call is loud, metallic *chatter-zeer*; song rapid, electric *kdik-kdik-kdik-pika-pika-pika-kzeeeer*.

NESTING Open cup of twigs, roots, stems in hawthorn, elm, stump, fence, or post; 2–5 eggs; 1 brood; May–August.

FEEDING Catches flying insects from elevated perch or gleans insects from foliage; eats berries and fruit, except in spring.

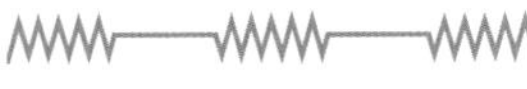

FLIGHT: strong, direct, and very agile with vigorous, rapid wing beats; hovers and sails.

WHITE-TIPPED
The white-tipped tails of these two Eastern Kingbirds are conspicuous as they sit on a budding twig.

OCCURRENCE
Breeds across much of North America in a variety of open habitats, including urban areas, parks, golf courses, fields with scattered shrubs, beaver ponds, and along forest edges. Long distance migrant; winters in South America, south to Argentina.

Length **7–9in (18–23cm)**	Wingspan **13–15in (33–38cm)**	Weight **1 1/16–2oz (30–55g)**
Social **Solitary/Pairs**	Lifespan **Up to 7 years**	Status **Secure**

DATE SEEN	WHERE	NOTES

Order **Passeriformes**	Family **Tyrannidae**	Species ***Myiarchus cinerascens***

Ash-throated Flycatcher

rusty outer edges to outer flight feathers

brown outer tail feathers

rounded wings

ADULT

IN FLIGHT

bushy gray-brown crest

short, relatively thin bill

pale gray throat

rusty edges to outer tail feathers

ADULT

all dark bill

grayish white chest

white wing bars

pale yellow belly

long tail

ADULT

FLIGHT: continuous flapping; rapid and direct; acrobatic maneuvers; hovers.

Of the three western species of *Myiarchus* flycatchers in the US, this is the most widespread and versatile, although it does prefer dry country. Deserts, mesquite, riverine and open woodlands, and juniper scrub are among its breeding habitats, though higher densities are found by rivers than in the open. Man-made structures such as pipes, the eaves of houses, and nest boxes often replace natural cavities for nesting. This species often fills cavities with material such as hair and feathers, to create a smaller chamber.

VOICE Call *huit* also *wheer*, *whip*, or *prrt;* dawn song *ha-wheer* or burry *ka-brick*.

NESTING Any natural or artificial cavity, adds dry grass, stems, twigs, and other materials such as hair or feathers; 2–7 eggs; 1–2 broods; March–July.

FEEDING Eats mainly insects; occasionally fruit, small reptiles, and mammals.

RUSTY FIELD MARKS
Rufous outer tail and wing feathers are useful field marks in identifying this species.

SIMILAR SPECIES

GREAT CRESTED FLYCATCHER eastern; see p.450

bulkier overall

yellow belly

BROWN-CRESTED FLYCATCHER different habitat; see p.450

darker gray above

lighter yellow below

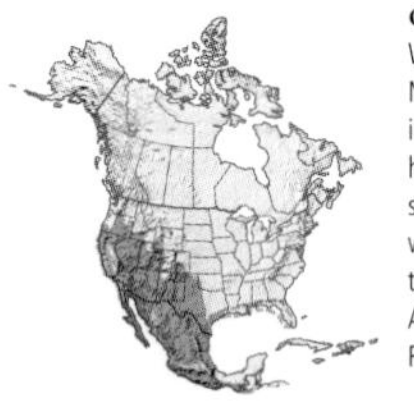

OCCURRENCE
Widespread in western North America. Breeds in lowland to mid-elevation habitats, in arid and semi-arid scrub, open woodland, or waterside forests. Migrates to Mexico and Central America to Costa Rica. Resident in Mexico.

Length **7–8in (18–20cm)**	Wingspan **12–13in (30–33cm)**	Weight **1 1/16–1 7/16oz (20–40g)**
Social **Solitary**	Lifespan **Up to 11 years**	Status **Secure**

DATE SEEN	WHERE	NOTES

Families **Laniidae, Vireonidae**

SHRIKES & VIREOS

SHRIKES

Two of the thirty species of shrikes (Laniidae) occur in Canada and the United States. The Loggerhead Shrike is truly North American, but the other North American species, the Northern (or Gray) Shrike, is also widespread in Europe and western Asia. Shrikes have a strongly hooked bill, almost like a bird of prey. In fact, shrikes capture not only insects, but also birds, rodents, and lizards, which they impale on a thorn in a shrub (a larder). Shrikes pounce down on their prey from high perches in trees or on fenceposts, catching it on or near the ground. Many shrike species are declining.

SEPARATE SPECIES
The Blue-headed Vireo is one of three species, formerly known as just one species, the Solitary Vireo.

VIREOS

Vireos are a family of songbirds restricted to the New World, with about 15 species occurring in the United States and Canada. Their classification has long been problematic—traditionally they were associated with warblers, but recent molecular studies suggest that they are actually related to crow-like birds. Vireo plumage is drab, often predominantly greenish or grayish above and whitish below, augmented by eye-rings, ("spectacles,") eyestripes, and wing bars. Most vireos have a preference for broadleaved habitats, where they move about deliberately, hopping and climbing as they slowly forage for their prey. They are mainly insect-eaters. Most species are mid- to long-distance migrants, retreating to warmer climes in winter, when insects are dormant. Vireos are most often detected by the male's loud and clear territorial song, which is repetitive and persistent.

KEEN SONGSTER
The White-eyed Vireo sings almost continuously, even on the hottest of summer days.

Family **Corvidae**

JAYS & CROWS

ALTHOUGH JAYS AND CROWS belong to a highly diverse family, the Corvidae, most members share some important characteristics. They are remarkably social, some species even breeding cooperatively, but at the same time they can be quiet and stealthy. Always opportunistic, corvids use strong bills and toes to obtain a varied, omnivorous diet. Ornithologists have shown that ravens, magpies, and crows are among the most intelligent birds. They exhibit self-awareness when looking into mirrors, can make tools, and successfully tackle difficult counting and problem-solving. As a rule, most corvid plumage comes in shades of blue, black, and white. The plumage of adult corvids does not vary by season. Corvidae are part of an ancient bird lineage (Corvoidea) that originated in Australasia. Crows and jays were among the birds most affected by the spread of West Nile virus in the early 2000s, but most populations seem to have recovered quickly.

BLACK AND BLUE
Many corvids (especially jays such as this Steller's Jay) have plumage in shades of black, blue, and gray.

Order **Passeriformes**	Family **Laniidae**	Species ***Lanius ludovicianus***

Loggerhead Shrike

FLIGHT: fast with rapid wing beats, sometimes interspersed with glides; swoops from perches.

Although a songbird, the Loggerhead Shrike is superficially raptor-like in several ways, particularly its prominent black face mask and powerful, hooked bill. It sits atop posts or tall trees, swooping down to catch prey on the ground. It has the unusual habit of then impaling its prey on thorns, barbed wire, or sharp twigs, which is thought to be the reason for the nickname "butcher bird." Unfortunately, the Loggerhead Shrike is declining, principally because of human alteration of its habitat.

VOICE Quiet warbles, trills, and harsh notes; song harsh notes singly or in series: *chaa chaa chaa.*

NESTING Open cup of vegetation, placed in thorny tree; 5 eggs; 1 brood; March–June.

FEEDING Kills large insects and small vertebrates—rodents, birds, reptiles—with powerful bill.

GEARED FOR HUNTING
The Loggerhead Shrike perches upright on tall shrubs or small trees, where it scans for prey.

SIMILAR SPECIES

NORTHERN SHRIKE see p.263
smaller bill
lighter upperparts

NORTHERN MOCKINGBIRD see p.316
darker upperparts
longer tail

OCCURRENCE
Found in semi-open country with scattered perches, but its distribution is erratic, occurring in relatively high densities in certain areas, but absent from seemingly suitable habitat. Occurs in congested residential areas in some regions (south Florida), but generally favors fairly remote habitats.

Length **9in (23cm)**	Wingspan **12in (31cm)**	Weight **1¼–2⅛oz (35–60g)**
Social **Solitary**	Lifespan **Unknown**	Status **Declining**

DATE SEEN	WHERE	NOTES

Order **Passeriformes**	Family **Laniidae**	Species ***Lanius excubitor***

Northern Shrike

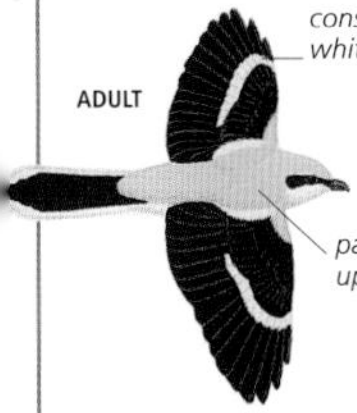

ADULT

conspicuous white wing bar

pale gray upperparts

IN FLIGHT

strongly hooked bill

delicately barred breast

brownish underparts

long tail

IMMATURE

large head

narrow black mask

pale gray upperparts

black wings

gray-white underparts

black tail, with white outer tail feathers

ADULT

FLIGHT: short flights between hunting perches; pounces on prey.

This northern version of the familiar Loggerhead Shrike is an uncommon winter visitor to the northern US and southern Canada. In some winters, this species is widespread across the mid-latitudes of North America, in other winters it is nearly absent. The Northern Shrike is paler, larger bodied, and larger billed than the Loggerhead Shrike, which enables it to attack and subdue larger prey than the Loggerhead. Many Northern Shrike populations worldwide are in decline, but to date there is no sign of a similar decline in North America.

VOICE Variety of short warbles, trills, and harsh notes; generally silent on wintering grounds.

NESTING Open, bulky cup in low tree or large shrub, lined with feathers and hair; 4–6 eggs; 1 brood; May–June.

FEEDING Swoops down on prey, such as rodents, small birds, and insects, which it impales on thorns or pointed branches.

BLACK-AND-WHITE DISPLAY
The Northern Shrike flashes its distinctive black-and-white markings while in flight.

SIMILAR SPECIES

LOGGERHEAD SHRIKE see p.262

shorter bill

darker, smaller overall

NORTHERN MOCKINGBIRD see p.316

straight, white-edged tail

thin bill

less black in wings

OCCURRENCE
Breeds in sub-Arctic coniferous forests, across Canada and Alaska. Winters in more southerly open country with sufficient perches. Avoids built-up and residential districts, but spends much time perching on fenceposts and roadside signs.

Length **10in (25cm)**	Wingspan **14in (35cm)**	Weight **1¾–2⅝oz (50–75g)**
Social **Solitary**	Lifespan **Unknown**	Status **Vulnerable**

DATE SEEN	WHERE	NOTES

Order **Passeriformes**	Family **Vireonidae**	Species ***Vireo bellii***

Bell's Vireo

This pale, grayish, and nondescript vireo is hard to see as it moves through dense brushy vegetation searching for food. Its most distinctive feature is a long tail, which it flicks as it moves. In the arid western parts of its range, in northern Mexico and Arizona, Bell's Vireo is usually found close to rivers or streams. The Eastern subspecies (*V. b. belli*) is distinctly brighter in plumage than the three western subspecies, one of which, the Least Bell's Vireo (*V. b. pusillus*) of southern California, is endangered.

VOICE Call high, raspy, and nasal; males highly vocal and sing all day long during the breeding season; song quite fast for a vireo.

NESTING Deep, rounded cup constructed of coarse materials, lined with fine grasses and hair, and bound with spider webs, in dense shrubbery woven to twigs by the rim; 3–5 eggs; 2 broods; April–May.

FEEDING Actively gleans its insect and spider prey from leaves and twigs, hopping from branch to branch in brushy vegetation.

FLIGHT: slightly undulating flight with rapid wing beats followed by short glides.

TAIL FLICKING
Unlike other vireos, Bell's Vireo is known for flicking its long tail as it sings.

SIMILAR SPECIES

WARBLING VIREO see p.270
white eyebrow
no wing bar

PHILADEPHIA VIREO see p.271
greenish upperparts

OCCURRENCE
Fairly common breeder in the bushy habitats of the central US, and the riverine thickets of the southwestern US, southward into northern Mexico. Winters along the Pacific slopes of Mexico.

Length **4¾in (12cm)**	Wingspan **7in (18cm)**	Weight **5/16oz (9g)**
Social **Solitary**	Lifespan **Up to 8 years**	Status **Vulnerable**

DATE SEEN	WHERE	NOTES

Order **Passeriformes**	Family **Vireonidae**	Species ***Vireo vicinior***

Gray Vireo

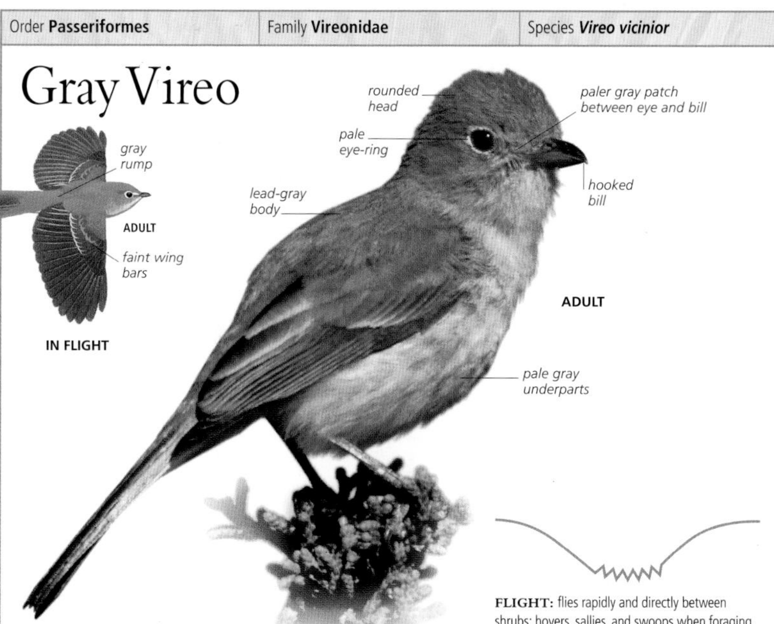

FLIGHT: flies rapidly and directly between shrubs; hovers, sallies, and swoops when foraging.

A drab, inconspicuous vireo of the hot and arid southwestern US, the Gray Vireo is reminiscent of a miniature shrike in terms of posture and shape. Found mainly in dense, shrubby vegetation such as pinyon and juniper, it is most often detected by its distinctive voice. In its restricted habitat, it can be confused with other small, gray birds such as gnatcatchers, titmice, and the Bushtit.

VOICE Varied calls, include trills and chatters; song given by male, harsh three- to four-note phrase.

NESTING Cup of dry plant materials and spider webs, suspended from twigs by rim, fairly low in shrub or tree, lined with fine fibers; 3–4 eggs; 1 brood; April–May.

FEEDING Gleans insects and spiders from leaves, twigs, and branches; also catches flies in flight; in winter, primarily eats fruit.

PERCHED SINGER
From the top of a shrub, a male sings to declare his ownership of the surrounding territory.

UNCOMMON BIRD
The Gray Vireo is an uncommon little bird and can be difficult to spot in its scrubby habitat.

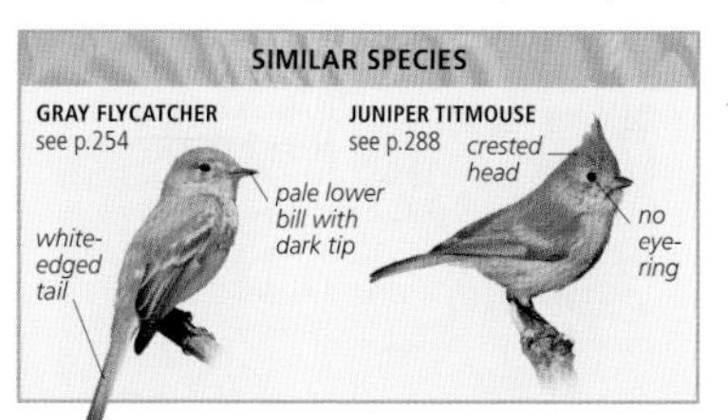

OCCURRENCE
Breeds in the hot and arid, shrubby scrublands of the southwestern US, in parts of Nevada, Colorado, Utah, Arizona, New Mexico, and Texas; short-distance migrant. Winters largely in Mexico, in similarly arid areas.

Length **5½in (14cm)**	Wingspan **8in (20cm)**	Weight **7/16oz (13g)**
Social **Solitary/Pairs**	Lifespan **Up to 5 years**	Status **Localized**

DATE SEEN	WHERE	NOTES

Order **Passeriformes**	Family **Vireonidae**	Species ***Vireo plumbeus***

Plumbeous Vireo

gray-and-white tail

two white wing bars

gray overall

ADULT

IN FLIGHT

gray upperparts

white "spectacles"

bill thick at base

white breast

gray edges on wing feathers

white belly

ADULT

FLIGHT: short, direct movement with strong wing beats.

This gray-and-white bird, with its conspicuous white "spectacles" and wing bars was recognized as a distinct species only in 1997. In that year, the bird formerly known as "Solitary Vireo" was split into three vireo species—Cassin's, Blue-headed, and Plumbeous—based on genetic, plumage, and voice differences. The range of the Plumbeous Vireo has been expanding west since the 1940s and it can now be found alongside the greenish-toned Cassin's Vireo.

VOICE Call a harsh scold; male song a series of rough, slurred, two- or three-note phrases.

NESTING Loose, round cup of fibers, bound with spider webs, lined with fine material, suspended by rim from twigs; 3–5 eggs; 1 brood; April–June.

FEEDING Plucks insects from leaves or twigs, slowly hopping through foliage; often sallies to catch prey.

NEST COVER
This species tends to build its nest at the end of a branch and may cover it with lichens.

BIG VOICE
Like other vireos, the male Plumbeous Vireo will often sing continuously.

SIMILAR SPECIES

GRAY VIREO see p.265
lighter wing bars

CASSIN'S VIREO see p.267
duller eye-ring
greenish upperparts
greenish flanks

OCCURRENCE
Breeds largely in coniferous or mountainous forests of the interior Southwest and down the Sierra Madre; found in Mexico through to Central America; also occurs close to rivers and streams in Arizona and New Mexico. Winters mostly on the Pacific Slope of Mexico.

Length **5¾in (14.5cm)**	Wingspan **10in (25cm)**	Weight **⅝oz (18g)**
Social **Solitary**	Lifespan **Unknown**	Status **Secure**

DATE SEEN	WHERE	NOTES

Order **Passeriformes**	Family **Vireonidae**	Species ***Vireo cassinii***

Cassin's Vireo

two whitish wing bars

ADULT

IN FLIGHT

dark patch between eye and bill

hooked bill

white "spectacles"

gray head

greenish gray back

ADULT

short tail

pale yellowish flanks

whitish belly

FLIGHT: short, direct movement with strong wing beats; can hover briefly.

Cassin's Vireo is similar to the closely related Plumbeous and Blue-headed Vireos in appearance and song. It is conspicuous and vocal throughout its breeding grounds in the far west of the US and north into southwest Canada. In winter, virtually the entire population migrates to Mexico. Cassin's Vireo was named in honor of John Cassin, who published the first comprehensive study of North American birds in 1865.

VOICE Call a harsh, scolding chatter; male's song a broken series of whistles, which ascend then descend; lower in tone than Blue-headed Vireo and higher than the Plumbeous.

NESTING Cup of fibers, lined with fine plant down; suspended from twigs; 2–5 eggs; 1–2 broods; April–July.

FEEDING Picks insects and spiders from leaves and twigs as it hops from branch to branch; occasionally sallies out or hovers.

TIRELESS SINGER
Cassin's Vireo is well known for its loud and incessant singing throughout the spring and into the summer.

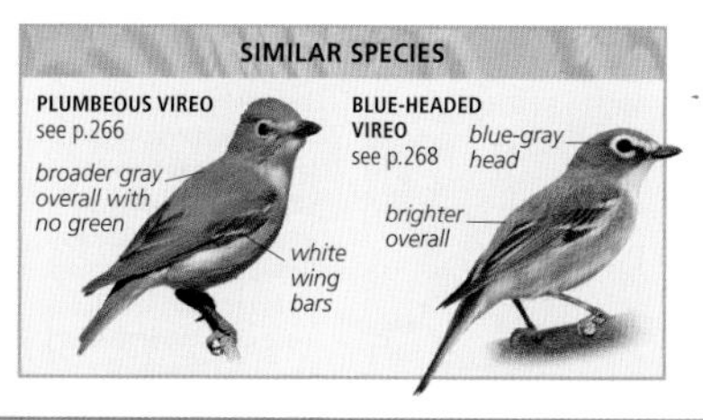

OCCURRENCE
Breeds in coniferous and mixed forests in the hills and mountains of British Columbia, Alberta, and, in the US, the Pacific Northwest through to southern California. Winters in western Mexico.

Length **5½in (14cm)**	Wingspan **9½in (24cm)**	Weight **9/16oz (16g)**
Social **Solitary/Pairs**	Lifespan **Unknown**	Status **Secure**

DATE SEEN	WHERE	NOTES

Order **Passeriformes**	Family **Vireonidae**	Species ***Vireo solitarius***

Blue-headed Vireo

Closely related to the Cassin's Vireo and Plumbeous Vireo, the fairly common Blue-headed Vireo is the brightest and most colorful of the three. Its blue-gray, helmeted head, adorned with striking white "spectacles" around its dark eyes also helps to distinguish it from other vireos in its range. This stocky and slow moving bird is heard more often than it is seen in its forest breeding habitat. However, during migration it can be more conspicuous and, is the first vireo to return in spring.

VOICE Call a harsh, scolding chatter; male's song a series of rich, sweet, high phrases of two to six notes slurred together.

NESTING Shallow, rounded cup loosely constructed of animal and plant fibers, lined with finer material and suspended from twigs by the rim; 3–5 eggs; 2 broods; May–July.

FEEDING Gleans insects from branches and leaves, usually high in shrubs and trees; often makes short sallies after prey.

FLIGHT: slow, heavy, undulating flight with a series of deep wing beats followed by short pauses.

SPECTACLED VIREO
Its rather thick head with conspicuous "spectacles" and gray color are distinctive field marks.

SIMILAR SPECIES

BLACK-CAPPED VIREO ◔ see p.450
smaller overall
thin bill

CASSIN'S VIREO see p.267
duller overall

OCCURRENCE
Breeds in large tracts of undisturbed coniferous and mixed forests with a rich understory, largely across eastern North America. It winters in woodlands across the southeastern US from Virginia to Texas, as well as in Mexico and northern Central America to Costa Rica.

Length **5½in (14in)**	Wingspan **9½in (24cm)**	Weight **9/16oz (16g)**
Social **Solitary/Pairs**	Lifespan **Up to 7 years**	Status **Secure**

DATE SEEN	WHERE	NOTES

Order **Passeriformes**	Family **Vireonidae**	Species ***Vireo huttoni***

Hutton's Vireo

short, rounded wings

ADULT

IN FLIGHT

large, rounded head

pale patch

broken eye-ring

white wing bars

thick, hooked bill

ADULT

blue-gray legs

This unobtrusive bird is understood at present to be a geographically variable species with about a dozen subspecies. These subspecies can be grouped into two populations. The first is a coastal population occurring from British Columbia to Baja California; the second is an interior population found from the Southwest and south to Central America. These two isolated populations, widely separated by desert, may actually represent different species. Very similar in appearance to the Ruby-crowned Kinglet with which it flocks in winter, Hutton's Vireo is distinguishable by its larger size and thicker bill. Unlike other vireos, this bird is largely nonmigratory.

VOICE Varied calls include harsh mewing and nasal, raspy *spit*; male's song a repetition of a simple phrase.

NESTING Deep cup constructed from plant and animal fibers, lined with finer materials, often incorporating lichens, suspended from twigs by the rim; 3–5 eggs; 1–2 broods; February–May.

FEEDING Hops diligently from branch to branch searching for caterpillars, spiders, and flies; also eats berries; gleans from leaves usually while perched, but occasionally sallies or hovers.

FLIGHT: weak and bouncy with rapid wing beats.

FOLLOW THE SONG
This kinglet-sized vireo is easily overlooked and is often detected by its song.

SIMILAR SPECIES

PACIFIC-SLOPE FLYCATCHER see p.255
wide, flat bill
unbroken eye-ring
long tail

RUBY-CROWNED KINGLET ♂ see p.300
thin bill
smaller overall

OCCURRENCE
Year-round resident in mixed evergreen forests; particularly common in live oak woods. Breeds in mixed oak-pine woodlands along the Pacific coast from British Columbia southward to northern Baja California, and from southwest California and New Mexico to Mexico and Guatemala.

Length **5in (13cm)**	Wingspan **8in (20cm)**	Weight **3/8oz (11g)**
Social **Solitary/Pairs**	Lifespan **Up to 13 years**	Status **Secure**

DATE SEEN	WHERE	NOTES

Order **Passeriformes**	Family **Vireonidae**	Species ***Vireo gilvus***

Warbling Vireo

FLIGHT: fast and undulating; rapid wing beats followed by brief, closed-wing glides.

Widely distributed across North America, this rather drab vireo is better known for its cheerful warbling song than for its plumage, and coincidentally, its thin bill and longish tail give this rather active vireo a somewhat warbler-like appearance. The eastern subspecies (*V. g. gilvus*), which is heavier and has a larger bill, and the western subspecies (*V. g. swainsonii*) are quite different and may in fact be separate species. Out of all the vireos, the Warbling Vireo is most likely to breed in human developments, such as city parks, suburbs, and orchards.

VOICE Harsh, raspy scold call; male's persistent song a high, rapid, and highly variable warble.

NESTING Rough cup placed high in a deciduous tree, hung from the rim between forked twigs; 3–5 eggs; 2 broods; March–July.

FEEDING Gleans a variety of insects, including grasshoppers, aphids, and beetles from leaves; eats fruit in winter.

PLAIN-LOOKING SONGSTER
The Warbling Vireo makes up for its plain appearance by its colorful voice, full of rounded notes and melodious warbles.

SIMILAR SPECIES

OCCURRENCE
Extensive distribution across most of temperate North America, from Alaska, around the northern limit of the northerly zone, and through western, central, and eastern North America. Breeds in deciduous and mixed forests, particularly near water. Winters in southern Mexico and Central America.

Length **5½in (14cm)**	Wingspan **8½in (21cm)**	Weight **7/16oz (12g)**
Social **Solitary/Pairs**	Lifespan **Up to 13 years**	Status **Secure**

DATE SEEN	WHERE	NOTES

Order **Passeriformes**	Family **Vireonidae**	Species ***Vireo philadelphicus***

Philadelphia Vireo

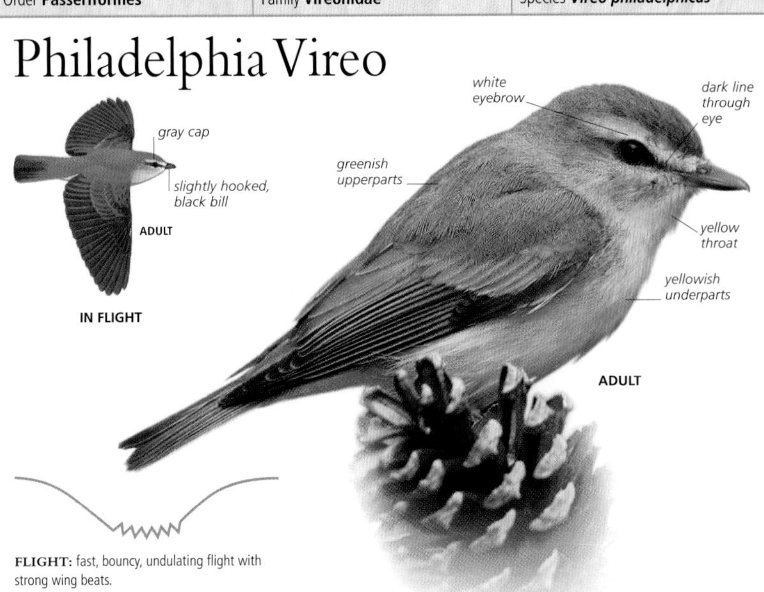

FLIGHT: fast, bouncy, undulating flight with strong wing beats.

Despite being widespread, the Philadelphia Vireo remains rather poorly studied. It shares its breeding habitat with the similar looking, but larger and more numerous, Red-eyed Vireo, and, interestingly, it modifies its behavior to avoid competition. It is the most northerly breeding vireo, with its southernmost breeding range barely reaching the US. Its scientific and English names derive from the fact that the bird was first discovered near Philadelphia in the mid-19th century.

VOICE Song a series of two and four note phrases, remarkably similar to the song of the Red-eyed Vireo.

NESTING Rounded cup of plant fibers bound by spider webs, hanging between forked twigs that narrows at the rim; 3–5 eggs; 1–2 broods; June–August.

FEEDING Gleans caterpillars, bees, flies, and bugs from leaves; usually forages high in trees, moving with short hops and flights.

DISTINGUISHED APPEARANCE
The Philadelphia Vireo's gentle expression and pudgy appearance help separate it from its neighbor, the Red-eyed Vireo.

SIMILAR SPECIES

BELL'S VIREO see p.264
faint wing bar
longer tail

WARBLING VIREO see p.270
plainer face
less yellow below

OCCURRENCE
Breeds in deciduous woodlands, mixed woodlands, and woodland edges, in a wide belt across Canada, reaching the Great Lakes and northern New England. The Philadelphia Vireo winters from Mexico to Panama and northern Colombia.

Length **5¼in (13.5cm)**	Wingspan **8in (20cm)**	Weight **7/16oz (12g)**
Social **Solitary/Pairs**	Lifespan **Up to 8 years**	Status **Secure**

DATE SEEN	WHERE	NOTES

Order **Passeriformes**	Family **Vireonidae**	Species ***Vireo olivaceus***

Red-eyed Vireo

generally olive above

head held at downward angle

ADULT

IN FLIGHT

gray crown

heavy eye-line

white eyestripe with black upper border

long bill

bird appears long and slender

deep red eye

ADULT

whitish underparts

bluish legs and toes

FLIGHT: fast, strong, and undulating with the body angled upwards.

Probably the most common songbird of northern and eastern North America, the Red-eyed Vireo is perhaps the quintessential North American vireo, although it is heard far more often than it is seen. It sings persistently and monotonously all day long and late into the season, long after other species have stopped singing. It generally stays high in the canopy of the deciduous and mixed woodlands where it breeds. The entire population migrates to central South America in winter. To reach their Amazonian winter habitats, Red-eyed Vireos migrate in fall (August–October) through Central America, Caribbean Islands, and northern South America to Ecuador, Peru, and Brazil.

VOICE Nasal mewing call; male song consists of slurred three-note phrases.

NESTING Open cup nest hanging on horizontal fork of tree branch; built with plant fibers bound with spider's web; exterior is sometimes decorated with lichen; 3–5 eggs; 1 brood; May–July.

FEEDING Gleans insects from leaves, hopping methodically in the canopy and sub-canopy of deciduous trees; during fall and winter, primarily feeds on fruit.

HOPPING BIRD
The Red-eyed Vireo's primary form of locomotion is hopping; at ground level and in trees.

BROWN EYES
Immature Red-eyed Vireos have brown eyes, but those of the adult birds are red.

OCCURRENCE
Breeds across North America from the Yukon and British Columbia east to the Canadian maritimes, southward from Washington to south central Texas, and west to Canada in central and northern states. Inhabits the canopy of deciduous forests and pine hardwood forests.

Length **6in (15cm)**	Wingspan **10in (25cm)**	Weight **⅝oz (17g)**
Social **Solitary/Pairs**	Lifespan **Up to 10 years**	Status **Secure**

DATE SEEN	WHERE	NOTES

Order **Passeriformes**	Family **Corvidae**	Species ***Perisoreus canadensis***

Gray Jay

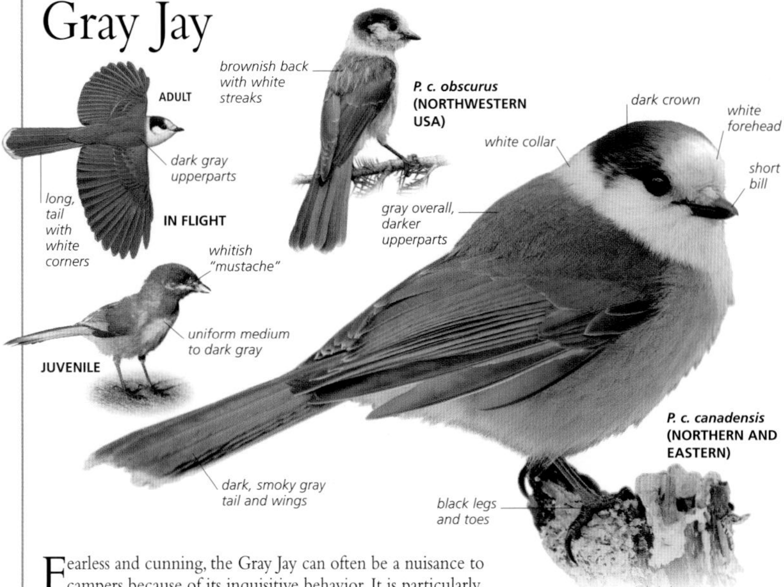
ADULT
IN FLIGHT
dark gray upperparts
long, tail with white corners
brownish back with white streaks
P. c. obscurus (NORTHWESTERN USA)
JUVENILE
whitish "mustache"
uniform medium to dark gray
dark crown
white forehead
white collar
short bill
gray overall, darker upperparts
P. c. canadensis (NORTHERN AND EASTERN)
dark, smoky gray tail and wings
black legs and toes

Fearless and cunning, the Gray Jay can often be a nuisance to campers because of its inquisitive behavior. It is particularly adept at stealing food and shiny metal objects, which has earned it the colloquial name of "Camp Robber." One of the interesting aspects of its behavior is the way it stores food for later use, by sticking it to trees with its viscous saliva. This is thought to be one of the reasons that enable it to survive the long northern winters. Gray Jays can often gather in noisy groups of three to six birds in order to investigate intruders encroaching upon their territory.

VOICE Mostly silent, but also produces variety of odd clucks and screeches; sometimes Blue Jay-like *jay!* and eerie whistles, including bisyllabic *whee-oo* or *ew*.

NESTING Bulky platform of sticks with cocoons on south side of coniferous tree; 2–5 eggs; 1 brood; February–May.

FEEDING Forages for insects and berries; also raids birds' nests.

FLIGHT: hollow-sounding wing beats followed by slow, seemingly awkward, rocking glides.

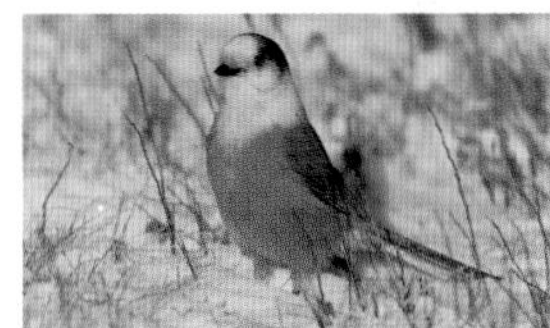

BUILT FOR COLD
The Gray Jay's short extremities and dense, fluffy plumage are perfect for long, harsh winters.

SIMILAR SPECIES

CLARK'S NUTCRACKER see p.278

NORTHERN MOCKINGBIRD see p.316

white wing patch
longer bill
no dark crown
longer tail
white wing patch

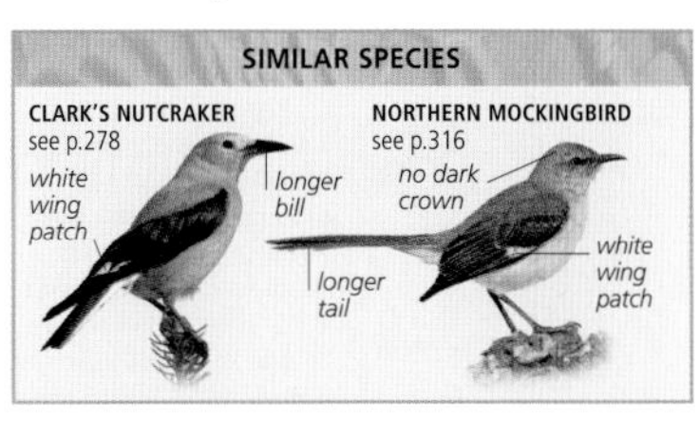

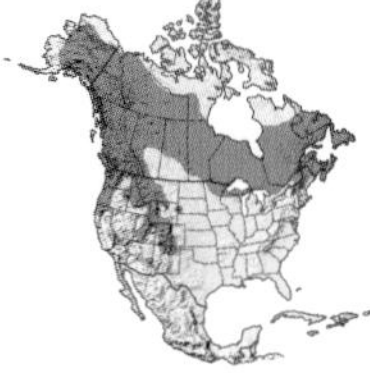

OCCURRENCE
Northern forests, especially lichen-festooned areas with firs and spruce. Found in coniferous forests across northern North America from Alaska to Newfoundland, the Maritimes, and northern New York and New England; south to western mountains; an isolated population in the Black Hills.

Length **10–11½in (25–29cm)**	Wingspan **18in (46cm)**	Weight **2⅛–2⅞oz (60–80g)**
Social **Family groups**	Lifespan **Up to 10 years**	Status **Secure**

DATE SEEN	WHERE	NOTES

Order **Passeriformes**	Family **Corvidae**	Species ***Cyanocitta stelleri***

Steller's Jay

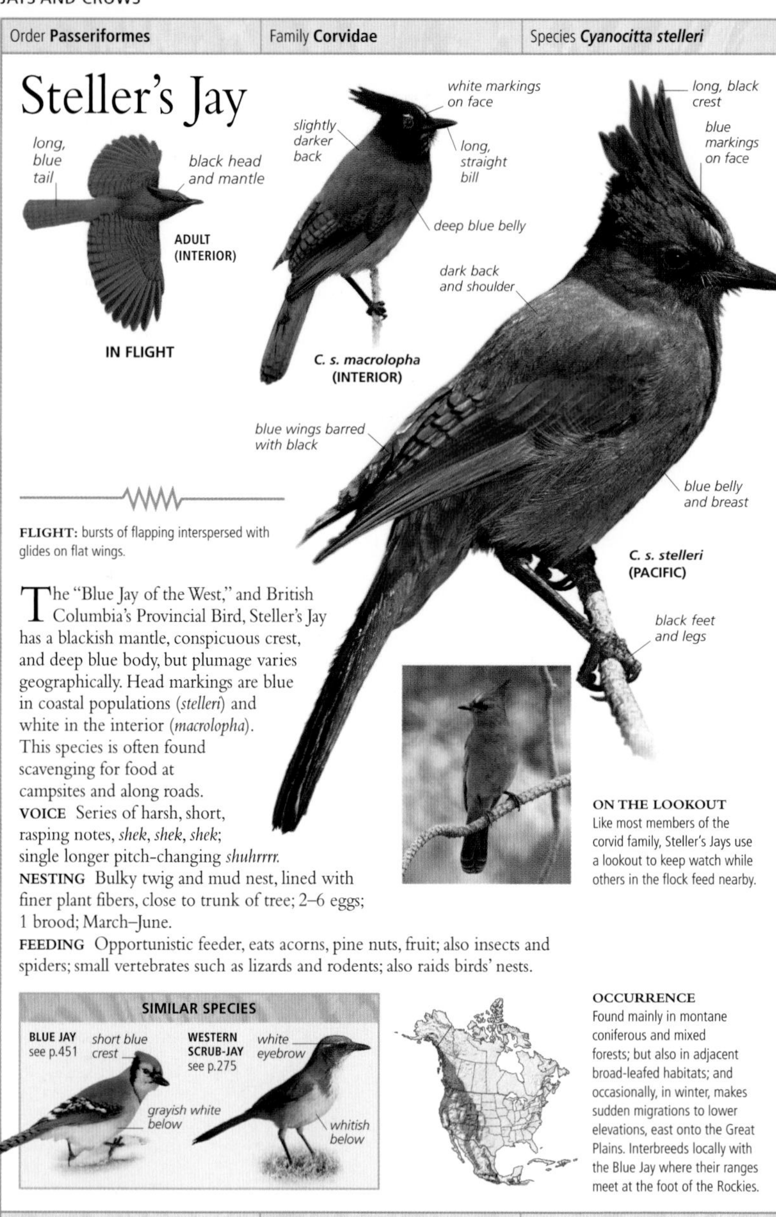

FLIGHT: bursts of flapping interspersed with glides on flat wings.

The "Blue Jay of the West," and British Columbia's Provincial Bird, Steller's Jay has a blackish mantle, conspicuous crest, and deep blue body, but plumage varies geographically. Head markings are blue in coastal populations (*stelleri*) and white in the interior (*macrolopha*). This species is often found scavenging for food at campsites and along roads.

VOICE Series of harsh, short, rasping notes, *shek, shek, shek*; single longer pitch-changing *shuhrrrr.*

NESTING Bulky twig and mud nest, lined with finer plant fibers, close to trunk of tree; 2–6 eggs; 1 brood; March–June.

FEEDING Opportunistic feeder, eats acorns, pine nuts, fruit; also insects and spiders; small vertebrates such as lizards and rodents; also raids birds' nests.

ON THE LOOKOUT
Like most members of the corvid family, Steller's Jays use a lookout to keep watch while others in the flock feed nearby.

SIMILAR SPECIES

BLUE JAY see p.451 short blue crest; grayish white below

WESTERN SCRUB-JAY see p.275 white eyebrow; whitish below

OCCURRENCE
Found mainly in montane coniferous and mixed forests; but also in adjacent broad-leafed habitats; and occasionally, in winter, makes sudden migrations to lower elevations, east onto the Great Plains. Interbreeds locally with the Blue Jay where their ranges meet at the foot of the Rockies.

Length **11–12½in (28–32cm)**	Wingspan **19in (48cm)**	Weight **3½–5oz (100–150g)**
Social **Small flocks**	Lifespan **Up to 15 years**	Status **Secure**

DATE SEEN	WHERE	NOTES

Order **Passeriformes**	Family **Corvidae**	Species ***Aphelocoma californica***

Western Scrub-Jay

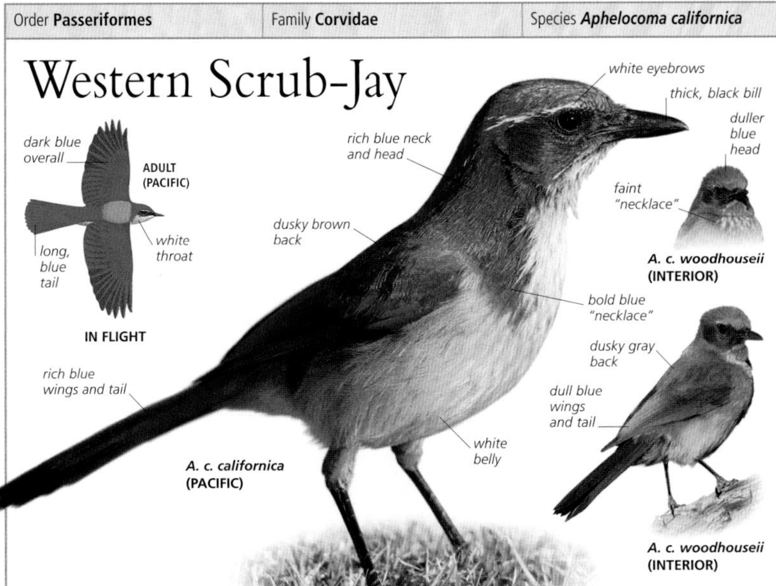

This species comprises three subspecies, two of which occur in the US, and the third, *A. c. sumichrasti*, in Mexico. The "Pacific" Scrub-Jay (*A. c. californica)* has bright-blue upperparts with a brownish shoulder, and whitish underparts with a bold blue breastband. The "Interior" Scrub-Jay (*A. c. woodhouseii)* has duller upperparts with a grayish shoulder, and dusky underparts with a very faint breastband; it also has a longer, straighter bill than the "Pacific." The "Interior" Scrub-Jay is shy and furtive, and is seen fleeing into bushes—if it is seen at all—whereas the "Pacific" subspecies is tame and bold, and is even found in backyards.

VOICE Varied, usually harsh, questioning, rising *rehnk*, vaguely robin-like *quill*, *quill*, and dry, hollow rattle.

NESTING Open cup of twigs lined with fibers and hair, concealed in shrub or tree; 2–6 eggs; 1 brood; March–July.

FEEDING Feeds on insects, fruits, acorns, and pine nuts.

FLIGHT: swift; slightly undulating; flurries of wing beats followed by weak glides.

HOME SWEET HOME
Western Scrub-Jays, especially the "Interior" subspecies, prefer to live in juniper scrubs.

SIMILAR SPECIES

STELLER'S JAY see p.274
black crest
sooty-black back and neck
dark-blue underparts

MEXICAN JAY see p.451
paler blue upperparts
grayer breast and throat

OCCURRENCE
The "Pacific" Scrub-Jay is found in suburbia and oak and riverine woodlands; the "Interior" subspecies is found in lower-elevation mountainous oak-pinyon-juniper scrub; the "Interior" occasionally makes sudden trips into the lowlands in winter, east into the Great Plains.

Length **10–12in (26–31cm)**	Wingspan **15½in (40cm)**	Weight **2⅞–3½oz (80–100g)**
Social **Small flocks**	Lifespan **Up to 15 years**	Status **Secure**

DATE SEEN	WHERE	NOTES

Order **Passeriformes**	Family **Corvidae**	Species ***Gymnorhinus cyanocephalus***

Pinyon Jay

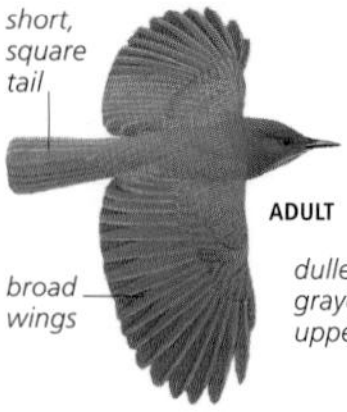

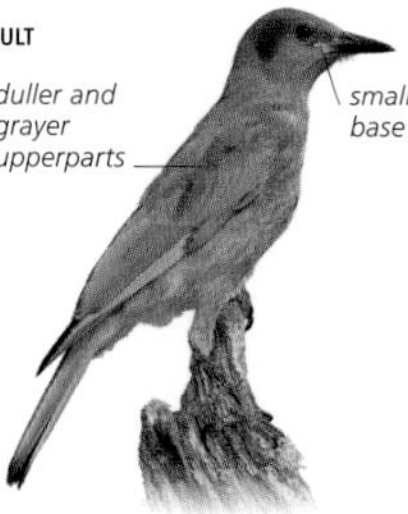

short, square tail
ADULT
broad wings
IN FLIGHT

duller and grayer upperparts
small, pink base of bill
JUVENILE

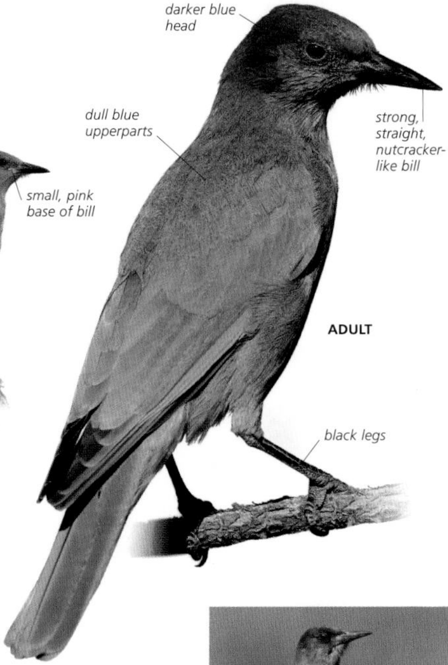

darker blue head
dull blue upperparts
strong, straight, nutcracker-like bill
ADULT
black legs

FLIGHT: direct with constant, stiff flapping; often in tight, wheeling flocks.

Named after the pinyon pine, Pinyon Jays have coevolved along with the nuts of this pine called piñones. As a result of this, the species is restricted mostly to western pinyon-juniper hills. Unlike most other members of the family Corvidae, the base of the Pinyon Jay's bill is featherless. This allows it to feed on the pith deep within pine cones, while keeping the feathers that cover its nostrils clean. Pinyon Jays form long-term partnerships, and nest in colonies that sometimes number in the hundreds.

VOICE Far-carrying, upslurred *howah, howah, howah* in flight.

NESTING Well-insulated, three layered cup on south side of tree or shrub; 3–5 eggs; 1–2 broods; February–May, sometimes also in fall if pine cones are plentiful.

FEEDING Feeds on piñones, other nuts, fruits, and insects; will also raid nests for eggs and hawk for insects.

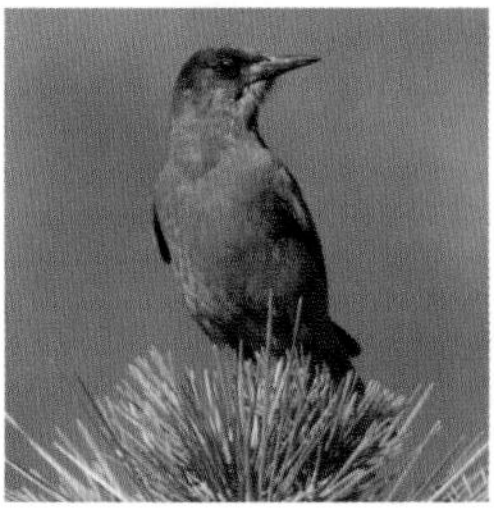

PINE SPECIALIST
Pinyon Jays specialize in eating pine nuts from Ponderosas and their namesake pinyons.

SIMILAR SPECIES

WESTERN SCRUB-JAY see p.275

white eyebrow
longer tail
paler underparts and throat

CLARK'S NUTCRACKER see p.278

gray in plumage

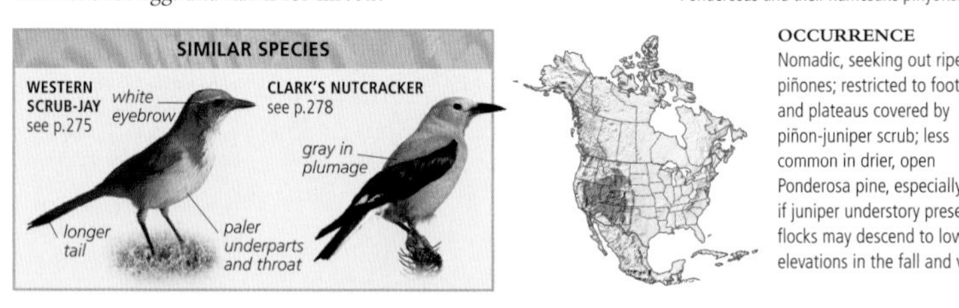

OCCURRENCE
Nomadic, seeking out ripe piñones; restricted to foothills and plateaus covered by piñon-juniper scrub; less common in drier, open Ponderosa pine, especially if juniper understory present; flocks may descend to lower elevations in the fall and winter.

Length **10–11in (25–28cm)**	Wingspan **19in (48cm)**	Weight **3½oz (100g)**
Social **Colonies**	Lifespan **Up to 15 years**	Status **Vulnerable**

DATE SEEN	WHERE	NOTES

Order **Passeriformes**	Family **Corvidae**	Species ***Pica hudsonia***

Black-billed Magpie

Loud, flashy, and conspicuous, the Black-billed Magpie is abundant in the northwestern quarter of the continent, from Alaska to interior US. It has adapted to suburbia, confidently strutting across front lawns locally. Until recently, it was considered the same species as the Eurasian Magpie (*P. pica*), and even though they look nearly identical, scientific evidence points instead to a close relationship with the other North American magpie, the Yellow-billed Magpie. Its long tail enables it to make rapid changes in direction in flight. The male uses his tail to display while courting a female. Why the Black-billed Magpie does not occur widely in eastern North America is a biological mystery.

VOICE Common call a questioning, nasal *ehnk*; also raspy *shenk, shenk, shenk*, usually in series.

NESTING Large, domed, often made of thorny sticks; 5–8 eggs; 1 brood; March–June.

FEEDING Omnivorous; forages on ground, mainly for insects, worms, seeds, and carrion; even picks ticks from mammals.

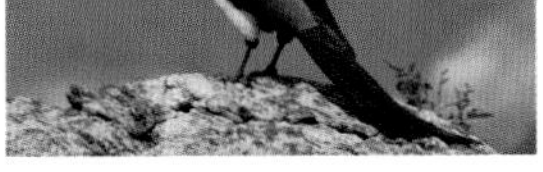

FLIGHT: direct, with slow, steady, and often shallow wing beats; occasional shallow glides.

IRIDESCENT SHEEN
In bright sunlight, beautiful iridescent blues, greens, golds, and purples appear on the wings and tail.

SIMILAR SPECIES

YELLOW-BILLED MAGPIE see p.451

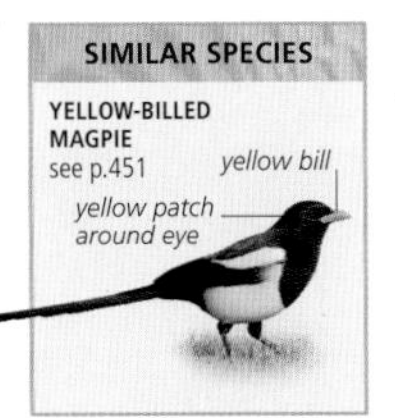

OCCURRENCE
Found in open habitats, foothills, and plains of the western US and Canada; nests in streamside vegetation; persecution has made it wary and restricted to wilderness in some areas, but in others it has adapted to suburbs of towns and cities.

Length **17–19½in (43–50cm)**	Wingspan **25in (63cm)**	Weight **6–7oz (175–200g)**
Social **Small flocks**	Lifespan **Up to 15 years**	Status **Secure**

DATE SEEN	WHERE	NOTES

Order **Passeriformes**	Family **Corvidae**	Species ***Nucifraga columbiana***

Clark's Nutcracker

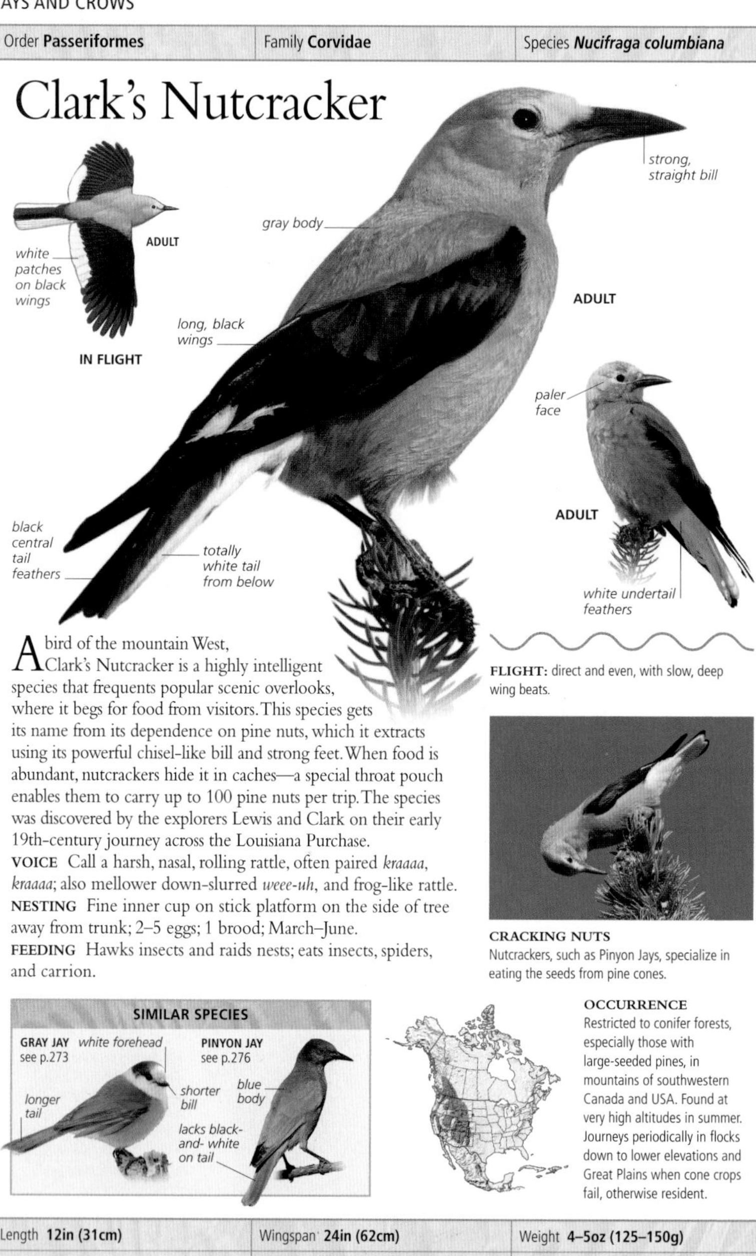

A bird of the mountain West, Clark's Nutcracker is a highly intelligent species that frequents popular scenic overlooks, where it begs for food from visitors. This species gets its name from its dependence on pine nuts, which it extracts using its powerful chisel-like bill and strong feet. When food is abundant, nutcrackers hide it in caches—a special throat pouch enables them to carry up to 100 pine nuts per trip. The species was discovered by the explorers Lewis and Clark on their early 19th-century journey across the Louisiana Purchase.

VOICE Call a harsh, nasal, rolling rattle, often paired *kraaaa, kraaaa*; also mellower down-slurred *weee-uh*, and frog-like rattle.

NESTING Fine inner cup on stick platform on the side of tree away from trunk; 2–5 eggs; 1 brood; March–June.

FEEDING Hawks insects and raids nests; eats insects, spiders, and carrion.

FLIGHT: direct and even, with slow, deep wing beats.

CRACKING NUTS
Nutcrackers, such as Pinyon Jays, specialize in eating the seeds from pine cones.

SIMILAR SPECIES

GRAY JAY see p.273
white forehead; longer tail; shorter bill

PINYON JAY see p.276
blue body; lacks black-and-white on tail

OCCURRENCE
Restricted to conifer forests, especially those with large-seeded pines, in mountains of southwestern Canada and USA. Found at very high altitudes in summer. Journeys periodically in flocks down to lower elevations and Great Plains when cone crops fail, otherwise resident.

Length **12in (31cm)**	Wingspan **24in (62cm)**	Weight **4–5oz (125–150g)**
Social **Pairs/Flocks**	Lifespan **Up to 17 years**	Status **Secure**

DATE SEEN	WHERE	NOTES

Order **Passeriformes**	Family **Corvidae**	Species ***Corvus brachyrhynchos***

American Crow

black overall

ADULT

IN FLIGHT

black overall with greenish sheen

long black bill

ADULT

strong legs and feet

shorter bill

dull black overall

JUVENILE

One of the most widespread and familiar of North American birds, the American Crow is common in almost all habitats—from wilderness to urban centers. Like most birds with large ranges, there is substantial geographical variation in this species. Birds are black across the whole continent, but size and bill shape vary from region to region. Birds from western Canada and western USA (*C. b. hesperis*) are on average smaller and have a lower-pitched voice; birds from southern Florida (*C. b. pascuus*) are more solitary and more wary.

VOICE Call a loud, familiar *caw!*; juveniles' call higher-pitched.

NESTING Stick base with finer inner cup; 3–7 eggs; 1 brood; April–June.

FEEDING Feeds omnivorously on fruit, carrion, garbage, insects, spiders; raids nests.

FLIGHT: direct and level with slow, steady flapping; does not soar.

LOOKING AROUND
Extremely inquisitive, American Crows are always on the lookout for food or something of interest.

SIMILAR SPECIES

FISH CROW higher, more nasal call; *slightly smaller overall*; *smaller head*

CHIHUAHUAN RAVEN see p.452; *larger bill*; *larger overall*; *wedge-shaped tail*

OCCURRENCE
Often seen converging at dusk toward favored roosting areas; most numerous in relatively open areas with large and widely spaced trees; has become abundant in some cities; a partial migrant, some populations are more migratory than others.

Length **15½–19½in (39–49cm)**	Wingspan **3ft (1m)**	Weight **15–22oz (425–625g)**
Social **Social**	Lifespan **Up to 15 years**	Status **Secure**

DATE SEEN	WHERE	NOTES
4/23/19	SU campus	

Order **Passeriformes**	Family **Corvidae**	Species ***Corvus corax***

Common Raven

The Common Raven, twice the size of the American Crow, is a bird of Viking legend, literature, scientific wonder, and the Yukon Official Bird. Its Latin name, *Corvus corax*, means "crow of crows." Ravens are perhaps the most brilliant of all birds: they learn quickly, adapt to new circumstances with remarkable mental agility, and communicate with each other through an array of vocal and motional behaviors. They are master problem solvers and deceivers, tricking each other with ingenious methods.

VOICE Varied and numerous vocalizations, including hoarse, rolling *krruuk*, twangy peals, guttural clicks, resonant *bonks*.

NESTING Platform of sticks with fine inner material on trees, cliffs, or man-made structure; 4–5 eggs; 1 brood; March–June.

FEEDING Feeds omnivorously on carrion, small crustaceans, fish, rodents, fruit, grain, and garbage; also raids nests.

FLIGHT: slow, steady, powerful, direct; can also be quite acrobatic; commonly soars.

SHARING INFORMATION
Ravens in flocks can communicate information about food sources.

SIMILAR SPECIES

AMERICAN CROW lacks shaggy throat feathers; see p.279
smaller bill
much smaller overall
lacks wedge-shaped tail

CHIHUAHUAN RAVEN see p.452
slightly smaller overall

OCCURRENCE
Found in almost every kind of habitat, including tundra, mountains, northern forest, woodlands, prairies, arid regions, coasts, and around human settlements; has recently recolonized areas at southern edge of range, from which it was once expelled by humans.

Length **23½–27in (60–69cm)**	Wingspan **4½ft (1.4m)**	Weight **2½–3¼lb (1–1.5kg)**
Social **Solitary/Pairs/Small flocks**	Lifespan **Up to 15 years**	Status **Secure**

DATE SEEN	WHERE	NOTES

Family **Bombycillidae**

WAXWINGS

Waxwings have a crest, a black mask, silky smooth rosy-brown plumage, secondary wing feathers with waxy red tips, and bright yellow tail bands. Of the three species of waxwing one (the Cedar Waxwing) breeds only in North America. Waxwings are fond of fruit, including mistletoe berries, of which they help to spread the seeds. Waxwings are nomadic, and emigrate after years of food abundance, nesting in areas distant from their regular breeding ranges. Bohemian Waxwings are notorious wanderers, and in "irruption" years many thousands can be seen far away from their normal Alaskan and north Canadian breeding areas.

CEDAR WAXWING
The Cedar Waxwing breeds across North America, from coast to coast.

Families **Paridae, Remizidae**

CHICKADEES & TITMICE

CHICKADEES

Chickadees are among the best-known and most widespread birds in North America. The name "chickadee" is derived from the calls of several species. These birds form flocks in winter. Some species can lower their body temperature in extreme cold.

TAME BIRDS
Black-capped Chickadees have distinctive black-and-white markings and are often very tame.

TITMICE & VERDIN

Distinguished from chickadees by their crests and lack of black throats (except the Bridled Titmouse from the Southwest), titmice species usually have more restricted North American distributions than chickadees. A denizen of southwestern deserts and shrublands, the Verdin is chickadee-like in behavior but belongs to the Remizidae, an Old World Family.

Families **Hirundinidae, Aegithalidae, Alaudidae, Reguliidae**

SWALLOWS, LARKS, & KINGLETS

SWALLOWS

Ornithologists usually call the short-tailed species in this group "martins," and the longer-tailed species "swallows." This nomenclature also has a geographic component. For example, one species is called Bank Swallow in America, but Sand Martin in the United Kingdom. As a family, swallows are cosmopolitan. North American species are migratory, and winter in Central and South America. Barn Swallows have been observed migrating over the Atacama Desert, and as far south as the Diego Ramírez Islands, not far from the Antarctic Peninsula.

LARKS

The only widespread North American species of lark, the Horned Lark, also occurs in the Old World, where it is named the Shore Lark. Larks are brownish birds, usually streaked, and live in open habitats, where they live on the ground. Display flights take the birds high up in the air, and are accompanied with musical songs.

KINGLETS

The five species of kinglets belong to one genus, *Regulus*. They are small, greenish birds, and males have a conspicuous crest of a different color. Two species are widespread in North American coniferous forests. Energetic and hardy, kinglets lay large clutches, eat insects and can survive harsh winters. The Ruby-crowned Kinglet has a very loud and ringing song for a bird weighing only 3/16 to 3/8 of an ounce (5-10 grams).

SURFACE SKIMMER
This Tree Swallow flies low over fresh water to catch insects .

Order **Passeriformes**	Family **Bombycillidae**	Species ***Bombycilla garrulus***

Bohemian Waxwing

yellow edges to outer flight feathers

ADULT

IN FLIGHT

wispy crest

black throat

gray upperparts

FEMALE

yellow tail band

reduced wing markings

FEMALE (1ST WINTER)

variable crest

gray-brown upperparts

gray underparts

MALE

chestnut undertail feathers

ornate wing markings

FLIGHT: quick wing beats interspersed with glides; often flies in tightly bunched flocks.

The Bohemian Waxwing is the wilder and rarer of the two waxwing species in North America. It breeds mainly in Alaska and western Canada. The species is migratory, but the extent of its wintertime movement is notoriously variable, depending on the availability of wild fruits. In most winters, relatively few Bohemian Waxwings visit the lower 48 states, but in special "irruption" years, tens of thousands may reach as far south as Colorado.

VOICE Call actually a dull trill, but effect of hundreds of birds calling together is remarkable and sounds like a high-pitched chorus; flocks vocalize constantly.

NESTING Dishevelled cup of sticks and grasses, placed in tree; 4–6 eggs; number of broods unknown; June–July.

FEEDING Catches insects on the wing in summer; flocks devour berries of native and exotic trees and shrubs throughout the year.

STRIKING TAIL
The Bohemian Waxwing's yellow tail band and chestnut undertail are evident here.

SIMILAR SPECIES

CEDAR WAXWING see p.283
plainer wing markings; warmer tones overall

CEDAR WAXWING ◔ see p.283
unmarked wings; smaller overall

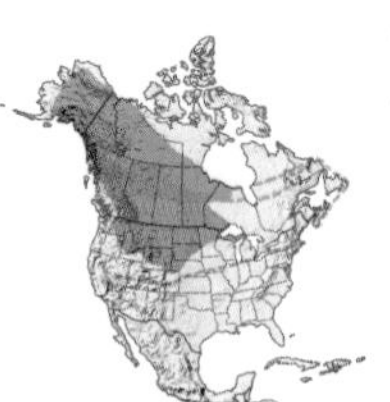

OCCURRENCE
Breeds in sub-Arctic coniferous forest, favoring disturbed areas such as beaver ponds and logging sites. Flocks gather at forest edges, hedges, and residential areas in winter. Hundreds or thousands of birds appear in an area, then disappear once food is depleted.

Length **8½in (21cm)**	Wingspan **14½in (37cm)**	Weight **1⁹⁄₁₆–2½oz (45–70g)**
Social **Flocks**	Lifespan **Up to 12 years**	Status **Localized**

DATE SEEN	WHERE	NOTES

Order **Passeriformes**	Family **Bombycillidae**	Species ***Bombycilla cedrorum***

Cedar Waxwing

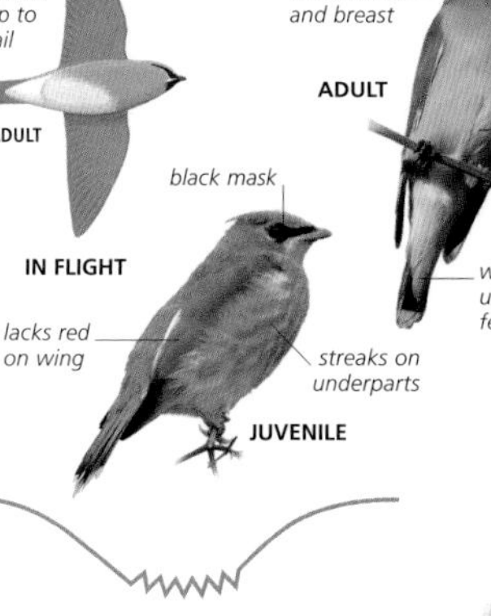

FLIGHT: straight and direct with alternate glides; usually in small to medium flocks.

Flocks of Cedar Waxwings, a nomadic species, move around the US looking for berries, which are their main source of food. Common in a specific location one year, they may disappear the next and occur elsewhere. Northern breeders tend to be more migratory than southern ones. In winter, their nomadic tendencies can send Cedar Waxwings as far south as South America. They can often be heard and identified by their calls, long before the flock settles to feed.

VOICE Basic vocalization a shrill trill: *shr-r-r-r-r-r* or *tre-e-e-e-e-e*, which appears to serve the function of both call note and song.

NESTING Open cup placed in fork of tree, often lined with grasses, plant fibers; 3–5 eggs; 1–2 broods; June–August.

FEEDING Eats in flocks at trees and shrubs with ripe berries throughout the year; also catches flying insects in summer.

BATHING ADULT
Cedar Waxwings love to take baths, and use birdbaths in suburban gardens.

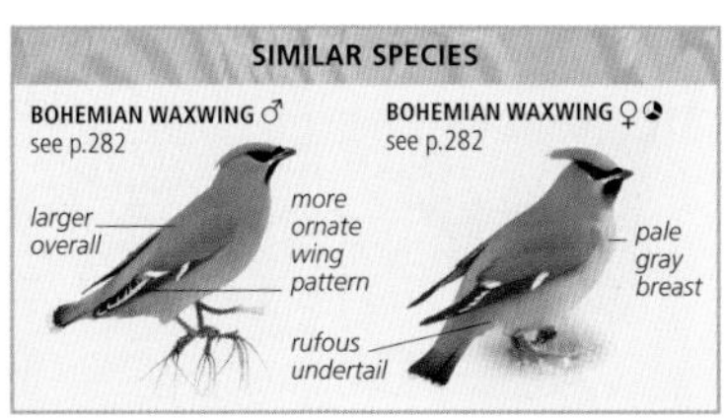

OCCURRENCE
Across northern US and southern Canada, in wooded areas. Breeds in woodlands, especially near streams and clearings. Winters anywhere where trees and shrubs have ripe fruits, especially in Mexico and South America. Spends a lot of time in treetops, but sometimes comes down to shrub level.

Length **7½in (19cm)**	Wingspan **12in (30cm)**	Weight **1¹⁄₁₆–1¼oz (30–35g)**
Social **Flocks**	Lifespan **Up to 7 years**	Status **Secure**

DATE SEEN	WHERE	NOTES

Order **Passeriformes**	Family **Paridae**	Species ***Parus atricapillus***

Black-capped Chickadee

The Black-capped Chickadee, the State Bird of Maine and Massachusetts, is the most widespread chickadee in North America, equally at home in the cold far north and in warm Appalachian valleys. To cope with the harsh winters in the northern parts of its range, this species can decrease its body temperature, entering a controlled hypothermia to conserve energy. There is variation in appearance depending on geographical location, northern birds being slightly larger and possessing brighter white wing edgings than southern birds. Although it is largely nonmigratory, winter chickadee flocks occasionally travel south of their traditional range.

VOICE Raspy *tsick-a-dee-dee-dee* call; song loud, clear whistle *bee-bee* or *bee-bee-be*, first note higher in pitch.

NESTING Cavity in rotting tree stump, lined with hair, fur, feathers, plant fibers; 6–8 eggs; 1 brood; April–June.

FEEDING Forages for insects and their eggs, and spiders in trees and bushes; mainly seeds in winter; may take seeds from an outstretched hand.

FLIGHT: swift and undulating, with fast wing beats.

ROUGH-EDGED BIB
The Black-capped Chickadee has a less well-defined lower bib margin than the Carolina Chickadee.

OCCURRENCE
Variety of wooded habitats, from vast forests in the far north to small woodlands in urban parks and suburbs. In years of poor seed crops in northern parts of the range, large numbers migrate southward as far as the Carolina Chickadee's range.

Length **5¼in (13.5cm)**	Wingspan **8½in (22cm)**	Weight **⅜oz (11g)**
Social **Mixed flocks**	Lifespan **Up to 12 years**	Status **Secure**

DATE SEEN	WHERE	NOTES

Order **Passeriformes**	Family **Paridae**	Species ***Parus gambeli***

Mountain Chickadee

FLIGHT: bouncy, with fast wing beats; interrupted by brief glides.

The Mountain Chickadee is aptly named as it is found at high elevations, up to 12,000ft (3,600m). Like other chickadees, it stores pine and spruce seeds. Social groups defend their winter territories and food resources, and migrate to lower elevations when seeds are scarce. Birds in the Rocky Mountains have a conspicuous white eyebrow and buff-tinged flanks; those in the mountains of California have grayish flanks and a fainter eyebrow.

VOICE Call raspy *tsick-jee-jee-jee*; whistle song of descending notes *bee-bee-bay*.

NESTING Natural tree cavity or old woodpecker hole, lined with moss and fur; 7–9 eggs; 1–2 broods; May–June.

FEEDING Forages high in trees for insects and spiders; eats seeds and berries; stores seeds in fall in preparation for winter.

VARIABLE EYEBROW
The white eyebrow is evident, but it may become duller in worn spring and summer plumage.

TYPICAL PERCH
The species spends much time perched in conifer trees, where it feeds.

SIMILAR SPECIES

BLACK-CAPPED CHICKADEE see p.284
no white eyebrow

MEXICAN CHICKADEE see p.453
no white eyebrow
larger black bib

OCCURRENCE
High elevations, preferring coniferous forests. May even be seen higher than the limit of tree growth. Some birds, especially the young, move down to the foothills and valleys in winter and may visit feeders. Some also wander away from the mountains and out onto the Great Plains.

Length **5¼in (13.5cm)**	Wingspan **8½in (22cm)**	Weight **⅜oz (11g)**
Social **Winter flocks**	Lifespan **Up to 10 years**	Status **Secure**

DATE SEEN	WHERE	NOTES

Order **Passeriformes**	Family **Paridae**	Species ***Parus hudsonicus***

Boreal Chickadee

ADULT

gray cheeks

gray tail

IN FLIGHT

brown cap

grayish brown back

black bib

gray wings

rich brown flanks and belly

ADULT

FLIGHT: bouncy, fast wing beats with brief glides.

The Boreal Chickadee was previously known by other names, including Hudsonian Chickadee, referring to its northern range, and the Brown-capped Chickadee. In the past, this species made large, irregular journeys south of its breeding range during winters of food shortage, but this pattern of invasions has not occurred in recent decades. Its back color is an interesting example of geographic variation—grayish in the West and brown in the central and eastern portions of its range.

VOICE Call a low-pitched, buzzy, a rather slow *tsee-day-day*; also a high-pitched trill, *dididididididi*; no whistled song.

NESTING Cavity lined with fur, hair, plant down; in natural, excavated, or old woodpecker hole; 4–9 eggs; 1 brood; May–June.

FEEDING Gleans insects, conifer seeds; hoards larvae and seeds in bark crevices in fall in preparation for winter.

IDENTIFICATION TIP
A brown back or flank helps distinguish a Boreal Chickadee from a Black-capped Chickadee.

SIMILAR SPECIES

CHESTNUT-BACKED CHICKADEE see p.287

ACROBATIC FORAGER
This acrobatic feeder is able to cling on to conifer needles as it searches for insects and spiders.

OCCURRENCE
Found across the vast northern spruce-fir forests from Alaska to Newfoundland, and from the treeline at the tundra south to the northeastern and northwestern states. The southern edge of the range appears to be retracting, for unknown reasons.

Length **5½in (14cm)**	Wingspan **8½in (21cm)**	Weight **⅜oz (10g)**
Social **Flocks**	Lifespan **Up to 5 years**	Status **Secure**

DATE SEEN	WHERE	NOTES

Order **Passeriformes**	Family **Paridae**	Species ***Parus rufescens***

Chestnut-backed Chickadee

FLIGHT: bouncy, fast wing beats with brief glides.

The Chestnut-backed is the smallest North American chickadee. Northern populations have more brightly colored sides and flanks than other North American chickadees—rich chestnut or rufous, matching the bright back and rump. Birds found southward into central California have paler and less extensive rufous underparts. Farther south still, in southern California, the sides and flanks are dull olive-brown or gray. The Chestnut-backed Chickadee may nest in loose colonies, unlike any other chickadee species.

VOICE A fast, high-pitched *sic-zee-zee, seet-seet-seet*, sharp *chek-chek*, crisp *twit-twit-twit*, and many variations; no whistled song.

NESTING Excavates hole, or uses natural cavity or old woodpecker hole; lined with moss, hair, fur; 5–8 eggs; 1 brood; April–June.

FEEDING Forages high in conifers for caterpillars and other insects; eats seeds and berries in winter.

A DASH OF WHITE
Bright white edges on the wing feathers are often a conspicuous field mark of this species.

SIMILAR SPECIES

BOREAL CHICKADEE
see p.286
grayish brown back
gray cheeks
rich brown flanks and belly

DARK CAP
In good light, this chickadee's brown cap is apparent; in poor light, the cap may look black.

OCCURRENCE
Year-round resident in humid coniferous forests of western Canada and the Pacific Northwest; in drier mixed and deciduous woodlands, and even in urban and suburban habitats south of San Francisco. Northern coastal populations have one of the most specialized habitats of North American chickadees.

Length **4¾in (12cm)**	Wingspan **7½in (19cm)**	Weight **⅜oz (10g)**
Social **Flocks**	Lifespan **Up to 9 years**	Status **Secure**

DATE SEEN	WHERE	NOTES

Order **Passeriformes**	Family **Paridae**	Species ***Parus ridgwayi***

Juniper Titmouse

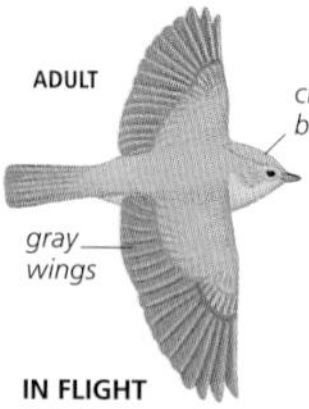
ADULT
crest may not be evident
gray wings
IN FLIGHT

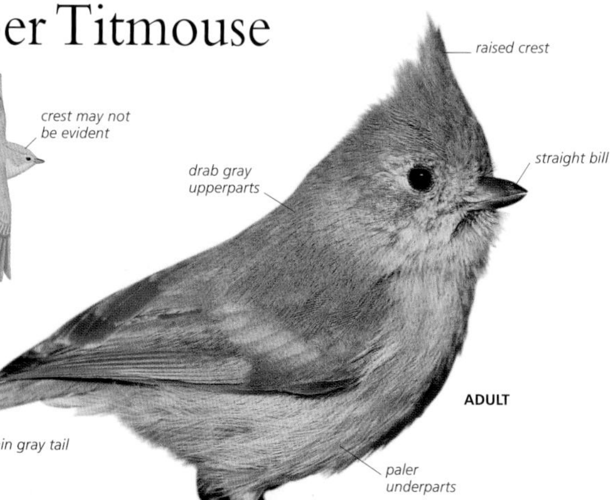
raised crest
straight bill
drab gray upperparts
ADULT
plain gray tail
paler underparts

Like its relative the Oak Titmouse, the Juniper Titmouse is a plain bird; in fact, its drabness is a useful field mark. Although distributed over a larger range, it is not as well known or studied as the Oak Titmouse, perhaps because it is less likely to be encountered in urban or suburban areas. In its juniper and pinyon woodland habitat, however, it is not rare, but easily overlooked.

VOICE Call a rapidly repeated *shick-dee*; song a fast, rolling, or trilled series of short phrases such as *we-dee we-dee we-dee*; both calls and song have many variations.

NESTING Natural tree cavities or abandoned woodpecker holes, lined with shredded bark, moss, hair; 5–6 eggs; 1 brood; April–May.

FEEDING Forages acrobatically among branches, trunks, and among foliage for insects, spiders, and insect larvae; sometimes eats berries and seeds on the ground.

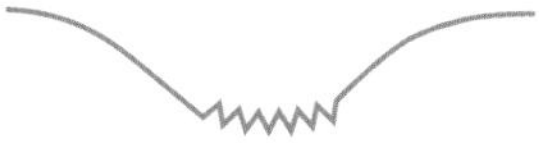

FLIGHT: swift and bounding; periods of fast wing beats alternating with short glides.

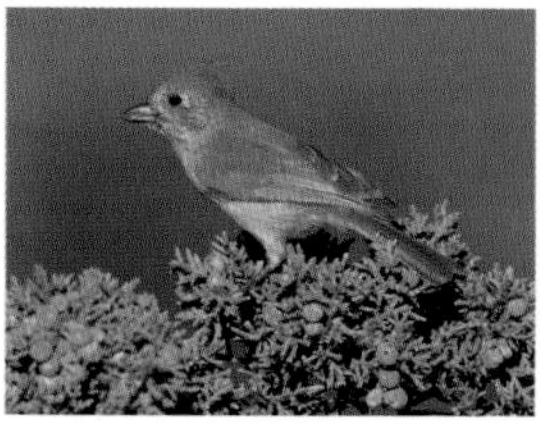

LIVING UP TO ITS NAME
A Juniper Titmouse can usually be found in juniper woodlands, perched on its namesake tree.

SIMILAR SPECIES
GRAY VIREO
see p.265
lacks crest
OAK TITMOUSE
see p.453
slightly darker overall

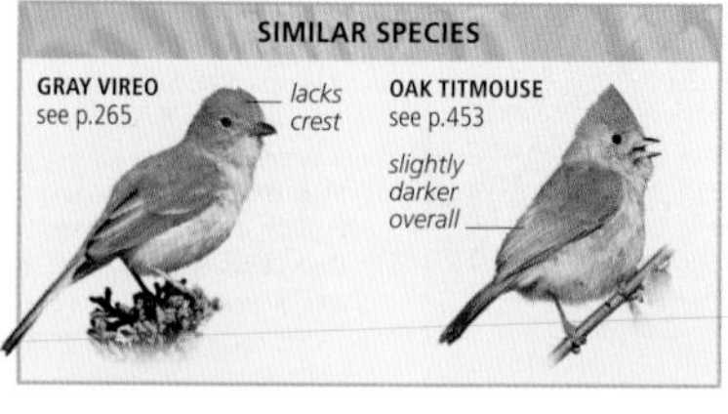

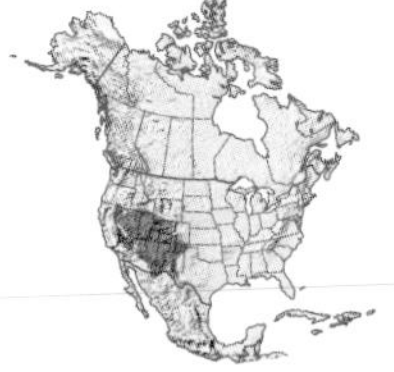

OCCURRENCE
Year-round resident of dry juniper and pinyon-juniper woodlands of the West. Inhabits moderate elevations, up to 8,000ft (2,400m) in the southern portions of the range. Its population is irregularly and locally distributed, although it may be more common in its habitat than is generally recognised.

Length **5¾in (14.5cm)**	Wingspan **9in (23cm)**	Weight **⅝oz (17g)**
Social **Family groups**	Lifespan **Up to 8 years**	Status **Secure**

DATE SEEN	WHERE	NOTES

Order **Passeriformes**	Family **Remizidae**	Species ***Auriparus flaviceps***

Verdin

ADULT

red flash in wings

IN FLIGHT

dark gray plumage overall

variable yellow on head

sharp, black pointed bill

reddish "shoulder" patch

ADULT

gray tail

dark bluish gray legs and feet

paler gray overall

distinctive pointed bill

short wings

JUVENILE

This yellow-headed, gray-bodied, active little bird is one of the most characteristic species of the hot southwestern deserts. The Verdin is constantly on the move, flitting from shrub to shrub, inspecting flowers and cobwebs, and flying short distances across clearings. In behavior and habitat preferences, Verdins resemble chickadees, bushtits, or perhaps even wrens. In fact, the Verdin's evolutionary relationships are unclear, but the species is now thought to be the only American representative of a bird family that is otherwise restricted to Eurasia, the Penduline Tits, or Remizidae, an interesting biological puzzle.

VOICE Call a bright, simple *beef*, made frequently as the bird forages, all day long and throughout the year.

NESTING Large-sized sphere with side entrance, made of twigs and leaves in thorny shrub; 4–5 eggs; 1–2 broods; April–July.

FEEDING Gleans small insects from leaves and flowers; also drinks nectar from flowers, and sometimes visits hummingbird feeders.

FLIGHT: weak, floppy, undulating; Verdins forage in shrubbery, sometimes fly across clearings.

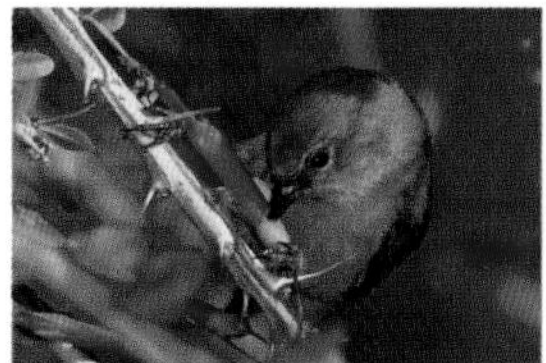

NECTAR FEEDER
The Verdin will often drink nectar from tubular flowers, particularly in winter.

SIMILAR SPECIES

LUCY'S WARBLER ♀ see p.461
chestnut rump
longer, thinner bill

LUCY'S WARBLER ♂ see p.461
gray face
chestnut rump

OCCURRENCE
Permanent resident in thorny vegetation of southwestern and Mexican deserts at low elevations, also in tamarisks in dry creek beds, and shrubs at the edge of desert oases. Many birds wander out into even sparser desert habitats.

Length **4½in (11.5cm)**	Wingspan **6½in (16cm)**	Weight **3/16–1/4oz (5–7g)**
Social **Solitary**	Lifespan **Up to 5 years**	Status **Secure**

DATE SEEN	WHERE	NOTES

Order **Passeriformes**	Family **Hirundinidae**	Species ***Riparia riparia***

Bank Swallow

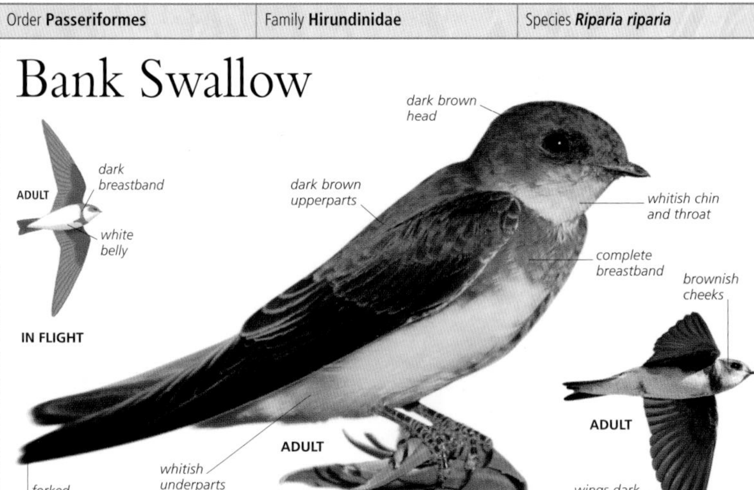

The Bank Swallow, known in the UK as the Sand Martin, is the slimmest and smallest of North American swallows. As its scientific name *riparia* (meaning "riverbanks") and common names suggest, the Bank Swallow nests in the banks and bluffs of rivers, streams, and lakes. It also favors sand and gravel quarries in the East. It is widely distributed across North America, breeding from south of the tundra–taiga line south to the central US. Nesting colonies can range from as few as 10 pairs to as many as 2,000, which are quite busy and noisy when all the birds are calling or coming in to simultaneously feed the young.

VOICE Call a soft *brrrrr* or *breee* often issued in pairs; song a harsh twittering or continuous chatter.

NESTING Both sexes excavate burrows in sandy banks containing a flat platform of grass, feathers, and twigs; 2–6 eggs; 1 brood; April–August.

FEEDING Catches insects, such as flies, moths, dragonflies, and bees in flight, but occasionally skims aquatic insects or their larvae off the water or terrestrial insects from the ground.

FLIGHT: fast, frantic, butterfly-like flight with glides, twists, and turns; shallow, rapid wing beats.

WAITING FOR MOM OR DAD
Hungry youngsters still expect to be fed, even when they're ready to fledge.

SIMILAR SPECIES

TREE SWALLOW larger; gray-brown upperparts with greenish tinge; see p.291
incomplete breastband

NORTHERN ROUGH-WINGED SWALLOW larger overall; see p.294
uniformly colored upperparts

OCCURRENCE
Widespread in North America. Breeds in lowland habitats associated with rivers, streams, lakes, reservoirs, and coasts, as well as in sand and gravel quarries. Often prefers man-made sites; winters in grasslands, open farm habitat, and freshwater areas in South America, south to Chile and Argentina.

Length **4¾–5½in (12–14cm)**	Wingspan **10–11in (25–28cm)**	Weight **3/8–11/16oz (10–19g)**
Social **Colonies**	Lifespan **Up to 9 years**	Status **Secure**

DATE SEEN	WHERE	NOTES

Order **Passeriformes**	Family **Hirundinidae**	Species ***Tachycineta bicolor***

Tree Swallow

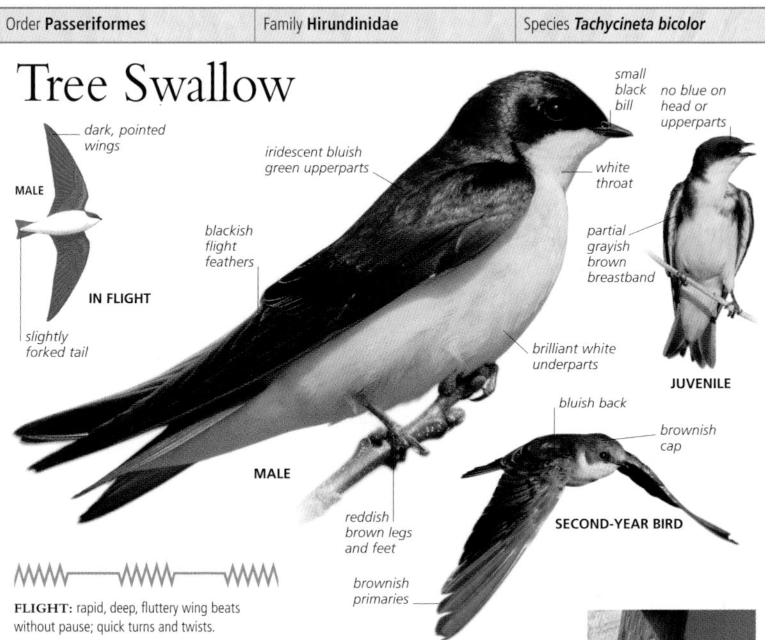

FLIGHT: rapid, deep, fluttery wing beats without pause; quick turns and twists.

One of the most common North American swallows, the Tree Swallow is found from coast to coast in the northern two-thirds of the continent all the way north to Alaska. As its Latin name *bicolor* suggests, it is a two-toned bird, with iridescent bluish green upperparts and white underparts. Juveniles can be confused with the smaller Bank Swallow, which has a more complete breastband. The Tree Swallow lives in a variety of habitats, but its hole-nesting habit makes it dependent on crevices in old trees, abandoned woodpecker cavities, and on artificial "housing" such as nest boxes. The size of the population fluctuates according to the availability of nesting sites.

VOICE Ranges from variable high, chirping notes to chatters and soft trills; also complex high and clear 2-note whistle phrases.

NESTING Layer of fine plant matter in abandoned woodpecker hole or nest box, lined with feathers; 4–6 eggs; 1 brood; May–July.

FEEDING Swoops after flying insects from dawn to dusk; also takes bayberries.

KEEPING LOOKOUT
This species uses artificial nest boxes, which the males defend as soon as they arrive.

SIMILAR SPECIES

BANK SWALLOW paler brown rump; see p.290
distinct dusky breastband

VIOLET-GREEN SWALLOW white flank patch; see p.292
white eye patch
violet-green upperparts

OCCURRENCE
Typically breeds close to water in open habitat, such as fields, marshes, lakes, and swamps, especially those with standing dead wood for cavity-nesting. Winters in roosts of hundreds of thousands of birds in marshes, in the southern US, and from Mexico to Panama; also Cuba.

Length **5–6in (13–15cm)**	Wingspan **12–14in (30–35cm)**	Weight **⅝–⅞oz (17–25g)**
Social **Large flocks**	Lifespan **Up to 11 years**	Status **Secure**

DATE SEEN	WHERE	NOTES

Order **Passeriformes**	Family **Hirundinidae**	Species ***Tachycineta thalassina***

Violet-green Swallow

long wings

ADULT

white underparts

IN FLIGHT

brown on head and sides of face

FEMALE

faint purplish neck patch

green head

emerald green back

white, crescent-like patch on throat and face

purple rump and tail

MALE

wing tips extend beyond tail when perched

FLIGHT: fluttering; close to the ground or circling at great heights with rapid wing beats; less soaring.

Although common in western North America from eastern Alaska south to Baja California, the Violet-green Swallow is poorly studied. Indeed, it is arguably the least well known of any North American swallow. It often occurs in mountain conifer forests where it breeds in woodpecker holes, in cliff crevices, and also birdhouses. A distinguishing feature of this swallow is the white patch that extends from its throat to its cheeks, and forms a line over its eyes. Its Latin name *thalassina* means "sea-green." Its common name refers to the same color, along with the violet of its rump. In its mountain habitat, the Violet-green Swallow can be encountered together with the White-throated Swift.

VOICE Primary call a twittering *chee-chee* of brief duration; alarm call a dry, brief *zwrack*.

NESTING Nest of grass, twigs, straw, and feathers in a natural or woodpecker cavity in a tree, also cliff or nesting box; 4–6 eggs; 2 broods; March–August.

FEEDING Catches flying insects, such as bees, wasps, moths, and flies; usually at higher levels than other species of swallows.

AT THE NEST HOLE
The female of this species can be distinguished from the male by her darker face.

SIMILAR SPECIES

WHITE-THROATED SWIFT see p.219
white sides of rump

TREE SWALLOW ♂ see p.291
iridescent greenish blue upperparts
blackish brown crown

OCCURRENCE
In the western US and Canada, breeds in coniferous, and mixed woodlands, especially Ponderosa and Monterey Pine and Quaking Aspen; also wooded canyons. Frequents waterways during migration; prefers high elevations in general. Breeds in Mexico, winters south to Costa Rica.

Length **5in (13cm)**	Wingspan **11in (28cm)**	Weight **½oz (14g)**
Social **Solitary/Colonies**	Lifespan **Unknown**	Status **Secure**

DATE SEEN	WHERE	NOTES

Order **Passeriformes**	Family **Hirundinidae**	Species ***Progne subis***

Purple Martin

FLIGHT: direct, powerful flight with deep wing beats; soars and glides when foraging.

The Purple Martin, the largest species of North American swallow, is one of the most popular of all backyard birds. Thousands of Purple Martin-lovers belong to two national organizations that publish magazines and newsletters devoted to the species. Found mostly in the eastern half of the continent, with local populations scattered across the West, this glossy-blue swallow is common in some areas but quite scarce in others. In the West it nests in abandoned woodpecker holes, but in the East the Purple Martin now depends almost entirely on the provisioning of "apartment-type" birdhouses for breeding.

VOICE Alarm call a *zwrack* or *zweet*; other calls are a variety of rolling, bubbling sounds; song a series of gurgles, chortles, and croaking phrases.

NESTING Loose mat of vegetation and mud in birdhouse compartments, rarely in natural cavities; 4 eggs; 1 brood; April–August.

FEEDING Captures flying insects at 150–500ft (45–150m) in the air; sometimes gleans insects from foliage or the ground.

FLOCK TOGETHER
Purple Martins are social birds: they breed in colonies and roost in flocks.

OCCURRENCE
In North America, eastern birds found almost exclusively in towns and cities where nest boxes are provided; western populations occur in more rural areas such as mountain and coastal forests where woodpecker holes are abundant; also uses Saguaro cactus for nesting in the Southwest. Winters in Brazil.

Length **7–8in (18–20cm)**	Wingspan **15–16in (38–41cm)**	Weight **1 7/16–2 1/8oz (40–60g)**
Social **Large flocks/Colonies**	Lifespan **Up to 13 years**	Status **Secure**

DATE SEEN	WHERE	NOTES

Order **Passeriformes**	Family **Hirundinidae**	Species ***Stelgidopteryx serripennis***

Northern Rough-winged Swallow

Given the name *serripennis,* "saw-like," by Audubon in 1888, and characterized by the serrations on its outer wing feathers, this species is otherwise somewhat drab in color and aspect. The Northern Rough-winged Swallow has a broad distribution in North America, across southern Canada and throughout the US. Often overlooked by birdwatchers, this brown-backed, dusky-throated swallow can be spotted hunting insects over water. In size and habit, the Northern Rough-winged Swallow shares many similarities with the Bank Swallow, including breeding habits and color, but the latter's notched tail and smaller size help tell them apart.

VOICE Steady repetition of short, rapid *brrrt* notes inflected upward; sometimes a buzzy *jee-jee-jee* or high-pitched *brzzzzzt.*

NESTING Loose cup of twigs and straw in a cavity or burrow in a bank, such as road cuts; 4–7 eggs; 1 brood; May–July.

FEEDING Captures flying insects, including flies, wasps, bees, damselflies, and beetles in the air; more likely to feed over water and at lower altitudes than other swallows.

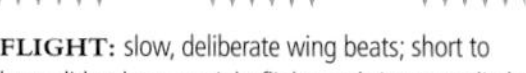

FLIGHT: slow, deliberate wing beats; short to long glides; long, straight flight, ends in steep climb.

BROWN BIRD
This swallow is brownish above, pale grayish below, with a brown smudge on the sides of its neck.

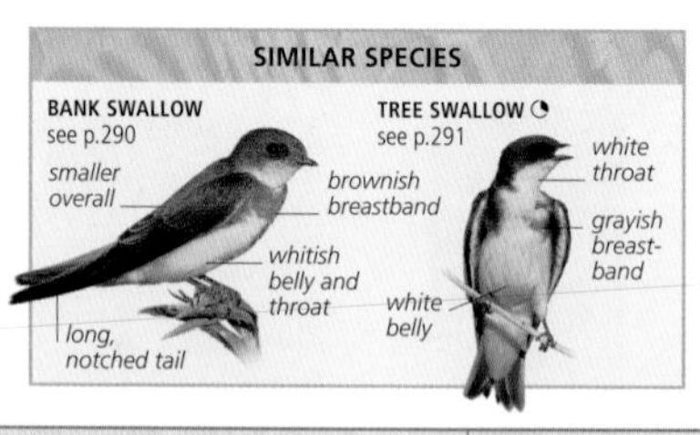

OCCURRENCE
In North America widespread from coast to coast. Nests at a wide variety of altitudes, prefers exposed banks of clay, sand, or gravel such as gorges, shale banks, and gravel pits. Forages along watercourses where aerial insects are plentiful. Breeds south to Costa Rica. Winters in Central America.

Length **4¾–6in (12–15cm)**	Wingspan **11–12in (28–30cm)**	Weight **⅜–⅝oz (10–18g)**
Social **Solitary**	Lifespan **Unknown**	Status **Secure**

DATE SEEN	WHERE	NOTES

Order **Passeriformes**	Family **Hirundinidae**	Species ***Hirundo rustica***

Barn Swallow

The most widely distributed and abundant swallow in the world, the Barn Swallow is found just about everywhere in North America south of the Arctic timberline. Originally a cave-nester before Europeans settlers came to the New World, the Barn Swallow readily adapted to nesting under the eaves of houses, under bridges, and inside buildings such as barns. It is now rare to find this elegant swallow breeding in a natural site. Steely blue upperparts, reddish underparts, and a deeply forked tail identify the Barn Swallow. North American breeders have deep, reddish orange underparts, but birds from Eurasia are white-bellied.

VOICE High-pitched, squeaky *chee-chee* call; song a long series of chatty, pleasant churrs, squeaks, chitterings, and buzzes.

NESTING Deep cup of mud and grass-stems attached to vertical surfaces or on ledges; 4–6 eggs; 1–2 broods; May–September.

FEEDING Snatches flying insects, such as flies, mosquitoes, wasps, and beetles in the air at lower altitudes than other swallows; sometimes eats wild berries and seeds.

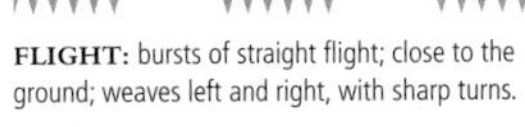

FLIGHT: bursts of straight flight; close to the ground; weaves left and right, with sharp turns.

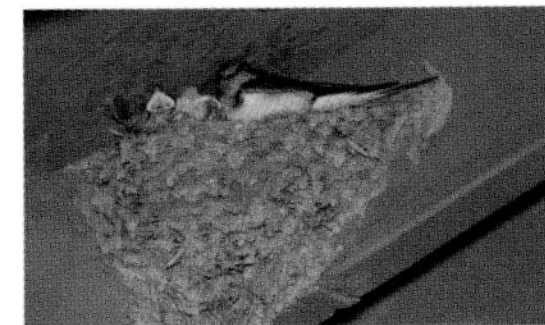

WELL PROTECTED
Whether in a barn or other structure, this swallow's nest is totally protected from wind and rain.

SIMILAR SPECIES

TREE SWALLOW ♂
see p.291

OCCURRENCE
Breeds across North America; south to central Mexico. Prefers agricultural regions and towns. Winters near sugarcane fields, grain fields, and marshes, south in South America as far as Patagonia. Hundreds of thousands winter in marshes of northern Argentina.

Length **6–7½in (15–19cm)**	Wingspan **11½–13in (29–33cm)**	Weight **⅝–11/16oz (17–20g)**
Social **Small colonies/Flocks**	Lifespan **Up to 8 years**	Status **Secure**

DATE SEEN	WHERE	NOTES

Order **Passeriformes**	Family **Hirundinidae**	Species ***Petrochelidon pyrrhonata***

Cliff Swallow

The Cliff Swallow is one of North America's most social land birds, sometimes nesting in colonies of over 3,500 pairs, especially in the western US. It is more locally distributed in the East. It can be distinguished from other North American swallows by its square tail and orange rump, but it resembles its close relative, the Cave Swallow, in color, pattern, and in affixing its mud nests to the sides of highway culverts, bridges, and buildings. The considerable increase in such structures has allowed the species to expand its range from the west to breed almost everywhere on the continent south of the tundra.

VOICE Gives *purr* and *churr* calls when alarmed; song a low, squeaky, 6-second twitter given in flight and near nests.

NESTING Domed nests of mud pellets on cave walls, buildings, culverts, bridges, and dams; 3–5 eggs; 1–2 broods; April–August.

FEEDING Catches flying insects (often swarming varieties) while on the wing; sometimes forages on the ground; ingests grit to aid digestion.

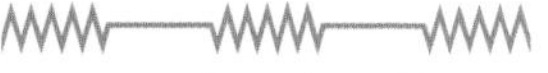

FLIGHT: strong, fast wing beats; glides more often but less acrobatically than other swallows.

GATHERING MUD
The Cliff Swallow gathers wet mud from puddles, pond edges, and streamsides to build its nest.

SIMILAR SPECIES

INDIVIDUAL HOMES
In a Cliff Swallow colony, each nest has a single opening.

OCCURRENCE
Breeds in North America from Alaska to Mexico. Prefers walls, culverts, buildings, cliffs, and undersides of piers on which to affix mud nests. Migrates to South America, where hundreds of thousands winter in the marshes of northern Argentina.

Length **5in (13cm)**	Wingspan **11–12in (28–30cm)**	Weight **$^{11}/_{16}$–$1^{1}/_{4}$oz (20–35g)**
Social **Colonies**	Lifespan **Up to 11 years**	Status **Secure**

DATE SEEN	WHERE	NOTES

Order **Passeriformes**	Family **Aegithalidae**	Species ***Psaltriparus minimus***

Bushtit

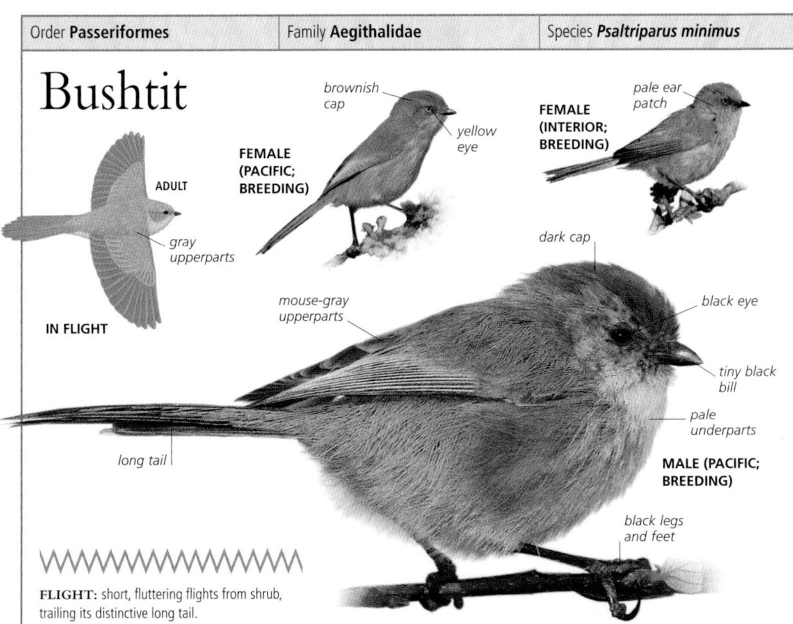

FLIGHT: short, fluttering flights from shrub, trailing its distinctive long tail.

For much of the year, the Bushtit roams the foothills and valleys of the western US, in flocks that usually number just a handful, but occasionally total many hundreds. This little bird is constantly on the move, foraging busily in the foliage of shrubs and small trees. One moment a flock is there; the next, it has moved on. Even during the breeding season, when most other perching birds become territorial, the Bushtit retains something of its social nature—raising the young is often a communal affair, with both siblings and single adults helping in the rearing of a pair's chicks.

VOICE Basic call a 2–3-part soft lisp, *ps psss pit*, interspersed with hard *spit* and *spick* notes, like little sparks.

NESTING Enormous pendant structure of cobwebs and leaves, hung from branch; 4–10 eggs; 2 broods; April–July.

FEEDING Gleans spiders and insects from vegetation; acrobatic while feeding, often hangs upside-down.

FORAGING
Constantly aflutter, the Bushtit flits through foliage, looking for insects and other small arthropods.

SIMILAR SPECIES

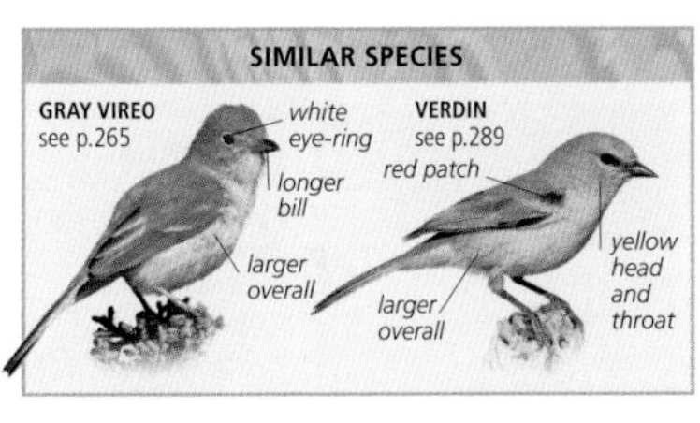

OCCURRENCE
Away from the coast, common in open woodlands and areas of shrubs, mainly on hillsides in summer, some birds move down to low-elevation valleys in the fall. Coastal populations commonly seen in cities and gardens as well as on hillsides, occur in native and non-native plant communities.

Length **4½in (11.5cm)**	Wingspan **6in (15.5cm)**	Weight **3/16–7/32oz (4.5–6g)**
Social **Flocks**	Lifespan **Up to 8 years**	Status **Secure**

DATE SEEN	WHERE	NOTES
4/23/19	In SU Quad	can hang upside-down

Order **Passeriformes**	Family **Alaudidae**	Species ***Eremophila alpestris***

Horned Lark

FLIGHT: undulating, with wings folded in after every few beats.

The Horned Lark is a bird of open country, especially places with extensive bare ground. The species is characteristic of arid, alpine, and Arctic regions; in these areas, it flourishes in the bleakest of habitats imaginable, from sun-scorched, arid lakeshores in the Great Basin, to windswept tundra north of the timberline. In some places, the only breeding bird species are the Horned Lark and the equally resilient Common Raven. In Europe and Asia, this species is known as the Shorelark.

VOICE Flight call a sharp *sweet* or *soo-weet*; song, either in flight or from the ground, pleasant, musical tinkling series, followed by *sweet... swit... sweet... s'sweea'weea'witta'swit.*

NESTING In depression in bare ground, somewhat sheltered by grass or low shrubs, lined with plant matter; 2–5 eggs; 1–3 broods; March–July.

FEEDING Survives exclusively on seeds of grasses and sedges in winter; eats mostly insects in summer.

GROUND FORAGER
With its short legs bent under its body, an adult looks for insects and seeds.

VERY VOCAL
The Horned Lark is a highly vocal bird, singing from the air, the ground, or low shrubs.

OCCURRENCE
Breeds widely, in any sort of open, even barren habitat with extensive bare ground, especially shortgrass prairies and deserts. Winters wherever there are snow-free openings, including along beaches and roads. Winters from southern Canada southward to Florida and Mexico.

Length **7in (18cm)**	Wingspan **12in (30cm)**	Weight **1¹⁄₁₆oz (30g)**
Social **Winter flocks**	Lifespan **Up to 8 years**	Status **Secure**

DATE SEEN	WHERE	NOTES

Order **Passeriformes**	Family **Reguliidae**	Species ***Regulus satrapa***

Golden-crowned Kinglet

whitish wing bars

MALE

IN FLIGHT

yellow crown patch, with black border

FEMALE

orange-and-yellow patch on crown, with black border

broad whitish stripe above eye

olive-green upperparts

short, straight bill

MALE

white wing bar

notched tail

pale buff to whitish underparts

FLIGHT: quick and erratic, but not direct; high in the air; can hover while foraging.

This hardy little bird, barely more than a ball of feathers, breeds in northern and mountainous coniferous forests in the US, after a considerable hiatus in mountain forests of Mexico and Guatemala. Planting of spruce trees in parts of the US Midwest has allowed this species to increase its range in recent years to Ohio, Indiana, Illinois, and Pennsylvania.

VOICE Call a thin, high-pitched and thread-like *tsee* or *see see*; song a series of high-pitched ascending notes for 2 seconds; complex song *tsee-tsee-tsee-tsee-teet-leetle*, followed by brief trill.

NESTING Deep, cup-shaped nest with rims arching inward, made of moss, lichen, and bark, and lined with finer strips of the same; 8–9 eggs; 1–2 broods; May–August.

FEEDING Gleans flies, beetles, mites, spiders, and their eggs from tips of branches, under bark, tufts of conifer needles; eats seeds, and persimmon fruits.

EXPANDING RANGE
This bird has expanded its range southward following spruce forestation.

SIMILAR SPECIES

RUBY-CROWNED KINGLET
see p.300

HIGHER VOICE
The Golden-crowned has a higher-pitched and less musical song than the Ruby-crowned.

OCCURRENCE
Breeds in remote northern and subalpine spruce or fir forests, mixed coniferous–deciduous forests, single-species stands, and pine plantations; winters in a wide variety of habitats—coniferous and deciduous forests, pine groves, low-lying hardwood forests, swamps, and urban and suburban habitats.

Length **3¼–4¼in (8–11cm)**	Wingspan **5½–7in (14–18cm)**	Weight **⁵⁄₃₂–⁹⁄₃₂oz (4–8g)**
Social **Solitary/Pairs**	Lifespan **Up to 5 years**	Status **Secure**

DATE SEEN	WHERE	NOTES

Order **Passeriformes**	Family **Reguliidae**	Species ***Regulus calendula***

Ruby-crowned Kinglet

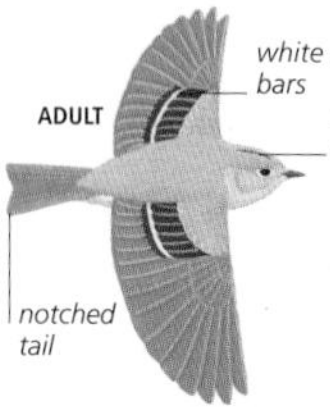

red patch on crown
incomplete white eye-ring
olive-green upperparts
white wing bars
ADULT
patch on crown often concealed
notched tail
IN FLIGHT
no red patch on crown
two white wingbars
MALE
olive underparts
FEMALE
MALE
small upturned bill
brown legs with paler brown feet

The Ruby-crowned Kinglet is perhaps one of the most easily recognizable songbirds in North America because of its very small size, incomplete white eye-ring, two white wing bars, and habit of incessantly flicking its wings while foraging. This bird is renowned for its loud, complex song and for laying up to 12 eggs in a clutch—probably the highest of any North American songbird. Despite local declines resulting from logging and forest fires, the Ruby-crowned Kinglet is common across the continent. It will sometimes be found in mixed-species flocks in winter, together with nuthatches and titmice.

VOICE Call a low, husky *jidit*; song, remarkably loud for such a small bird, begins with 2–3 high, clear notes *tee* or *zee* followed by 5–6 lower *tu* or *turr* notes, and ends with ringing galloping notes *tee-da-leet, tee-da-leet, tee-da-leet*.

NESTING Globular or elongated nest hanging from or on large branch with an enclosed or open cup, made of mosses, feathers, lichens, spider's silk, bark, hair, and fur; 5–12 eggs; 1 brood; May–October.

FEEDING Gleans a wide variety of insects, spiders, and their eggs among the leaves on the outer tips of higher, smaller branches; eats fruit and seeds; often hovers to catch prey.

FLIGHT: short bursts of rapid wing beats, but overall quick and direct flight.

CONCEALED COLOR
This bird's red patch is often concealed unless the bird is agitated or excited.

SIMILAR SPECIES

ALWAYS FLICKING
Ruby-crowned Kinglets are easily identified by their habit of constantly flicking their wings.

OCCURRENCE
Within the northern forest zone, breeds near water in Black Spruce and tamarack forests, muskegs, forests with mixed conifers and northern hardwoods; in the mountainous West, spruce-fir, Lodgepole Pine, and Douglas Fir forests. Winters in a broad range of forests, thickets, and borders.

Length **3½–4¼in (9–11cm)**	Wingspan **6–7in (15–18cm)**	Weight **³⁄₁₆–⅜oz (5–10g)**
Social **Winter flocks**	Lifespan **Up to 5 years**	Status **Secure**

DATE SEEN	WHERE	NOTES

Families **Troglodytidae, Polioptilidae**

WRENS & GNATCATCHERS

WITH ONE EXCEPTION, the Eurasian Winter Wren, wrens are all small American songbirds. Most are brown with light and dark streaking. The scientific family name, Troglodytidae, which derives from a Greek word meaning "cave-dweller," seems apt in light of the furtive habits of wrens, which are heard more often than they are seen. Wrens are renowned for their remarkable songs, and, in some species, for their precisely synchronized duets. Of the 13 species of gnatcatchers, small songbirds with subdued plumage and discreet habits, three occur in Canada and the USA.

COCKED TAIL
As they sing, Winter Wrens often hold their tails upward in a near-vertical position.

Families **Sittidae, Certhiidae**

NUTHATCHES & TREECREEPER

EASILY RECOGNIZED BY their distinctive shape and feeding technique, nuthatches are common North American woodland birds. They are plump-bodied and short-tailed, with blue-gray backs, and often have a contrasting darker crown. These birds use their bills to probe for insects in the crevices of tree trunks and branches. Strong feet and long claws allow them to move along the underside of branches. This contrasts with many other birds, which only move upward on a tree trunk. This characteristic movement is one of the easiest ways to identify nuthatches. Only one species of treecreeper is found in North America. Often overlooked, treecreepers forage by searching methodically in bark crevices.

ACROBATIC POSE
Downward-facing nuthatches such as this one often lift their heads in a characteristic pose.

Family **Mimidae**

THRASHERS & RELATIVES

THE FAMILY NAME for catbirds, mockingbirds, and thrashers is from the Latin for "to imitate," and no other word better defines the ten species of these birds that are found in North America. The Northern Mockingbird is especially well known for its ability to incorporate the songs of other species into its own song. Members of the Mimidae have long, curved bills and reclusive habits. Some members of this group are able to recognize and remove the eggs of brood parasites such as the Brown-headed Cowbird. The Gray Catbird is recognized by its cat-like *meeow* calls and its overall gray plumage.

DISTINCTIVE BILL
This Long-billed Thrasher is characterized by its slender, curved bill, long, thin legs, and long, rounded tail.

Order **Passeriformes**	Family **Troglodytidae**	Species ***Campylorhynchus brunneicapillus***

Cactus Wren

FLIGHT: straight, with fast wing beats and short glides; usually close to the ground.

Arizona's State Bird, the Cactus Wren is the largest and most brightly colored of the North American wrens. Unfortunately, its population has been declining as its habitat is destroyed by agricultural development and wildfires. Its distinctively pale and weakly spotted subspecies, the "San Diego," is especially susceptible to loss of habitat. The Cactus Wren is known for building large, ball-shaped nests, often in cacti, which act as superbly effective deterrents to predators.

VOICE Call a loud *chack*; song a grating *kchar kchar kchar kchar*, with a harsh cluck-like quality; sings repeatedly from top of cactus or shrub, especially in the morning.

NESTING Bulky globular mass of woven grasses and stems with entrance hole on side; 3–5 eggs; 1–2 broods; March–August.

FEEDING Plucks insects and spiders from ground or shrubs.

SAFE HOUSE
The large globular nests that Cactus Wrens build contain a small passage that leads to the nest chamber.

NEST CONSTRUCTION
Strongly woven with pieces of plant matter, the nest protects the young from the hot sun.

OCCURRENCE
Occupies deserts and arid hillsides dominated by cacti and thorny shrubs in the Southwest. Also suburbs where artificial plantings provide nest sites. The "San Diego" subspecies (*sandiegensis*) is found in sagebrush along the coast of southern California and northwestern Baja California.

Length **8½in (22cm)**	Wingspan **11in (28cm)**	Weight **1¼oz (35g)**
Social **Family groups**	Lifespan **Up to 7 years**	Status **Declining**

DATE SEEN	WHERE	NOTES

Order **Passeriformes**	Family **Troglodytidae**	Species ***Salpinctes obsoletus***

Rock Wren

rusty rump

bright buff feather tips

ADULT

IN FLIGHT

faint eyestripe

grayish brown upperparts

thin, brown streaks

pale lemon-yellow belly

black-and-white barring on undertail

pale buff lower flanks

ADULT

FLIGHT: straight, with fast wing beats; sometimes glides from high perch.

An inhabitant of various rocky landscapes—it often sings from the edge of a high precipice—the Rock Wren's voice, while not particularly loud, carries surprisingly far through the dry air of the West. It is perpetually busy running, fluttering, and darting in and out of crevices in search of food. A well-known behavioral quirk of the Rock Wren is to bob and sway conspicuously when a human approaches. However, its oddest habit is to "pave" the area in front of its nest entrance with a walkway of pebbles—the purpose of this is unknown.

VOICE Call a sharp *ch'keer,* varied series of warbles, trills, chatters, and repeated musical phrases such as *chuwee chuwee, teedee teedee,* reminiscent of a mockingbird or a thrasher; sings at all elevations.

NESTING Cup of various grasses lined with soft materials, in rock crevice or under overhang; 4–8 eggs; 1–2 broods; April–August.

FEEDING Probes in rock crevices on ground and in dirt banks for a variety of insects and spiders.

A CHANGE OF SCENERY
Rock Wrens occasionally venture out into open grasslands and perch on man-made structures, well away from their usual surroundings.

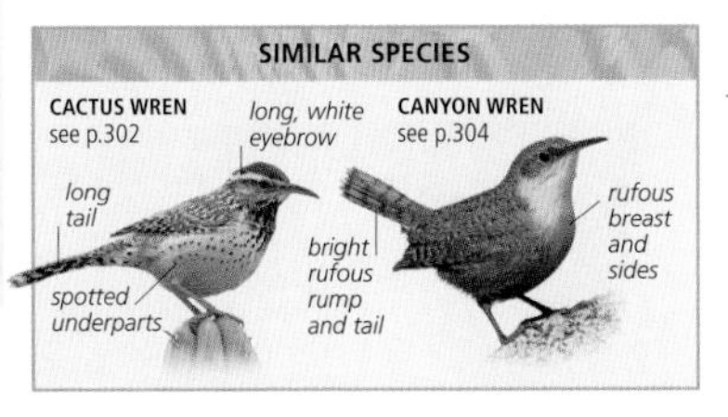

OCCURRENCE
Inhabits arid country with rocky cliffs and canyons, as well as man-made quarries and gravel piles; a wide variety of elevations from hot, low deserts to windswept mountain tops as high as 10,000ft (3,000m). Northern birds migrate to southern states for winter.

Length **6in (15cm)**	Wingspan **9in (23cm)**	Weight **⅝oz (17g)**
Social **Solitary/Pairs**	Lifespan **Unknown**	Status **Secure**

DATE SEEN	WHERE	NOTES

Order **Passeriformes**	Family **Troglodytidae**	Species ***Catherpes mexicanus***

Canyon Wren

The Canyon Wren's loud, clear whistles echo across canyons in the West, but the singer usually stays out of sight, remaining high among the crevices of its cliffside home. When it can be observed, the most striking aspect of its behavior is its extraordinary ability to walk up, down, and sideways on vertical rock walls. This remarkable agility is achieved through its strong toes and long claws; these features enable Canyon Wrens to find a grip in the tiniest of depressions and fissures in the rock.

VOICE Series of 10–15 loud, ringing whistles, descending in pitch, gradually slowing, and ending with several thin buzzes.

NESTING Cup of sticks lined with soft material such as plant down, in crevice or hole; 4–6 eggs; 1–2 broods; April–August.

FEEDING Uses extremely long bill to probe crevices for insects and spiders; can flatten itself by spreading legs to enter low overhangs.

FLIGHT: steady, straight, and fluttery; broad, rounded wings let it glide to a lower perch.

BLENDING IN
Except for the white throat, the Canyon Wren's plumage matches its rocky habitat.

CLIFF-HOPPER
This bird can half-fly and half-hop up steep cliffs by flapping its broad wings for extra lift.

OCCURRENCE
Maintains year-round territory on rocky hillsides, outcroppings, and vertical rock-walled canyons through much of the west of the continent and southward to Mexico. Sometimes nests in holes in stone buildings, old sheds, and other structures, apparently unconcerned by nearby human activity.

Length **5¾in (14.5cm)**	Wingspan **7½in (19cm)**	Weight **⅜oz (11g)**
Social **Solitary/Pairs**	Lifespan **Unknown**	Status **Secure**

DATE SEEN	WHERE	NOTES

Order **Passeriformes**	Family **Troglodytidae**	Species ***Cistothorus palustris***

Marsh Wren

ADULT

boldly striped black-and-white back

rusty rump

plain, rusty wing patches

IN FLIGHT

barred tail feathers

heavily streaked, black-and-white back

rusty flanks and uppertail feathers

whitish eyebrow

brown forehead and cap

dull whitish, buff underparts

long bill

ADULT

FLIGHT: straight, with rapid wing beats over short distances, from one reed patch to another.

The Marsh Wren, a common resident of saltwater and freshwater marshes, is known for singing loudly through both day and night. The males perform fluttery, aerial courtship flights while singing, and are polygamous, mating with two or more females. Like the Sedge Wren, the male builds several dummy nests before his mate constructs one herself. The Marsh Wren nests in taller vegetation than the Sedge Wren and over deeper water. Eastern (*C. p. palustris*) and Western (*C. p. paludicola*) Marsh Wrens differ in voice and behavior, and some ornithologists classify them as separate species.

VOICE Calls a low *chek* and a raspy *churr*; song a loud *chuk chuk chuk*, then fast *tih-tih-tih-rih-tih-tih*, an enthusiastic singer.

NESTING Oblong structure with side entrance, woven of reeds and lined with soft materials; 4–5 eggs; 2 broods; March–July.

FEEDING Forages acrobatically for insects, such as mosquitoes, dragonflies, and beetles, within dense clusters of cattails and reeds.

DELICATELY PERCHED
This wren perches on vertical reeds and often holds itself up by spreading its legs across two stalks.

SIMILAR SPECIES

SEDGE WREN see p.455

streaked cap

barred wings

buffy underparts

HOUSE WREN see p.308

plain back

grayish brown underparts

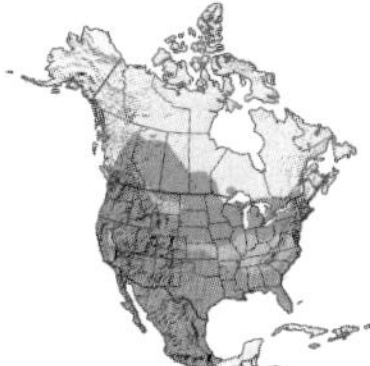

OCCURRENCE
Breeds across North America from Canada to the mountains of the western and central northern states. Inhabits freshwater and saltwater marshes with tall vegetation, above water, sometimes more than 3ft (1m) deep. It is irregularly distributed in its range. Winters in grassy marshes and wetlands.

Length **5in (13cm)**	Wingspan **6in (15cm)**	Weight **³⁄₈oz (11g)**
Social **Loose colonies**	Lifespan **Unknown**	Status **Localized**

DATE SEEN	WHERE	NOTES

Order **Passeriformes**	Family **Troglodytidae**	Species ***Thryomanes bewickii***

Bewick's Wren

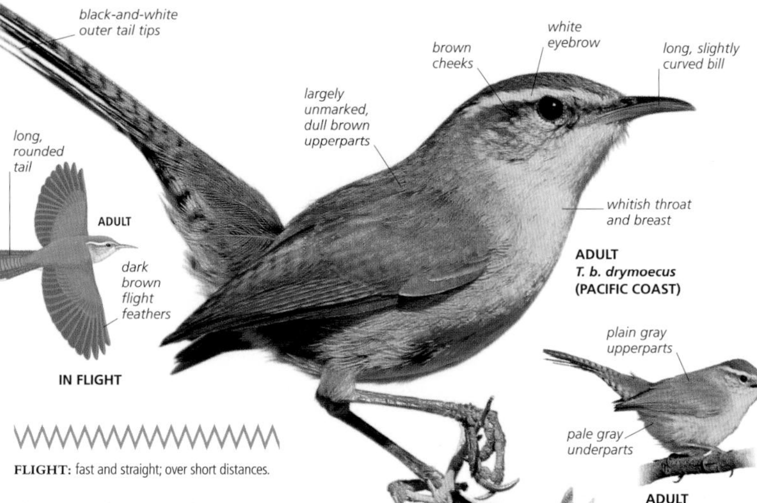

FLIGHT: fast and straight; over short distances.

ADULT
T. b.eremophilus
(INTERIOR WEST AND MEXICO)

Similar in the West to the House Wren in the East, but less common and occupying a smaller range, Bewick's Wren is also familiar around human habitations. It nests in any sort of hole or crevice in barns, houses, abandoned machinery, woodpiles, and even trash heaps in farms and towns. Bewick's Wren has undergone large-scale changes in geographic distribution: in the 19th century its range expanded northward to the eastern and midwestern US, but it gradually disappeared from those regions in the 20th century. It has been suggested that the more aggressive House Wren slowly replaced Bewick's Wren in these areas.

VOICE Loud, complex, and varied mixture of cheeps, buzzes, and clear notes; vocalizations differ according to geographic location; also mimics other birds.

NESTING Cup of sticks lined with leaves, and other soft materials, in natural or human-made cavity, including nest boxes; 5–10 eggs; 2 broods; March–June.

FEEDING Forages for insects in brush, shrubs, crannies of buildings, and leaf litter on ground.

TALENTED MIMIC
Bewick's is sometimes known as the "Mocking Wren," because it can imitate other species' songs.

SIMILAR SPECIES

CAROLINA WREN
see p.455

TYPICAL POSTURE
Bewick's Wren may often be spotted with its distinctive tail cocked vertically.

OCCURRENCE
Year-round resident in brushy areas, open woodlands, and around human structures; from southern British Columbia southward to Baja California, east to Arkansas, and as far south as Oaxaca in Mexico. May withdraw slightly southward from northernmost portions of range in winter.

Length **5in (13cm)**	Wingspan **7in (18cm)**	Weight **3/8oz (11g)**
Social **Solitary/Pairs**	Lifespan **At least 8 years**	Status **Secure**

DATE SEEN	WHERE	NOTES

Order **Passeriformes**	Family **Troglodytidae**	Species ***Troglodytes troglodytes***

Winter Wren

distinct tan eyebrow

stubby tail, usually cocked straight up

dark brown, barred back

small thin bill

ADULT

short, barred tail

ADULT

barred, rounded wings

IN FLIGHT

flanks strongly barred

The Winter Wren has one of the loudest songs of any North American bird of a similar size: the male's song carries far through its forest haunts. It is widespread, found throughout Eurasia, and from the Aleutians and Alaska eastward to Newfoundland, and as far south as California in the West and the Appalachians in the East, where the subspecies *T. t. pullus* resides. Its winter range is also western (to California) and eastern (to Texas), with a wide hiatus in between. It forages in tangles of fallen trees and shrubs, appearing mouse-like as it creeps amid the shadows. In Europe, as its family's sole species, it is simply called "the Wren."

VOICE Call a double *chek-chek* or *chimp-chimp*; song a loud, extremely long, complex series of warbles, trills, and single notes.

NESTING Well-hidden in a cavity near ground with dead wood and crevices; nest a messy mound lined with feathers; 4–7 eggs; 1–2 broods; April–July.

FEEDING Forages for insects in low, dense undergrowth, often in wet areas along streams; sometimes thrusts its head into water to capture prey.

FLIGHT: fast and direct, with rapid beats of its short, broad wings.

VOCAL VIRTUOSO
The Winter Wren is a skulker, but in the breeding season singing males show up on lower perches.

SIMILAR SPECIES

HOUSE WREN
see p.308

NERVOUS REACTION
When alarmed, this wren cocks its tail almost vertically, before escaping into a mossy thicket.

OCCURRENCE
Breeds in northern and mountain forests dominated by evergreen trees with a dense understory, fallen trees, and banks of streams. In the Appalachians, breeds in treeless areas with grass near cliffs. Northernmost birds migrate south to winter in woodlands, brush piles, tangles, and secluded spots.

Length **4in (10cm)**	Wingspan **5½in (14cm)**	Weight **5/16oz (9g)**
Social **Solitary/Family groups**	Lifespan **At least 4 years**	Status **Secure**

DATE SEEN	WHERE	NOTES

Order **Passeriformes**	Family **Troglodytidae**	Species ***Troglodytes aedon***

House Wren

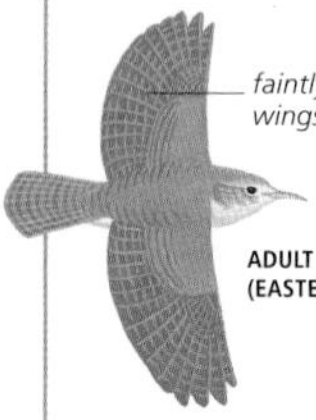
faintly barred wings
ADULT (EASTERN)
IN FLIGHT

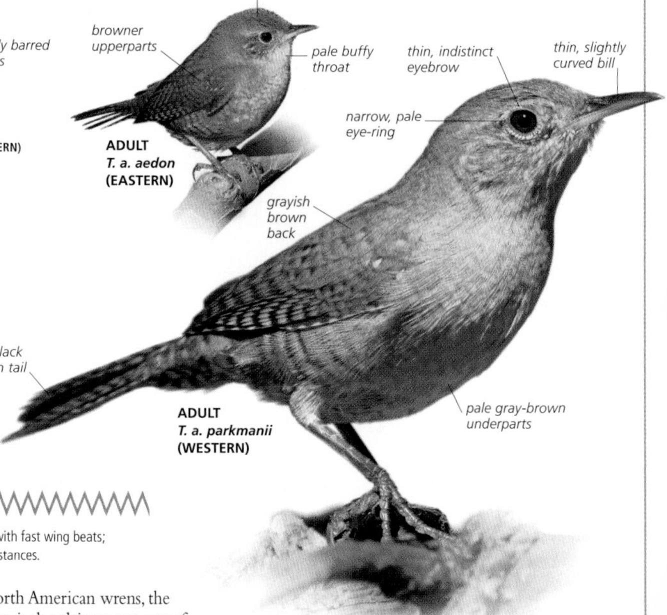
plain brown crown
browner upperparts
pale buffy throat
ADULT
T. a. aedon
(EASTERN)
thin, indistinct eyebrow
thin, slightly curved bill
narrow, pale eye-ring
grayish brown back
narrow, black barring on tail
pale gray-brown underparts
ADULT
T. a. parkmanii
(WESTERN)

FLIGHT: straight, with fast wing beats; typically over short distances.

Of all the North American wrens, the House Wren is the plainest, yet one of the most familiar and endearing, especially when making its home in a backyard nest box. However, it can be a fairly aggressive species, driving away nearby nesting birds of its own and other species by destroying nests, puncturing eggs, and even killing young. In the 1920s, distraught bird lovers mounted a campaign calling for the eradication of House Wrens, though the campaign did not last long as most people were in favor of letting nature take its course.

VOICE Call a sharp *chep* or *cherr*; song opens with several short notes, followed by bubbly explosion of spluttering notes.

NESTING Cup lined with soft material on stick platform in natural, man-made cavities, such as nest boxes; 5–8 eggs; 2–3 broods; April–July.

FEEDING Forages for insects and spiders in trees and shrubs, gardens, and yards.

SIMILAR SPECIES

WINTER WREN see p.307

dark brown overall
shorter tail
heavily barred flanks

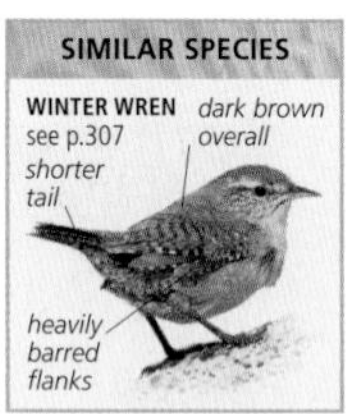

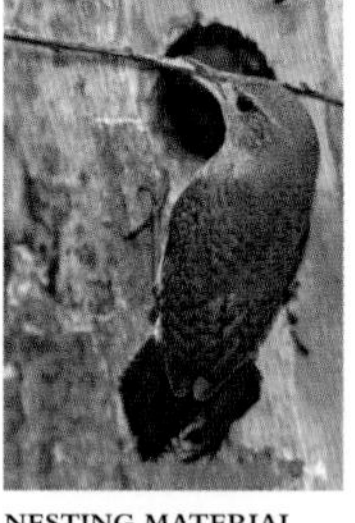

NESTING MATERIAL
This small bird has brought an unusually large twig to its nest inside an old woodpecker hole.

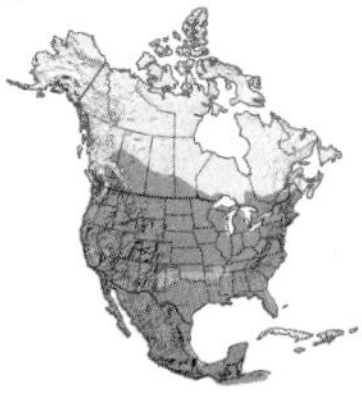

OCCURRENCE
Breeds in cities, towns, parks, farms, yards, gardens, and woodland edges. Rarely seen during migration period (late July to early October). Winters south of its breeding range, from southern US to Mexico, in woodlands, shrubby areas, and weedy fields. Nests, or is resident as far south as Tierra del Fuego.

Length **4½in (11.5cm)**	Wingspan **6in (15cm)**	Weight **⅜oz (11g)**
Social **Solitary**	Lifespan **Up to 9 years**	Status **Secure**

DATE SEEN	WHERE	NOTES

Order **Passeriformes**	Family **Polioptilidae**	Species ***Polioptila caerulea***

Blue-gray Gnatcatcher

MALE
white outer tail feathers
pale gray overall
IN FLIGHT
paler upperparts
lacks black line
FEMALE
blue-gray nape
black line above eye; absent in winter
white eye-ring
blue-gray upperparts
white throat
black central tail feathers
pale patch on wing
pale gray underparts
MALE

FLIGHT: short, straight, and fluttering; usually in short bursts from tree-top to tree-top.

If it did not give its continual wheezy call, the Blue-gray Gnatcatcher might often be missed, as it spends much of its time foraging high up in tall trees. In winter it becomes even harder to find as it is generally silent. This species is the most northern of the North American gnatcatchers and is also the only one to migrate. It can exhibit aggressive behavior and is capable of driving off considerably larger birds than itself. The range of the Blue-gray Gnatcatcher appears to be expanding and populations are increasing.

VOICE Call soft, irregular *zhee, zhee*, uttered constantly while foraging; song soft combination of short notes and nasal wheezes.

NESTING Cup of plant fibers, spider webs, mosses; usually high on branch; lined with soft plant material; 4–5 eggs; 1–2 broods; April–June.

FEEDING Forages for small insects and spiders by acrobatically flitting from twig to twig, while twitching long tail.

LISTEN CLOSELY
The rather faint complex song is best heard when the bird is singing from a low perch.

SIMILAR SPECIES

BLACK-TAILED GNATCATCHER
see p.310
black cap
tail white only at tip

TENNESSEE WARBLER
see p.347
no eye-ring
greenish upperparts
short tail
white underparts

OCCURRENCE
In eastern North America, breeds in deciduous or pine woodlands; in the West, in scrubby habitats, often near water. Winters in brushy habitats in southern US, Mexico, and Central America. Also breeds in Mexico, Belize, and the Bahamas.

Length **4¼in (11cm)**	Wingspan **6in (15cm)**	Weight **7/32oz (6g)**
Social **Solitary/Flocks**	Lifespan **At least 4 years**	Status **Secure**

DATE SEEN	WHERE	NOTES

Order **Passeriformes**	Family **Polioptilidae**	Species ***Polioptila melanura***

Black-tailed Gnatcatcher

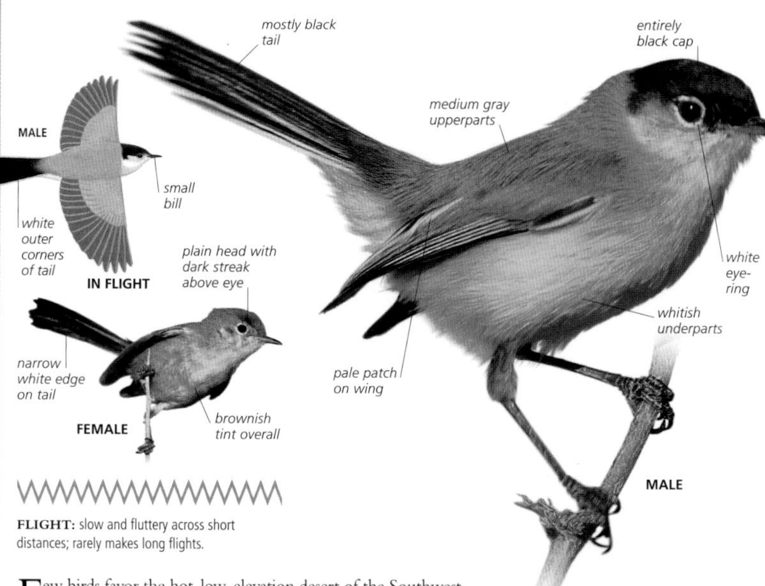

FLIGHT: slow and fluttery across short distances; rarely makes long flights.

Few birds favor the hot, low-elevation desert of the Southwest as much as the Black-tailed Gnatcatcher. This tiny species spends most of its time flitting about among shrubs and foliage, perpetually flicking its tail from side to side. It is monogamous, and after pairs have established a nesting territory, they defend it aggressively throughout the year.

VOICE Various scolding notes *zhee-zhee-zhee*, *chih-chih-chih*, and *chee-chee-chee*; song, rarely heard, soft *tse-dee-dee-dee*.

NESTING Cup of plant fibers and spider webs, placed in shrub usually close to the ground; often lined with fine fibers; 3–4 eggs; 2 broods; April–July.

FEEDING Forages for insects, such as beetles and moths, among branches and leaves of shrubs; occasionally eats fruits and seeds.

DISTINGUISHING FEATURE
The male Black-tailed Gnatcatcher's black cap distinguishes it from the other gnatcatchers.

SIMILAR SPECIES

BLUE-GRAY GNATCATCHER see p.309
blue-tinted upperparts; *white throat*

VIRGINIA'S WARBLER see p.350
dark reddish cap; *pale gray upperparts*; *yellow undertail feathers*

OCCURRENCE
Resident in hot, low-elevation southwestern deserts in thorny scrub, acacia, Mesquite, Saguaro, creosote bush, saltbush, and other shrubs. Mostly found in dry riverbeds, but also in brushy groves along waterways. Range extends south into Mexico.

Length **4½in (11.5cm)**	Wingspan **5½in (14cm)**	Weight **7/32oz (6g)**
Social **Solitary/Pairs**	Lifespan **Unknown**	Status **Localized**

DATE SEEN	WHERE	NOTES

Order **Passeriformes**	Family **Sittidae**	Species ***Sitta pygmaea***

Pygmy Nuthatch

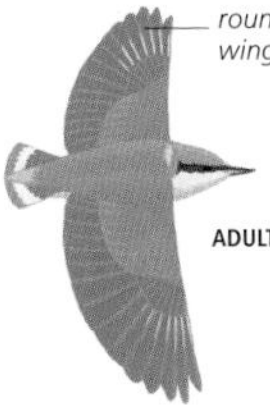

rounded wings

ADULT

IN FLIGHT

pointed, chisel-like bill

grayish brown cap

black eyestripe

blue-gray upperparts

dusky underparts

very short tail

grayish flanks

ADULT

sharp claws

Pygmy Nuthatches are found in noisy and busy flocks throughout the year in their pine forest home of the American West. They are cooperative breeders, with young birds from the previous year's brood often helping adult birds raise the next year's young. They have a particular preference for Ponderosa and Jeffery Pines and are often absent from mountain ranges that lack their favourite trees. Pygmy Nuthatches are heard more often than they are seen, probably because they like to stick to the treetops.

VOICE Highly vocal species; calls piercing *peep* and *pip* notes, given singly or in frenzied series; in series, call resembles vocalizations of some Red Crossbills; calls of birds in flocks are somewhat bell-like.

NESTING Excavates cavity in pine tree; nest is a mass of plant material and feathers; 5–9 eggs; 1–2 broods; April–July.

FEEDING Forages on pine trees; mainly eats insects, caterpillars, moths, and grubs.

FLIGHT: jerky, undulating motion; appears bobtailed and rotund in flight.

SQUEEZING OUT OF A NEST
All nuthatches nest in tree cavities, which they wholly or partially excavate themselves.

SIMILAR SPECIES

BROWN-HEADED NUTHATCH richer brown crown; paler overall

PINE FORAGER
A Pygmy Nuthatch hangs upside down, carrying a tiny piece of food.

OCCURRENCE
Patchily distributed in pine forests of western North America, from British Columbia south to California, Arizona, New Mexico, and Texas; also in Mexico. Most numerous in dry mountain forests up to 650ft (2,000m), but in California ranges down to sea level. Generally patch distribution.

Length **4¼in (11cm)**	Wingspan **8in (20cm)**	Weight **⅜oz (11g)**
Social **Small flocks**	Lifespan **Up to 2 years**	Status **Secure**

DATE SEEN	WHERE	NOTES

Order **Passeriformes**	Family **Sittidae**	Species ***Sitta canadensis***

Red-breasted Nuthatch

FLIGHT: short, swift dashes across forest clearings; irregular, undulating motion.

This aggressive, inquisitive nuthatch, with its distinctive black eyestripe, breeds in conifer forests across North America. The bird inhabits mountains in the West; in the East, it is found in lowlands and hills. However, sometimes it breeds in conifer groves away from its core range. Each fall, birds move from their main breeding grounds, but the extent of this exodus varies from year to year, depending on population cycles and food availability.

VOICE Call a one-note tooting sound, often repeated, with strong nasal yet musical quality: *aaank*, *enk*, *ink*, rather like a horn.

NESTING Excavates cavity in pine tree; nest of grass lined with feathers, with sticky pine resin applied to entrance; 5–7 eggs, 1 brood; May–July.

FEEDING Probes bark for beetle grubs; also eats insect larvae found on conifer needles; seeds in winter.

TASTY GRUB
This nuthatch has just extracted its dinner from the bark of a tree, a favorite foraging habitat.

SIMILAR SPECIES

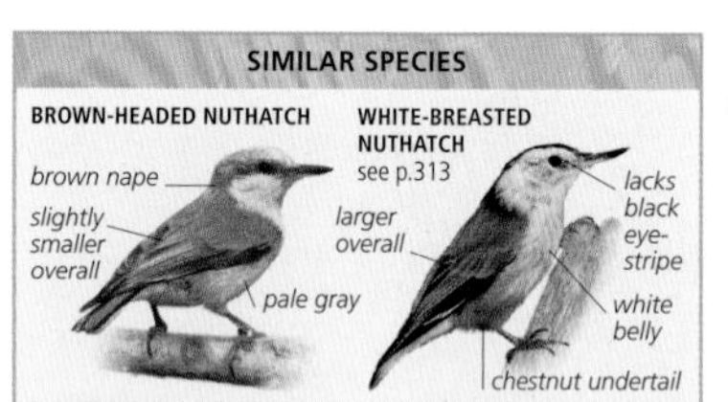

OCCURRENCE
Found year-round in coniferous and mixed hardwood forests. During breeding season, absent from southeastern pine forests, except in the Appalachians. In the west, shares its habitat with Pygmy Nuthatch, but ranges to higher elevations.

Length **4¼in (11cm)**	Wingspan **8½in (22cm)**	Weight **⅜–7⁄16oz (10–13g)**
Social **Solitary/Pairs**	Lifespan **Up to 7 years**	Status **Secure**

DATE SEEN	WHERE	NOTES

Order **Passeriformes**	Family **Sittidae**	Species ***Sitta carolinensis***

White-breasted Nuthatch

FLIGHT: weak, with quick wing beats followed by glide; often short, from tree to tree.

The amiable White-breasted Nuthatch inhabits residential neighborhoods across the US and southern Canada, and often visits birdfeeders in winter. The largest of our nuthatches, it spends more time probing furrows and crevices on trunks and boughs than other nuthatches do. It walks irregularly on trees: forward, backward, upside-down, or horizontally. Of the 11 subspecies in its Canada-to-Mexico range, five occur in Canada and in the US. They differ in call notes and, to a lesser extent, in plumage.

VOICE Calls vary geographically: eastern birds nasal *yank yank*; interior birds stuttering *st't't't't'*; Pacific slope birds tremulous *yiiiirk*; song of all populations a mellow *tu tu tu tu*, like a flicker, but softer.

NESTING Tree cavity, once used by woodpeckers, lined with grass and hair, adds mud to cavity opening; 5–9 eggs, 1 brood; April–June.

FEEDING Scours bark methodically for insects such as beetle larvae.

UNUSUAL DESCENT
Nuthatches are unusual in that they routinely descend branches and trunks head-first.

SIMILAR SPECIES

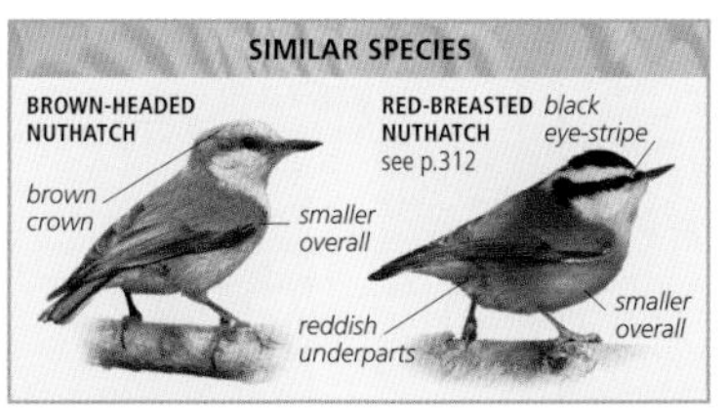

OCCURRENCE
More liberal than other nuthatches in use of forest types; overlaps with the smaller species in coniferous forest ranges, but also common in broadleaf deciduous or mixed forests; weakly migratory: little movement in most falls, but moderate departures from breeding grounds in some years.

Length **5¾in (14.5cm)**	Wingspan **11in (28cm)**	Weight **11/16–7/8oz (19–25g)**
Social **Solitary/Pairs**	Lifespan **Up to 9 years**	Status **Secure**

DATE SEEN	WHERE	NOTES

Order **Passeriformes**	Family **Certhiidae**	Species ***Certhia americana***

Brown Creeper

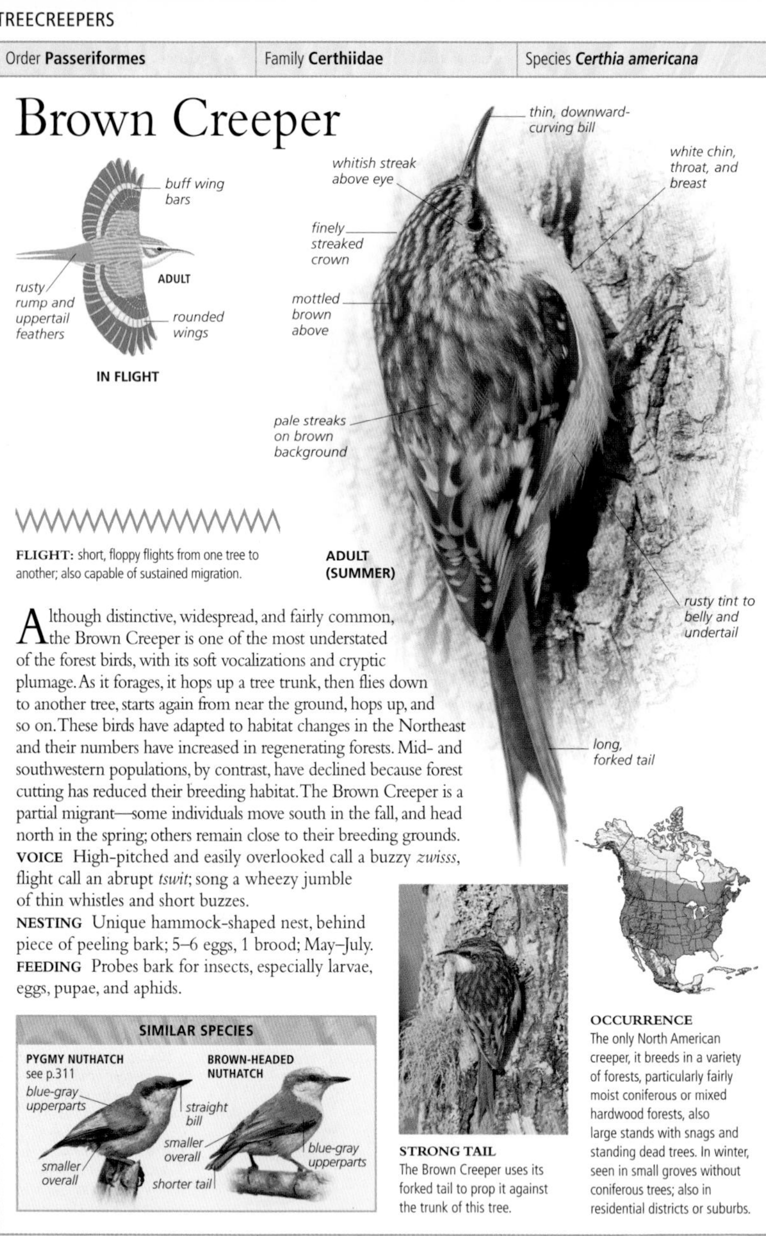

FLIGHT: short, floppy flights from one tree to another; also capable of sustained migration.

Although distinctive, widespread, and fairly common, the Brown Creeper is one of the most understated of the forest birds, with its soft vocalizations and cryptic plumage. As it forages, it hops up a tree trunk, then flies down to another tree, starts again from near the ground, hops up, and so on. These birds have adapted to habitat changes in the Northeast and their numbers have increased in regenerating forests. Mid- and southwestern populations, by contrast, have declined because forest cutting has reduced their breeding habitat. The Brown Creeper is a partial migrant—some individuals move south in the fall, and head north in the spring; others remain close to their breeding grounds.

VOICE High-pitched and easily overlooked call a buzzy *zwisss*, flight call an abrupt *tswit*; song a wheezy jumble of thin whistles and short buzzes.

NESTING Unique hammock-shaped nest, behind piece of peeling bark; 5–6 eggs, 1 brood; May–July.

FEEDING Probes bark for insects, especially larvae, eggs, pupae, and aphids.

SIMILAR SPECIES

PYGMY NUTHATCH see p.311

BROWN-HEADED NUTHATCH

STRONG TAIL
The Brown Creeper uses its forked tail to prop it against the trunk of this tree.

OCCURRENCE
The only North American creeper, it breeds in a variety of forests, particularly fairly moist coniferous or mixed hardwood forests, also large stands with snags and standing dead trees. In winter, seen in small groves without coniferous trees; also in residential districts or suburbs.

Length **5¼in (13.5cm)**	Wingspan **8in (20cm)**	Weight **¼–⅜oz (7–10g)**
Social **Solitary**	Lifespan **Up to 4 years**	Status **Secure**

DATE SEEN	WHERE	NOTES

Order **Passeriformes**	Family **Mimidae**	Species ***Dumetella carolinensis***

Gray Catbird

gray overall

ADULT

long, black tail

IN FLIGHT

dark gray to black head

straight, blackish bill

gray upperparts

large, black eye

gray underparts

bright brick-red undertail feathers

ADULT

In addition to the feline-like, mewing calls that earned it its common name, the Gray Catbird not only has an extraordinarily varied vocal repertoire, but it can also sing two notes simultaneously. It has been reported to imitate the vocalizations of over 40 bird species, at least one frog species, and several sounds produced by machines and electronic devices. Despite their shy, retiring nature, Gray Catbirds tolerate human presence and will rest in shrubs in suburban and urban lots. Another fascinating skill is the Gray Catbird's ability to recognize and remove eggs of the brood parasite, the Brown-headed Cowbird.

VOICE *Mew* call, like a young kitten; song a long, complex series of unhurried, often grouped notes, sometimes interspersed with whistles and squeaks.

NESTING Large, untidy cup of woven twigs, grass, and hair lined with finer material; 3–4 eggs; 1–2 broods; May–August.

FEEDING Feeds on a wide variety of berries and insects, usually whatever is most abundant in season.

FLIGHT: short flights between habitat patches with constant, medium-speed wing beats.

ANGLED ATTITUDE
Between bouts of feeding, a Gray Catbird often rests with its body and tail at a 50-degree angle.

LARGE BLACK EYES
Peering from the foliage, a Gray Catbird investigates its surroundings.

SIMILAR SPECIES

NORTHERN MOCKINGBIRD
see p.316
white wing patch
lighter gray
longer tail edged in white

CRISSAL THRASHER
see p.456
longer, curved bill
brown-gray overall

OCCURRENCE
Breeds in mixed young to mid-aged forests with abundant undergrowth, from British Columbia east to Maritimes and Newfoundland, and in the US diagonally west-east from Washington State to New Mexico, east to the Gulf Coast, north to New England. Northern population migratory.

Length **8–9½in (20–24cm)**	Wingspan **10–12in (25–30cm)**	Weight **1¼–2⅛oz (35–60g)**
Social **Solitary/Pairs**	Lifespan **Up to 11 years**	Status **Secure**

DATE SEEN	WHERE	NOTES

Order **Passeriformes**	Family **Mimidae**	Species ***Mimus polyglottos***

Northern Mockingbird

ADULT

white patches on wing

IN FLIGHT

shorter tail

speckled breast and belly

JUVENILE

gray head

pointed, curved bill

yellow eye

long tail with white outer tail feathers

white undertail feathers

ADULT

white patch on wing feathers

FLIGHT: usually direct and level on constant, somewhat fluttering, quick wing beats.

The ability of the Northern Mockingbird to imitate sounds is truly impressive: some individuals can incorporate over 100 different phrases of as many different birds in their songs. Phrases are usually repeated, often quite a few times, and somewhat modified at each repetition. This species, once thought to be headed for extinction due to the caged-bird trade in the 1700s and 1800s, has largely recovered since then. In fact, the Northern Mockingbird's range has expanded in the last few decades, due partly to its high tolerance for humans and their habitats. A diagnostic field characteristic of the Northern Mockingbird is its tendency to "wing flash," showing its white outer wing feather patches when holding its wings overhead.

VOICE Long, complex repertoire often imitating other birds, non-bird noises, and the sounds of mechanical devices.

NESTING Bulky cup of twigs, lined, in shrub or tree; 3–5 eggs; 1–3 broods; March–August.

FEEDING Eats a wide variety of fruit, berries, and insects, including ants, beetles, and grasshoppers.

BERRY PICKER
Northern Mockingbirds love berries, and make good use of them during the fall.

SIMILAR SPECIES

LOGGERHEAD SHRIKE see p.262
brown mask
black wings

CLARK'S NUTCRACKER see p.278
white patch low on wing
darker gray belly
whiter sides to tail

OCCURRENCE
Widespread in the US from coast to coast south of the timberline, primarily along edges of disturbed habitats, including young forests and especially suburban and urban areas with shrubs or hedges.

Length **8½–10in (22–25cm)**	Wingspan **13–15in (33–38cm)**	Weight **1 9/16–2oz (45–55g)**
Social **Pairs**	Lifespan **Up to 20 years**	Status **Secure**

DATE SEEN	WHERE	NOTES

Order **Passeriformes**	Family **Mimidae**	Species ***Oreoscoptes montanus***

Sage Thrasher

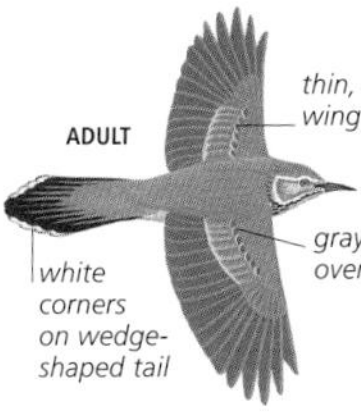

ADULT

thin, white wing bars

gray overall

white corners on wedge-shaped tail

IN FLIGHT

pale yellowish eye

whitish ring around back of cheek

dusky, brownish gray upperparts

short, straight bill

thin "mustache"

thin, brown streaking on off-white throat, breast, and belly

ADULT

FLIGHT: prefers to run; may dart low between patches of habitat using short, rapid wing beats.

This plain-colored little bird is the smallest of the North American thrashers. Together with several other members of this group, the Sage Thrasher recognizes and removes the eggs of brood parasites, especially those of the Brown-headed Cowbird. Unfortunately, it may also be the least studied of the thrasher group, perhaps because the dense nature of its habitat makes study difficult. The English name, "Sage Thrasher," truly describes this bird's western habitat.

VOICE Song varies in duration: low, repeated, very musical notes or phrases that may blend together in a melodious song.

NESTING Large cup with stick frame lined with grass, horse hair, sheep's wool, and fur; 3–6 eggs; 1-2 broods; April–July.

FEEDING Eats insects, especially ants and beetles, on the ground; will also consume berries when seasonally available.

JUICY MEAL
This thrasher forages mostly on or near the ground; it feeds on insects and berries.

SHOW-OFF TENDENCIES
Males attract mates and defend their territory with raised wings, in a fluttering display.

SIMILAR SPECIES

LONG-BILLED THRASHER see p.455
long, curved bill
dull brown back
dark streaks on white underparts

CURVE-BILLED THRASHER see p.319
orange eye
more gray back
pale gray spots

OCCURRENCE
Very closely associated with sagebrush habitat in low-elevation, semi-arid valleys of the western US. Winters from southwestern US to Baja California and continental Mexico, southwards to Sonora and Coquila.

Length **8–9in (20–23cm)**	Wingspan **10–13in (25–33cm)**	Weight **1$^{7}/_{16}$–1$^{3}/_{4}$oz (40–50g)**
Social **Solitary/Pairs**	Lifespan **Unknown**	Status **Localized**

DATE SEEN	WHERE	NOTES

Order **Passeriformes**	Family **Mimidae**	Species ***Toxostoma rufum***

Brown Thrasher

The Brown Thrasher is usually difficult to view clearly because it keeps to dense underbrush. Like most other thrashers, this species prefers running or hopping to flying. When nesting, it can recognize and remove the eggs of brood parasites like the Brown-headed Cowbird. The current population decline is most likely the result of fragmentation of large, wooded habitats into patches, which lack the forest interior habitat this species needs.

VOICE Calls varied, including rasping sounds; song a long series of musical notes, sometimes imitating other species; repeats phrase twice before moving onto the next one.

NESTING Bulky cup of twigs, close to ground, lined with leaves, grass, bark; 3–5 eggs; 1 brood; April–July.

FEEDING Mainly insects (especially beetles) and worms gathered from leaf litter on the forest floor; will peck at cultivated grains, nuts, berries, and fruit.

FLIGHT: slow and heavy with deep wing beats; below treetops, especially in and around ground.

STREAKED BREAST
Displaying its heavily streaked underparts, this Brown Thrasher is perched and ready to sing.

OCCURRENCE
Widespread across central and eastern North America, from Canada to Texas and Florida, in a variety of densely wooded habitats, particularly those with thick undergrowth, but will use woodland edges, hedges, and riverine trees. A partial migrant, it winters in the southern part of its range.

SIMILAR SPECIES

Length **10–12in (25–30cm)**	Wingspan **11–14in (28–36cm)**	Weight **$2\frac{1}{8}$–$2\frac{7}{8}$oz (60–80g)**
Social **Solitary/Flocks**	Lifespan **Up to 13 years**	Status **Declining**

DATE SEEN	WHERE	NOTES

Order **Passeriformes**	Family **Mimidae**	Species ***Toxostoma curvirostre***

Curve-billed Thrasher

long, dark tail
ADULT
long, curved bill
whitish corners to tail
IN FLIGHT

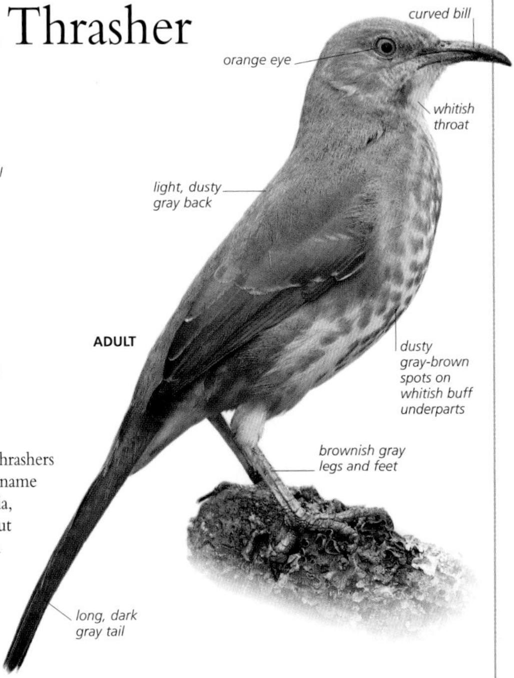

curved bill
orange eye
whitish throat
light, dusty gray back
ADULT
dusty gray-brown spots on whitish buff underparts
brownish gray legs and feet
long, dark gray tail

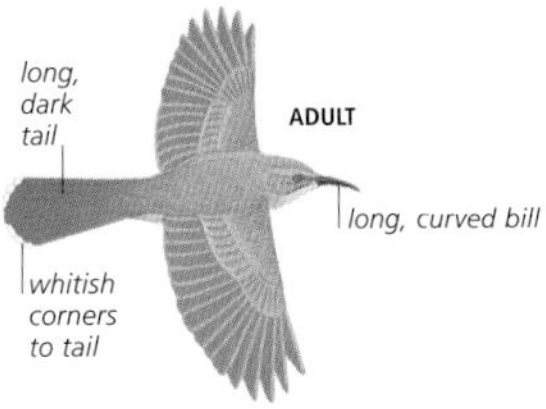

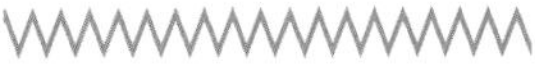

FLIGHT: rapid and quite erratic, usually between patches of habitat.

Several species of North American thrashers would equally deserve the English name of "curved-billed," including California, Long-billed, Crissal, and Le Conte's, but *curvirostre* was described by the English ornithologist William Swainson back in 1827, years before these other species. So, following a general rule in giving birds a common name, "Curve-billed" stuck. The arid-country loving Curve-billed is somewhat unkempt looking, with a thick bill and powerful legs. Less of a mimic than other thrashers, it is nevertheless quite vocal, and its two-note *twit-twit* call is a characteristic sound of the southwestern semi-deserts.

VOICE Two-note *qwit-qweet*; song a series of clear, warbled whistles broken into distinct phrases; some mimicry of other species' calls.

NESTING Bulky, rather messy-looking cup of thorny sticks, in cactus or shrub, lined with grass, feathers, and hair; 3–5 eggs; 2 broods; February–July.

FEEDING Forages on ground and in leaf litter for insects and snails; eats fruit and berries in the fall.

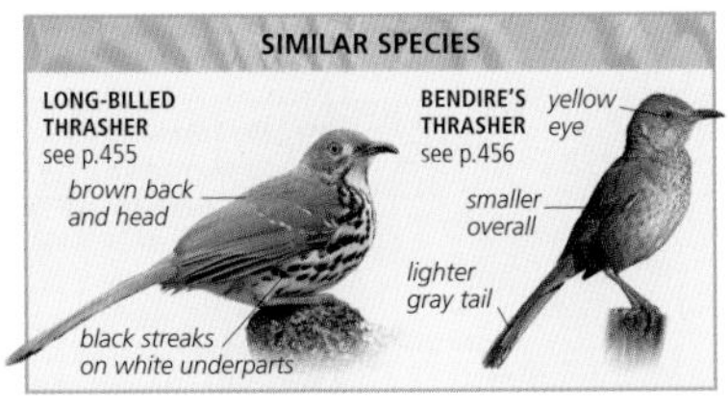

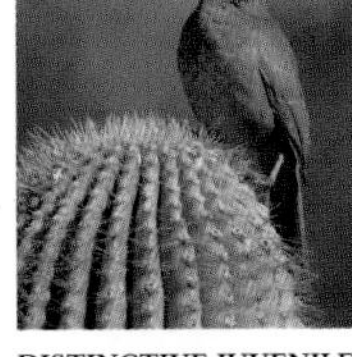

DISTINCTIVE JUVENILE
Juvenile birds show less spotting on their underparts and paler eyes than the adults.

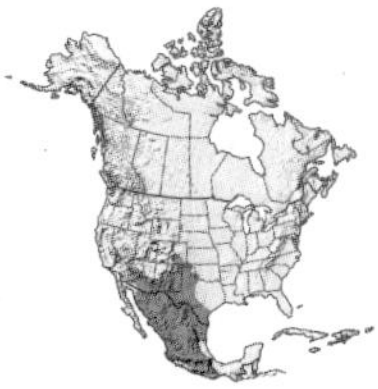

OCCURRENCE
In the US, the Curve-billed Thrasher inhabits open, scrubby, arid to semi-arid areas, where it is often found along edges between brush and clearings. Its Mexican range extends south to Veracuz and Oaxaca. It is largely resident throughout its US and Mexican range.

SIMILAR SPECIES

LONG-BILLED THRASHER see p.455

BENDIRE'S THRASHER see p.456

brown back and head
black streaks on white underparts
yellow eye
smaller overall
lighter gray tail

Length **10–13in (25–33cm)**	Wingspan **12–15in (30–38cm)**	Weight **2⅛–2⅞oz (60–80g)**
Social **Pairs**	Lifespan **Up to 11 years**	Status **Localized**

DATE SEEN	WHERE	NOTES

Order **Passeriformes**	Family **Sturnidae**	Species ***Sturnus vulgaris***

European Starling

This distinctive non-native species is perhaps the most successful bird in North America—and probably the most maligned. In the 1890s, 100 European Starlings were released in New York City's Central Park; these were the ancestors of the many millions of birds that now live all across the US. This adaptable and aggressive bird competes with native species for nest sites, and the starling usually wins—even against larger species such as the Northern Flicker.

VOICE Highly varied; gives whooshing *sssssheer*, often in flight; also whistled *wheeeooo*; song an elaborate pulsing series with slurred whistles and clicking notes; imitates other species' vocalizations.

NESTING Natural or artificial cavity of any sort; 4–6 eggs; 1–2 broods; March–July.

FEEDING Omnivorous; picks at anything that might be edible; insects and berries are common food items; also visits birdfeeders and trash cans; often feeds on grubs in lawns.

FLIGHT: individuals fly in direct, buzzy manner; flocks bunch up tightly in flight.

INSECT EATER
Despite its parents' omnivorous diet, the nestlings are fed almost exclusively on insects and larvae.

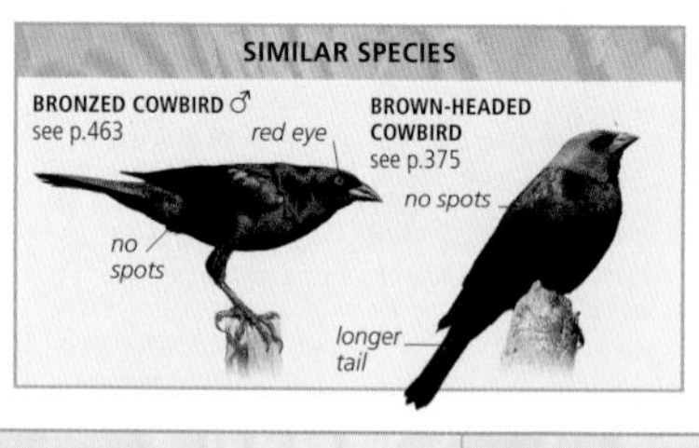

OCCURRENCE
In North America from southern Canada to the US–Mexico border; also Puerto Rico and other Caribbean islands. Common to abundant in cities, towns, and farmlands; also occurs in relatively "wild" settings far from human habitation. Forms flocks at all times, huge in winter.

Length **8½in (21cm)**	Wingspan **16in (41cm)**	Weight **2⅝–3⅜oz (75–95g)**
Social **Colonies**	Lifespan **Up to 17 years**	Status **Secure**

DATE SEEN	WHERE	NOTES
4/23/19	SU campus	In flocks

THRUSHES

MOST THRUSHES ARE medium-sized brown- or olive-brown-backed birds with varying amounts of spotting underneath. Although undistinguished in color, they more than make up for their drab plumage with beautiful flutelike songs. Characteristically, thrushes and their relatives have a juvenile plumage with marked spotting and scalloping. The Varied Thrush is the sole member of the genus *Ixoreus*, and differs dramatically from other thrushes, with a bold black-and-rust pattern. It is one of the most distinctive birds in North America. Other birds that stand out from amongst other thrushes are the brightly colored bluebirds, which have been the target of successful conservation efforts, and the duller Townsend's Solitaire.

ORCHARD DWELLER
Bluebirds, for example this Mountain Bluebird, favor orchards far more than other thrushes.

GROUND BIRDS
Though they perch to sing, thrushes, including this Varied Thrush, spend a lot of their time on or near the ground.

WAGTAILS, PIPITS, & DIPPERS

GROUND-DWELLING SONGBIRDS are represented by more than 50 species worldwide. Only two of these species are regularly found in North America.

WAGTAILS

Wagtails are named for their habit of constantly bobbing their long, slender tails up and down. Their plumage contrasts bright colors with black. Although primarily a European genus, two wagtail species are considered regular North American breeders, and two others are routinely sighted along the Bering Sea coast and Aleutian Islands.

PIPITS

Unlike wagtails, the two species of pipit that breed in North America also winter there. Very much birds of open, treeless country, both pipit species are more likely to be seen on their widespread wintering grounds than in their breeding range.

DIPPERS

The only North American species of dipper is exclusively western, and occurs from Alaska south to Mexico and Panama. It is the only songbird that feeds underwater.

COUNTRY-LOVERS
Pipits, such as this female American Pipit, live in open countryside.

Order **Passeriformes**	Family **Turdidae**	Species ***Ixoreus naevius***

Varied Thrush

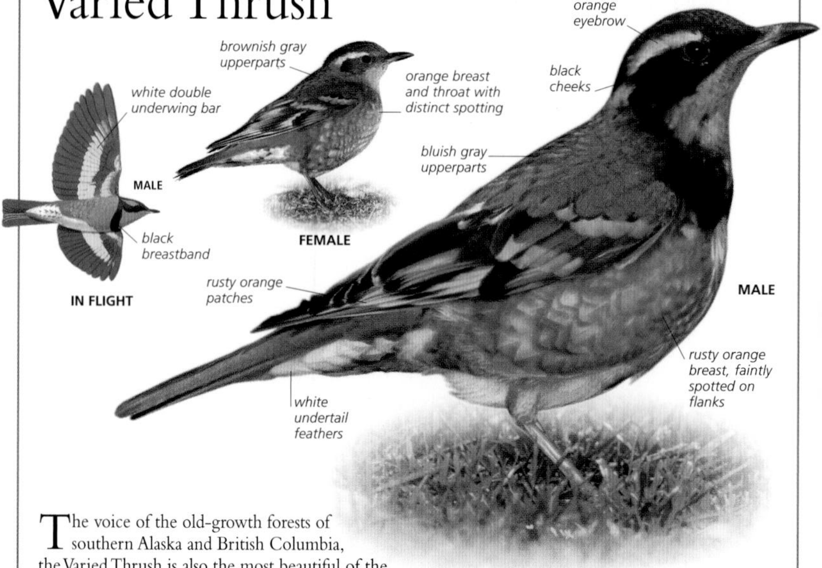

white double underwing bar
MALE
black breastband
IN FLIGHT
brownish gray upperparts
orange breast and throat with distinct spotting
FEMALE
orange eyebrow
black cheeks
bluish gray upperparts
rusty orange patches
white undertail feathers
MALE
rusty orange breast, faintly spotted on flanks

The voice of the old-growth forests of southern Alaska and British Columbia, the Varied Thrush is also the most beautiful of the North American thrushes. Its song is so haunting and ethereal that to hear it can give the listener goosebumps. To see the bird is another matter, as it is often rather shy, except when bringing food to its nestlings. The Varied Thrush's orange and black head, deep bluish black back, and its two rusty wing bars are an unmistakable combination of markings.

VOICE Song is a single note that rises or falls in tone; repeats its song after about 10 seconds; sings for long periods of time from one perch, then moves to another to start anew.

NESTING Bulky cup of twigs, dead leaves, pieces of bark, stems of grass and weeds, lined with fine grass stems, mainly in conifer trees, against trunk; 3–4 eggs; 1–2 broods; April–August.

FEEDING Feeds on insects and caterpillars while breeding; fruit and berries in winter.

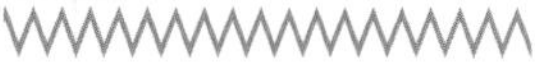

FLIGHT: rapid wing beats; fast and direct.

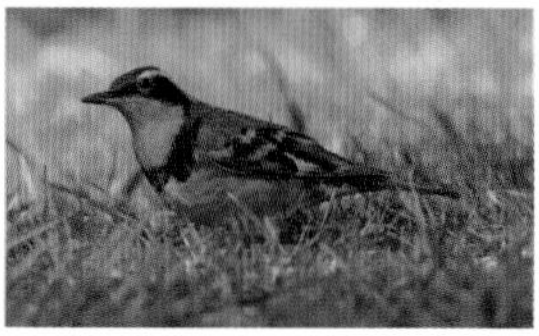

SUMMER DIET
During its breeding season, this thrush forages for insects, often outside the forest interior.

SIMILAR SPECIES

FOREST DWELLER
The Varied Thrush is often difficult to find, because it inhabits dark forests.

OCCURRENCE
Breeds from Alaska south to Montana; prefers moist coniferous forests throughout breeding range; likely to be found in mature forests. Winters south of its breeding range; habitat varies between ravines and thickets to suburban lawns. Habitat in migration much like winter choices.

Length **7–10in (18–25cm)**	Wingspan **13–15in (33–38cm)**	Weight **2¼–3½oz (65–100g)**
Social **Solitary/Flocks**	Lifespan **At least 5 years**	Status **Declining**

DATE SEEN	WHERE	NOTES

Order **Passeriformes**	Family **Turdidae**	Species ***Sialia mexicana***

Western Bluebird

Very similar to its close relative, the Eastern Bluebird, but with a distribution restricted to the western part of the continent, the male Western Bluebird is endowed with a spectacular plumage—brilliant blue upperparts and deep chestnut-orange underparts. Unlike the Eastern Bluebird, the Western Bluebird has a brown back and a complete blue hood. Females and juveniles are harder to distinguish, but their ranges are quite different.

FLIGHT: slow and easy-looking, with shallow wing beats.

VOICE Vocalizations similar to those of the Eastern Bluebird; calls soft *few, few* or *fewrr-fewrr*; song a pleasant, soft series of churring notes, all strung together, often given at dawn.

NESTING Shallow cup of dry grass and feathers in natural tree cavity or old woodpecker cavity; 4–6 eggs; 1–2 broods; March–July.

FEEDING Feeds mainly on insects in breeding season; eats berries, such as juniper, in winter.

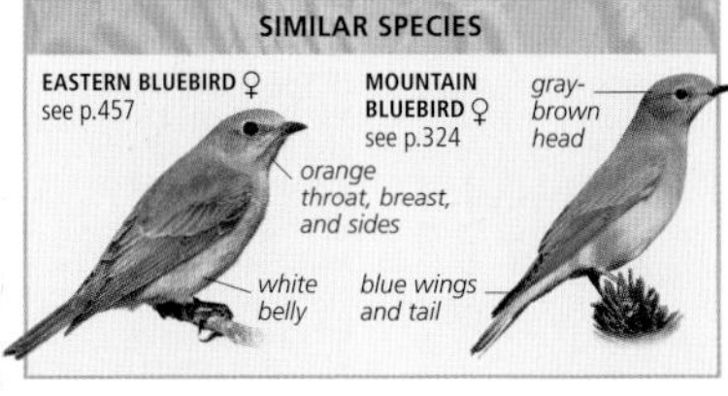

PERCHED MALE
The Western Bluebird hunts from low perches, from which it takes insects from the ground or air.

OCCURRENCE
During breeding season, open woodlands (coniferous and deciduous) and forest edges. In winter, moves to lower elevations and occupies open and semi-open areas, such as pinyon-juniper forests and deserts. Partial migrant; northern birds move south where southern breeders reside.

Length **6–7in (15–18cm)**	Wingspan **11½–13in (29–33cm)**	Weight **$\frac{7}{8}$–$1\frac{1}{16}$oz (25–30g)**
Social **Winter flocks**	Lifespan **Up to 7 years**	Status **Secure**

DATE SEEN	WHERE	NOTES

Order **Passeriformes**	Family **Turdidae**	Species ***Sialia currucoides***

Mountain Bluebird

A bird of the American West, especially sub-alpine meadows, the Mountain Bluebird is as striking as the other two *Sialia* species, but, unlike them, lacks any reddish chestnut in its plumage. It is also more slender-looking, and flies in an almost lazy manner. More often than its two relatives, it feeds by hovering, kestrel-like, over meadows, before pouncing on insects. Males guard their mates from pair-bond time to egg-hatching time.

VOICE Calls rolled, soft churring; one song, loud but infrequent, similar to the American Robin's song—*sing-song cheerily cheer-up cheerio*; the other, soft and repetitive whistle.

NESTING Cavity nest of grass, weeds, and bark; 5–6 eggs; 2 broods; May–July.

FEEDING Insects, including crickets, grasshoppers, bees, and caterpillars, dominate its diet year round; also berries.

FLIGHT: slow unhurried, almost leisurely, with shallow wing beats.

BERRY LOVER
Berries are an important part of the bird's diet along with insects and caterpillars.

OCCURRENCE
Breeds in western North America, in grassland or open canyons with scattered trees, or alpine parklands. In winter, prefers open habitats and avoids dry areas. Winter habitat includes juniper forest and Ponderosa Pine in the south of its territory.

SIMILAR SPECIES

EASTERN BLUEBIRD ♀ see p.457
brownish back
white belly

WESTERN BLUEBIRD ♀ see p.323
grayish throat
pale orange on breast and flanks

TOWNSEND'S SOLITAIRE see p.325
white eye-ring
gray overall
longer tail

Length **6–8in (15–20cm)**	Wingspan **11–12½in (28–32cm)**	Weight **1¹⁄₁₆oz (30g)**
Social **Flocks**	Lifespan **At least 5 years**	Status **Secure**

DATE SEEN	WHERE	NOTES

Order **Passeriformes**	Family **Muscicapidae**	Species ***Myadestes townsendi***

Townsend's Solitaire

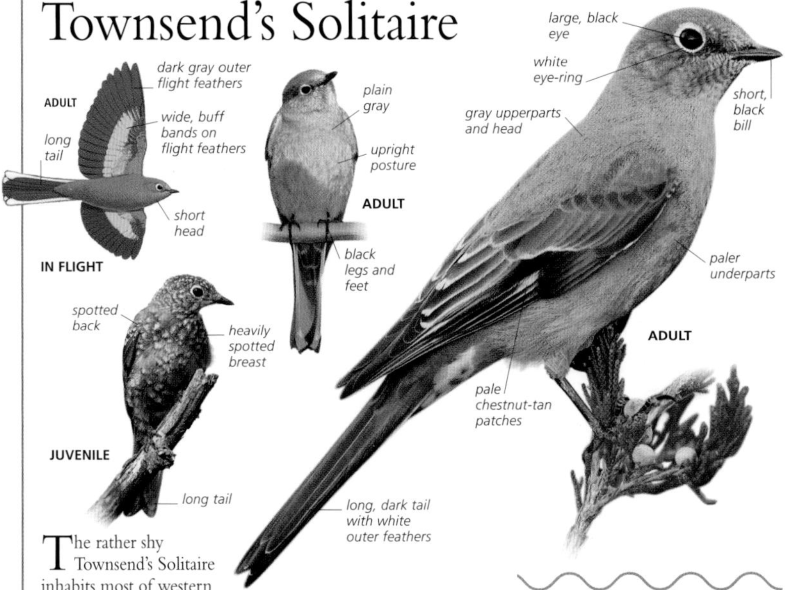

dark gray outer flight feathers
ADULT
wide, buff bands on flight feathers
long tail
short head
IN FLIGHT
plain gray
upright posture
ADULT
black legs and feet
large, black eye
white eye-ring
gray upperparts and head
short, black bill
paler underparts
ADULT
pale chestnut-tan patches
spotted back
heavily spotted breast
JUVENILE
long tail
long, dark tail with white outer feathers

The rather shy Townsend's Solitaire inhabits most of western North America, especially high-elevation coniferous forests of the Sierras and Rockies. Its drab gray plumage, with a chestnut-tan wing pattern, remains the same throughout the year, and the sexes look alike. From a perch high on a branch, Townsend's Solitaire darts after flying insects and snaps its bill shut after catching its prey, unlike other thrush-like birds.

VOICE Calls are single-note, high-pitched whistles; sings all year, but especially when establishing territories; main song robin-like, full of rolled or trilled sounds, interspersed with squeaky notes.

NESTING Cup of pine needles, dry grass, weed stems, and bark on ground or under overhang; 4 eggs; 1–2 broods; May–August.

FEEDING Forages for a wide variety of insects and spiders during breeding season; feeds on fruits and berries after breeding, particularly junipers.

FLIGHT: unhurried motion, usually over short distances, with slow, steady wing beats.

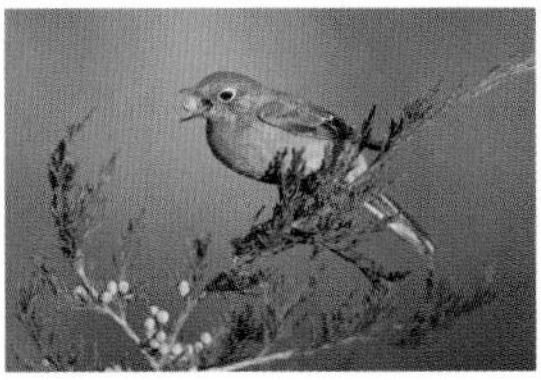

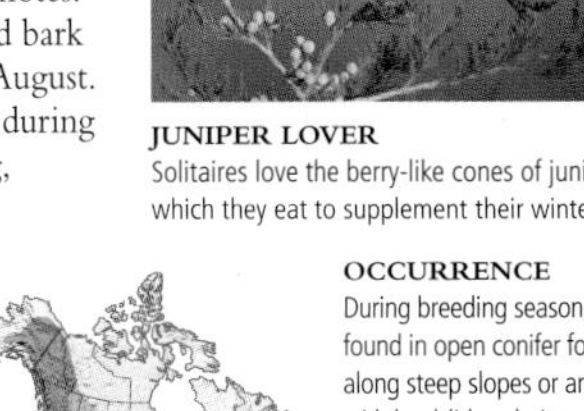

JUNIPER LOVER
Solitaires love the berry-like cones of junipers, which they eat to supplement their winter diet.

SIMILAR SPECIES

GRAY PLUMAGE
Townsend's Solitaire is a drab gray overall, but has a conspicuous white eye-ring.

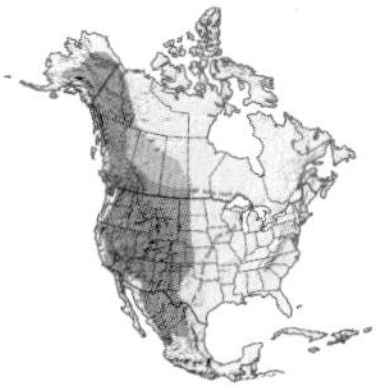

OCCURRENCE
During breeding season, found in open conifer forests along steep slopes or areas with landslides; during winter, at lower elevations, in open woodlands where junipers are abundant. Partial-migrant northern populations move south in winter, as far as central Mexico.

Length **8–8½in (20–22cm)**	Wingspan **13–14½in (33–37cm)**	Weight **1¹⁄₁₆–1¼oz (30–35g)**
Social **Solitary**	Lifespan **Up to 5 years**	Status **Secure**

DATE SEEN	WHERE	NOTES

Order **Passeriformes**	Family **Turdidae**	Species ***Catharus fuscescens***

Veery

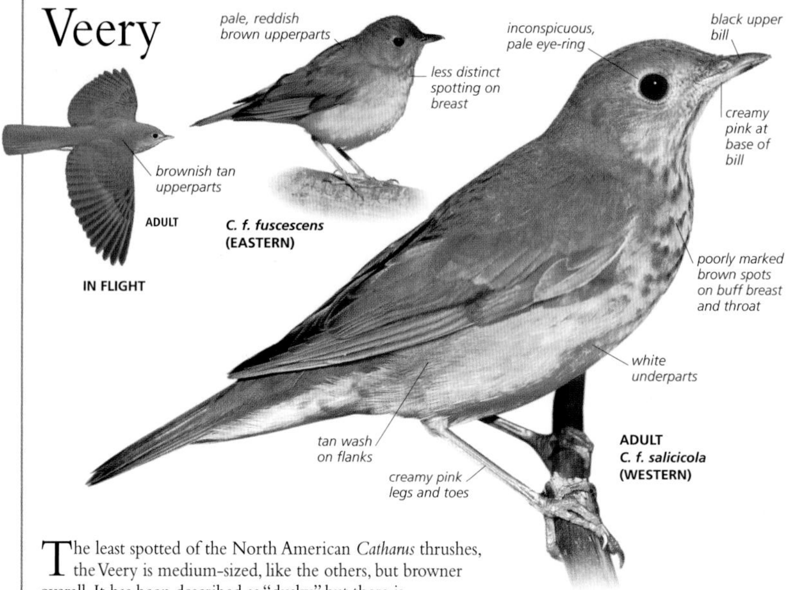

pale, reddish brown upperparts
less distinct spotting on breast
inconspicuous, pale eye-ring
black upper bill
creamy pink at base of bill
brownish tan upperparts
ADULT
C. f. fuscescens (EASTERN)
IN FLIGHT
poorly marked brown spots on buff breast and throat
white underparts
tan wash on flanks
creamy pink legs and toes
ADULT
C. f. salicicola (WESTERN)

The least spotted of the North American *Catharus* thrushes, the Veery is medium-sized, like the others, but browner overall. It has been described as "dusky," but there is a geographical variation in duskiness; four subspecies have been described to reflect this. Eastern birds (*C. f. fuscescens*) are ruddier than their western relatives (*C. f. salicicola*). The Veery is a long-distance migrant, spending the northern winter months in Venezuela, Colombia, the Guianas, and Brazil in a variety of tropical habitats.

VOICE A series of descending *da-vee-ur, vee-ur, veer, veer,* somewhat bi-tonal, sounding like the name Veery; call a rather soft *veer*.

NESTING Cup of dead leaves, bark, weed stems, and moss on or near ground; 4 eggs; 1–2 broods; May–July.

FEEDING Forages on the ground for insects, spiders, snails; eats fruit and berries after breeding.

FLIGHT: rapid and straight, with intermittent hops and glides; makes long hops when on ground.

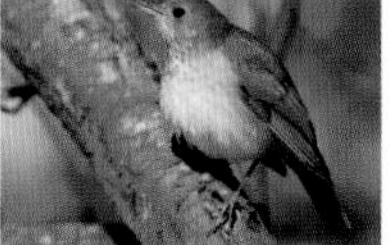

DAMP DWELLINGS
The Veery breeds in damp habitats, such as moist wooded areas or in trees near or in swamps.

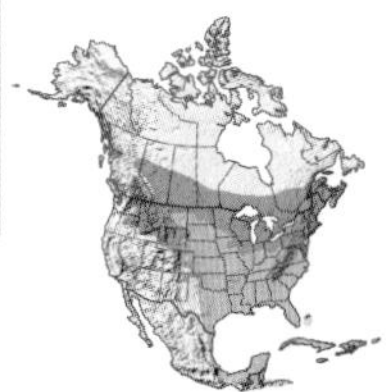

OCCURRENCE
In summer, mainly found in damp deciduous forests, but in some places habitat near rivers preferred. In winter, choice of habitat flexible; found in tropical broadleaf evergreen forest, on forest edges, in open woodlands, and in second-growth areas regenerating after fires or clearing.

SIMILAR SPECIES

GRAY-CHEEKED THRUSH
see p.457
gray face
bold black-brown breast spots
BICKNELL'S THRUSH
bold brown breast spots
grayish brown upperparts
SWAINSON'S THRUSH
see p.327
buffy-colored face
bold brown-black breast spots

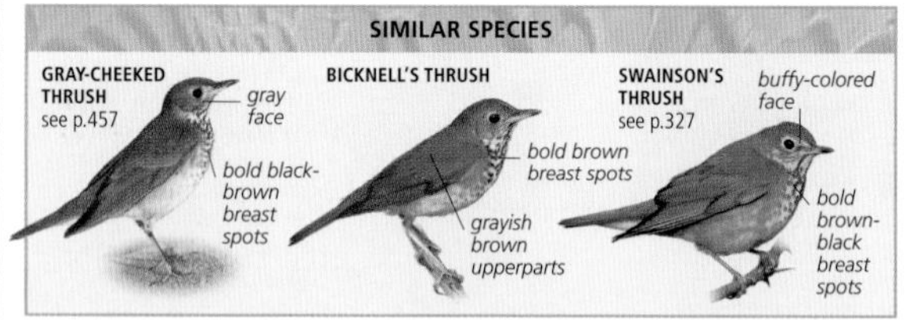

Length **7in (18cm)**	Wingspan **11–11½in (28–29cm)**	Weight **1 1/16–2oz (28–54g)**
Social **Pairs**	Lifespan **Up to 10 years**	Status **Declining**

DATE SEEN	WHERE	NOTES

Order **Passeriformes**	Family **Turdidae**	Species ***Catharus ustulatus***

Swainson's Thrush

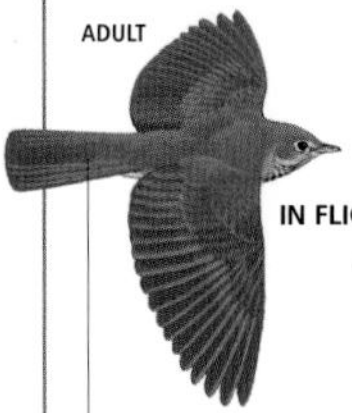

buffy eye-ring
ADULT
IN FLIGHT
olive-brown rump and tail
olive-brown upperparts
buff breast
distinct blackish spots
ADULT
C. c. swainsoni
(EASTERN)
russet back
more rufous in upperparts
smaller, less distinct, sparser spotting
ADULT
C. c. ustulatus
(WESTERN)

Swainson's Thrush can be distinguished from other spotted thrushes by its buffy face and the rising pitch of its flute-like, melodious song. This species is also distinctive as it feeds higher up in the understory than most of its close relatives. The western subspecies of Swainson's Thrush is russet-backed and migrates to Central America for the winter, while the other populations are olive-backed and winter in South America.

VOICE Single-note call *whit* or *whooit*; main song delivered by males, several phrases, each one spiraling upward; flute-like song is given during breeding and migration.

NESTING Open cup of twigs, moss, dead leaves, bark, and mud, on branches near trunks of small trees or in shrubs; 3–4 eggs; 1–2 broods; April–July.

FEEDING Forages in the air, using fly-catching methods to capture a wide range of insects during breeding season; berries during migration and in winter.

FLIGHT: rapid and straight, with intermittent flaps and glides.

DISTINCTIVE SONG
This bird's song distinguishes it from other thrushes.

TREE DWELLER
Shy and retiring, Swainson's Thrush feeds higher in trees more other *Catharus* thrushes.

SIMILAR SPECIES

VEERY see p.326
tawny brown back
lightly spotted breast

HERMIT THRUSH see p.328
grayish cheeks
streaks on sides of breast
rust-colored tail

OCCURRENCE
Breeds mainly in coniferous forests, especially spruce and fir, except in California, where it prefers deciduous riverine woodlands and damp meadows with shrubbery. During spring and fall migrations, dense understory preferred. Winter habitat is mainly old growth forest.

Length **6½–7½in (16–19cm)**	Wingspan **11½–12in (29–31cm)**	Weight **⅞–1$^{9}/_{16}$oz (25–45g)**
Social **Pairs/Flocks**	Lifespan **Up to 11 years**	Status **Declining**

DATE SEEN	WHERE	NOTES

Order **Passeriformes**	Family **Turdidae**	Species ***Catharus guttatus***

Hermit Thrush

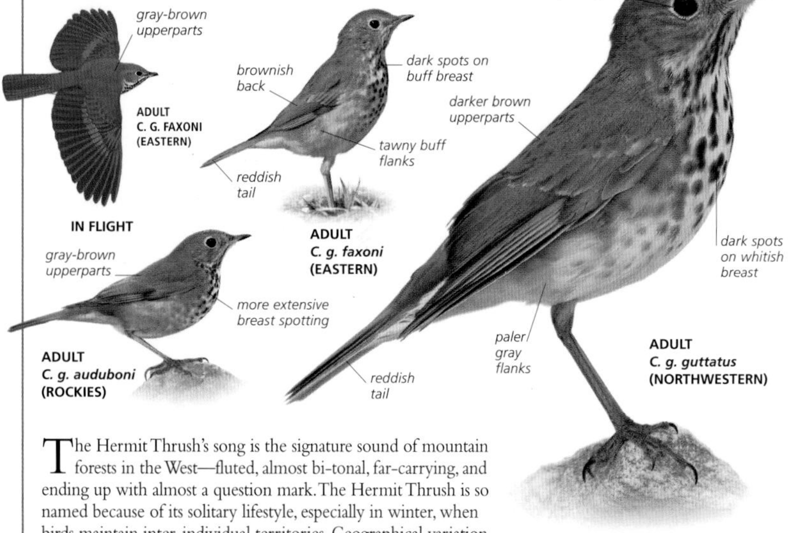

gray-brown upperparts

ADULT C. G. FAXONI (EASTERN)

IN FLIGHT

brownish back

dark spots on buff breast

tawny buff flanks

reddish tail

ADULT *C. g. faxoni* (EASTERN)

thin white eye-ring

darker brown upperparts

dark spots on whitish breast

paler gray flanks

reddish tail

ADULT *C. g. guttatus* (NORTHWESTERN)

gray-brown upperparts

more extensive breast spotting

ADULT *C. g. auduboni* (ROCKIES)

The Hermit Thrush's song is the signature sound of mountain forests in the West—fluted, almost bi-tonal, far-carrying, and ending up with almost a question mark. The Hermit Thrush is so named because of its solitary lifestyle, especially in winter, when birds maintain inter-individual territories. Geographical variation within the vast range of the species has led to the recognition of nine subspecies (three are illustrated here). Western birds generally winter south of the US, in Mexico, Guatemala, and El Salvador.

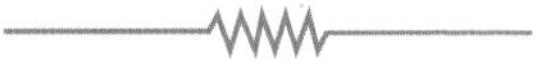

FLIGHT: rapid and straight, with intermittent flaps and glides.

VOICE Calls *tchek*, soft, dry; song flute-like, ethereal, falling, repetitive, and varied; several phrases delivered on a different pitch.

NESTING Cup of grasses, mosses, twigs, leaves, mud, hair, on ground or in low tree branches; 4 eggs; 1–2 broods; May–July.

FEEDING Mainly forages on ground for insects, larvae, earthworms, and snails; in winter, also eats fruit.

URBAN VISITOR
This thrush is frequently seen in wooded areas in urban and suburban parks.

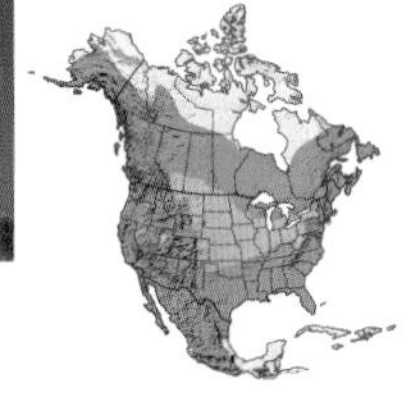

OCCURRENCE
Occurs in coniferous forests and mixed conifer–deciduous woodlands; prefers to nest along the edges of a forest interior, like a bog. During migration, found in many wooded habitats. Found in forest and other open woodlands during winter.

Length **6–7in (15–18cm)**	Wingspan **10–11in (25–28cm)**	Weight **$\frac{7}{8}$–$1\frac{1}{16}$oz (25–30g)**
Social **Solitary**	Lifespan **Up to 9 years**	Status **Secure**

DATE SEEN	WHERE	NOTES

Order **Passeriformes**	Family **Turdidae**	Species ***Turdus migratorius***

American Robin

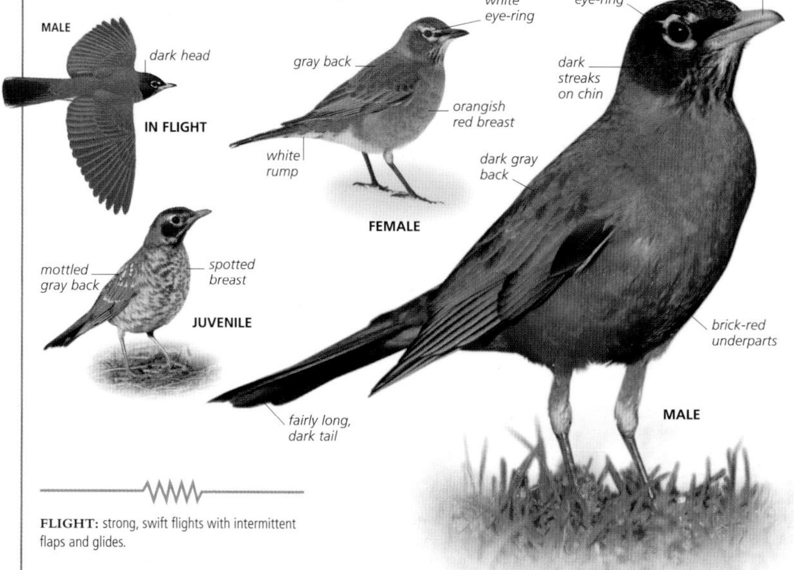
MALE
dark head
IN FLIGHT
gray back
more complete white eye-ring
orangish red breast
white rump
FEMALE
broken white eye-ring
yellow bill
dark streaks on chin
dark gray back
mottled gray back
spotted breast
JUVENILE
brick-red underparts
fairly long, dark tail
MALE

FLIGHT: strong, swift flights with intermittent flaps and glides.

The American Robin, the largest and most abundant of the North American thrushes, is probably also the most familiar bird across the entire continent, its presence on suburban lawns is a clear sign of spring. Unlike other species, it has adapted and prospered in human-altered habitats. It breeds in the entire US and Canada, winters across the US, and migrates out of most of Canada in fall. The decision to migrate is largely governed by changes in the availability of food. As the breeding season approaches, it is the males that sing first, either late in winter or early spring. The bird's brick-red breast—more vivid in males than in females—is its most distinguishing feature.

VOICE Calls a high pitch *tjip* and a multi-note, throaty *tjuj-tjuk*; primary song a melodious *cheer-up*, *cheer-up*, *cheer-wee*, one of the first birds to be heard during dawn chorus, and one of the last to cease singing in the evening.

NESTING Substantial cup of grass, weeds, twigs, strengthened with mud, in trees or shrub, in fork tree, or on branch on tree; 4 eggs; 2–3 broods; April–July.

FEEDING Forages in leaf litter, mainly for earthworms and small insects; mostly consumes fruit in the winter season.

SIMILAR SPECIES

VARIED THRUSH
see p.322
orange eyebrow
bluish gray upperparts
wide black "necklace"

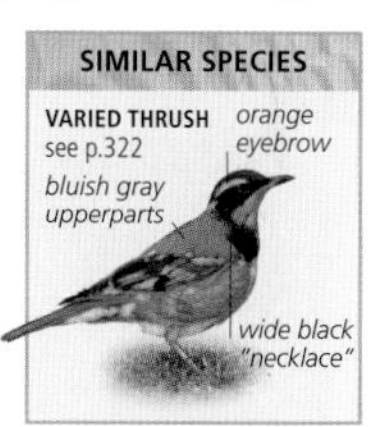

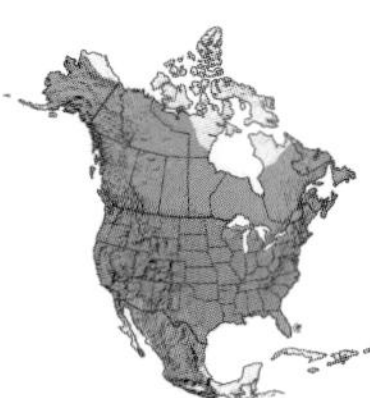

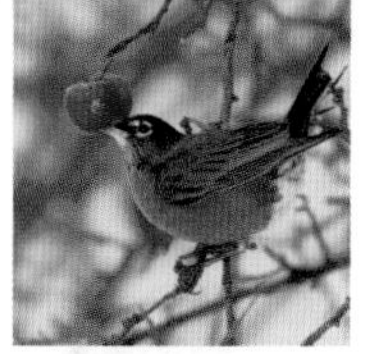

SEASONAL DIET
Robins are particularly dependent on the availability of fruit during the winter months.

OCCURRENCE
Breeding habitat a mix of forest, woodland, suburban gardens, lawns, municipal parks, and farms. A partial migrant; found in woodlands with berry-bearing trees. Nonmigrating populations' winter habitat is similar to breeding habitat. Reaches Guatemala in winter.

Length **8–11in (20–28cm)**	Wingspan **12–16in (30–41cm)**	Weight **2⅝oz (75g)**
Social **Flocks**	Lifespan **Up to 13 years**	Status **Secure**

DATE SEEN	WHERE	NOTES
1/23/19	SU campus	saw both males & females

Order **Passeriformes**	Family **Cinclidae**	Species ***Cinclus mexicanus***

American Dipper

The most aquatic North American songbird, the American Dipper is at home in the cold, rushing streams of the American West. It is known for its feeding technique of plunging into streams for insect larvae under stones or in the streambed. When not foraging, it watches from a rock or log, bobbing up and down, constantly flashing its nictitating membrane (the transparent third eyelid that protects the eye when the bird is underwater). Susceptible to changes in water chemistry and turbulence, which alter the abundance of its main food, caddisfly larvae, this bird has been proposed as an indicator for stream quality.

VOICE Call a harsh *bzzt*, given singly or in rapid series; song a loud, disorganized series of pleasing warbles, whistles, and trills.

NESTING Domed nest with side entrance, placed underneath bridge or behind waterfall; 4–5 eggs; 1–2 broods; March–August.

FEEDING Forages for insects and insect larvae, especially caddisflies; sometimes eats small fish and fish eggs.

FLIGHT: low over water, twisting and turning with the stream with rapid, buzzy wing beats.

BOBBING MOTION
The American Dipper often pauses on rocks in streams, where it bobs up and down.

SIMILAR SPECIES

RUSTY BLACKBIRD see p.377
yellow eye
longer tail

BREWER'S BLACKBIRD ♀ see p.378
sharper bill
more slender body
long tail

OCCURRENCE
Found from Alaska, the Yukon, and British Columbia, south to California, Arizona, New Mexico, Mexico, and Panama. On Pacific slope, breeds down to sea level; in interior West, breeds mainly in mountains and foothills; retreats to lower elevations in winter.

Length **7½in (19cm)**	Wingspan **11in (28cm)**	Weight **1¾–2¼oz (50–65g)**
Social **Solitary**	Lifespan **Up to 7 years**	Status **Secure**

DATE SEEN	WHERE	NOTES

Order **Passeriformes**	Family **Passeridae**	Species ***Passer domesticus***

House Sparrow

This is the familiar "sparrow" of towns, cities, suburbs, and farms. The House Sparrow is not actually a sparrow as understood in North America, but rather a member of a Eurasian family called the weaver-finches. It was first introduced in Brooklyn, New York, in 1850. From this modest beginning, and with the help of several other introductions up until the late 1860s, this hardy and aggressive bird eventually spread right through the North American continent. In a little more than 150 years, the House Sparrow has evolved and shows the same sort of geographic variation as some widespread native birds. It is pale in the arid Southwest, and darker in wetter regions.

VOICE Variety of calls, including a *cheery chirp*, a dull *jurv* and a rough *jigga*; song consists of *chirp* notes repeated endlessly.

NESTING Untidy mass of dried vegetable material in either natural or artificial cavities; 3–5 eggs; 2–3 broods; April–August.

FEEDING Mostly seeds; sometimes gleans insects and fruits.

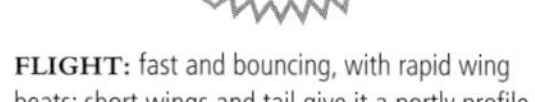

FLIGHT: fast and bouncing, with rapid wing beats; short wings and tail give it a portly profile.

APTLY NAMED

This sparrow is seen near human structures—roofs, outbuildings, loading docks, curbs, and streetlights.

SIMILAR SPECIES

OCCURRENCE

Flourishes in the downtown sections of cities and anywhere near human habitations, including agricultural outbuildings in remote areas of the continent. Found in Mexico, Central and South America, and the West Indies. Widespread also in Eurasia, SE Asia, North Africa, and Arabia.

Length **6in (15.5cm)**	Wingspan **9½in (24cm)**	Weight **⅝–1¹⁄₁₆oz (18–30g)**
Social **Flocks**	Lifespan **Up to 7 years**	Status **Declining**

DATE SEEN	WHERE	NOTES

Order **Passeriformes**	Family **Motacillidae**	Species ***Anthus rubescens***

American Pipit

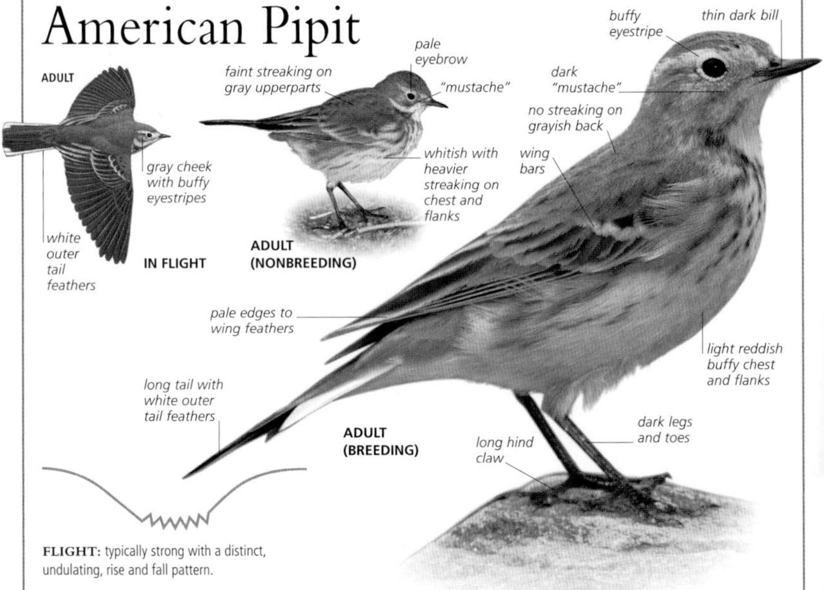
ADULT
gray cheek with buffy eyestripes
white outer tail feathers
IN FLIGHT
faint streaking on gray upperparts
pale eyebrow
"mustache"
whitish with heavier streaking on chest and flanks
ADULT (NONBREEDING)
buffy eyestripe
thin dark bill
dark "mustache"
no streaking on grayish back
wing bars
pale edges to wing feathers
light reddish buffy chest and flanks
long tail with white outer tail feathers
ADULT (BREEDING)
long hind claw
dark legs and toes

FLIGHT: typically strong with a distinct, undulating, rise and fall pattern.

The American Pipit is divided into four subspecies, three of which breed in North America, and the fourth in Siberia. In nonbreeding plumage, the American Pipit is a drab-looking, brownish gray bird that forages for insects along waterways and lakeshores, or in cultivated fields with short stems. In the breeding season, molting transforms it into a beauty—with gray upperparts and reddish underparts. American Pipits are known for pumping their tails up and down. When breeding, males display by rising into the air, then flying down with wings open and singing. Its migration takes the American Pipit as far south as Guatemala.

VOICE Alarm call a *tzeeep*; song repeated *tzwee-tzooo* from the air.

NESTING Cup in shallow depression on ground, outer frame of grass, lined with fine grass and hair; 4–6 eggs; 1 brood; June–July.

FEEDING Picks insects; also eats seeds during migration.

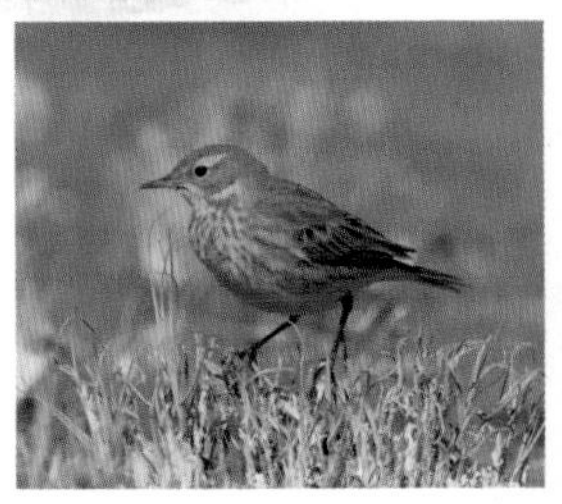

WINTER DRAB
Foraging in short vegetation, this bird is almost the same color as its surroundings.

SIMILAR SPECIES
HORNED LARK
see p.298
less white on tail edge
less streaking on throat and chest
SPRAGUE'S PIPIT
see p.459
heavy streaking on back
pale cheeks and throat
pale legs

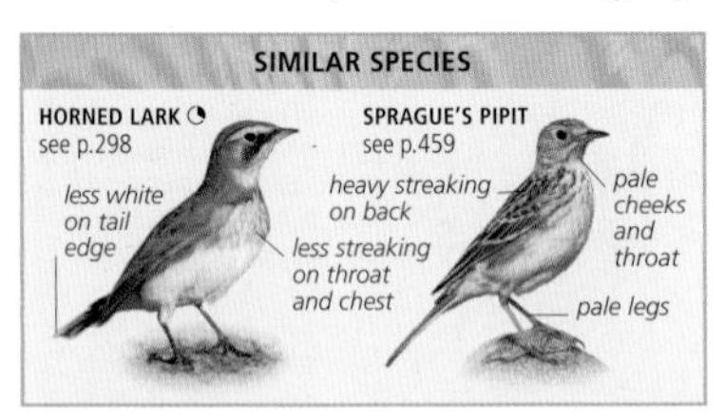

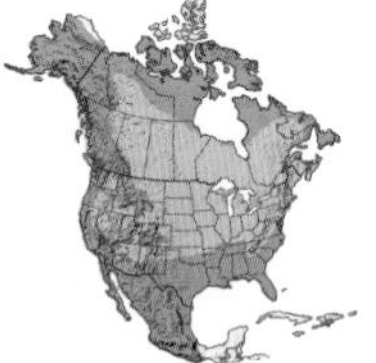

OCCURRENCE
Breeds in Arctic tundra in the north, and alpine tundra in the Rockies; also breeds on treeless mountaintops in Maine and New Hampshire. Winters in open coastal areas and harvested agricultural fields across the US. Some North American migrants fly to Asia for the winter.

Length **6–8in (15–20cm)**	Wingspan **10–11in (25–28cm)**	Weight **11/16oz (20g)**
Social **Flocks**	Lifespan **Up to 6 years**	Status **Secure**

DATE SEEN	WHERE	NOTES

FINCHES

THE NAME "FINCHES" applies to the Fringillidae, a family of seed-eating songbirds that includes 16 species in North America. They vary in size and shape from the small and fragile-looking redpolls to the robust and chunky Evening Grosbeak. Finch colors range from whitish with some pink (redpolls) to gold (American Goldfinch), bright red (crossbills), and yellow, white, and black (Evening Grosbeak). However, irrespective of body shape, size, and color, all have conical bills with razor-sharp edges. Finches do not crush seeds. Instead, they cut open the hard hull, then seize the seed inside with their tongue and swallow it. The bills of conifer-loving crossbills are crossed at the tip, a unique arrangement that permits them to open tough-hulled pine cones. Roughly 50 percent of crossbills are "left-billed" and 50 percent "right-billed"—lefties are right-footed, and vice versa. Most finches are social. Although they breed in pairs, after nesting finches form flocks, some of which are huge. Most finch populations fluctuate in size, synchronized with seed production and abundance. All finches are vocal, calling constantly while flying, and singing in the spring. Calls are usually sharp, somewhat metallic sounds, although the American Goldfinch's tinkling calls are sweeter. Songs can be quite musical, clear-sounding melodies, like that of the Cassin's Finch. Finches make open cup-shaped nests of grasses and lichens, in trees or shrubs, and are remarkably adept at hiding them.

CROSSBILL
Perched on a pine tree branch, a female Red Crossbill grinds a seed in her bill to break open the hull and reach the fat-rich kernel inside.

NOT REALLY PURPLE
The inaccurately named Purple Finch actually has a lovely wine-red color.

GARDEN GLOW
Even pink flower buds cannot compete with the yellow of a male American Goldfinch.

Order **Passeriformes**	Family **Fringillidae**	Species ***Carduelis pinus***

Pine Siskin

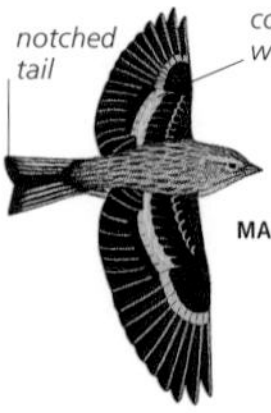

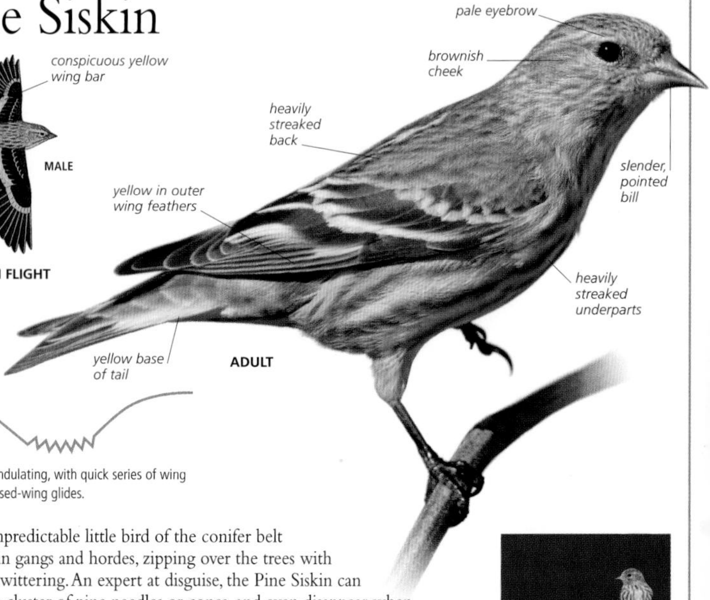

notched tail
conspicuous yellow wing bar
MALE
IN FLIGHT

pale eyebrow
brownish cheek
heavily streaked back
slender, pointed bill
yellow in outer wing feathers
heavily streaked underparts
yellow base of tail
ADULT

FLIGHT: undulating, with quick series of wing beats and closed-wing glides.

This unpredictable little bird of the conifer belt runs in gangs and hordes, zipping over the trees with incessant twittering. An expert at disguise, the Pine Siskin can resemble a cluster of pine needles or cones, and even disappear when a Sharp-shinned Hawk appears. Often abundant wherever there are pines, spruces, and other conifers, Pine Siskins may still disappoint birdwatchers by making a mass exodus from a region if the food supply is not to their liking. A vicious fighter at feeding tables, nomadic by nature, with high energy and fearlessness, the Pine Siskin is a fascinating species.

VOICE Rising *toooeeo*, mostly when perched; also raspy *chit-chit-chit* in flight.

NESTING Shallow cup of grass and lichens near the end of a conifer branch; 3–4 eggs; 1–2 broods; February–August.

FEEDING Eats conifer seeds; gleans insects and spiders; also seen feeding on roadsides, lawns, and weed fields.

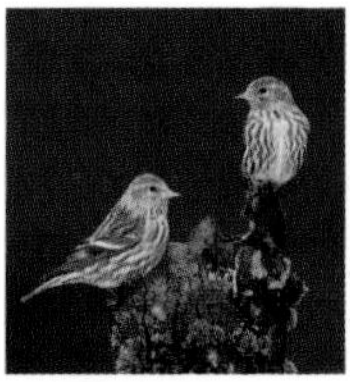

FOREST DWELLER
The streaked Pine Siskin inhabits northern and western coniferous forests.

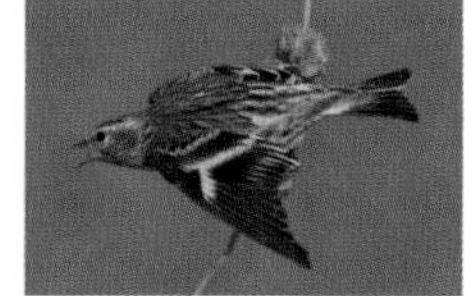

QUARRELSOME
A bird warns off a neighbor at a food source, displaying its yellow wing stripe.

SIMILAR SPECIES

COMMON REDPOLL
see p.337

tiny, pale bill
heavier streaking

YELLOW-RUMPED WARBLER ♀
see p.355

yellow rump
yellow patches

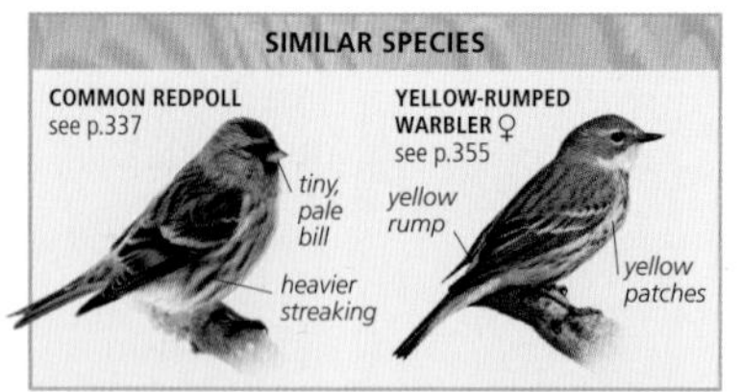

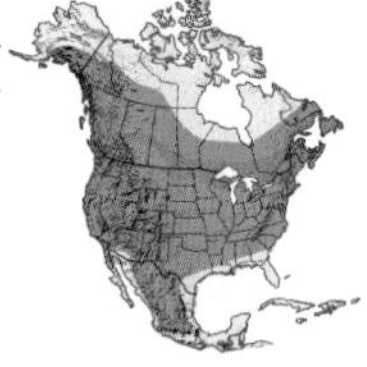

OCCURRENCE
Widespread across North America; occurs in coniferous and mixed coniferous forests, but also seen in parkland and suburbs. In some winters may appear south of regular breeding range to Missouri and Tennessee, also Mexico. Prefers open areas to continuous forest.

Length **4¼–5½in (11–14cm)**	Wingspan **7–9in (18–23cm)**	Weight **7/16–5/8oz (12–18g)**
Social **Flocks**	Lifespan **Up to 10 years**	Status **Secure**

DATE SEEN	WHERE	NOTES

Order **Passeriformes**	Family **Fringillidae**	Species ***Carduelis tristis***

American Goldfinch

Sometimes described as a giant yellow-and-black bumblebee, a male American Goldfinch is a spectacular summer sight. Goldfinches reveal their presence before they are seen by their tinkling, bell-like calls. If there are weeds in seed around, goldfinches will find them and feed energetically on the manna. This all-American species is the State Bird of Washington State.

VOICE Loud, rising, quizzical *pter-yee?* by males; 3–5-note *tit-tse-tew-tew* by both sexes, usually in flight; song complex, warbling, tinkling, and melodious.

NESTING Neat open cup of grass, shaded by leaves, in a tree or tall shrub; 4–5 eggs; 1–2 broods; June–September.

FEEDING Feed mainly on seeds from annuals; also birch and alder; some insects; love sunflower and thistle seed, whether on flower heads or at feeders.

FLIGHT: deeply undulating; wing beats alternating with closed-wing dips.

SIMILAR SPECIES

LESSER GOLDFINCH see p.336
greenish back; conspicuous wing bars

LAWRENCE'S GOLDFINCH see p.459
yellow wing bars; black face; yellow breast

WILSON'S WARBLER see p.369
black cap; yellow face

OCCURRENCE
In low shrubs, deciduous woodlands, farmlands, orchards, suburbs, and gardens across much of North America, from southern Canada to California and Georgia; in winter south to northern Mexico and Florida; winter habitats similar to those used at other times.

Length **4¼–5in (11–13cm)**	Wingspan **7–9in (18–23cm)**	Weight **⅜–¹¹⁄₁₆oz (11–20g)**
Social **Small flocks**	Lifespan **Up to 11 years**	Status **Secure**

DATE SEEN	WHERE	NOTES

Order **Passeriformes**	Family **Fringillidae**	Species ***Carduelis psaltria***

Lesser Goldfinch

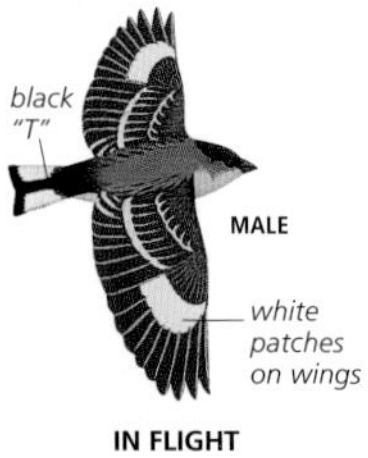
black "T"
MALE
white patches on wings
IN FLIGHT

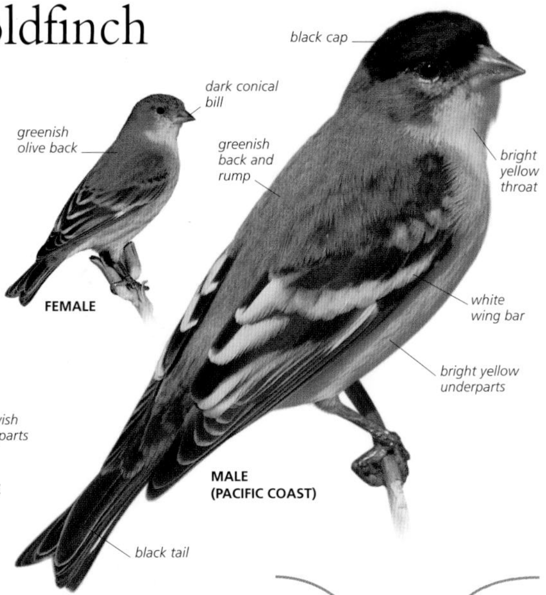
dark conical bill
greenish olive back
FEMALE
black cap
greenish back and rump
bright yellow throat
white wing bar
bright yellow underparts
MALE (PACIFIC COAST)
black tail

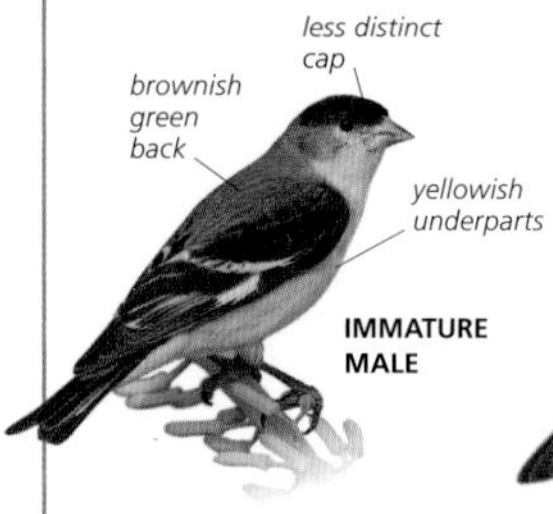
less distinct cap
brownish green back
yellowish underparts
IMMATURE MALE

The Lesser Goldfinch is a highly vocal bird, commonly found in gardens, suburbs, and farmlands, in addition to its natural habitats of open fields and scrub. Single birds and small flocks are often seen zooming around and flying overhead, calling noisily or singing in flight. The male has a brighter yellow breast and belly than the female. It also has a black cap, unlike the female, and its nape and back color varies from black in Texas and Mexico, to green along the Pacific coast.

VOICE Call descending *peeyee* and 2-note *tee-eee*, with second note higher; also rapid *dididit*; song warbles and trills.

NESTING Well-concealed cup, 10–30ft (3–9m) up in densely foliaged trees; 4 eggs; 1 brood; April–September.

FEEDING Eats a range of weed seeds; also eats insects, especially aphids, when available.

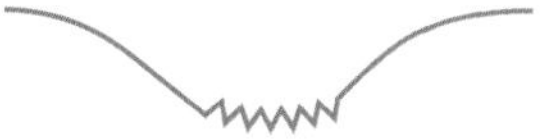

FLIGHT: undulating with dips; similar to other goldfinches.

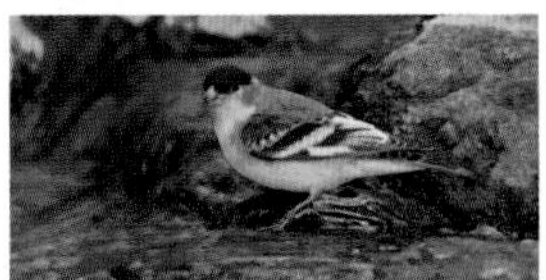

GREENISH BACK
A western version of the American Goldfinch, the male Lesser Goldfinch is also greenish above.

SIMILAR SPECIES

AMERICAN GOLDFINCH
see p.335

black forehead
all yellow
white rump

LAWRENCE'S GOLDFINCH
see p.459

gray back
yellow breast
yellow wing bars

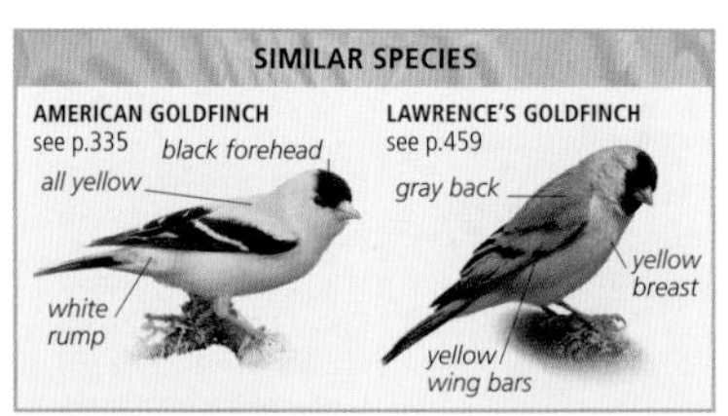

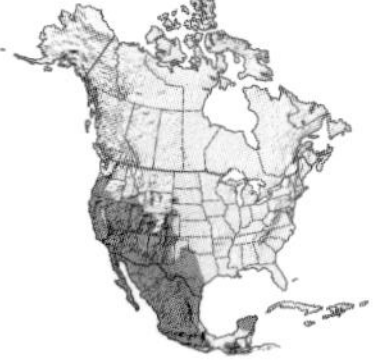

OCCURRENCE
This western species is not picky in its choice of habitat, which includes deciduous and coniferous woodlands, thickets, desert oases, parks and gardens; occurs from California to Texas in the breeding season and south to Mexico in winter.

Length **3½–4¼in (9–11cm)**	Wingspan **6–6¾in (15–17cm)**	Weight **⅜oz (10g)**
Social **Flocks**	Lifespan **Up to 6 years**	Status **Secure**

DATE SEEN	WHERE	NOTES

Order **Passeriformes**	Family **Fringillidae**	Species ***Carduelis flammea***

Common Redpoll

Every other year, spruce, birch, and other trees in the northern forest zone fail to produce a good crop of seeds, forcing the Common Redpoll to look for food farther south than usual—as far south as the northern US states. The Common Redpoll is oddly tame around people and is easily attracted to winter feeders. The degree of whiteness in its plumage varies greatly among individuals, related to sex and age. The taxonomy of the Common Redpoll includes four subspecies around the world, and there are suggestions that some may be distinct species.

VOICE Flight call dry *zit-zit-zit-zit* and rattling *chirr*; also high *too-ee* call while perched; song series of rapid trills.

NESTING Cup of small twigs in spruces, larches, willows, alders; 4–6 eggs; 1–2 broods; May–June.

FEEDING Feeds on small seeds from conifers, sedge, birch, willow, alder; also insects and spiders.

FLIGHT: deeply undulating, with dips between bouts of wing beats.

FRIENDLY FLOCK
Common Redpolls are only weakly territorial, sometimes even nesting close together.

OCCURRENCE
Mainly in extreme northern North America from Alaska to Québec and Labrador, in low forest, sub-Arctic, and shrubby tundra habitats. More southern winter appearances typically occur every other year, rarely south of northern US states, from the Dakotas east to New York and New England.

Length **4¾–5½in (12–14cm)**	Wingspan **6½–6¾in (16–17cm)**	Weight **⅜–¹¹⁄₁₆oz (11–19g)**
Social **Flocks**	Lifespan **Up to 10 years**	Status **Secure**

DATE SEEN	WHERE	NOTES

Order **Passeriformes**	Family **Fringillidae**	Species ***Leucosticte tephrocotis***

Gray-crowned Rosy-Finch

brown upperparts

ADULT (WESTERN)

IN FLIGHT

more extensive gray on head

dark chin

ADULT (WESTERN)

gray behind eye

dark crown

pinkish shoulder patch

chocolate-brown overall

ADULT (BERING SEA)

rusty brown underparts

ADULT (INTERIOR)

notched tail

whitish undertail feathers

The often lifeless and windswept rocks and crags of high western mountains are the domain of these brown-and-pink birds, which are seldom in contact with humanity. The Gray-crowned Rosy-Finch is one of several mountain finch species that extend across the Bering Strait into eastern Asia. Geographically variable in size and coloration, with exceptionally large forms occurring on the Pribilof and Aleutian Islands, the Gray-crowned Rosy-Finch is the most abundant of the North American rosy-finches.

VOICE High-pitched *peew*, given singly or in short series; song repetitive series of *twee* notes.

NESTING Bulky assemblage of grasses, lichens, and twigs in cracks or under rock overhangs; 3–5 eggs; 1–2 broods; May–June.

FEEDING Feeds on the ground on a variety of seeds, with insects and their larvae comprising a larger part of the diet in summer.

FLIGHT: undulating but often irregular with glides.

ROCK LOVER
This dark rusty-brown species watches its surroundings from a rocky perch near an icy field.

SIMILAR SPECIES

BLACK ROSY-FINCH see p.460

darker cheeks

BROWN-CAPPED ROSY-FINCH see p.460

rosy underparts

OCCURRENCE
Most widely distributed of the three North American rosy-finch species, occurring from Alaska south to the Rockies; breeds in alpine habitats like rocky screes above snow line and Arctic tundra; in winter also occurs at lower elevations; sometimes at feeders.

Length **5½–8½in (14–21cm)**	Wingspan **13in (33cm)**	Weight **⅞–2⅛oz (25–60g)**
Social **Flocks**	Lifespan **Unknown**	Status **Localized**

DATE SEEN	WHERE	NOTES

Order **Passeriformes**	Family **Fringillidae**	Species ***Carpodacus purpureus***

Purple Finch

FLIGHT: rapid wing beats, alternating with downward glides.

One of three difficult-to-distinguish members of the genus *Carpodacus* in North America, the Purple Finch is best known as a visitor to winter feeding stations. The western subspecies (*californicus*) is slightly darker and duller than the eastern form (*purpureus*). Only moderately common, the raspberry-red males pose less of an identification challenge than the brown-streaked females. Even on their breeding grounds in open and mixed coniferous forest, Purple Finches are more often heard than seen.

VOICE Flight call single, rough *pikh*; songs rich series of notes, up and down in pitch.

NESTING Cup of sticks and grasses on a conifer branch; 4 eggs; 2 broods; May–July.

FEEDING Eats buds, seeds, flowers of deciduous trees; insects and caterpillars in summer; also seeds and berries.

RASPBERRY TINTED
On a lichen-covered branch this male's delicate coloring is quite striking.

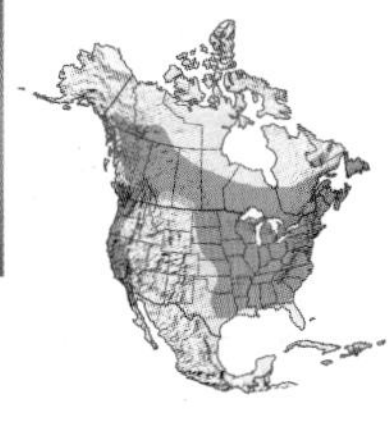

OCCURRENCE
Resident from Baja California north along the Pacific coast and the Cascade Mountains to Yukon Territory. Breeds in northern mixed conifer and hardwood forests in the East, where it is partially migratory, moves as far south as the Gulf Coast.

SIMILAR SPECIES

HOUSE FINCH ♀ western; see p.341

CASSIN'S FINCH ♀ see p.340

RED-WINGED BLACKBIRD ♀ see p.376

Length **4¾–6in (12–15cm)**	Wingspan **8½–10in (22–26cm)**	Weight **$^{11}/_{16}$–$1^{1}/_{16}$oz (20–30g)**
Social **Flocks**	Lifespan **Unknown**	Status **Declining**

DATE SEEN	WHERE	NOTES

Order **Passeriformes**	Family **Fringillidae**	Species ***Carpodacus cassinii***

Cassin's Finch

Named after the 19th-century ornithologist John Cassin, this finch has a rich, melodious song that incorporates phrases from the songs of several different Rocky Mountain species. From below, the male Cassin's Finch resembles a sparrow, but when it alights on a tree stump, its full, purple-red plumage is immediately evident. This species closely resembles the other two species in the genus *Carpodacus*, the Purple and House finches, whose ranges it overlaps, so it may take time and practice to be certain of this species' identity in the field. The female Cassin's Finch is not distinctive—it resembles a generic fledgling or a sparrow.

VOICE Call *tee-uhh* or *piddlit*; song rich and warbling; may include high-frequency whistles and imitations of other species.

NESTING Open cup on lateral branch of conifer, also in aspen or sagebrush; 4–5 eggs; 1 brood; May–July.

FEEDING Eats berries, pine seeds, aspen buds, insects, larvae; feeds mainly on ground but frequents feeding stations in winter.

FLIGHT: rapid wing beats, then a glide, in a regular sequence.

ARBOREAL FINCH
Cassin's Finch likes to perch on an elevated twig or branch, often in coniferous forests.

OCCURRENCE
Found in coniferous forests in mountains of western US; may occur in sagebrush–juniper plains or open areas with Ponderosa or Lodgepole pine. Migratory both toward lower elevations and southward. Winters throughout its breeding range.

Length **5½–6½in (14–16cm)**	Wingspan **10–10½in (25–27cm)**	Weight **⅞–1¼oz (25–35g)**
Social **Flocks**	Lifespan **Up to 10 years**	Status **Secure**

DATE SEEN	WHERE	NOTES

Order **Passeriformes**	Family **Fringillidae**	Species ***Carpodacus mexicanus***

House Finch

FLIGHT: bouncy, undulating flight typical of finches; usually flies above treetop level.

Historically, the House Finch was a western bird, and was first reported in the eastern side of the US on Long Island, New York in 1941. These birds are said to have originated from the illegal bird trade. The population of the eastern birds started expanding in the 1960s, so much so that by the late 1990s, their population had expanded westward to link up with the original western population. The male House Finch is distinguished from the Purple and Cassin's finches by its brown streaked underparts, while the females have plainer faces and generally blurrier streaking.

VOICE Call note *queet*; varied jumble of notes, often starting with husky notes to whistled and burry notes, and ending with a long *wheeerr.*

NESTING Females build nests from grass stems, thin twigs, and thin weeds in trees and on man-made structures; 1–6 eggs; 2–3 broods; March–August.

FEEDING Eats, almost exclusively, vegetable matter, such as buds, fruits, and seeds; readily comes to feeders.

RED IN THE FACE
The breeding male House-Finch can be identified by its stunning brick-red plumage.

OCCURRENCE
Found in urban, suburban, and settled areas; in the West also in wilder areas, such as savannas, desert grasslands, and chaparral, particularly near people; in the East almost exclusively in settled areas, including the centers of large cities. Resident, some birds move after breeding.

Length **5–6in (12.5–15cm)**	Wingspan **8–10in (20–25cm)**	Weight **9/16–1oz (16–27g)**
Social **Flocks**	Lifespan **Up to 12 years**	Status **Secure**

DATE SEEN	WHERE	NOTES
4/23/19	Outside of Library	Male

Order **Passeriformes**	Family **Fringillidae**	Species ***Pinicola enucleator***

Pine Grosbeak

FLIGHT: undulating, buoyant, calm wing beats interrupted by glides.

The largest member of the family Fringillidae in North America, and easily distinguished by the male's unmistakable thick, stubby bill, the Pine Grosbeak is a resident of conifer forests at high elevations in the Rockies in the West. The bird is also found across northern Eurasia, where nine subspecies have been identified, four of which are found in North America. Due to extensive color variation of individual plumages, the age and sex of given individuals are not always easily determined.

VOICE Contact calls of eastern birds *tee-tew*, or *tee-tee-tew*; western forms give more complex *tweedle*; warbling song.

NESTING Well-hidden, open cup nest usually in spruce or larch trees; 2–5 eggs, 1 brood; June–July.

FEEDING Eats spruce buds, maple seeds, and mountain ash berries throughout the year; consumes insects in summer.

FRUIT LOVER
This species can often be seen hanging from branches, gorging on ripe fruit.

SIMILAR SPECIES

RED CROSSBILL see p.343 — *brownish back*; *mandibles crossed*

WHITE-WINGED CROSSBILL see p.344 — *mandibles crossed*; *white bars on wing*

OCCURRENCE
Found in the boreal zone from Alaska to Québec and Newfoundland, in open, northern coniferous forests in summer, usually near fresh water. Winters throughout its breeding range, but may move southward to southern Canada and the northeastern US.

Length **8–10in (20–25cm)**	Wingspan **13in (33cm)**	Weight **2–2½oz (55–70g)**
Social **Flocks**	Lifespan **Up to 10 years**	Status **Secure**

DATE SEEN	WHERE	NOTES

Order **Passeriformes**	Family **Fringillidae**	Species ***Loxia curvirostra***

Red Crossbill

The Red Crossbill has evolved one of the most efficient mechanisms to unlock the seeds of conifers. The highly adapted bill is used to bite between the scales of a conifer cone and pry them apart, then the seed is lifted out with its tongue. Eight different "forms" have been recognized, all of the same color but different in body size, bill shape and size. Each "form" has a different flight call and rarely interbreeds with other "forms" even where they overlap. These "forms" may actually be different species.

VOICE Common call *jit* repeated 2–5 times; song complex, continuous warbling of notes, whistles, and buzzes.

NESTING Cup nest on lateral conifer branch; 3–5 eggs; 2 broods; can breed year-round.

FEEDING Feeds on pine seeds; also insects and larvae, particularly aphids; also other seeds.

FLIGHT: strong and deeply undulating.

PROCESSING SEEDS
The Red Crossbill manipulates seeds with its tongue before swallowing them.

SIMILAR SPECIES

WHITE-WINGED CROSSBILL see p.344
conspicuous wing bars
pinker plumage

SCARLET TANAGER
vivid red plumage
no black stripe

OCCURRENCE
Range covers coniferous or mixed-coniferous and deciduous forests from Newfoundland to British Columbia and southern Alaska; also mountain forests in the Rockies, south to Mexico; irregular movements, depending on the availability of pine cones.

Length **5–6¾in (13–17cm)**	Wingspan **10–10½in (25–27cm)**	Weight **⅞–1¼oz (25–35g)**
Social **Flocks**	Lifespan **Up to 10 years**	Status **Secure**

DATE SEEN	WHERE	NOTES

Order **Passeriformes**	Family **Fringillidae**	Species ***Loxia leucoptera***

White-winged Crossbill

FLIGHT: strong and undulating with quick wing beats alternating with glides.

Cone debris, needles, and whole cones clatter down from a spruce in the otherwise silent winter forest. Some twittering is heard, and then a chorus of metallic, yanking notes reveals that a flock of a dozen White-winged Crossbills has been causing all the commotion. In an instant, the entire flock erupts into the air, calling loudly in flight, only to disappear completely in the distance. Few other creatures of the northern forests go about their business with such determined energy, and no others accent a winter woodland with hot pink and magenta—the colors of the White-winged Crossbill's head and breast.

VOICE Calls are sharp, chattering *plik*, or deeper *tyoop*, repeated in series of 3–7 notes; song melodious trilling.

NESTING Open cup nest, usually high on end of a spruce branch; 3–5 eggs; 2 broods; July, January–February.

FEEDING Eats seeds from small-coned conifers; spruces, firs, larches; feeds on insects when available.

EATING SNOW
The White-winged Crossbill frequently eats snow to provide essential moisture.

SIMILAR SPECIES

PINE GROSBEAK
see p.342
blunt bill
longer tail

RED CROSSBILL
see p.343
no wing bars
redder plumage

OCCURRENCE
Nomadic; most common in the spruce zone of Alaska and Canada but has bred as far south as Colorado in the West; in the East, from Québec and Newfoundland southward to New York and New England.

Length **5½–6in (14–15cm)**	Wingspan **10–10½in (26–27cm)**	Weight **11/16–1 1/16oz (20–30g)**
Social **Flocks**	Lifespan **Up to 10 years**	Status **Secure**

DATE SEEN	WHERE	NOTES

Order **Passeriformes**	Family **Fringillidae**	Species ***Coccothraustes vespertinus***

Evening Grosbeak

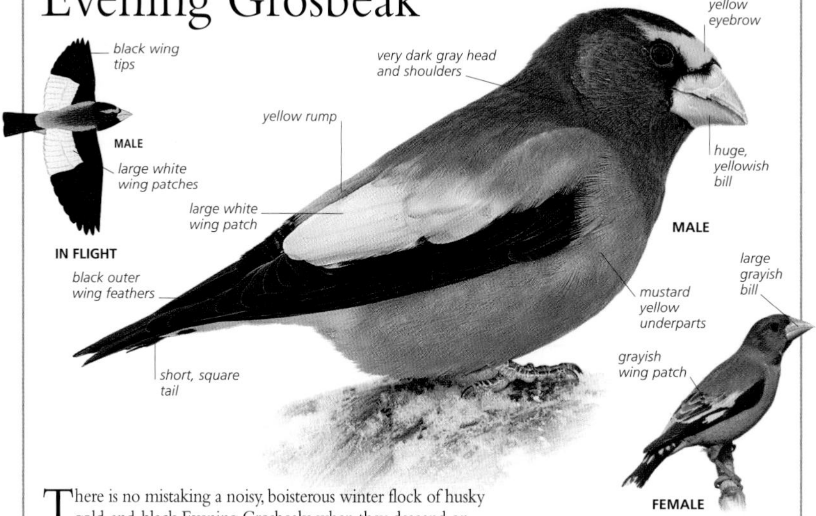
black wing tips
MALE
large white wing patches
IN FLIGHT
conspicuous yellow eyebrow
very dark gray head and shoulders
yellow rump
huge, yellowish bill
large white wing patch
MALE
black outer wing feathers
mustard yellow underparts
short, square tail
large grayish bill
grayish wing patch
FEMALE

There is no mistaking a noisy, boisterous winter flock of husky gold-and-black Evening Grosbeaks when they descend on a birdfeeder. The bird's outsize yellow bill seems to be made as much for threatening would-be rivals as it is designed for efficiently cracking sunflower seeds. In the breeding season, by contrast, the Evening Grosbeak is secretive and seldom detected, neither singing loudly nor displaying ostentatiously and nesting high in a tree. Once a bird of western North America, it has extended its range eastward in the past 200 years, and now breeds as far as Newfoundland. This may be a result of the planting of ornamental box elder, which carries its abundant seeds winter-long, ensuring a ready food supply for the bird.

VOICE Call descending *feeew*; also buzzy notes and beeping chatter.

NESTING Loose, grass-lined twig cup, usually on conifer branch; 3–4 eggs; 1–2 broods; May–July.

FEEDING Eats seeds of pines and other conifers; also maple and box elder seeds; also insects and their larvae, particularly spruce budworms, which are actually Tortricid moths.

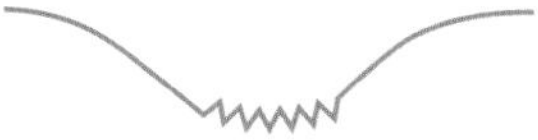

FLIGHT: undulating, with dips between bouts of wing beats, may hover briefly.

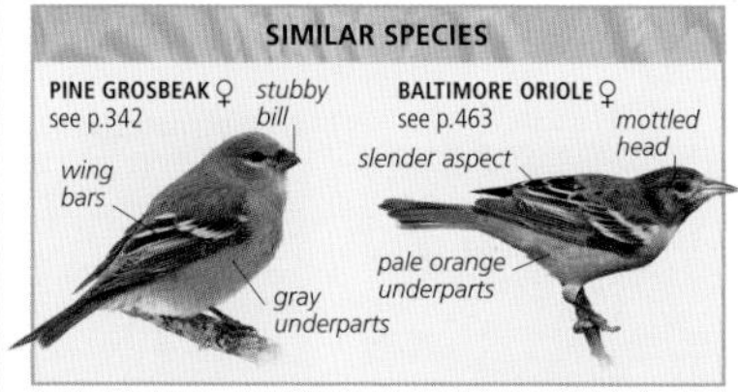

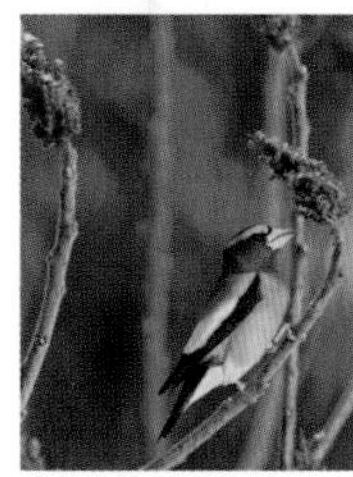

CAPABLE BILL
This bird's extremely robust bill can deal with all kinds of winter fruits and seeds.

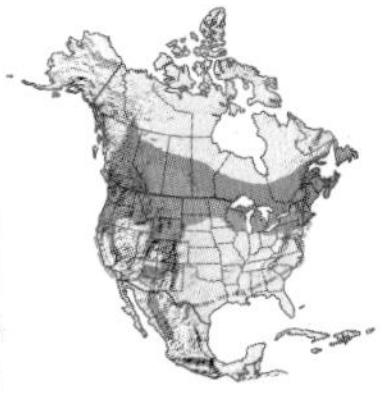

OCCURRENCE
Breeds in mixed conifer and spruce forests from the Rocky Mountain region to eastern Canada, and in western mountain ranges south to Mexico. Winters in coniferous or deciduous woodlands, often in suburban locations; may move south from northern range, depending on food supply.

SIMILAR SPECIES

PINE GROSBEAK ♀ see p.342

BALTIMORE ORIOLE ♀ see p.463

stubby bill
wing bars
gray underparts
slender aspect
mottled head
pale orange underparts

Length **6½–7in (16–18cm)**	Wingspan **12–14in (30–36cm)**	Weight **2–2½oz (55–70g)**
Social **Flocks**	Lifespan **Up to 15 years**	Status **Secure**

DATE SEEN	WHERE	NOTES

WOOD-WARBLERS

THE FAMILY PARULIDAE, comprising more than 100 species, is restricted to the Americas. These are among the most colorful of North American birds. The family is also remarkable for its diversity in plumage color, song, feeding behavior, breeding biology (ground nesting or tree nesting), sexual dimorphism, and habitat choice. However, wood-warblers generally share a similar shape: they are small, slender birds with thin, pointed bills, which they mostly use for catching insect prey. The thicker-billed Yellow-breasted Chat is an exception to the usual warbler body shape. In addition, the Chat's song is quite unlike other warblers'. Molecular data suggest what some birders have suspected—that it is not a warbler—but the evidence is still inconclusive. Most species of North American wood-warblers are found in the East, especially in forests. Some western warbler species occur in dense, moist habitats, including the rainforests of British Colombia, Washington, and Oregon. By contrast, other western species live in arid habitats, such as the mesquite woodlands of the Southwest. Migration routes vary between eastern and western warbler species. Most western warblers have short migration routes southward to winter ranges in Mexico. Most eastern species are long-distance migrants that fly in southerly directions toward either Florida and the Caribbean or toward Mexico and Central America. Some species even travel as far as South America.

FEEDING STRATEGIES
Some warblers, such as this Black-and-white, probe the cracks in tree trunks for food.

PLASTIC PLUMAGE
Many male *Dendroica* warblers (like this Blackburnian) are only brightly colored when breeding. This species is rare in the West.

STATIC PLUMAGE
In some warbler species, such as this Golden-winged, males keep their stunning plumage year-round. Golden-winged Warblers are rare in the West.

Order **Passeriformes**	Family **Parulidae**	Species ***Vermivora peregrina***

Tennessee Warbler

gray head
white eyestripe
MALE (BREEDING)
IN FLIGHT
olive-green upperparts
olive-gray head
FEMALE
whitish belly
blue-gray crown
spiky bill
olive back and wings
olive-gray back
white undertail feathers
grayish white underparts
yellowish throat and breast
MALE (BREEDING)
MALE (FALL)

The Tennessee Warbler was named on the basis of a specimen found in that state on migration, as this species breeds almost entirely in Canada and winters in Central America. These warblers inhabit fairly remote areas and their nests are difficult to find. It is one of a number of species that takes advantage of outbreaks of spruce budworms (actually Tortricid moths); their populations tend to increase in years when budworms themselves increase.

VOICE Call a sharp *tzit*; flight call a thin slightly rolling *seet*; song usually three-part staccato series, *chip-chip-chip*, each series increasing in pitch and usually in tempo.

NESTING Nest woven of fine plant matter, in ground depression, concealed from above by shrubbery; 4–7 eggs; 1 brood; June.

FEEDING Searches outer branches of trees for caterpillars, bees, wasps, beetles, and spiders; also eats fruits in winter and drinks nectar by piercing base of flowers.

FLIGHT: fast, slightly undulating, and direct with rapid wing beats.

UNIQUE UNDERPARTS
The breeding male is the only North American wood-warbler with unmarked grayish white underparts.

SIMILAR SPECIES

PHILADELPHIA VIREO
see p.271
white eyebrow
yellowish underparts

ORANGE-CROWNED WARBLER
see p.348
shorter wings
greenish yellow rump
muted markings

OCCURRENCE
Breeds in a variety of habitats, especially woodlands with dense understory and thickets of willows and alders. Very common in suburban parks and gardens during migration, particularly in the Midwest. Winters from southern Mexico to northern Ecuador and northern Venezuela; also Cuba.

Length **4¾in (12cm)**	Wingspan **7¾in (19.5cm)**	Weight **9/32–5/8oz (8–17g)**
Social **Flocks**	Lifespan **Up to 6 years**	Status **Secure**

DATE SEEN	WHERE	NOTES

Order **Passeriformes**	Family **Parulidae**	Species ***Vermivora celata***

Orange-crowned Warbler

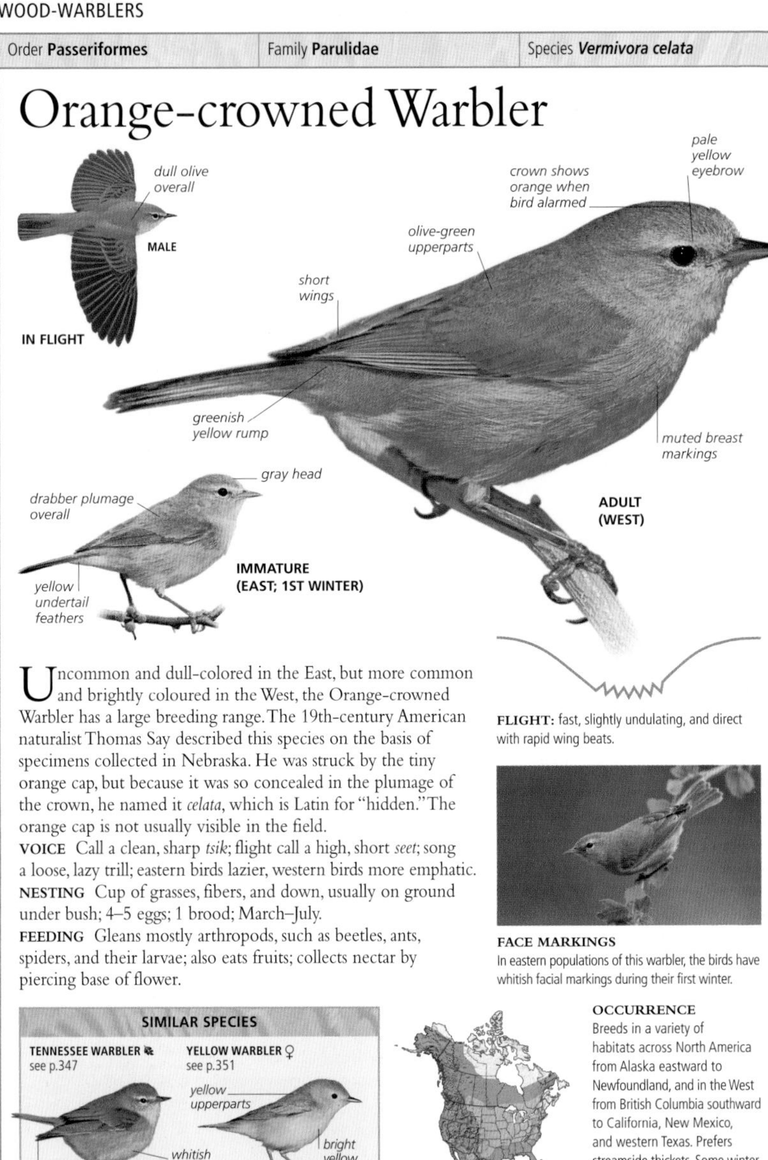

Uncommon and dull-colored in the East, but more common and brightly coloured in the West, the Orange-crowned Warbler has a large breeding range. The 19th-century American naturalist Thomas Say described this species on the basis of specimens collected in Nebraska. He was struck by the tiny orange cap, but because it was so concealed in the plumage of the crown, he named it *celata*, which is Latin for "hidden." The orange cap is not usually visible in the field.

VOICE Call a clean, sharp *tsik*; flight call a high, short *seet*; song a loose, lazy trill; eastern birds lazier, western birds more emphatic.

NESTING Cup of grasses, fibers, and down, usually on ground under bush; 4–5 eggs; 1 brood; March–July.

FEEDING Gleans mostly arthropods, such as beetles, ants, spiders, and their larvae; also eats fruits; collects nectar by piercing base of flower.

FLIGHT: fast, slightly undulating, and direct with rapid wing beats.

FACE MARKINGS
In eastern populations of this warbler, the birds have whitish facial markings during their first winter.

SIMILAR SPECIES

TENNESSEE WARBLER ♂ see p.347

longer wings; whitish underparts

YELLOW WARBLER ♀ see p.351

yellow upperparts; bright yellow breast and belly

OCCURRENCE
Breeds in a variety of habitats across North America from Alaska eastward to Newfoundland, and in the West from British Columbia southward to California, New Mexico, and western Texas. Prefers streamside thickets. Some winter in the West, while others go to Mexico and Guatemala.

Length **5in (13cm)**	Wingspan **7¼in (18.5cm)**	Weight **¼–⅜oz (7–11g)**
Social **Winter flocks**	Lifespan **Up to 6 years**	Status **Secure**

DATE SEEN	WHERE	NOTES

Order **Passeriformes**	Family **Parulidae**	Species ***Vermivora ruficapilla***

Nashville Warbler

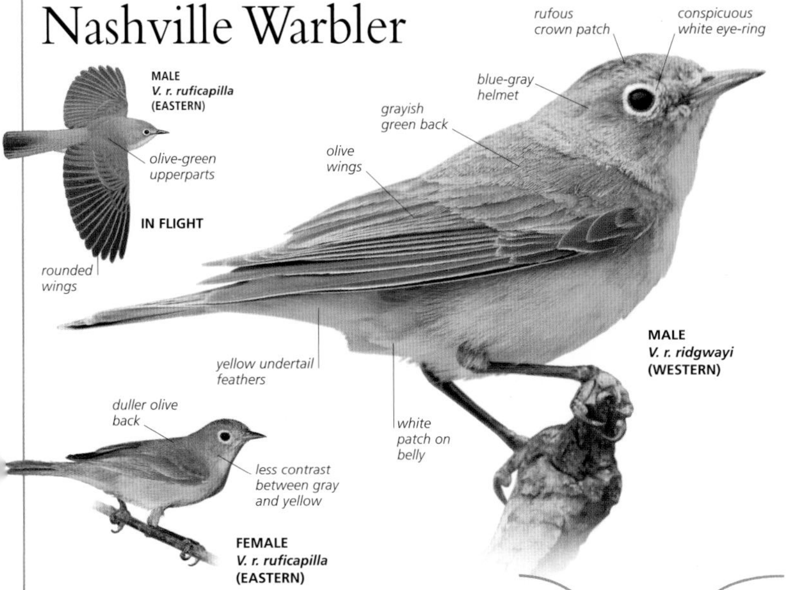
rufous
crown patch
conspicuous
white eye-ring
MALE
V. r. ruficapilla
(EASTERN)
blue-gray
helmet
grayish
green back
olive-green
upperparts
olive
wings
IN FLIGHT
rounded
wings
MALE
V. r. ridgwayi
(WESTERN)
yellow undertail
feathers
duller olive
back
white
patch on
belly
less contrast
between gray
and yellow
FEMALE
V. r. ruficapilla
(EASTERN)

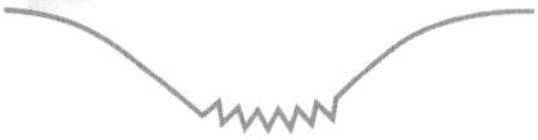

FLIGHT: fast, slightly undulating, and direct, with rapid wing beats.

Although often confused with the ground-walking, chunky Connecticut Warbler, the Nashville Warbler is much smaller, hops about up in trees, and has a yellow throat. Nashville has two subspecies: *V. r. ruficapilla* in the East and *V. r. ridgwayi* in the West. Differences in voice, habitat, behavior, and plumage hint that they may in fact be separate species. *V. r. ridgwayi* can be distinguished by more extensive white on the belly and a grayish green back.

VOICE Call sharp *tik*, sharper in West; flight call high, thin *siit*; eastern song two parts: first part lazy, second faster trill *tee-tsee tee-tsee tee-tsee tititititi*; western song slightly lower and fuller with lazier second part, a seldom trilled *tee-tsee tee-tsee tee-tsee weesay weesay way*.

NESTING Cup hidden on ground in dense cover; 3–6 eggs; 1 brood; May–July.

FEEDING Gleans insects and spiders from trees.

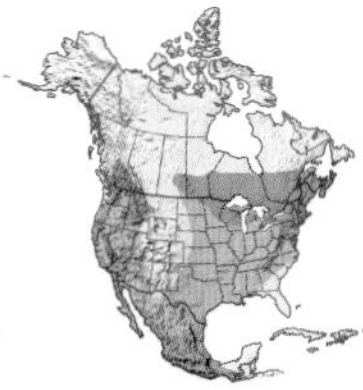

OCCURRENCE
Western *ridgwayi* breeds in brushy montane habitats in the Sierras and northern Rockies and winters in coastal California and from southern Texas to Guatemala; Eastern *ruficapilla* breeds in wet habitats from Saskatchewan east to Newfoundland and south to Virginia; it winters in Mexico.

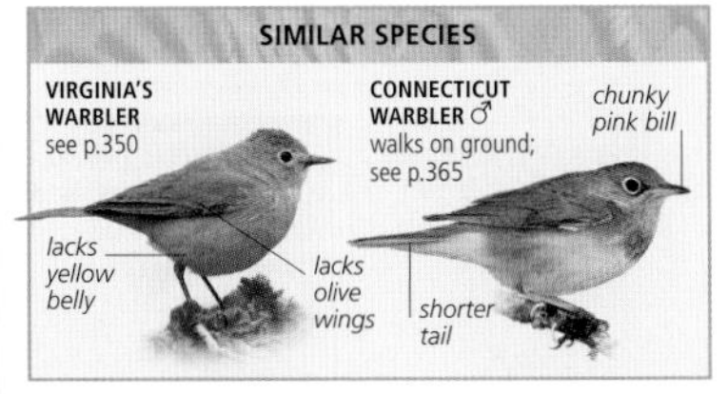

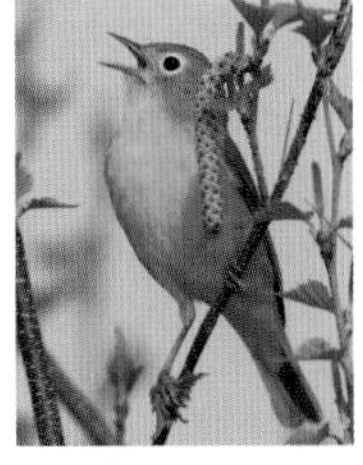

FIELD MARKS
The white eye-ring and belly are evident on this singing male.

SIMILAR SPECIES

VIRGINIA'S WARBLER
see p.350

CONNECTICUT WARBLER ♂
walks on ground; see p.365

chunky
pink bill
lacks
yellow
belly
lacks
olive
wings
shorter
tail

Length **4¾in (12cm)**	Wingspan **7½in (19cm)**	Weight **¼–7/16oz (7–13g)**
Social **Migrant/Winter flocks**	Lifespan **Up to 7 years**	Status **Secure**

DATE SEEN	WHERE	NOTES

Order **Passeriformes**	Family **Parulidae**	Species ***Vermivora virginiae***

Virginia's Warbler

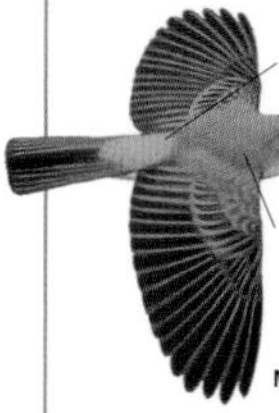

conspicuous yellow rump
plain gray overall
MALE
IN FLIGHT

yellow rump
dark gray wings
MALE

rufous on crown
complete white eye-ring
yellow undertail feathers
yellow breast
pale gray underparts
MALE

FLIGHT: fast, slightly undulating, and direct, with rapid wing beats.

This western warbler can be quite shy, and its preference for a dense brushy habitat and unforgiving terrain make it all the more difficult to see. Virginia's Warbler and Nashville's Warbler share the habit of constantly bobbing their tail. Although Virginia's Warblers nest on the ground, singing males frequent the tops of junipers and pines. In the Davis Mountains of west Texas, a small population of Virginia's Warblers has recently interbred with the rare Colima Warbler.

VOICE Call hard, sharp, yet hollow *ssink*; song lazy, sweet warble: *sweet sweet sweet sweet teedle-eedle-eedle-eedle tyew tyew.*

NESTING Cup of grassy material on steep slope, hidden in hole or vegetation; 3–5 eggs; 1 brood; May–July.

FEEDING Gleans a variety of insects, especially caterpillars, from branches and leaves.

CONSPICUOUS BREAST PATCH
The yellow breast patch on a singing male stands out against its overall gray plumage.

SIMILAR SPECIES

NASHVILLE WARBLER (WESTERN) ♀ see p.349
blue-gray helmet
olive wings
more extensive yellow

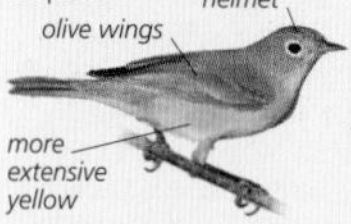

COLIMA WARBLER see p.460
brownish back
orange upper- and undertail feathers
brownish flanks

OCCURRENCE
Breeds in dense dry shrub on steep slopes, often with open pine canopy, in the southern Rockies, Great Basin, and the Black Hills; occupies similar habitats during migration and in winter. WIntering range extends southward to Oaxaca in Mexico.

Length **4¾in (12cm)**	Wingspan **7½in (19cm)**	Weight **¼–⅜oz (7–10g)**
Social **Flocks**	Lifespan **Up to 4 years**	Status **Secure**

DATE SEEN	WHERE	NOTES

Order **Passeriformes**	Family **Parulidae**	Species ***Dendroica petechia***

Yellow Warbler

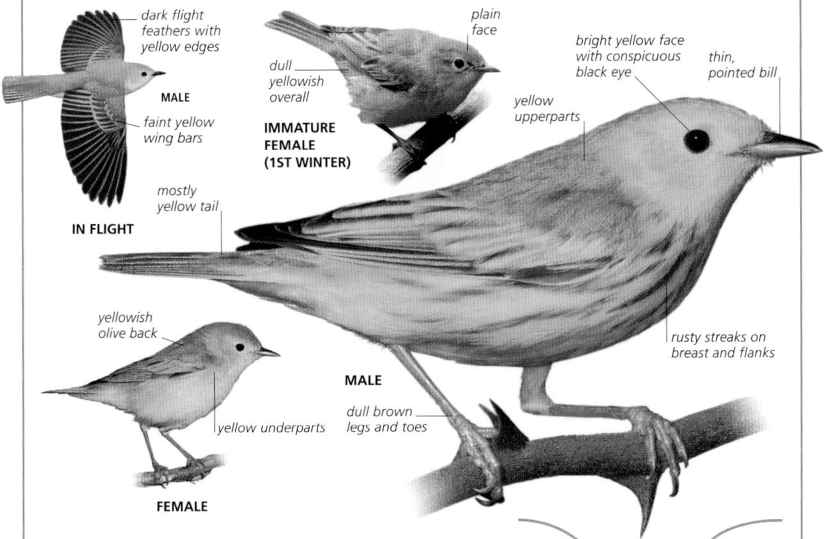

dark flight feathers with yellow edges
MALE
faint yellow wing bars
IN FLIGHT
mostly yellow tail
dull yellowish overall
plain face
IMMATURE FEMALE (1ST WINTER)
bright yellow face with conspicuous black eye
thin, pointed bill
yellow upperparts
rusty streaks on breast and flanks
MALE
dull brown legs and toes
yellowish olive back
yellow underparts
FEMALE

By May, the song of the Yellow Warbler can be heard across North America as the birds arrive for the summer. This species is extremely variable geographically, with about 40 subspecies, especially on its tropical range (West Indies and Central and South America). The Yellow Warbler is known to build another nest on top of an old one when cowbird eggs appear in it, which can result in up to six different tiers. The Yellow Warbler does not walk, but rather hops from branch to branch.

VOICE Call a variable *chip*, sometimes given in series; flight call buzzy *zeep*; song variable series of fast, sweet notes; western birds often add an emphatic ending.

NESTING Deep cup of plant material, grasses in vertical fork of deciduous tree or shrub; 4–5 eggs; 1 brood; May–July.

FEEDING Eats mostly insects and insect larvae, plus some fruit.

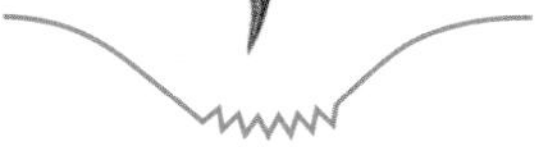

FLIGHT: fast, slightly undulating, and direct, with rapid wing beats.

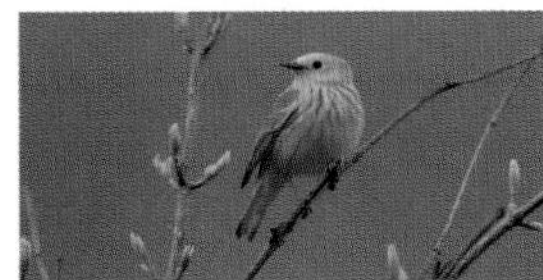

ONE OF A KIND
This species has more yellow in its plumage than any other North American wood-warbler.

SIMILAR SPECIES

ORANGE-CROWNED WARBLER
see p.348
olive-green overall
WILSON'S WARBLER ♀
see p.369
dark crown
longer tail

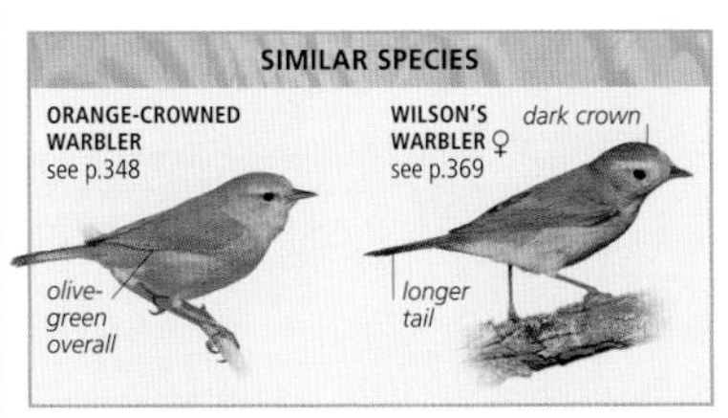

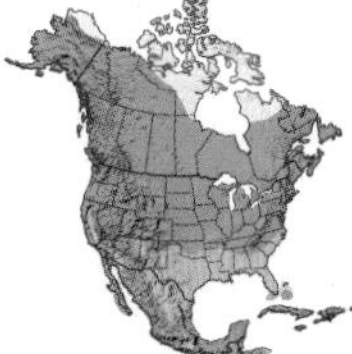

OCCURRENCE
Widespread in most shrubby and second-growth habitats of North America. Migrates to southern US and southward to Mexico, Central America, and South America. Resident populations live in Florida and the West Indies.

Length **5in (13cm)**	Wingspan **8in (20cm)**	Weight **9/32–½oz (8–14g)**
Social **Flocks**	Lifespan **Up to 9 years**	Status **Secure**

DATE SEEN	WHERE	NOTES

Order **Passeriformes**	Family **Parulidae**	Species ***Dendroica striata***

Blackpoll Warbler

white tail spots
two white wing bars
MALE
IN FLIGHT

greenish upperparts with fine black streaks
faint, fine streaking on underparts
FEMALE (BREEDING)

greenish overall
streaking on breast
MALE (FALL)
pale feet contrasting with darker legs

black cap
white cheek
bold black streaks on gray back
streaked underparts
white undertail feathers
orange legs
MALE (BREEDING)

The Blackpoll Warbler is well known for undergoing a remarkable fall migration that takes it over the Atlantic Ocean from the northeastern US to northern Venezuela. Before departing, it almost doubles its body weight with fat to serve as fuel for the nonstop journey. With the return of spring, most of these birds travel the shorter Caribbean route back north.

VOICE Call piercing *chip*; flight call high, buzzy yet sharp *tzzzt*; common song crescendo of fast, extremely high-pitched ticks, ending with a decrescendo *tsst tsst TSST TSST TSST tsst tsst;* less commonly, ticks run into even faster trill.

NESTING Well-hidden cup placed low against conifer trunk; 3–5 eggs; 1–2 broods; May–July.

FEEDING Gleans arthropods, such as worms and beetles, but will take small fruit in fall and winter.

FLIGHT: fast, slightly undulating, and direct, with rapid wing beats.

REACHING THE HIGH NOTES
The song of the male Blackpoll is so high-pitched that it is inaudible to many people.

SIMILAR SPECIES

BAY-BREASTED WARBLER
see p.461
greenish sides to neck
warm wash to flanks

BLACK-AND-WHITE WARBLER ♂
see p.361
black cheek
distinct black-and-white stripes

OCCURRENCE
Breeds in spruce-fir forests across the northern boreal forest zone from Alaska eastward to Newfoundland, southward to coastal coniferous forests in the Maritimes and northern New England. Migrants fly over the Atlantic Ocean to a landfall in the Caribbean and northern South America.

Length **5½in (14cm)**	Wingspan **9in (23cm)**	Weight **⅜–⅝oz (10–18g)**
Social **Flocks**	Lifespan **Up to 8 years**	Status **Secure**

DATE SEEN	WHERE	NOTES

Order **Passeriformes**	Family **Parulidae**	Species ***Dendroica magnolia***

Magnolia Warbler

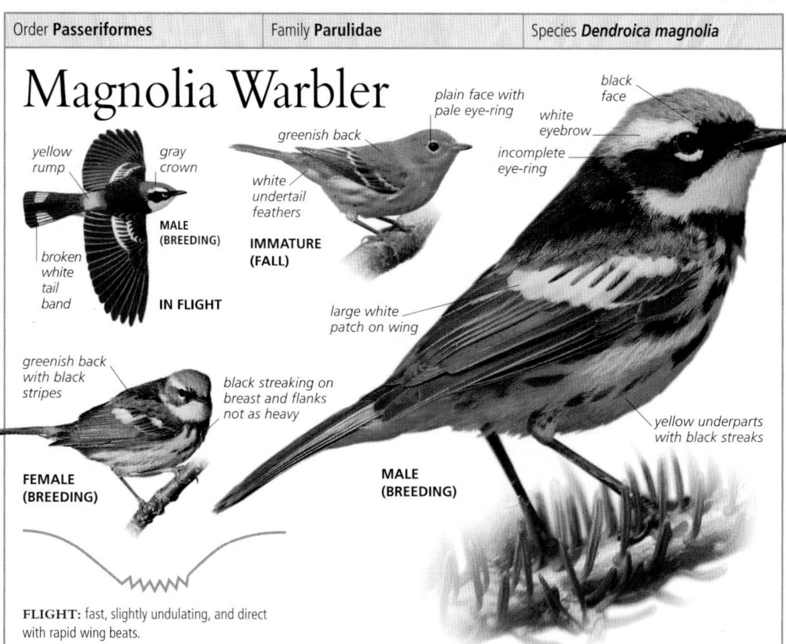

FLIGHT: fast, slightly undulating, and direct with rapid wing beats.

The bold, flashy, and common Magnolia Warbler is hard to miss as it flits around at eye level, fanning its uniquely marked tail. This species nests in young forests and winters in almost any habitat, so its numbers have not suffered in recent decades, unlike some of its relatives. Although it really has no preference for its namesake plant, the 19th-century ornithologist Alexander Wilson discovered a Magnolia Warbler feeding in a magnolia tree during migration, which is how it got its name.

VOICE Call a tinny *jeinf*, not particularly warbler-like; also short, simple whistled series *wee'-sa wee'-sa WEET-a-chew*; short, distinctive, flight call a high, trilled *zeep*.

NESTING Flimsy cup of black rootlets placed low in dense conifer against trunk; 3–5 eggs; 1 brood; June–August.

FEEDING Gleans mostly caterpillars, beetles, and spiders.

SPRUCE WARBLER
The conspicuous male Magnolia Warbler can be found singing its distinctive, loud song, often throughout the day, in a spruce tree.

SIMILAR SPECIES

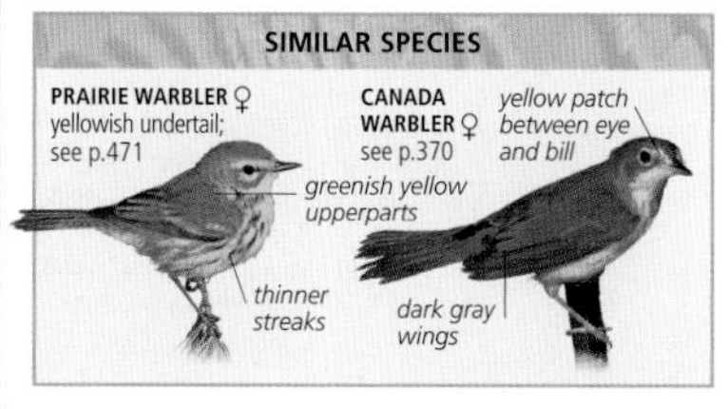

OCCURRENCE
Breeds in dense, young mixed and coniferous forests from Yukon east to Newfoundland and south into Appalachians of Tennessee; migrates across the Gulf and Caribbean; winters in varied habitats in Caribbean and from southeast Mexico to Panama; rare vagrant in the West.

Length **5in (13cm)**	Wingspan **7½in (19cm)**	Weight **7/32–7/16oz (6–12g)**
Social **Migrant/Winter flocks**	Lifespan **Up to 6 years**	Status **Secure**

DATE SEEN	WHERE	NOTES

Order **Passeriformes**	Family **Parulidae**	Species ***Dendroica tigrina***

Cape May Warbler

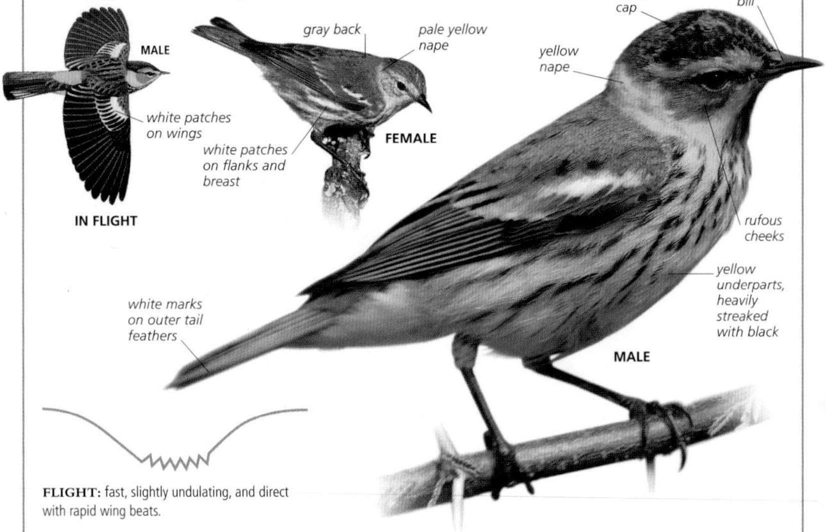

MALE
white patches on wings
IN FLIGHT
gray back
pale yellow nape
FEMALE
white patches on flanks and breast
black cap
thin, pointed bill
yellow nape
rufous cheeks
yellow underparts, heavily streaked with black
white marks on outer tail feathers
MALE

FLIGHT: fast, slightly undulating, and direct with rapid wing beats.

The Cape May Warbler is a spruce budworm (a moth actually, not a worm) specialist, and its populations increase during outbreaks of this pest. Cape May Warblers chase other birds aggressively from flowering trees, where they use their semitubular tongue to suck the nectar from blossoms. In its summer spruce forest habitat, the Cape May Warbler plucks insects from clumps of needles. The "Cape May" Warbler was named this way because the first specimen was collected here, but it doesn't breed at Cape May!

VOICE Song a high, even-pitched series of whistles *see see see see.*

NESTING Cup placed near trunk, high in spruce or fir near top; 4–9 eggs; 1 brood; June–July.

FEEDING Gleans arthropods, especially spruce budworms, and also flies, adult moths, and beetles from mid-high levels in canopy; also fruit and nectar during the nonbreeding season.

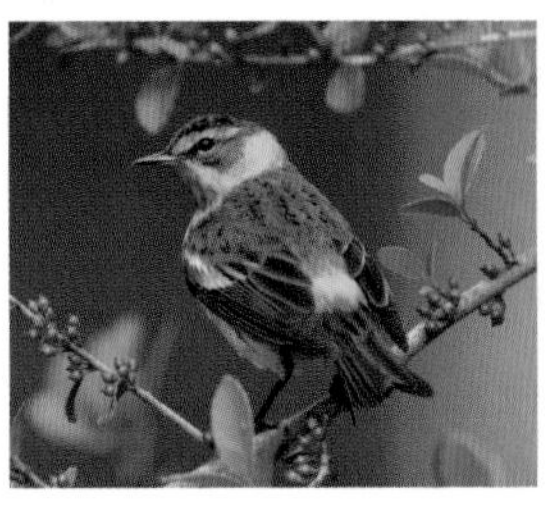

SPRING FLASH
Magnificently colored, a male shows its chestnut cheek, yellow "necklace," and yellow rump.

SIMILAR SPECIES

YELLOW-RUMPED WARBLER (MYRTLE) ♀ see p.355

PALM WARBLER (WESTERN) see p.360

thicker, heavier bill
yellow rump
yellow flank patches
browner overall
yellow undertail feathers

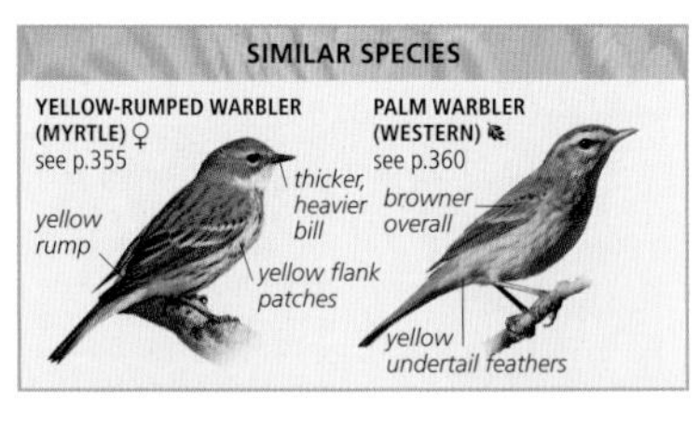

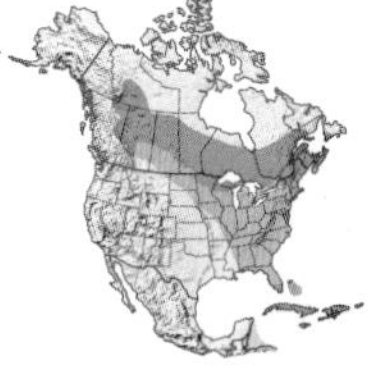

OCCURRENCE
Breeds from the Yukon and British Columbia to the Great Lakes, the Maritimes, and New England in mature spruce–fir forests. Migrants occur in a variety of habitats. Winters especially in gardens in Central America, as far south as Honduras.

Length **5in (13cm)**	Wingspan **8in (20cm)**	Weight **$\frac{5}{16}$–$\frac{7}{16}$oz (9–13g)**
Social **Migrant flocks**	Lifespan **Up to 4 years**	Status **Secure**

DATE SEEN	WHERE	NOTES

Order **Passeriformes**	Family **Parulidae**	Species ***Dendroica coronata***

Yellow-rumped Warbler

white wing bars
MALE (MYRTLE)
IN FLIGHT

whitish eyebrow
same pattern as male, but duller
whitish throat
yellow flanks
FEMALE
D. c. coronata
(MYRTLE)

large, white wing patch
solid black breast
unmarked undertail
MALE
D. c. auduboni
(AUDUBON'S)

yellowish throat
grayish overall
FEMALE
D. c. auduboni
(AUDUBON'S)

The abundant and widespread Yellow-rumped Warbler is not choosy about its wintering habitats. It was often considered to consist of two species, "Myrtle" (*D. c. coronata*) in the East, and "Audubon's" (*D. c. auduboni*) in the West. Because they interbreed freely in a narrow zone of contact in British Columbia and Alberta, the American Ornithologists Union merged them. The two forms differ in plumage and voice, and their hybrid zone appears stable.

VOICE Myrtle's call a flat, husky *tchik*; Audubon's a higher-pitched, relatively musical, rising *jip*; flight call of both a clear, upslurred *sviiit*; song loose, warbled trill with an inflected ending; Myrtle's song higher and faster, Audubon's lower and slower.

NESTING Bulky cup of plant matter in conifer; 4–5 eggs; 1 brood; March–August.

FEEDING Feeds mostly on flies, beetles, wasps, and spiders during breeding; takes fruit and berries at other times of the year, often sallies to catch prey.

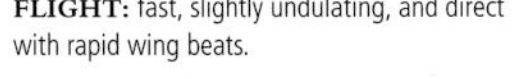

FLIGHT: fast, slightly undulating, and direct with rapid wing beats.

WIDESPREAD WARBLER
Yellow-rumped Warblers are widespread and are likely to be spotted often.

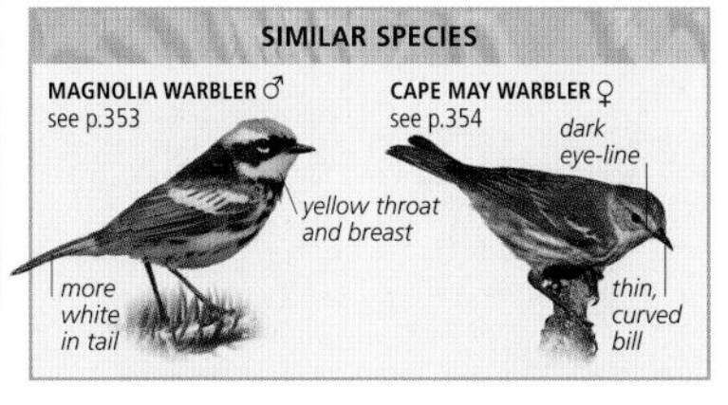

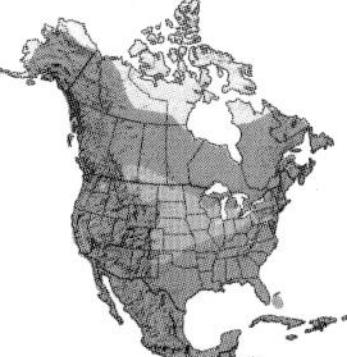

OCCURRENCE
Both eastern and western populations are widespread across the continent from Alaska eastward to Québec and Labrador, and westward in the mountains south to Arizona, New Mexico, and Northern Mexico. Prefers coniferous and mixed hardwood coniferous forests.

Length **5in (13cm)**	Wingspan **9in (23cm)**	Weight **3⁄8–5⁄8oz (10–17g)**
Social **Flocks**	Lifespan **Up to 7 years**	Status **Secure**

DATE SEEN	WHERE	NOTES

Order **Passeriformes**	Family **Parulidae**	Species ***Dendroica nigrescens***

Black-throated Gray Warbler

MALE
white wing bars
gray overall
IN FLIGHT

pattern more subdued than male
white throat
black band across breast
FEMALE

bold white cheeks
no eye-ring
yellow spot between eye and bill
plain gray back
white outer tail feathers
MALE
white undertail feathers
one or two white wing bars
heavy, black streaks on underparts

FLIGHT: fast, slightly undulating, and direct with rapid wing beats.

The Black-throated Gray Warbler, a somewhat chickadee-like bird, inhabits the understory of forests and woodlands of oak and mixed woodlands in dry to arid western North America. Remarkably, considering that it is fairly common, not much is known about its life history, except that it has a rather leisurely foraging style, that its nest is built by both males and females, placed only a feet few away from the ground, and that it lingers in its breeding range until late fall, sometimes even wintering in California and Arizona.

VOICE Call a hard, flat *chep*; flight call a rising *siiit*; song a series of mid-range, paired, buzzy notes, slightly rising then dropping in pitch with the last note, *buzz-zu buzz-zu buzz-zu buzz-zo buzz-zo buzz-zee BEE-chu!*

NESTING Deep and compact cup of grass, lined with feathers, in brush; 3–5 eggs; 2 broods; May–July.

FEEDING A rather deliberate forager, gleans insects, especially caterpillars, from foliage at mid-levels.

LIVELY SONG
The buzzy song of this species is typical of the "black-throated" warbler group.

OCCURRENCE
Ranges from British Columbia south to California. Breeds in open coniferous and mixed woodlands with dense scrubby understory of pinyon, juniper, and/or oak; migrants use a greater variety of habitats; winters in dry scrub and woodlands southward away from its breeding range.

Length **5in (13cm)**	Wingspan **7½in (19cm)**	Weight **¼–⅜oz (7–10g)**
Social **Flocks**	Lifespan **Unknown**	Status **Secure**

DATE SEEN	WHERE	NOTES

Order **Passeriformes**	Family **Parulidae**	Species ***Dendroica virens***

Black-throated Green Warbler

olive-green back
MALE
two white wing bars
IN FLIGHT
same as male, but duller
greenish flanks
FEMALE
greenish cap
yellow face
black bib and chin
heavily streaked underparts
white outer tail feathers
yellowish flanks
MALE

FLIGHT: fast, slightly undulating, and direct with rapid wing beats; typical warbler flight.

This species is easy to distinguish as its bright yellow face is unique among birds inhabiting northeastern North America. It is a member of the *virens* "superspecies," a group of non-overlapping species that are similar in plumage and vocalizations—the Black-throated Green, Golden-cheeked, Townsend's, and Hermit Warblers. Sadly, this species is vulnerable to habitat loss in parts of its wintering range.

VOICE Flat *tchip* call; flight call a rising *siii*; two high-pitched, buzzy songs, fast *zee zee zee zee zoo zee*; and lower, slower *zu zee zu-zu zee.*

NESTING Cup of twigs and grasses around 10–65ft (3–20m) on horizontal branch near trunk in the North, away from trunk in the South; 3–5 eggs; 1 brood; May–July.

FEEDING Gleans arthropods, especially caterpillars; also takes small fruit, including poison ivy berries, in nonbreeding season.

YELLOW-AND-BLACK GEM
From a high perch in a spruce tree, a male advertises his territory with persistent singing.

SIMILAR SPECIES

GOLDEN-CHEEKED WARBLER ♂ see p.462
black crown
thin, black eye-line

GOLDEN-CHEEKED WARBLER ♀ see p.462
darker crown
darker upper breast

OCCURRENCE
Breeds in many forest types, especially a mix of conifers and hardwoods, from British Columbia east to Newfoundland and the southeastern US along the Appalachians. Migrants and wintering birds use a variety of habitats. Winters from southern Texas into Venezuela; small numbers in Caribbean.

Length **5in (13cm)**	Wingspan **8in (20cm)**	Weight **9/32–3/8oz (8–11g)**
Social **Migrant/Winter flocks**	Lifespan **Up to 6 years**	Status **Secure**

DATE SEEN	WHERE	NOTES

Order **Passeriformes**	Family **Parulidae**	Species ***Dendroica townsendi***

Townsend's Warbler

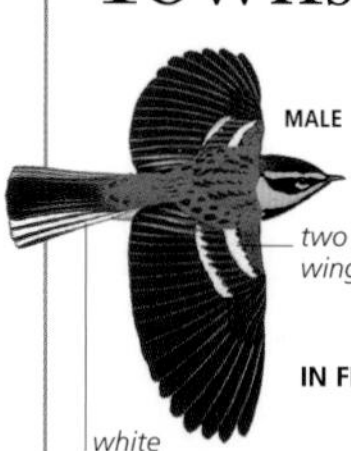

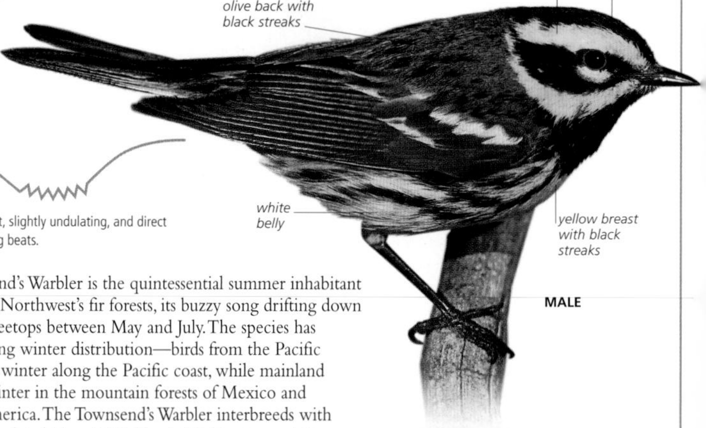

MALE

two white wing bars

IN FLIGHT

white outer tail feathers

streaks on undertail

poorly marked streaks on flanks

head patterned like male's, but duller

yellow breast

FEMALE

striking head with black-and-yellow streaks

black crown

olive back with black streaks

white belly

yellow breast with black streaks

MALE

FLIGHT: fast, slightly undulating, and direct with rapid wing beats.

Townsend's Warbler is the quintessential summer inhabitant of the Northwest's fir forests, its buzzy song drifting down from the treetops between May and July. The species has an interesting winter distribution—birds from the Pacific Northwest winter along the Pacific coast, while mainland breeders winter in the mountain forests of Mexico and Central America. The Townsend's Warbler interbreeds with the closely related Hermit Warbler in Washington and Oregon, resulting in varied-looking hybrids.

VOICE Song a series of buzzy notes that accelerate and increase in pitch; two examples are *wheezy wheezy wheezy zeee* and *zuuu dit-dit-dit zuuu dit-dit-dit zo ZEE zu ZAY.*

NESTING Bulky shallow cup of plant matter, hidden by needles on branch far from trunk, high in conifer trees; 3–7 eggs; 1 brood; May–July.

FEEDING Gleans insects, spiders, and caterpillars; will also take honeydew secreted by aphids and other insects.

PALER JUVENILE
Young Townsend's Warblers are paler than adults but show the same color pattern as adult females.

SIMILAR SPECIES

BLACK-THROATED GREEN WARBLER ♂ see p.357
larger bib
no yellow on breast

BLACK-THROATED GREEN WARBLER ♀ see p.357
paler cheek patch
lacks bright yellow breast

OCCURRENCE
Breeds from southern Alaska to Wyoming in mature fir, coniferous, and mixed coniferous–deciduous forests; elevations range from sea level to subalpine. Winters in Mexico and Central America in different habitats including coastal, woodland, and suburban parks and gardens.

Length **5in (13cm)**	Wingspan **8in (20cm)**	Weight **¼–⅜oz (7–11g)**
Social **Flocks**	Lifespan **Up to 4 years**	Status **Secure**

DATE SEEN	WHERE	NOTES

Order **Passeriformes**	Family **Parulidae**	Species ***Dendroica occidentalis***

Hermit Warbler

MALE
two white wing bars
IN FLIGHT
white outer tail feathers
more olive upperparts
olive-green crown
FEMALE
pale throat
bright yellow head
narrow dark patch
plain face
grayish back
black throat
unstreaked white underparts
MALE

The yellow-headed Hermit Warbler is the southern counterpart of the Townsend's Warbler, which has a yellow head patterned with black and a yellow breast. In spite of differences in their markings, the two species interbreed where their ranges meet, in parts of Washington and Oregon. Their songs are nearly indistinguishable in the contact zone. Most hybrids resemble Hermit Warblers with greenish backs and yellow breasts. The Hermit Warbler lives in the canopy of tall conifers, including tall pines and Douglas firs, and also in mixed conifer-hardwood forests. Its canopy-dwelling behavior makes this species difficult to observe.

VOICE Series of clear notes with downslurred ending *wee-see wee-see wee-see seu*; another buzzier note, increasing in tempo and pitch: *zuuuu zoooh zeee zee-zee ZEEP*; similar to Black-throated Green Warbler of northeastern coniferous forests.

NESTING Cup of fine material in conifer on main horizontal branch near trunk; 4–5 eggs; 1 brood; May–July.

FEEDING Gleans a variety of insects, spiders, and caterpillars from branches and leaves; also catches insects in flight.

FLIGHT: fast, slightly undulating, and direct with rapid wing beats, from treetop to treetop.

EXCEPTIONAL VIEW
Hermit Warblers spend nearly all their time in tree canopies and are rarely seen on the ground.

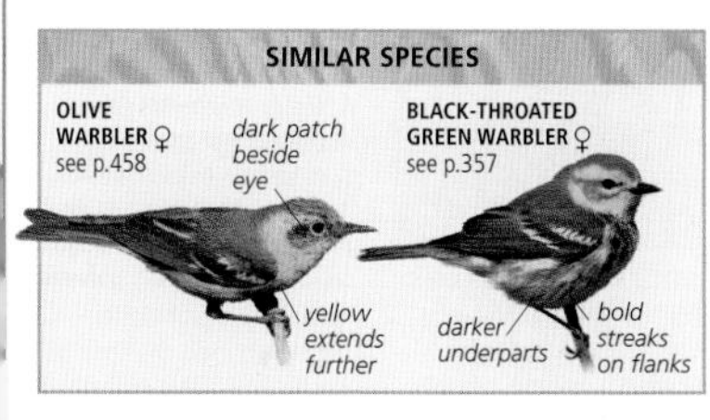

OCCURRENCE
A conifer forest specialist preferring cool, old forests along the Pacific slope of its coastal ranges and sierras from Washington State to California. Winters in southern California, as well as Mexico, Guatemala, Honduras, and Nicaragua.

Length **5in (13cm)**	Wingspan **8in (20cm)**	Weight **9/32–3/8oz (8–11g)**
Social **Flocks**	Lifespan **Up to 4 years**	Status **Secure (p)**

DATE SEEN	WHERE	NOTES

Order **Passeriformes**	Family **Parulidae**	Species ***Dendroica palmarum***

Palm Warbler

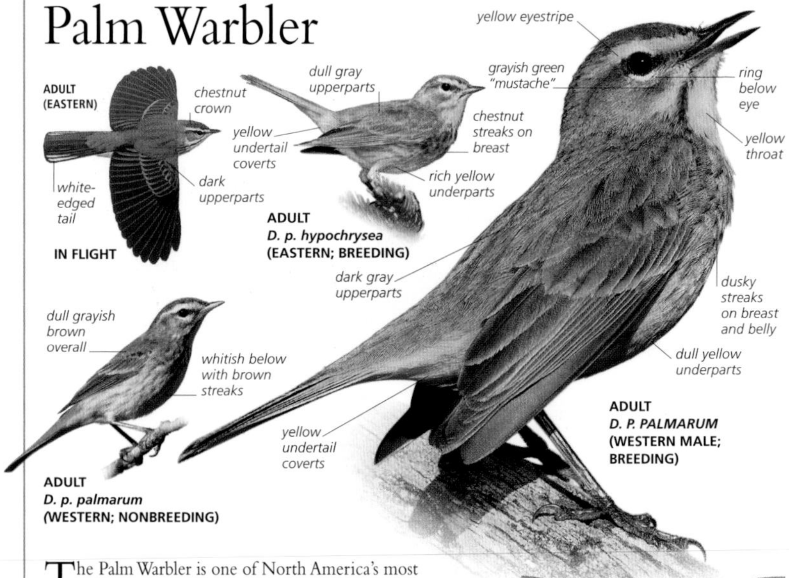

ADULT
(EASTERN)
chestnut crown
white-edged tail
dark upperparts
IN FLIGHT
dull gray upperparts
yellow undertail coverts
chestnut streaks on breast
rich yellow underparts
ADULT
D. p. hypochrysea
(EASTERN; BREEDING)
yellow eyestripe
grayish green "mustache"
ring below eye
yellow throat
dark gray upperparts
dusky streaks on breast and belly
dull yellow underparts
ADULT
D. P. PALMARUM
(WESTERN MALE; BREEDING)
yellow undertail coverts
dull grayish brown overall
whitish below with brown streaks
ADULT
D. p. palmarum
(WESTERN; NONBREEDING)

The Palm Warbler is one of North America's most abundant warblers. Its tail-pumping habits make it easy to identify in any plumage. It was named *palmarum* (meaning "palm") in 1789 because it was first recorded among palm thickets on the Caribbean island of Hispaniola. The western subspecies (*D. p. palmarum*) is found in western and central Canada, but is rare along the west coast in winter. It is grayish brown above and lacks the chestnut streaks of the eastern subspecies (*D. p. hypochrysea*), which has a yellower face, and breeds in southeastern Canada and northeastern US.

VOICE Call a husky *chik* or *tsip*; flight call a light *ziint*; slow, loose, buzzy trill: *zwi zwi zwi zwi zwi zwi zwi zwi*.

NESTING Cup of grasses on or near ground in open area of conifers at forest edge of a bog; 4–5 eggs; 1 brood; May–July.

FEEDING Eats insects, sometimes caught in flight; also takes seeds and berries.

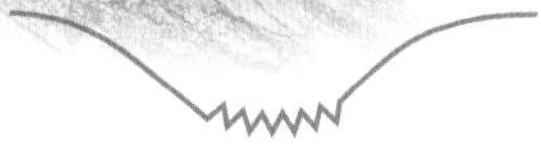

FLIGHT: fast, slightly undulating, and direct with rapid wing beats.

OCCURRENCE
In North America, breeds in spruce bogs within the northern forest zone, across Canada from the Yukon to the Maritimes and Labrador, and in the US from Minnesota to Maine. Often migrates through central portions of eastern US; winters in southeastern US, Florida, and Central America.

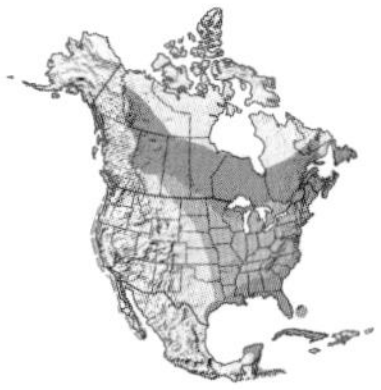

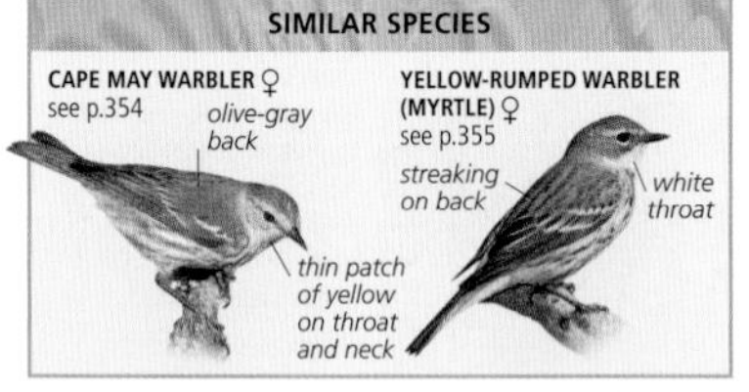

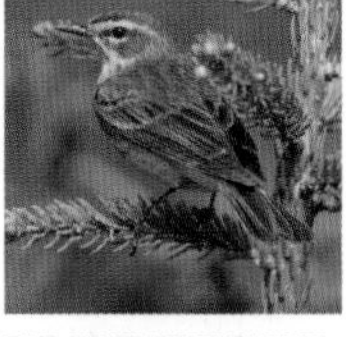

FAR FROM THE PALMS
This male Palm Warbler is far north of the coastal palms where its kin spend the winter.

SIMILAR SPECIES

CAPE MAY WARBLER ♀
see p.354

olive-gray back
thin patch of yellow on throat and neck

YELLOW-RUMPED WARBLER (MYRTLE) ♀
see p.355

streaking on back
white throat

Length **5½in (14cm)**	Wingspan **8in (20cm)**	Weight **¼–7/16oz (7–13g)**
Social **Flocks**	Lifespan **Up to 6 years**	Status **Secure**

DATE SEEN	WHERE	NOTES

Order **Passeriformes**	Family **Parulidae**	Species ***Mniotilta varia***

Black-and-white Warbler

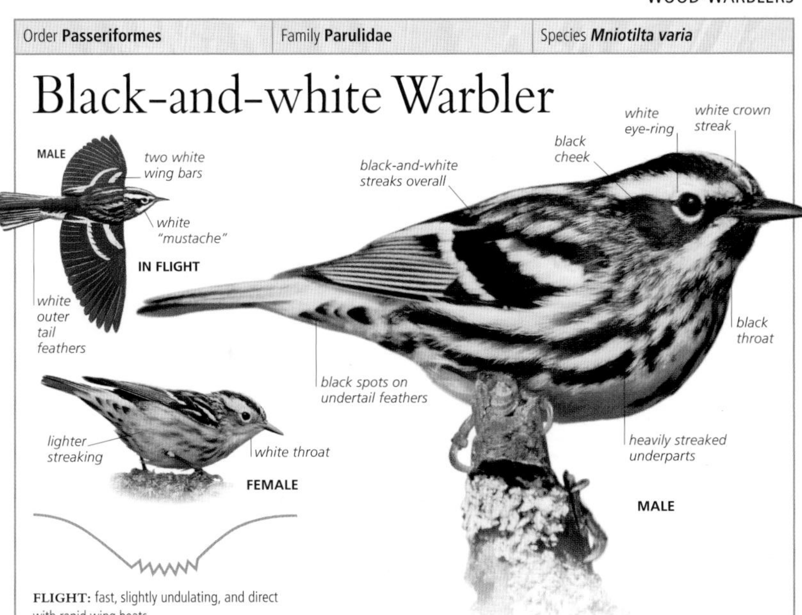

FLIGHT: fast, slightly undulating, and direct with rapid wing beats.

The Black-and-white Warbler is best known for its creeper-like habit of feeding in vertical and upside-down positions as it pries into bark crevices, where its relatively long, curved bill allows it to reach tiny nooks and crannies. These habits, combined with streaked plumage, make this bird one of the most distinctive warblers in North America. It is a long-distance migrant, with some birds wintering in parts of northern South America.

VOICE Sharp *stik* call; flight call a very high, thin *ssiit*, often doubled; song a thin, high-pitched, wheezy series *wheesy wheesy wheesy wheesy wheesy wheesy.*

NESTING Cup on ground against stump, fallen logs, or roots; 4–6 eggs; 1 brood; April–August.

FEEDING Creeps along branches and trunks, probing into bark for insects and insect larvae.

SQUEAKY WHEEL
The high-pitched, wheezy song of this warbler is said to be reminiscent of a squeaky wheel.

UPSIDE-DOWN
Black-and-white Warblers often creep head-first along trunks and branches of trees.

SIMILAR SPECIES

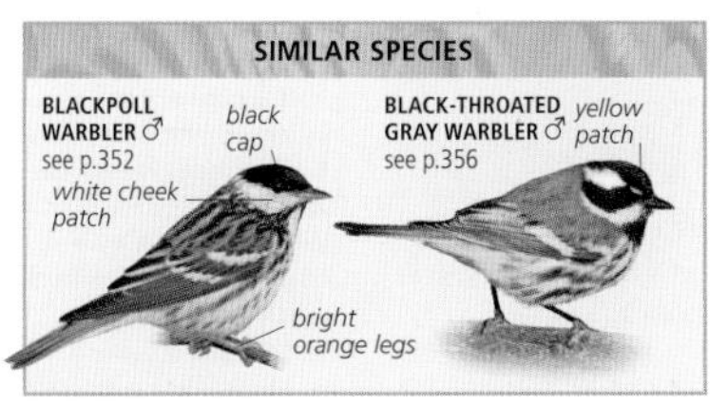

OCCURRENCE
Breeds in deciduous and mixed mature and second-growth woodlands; migrants occur on a greater variety of habitats; winters in a wide range of wooded habitats in southern US, Mexico and into Central and South America. Rare along West Coast in winter.

Length **5in (13cm)**	Wingspan **8in (20cm)**	Weight **5/16–1/2oz (9–14g)**
Social **Migrant/Winter flocks**	Lifespan **Up to 11 years**	Status **Secure**

DATE SEEN	WHERE	NOTES

Order **Passeriformes**	Family **Parulidae**	Species ***Setophaga ruticilla***

American Redstart

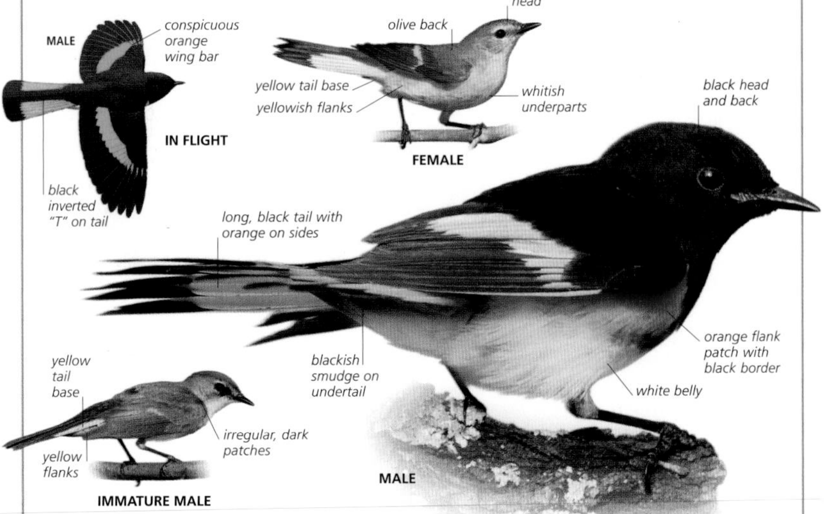

MALE
conspicuous orange wing bar
IN FLIGHT
black inverted "T" on tail
grayish head
olive back
yellow tail base
yellowish flanks
whitish underparts
FEMALE
black head and back
long, black tail with orange on sides
orange flank patch with black border
white belly
blackish smudge on undertail
MALE
yellow tail base
yellow flanks
irregular, dark patches
IMMATURE MALE

The American Redstart is a vividly colored, energetic and acrobatic warbler with a reasonably broad range across North America. One of its behavioral quirks is to fan its tail and wings while foraging, supposedly using the flashes of bold color to scare insects into moving, making them easy prey. It possesses well-developed rictal bristles, hair-like feathers extending from the corners of the mouth, which help it to detect insects.

VOICE Harsh *tsiip* call; flight call a high, thin *sveep*; song a confusingly variable, high, thin, yet penetrating series of notes; one version burry, emphatic, and downslurred *see-a see-a see-a see-a ZEE-urrrr*.

NESTING Cup of grasses and rootlets, lined with feathers; placed low in deciduous tree; 2–5 eggs; 1–2 broods; May–July.

FEEDING Gleans insects and spiders from leaves at mid-levels in trees; also catches moths, flies in flight; will also eat fruit.

FLIGHT: fast, slightly undulating, and direct with rapid wing beats.

COMMON SONG
This bird's short, ringing song is a common sound in the moist deciduous woods of the East and North.

MALE CAREGIVER
As with most warblers, male Redstarts help raise the young, though they may be polygamous.

OCCURRENCE
Breeds in moist deciduous and mixed woodlands; migrants and wintering birds use a wide range of habitats. Winters from Baja California and south Florida through Middle America and the Caribbean to northern South America. Rare along coast of Southern California, and Baja California in winter.

Length **5in (13cm)**	Wingspan **8in (20cm)**	Weight **7/32–3/8oz (6–11g)**
Social **Flocks**	Lifespan **Up to 10 years**	Status **Secure**

DATE SEEN	WHERE	NOTES

Order **Passeriformes**	Family **Parulidae**	Species ***Seiurus aurocapillus***

Ovenbird

plain olive overall

ADULT

IN FLIGHT

orange-and-black striped crown

bold white eye-ring

olive upperparts

white throat

black streaked underparts

ADULT

FLIGHT: fast, slightly undulating, and direct with rapid wing beats.

Like members of the unrelated, tropical ovenbird family (Furnariidae), this little bird is so-called for the domed, oven-like nests it builds on the ground; unique structures for a North American bird. The Ovenbird is also noted for its singing. Males flit about boisterously, often at night, incorporating portions of their main song into a jumble of spluttering notes. In the forest, one male singing loudly to declare his territory can set off a whole chain of responses from his neighbors, until the whole forest rings.

VOICE Call variably pitched, sharp *chik* in series; flight call high, rising *siiii*; song loud, ringing crescendo of paired notes *chur-tee' chur-tee' chur-tee' chur-tee' chur-TEE chur-TEE chur-TEE.*

NESTING Domed structure of leaves and grass on ground with side entrance; 3–6 eggs; 1 brood; May–July.

FEEDING Forages mainly on the forest floor for insects and other invertebrates.

STRUTTING ITS STUFF
The Ovenbird is noted for the way it struts across the forest floor like a tiny chicken.

SIMILAR SPECIES

NORTHERN WATERTHRUSH much slimmer; see p.364

dark brown upperparts

no eye-ring

LOUISIANA WATERTHRUSH see p.471

white eyebrow

dark brown upperparts

OCCURRENCE
Breeds in closed-canopy mixed and deciduous forests with suitable amount of fallen plant material for nest building and foraging; migrants and wintering birds use similar habitats.

Length **6in (15cm)**	Wingspan **9½in (24cm)**	Weight **9/16–7/8oz (16–25g)**
Social **Solitary/Flocks**	Lifespan **Up to 7 years**	Status **Declining**

DATE SEEN	WHERE	NOTES

Order **Passeriformes**	Family **Parulidae**	Species ***Seiurus noveboracensis***

Northern Waterthrush

FLIGHT: fast, slightly undulating, and direct with rapid wing beats.

The tail-bobbing Northern Waterthrush is often heard giving a *spink!* call as it swiftly flees from observers. Although this species may be mistaken for the closely related Louisiana Waterthrush, there are clues that are helpful in its identification. While the Northern Waterthrush prefers still water, its relative greatly prefers running water; in addition, its song is quite unlike that of the Louisiana Waterthrush.

VOICE Call a sharp, rising, ringing *spink!*; flight call a rising, buzzy *ziiiit*; song a loud series of rich, accelerating, staccato notes, usually decreasing in pitch *teet, teet, toh-toh toh-toh tyew-tyew!*.

NESTING Hair-lined, mossy cup placed on or near ground, hidden in roots of fallen or standing tree or in riverbank; 4–5 eggs; 1 brood; May–August.

FEEDING Mostly eats insects, such as ants, mosquitoes, moths, and beetles, both larvae and adult, plus slugs, and snails; when migrating, also eats small crustaceans, and even tiny fish.

YELLOW FORM
Many Northern Waterthrushes have yellow underparts, like this one, while others have white.

SIMILAR SPECIES

OVENBIRD much rounder; fatter; see p.363
olive upperparts
bold eye-ring

LOUISIANA WATERTHRUSH see p.471
eyebrow widens behind eye
thicker, longer bill
orange wash to flanks

OCCURRENCE
Breeds right across northern North America in dark, still-water swamps and bogs; also in the still edges of rivers and lakes; migrant birds use wet habitats; winters in shrubby marshes, mangroves, and occasionally in crops, such as rice fields and citrus groves.

Length **6in (15cm)**	Wingspan **9½in (24cm)**	Weight **½–⅞oz (14–23g)**
Social **Solitary**	Lifespan **Up to 9 years**	Status **Secure**

DATE SEEN	WHERE	NOTES

Order **Passeriformes**	Family **Parulidae**	Species ***Oporornis agilis***

Connecticut Warbler

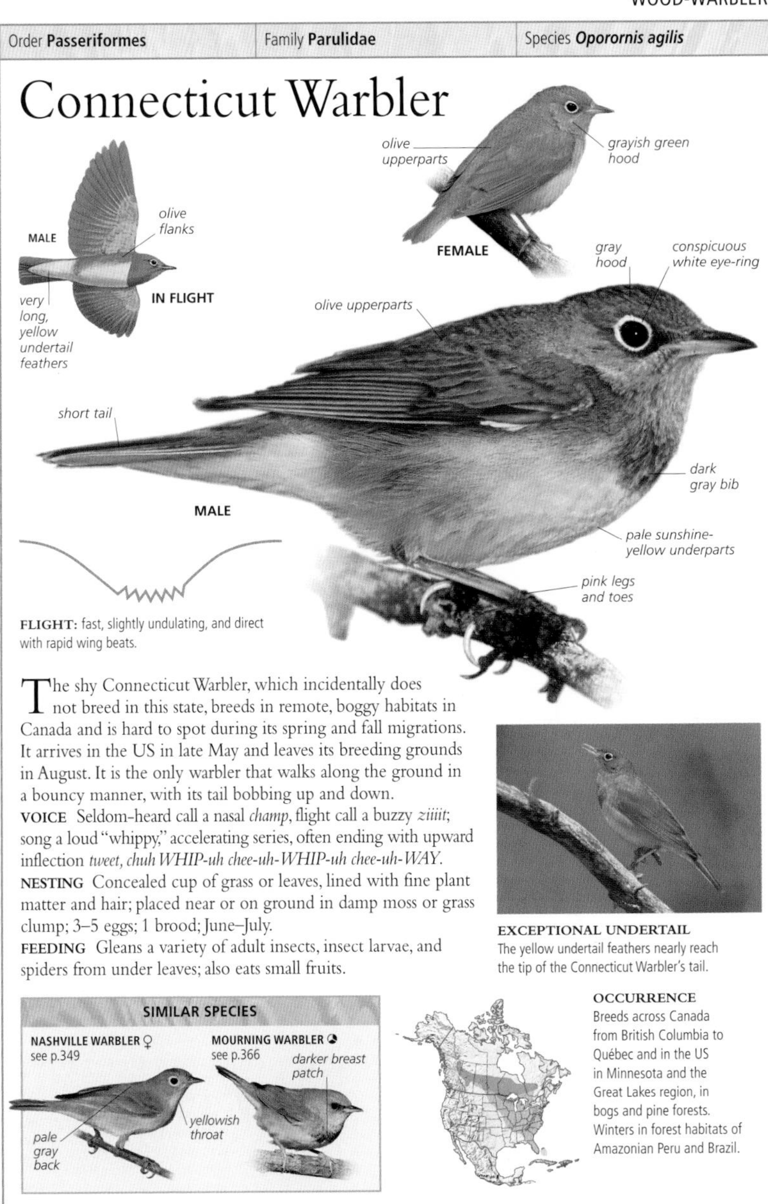

FLIGHT: fast, slightly undulating, and direct with rapid wing beats.

The shy Connecticut Warbler, which incidentally does not breed in this state, breeds in remote, boggy habitats in Canada and is hard to spot during its spring and fall migrations. It arrives in the US in late May and leaves its breeding grounds in August. It is the only warbler that walks along the ground in a bouncy manner, with its tail bobbing up and down.

VOICE Seldom-heard call a nasal *champ*, flight call a buzzy *ziiiit;* song a loud "whippy," accelerating series, often ending with upward inflection *tweet, chuh WHIP-uh chee-uh-WHIP-uh chee-uh-WAY.*

NESTING Concealed cup of grass or leaves, lined with fine plant matter and hair; placed near or on ground in damp moss or grass clump; 3–5 eggs; 1 brood; June–July.

FEEDING Gleans a variety of adult insects, insect larvae, and spiders from under leaves; also eats small fruits.

EXCEPTIONAL UNDERTAIL
The yellow undertail feathers nearly reach the tip of the Connecticut Warbler's tail.

SIMILAR SPECIES

NASHVILLE WARBLER ♀ see p.349
pale gray back; yellowish throat

MOURNING WARBLER see p.366
darker breast patch

OCCURRENCE
Breeds across Canada from British Columbia to Québec and in the US in Minnesota and the Great Lakes region, in bogs and pine forests. Winters in forest habitats of Amazonian Peru and Brazil.

Length **6in (15cm)**	Wingspan **9in (23cm)**	Weight **⁷⁄₁₆–¹¹⁄₁₆oz (13–20g)**
Social **Solitary**	Lifespan **Up to 4 years**	Status **Secure (p)**

DATE SEEN	WHERE	NOTES

Order **Passeriformes**	Family **Parulidae**	Species ***Oporornis philadelphia***

Mourning Warbler

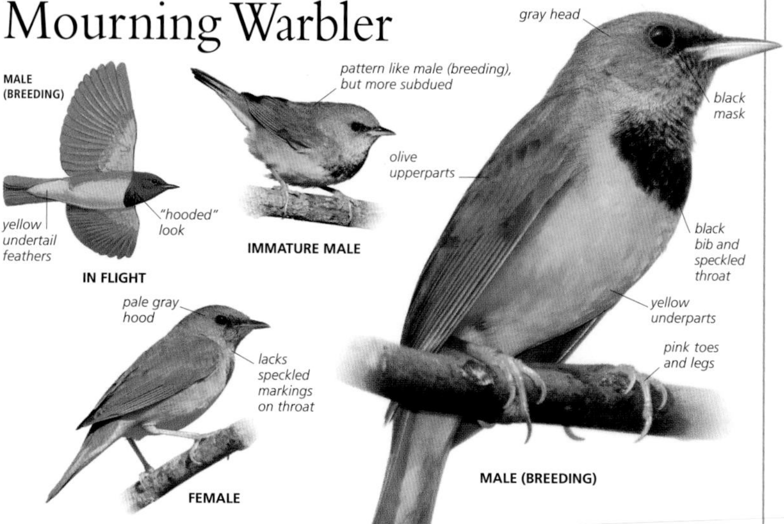
MALE (BREEDING)
yellow undertail feathers
"hooded" look
IN FLIGHT
pattern like male (breeding), but more subdued
olive upperparts
IMMATURE MALE
pale gray hood
lacks speckled markings on throat
FEMALE
gray head
black mask
black bib and speckled throat
yellow underparts
pink toes and legs
MALE (BREEDING)

The pleasant song of the Mourning Warbler is often used in commercials and movies as a background sound of idyllic suburban settings. It is doubtful, however, that you would find this gray-headed, black-throated warbler in a backyard, as it prefers dense, herbaceous tangles—both for breeding and during migration. These birds are late spring migrants and the leaves are fully out when they arrive in the eastern US, making it difficult to see them. The easiest way to see a Mourning Warbler is to track a male by its song.

VOICE Call a flat *tchik*; flight call a high, thin, clear *svit*; song a very burry series of paired notes with low-pitched ending: *churrr-ee churrr-ee churrr-ee churr-ee churrr-ee-oh.*

NESTING Well-concealed cup of leaves, lined with grass, on or near ground in dense tangle; 2–5 eggs; 1 brood; June–August.

FEEDING Mainly gleans insects and spiders in low foliage; eats some plant material in winter.

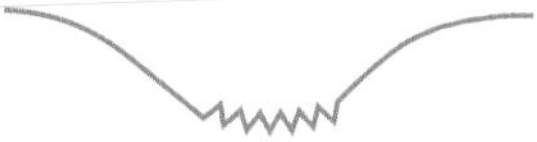

FLIGHT: fast, slightly undulating, and direct with rapid wing beats.

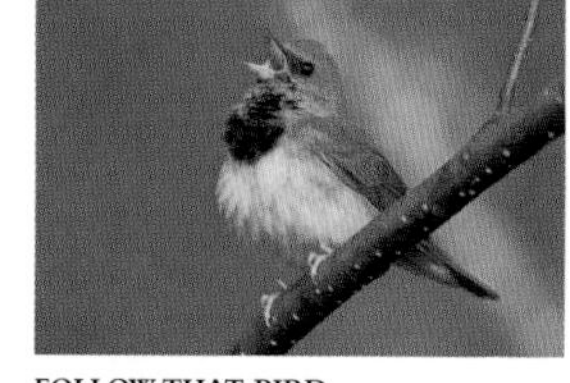

FOLLOW THAT BIRD
Tracking down a singing male is the easiest way to find this skulking species.

SIMILAR SPECIES
MACGILLIVRAY'S WARBLER ♀
see p.367
incomplete eye-ring
longer tail
COMMON YELLOWTHROAT ♀
see p.368
smaller, black bill
longer tail

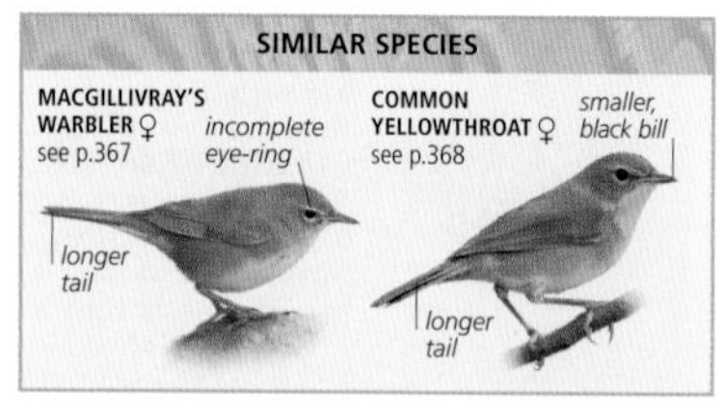

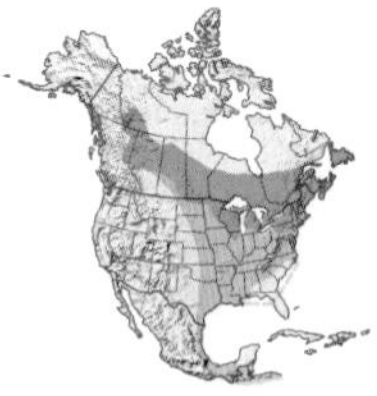

OCCURRENCE
Breeds in dense thickets of disturbed woodlands from the Yukon and British Columbia, east to Québec and Newfoundland, south to the Great Lakes, New England, New York, and the Appalachians. Winters in dense thickets in Central and South America.

Length **5in (13cm)**	Wingspan **7.5in (19cm)**	Weight **3/8–7/16oz (10–13g)**
Social **Solitary**	Lifespan **Up to 8 years**	Status **Secure**

DATE SEEN	WHERE	NOTES

Order **Passeriformes**	Family **Parulidae**	Species ***Oporornis tolmiei***

MacGillivray's Warbler

MALE

olive upperparts

grayish head

incomplete, white eye-ring

FEMALE

pale gray throat

olive upperparts

IN FLIGHT

yellow undertail feathers

incomplete eye-ring

black patch between eye and bill

gray head

irregular, black bib

MALE

yellow underparts

pinkish legs and toes

FLIGHT: fast, slightly undulating, and direct with rapid wing beats.

This western counterpart to the Mourning Warbler is distinguished from it by the incomplete white eye-ring. Ornithologists have suggested that the English name of this species should be "Tolmie's Warbler," as it was described and given its Latin name, *tolmiei*, in April 1839, to honor the Scottish-born physician W. F. Tolmie. But a month later, John James Audubon, apparently unaware of the name *tolmiei*, named the same species *macgillivrayi*, to honor the naturalist William MacGillivray. This problem was easily solved, as the rule of priority establishes the earliest scientific name as the valid one, so the name *tolmiei* was retained. However, the English name, MacGillivray, has also stuck.

VOICE Call a sharp *tssik*; flight call a high, thin, clear *svit*; song a loud, staccato, rolling series; ends lower or higher than rest of song.

NESTING Cup of plant material just off the ground in deciduous shrubs and thickets; 3–5 eggs; 1 brood; May–August.

FEEDING Gleans beetles, flies, bees, caterpillars from low foliage.

FAIRLY EASY TO FIND
This species is easy to spot, often popping up onto a branch in response to some disturbance.

SIMILAR SPECIES

MOURNING WARBLER ♀ see p.366

no bold eye markings

shorter tail

COMMON YELLOWTHROAT ♀ see p.368

smaller, black bill

longer tail

OCCURRENCE
Breeds in thickets within mixed and coniferous forests, often along streams from southeast Alaska and British Columbia south to California and Baja California, and across the western states. Winters in varied habitats with sufficient thickets in Mexico and in Central America.

Length **5in (13cm)**	Wingspan **7.5in (19cm)**	Weight **5/16–7/16oz (9–12g)**
Social **Solitary**	Lifespan **Up to 4 years**	Status **Secure**

DATE SEEN	WHERE	NOTES

Order **Passeriformes**	Family **Parulidae**	Species ***Geothlypis trichas***

Common Yellowthroat

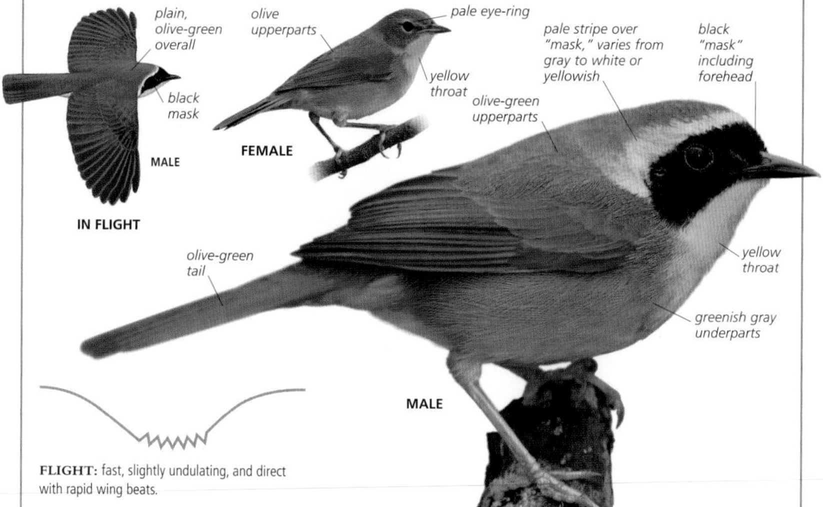

plain, olive-green overall

black mask

MALE

IN FLIGHT

olive upperparts

pale eye-ring

yellow throat

FEMALE

pale stripe over "mask," varies from gray to white or yellowish

black "mask" including forehead

olive-green upperparts

olive-green tail

yellow throat

greenish gray underparts

MALE

FLIGHT: fast, slightly undulating, and direct with rapid wing beats.

This common and easy-to-see warbler is noticeable partly because of its loud, simple song. This species varies in voice and plumage across its range and 14 subspecies have been described. In the western US, the birds have yellower underparts, brighter white head stripes, and louder, simpler songs than eastern birds. The male often flies upwards rapidly, delivering a more complex version of its otherwise simple song.

VOICE Call a harsh, buzzy *tchak*, repeated into chatter when agitated; flight call a low, flat, buzzy *dzzzit*; song a variable but distinctive series of rich (often three-note) phrases: *WITCH-uh-tee WITCH-uh-tee WITCH-uh-tee WHICH*; more complex flight song.

NESTING Concealed, bulky cup of grasses just above ground or water; 3–5 eggs; 1 brood; May–August.

FEEDING Eats insects and spiders in low vegetation; also seeds.

UNFORGETTABLE CALL
The song of the male Common Yellowthroat is an extremely helpful aid in its identification.

SIMILAR SPECIES

KENTUCKY WARBLER ♂ much larger

yellow eyebrow

bright yellow belly

shorter tail

MOURNING WARBLER ♀ see p.366

gray head

pink-based bill

bright yellow on belly

OCCURRENCE
Found south of the tundra, from Alaska and the Yukon to Québec and Newfoundland, and south to California, Texas, and to southeastern US. Habitats dense herbaceous understory, from marshes and grasslands to pine forest and hedgerows. Winters from Mexico to Panama and the Antilles.

Length **5in (13cm)**	Wingspan **6¾in (17cm)**	Weight **29oz (825g)**
Social **Migrant/Winter flocks**	Lifespan **Up to 11 years**	Status **Secure**

DATE SEEN	WHERE	NOTES

Order **Passeriformes**	Family **Parulidae**	Species ***Wilsonia pusilla***

Wilson's Warbler

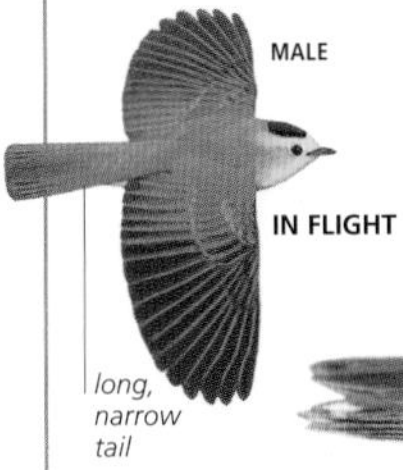

MALE

IN FLIGHT

long, narrow tail

FEMALE

olive or blackish crown

yellow eyebrow and chin

olive upperparts

black cap

large black eye

yellow brightest on face

MALE

FLIGHT: fast, slightly undulating, and direct with rapid wing beats.

The tiny Wilson's Warbler is perhaps the most common spring migrant of all the wood-warblers across many areas of the western US and Canada. In the East, however, it is much scarcer in spring. Wilson's Warblers have a wide range of habitats, yet their numbers are declining, especially in the West, as its riverine breeding habitats are gradually being destroyed by development. This species and the entire genus are named after the renowned early 19th-century ornithologist, Alexander Wilson.

VOICE Call a rich *chimp* or *champ;* flight call a sharp, liquid *tsik;* song a variable, chattering trill, often increases in speed *che che che che chi-chi-chi-chit.*
NESTING Cup of leaves and grass placed on or near ground in mosses or grass, higher along Pacific coast; 4–6 eggs; 1 brood; April–June.
FEEDING Captures insects in foliage, leaf litter, or during flight; also takes berries and honeydew.

BRIGHT WESTERN BIRD
In its western range, male Wilson's Warblers have a glowing yellow-orange face; eastern birds are duller.

EASY IDENTIFICATION
The black cap and yellow face of the otherwise olive-colored Wilson's Warbler are good field marks.

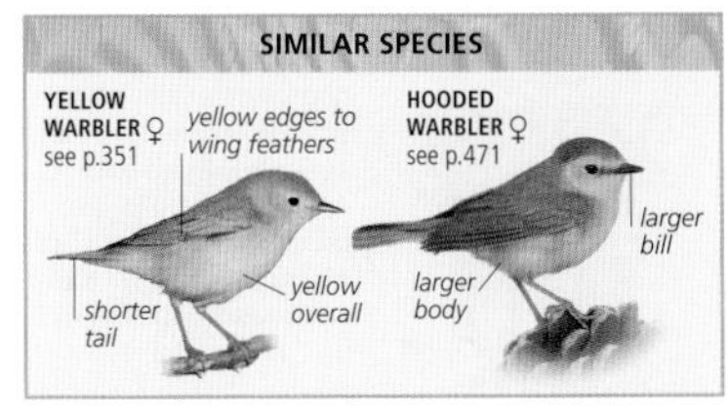

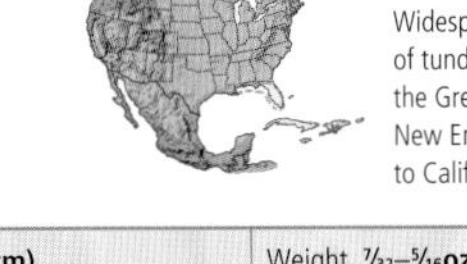

OCCURRENCE
Breeds in wet shrubby thickets with no canopy, often along streams and lakes; Pacific slope birds use more varied habitats, including moist forests. Widespread in forests south of tundra, from Newfoundland, the Great Lakes, and northern New England; British Columbia to California and New Mexico.

Length **4¾in (12cm)**	Wingspan **7in (17.5cm)**	Weight **7/32–5/16oz (6–9g)**
Social **Flocks**	Lifespan **Up to 6 years**	Status **Declining**

DATE SEEN	WHERE	NOTES

Order **Passeriformes**	Family **Parulidae**	Species ***Wilsonia canadensis***

Canada Warbler

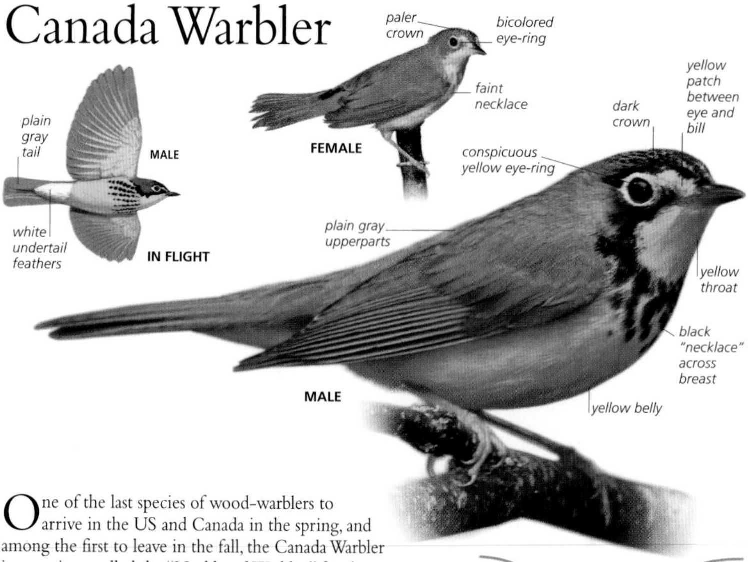
paler crown
bicolored eye-ring
faint necklace
FEMALE
plain gray tail
MALE
white undertail feathers
IN FLIGHT
yellow patch between eye and bill
dark crown
conspicuous yellow eye-ring
plain gray upperparts
yellow throat
black "necklace" across breast
MALE
yellow belly

One of the last species of wood-warblers to arrive in the US and Canada in the spring, and among the first to leave in the fall, the Canada Warbler is sometimes called the "Necklaced Warbler," for the conspicuous black markings on its chest. This uncommon bird is sadly declining, probably because of the maturation and draining of its preferred breeding habitat, consisting of old mixed hardwood forests with moist undergrowth.

VOICE Call a thick *tchip;* flight call a variable, clear *plip;* song a haphazard jumble of sweet notes, often beginning with or interspersed with *tchip,* followed by a pause.

NESTING Concealed cup of leaves, in moss or grass, on or near ground; 4–5 eggs; 1 brood; May–June.

FEEDING Gleans at mid-levels for many species of insects; also flycatches and forages on ground.

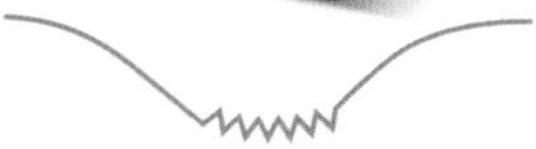

FLIGHT: fast, slightly undulating, and direct with rapid wing beats.

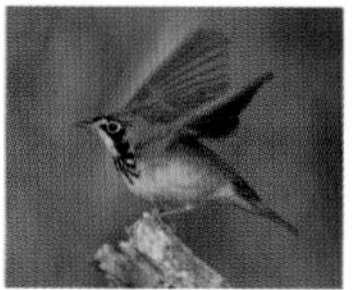

TAKING FLIGHT
This species often waits for prey to fly by, before launching into flight to pursue it.

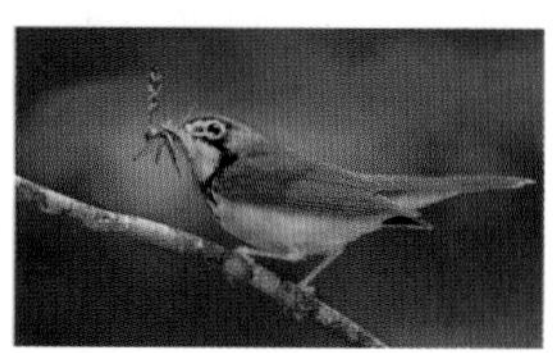

FAMILIAR MEAL
Flying insects, including crane flies, make up the bulk of the Canada Warbler's diet.

SIMILAR SPECIES

MAGNOLIA WARBLER ♀
see p.353
white eyebrow
streaked flanks
KIRTLAND'S WARBLER ♂
streaked mantle and flanks

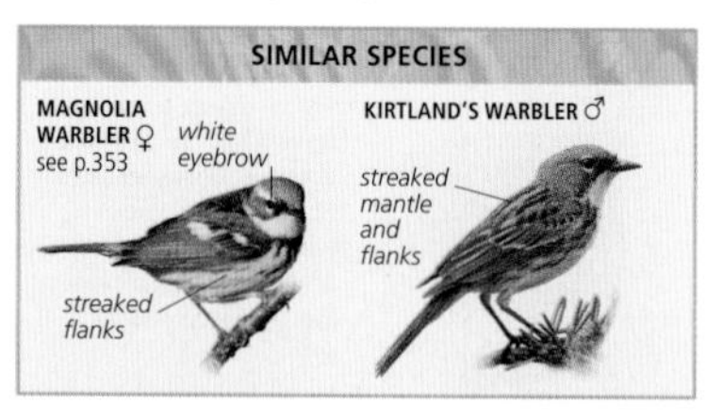

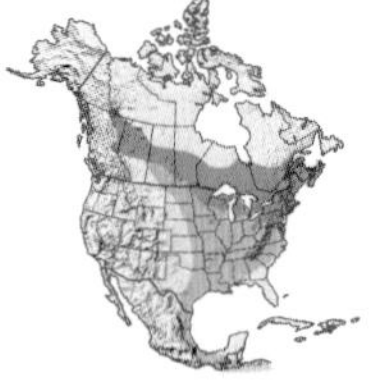

OCCURRENCE
Breeds in moist deciduous, mixed, and coniferous forests with well-developed understory, especially swampy woods; migrants use well-vegetated habitats; winters in dense, wet thickets and a variety of tropical woodlands in South America.

Length **5in (13cm)**	Wingspan **8in (20cm)**	Weight **9/32–1/2oz (8–15g)**
Social **Flocks**	Lifespan **Up to 8 years**	Status **Declining**

DATE SEEN	WHERE	NOTES

Order **Passeriformes**	Family **Parulidae**	Species ***Icteria virens***

Yellow-breasted Chat

FLIGHT: fast and direct with rapid wing beats and drooping tail; tends to stay under cover.

This unique species has puzzled ornithologists and scientists for a long time, and still does, as molecular (DNA) studies have given conflicting results about whether it actually belongs to the wood-warbler family or not. Sometimes it skulks in dense vegetation and is difficult to spot; at other times it sits in full view, singing atop small trees. One of its behavioral quirks is to suddenly fly upward, then glide slowly back down to earth, while singing.

VOICE Seldom-heard calls include a low, soft *tuk* and nasal, downslurred *tiyew*; song is a mixture of monosyllabic grunts, clucks, and whistles in repeated, decelerating series, with pauses between different series; sometimes sings at night; also mimics other birds.

NESTING Concealed and bulky structure of dead plant matter, in thicket near eye-level; 3–5 eggs; 1–2 broods; May–August.

FEEDING Eats insects; also fruit and berries.

CLUCKS AND WHISTLES This bird has a remarkably varied vocal repertoire, including loud clucks and whistles.

OCCURRENCE Breeds in dense shrubby areas, including forest edges; western birds mostly restricted to thickets along riverine corridors; migrants found in a variety of habitats. Winters in scrubby habitats from Mexico to Panama.

SIMILAR SPECIES

YELLOW-THROATED VIREO see p.450
yellow "spectacles"

COMMON YELLOWTHROAT ♂ see p.368
shorter tail
black mask

Length **7½in (19cm)**	Wingspan **9½in (24cm)**	Weight **11/16–1 1/16oz (20–30g)**
Social **Solitary**	Lifespan **Up to 9 years**	Status **Declining**

DATE SEEN	WHERE	NOTES

ORIOLES & BLACKBIRDS

THE ICTERIDS EXEMPLIFY the wonderful diversity that exists among birds. Most icterids are common and widespread, occurring from coast to coast. They are present in nearly every habitat in North America, from the arid Southwest and Florida to the boreal forest zone in the north, though not in the tundra. The species reveal a tremendous variety in color, nesting, and social behavior—from solitary orioles to vast colonies of comparatively drab blackbirds. One group of icterids, the cowbirds, are obligatory brood parasites. They make no nest, but lay their eggs in the nests of other birds, mostly small songbirds.

ORIOLES

Orioles are common seasonal migrants to North America. They are generally recognized by their contrasting black and orange plumage, although some species tend more toward yellow or chestnut shades. Orioles construct intricate hanging nests which display an impressive combination of engineering and weaving. Most oriole species have a loud and melodious song and show tolerance of humans, a combination that makes them popular throughout their range. Bullock's Oriole is the only oriole species that is widespread and common in the West; other western species are restricted to the Southwest or southern Texas. The migratory habits of orioles are mixed: Bullock's Oriole migrates south in the fall, while Audubon's and Altamira's Orioles are sedentary in southern Texas.

COWBIRDS

Cowbirds are strictly parasitic birds, and have been known to lay their eggs in the nests of nearly 300 different bird species in North and South America. The males of all three North American cowbird species are readily identified by their thick bills and dark, iridescent plumage. The females and immatures are drab by comparison.

SUBTLE BRILLIANCE
Although its plumage is dark, the Common Grackle displays a beautiful iridescence.

BLACKBIRDS & GRACKLES

This group of birds is largely covered with dark feathers, and their long, pointed bills and tails give them a streamlined appearance. Not as brilliantly colored as some of the other icterids, these are among the most numerous birds on the continent. After the breeding season they gather in huge flocks, and form an impressive sight.

MEADOWLARKS

Meadowlarks occur in both South and North America. The North American species have yellow breasts, but the South American species sport bright red breasts. Only the Western Meadowlark breeds commonly in the West. It is difficult to tell apart from its eastern counterpart, except by its song, yellow chest with a black bib, and a sweet singing voice.

BIG VOICE
A Meadowlark's melodious voice is a defining feature in many rural landscapes.

NECTAR LOVER
The magnificently colored Baltimore Oriole inserts its bill into the base of a flower, taking the nectar, but playing no part in pollination. This species is rare in the West.

Order **Passeriformes**	Family **Icteridae**	Species ***Icterus parisorum***

Scott's Oriole

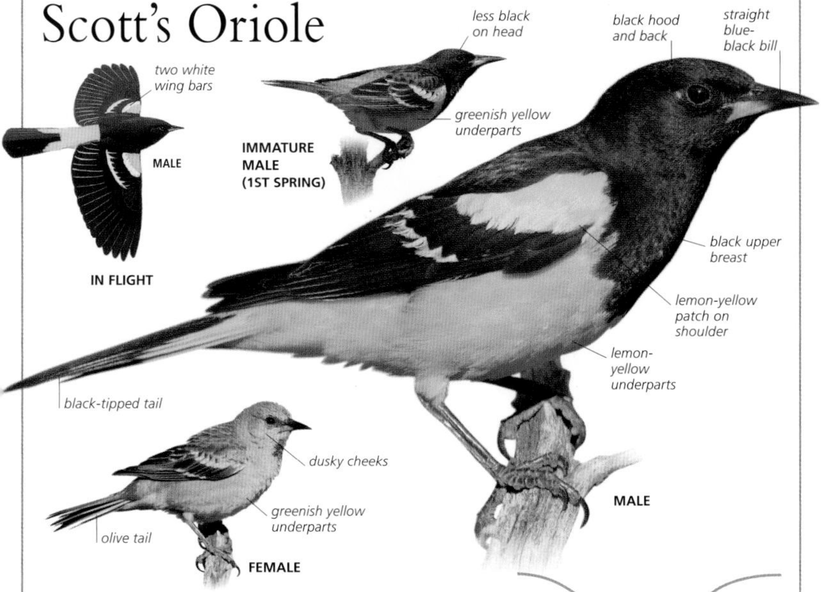

two white wing bars
MALE
IN FLIGHT
less black on head
greenish yellow underparts
IMMATURE MALE (1ST SPRING)
black hood and back
straight blue-black bill
black upper breast
lemon-yellow patch on shoulder
lemon-yellow underparts
black-tipped tail
MALE
dusky cheeks
greenish yellow underparts
olive tail
FEMALE

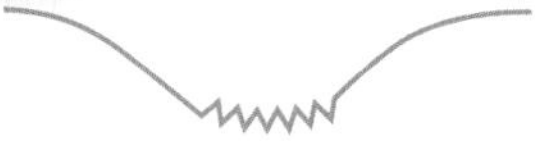

FLIGHT: quick wing beats; more bouncing between flapping than other orioles.

Scott's Oriole's Latin species name, parisorum, was coined by Prince Charles Bonaparte in 1838 for the Paris brothers, two French natural history specimen dealers. The bird's English name honors General Winfield Scott, commander-in-chief of the American troops in the Mexican War. This Oriole's bright yellow plumage is unusual among North American orioles, most of which are varying degrees of orange. It lives in semi-arid and rocky slopes, a fact that is largely responsible for its colloquial names of "Desert" or "Mountain" Oriole.

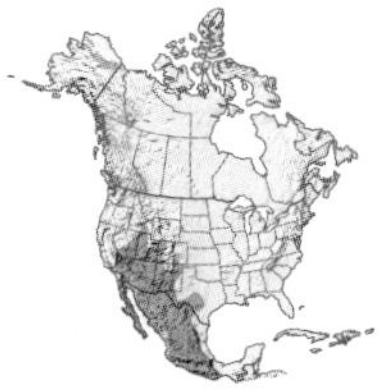

VOICE Call a sharp *chek*; song a musical series of loud whistles *tew-tew-treew*.
NESTING Shallow cup woven from thin plant strips, often yucca, hung from leaves or branches; 3–5 eggs; 1–2 broods; March–July.
FEEDING Eats insects, adults and larvae, such as flies, wasps, and beetles; feeds on nectar and fruit where available; visits feeders.

SIMILAR SPECIES

ORCHARD ORIOLE
see p.463
smaller, darker head
chestnut-colored belly
AUDUBON'S ORIOLE
greenish yellow back
black hood
all-black tail

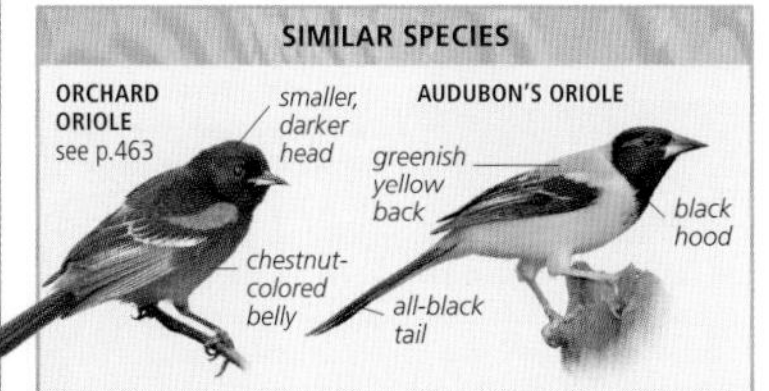

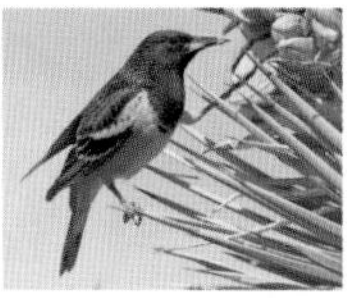

YUCCA LOVER
Found in all kinds of arid scrubland—yuccas are a favorite of Scott's Orioles.

OCCURRENCE
Breeds in mid-elevation, semi-arid open scrub on level ground or slopes with oak scrub, pinyon pine, and yucca. Winters in pine-oak scrub valleys of central Mexico. Individuals wander widely and have been reported as far away from their usual habitat as New York City.

Length **8–9in (20–23cm)**	Wingspan **11–13in (28–33cm)**	Weight **1⁷⁄₁₆oz (40g)**
Social **Pairs/Family groups**	Lifespan **Up to 6 years**	Status **Secure**

DATE SEEN	WHERE	NOTES

Order **Passeriformes**	Family **Icteridae**	Species ***Icterus bullockii***

Bullock's Oriole

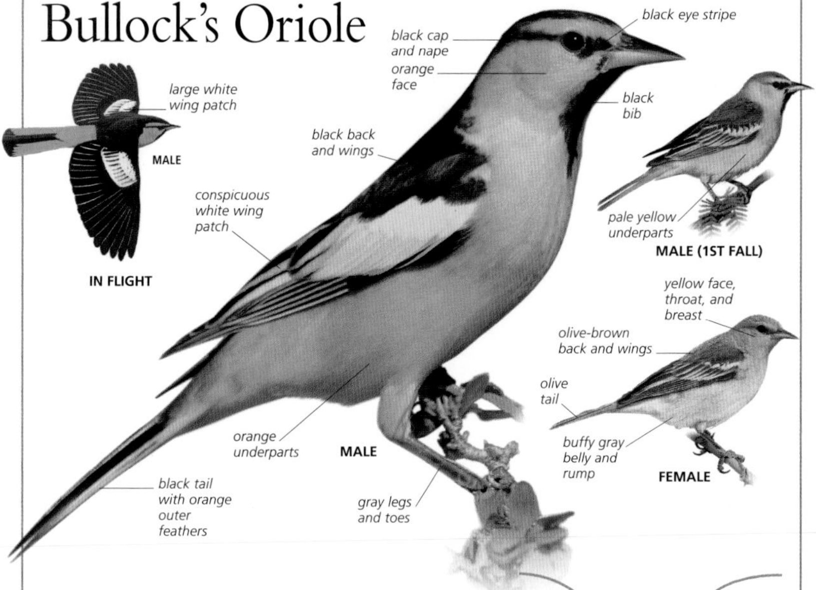

Bullock's Oriole is the western counterpart of the Baltimore in both behavior and habitat. The two were considered to belong to a single species, the Northern Oriole (*I. galbula*), because they interbreed where they overlap in the Great Plains. Recent studies, however, suggest that they are separate species. Unlike many other orioles, Bullock's is more resistant to brood parasites and removes cowbird eggs from its nest.

VOICE Varied string of one- and two-part notes often mumbled or slurred at the end; similar to, but less melodious, than the Baltimore Oriole's song.

NESTING Hanging basket of woven plant strips located at the tips of branches; 4–5 eggs; 1 brood; March–June.

FEEDING Forages for insects, in particular grasshoppers and caterpillars, but also ants, beetles, and spiders; nectar and fruit when available.

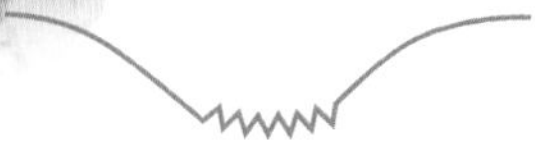

FLIGHT: full, powerful wing beats, resulting in a "heavier" flight aspect than similar species.

OCCURRENCE
Breeds commonly in riverine woodlands with willows and cottonwoods; also mixed hardwood forests, mesquite woodland, and groves of fruit trees. After breeding, Bullock's Orioles migrate southward and spend the winter from Mexico to Nicaragua.

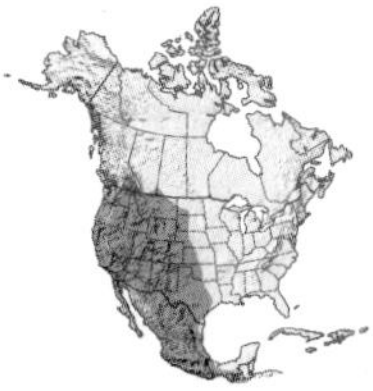

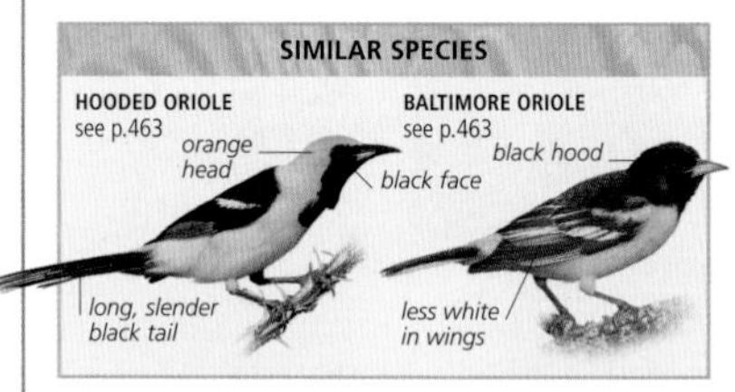

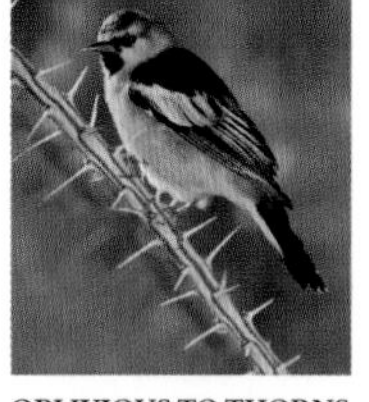

OBLIVIOUS TO THORNS
This male Bullock's Oriole perches on a branch with long thorns, but it is not perturbed.

SIMILAR SPECIES

HOODED ORIOLE
see p.463

BALTIMORE ORIOLE
see p.463

Length **6½–7½in (16–19cm)**	Wingspan **10–12in (25–30cm)**	Weight **$1\frac{1}{16}$–$1\frac{9}{16}$oz (30–45g)**
Social **Pairs/Flocks**	Lifespan **Up to 8 years**	Status **Secure**

DATE SEEN	WHERE	NOTES

Order **Passeriformes**	Family **Icteridae**	Species ***Molothrus ater***

Brown-headed Cowbird

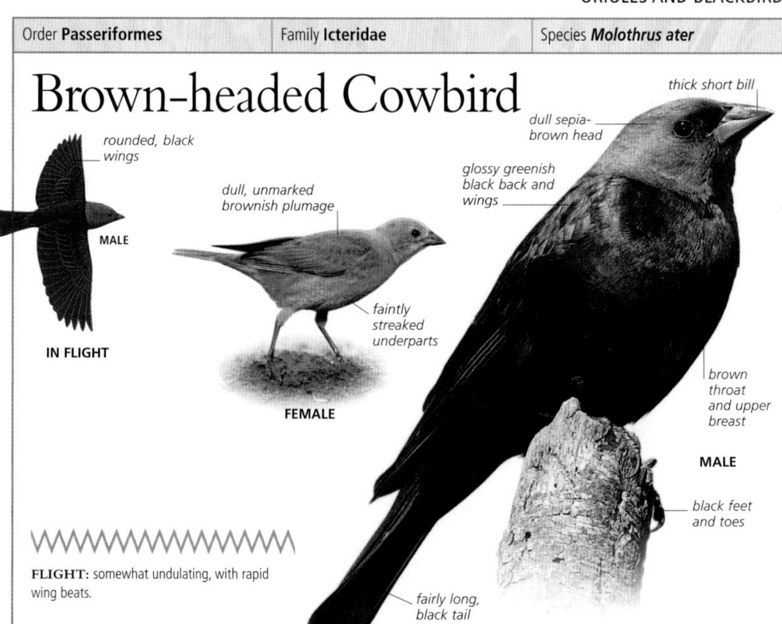

FLIGHT: somewhat undulating, with rapid wing beats.

North America's most common brood parasite, the Brown-headed Cowbird was once a bird of the Great Plains, following the vast herds of bison to feed on insects kicked up by their hooves. Now, most likely the result of forest clearance and suburban development, it is found continent-wide and north to the Yukon and Canada. It has become a serious threat to the breeding success of North American songbirds. It lays its eggs in the nests of more than 220 different species, and its young are raised to fledglings by more than 140 species, including the highly endangered Kirtland's Warbler.

VOICE High-pitched, squeaky whistles and bubbling notes, *dub-dub-come-tzeee*; also various clucks and *cheks*.

NESTING No nest, lays eggs in nests of other species; a female may lay an astounding 25–55 (or more) eggs per season; April–August.

FEEDING Primarily eats grass seeds and cereal grains, but also insects when available, especially grasshoppers and beetles.

AT A FEEDER
A female Brown-headed Cowbird enjoys a snack of seeds at a suburban feeder.

SIMILAR SPECIES

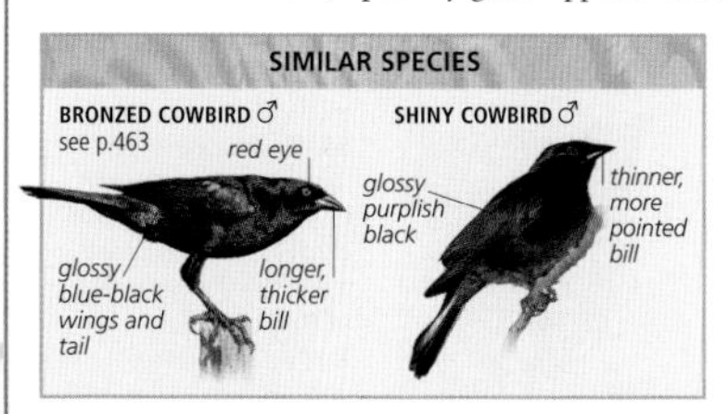

OCCURRENCE
Favors habitats modified by human activity, such as open wooded patches, low grass fields, fruit orchards, agricultural pastures with livestock, suburban gardens and areas. Widespread across North America in both Canada and the US. Western birds migrate south to Mexico.

Length **6–8in (15–20cm)**	Wingspan **11–13in (28–33cm)**	Weight **1 7/16–1 3/4oz (40–50g)**
Social **Large flocks**	Lifespan **Up to 16 years**	Status **Secure**

DATE SEEN	WHERE	NOTES

Order **Passeriformes**	Family **Icteridae**	Species ***Agelaius phoeniceus***

Red-winged Blackbird

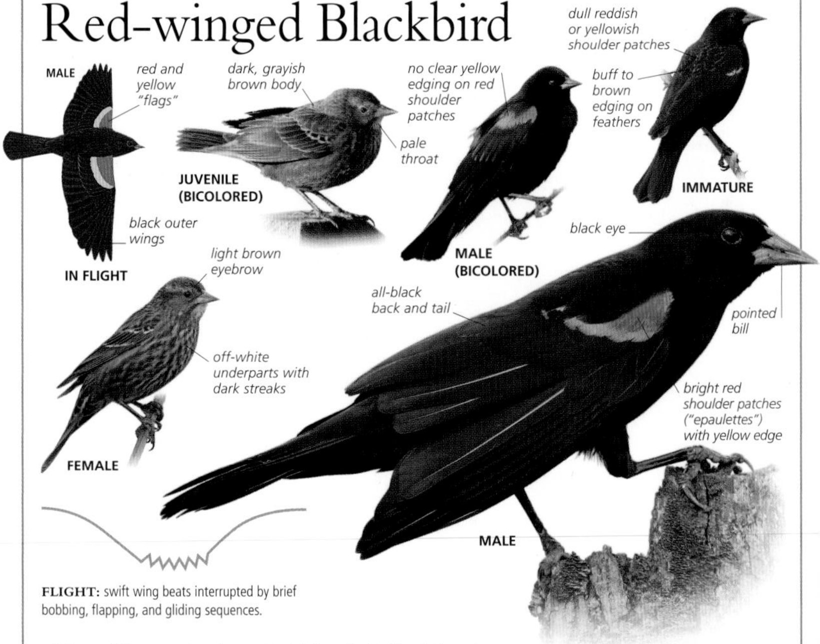

MALE
red and yellow "flags"
black outer wings
IN FLIGHT
dark, grayish brown body
pale throat
JUVENILE (BICOLORED)
no clear yellow edging on red shoulder patches
MALE (BICOLORED)
dull reddish or yellowish shoulder patches
buff to brown edging on feathers
IMMATURE
light brown eyebrow
off-white underparts with dark streaks
FEMALE
all-black back and tail
black eye
pointed bill
bright red shoulder patches ("epaulettes") with yellow edge
MALE

FLIGHT: swift wing beats interrupted by brief bobbing, flapping, and gliding sequences.

One of the most abundant native bird species in North America, the Red-winged Blackbird is also one of the most conspicuous in wetland habitats. The sight and sound of males singing from the tops of cattails is a sure sign that spring is near. This adaptable species migrates and roosts in flocks that may number in the millions. There are 22 subspecies, one of the most distinctive being the "Bicolored" Blackbird (*A. p. gubernator*) from Mexico.

VOICE Various brusk *chek*, *chit*, or *chet* calls; male song a *kronk-a-rhee* with a characteristic nasal, rolling and metallic "undulating" ending.

NESTING Cup of grasses and mud woven into dense standing reeds or cattails; 3–4 eggs; 1–2 broods; March–June.

FEEDING Forages for seeds and grains; largely insects when breeding.

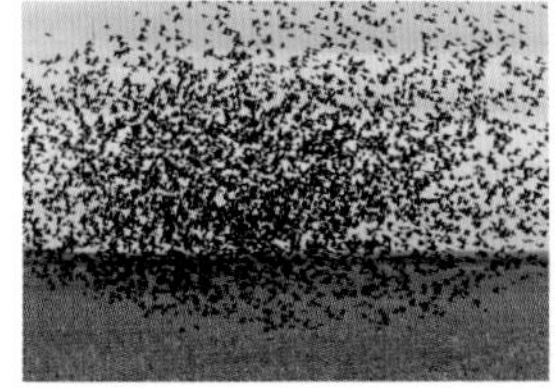

DENSE FLOCKS
The huge flocks of Red-winged Blackbirds seen in the fall and during migration are an amazing sight.

SIMILAR SPECIES

TRICOLORED BLACKBIRD ♂ see p.464

RUSTY BLACKBIRD see p.377

all-black body
white-edged red shoulder patches
longer tail
pale eye

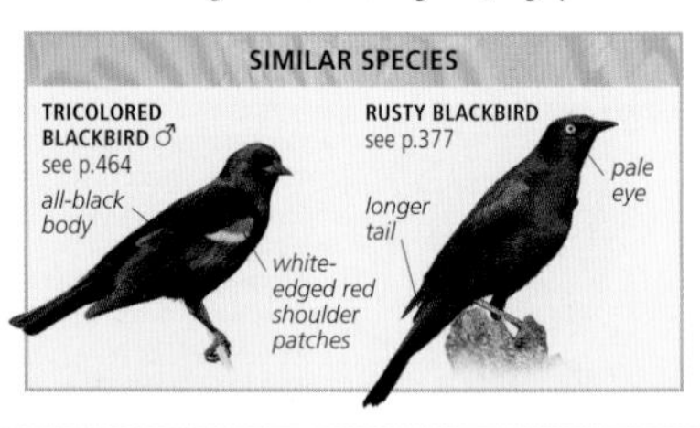

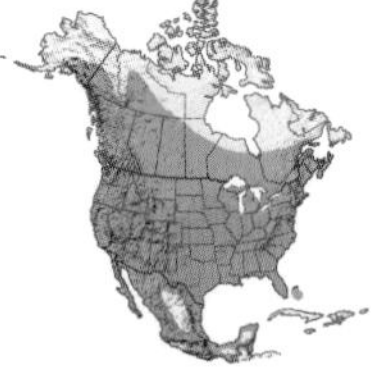

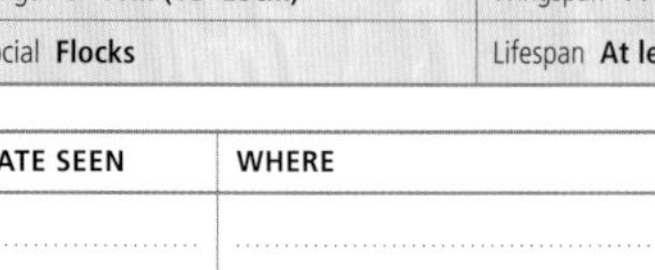

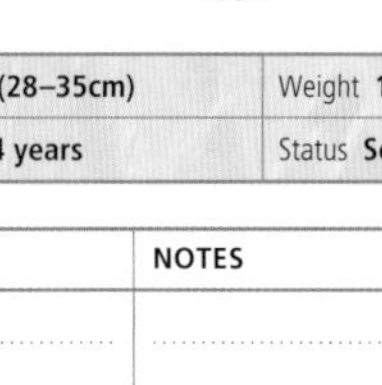

OCCURRENCE
Widespread across Canada and the US from Alaska to the Maritimes, and south to Mexico, Central America, and the Bahamas. Lives in wetlands, especially freshwater marshes with cattails, and also saltwater; wet meadows with tall grass and open woodlands with reeds. Migrates south in winter.

Length **7–10in (18–25cm)**	Wingspan **11–14in (28–35cm)**	Weight **1$^{9}/_{16}$–2½oz (45–70g)**
Social **Flocks**	Lifespan **At least 14 years**	Status **Secure**

DATE SEEN	WHERE	NOTES

Order **Passeriformes**	Family **Icteridae**	Species ***Euphagus carolinus***

Rusty Blackbird

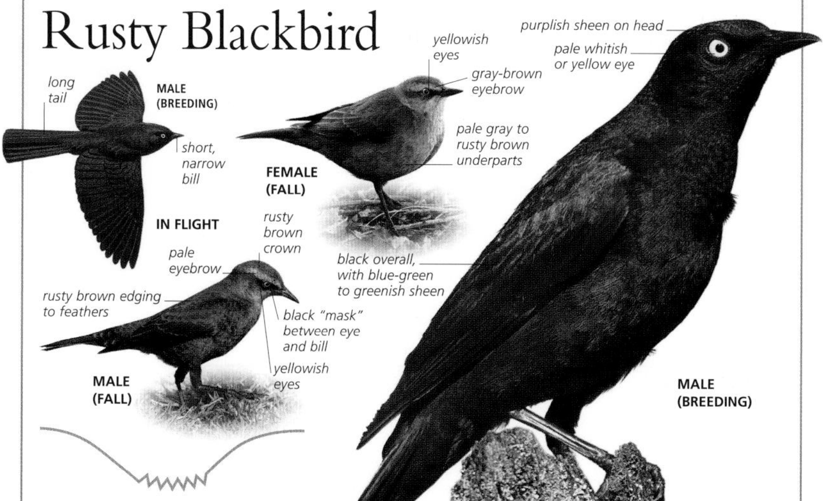

long tail
MALE (BREEDING)
short, narrow bill
IN FLIGHT
yellowish eyes
gray-brown eyebrow
pale gray to rusty brown underparts
FEMALE (FALL)
rusty brown crown
pale eyebrow
rusty brown edging to feathers
black "mask" between eye and bill
yellowish eyes
MALE (FALL)
purplish sheen on head
pale whitish or yellow eye
black overall, with blue-green to greenish sheen
MALE (BREEDING)

FLIGHT: strong, direct, with slight undulations between flapping and brief gliding.

The Rusty Blackbird is perhaps the least known of all North American blackbirds. This is mainly because it breeds in remote, inaccessible swampy areas, and is much less of a pest to agricultural operations than some of the other members of its family. Unlike most other blackbirds, the plumage on the male Rusty Blackbird changes to a dull, reddish brown during the fall—giving the species its common name. It is also during the fall migrations that this species is most easily observed, moving south in long flocks that often take several minutes to pass overhead.

VOICE Both sexes use *chuk* call during migration flights; male song a musical *too-ta-lee*.

NESTING Small bowl of branches and sticks, lined with wet plants and dry grass, usually near water; 3–5 eggs; 1 brood; May–July.

FEEDING Eats seasonally available insects, spiders, grains, seeds of trees, and fleshy fruits or berries.

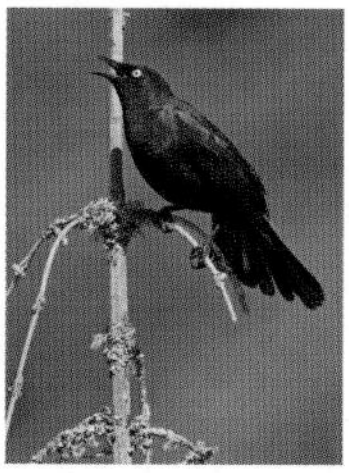

WIDE OPEN
Seldom seen, the male's courtship display includes gaping and tail-spreading.

SIMILAR SPECIES
BREWER'S BLACKBIRD
see p.378
purplish sheen on head
longer tail
COMMON GRACKLE
see p.379
bluish sheen on head
bill thicker at base
large tail
glossy bronze body

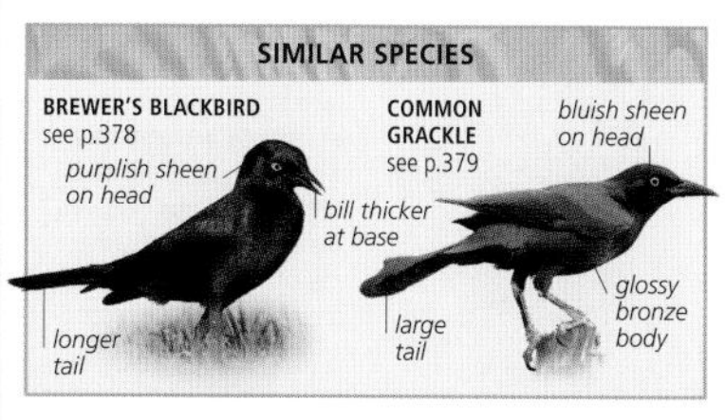

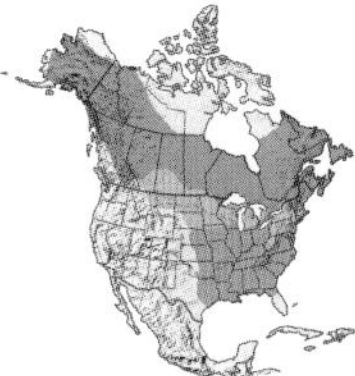

OCCURRENCE
Breeds in moist to wet forests up to the timberline in the far north from Alaska to NE Canada; but barely in the continental US (farther north than any other species of North American blackbird); winters in eastern US, in several kinds of swampy forests.

Length **8–10in (20–25cm)**	Wingspan **12–15in (30–38cm)**	Weight **1⁹⁄₁₆–2⁷⁄₈oz (45–80g)**
Social **Pairs/Winter flocks**	Lifespan **At least 9 years**	Status **Secure**

DATE SEEN	WHERE	NOTES

Order **Passeriformes**	Family **Icteridae**	Species ***Euphagus cyanocephalus***

Brewer's Blackbird

FLIGHT: several wing beats followed by short glides with shallow rise and fall pattern.

The Brewer's Blackbird, unlike the swamp-loving Rusty Blackbird, seems to prefer areas disturbed by humans to natural ones throughout much of its range. It is likely that the relatively recent eastward range expansion of Brewer's Blackbird has been aided by changes in land practices. Interestingly, when the Brewer's Blackbird range overlaps with that of the Common Grackle, it wins out in rural areas, but loses out in urban areas. This species can be found feasting on waste grains left behind after the harvest.

VOICE Buzzy *tshrrep* song ascending in tone.

NESTING Bulky cup of dry grass, stem and twig framework lined with soft grasses and animal hair; 3–6 eggs; 1–2 broods; April–July.

FEEDING Forages on the ground for many species of insects during breeding season, also snails; seeds, grain, and occasional fruit in fall and winter.

BROWN-EYED BIRD
Brown eyes distinguish the female Brewer's from the yellow-eyed, female Rusty Blackbird.

SIMILAR SPECIES

RUSTY BLACKBIRD
see p.377
bill thinner at base
shorter tail

COMMON GRACKLE
see p.379
glossy bronze body
long, wedge-shaped tail

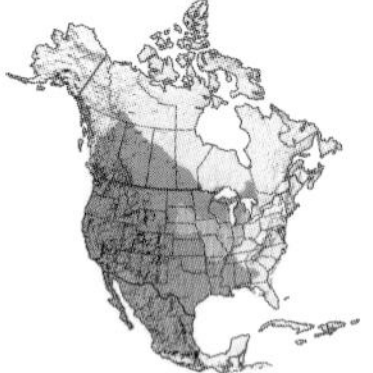

OCCURRENCE
Breeds and winters in open areas, readily adapting to, and preferring, disturbed areas and human developments, such as parks, gardens, clear-felled forests, and fallow fields edged with dense trees or shrubs.

Length **10–12in (25–30cm)**	Wingspan **13–16in (33–41cm)**	Weight **1¾–2½oz (50–70g)**
Social **Flocks/Colonies**	Lifespan **Up to 13 years**	Status **Secure**

DATE SEEN	WHERE	NOTES

Order **Passeriformes**	Family **Icteridae**	Species ***Quiscalus quiscula***

Common Grackle

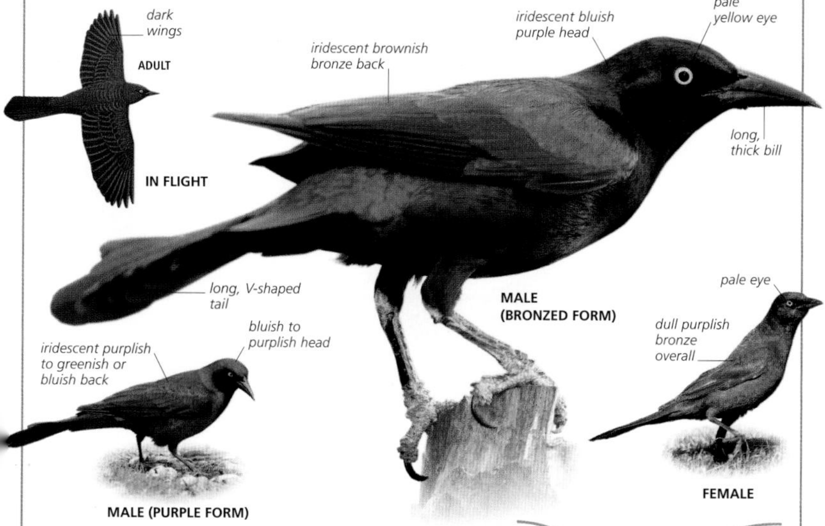
dark wings
ADULT
IN FLIGHT
iridescent brownish bronze back
iridescent bluish purple head
pale yellow eye
long, thick bill
long, V-shaped tail
MALE (BRONZED FORM)
bluish to purplish head
iridescent purplish to greenish or bluish back
MALE (PURPLE FORM)
pale eye
dull purplish bronze overall
FEMALE

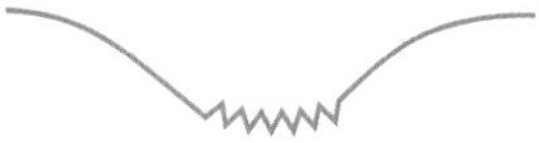

FLIGHT: straight, level, and direct without the up and down undulation of blackbird species.

This adaptable species has expanded its range rapidly in the recent past, thanks to human land clearing practices. The Common Grackle is so well suited to urban and suburban habitats that it successfully excludes other species from them. During migration and winter, Common Grackles form immense flocks, some of which may be made up of more than one million individuals. This tendency, combined with its preference for cultivated areas, has made this species an agricultural pest in some regions.

VOICE Call a low, harsh *chek*; loud song series of odd squeaks and whistles.

NESTING Small bowl in trees, with a frame of sticks filled with mud and grasses; 4–6 eggs; 1–2 broods; April–July.

FEEDING Eats beetles, flies, spiders, and worms, as well as small vertebrates; also seeds and grain, especially in nonbreeding season; an omnivore.

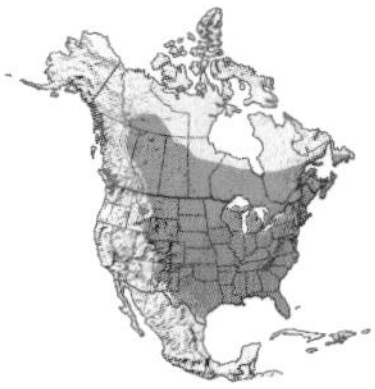

OCCURRENCE
The Common Grackle lives in a wide variety of open woodlands, suburban woodlots, city parks, gardens, and hedgerows. It is absent west of the Great Plains. Wintering range extends south to the Gulf Coast.

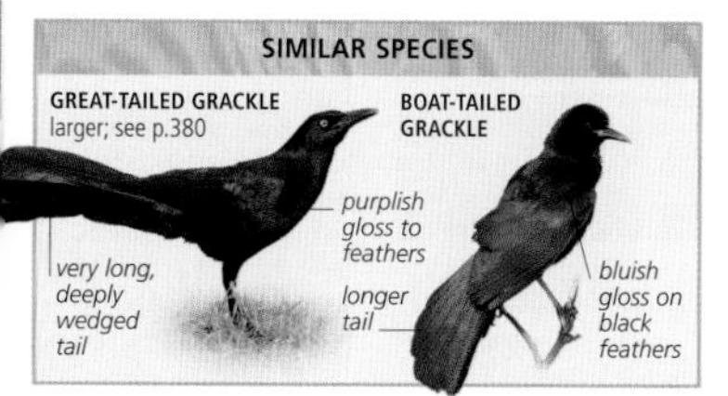

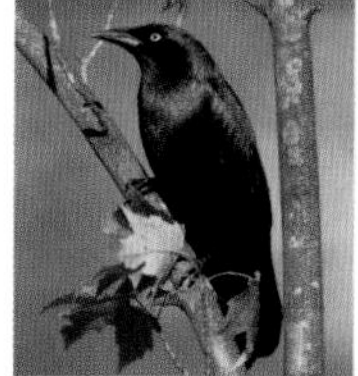

HIGHLY ADAPTABLE
This grackle is comfortable near human developments, resulting in the expansion of its range.

SIMILAR SPECIES

GREAT-TAILED GRACKLE
larger; see p.380
very long, deeply wedged tail
purplish gloss to feathers
BOAT-TAILED GRACKLE
longer tail
bluish gloss on black feathers

Length **11–13½in (28–34cm)**	Wingspan **15–18in (38–46cm)**	Weight **3⅛–4oz (90–125g)**
Social **Flocks**	Lifespan **Up to 20 years**	Status **Secure**

DATE SEEN	WHERE	NOTES

Order **Passeriformes**	Family **Icteridae**	Species ***Quiscalus mexicanus***

Great-tailed Grackle

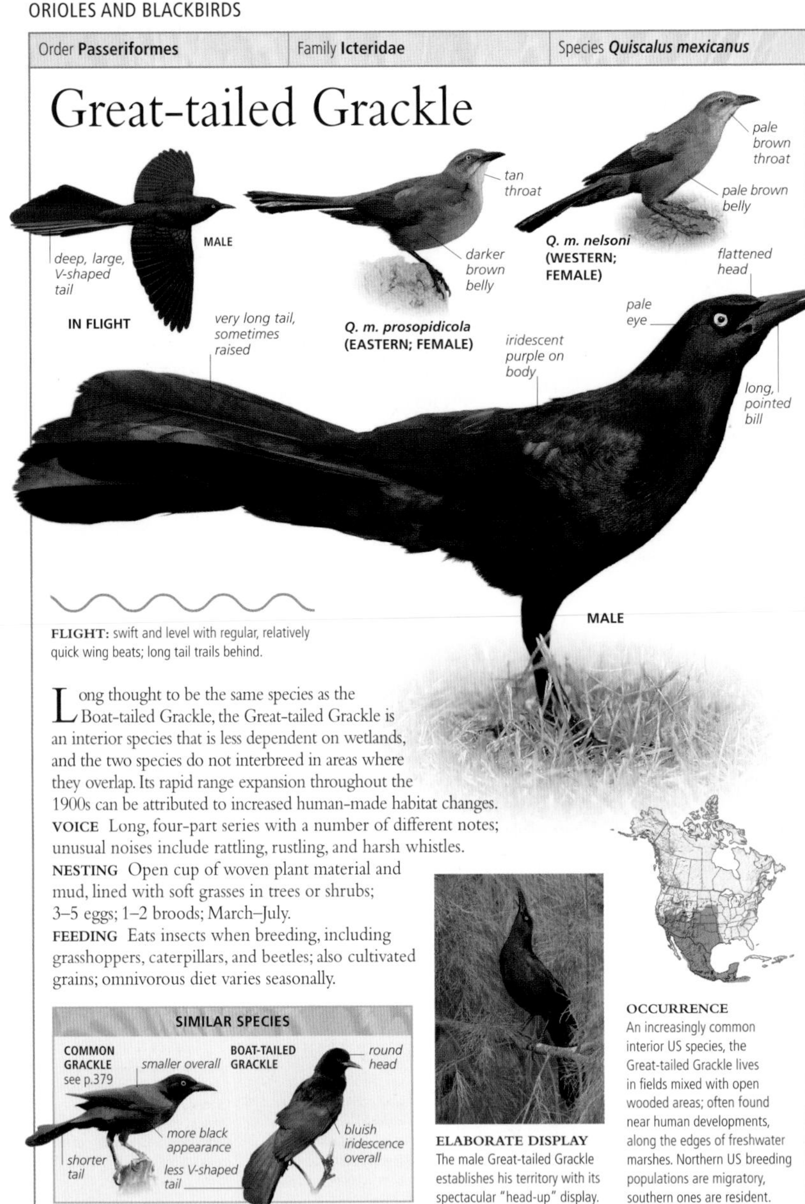

FLIGHT: swift and level with regular, relatively quick wing beats; long tail trails behind.

Long thought to be the same species as the Boat-tailed Grackle, the Great-tailed Grackle is an interior species that is less dependent on wetlands, and the two species do not interbreed in areas where they overlap. Its rapid range expansion throughout the 1900s can be attributed to increased human-made habitat changes.

VOICE Long, four-part series with a number of different notes; unusual noises include rattling, rustling, and harsh whistles.

NESTING Open cup of woven plant material and mud, lined with soft grasses in trees or shrubs; 3–5 eggs; 1–2 broods; March–July.

FEEDING Eats insects when breeding, including grasshoppers, caterpillars, and beetles; also cultivated grains; omnivorous diet varies seasonally.

SIMILAR SPECIES

COMMON GRACKLE see p.379 smaller overall; more black appearance; shorter tail; less V-shaped tail

BOAT-TAILED GRACKLE round head; bluish iridescence overall

ELABORATE DISPLAY
The male Great-tailed Grackle establishes his territory with its spectacular "head-up" display.

OCCURRENCE
An increasingly common interior US species, the Great-tailed Grackle lives in fields mixed with open wooded areas; often found near human developments, along the edges of freshwater marshes. Northern US breeding populations are migratory, southern ones are resident.

Length **13–19in (33–48cm)**	Wingspan **18–24in (46–61cm)**	Weight **4–10oz (125–275g)**
Social **Flocks**	Lifespan **Up to 13 years**	Status **Secure**

DATE SEEN	WHERE	NOTES

Order **Passeriformes**	Family **Icteridae**	Species ***Sturnella neglecta***

Western Meadowlark

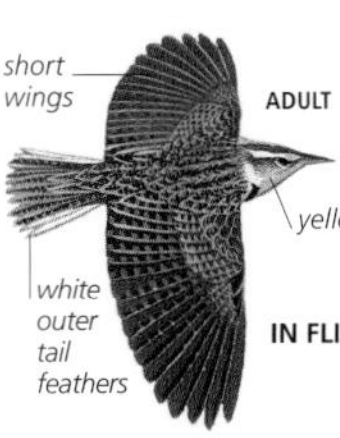

short wings
ADULT
yellow throat
white outer tail feathers
IN FLIGHT

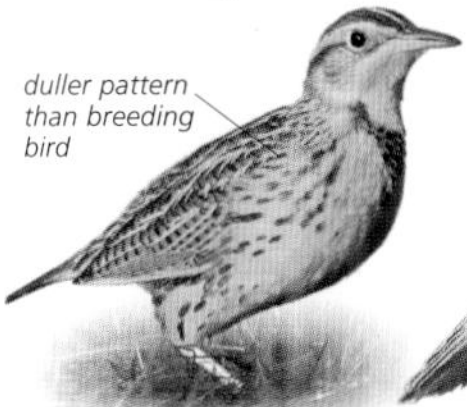

duller pattern than breeding bird
ADULT (NONBREEDING)

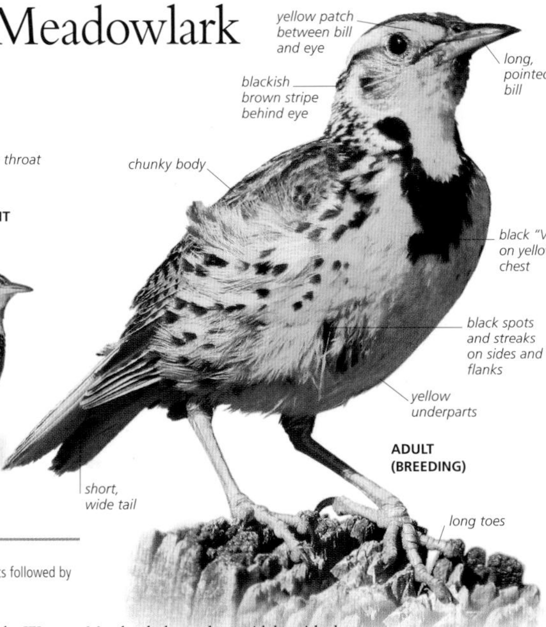

yellow patch between bill and eye
long, pointed bill
blackish brown stripe behind eye
chunky body
black "V" on yellow chest
black spots and streaks on sides and flanks
yellow underparts
ADULT (BREEDING)
short, wide tail
long toes

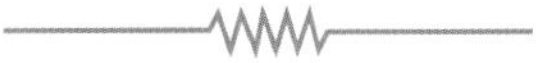

FLIGHT: several rapid wing beats followed by a short glide.

Although the range of the Western Meadowlark overlaps widely with that of its Eastern counterpart, hybrids between the two species are very rare and usually sterile. The large numbers of Western Meadowlarks in the western Great Plains, the Great Basin, and the Central Valley of California, combined with the male's tendency to sing conspicuously from the tops of shrubs, when fenceposts are not available, make this species attractive to birdwatchers. Where the two meadowlarks overlap they are best identified by their song.

VOICE Series of complex, bubbling, whistled notes descending in pitch.

NESTING Domed grass cup, well hidden in tall grasses; 3–7 eggs; 1 brood; March–August.

FEEDING Feeds mostly on insects, including beetles, grubs, and grasshoppers; also grains and grass seeds.

OCCURRENCE
Common in western North America, across much of southern Canada and the western US, south to Mexico. Breeds primarily in open grassy plains, but also uses agricultural fields with overgrown edges and hayfields. Partial migrant in US, winters south to Mexico.

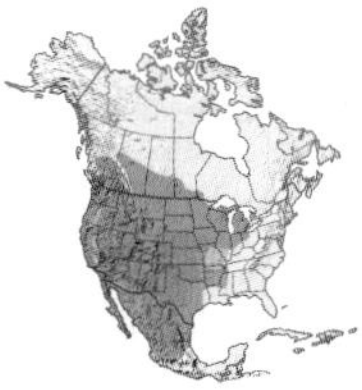

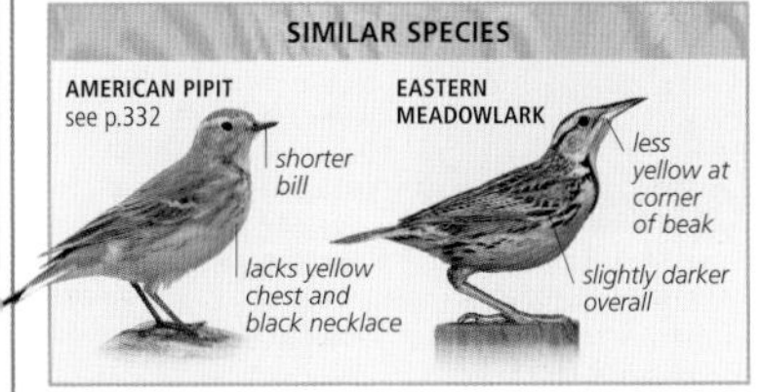

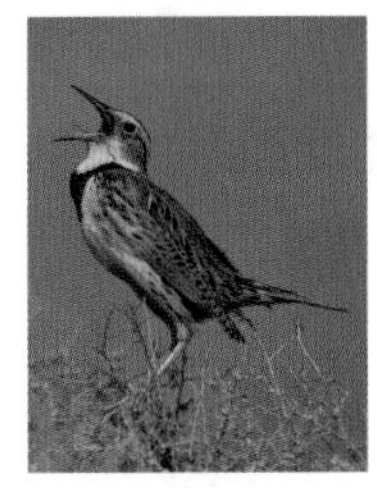

A SHRUB WILL DO
With few fenceposts in the Western Meadowlark's habitat, it perches on a shrub to sing.

SIMILAR SPECIES

AMERICAN PIPIT
see p.332
shorter bill
lacks yellow chest and black necklace
EASTERN MEADOWLARK
less yellow at corner of beak
slightly darker overall

Length **7–10in (18–26cm)**	Wingspan **13–15in (33–38cm)**	Weight **2⅞–4oz (80–125g)**
Social **Pairs/Winter flocks**	Lifespan **Up to 10 years**	Status **Secure**

DATE SEEN	WHERE	NOTES

Order **Passeriformes**	Family **Icteridae**	Species ***Xanthocephalus xanthocephalus***

Yellow-headed Blackbird

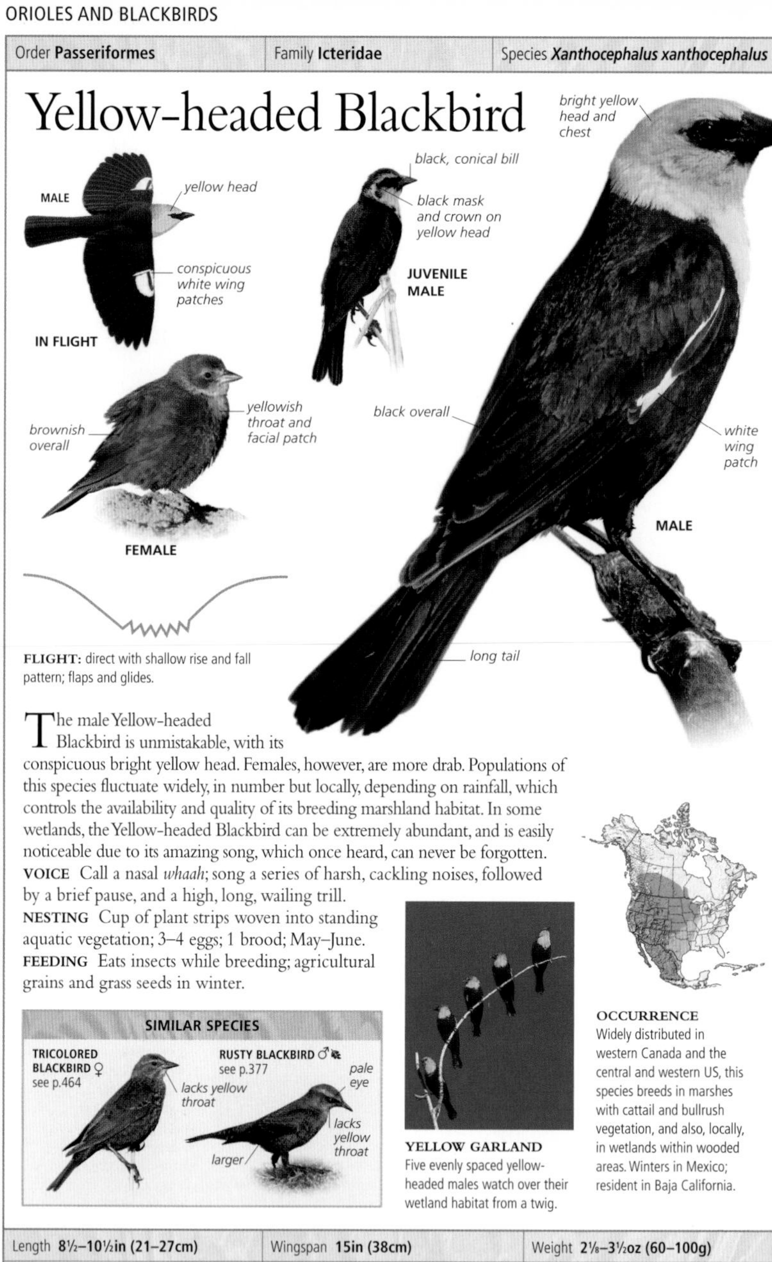

FLIGHT: direct with shallow rise and fall pattern; flaps and glides.

The male Yellow-headed Blackbird is unmistakable, with its conspicuous bright yellow head. Females, however, are more drab. Populations of this species fluctuate widely, in number but locally, depending on rainfall, which controls the availability and quality of its breeding marshland habitat. In some wetlands, the Yellow-headed Blackbird can be extremely abundant, and is easily noticeable due to its amazing song, which once heard, can never be forgotten.

VOICE Call a nasal *whaah*; song a series of harsh, cackling noises, followed by a brief pause, and a high, long, wailing trill.

NESTING Cup of plant strips woven into standing aquatic vegetation; 3–4 eggs; 1 brood; May–June.

FEEDING Eats insects while breeding; agricultural grains and grass seeds in winter.

SIMILAR SPECIES

TRICOLORED BLACKBIRD ♀ see p.464

lacks yellow throat

RUSTY BLACKBIRD ♂ see p.377

pale eye

lacks yellow throat

larger

YELLOW GARLAND

Five evenly spaced yellow-headed males watch over their wetland habitat from a twig.

OCCURRENCE

Widely distributed in western Canada and the central and western US, this species breeds in marshes with cattail and bullrush vegetation, and also, locally, in wetlands within wooded areas. Winters in Mexico; resident in Baja California.

Length **8½–10½in (21–27cm)**	Wingspan **15in (38cm)**	Weight **2⅛–3½oz (60–100g)**
Social **Flocks/Colonies**	Lifespan **Up to 9 years**	Status **Localized**

DATE SEEN	WHERE	NOTES

Order **Passeriformes**	Family **Icteridae**	Species ***Dolichonyx oryzivorus***

Bobolink

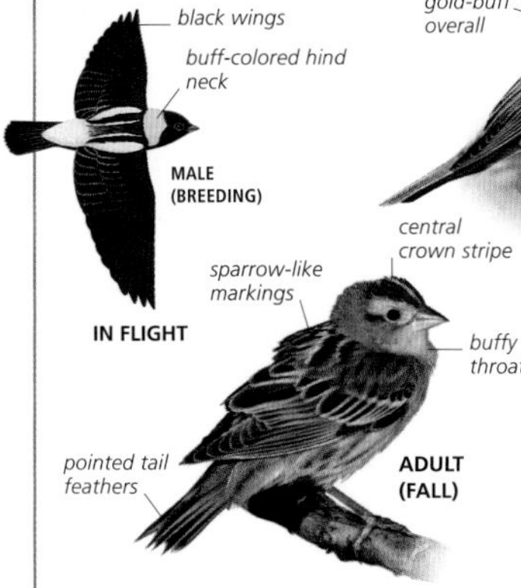

black wings
buff-colored hind neck
MALE (BREEDING)
IN FLIGHT

gold-buff overall
blackish brown crown
pinkish bill
FEMALE (BREEDING)

central crown stripe
sparrow-like markings
buffy throat
pointed tail feathers
ADULT (FALL)

black face and crown
white shoulder feathers
black underparts
white rump
black tail with pointed feathers
MALE (BREEDING)

FLIGHT: typically direct flight; series of rapid wing beats; glides of varying length.

The Bobolink is a common summer resident of open fallow fields through much of the northern US and southern Canada. In spring, the males perform a conspicuous circling or "helicoptering" display, which includes singing, to establish territory and to attract females. Bobolink populations have declined on its breeding grounds and in wintering areas because of habitat loss and changing agricultural practices.

VOICE Calls like the end of its name *link*; song a long, complex babbling series of musical notes varying in length and pitch.

NESTING Woven cup of grass close to or on the ground, well hidden in tall grass; 3–7 eggs; 1 brood; May–July.

FEEDING Feeds mostly on insects, spiders, grubs in breeding season, but seasonally variable; also cereal grains and grass seeds.

TAKING A BREAK
This male has fled the sun of the open fields to seek shelter in the shade of a tree.

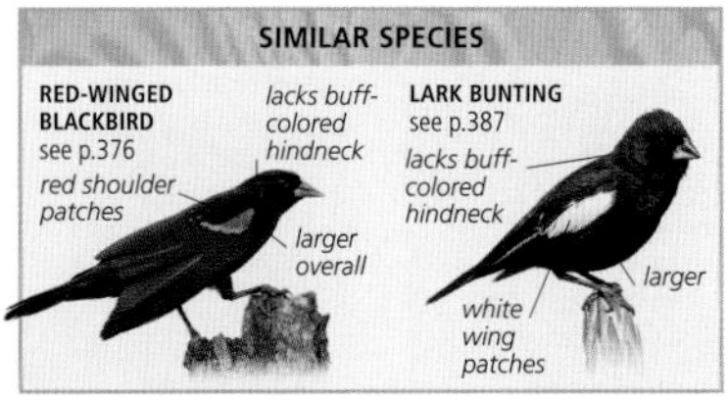

SIMILAR SPECIES

RED-WINGED BLACKBIRD see p.376
red shoulder patches
lacks buff-colored hindneck
larger overall

LARK BUNTING see p.387
lacks buff-colored hindneck
white wing patches
larger

OCCURRENCE
Breeds in open fields with a mixture of tall grasses and other herbaceous vegetation, especially old hayfields. In Canada from British Columbia to the East Coast; in the US from Idaho to New England. Migrates through the southern US and the Caribbean; winters in northern South America.

Length **6–8in (15–20cm)**	Wingspan **10–12in (25–30cm)**	Weight **1 1/16–2oz (30–55g)**
Social **Winter flocks**	Lifespan **Up to 10 years**	Status **Declining**

DATE SEEN	WHERE	NOTES

Family **Emberizidae**

LONGSPURS & AMERICAN SPARROWS

THE EMBERIZIDAE IS A FAMILY of finch-like birds that includes longspurs, buntings, and American sparrows. These birds occur everywhere in the world except for Australia and Antarctica. Emberizid finches are a diverse group, with over 300 species worldwide, including about 50 in North America. Although the scientific names of these birds are straightforward, their common names are not, and it is easy to become confused. Early settlers in North America thought these birds resembled European sparrows, and most North American emberizids are named "sparrows," despite having no close relationship with the European species *Passer domesticus*, which was deliberately introduced to the US. Distinguishing between different North American sparrows can be a daunting job. Many are small, brownish birds, with streaking in their plumage. They usually remain hidden in dense vegetation, and are not easy to see. Clues such as voice, habitat, behavior, and body shape are essential in their identification. Emberizids tend to forage for seeds on or near the ground, using their stout, conical bills to crush the seeds. Some North American sparrow species are year-round residents, but most are either migrants or partial migrants, and some have both resident and migrant populations. Fox Sparrows and Song Sparrows provide superb examples of species in the making, with numerous subspecies and overlapping ranges: because of geographical and ecological diversification, we are able to observe evolution in action.

BEST VIEW
Singing males like this Chestnut-collared Longspur are easily seen in summer.

TYPICAL SPARROW
A White-crowned Sparrow shows the typical stout emberizid beak.

Family **Thraupidae**

TANAGERS

THE TANAGERS COMPRISE a large, diverse family of over 200 songbird species, found only in the Americas. Some tropical species are dull-colored, and feed on insects from the forest floor, while others are rainbow-colored fruit-eaters that congregate in the canopy of fruit-bearing trees. North American tanagers belong to the genus *Piranga*, a Tupi-Guarani name from South America. Males are brightly colored in reds or yellows, but females are dull greenish yellow. The Western Tanager migrates to Mexico.

MALE COLORS
Male Western Tanagers are some of North America's most colorful birds.

Family **Cardinalidae**

CARDINALS

THE FAMILY CARDINALIDAE includes the well-known Northern Cardinal, but also the Dickcissel, several grosbeaks, and "buntings." These buntings have the same common name as some emberizid finches, but are unrelated to them. All cardinalids are vocal, and some are spectacularly colored, especially the electric-blue Indigo Bunting and the multicolored Painted Bunting. The Pyrrhuloxia, with a parrot-like bill, is a close relative of the Northern Cardinal.

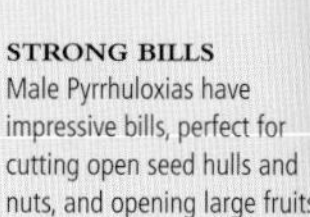

STRONG BILLS
Male Pyrrhuloxias have impressive bills, perfect for cutting open seed hulls and nuts, and opening large fruits.

Order **Passeriformes**	Family **Emberizidae**	Species ***Calcarius lapponicus***

Lapland Longspur

thin white edge to tail

MALE (BREEDING)

black face

IN FLIGHT

streaked crown

black streak on throat

FEMALE (BREEDING)

rich buffy hood

thick streaking on flanks

ADULT (NONBREEDING)

white eye-line

thick yellowish bill

bright rufous nape

rusty wing panel

white underparts

black flanks

MALE (BREEDING)

FLIGHT: deeply undulating, with birds often calling in troughs as they flap.

The genus name, *Calcarius*, refers to the long hind claw of this bird, hence "longspur" in American usage. The Lapland Longspur is one of the most numerous breeding birds in the Arctic tundra, from Labrador west to Alaska, and across northern Eurasia. In winter, they form huge flocks in open habitats of southern Canada and the US and are found on gravel roads and barren countryside immediately after heavy snowfall. DNA data suggest that the longspurs and *Plectrophenax* buntings may not belong to the family Emberizidae, but where remains an open question.

VOICE Flight call a dry rattle, *tyew*, unlike other longspurs; song a series of thin tinklings and whistles, melodious, often in flight.

NESTING Cup of grass and sedges placed in depression on ground next to a clump of vegetation; 4–6 eggs; 1 brood; May–July.

FEEDING Eats insects during breeding season; seeds in winter.

CONSPICUOUS SPECIES
This longspur is one of the most conspicuous breeding birds of the Arctic tundra.

SIMILAR SPECIES

SMITH'S LONGSPUR ♀
see p.464
white bars on wing
thin bill

CHESTNUT-COLLARED LONGSPUR ♀ ❄
see p.464
more white in tail
dark cheek patch

OCCURRENCE
Breeds in tundra right across the high Arctic of North America and Eurasia. Winters in open grasslands and barren fields, and on beaches across the northern and central US and parts of south-central and northeastern Canada.

Length **6½in (16cm)**	Wingspan **10½–11½in (27–29cm)**	Weight **⅞–1 1/16oz (25–30g)**
Social **Large flocks**	Lifespan **Up to 5 years**	Status **Secure**

DATE SEEN	WHERE	NOTES

Order **Passeriformes**	Family **Emberizidae**	Species ***Plectrophenax nivalis***

Snow Bunting

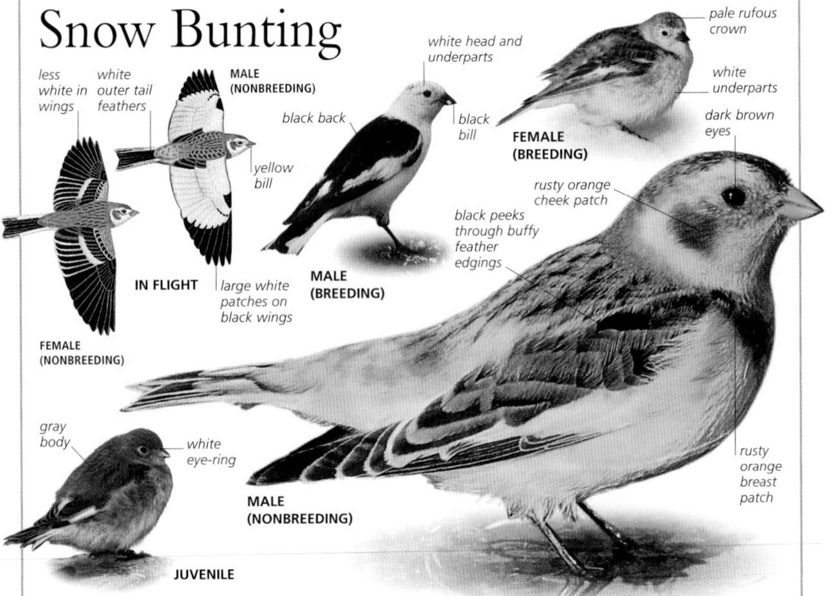

less white in wings
white outer tail feathers
MALE (NONBREEDING)
yellow bill
IN FLIGHT
large white patches on black wings
FEMALE (NONBREEDING)
white head and underparts
black back
black bill
MALE (BREEDING)
pale rufous crown
white underparts
dark brown eyes
FEMALE (BREEDING)
rusty orange cheek patch
black peeks through buffy feather edgings
rusty orange breast patch
MALE (NONBREEDING)
gray body
white eye-ring
JUVENILE

The bold white wing patches of the Snow Bunting make it immediately recognizable in a whirling winter flock of dark-winged longspurs and larks. In winter, heavy snowfall forces flocks onto roadsides, where they can be seen more easily. To secure and defend the best territories, some males arrive as early as April in their barren high-Arctic breeding grounds; these buntings breed further north than any other songbirds. The Snow Bunting is very similar in appearance to the rare McKay's Bunting, localized to western Alaska. Although McKay's Bunting generally has less black on the back, in the wings, and on the tail, the two species cannot always be conclusively identified. This is especially true as they sometimes interbreed, producing hybrids.

VOICE Flight call a musical, liquid rattle, also *tyew* notes and short buzz; song a pleasant series of squeaky and whistled notes.

NESTING Bulky cup of grass and moss, lined with feathers, and placed in sheltered rock crevice; 3–6 eggs; 1 brood; June–August.

FEEDING Eats seeds (sedge in Arctic), flies and other insects, and buds on migration.

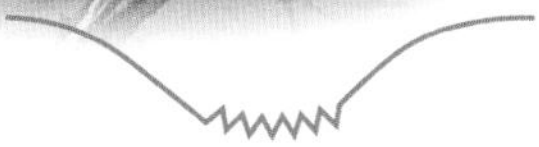

FLIGHT: deeply undulating; flocks "roll" along as birds at back overtake those in front.

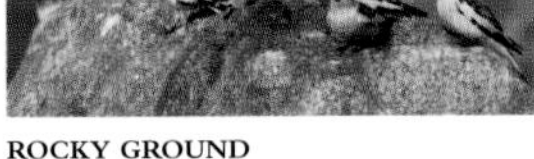

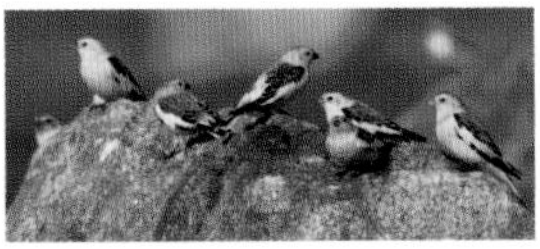

ROCKY GROUND
About the only perches in the Snow Bunting's barren breeding grounds are large boulders.

SIMILAR SPECIES

McKAY'S BUNTING
see p.465
mostly white tail, back, and wings

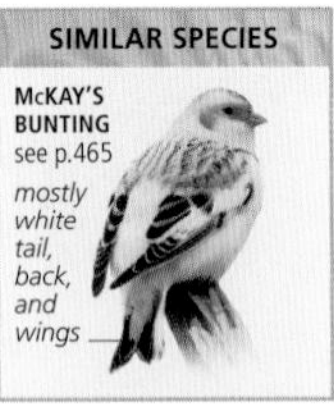

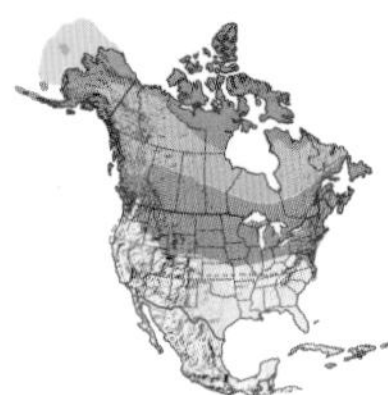

OCCURRENCE
Breeds in rocky areas, usually near sparsely vegetated tundra, right across the Arctic in both North America and Eurasia. North American birds winter in open country and on shores across southern Canada and the northern US, and in southern and western coastal areas of Alaska.

Length **6½–7in (16–18cm)**	Wingspan **12½–14in (32–35cm)**	Weight **1¼–2oz (35–55g)**
Social **Large flocks**	Lifespan **Unknown**	Status **Secure**

DATE SEEN	WHERE	NOTES

Order **Passeriformes**	Family **Emberizidae**	Species ***Calamospiza melanocorys***

Lark Bunting

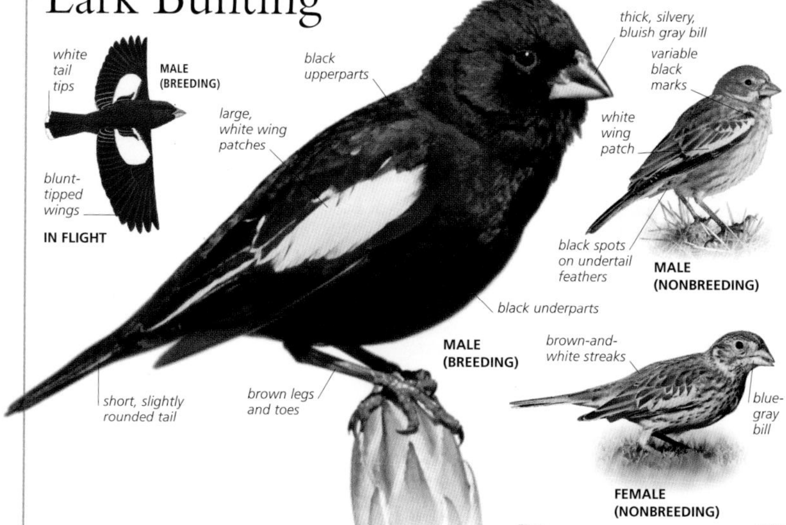

white tail tips

MALE (BREEDING)

blunt-tipped wings

IN FLIGHT

black upperparts

large, white wing patches

thick, silvery, bluish gray bill

variable black marks

white wing patch

black spots on undertail feathers

MALE (NONBREEDING)

black underparts

MALE (BREEDING)

short, slightly rounded tail

brown legs and toes

brown-and-white streaks

blue-gray bill

FEMALE (NONBREEDING)

The stocky Lark Bunting is perhaps the most frequently seen bird on the North American High Plains. Unlike the Chestnut-collared Longspur, which lives alongside it, it coped with the changes wrought on its habitat by humans, and occurs in extraordinarily high density throughout its range. Nomadic flocks of thousands of birds scour the high deserts, open grasslands, and sage brushlands for seeds. Breeding-plumage males are unmistakable: black with large white wing patches. Females and immature birds are duller, with more subdued wing patches.

VOICE Call a low, soft, whistled *hwoik*; song partly melodious, partly "scratchy," with repetitions of phrases, then whistles.

NESTING Open cup of grass, lined with fine plant material, in depression in ground; 4–5 eggs; 1 brood; May–August.

FEEDING Mainly seeds in winter, a variety of insects in summer.

FLIGHT: low and undulating, short glides alternating with stiff wing beats.

CAUGHT BY ANY MEANS

Lark Buntings hawk, glean, and forage insect prey throughout the breeding season.

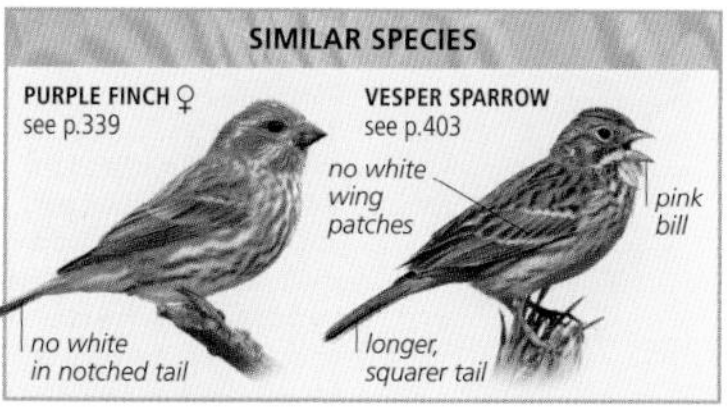

SIMILAR SPECIES

PURPLE FINCH ♀ see p.339
no white in notched tail

VESPER SPARROW see p.403
no white wing patches; pink bill; longer, squarer tail

OCCURRENCE

Breeds in grasslands and sage flats on High Plains from Alberta south to the Texas panhandle. Winters in similar habitats—and also in deserts, cultivated plains, and open shrubsteppes—across interior southwestern US and northern Mexico. Migrants use similar open-country habitats.

Length **7in (18cm)**	Wingspan **10½–11in (27–28cm)**	Weight **1 1/16–1¾oz (30–50g)**
Social **Large flocks**	Lifespan **Unknown**	Status **Secure**

DATE SEEN	WHERE	NOTES

Order **Passeriformes**	Family **Emberizidae**	Species ***Passerella iliaca***

Fox Sparrow

ADULT (RED)
dark rufous overall
IN FLIGHT

rusty streaks on back
gray nape
two white wing bars
darker upper mandible
belly marked with rufous chevrons
P. i. iliaca
(RED; EAST)

dark brown head and upperparts
densely spotted breast
rusty tail
P. i. unalaschensis
(SOOTY; ALASKA, BRITISH COLUMBIA)

gray head and back
long, rusty tail
belly marked with rufous chevrons
P. i. altivagans
(SLATE-COLORED; ROCKIES)

grayish brown head and upperparts
very large bill
fine streaks on throat
rusty wings and tail
P. i. stephensi
(THICK-BILLED; CALIFORNIA MOUNTAINS)

FLIGHT: alternates wing beats and glides; straight and fluttery, from cover to cover.

Larger, more robust, and more colorful than its close relatives, the Fox Sparrow is a beautiful species. When it appears in backyards, its presence can be detected by its foraging habits; it crouches low in leaf litter, and hops back and forth, noisily, to disturb leaves, under which it finds seeds or insects. It varies considerably over its huge western range, from thick-billed birds in the Sierras to sooty ones in the Northwest, and slate-colored birds in the Rockies.

VOICE Call is sharp, dry *tshak* or *tshuk;* flight call a high-pitched *tzeep!;* song is complex and musical with trills and whistles.
NESTING Dense cup of grasses or moss lined with fine material; usually placed low in shrub; 2–5 eggs; 1 brood; April–July.
FEEDING Forages for insects, seeds, and fruit.

FOXY RED
The Fox Sparrow gets its name from the rusty coloration of the eastern "Red" birds.

SIMILAR SPECIES

HERMIT THRUSH
see p.328
unstreaked flanks
different bill shape

SONG SPARROW
see p.389
thinner bill
longer tail
breast streaking less marked

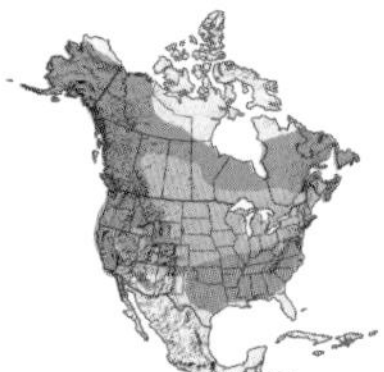

OCCURRENCE
Encompasses the entire boreal forest zone, from Alaska in the West to Québec, Labrador, and Newfoundland in the East. In the West, it occurs in coastal and near-coast thickets within coniferous or mixed woodlands. Winters in the Pacific West, south to Baja California; also from Texas to Massachusetts.

Length **6–7½in (15–19cm)**	Wingspan **10½–11½in (27–29cm)**	Weight **⅞–1$\frac{9}{16}$oz (25–45g)**
Social **Solitary/Small flocks**	Lifespan **Up to 9 years**	Status **Secure**

DATE SEEN	WHERE	NOTES

Order **Passeriformes**	Family **Emberizidae**	Species ***Melospiza melodia***

Song Sparrow

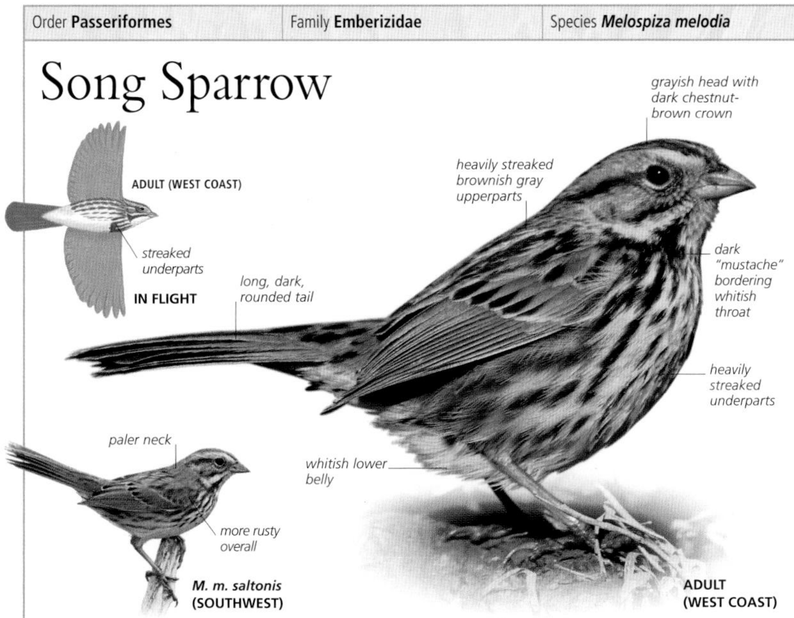

The familiar song of this species can be heard in backyards across the continent, including in winter, although it varies both individually and geographically. In the southeastern US, where it does not breed, migrant birds start singing in early spring before departing for northern areas. The Song Sparrow may be the North American champion of geographical variation—about 40 subspecies have been described. These vary from the large, dark birds of the Aleutian Islands (*M. m. maxima*) to the smaller, paler birds of southern Arizona (*M. m. saltonis*). Eastern birds, such as *M. m. melodia*, fall between the two in size.

VOICE A dry *tchip* call; flight call a clear *siiti*; song a jumble of variable whistles and trills, *deeep deeep deep-deep chrrrr tiiiiiiiiiiii tyeeur* most common.

NESTING Bulky cup on or near ground, in brush or marsh vegetation; 3–5 eggs; 1–3 broods; March–August.

FEEDING In summer, feeds mainly on insects; in winter, eats mainly seeds, but also fruit.

FLIGHT: low and direct, staying within cover whenever possible.

SIMILAR SPECIES

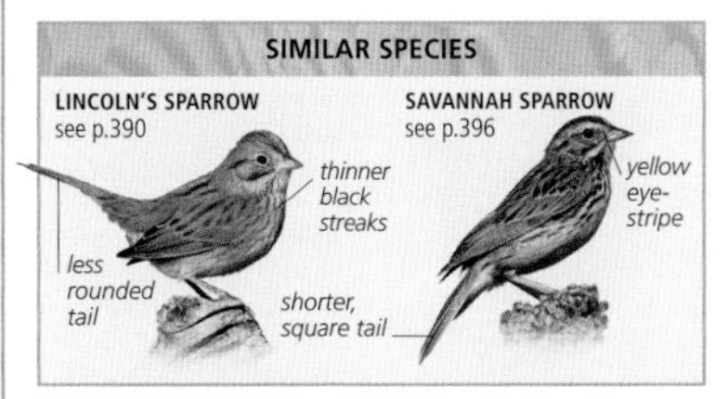

BREAST SPOT
The Song Sparrow often sings from exposed perches, showing off its characteristic breast spot.

OCCURRENCE
Widespread in a range of habitats (although not in dense forests) across Canada and the US, from the Atlantic to the Pacific Coasts and north to Alaska. Some populations move south of their breeding range in winter.

Length **5–7½in (13–19cm)**	Wingspan **8½–12in (21–31cm)**	Weight **7/16–1¾oz (13–50g)**
Social **Solitary/Flocks**	Lifespan **Up to 9 years**	Status **Secure**

DATE SEEN	WHERE	NOTES
4/23/19	Seattle U campus	Male, Singing

Order **Passeriformes**	Family **Emberizidae**	Species ***Melospiza lincolnii***

Lincoln's Sparrow

At first glance, Lincoln's Sparrow appears plain, but on close inspection it reveals itself to be a bird with subtly varying, but crisply outlined, markings. In the breeding season, it seeks out moist willow scrub at the tundra–taiga timberline; outside the breeding season, Lincoln's Sparrow occurs in scrubby habitats right across North America. It will occasionally visit backyard feeders in winter, but it is generally secretive and stays within fairly dense cover. Lincoln's Sparrow's rich, musical song is unmistakable, and it varies remarkably little from region to region. Audubon named this species in 1834 in honor of his collector Thomas Lincoln.

VOICE Call a variable, loud *tchip*, flight call a rolling *ziiiit*; song series of rich, musical trills, *ju-ju-ju dodododo didididididi whrrrrr.*

NESTING Grass cup, lined with fine grass, and hidden in depression in ground under overhanging sedges or grasses; 3–5 eggs; 1 brood; June–August.

FEEDING Mainly seeds in winter; in summer, mostly insects, such as beetles, mosquitoes, and moths.

FLIGHT: low and direct, staying within cover whenever possible.

RAISE THE ALARM

When disturbed, Lincoln's Sparrow often raises its central crown feathers, which form a crest.

SIMILAR SPECIES

SONG SPARROW see p.389
larger overall; *more coarse streaking*

SAVANNAH SPARROW see p.396
yellow stripe above eye; *short, square, notched tail*

OCCURRENCE

Breeds in muskeg and wet thickets across northern North America, also south into the western ranges of California and Arizona. Migrants and wintering birds use a variety of scrubby habitats. Winters in southern US (and farther south), and on Pacific Coast north to British Columbia.

Length **5¼–6in (13.5–15cm)**	Wingspan **7½–8½in (19–22cm)**	Weight **½–⅞oz (15–25g)**
Social **Solitary/Small flocks**	Lifespan **Up to 7 years**	Status **Secure**

DATE SEEN	WHERE	NOTES

Order **Passeriformes**	Family **Emberizidae**	Species ***Melospiza georgiana***

Swamp Sparrow

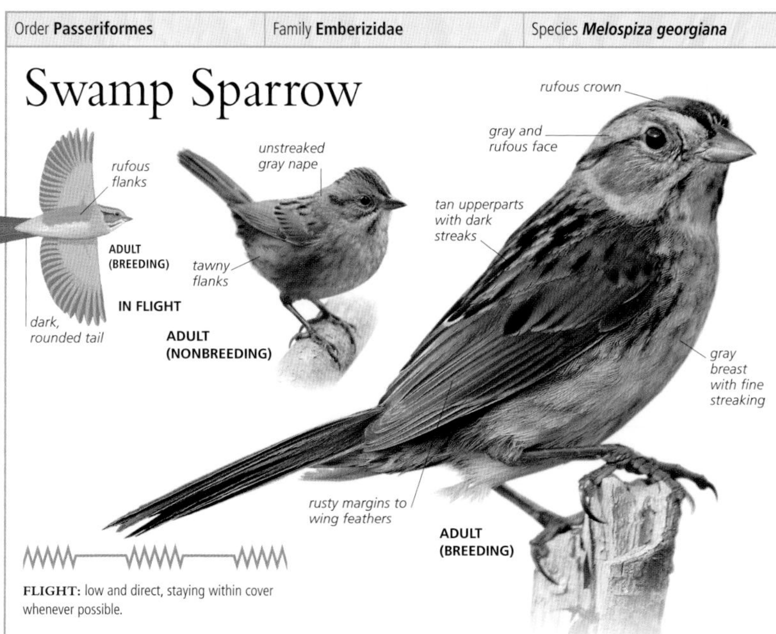

FLIGHT: low and direct, staying within cover whenever possible.

The Swamp Sparrow is a common breeder in wet habitats across eastern North America and Canada west to the southern Yukon and eastern British Columbia. It is abundant in its preferred habitat of tall reed and cattail marshes. A somewhat skittish bird, the Swamp Sparrow is often seen darting rapidly into cover, but usually repays the patient observer with a reappearance, giving its characteristic *chimp* call. Though often confused with both the Song Sparrow and Lincoln's Sparrow, the Swamp Sparrow never shows more than a very faint, blurry streaking on its gray breast, and sports conspicuous rusty-edged wing feathers. Its song is also quite different.

VOICE Call a slightly nasal, forceful *chimp*, flight call a high, buzzy *ziiiiii*; song a slow, monotonous, loose trill of chirps.

NESTING Bulky cup of dry plants placed 1–4ft (30–120cm) above water in marsh vegetation; 3–5 eggs; 1–2 broods; May–July.

FEEDING Mostly insects in the breeding season, especially grasshoppers; seeds in winter; occasionally fruit.

HIGH PERCH
This male Swamp Sparrow is checking his territory from atop a seeding cattail flower.

SIMILAR SPECIES

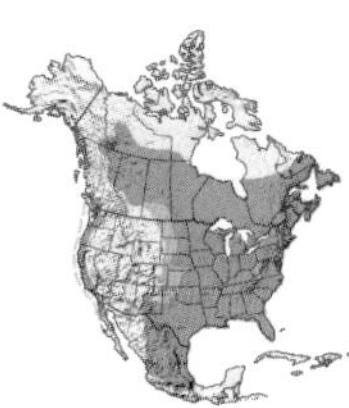

OCCURRENCE
Breeds in marshes, cedar bogs, damp meadows, and wet hayfields, from the Yukon east to Newfoundland and south to Nebraska and the Delmarva Peninsula; winters in marshes in eastern US and south through Mexico; rare but regular along Pacific coast.

Length **5–6in (12.5–15cm)**	Wingspan **7–7½in (18–19cm)**	Weight **½–⅞oz (15–25g)**
Social **Solitary/Small flocks**	Lifespan **Up to 6 years**	Status **Secure**

DATE SEEN	WHERE	NOTES

Order **Passeriformes**	Family **Emberizidae**	Species ***Zonotrichia leucophrys***

White-crowned Sparrow

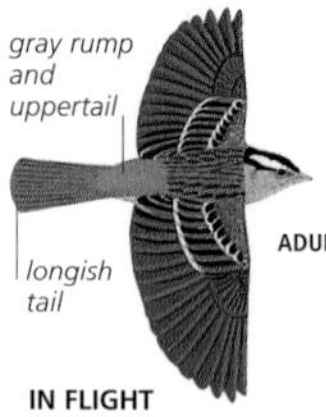
gray rump and uppertail
longish tail
ADULT

IN FLIGHT

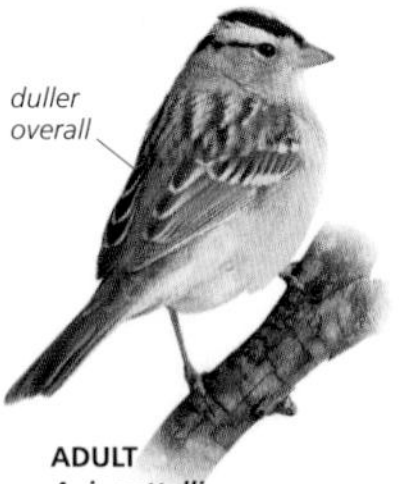
duller overall

ADULT
A. i. nuttalli
(PACIFIC COAST)

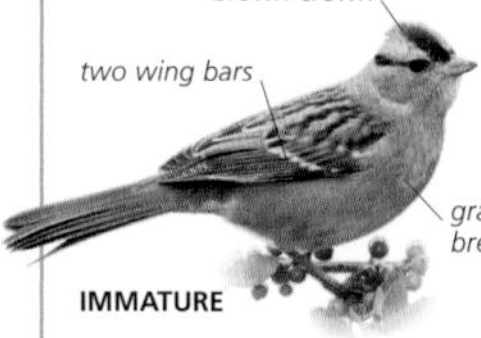
brown crown
two wing bars
gray breast

IMMATURE

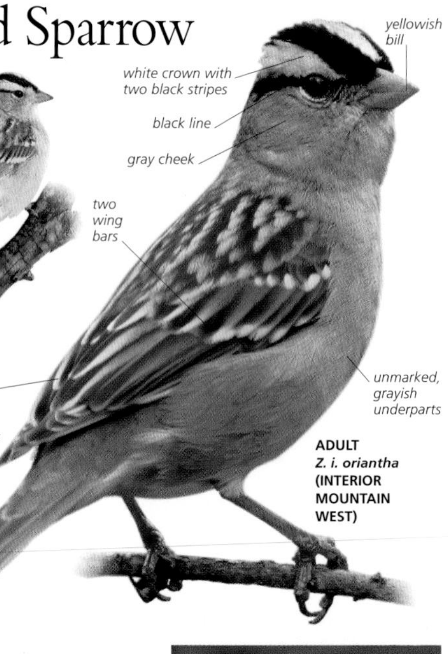
yellowish bill
white crown with two black stripes
black line
gray cheek
two wing bars
white streaking on brown upperparts
unmarked, grayish underparts

ADULT
Z. i. oriantha
(INTERIOR MOUNTAIN WEST)

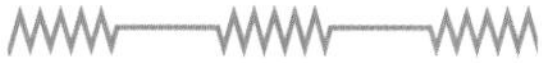

FLIGHT: low and direct, staying within cover whenever possible.

Widespread in the west, the White-crowned Sparrow has five subspecies. Pacific Coast birds are brown, with a yellowish bill, a gray patch between the eye and bill, and a gray-washed head stripe; western and northwestern birds are gray below, with a gray patch between the eye and bill, an orange bill, and a white head stripe. In parts of California, the White-crowned Sparrow is a common bird of gardens, parks, and suburbs.

VOICE Call a sharp *tink*; flight call a thin *seep*; song a buzzy whistle followed by buzzes, trills, and whistles.

NESTING Bulky cup of grass placed on or near the ground in bushes; 4–6 eggs; 1–3 broods; March–August.

FEEDING Forages for seeds, insects, fruit, buds, and even grass.

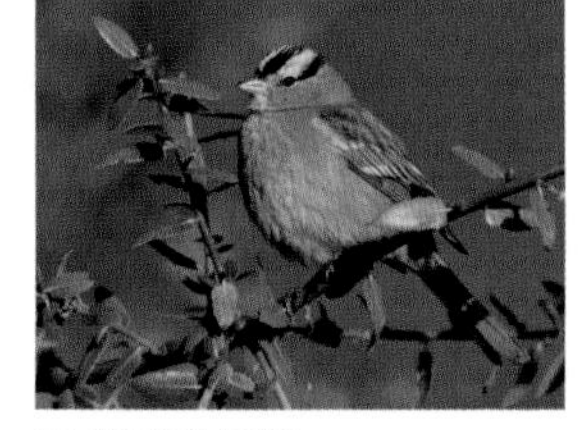

LOOKING RESTED
Perched on a shrub, this sparrow's white eyestreak is highly visible.

SIMILAR SPECIES

WHITE-THROATED SPARROW see p.393

yellow patch
gray bill
chunkier overall
more reddish

GOLDEN-CROWNED SPARROW ◔ yellowish forecrown; see p.394

plain face
gray bill

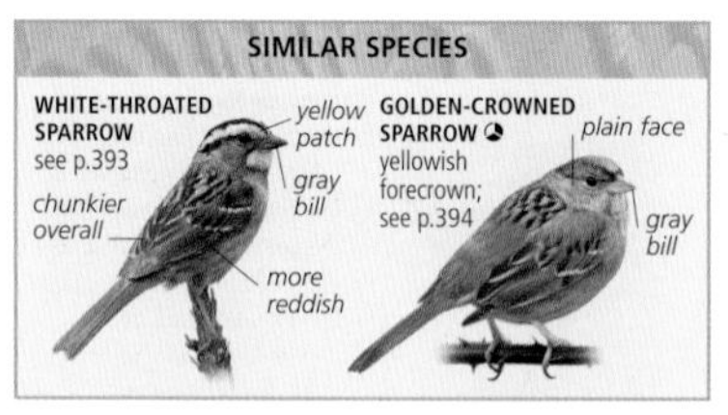

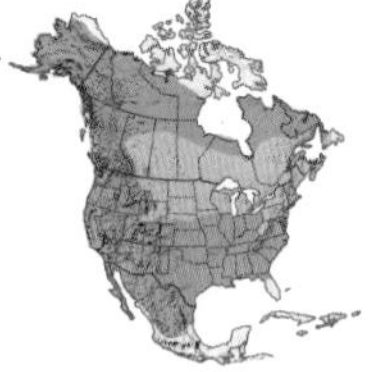

OCCURRENCE
Widespread across the boreal forest and the taiga–tundra border, from Alaska eastward to Québec and Labrador, and southward from British Columbia to coastal California and the intermontane West. In the North, breeds in willow thickets, wet forest; in the West, habitats are more varied and include suburbs.

Length **6½–7in (16–18cm)**	Wingspan **9½–10in (24–26cm)**	Weight **1¹⁄₁₆–1¼oz (20–35g)**
Social **Flocks**	Lifespan **Up to 13 years**	Status **Secure**

DATE SEEN	WHERE	NOTES

Order **Passeriformes**	Family **Emberizidae**	Species ***Zonotrichia albicollis***

White-throated Sparrow

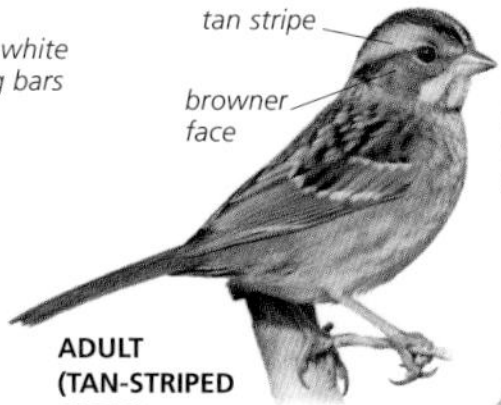

two white wing bars
ADULT
IN FLIGHT
tan stripe
browner face
ADULT (TAN-STRIPED FORM)
bold white stripe
bright rufous back and tail
yellow patch
white throat
gray bill
streaking on breast
IMMATURE (TAN-STRIPED FORM)
fairly long tail
gray underparts
ADULT (WHITE-STRIPED FORM)

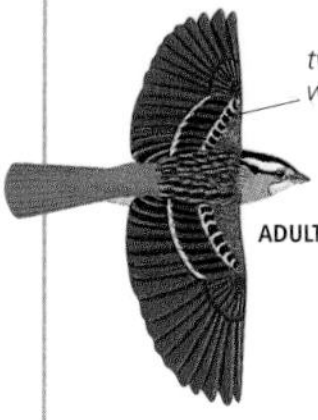

Common almost everywhere in eastern North America, but more localized in the west, White-throated Sparrows sing all year round. Their distinctive song can be remembered with the popular mnemonics *Oh sweet Canada Canada Canada*, or the less accurate *Old Sam Peabody*. This species has two different color forms, one with a white stripe above its eye, and the other with a tan stripe. In the nonbreeding season, large flocks roam the leaf litter of woodlands in search of food. Often the only indication of their presence is the occasional moving leaf or thin, lisping flight call.

VOICE Call loud, sharp *jink*; flight call lisping *tssssst!*; song clear whistle comprising 1–2 higher notes, then three triplets.

NESTING Cup placed on or near ground in dense shrubbery; 2–6 eggs; 1 brood; May–August.

FEEDING Mainly forages on the ground for seeds, fruit, insects, buds, and various grasses.

FLIGHT: low and direct, staying within cover whenever possible.

DIFFERENT COLOR FORMS
The presence of white or tan stripes on White-throated Sparrows is not related to their sex.

SIMILAR SPECIES

WHITE-CROWNED SPARROW slimmer overall; see p.392
no yellow patch
orange or pink bill

GOLDEN-CROWNED SPARROW see p.394
yellowish forecrown
plain, grayish breast

OCCURRENCE
Breeds in forests from eastern Yukon to Newfoundland, south to the Great Lakes region and northern Appalachians. Nonbreeders prefer wooded thickets and hedges. Winters across the eastern US and extreme south of the Southwest. Rare but regular along the Pacific Coast.

Length **6½–7½in (16–17.5cm)**	Wingspan **9–10in (23–26cm)**	Weight **¹¹⁄₁₆–1¼oz (20–35g)**
Social **Flocks**	Lifespan **Up to 10 years**	Status **Secure**

DATE SEEN	WHERE	NOTES

Order **Passeriformes**	Family **Emberizidae**	Species ***Zonotrichia atricapilla***

Golden-crowned Sparrow

white wing bars
ADULT (BREEDING)
IN FLIGHT
streaks on head
dull yellow crown
IMMATURE
bright yellow crown
thick black eyebrow
duller yellow on crown
much less black on face
ADULT (NONBREEDING)
long tail
light grayish brown underparts
ADULT (BREEDING)

The Golden-crowned Sparrow is in many respects the western counterpart of the White-throated Sparrow. It sings in a minor key and, as a result, has a reputation for sounding melancholy. Many late 19th-century Klondike gold prospectors called this bird "Weary Willie"—to them, its song sounded remarkably like *I'm so tired* or *No gold here.* It has been regarded as a pest in the past because of its habit of consuming crops in agricultural fields and gardens. Nonbreeding adults retain their distinctive golden crown in the winter, but it appears duller.

VOICE Call loud *tsik*; flight call soft, short *seeep*; song variable series of melancholy whistles, sometimes slurred or trilled.

NESTING Concealed bulky cup placed on ground at base of bush; 3–5 eggs; 1–2 broods; June–August.

FEEDING Predominantly forages on the ground for seeds, insects, fruit, flowers, and buds.

FLIGHT: low and direct, staying within cover whenever possible.

GROUND FORAGER
This sparrow can be found by listening for the noise it makes as it roots around in the leaf litter.

OCCURRENCE
Breeds in shrubby habitat along the tree line and open, boggy forests from Alaska east to the southwestern Northwest Territories, south to British Columbia and southwestern Alberta. Winters in dense thickets from south coastal British Columbia to northern Baja California.

Length **7in (18cm)**	Wingspan **9–10in (23–25cm)**	Weight **11/16–1¼oz (20–35g)**
Social **Flocks**	Lifespan **Up to 10 years**	Status **Secure**

DATE SEEN	WHERE	NOTES

Order **Passeriformes**	Family **Emberizidae**	Species ***Junco hyemalis***

Dark-eyed Junco

MALE (SLATE-COLORED)
white outer tail feathers
IN FLIGHT

bluish gray hood
dark area between eye and bill
dull, brownish back
pinkish flanks
J. h. mearnsi
(FEMALE; PINK-SIDED)

blackish hood
rust back
reddish flanks
J. h. oreganus
(MALE; OREGON)

black mask
reddish brown back
gray rump
pale gray underparts
J. h. caniceps
(MALE; GRAY-HEADED)

gray body with darker back
white belly
J. h. hyemalis
(MALE; SLATE-COLORED)

The Dark-eyed Junco's arrival at birdfeeders during winter snowstorms has earned it the colloquial name of "snowbird." The name "Dark-eyed Junco" is actually used to describe a group of birds that vary geographically in a such a strikingly diverse way that 16 subspecies have been described. "Slate-colored" populations are widespread across Canada and the northeastern US. "White-winged" birds nest in the Black Hills; "Pink-sided" ones breed in Idaho, Montana, and Wyoming; and "Oregon" birds breed in the West, from Alaska to British Columbia and the mountains of the western US in the Sierras south to Mexico. "Red-backed" populations (not illustrated) reside in the mountains of Arizona and New Mexico, and "Gray-headed" birds range between the "Red-backed" and "Pink-sided" populations.

VOICE Loud, smacking *tick* and soft *dyew* calls; flight call a rapid, twittering, and buzzy *zzeet*; song a simple, liquid, 1-pitch trill.

NESTING Cup placed on ground hidden under vegetation or next to rocks; 3–5 eggs; 1–2 broods; May–August.

FEEDING Eats insects and seeds; also berries.

FLIGHT: low and direct, staying within cover whenever possible.

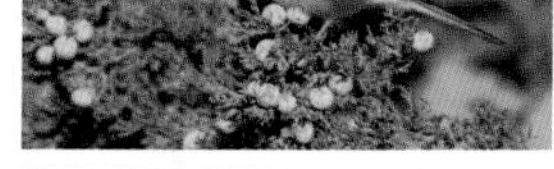

PINK-SIDED MALE
Like most juncos, this male is brighter with greater contrasts, darker eye areas, and more vivid colors.

SIMILAR SPECIES

YELLOW-EYED JUNCO
see p.465

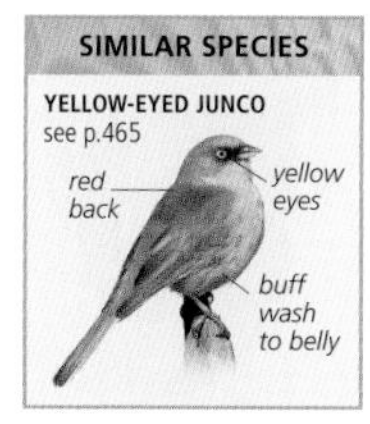

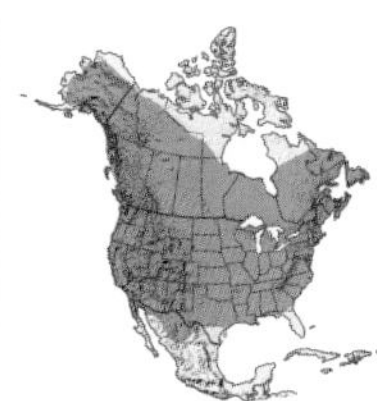

OCCURRENCE
Breeds in coniferous and mixed forests in Canada, northwestern and northeastern US, south in the east along the Appalachians to Georgia; in the west, in mountains from Alaska and British Columbia to New Mexico and northern Baja California. Winters from southern Canada to northern Mexico except Florida.

Length **6–6¾in (15–17cm)**	Wingspan **8–10in (20–26cm)**	Weight **⅝–1 1/16oz (18–30g)**
Social **Flocks**	Lifespan **Up to 11 years**	Status **Secure**

DATE SEEN	WHERE	NOTES

Order **Passeriformes**	Family **Emberizidae**	Species ***Passerculus sandwichensis***

Savannah Sparrow

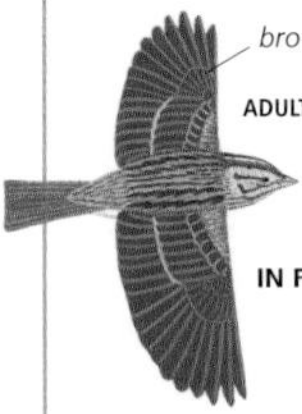

brown overall
ADULT
IN FLIGHT

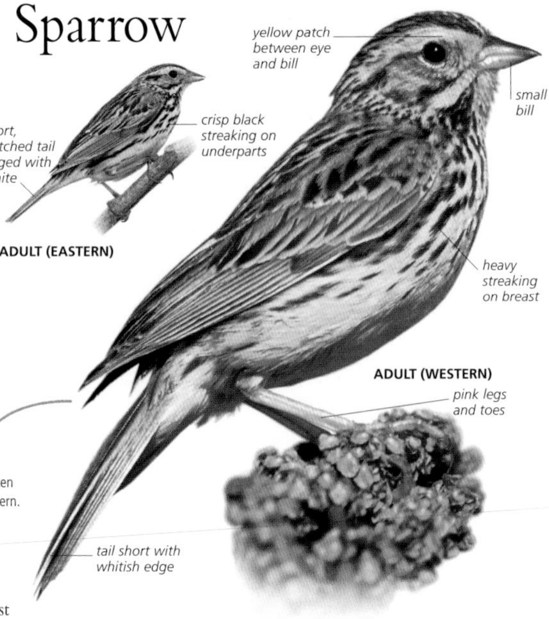

short, notched tail edged with white
crisp black streaking on underparts
ADULT (EASTERN)
yellow patch between eye and bill
small bill
heavy streaking on breast
ADULT (WESTERN)
pink legs and toes
tail short with whitish edge

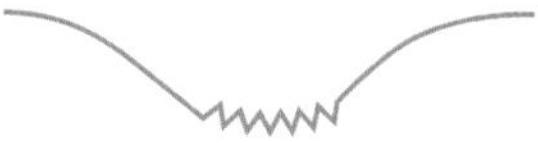

FLIGHT: square-tailed with an often undulating or "stair-step" flight pattern.

The Savannah Sparrow shows tremendous geographic variation—21 subspecies—across its vast range, but it is always brown, with dark streaks above and white with dark streaks below. The "Large-billed Sparrow" (*P. s. rostratus* and *P. s. atratus*) breeds in Baja California, and Sonora, Mexico. The most distinct of all subspecies, these birds occur as nonbreeders near California's Salton Sea. Their distinct song consists of three buzzy trills, and their flight calls are lower and more metallic than those of other populations.

VOICE Call a sharp, but full *stip*; flight call a thin, weak, downslurred *tseew*; song a *sit sit sit sit suh-EEEEE say*, from perch or in display flight with legs dangling.

NESTING Concealed cup of grass placed in depression on ground, protected by overhanging grass or sedges; 2–6 eggs; 1–2 broods; June–August.

FEEDING Forages on the ground, mostly for insects; in summer also eats seeds; in winter, berries and fruit when available; also small snails and crustaceans.

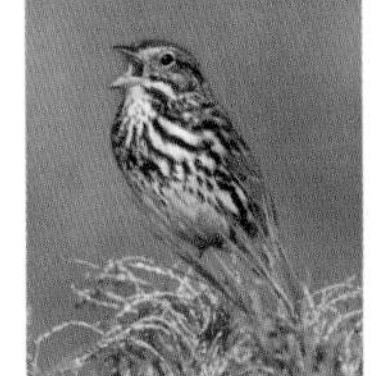

BELDING'S SPARROW
This darker, more heavily streaked subspecies inhabits coastal salt-marshes in southern California.

SIMILAR SPECIES

SONG SPARROW
see p.389

larger overall
longer, rounded tail

VESPER SPARROW
see p.403

rusty shoulder
dark tail

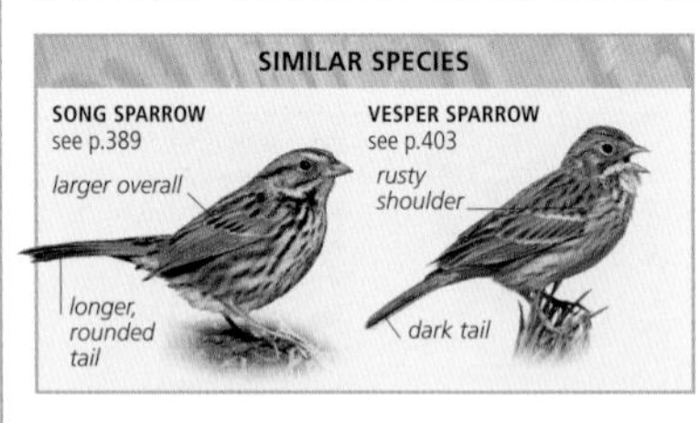

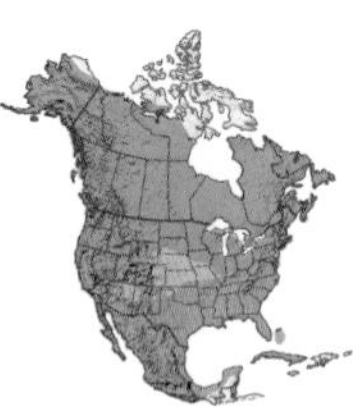

OCCURRENCE
Breeds in meadows, grasslands, pastures, bushy tundra, and some cultivated land across northern North America. Also along Pacific Coast and in Mexican interior. Nonbreeders use varied open habitats. Winters across southern US to Honduras, also Cuba, the Bahamas, and Cayman Islands.

Length **5½–6in (14–15cm)**	Wingspan **6¾in (17cm)**	Weight **½–1¹⁄₁₆oz (15–30g)**
Social **Solitary/Loose flocks**	Lifespan **Unknown**	Status **Secure**

DATE SEEN	WHERE	NOTES

Order **Passeriformes**	Family **Emberizidae**	Species ***Ammodramus leconteii***

Le Conte's Sparrow

FLIGHT: low and weak, with spiky tail pointed down; much fast flapping.

Intricately patterned in browns and buffs, Le Conte's Sparrow is usually very difficult to see. Not only is it tiny—one of the smallest of all North American sparrows—but in its grassland and marsh habitats of interior North America, it darts for cover, hiding under grasses instead of flushing when disturbed. The flight call and song of this elusive little bird are remarkably insect-like. Many people who hear it believe that the unseen caller is a grasshopper. Its nest is even harder to find, making this bird a real challenge to study as well as observe.

VOICE Call long, down-slurred *zheeep*; flight call similar to grasshopper; song insect-like, buzzy *tik'-uht-tizz-ZHEEEEEE-k*.

NESTING Concealed little cup placed on or near ground; 3–5 eggs; 1 brood; June–August.

FEEDING Forages on the ground and in grasses for insects, insect larvae, spiders, and seeds.

HIDEAWAY BIRD
Le Conte's Sparrow is usually found skulking in medium-to-tall grass.

SIMILAR SPECIES

OCCURRENCE
Breeds in marshes, wet meadows, and bogs from the southern Yukon east to Lake Superior and western Québec. Migrants and wintering birds are found in tall grass and marshes in southwestern Kansas to southern Indiana, and from central Texas to the Carolinas.

Length **4½–5in (11.5–13cm)**	Wingspan **6½–7in (16–18cm)**	Weight **7/16–9/16oz (12–16g)**
Social **Solitary/Loose flocks**	Lifespan **Unknown**	Status **Secure**

DATE SEEN	WHERE	NOTES

Order **Passeriformes**	Family **Emberizidae**	Species ***Ammodramus savannarum***

Grasshopper Sparrow

FLIGHT: low and weak, with spiky tail pointed down; much flapping.

A Grasshopper Sparrow singing briefly atop a weed is usually the first glimpse people get of a member of the secretive genus *Ammodramus*. Although its large head and spiky tail are characteristic of species in its genus, the Grasshopper Sparrow is the only *Ammodramus* sparrow to have a plain breast and two completely different songs. While it does eat grasshoppers, its common name derives from its grasshopper-like song. The Grasshopper Sparrow varies geographically, with about 12 subspecies.

VOICE Sharp *tik* call; flight call a long, high *tseeee*; song an insect-like trill *tik'-tok-TREEEE*, or series of quick buzzes.

NESTING Cup of grass placed in clump of grass; 3–6 eggs; 1–2 broods; April–August.

FEEDING Forages on ground for seeds and insects.

YELLOW STRIPE
The pale crown stripe is quite visible here as the bird faces the photographer.

SIMILAR SPECIES

LE CONTE'S SPARROW see p.397
orange eyebrow; brighter overall; gray cheek patch

BAIRD'S SPARROW see p.466
ocher crown; dark, lateral throat stripe

OCCURRENCE
Breeds in short grassland, pastures, and even mown areas across much of the US and in southern Canada. Locally distributed in the Southwest, also patchily through central US. Winters in similar habitats from southern US to Colombia; also in the West Indies.

Length **5in (13cm)**	Wingspan **8in (20cm)**	Weight **½–$^{11}/_{16}$oz (15–20g)**
Social **Solitary/Flocks**	Lifespan **Up to 7 years**	Status **Declining**

DATE SEEN	WHERE	NOTES

Order **Passeriformes**	Family **Emberizidae**	Species ***Spizella arborea***

American Tree Sparrow

rufous crown
black-and-yellow bill
gray eyebrow and nape
rusty stripe behind eye
rusty tones on shoulder and wings
streaked underparts
ADULT (BREEDING)
IN FLIGHT
JUVENILE
rust patch at shoulder
black and rust streaking on back
two wing bars
dark central breast spot
streaked back
tan, unstreaked flanks and underparts
ADULT (BREEDING)
ADULT (NONBREEDING)
long square tail

The first heavy snowfalls of winter often bring flocks of American Tree Sparrows to birdfeeders. This bird is commonly mistaken for the smaller Chipping Sparrow, but the two species look different in winter. The American Tree Sparrow's central breast spot, bicolored bill, and relatively large size are unique among *Spizella* sparrows. American Tree Sparrows are social birds and some winter flocks can number in the hundreds. Poorly named, this species actually breeds in boggy habitats of the Far North.

VOICE Call a bell-like *teedle-ee*; flight call a thin, slightly descending *tsiiiu*; song *seee seee di-di-di di-di-di dyew dyew.*

NESTING Neat cup on ground concealed within thicket; 4–6 eggs; 1 brood; June–July.

FEEDING Feeds on seeds, berries, and a variety of insects.

FLIGHT: lightly undulating, often flies to open perch when flushed.

WINTER HABITATS
In winter this species frequents barren habitats, like old fields and roadsides, as well as feeders.

SIMILAR SPECIES

CHIPPING SPARROW see p.400
lacks rusty eye-line
no central, black breast spot

FIELD SPARROW see p.466
all-pale bill
bold white eye-ring
smaller overall

OCCURRENCE
Breeds in scrubby thickets of birch and willows in the area between taiga and tundra across Alaska and north Canada. Nonbreeders choose open, grassy, brushy habitats. Winters across south Canada and the northern US. Casual to Pacific coast and southern US.

Length **6¼in (16cm)**	Wingspan **9½in (24cm)**	Weight **7/16–7/8oz (13–25g)**
Social **Flocks**	Lifespan **Up to 11 years**	Status **Secure**

DATE SEEN	WHERE	NOTES

Order **Passeriformes**	Family **Emberizidae**	Species ***Spizella passerina***

Chipping Sparrow

The Chipping Sparrow is a common and trusting bird, which breeds in backyards across most of North America. While they are easily identifiable in the summer, "Chippers" molt into a drab, nonbreeding plumage during fall, at which point they are easily confused with the Clay-colored and Brewer's Sparrows they flock with. Most winter reports of this species in the north are actually of the larger American Tree Sparrow. In winter, Chipping Sparrows lack their bright, rusty crown and are restricted to the southern states.

VOICE Call a sharp *tsip*; flight call a sharp, thin *tsiiit*; song an insect-like trill of chip notes, variable in duration and intensity.

NESTING Neat cup usually placed well off the ground in tree or shrub; 3–5 eggs; 1–2 broods; April–August.

FEEDING Eats seeds of grasses and annuals, plus some fruits; when breeding, also eats insects and other invertebrates.

FLIGHT: lightly undulating, often to open perch when flushed.

BACKYARD BIRD
Chipping Sparrows are common in gardens and backyards all across the continent.

SIMILAR SPECIES

CLAY-COLORED SPARROW see p.401
heavy streaks

BREWER'S SPARROW see p.402
streaked crown
partial "necklace"
pale underparts

OCCURRENCE
Found in a wide variety of habitats: open forest, woodlands, grassy park-like areas, seashores, and backyards. Breeds in North America south of the Arctic timberline southward to Mexico, and in Central America as far south as Nicaragua. Winters from southern states to Nicaragua.

Length **5½in (14cm)**	Wingspan **8½in (21cm)**	Weight **⅜–½oz (10–15g)**
Social **Large flocks**	Lifespan **Up to 9 years**	Status **Secure**

DATE SEEN	WHERE	NOTES

Order **Passeriformes**	Family **Emberizidae**	Species ***Spizella pallida***

Clay-colored Sparrow

FLIGHT: lightly undulating, often flies to open perch when flushed.

The small Clay-colored Sparrow is best known for its mechanical, buzzy song. This bird spends much of its foraging time away from its breeding habitat; consequently, males' territories are very small, allowing for dense breeding populations. Clay-colored Sparrows have shifted their breeding range eastward and northward over the last century, most likely because of changes in land practices. During the nonbreeding season, they form large flocks in open country, associating with other *Spizella* sparrows, especially Chippings and Brewer's.

VOICE Call a sharp *tsip*; flight call a short, rising *sip*; song a series of 2–7 mechanical buzzes on one pitch.

NESTING Cup of grass placed just off the ground in shrub or small tree; 3–5 eggs; 1–2 broods; May–August.

FEEDING Forages on or near the ground for seeds and insects.

CHRISTMAS PRESENT
The Clay-colored Sparrow is fond of low conifers for breeding, so Christmas tree farms form a perfect habitat.

OCCURRENCE
Breeds in open habitats: prairies, shrubland, forest edges, and Christmas tree farms along the US/Canadian border and northward to the southern Northwest Territory. Winters in a large variety of brushy and weedy areas from south Texas to Mexico. Migration takes it to the Great Plains.

Length **5½in (14cm)**	Wingspan **7½in (19cm)**	Weight **⅜–½oz (10–15g)**
Social **Large flocks**	Lifespan **Up to 5 years**	Status **Secure**

DATE SEEN	WHERE	NOTES

Order **Passeriformes**	Family **Emberizidae**	Species ***Spizella breweri***

Brewer's Sparrow

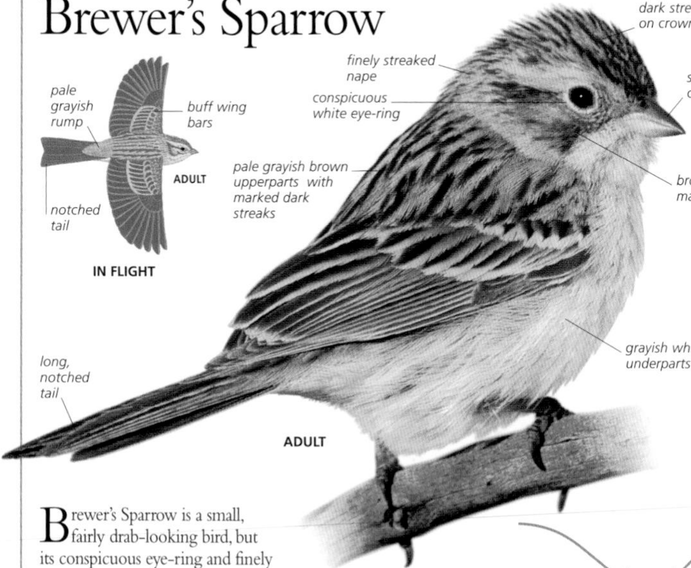
pale grayish rump
buff wing bars
ADULT
notched tail
IN FLIGHT
dark streaks on crown
finely streaked nape
small, conical bill
conspicuous white eye-ring
pale grayish brown upperparts with marked dark streaks
brown facial markings
grayish white underparts
long, notched tail
ADULT

Brewer's Sparrow is a small, fairly drab-looking bird, but its conspicuous eye-ring and finely streaked nape are good identification marks as is its varied, loud, and often sustained song. Most of these sparrows nest in arid sagebrush in the western US and Alberta, but an isolated population, subspecies *S. b. taverneri* ("Timberline Sparrow"), breeds in the Canadian Rockies and north Alaska. It is darker, more boldly marked, and longer-billed with a slower, more musical song. This species was named to honor Thomas Mayo Brewer, a naturalist from Massachusetts.

VOICE Call a sharp *tsip*; flight call a short, rising *sip*; song a long series of descending trills, rattles, and buzzes on different pitches: quite a production.

NESTING Compact cup on or near ground in small bush; 3–4 eggs; 1–2 broods; May–August.

FEEDING Forages on ground for insects and seeds.

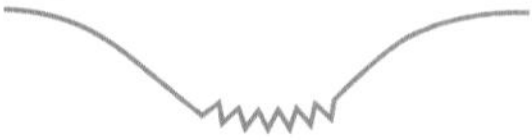

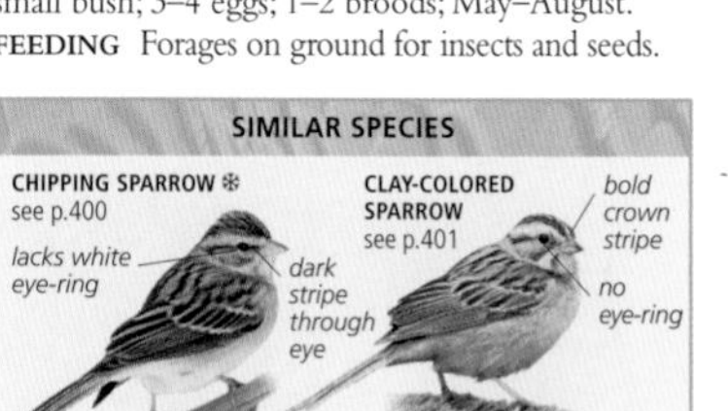

FLIGHT: lightly undulating; alternates rapidly between glides and active flight.

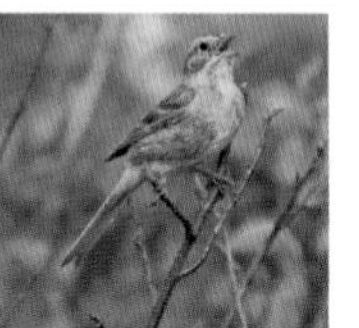

CONTINUOUS SINGING
Across its range in spring, male Brewer's Sparrows sing continuously to attract a mate.

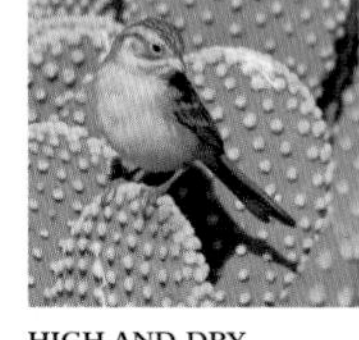

HIGH AND DRY
These sparrows are fond of the arid brushlands and deserts of the High Plains and Great Basin.

SIMILAR SPECIES

CHIPPING SPARROW ❄
see p.400
lacks white eye-ring
dark stripe through eye
CLAY-COLORED SPARROW
see p.401
bold crown stripe
no eye-ring

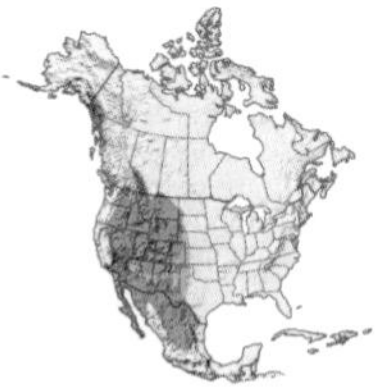

OCCURRENCE
The "Timberline" subspecies breeds in mountain valleys of eastern Alaska and the western Yukon. The "Brewer's" subspecies breeds in brushlands, shrublands, and thickets, especially sagebrush, in the intermontane West. Winters in desert scrub and weedy fields in the Southwest, and northwestern and central Mexico.

Length **5½in (14cm)**	Wingspan **7½in (19cm)**	Weight **5/16–½oz (9–14g)**
Social **Solitary/Flocks**	Lifespan **Unknown**	Status **Declining**

DATE SEEN	WHERE	NOTES

Order **Passeriformes**	Family **Emberizidae**	Species ***Pooecetes gramineus***

Vesper Sparrow

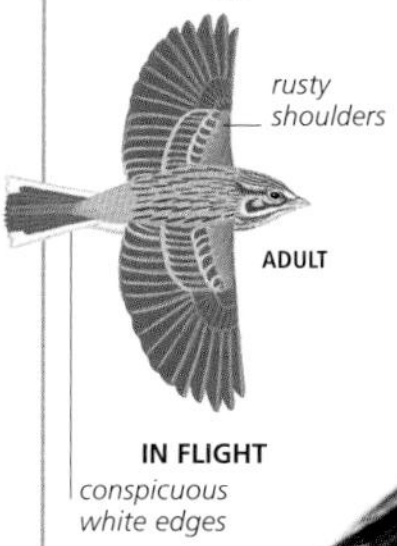

rusty shoulders
ADULT
IN FLIGHT
conspicuous white edges

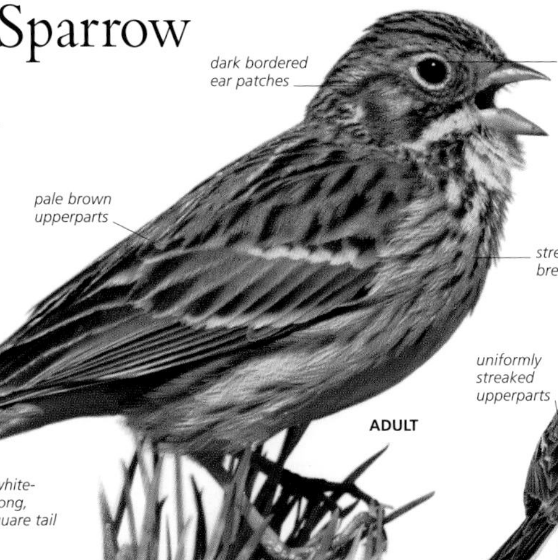

dark bordered ear patches
white eye-ring
pale brown upperparts
streaked breast
ADULT
boldly white-edged long, dark, square tail

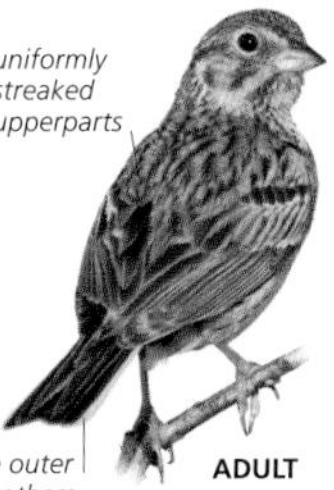

uniformly streaked upperparts
white outer tail feathers
ADULT

The Vesper Sparrow got its common name because its song was considered by some ornithologists to sound sweeter in the evening, when "vespers" are sung in the Catholic church. When Henry David Thoreau wrote of this species, he called it the "Bay-winged Bunting," a name given by Audubon because of its (sometimes concealed) rusty shoulder patches. The Vesper Sparrow needs areas with bare ground to breed, so it is one of the few species that can successfully nest in areas of intensive agriculture; the bird's numbers seem to be declining in spite of this.

VOICE Full *tchup* call, flight call thin *tseent*; song consists of 2 whistles of same pitch, followed by 2 higher-pitched ones, then trills, ends lazily.

NESTING Cup placed on patch of bare ground, against grass, bush, or rock; 3–5 eggs; 1 brood; April–August.

FEEDING Eats insects and seeds.

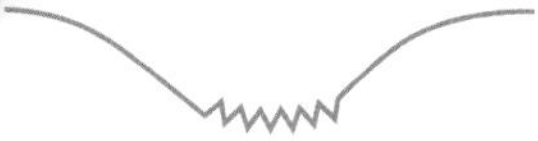

FLIGHT: strong, often perches when flushed; often moves on ground.

SIMILAR SPECIES

SAVANNAH SPARROW see p.396

SAVANNAH SPARROW Eastern

smaller bill
lacks white eye-ring
orange feet

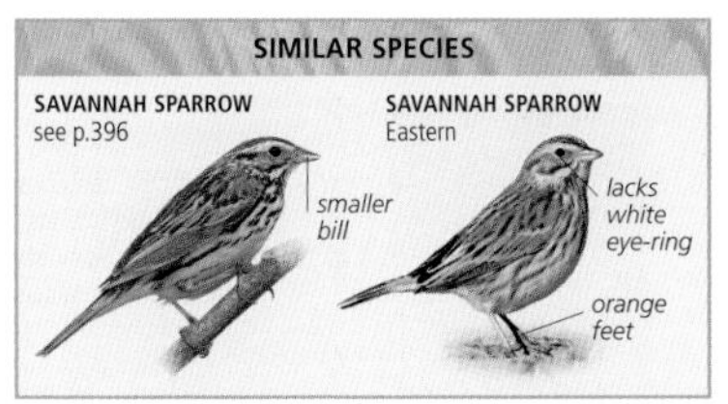

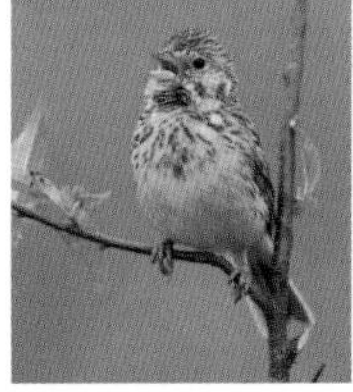

GIFTED SONGSTER
The sweet song of the Vesper Sparrow is a characteristic sound of northern open areas.

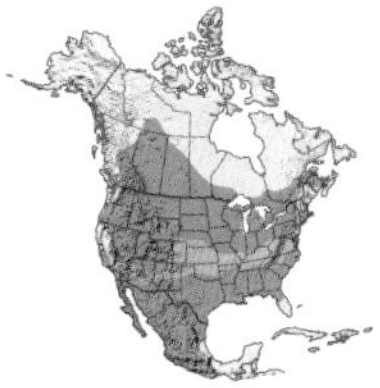

OCCURRENCE
In the West, found in sagebrush, open pine woodlands, and subalpine grasslands. Occurs from the Maritimes westward to the Northwest Territories, and southward to California and Arizona. Winters in sparsely vegetated, open habitats from southern US to southwest Mexico.

Length **6¼in (16cm)**	Wingspan **10in (25cm)**	Weight **11/16–1 1/16oz (20–30g)**
Social **Flocks**	Lifespan **Up to 7 years**	Status **Declining**

DATE SEEN	WHERE	NOTES

Order **Passeriformes**	Family **Emberizidae**	Species ***Chondestes grammacus***

Lark Sparrow

long, rounded tail with white corners

ADULT

IN FLIGHT

pale patch at base of outer wing feathers

JUVENILE

thick gray bill

central breast spot

unique bold facial pattern

brown upperparts

central breast spot

long tail

ADULT

FLIGHT: strong flight, in straight lines; often perches when flushed.

The bold harlequin facial pattern, single central breast spot, and long, rounded, black tail with white outer corners make the Lark Sparrow one of the most easily identifiable of North American sparrows. It is commonly found singing from the top of a fencepost or small tree in the western US. Conversely, Lark Sparrow numbers have declined precipitously in the East, where the species is mostly associated with western-like sandy soils. It is likely, however, that its presence in the East was only possible because of the clearing of forests, so the species may in fact simply be retreating to its natural range. Males are strongly territorial at their nesting sites.

VOICE Thin, up-slurred *tseep* call, flight call sharp *tink*; song series of trills, whistles, and rattles on varying pitches.

NESTING Cup usually placed on ground at base of plant, or off-ground in tree or bush; 3–5 eggs; 1–2 broods; April–August.

FEEDING Eats seeds and insects.

ON THE FENCE
The Lark Sparrow is a common roadside bird, often found perching on barbed wire fences.

OCCURRENCE
In the West, breeds in a variety of open habitats, such as sagebrush flats and grasslands from British Columbia and Saskatchewan to Baja California and central Mexico. Localized breeder in the East, associated with well-drained soils, east to Ohio. Winters from southern US to southwestern and central Mexico.

Length **6–6¾in (15–17cm)**	Wingspan **11in (28cm)**	Weight **11/16–1 1/16oz (20–30g)**
Social **Large flocks**	Lifespan **Up to 8 years**	Status **Secure**

DATE SEEN	WHERE	NOTES

Order **Passeriformes**	Family **Emberizidae**	Species ***Amphispiza bilineata***

Black-throated Sparrow

Because of perceived similarities in their songs, the Black-throated Sparrow has been called "the Song Sparrow of the desert." They are easily identified as they possess a bold white eyebrow in all plumages, which prevents confusion with other species. It is possible, however, for first-time observers to misidentify juvenile Black-throated Sparrows for Sage Sparrows. The Black-throated Sparrow is exclusively western. It lives in a variety of arid habitats, especially on hillsides covered with cactus, creosote, and ocotillo, but also in sagebrush and open pine woodlands.

VOICE Weak *tink* call; song consists of a few short, clear notes, followed by a high trill: *tink tink-tink treeeeee*, also *ti-ti-tink churrrrrrrrrr*.

NESTING Loose cup placed on or near ground in bush or grass; 3–4 eggs; 1–2 broods; March–September.

FEEDING Eats seeds, insects, and cactus fruit.

FLIGHT: direct with rapid wing beats, flies low between shrubs and trees.

CLEAR PLUMAGE
No other sparrow comes close to equaling this species' bold head and throat patterning.

SIMILAR SPECIES

SPRING SINGER
In spring the male declares his territory by singing from the top of a yucca or other high perch.

OCCURRENCE
Found in desert scrub, from the Great Basin east and south to Texas, south to Baja California and central Mexico. Breeds sporadically in eastern Washington state. Withdraws from the Great Basin and much of the arid Southwest in winter. Resident in Mexico. Casual to the Pacific coast and the East.

Length **5½in (14cm)**	Wingspan **7¾in (19.5cm)**	Weight **3/8–9/16oz (10–16g)**
Social **Solitary**	Lifespan **Up to 6 years**	Status **Secure**

DATE SEEN	WHERE	NOTES

Order **Passeriformes**	Family **Emberizidae**	Species ***Amphispiza belli***

Sage Sparrow

FLIGHT: weak; undulating over short distances; drops quickly to the ground.

With its tail cocked and held high above its back, the Sage Sparrow can be seen darting on the ground from bush to bush in sagebrush flats and dense shrub growth. There are five subspecies, which can be grouped into two main populations that vary in habitat, plumage, migratory habits, and song, and were once considered to be separate species. "Bell's Sparrow" (*A. b. belli*) from California, has much darker upperparts with an unstreaked upper shoulder, a thick, lateral throat stripe, and a plain, dark tail. The "Sage Sparrow" (*A. b. nevadensis*) from much of the West, has pale upperparts with dark upper-shoulder streaking, a thin, lateral throat stripe, and a white-edged tail. All five subspecies are declining, mainly because of habitat loss. One—*A. b. clementeae*, found only on San Clemente Island, off California—is listed as threatened.

VOICE Call sharp, short *tink*; Bell's song consists of jumbled squeaky notes; True Sage's song low-pitched *free FROOH dudu, free FROOH dudu.*

NESTING Cup placed just off ground in shrub or on the ground (never in case of Bell's Sparrow); 1–5 eggs; 1–3 broods; March–July.

FEEDING Eats seeds, insects, and fruit.

SAGE FLAT SPECIALIST
The Sage Sparrow requires a habitat with extensive expanses of sagebrush.

SIMILAR SPECIES

BELL'S SPARROW
"Bell's Sparrow" is much darker than the "Sage Sparrow," and has a completely black tail.

OCCURRENCE
"Bell's Sparrow" is a resident of steep hillsides with dense shrub growth, from northern California south to central Baja California. The "Sage Sparrow" breeds in Great Basin sagebrush flats, and winters in the interior Southwest. Casual in the Great Plains, accidental in the East.

Length **6–6½in (15-16cm)**	Wingspan **8½in (21cm)**	Weight **7/16–11/16oz (13–19g)**
Social **Solitary**	Lifespan **Up to 7 years**	Status **Declining**

DATE SEEN	WHERE	NOTES

Order **Passeriformes**	Family **Emberizidae**	Species ***Aimophila cassinii***

Cassin's Sparrow

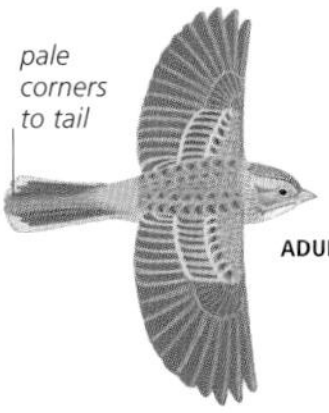

pale corners to tail

ADULT

IN FLIGHT

more buffy overall

brown streaked underparts

JUVENILE

streaked crown

small bill

pale eye-ring

scalloped upperparts

fine patterning on breast

ADULT

long rounded tail, with barred central feathers

Cassin's Sparrow, a rather drab little brown bird, more than makes up for its modest appearance with its impressive song, which it often delivers during a bout of skylarking. The end of the song (all of which seems to be in a minor key) is usually a whistled quadruplet that ends on a discordant, questioning note. The bird's occurrence outside its core range—the arid grasslands of central-southern US—depends on rainfall, so it may be rare in some locations one summer, but abundant in the same places the next.

VOICE Calls high *seeps* and *chips*, often in series; song *see-eee sii-ii-i-i-i-i-i-i-i zee-zooo' zee-ZWAAAY*, ending on questioning note.

NESTING Cup placed in grass on or near ground, often in prickly-pear cactus; 2–5 eggs; 1–2 broods; May–September.

FEEDING Scratches around on ground for seeds, flowers, buds, insects, insect larvae, and spiders.

FLIGHT: direct and low, somewhat weak, with fast wing beats in bursts.

COMMON TUNE
This sparrow's song is well known in the central-southern US, and an easy way to identify the bird.

SIMILAR SPECIES

BACHMAN'S SPARROW — smaller overall; grayer overall

BOTTERI'S SPARROW see p.467 — no eye-ring; larger bill; dark tail

OCCURRENCE
Breeds in arid grasslands with scattered shrubs, yuccas, and low trees, from western Nebraska southward to central Mexico. Winters from US–Mexican border southward to central Mexico.

Length **6in (15cm)**	Wingspan **9in (23cm)**	Weight **⅝–$^{11}/_{16}$oz (18–20g)**
Social **Solitary**	Lifespan **Unknown**	Status **Declining**

DATE SEEN	WHERE	NOTES

Order **Passeriformes**	Family **Emberizidae**	Species ***Aimophila ruficeps***

Rufous-crowned Sparrow

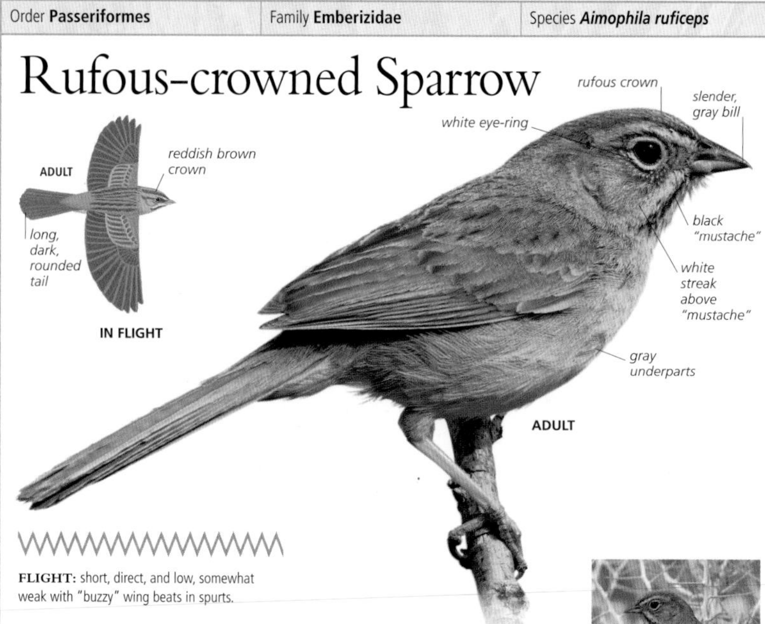

FLIGHT: short, direct, and low, somewhat weak with "buzzy" wing beats in spurts.

This sparrow is a common resident of dry canyons and sparsely wooded hillsides in the southwestern US, locally up to 5,000ft (1,500m). Its range is similar to that of the Greater Roadrunner. The Rufous-crowned Sparrow is a real skulker, running and hiding at the first sign of danger. For this reason, it is often first detected by its characteristic *deeer* call note, which it gives sometimes in a laughter-like series. The Rufous-crowned Sparrow is quite similar to the rarer Rufous-winged Sparrow, but they have very different calls, and live in separate habitats. Rufous-winged Sparrows live in flat desert.

VOICE Call a low, nasal *deeer*; song a jumble of chattering notes.

NESTING Cup of twigs and grass placed in bush or rocks on or near ground; 2–5 eggs; 1–3 broods; March–September.

FEEDING Forages on ground and in shrubs for seeds, insects, and insect larvae.

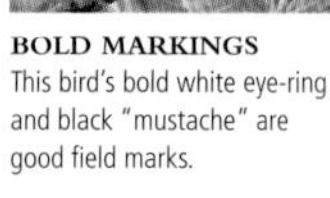

BOLD MARKINGS
This bird's bold white eye-ring and black "mustache" are good field marks.

CATCHING A GLIMPSE
Occasionally, this skulking bird will hop up to a perch to look at its surroundings.

OCCURRENCE
Resides in arid scrub and low trees on hillsides and in canyons in California, Colorado, Utah, Arizona, New Mexico, Oklahoma, Texas, and Arkansas; also in Mexico (Baja California, on mainland to Isthmus of Tehuantepec). In Mexico found in oak-pine woodlands.

Length **6in (15cm)**	Wingspan **7½in (19cm)**	Weight **½–⅞oz (15–25g)**
Social **Solitary**	Lifespan **Unknown**	Status **Secure**

DATE SEEN	WHERE	NOTES

Order **Passeriformes**	Family **Emberizidae**	Species ***Pipilo chlorurus***

Green-tailed Towhee

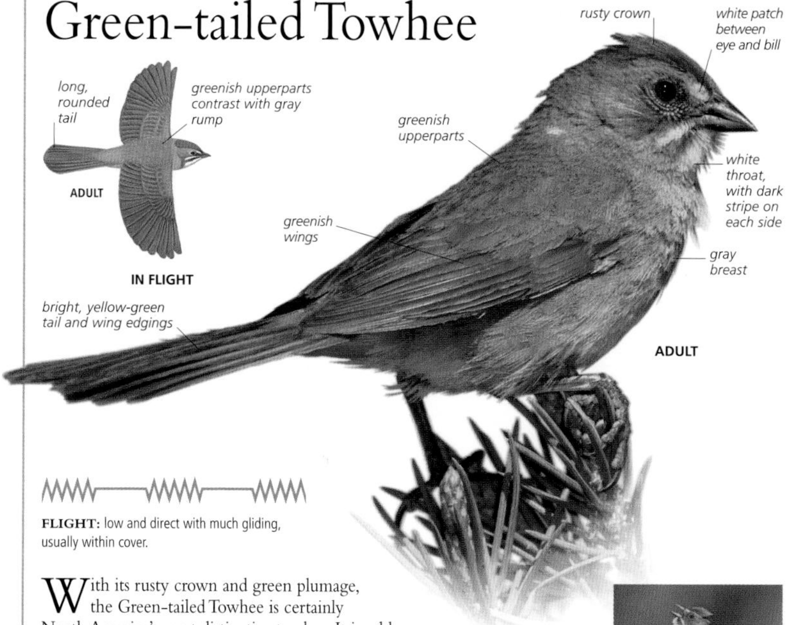
long, rounded tail
greenish upperparts contrast with gray rump
ADULT
IN FLIGHT
rusty crown
white patch between eye and bill
greenish upperparts
white throat, with dark stripe on each side
greenish wings
gray breast
bright, yellow-green tail and wing edgings
ADULT

FLIGHT: low and direct with much gliding, usually within cover.

With its rusty crown and green plumage, the Green-tailed Towhee is certainly North America's most distinctive towhee. It is seldom seen, however, because it tends to stay hidden on the ground in dense cover, both in the breeding season and in winter, although in that season, Green-tailed Towhees come out to feed on seeds on deserted, dusty roads. But generally you are more likely to hear this bird scratching about in the undergrowth than see it. Although the Olive Sparrow is superficially similar, the two seldom overlap in range or habitat.

VOICE Call a nasal mewing, rapid chips in excitement; flight call a high *tzhreeee*; song a slurred whistle followed by 1–2 trills.

NESTING Bulky cup of twigs and grasses placed on or near ground at base of sagebrush; 3–4 eggs; 1–2 broods; May–July.

FEEDING Forages under cover, often by "double-scratching" with both feet at the same time, for insects, insect larvae, seeds, and some fruit.

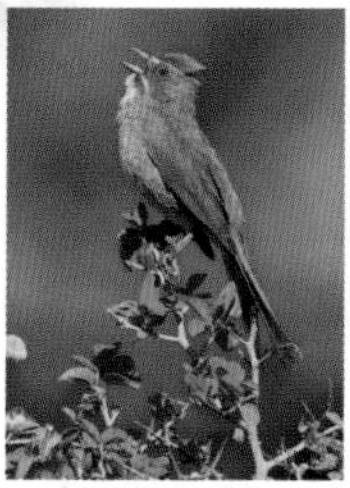

WHERE TO SEE IT
Finding a single male atop a bush or tree may be the easiest way to see this bird.

SIMILAR SPECIES

CHIPPING SPARROW see p.400

white wing bars
much smaller overall

OLIVE SPARROW see p.468

no rufous on crown
smaller overall
lacks bold throat markings

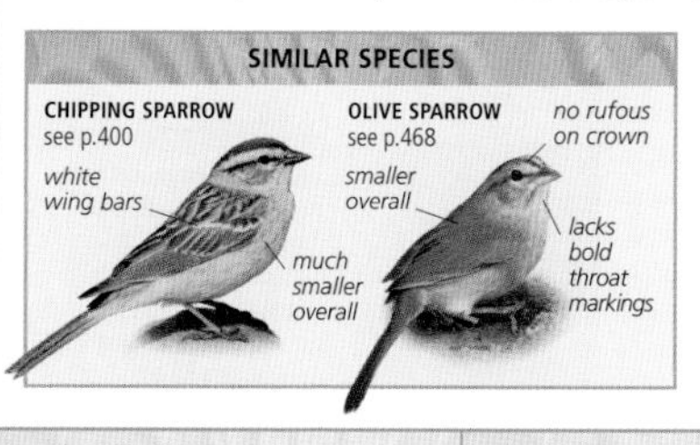

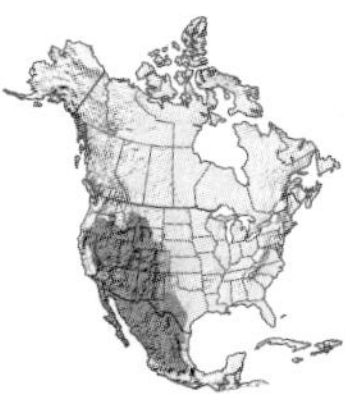

OCCURRENCE
Breeds in a variety of habitats, including chaparral, shrubby hillsides, sagebrush flats, and high-elevation creeks, in much of the western US and northern Baja California. Winters in desert thickets and shallow ravines from the US–Mexican border region southward to central Mexico.

Length **7¼in (18.5cm)**	Wingspan **9½in (24cm)**	Weight **11/16–1¼oz (20–35g)**
Social **Solitary/Small flocks**	Lifespan **Up to 8 years**	Status **Secure**

DATE SEEN	WHERE	NOTES

Order **Passeriformes**	Family **Emberizidae**	Species ***Pipilo maculatus***

Spotted Towhee

rounded tail

white wing bars

white tail tips

IN FLIGHT

MALE

brown tail

white spots on dark sepia-brown upperparts

blackish brown head

FEMALE

long tail, with white outer feathers

broad white spots on black upperparts

red eye

black head

rusty red flanks

rusty flanks

white underparts

MALE

FLIGHT: low and direct, with much gliding, usually within cover.

This large and colorful western sparrow can often be heard rummaging through dry leaves in the undergrowth in search of food, where it may produce roughly circular pits in the soil, using its feet like a garden rake. The Spotted Towhee is variable across its range, and has been separated into 20 subspecies. All of them are distinguished from the Eastern Towhee, the Spotted Towhee's eastern counterpart, by white spots and bars on their upperparts.

VOICE Depending on geographical location, call *zhreee* or a buzzy, nasal, descending *reeeer*; song ends with a trill.

NESTING Large cup in depression on ground, under cover, also low in thicket; 3–5 eggs; 1–2 broods; April–June.

FEEDING Scratches for food, including insects, fruits, seeds, and acorns; sometimes eats small snakes and lizards.

RUFOUS SIDES
The Spotted Towhee was once grouped with the Eastern Towhee under the name "Rufous-sided Towhee."

DIFFERENT DIALECTS
The vocalizations of the Spotted Towhees vary geographically.

SIMILAR SPECIES

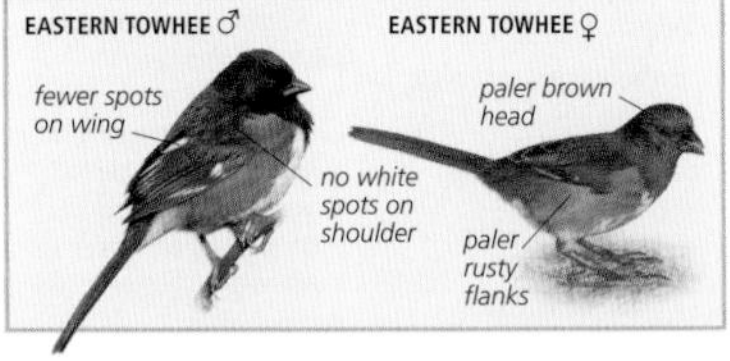

EASTERN TOWHEE ♂

fewer spots on wing

no white spots on shoulder

EASTERN TOWHEE ♀

paler brown head

paler rusty flanks

OCCURRENCE
Breeds mainly in thickets, shrubby hillsides, and woodlands, from southern British Columbia and Saskatchewan across the western US, southward to southern Oaxaca, Mexico, but occurs in dense forests in coastal British Columbia. Winters in the south-central US and western Midwest.

Length **8in (20cm)**	Wingspan **10½in (27cm)**	Weight **1¼–1 9/16oz (35–45g)**
Social **Solitary/Small flocks**	Lifespan **Up to 11 years**	Status **Secure**

DATE SEEN	WHERE	NOTES

Order **Passeriformes**	Family **Emberizidae**	Species ***Pipilo fuscus***

Canyon Towhee

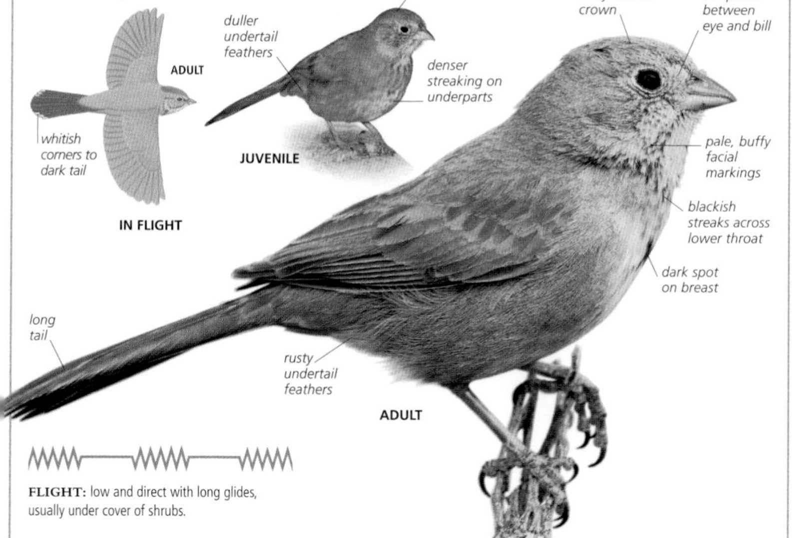
faint crown patch
duller undertail feathers
ADULT
denser streaking on underparts
whitish corners to dark tail
JUVENILE
IN FLIGHT
rusty brown crown
tan patch between eye and bill
pale, buffy facial markings
blackish streaks across lower throat
dark spot on breast
long tail
rusty undertail feathers
ADULT

FLIGHT: low and direct with long glides, usually under cover of shrubs.

The Canyon Towhee (once merged with the California Towhee as a single species, the "Brown Towhee") is a bird of the arid Southwest, where it occurs in a wide variety of bushy habitats. Its pale, sandy coloration helps it to blend in with the dusty ground on which it forages. Other species of birds inhabiting the arid Southwest, such as Curve-Billed, Le Conte's, Bendire's, and Crissal Thrashers also share this pale color scheme of sand-colored bodies and rusty undertail feathers. The Canyon Towhee, however, can be easily distinguished from the others by its stubby, conical bill.

VOICE Call a nasal *cheemp*; also various clicking and lisping notes, sometimes in series; song a variable slow trill.

NESTING Cup placed at about eye-level close to, or against trunk of tree or bush; 2–5 eggs; 1–2 broods; February–October.

FEEDING Forages on the ground for insects and seeds.

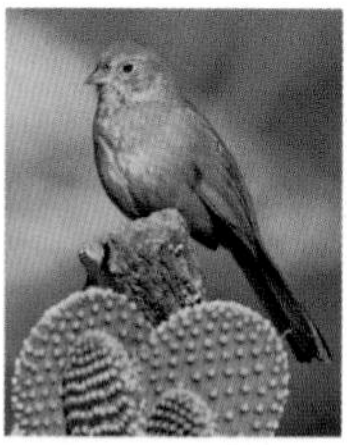

DESERT LOVER
The Canyon Towhee likes to perch high to survey its territory.

SIMILAR SPECIES

CALIFORNIA TOWHEE
see p.467
darker overall
no central breast spot
ABERT'S TOWHEE
see p.467
black mask
darker face
pale bill
unstreaked underparts

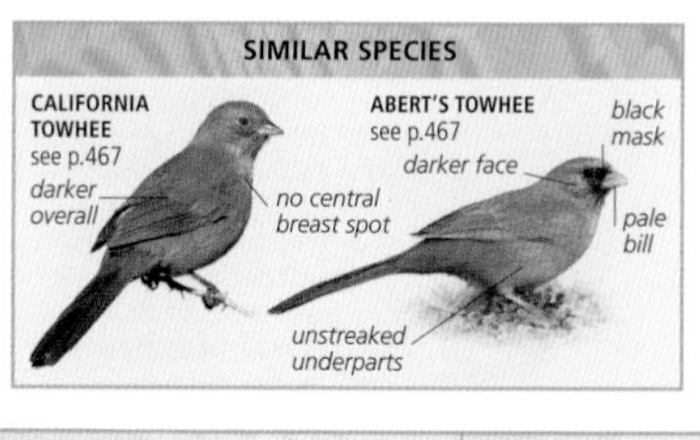

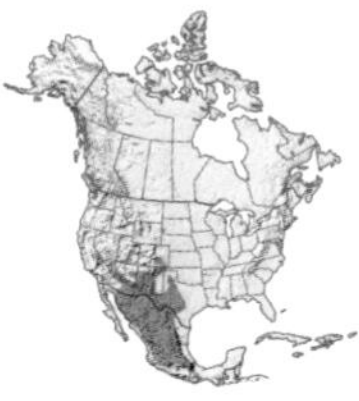

OCCURRENCE
Lives in a variety of habitats, including rocky hillside scrub, desert grasslands, and suburban areas from west Arizona, southeast Colorado, and central Texas to central Mexico. Largely resident, but some birds undertake local movements.

Length **8½in (21cm)**	Wingspan **11½in (29cm)**	Weight **1¼–1¾oz (35–50g)**
Social **Solitary/Small flocks**	Lifespan **Up to 7 years**	Status **Secure**

DATE SEEN	WHERE	NOTES

Order **Passeriformes**	Family **Thraupidae**	Species ***Piranga rubra***

Summer Tanager

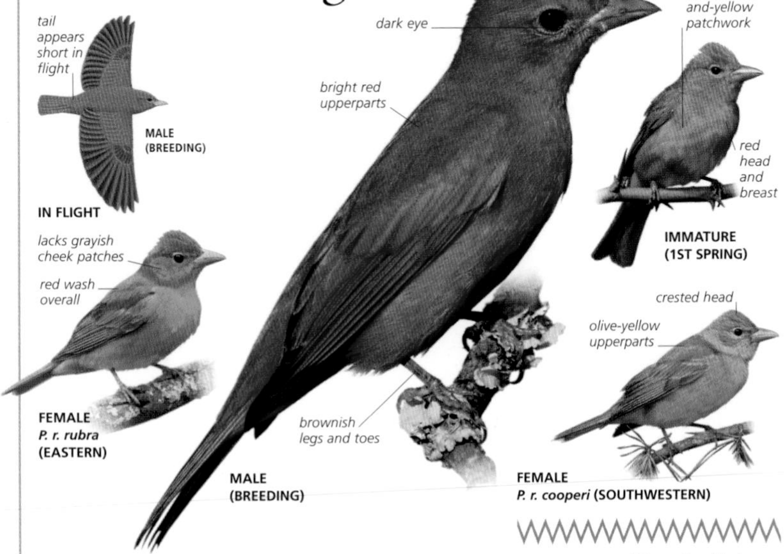

thick, long, yellowish bill
variable red-and-yellow patchwork
tail appears short in flight
MALE (BREEDING)
IN FLIGHT
dark eye
bright red upperparts
red head and breast
IMMATURE (1ST SPRING)
lacks grayish cheek patches
red wash overall
FEMALE P. r. rubra (EASTERN)
crested head
olive-yellow upperparts
brownish legs and toes
MALE (BREEDING)
FEMALE P. r. cooperi (SOUTHWESTERN)

FLIGHT: strong and direct with quick wing beats; occasionally glides.

The stunning male Summer Tanager is the only North American bird that is entirely bright red. Immature males in their first spring plumage are almost equally as striking, with their patchwork of bright yellow-and-red plumage. The two subspecies of the Summer Tanager are quite similar—*P. r. rubra* breeds in the East while *P. r. cooperi* breeds in the West. The latter is, on an average, paler, larger, and longer-billed.

VOICE Call an explosive *PIT-tuck!* or *PIT-a TUK*; flight call a muffled, airy *vreee*; song similar to American Robin, but more muffled and with longer pauses.

NESTING Loosely built cup of grasses usually placed high up in tree; 3–4 eggs; 1 brood; May–August.

FEEDING Eats bees, wasps, and other insects; also consumes fruit.

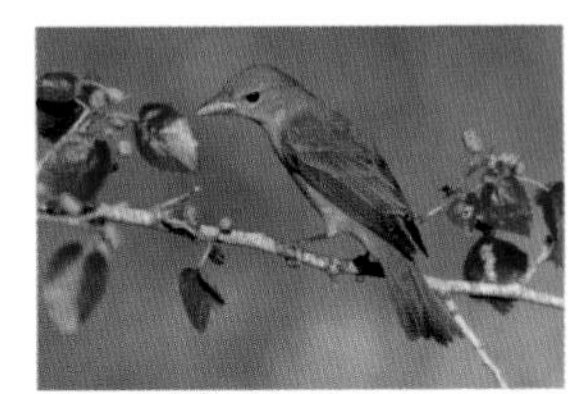

MAD FOR MULBERRIES
All *Piranga* tanagers are frugivores in season and mulberries are one of their favorites.

SIMILAR SPECIES
HEPATIC TANAGER ♀
see p.468
yellowish upperparts
reddish brown wings
SCARLET TANAGER ♀
greenish overall
smaller, grayish bill
darker, wings and tail

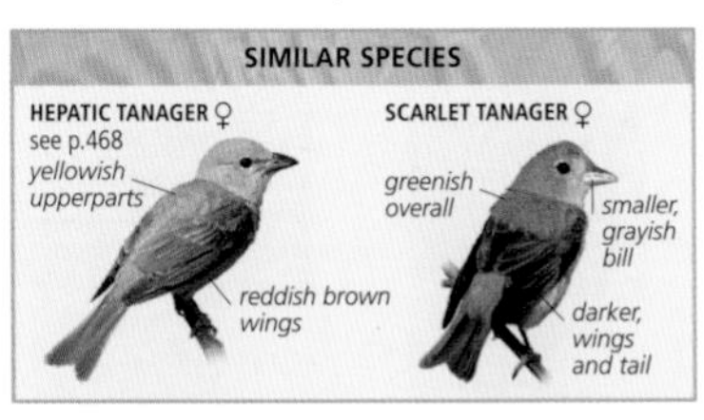

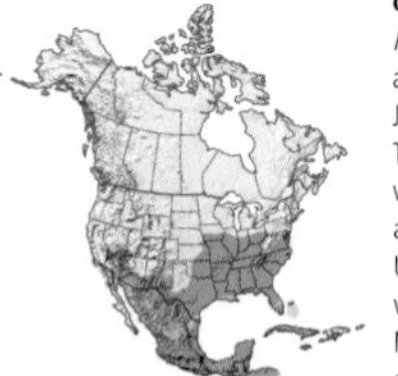

OCCURRENCE
P. r. rubra breeds in deciduous and mixed woodlands from New Jersey and Nebraska south to Texas; *P. r. cooperi* in cottonwood-willow habitats near streams and rivers from California and Utah to Texas and Mexico. Both winter from southern Texas and Mexico to Bolivia and Brazil, and the West Indies.

Length **8in (20cm)**	Wingspan **12in (31cm)**	Weight **⅞–1⁷⁄₁₆oz (25–40g)**
Social **Solitary**	Lifespan **Unknown**	Status **Secure**

DATE SEEN	WHERE	NOTES

Order **Passeriformes**	Family **Thraupidae**	Species ***Piranga ludoviciana***

Western Tanager

orange head and hood, blending into yellow
two wing bars
more olive and grayish overall
yellow collar
yellow upperwing bar
red wash on face
orange head
jet-black back
FEMALE (NONBREEDING)
MALE (BREEDING)
white lower wing bar
IN FLIGHT
black tail
bright yellow underparts
MALE (NONBREEDING)
bluish gray feet and legs
bright yellow rump
MALE (BREEDING)
olive-green upperparts
FEMALE (BREEDING)

FLIGHT: strong and direct; deliberate.

The hoarse song of the exquisitely plumaged male Western Tanager is a characteristic sound of coniferous forests in western North America. All *Piranga* tanagers have songs and whistled flight calls that closely resemble those of the *Pheucticus* grosbeaks. Recent studies hint that this is not a coincidence and that *Piranga* tanagers are actually part of the family Cardinalidae (cardinals and their allies), not Thraupidae (tanagers).

VOICE Distinctive call, a rolled *pruh-DHIT!* or *pur-duh-RIT!*; flight call a *hweee*; song similar to Scarlet Tanager, but less burry.

NESTING Loosely woven cup of grasses, lined with rootlets, high in tree; 3–5 eggs; 1 brood; May–August.

FEEDING Forages for insects, such as termites, flies, moths, and bees in breeding season; eats berries in nonbreeding season.

ORANGE AND YELLOW
Two Western Tanagers display their beautiful orange, yellow, and black plumage.

SIMILAR SPECIES

SCARLET TANAGER ♀
greener overall
lacks bold wing bars

BRIGHT BLEND
This colorful bird blends into its surroundings surprisingly well.

OCCURRENCE
Breeds farther north than any other tanager, in open coniferous and mixed forests of the West, from southeastern Alaska and southwestern Northwest Territories to northern Baja California and western Texas. Winters from southern California and southward to Mexico.

Length **7½in (19cm)**	Wingspan **11½in (29cm)**	Weight **⅞–1¼ oz (25–35g)**
Social **Solitary**	Lifespan **Up to 8 years**	Status **Secure**

DATE SEEN	WHERE	NOTES

Order **Passeriformes**	Family **Cardinalidae**	Species ***Pheucticus ludovicianus***

Rose-breasted Grosbeak

MALE (BREEDING)
IN FLIGHT
white rump
short tail with white corners
IMMATURE MALE (1ST FALL)
rosy or orange breast
white marks on head
large, pinkish bill
white wing bars
thick streaks on underparts
FEMALE
brown patches on back
streaked underparts
MALE (NONBREEDING)
black head and back
bold, white wing patches
rose-red breast
white belly
MALE (BREEDING)

FLIGHT: undulating but powerful flight with bursts of wing beats.

The huge bill of this species earned it the name "grosbeak." For many birdwatchers in the East, the arrival of a flock of dazzling male Rose-breasted Grosbeaks in early May signals the peak of spring songbird migration. Adult males in their tuxedo attire with rose-red ties are unmistakable, but females and immature males are more somber. In the fall, immature males often have orange breasts, and may be mistaken for female Black-headed Grosbeaks. The difference is in the pink wing lining usually visible on perched birds, pink bill, and streaking across the center of the breast.

VOICE Call a high, sharp, explosive *sink* or *eeuk*, flight call an airy *vreee*; song a liquid, flute-like warble, rather slow in delivery, almost relaxed.

NESTING Loose, open cup or platform, usually in deciduous saplings, mid- to high level; 2–5 eggs; 1–2 broods; May–July.

FEEDING Eats arthropods, fruit, seeds, and buds.

STUNNING MALE
A striking male Rose-breasted Grosbeak in springtime is quite unmistakable on a tree.

OCCURRENCE
Uncommon in the western US; breeds in western Canada in deciduous and mixed woods, parks, and orchards. Found across the northeastern US, and across Canada westward from Newfoundland through Ontario to southeastern Yukon. Winters from Mexico and the Caribbean, south to Guyana and Peru.

Length **8in (20cm)**	Wingspan **12½in (32cm)**	Weight **1¼–2oz (35–55g)**
Social **Solitary/Small flocks**	Lifespan **Up to 13 years**	Status **Secure**

DATE SEEN	WHERE	NOTES

Order **Passeriformes**	Family **Cardinalidae**	Species ***Pheucticus melanocephalus***

Black-headed Grosbeak

large, white wing patch
MALE (BREEDING)
IN FLIGHT

blackish brown cheek patch
white tip to feathers
pencil-thin streaks on breast
MALE (1ST FALL)

white eyebrow
brown head and upperparts
tawny breast
FEMALE
fine brown streaks on underparts

black head
thick gray-and-black bill
orange hind collar
black upperparts
orange breast
two white wing bars
orange rump
short tail, with white corners
MALE

FLIGHT: undulating but powerful, with few rapid wing beats followed by glides.

Well known and widespread across the West, this orange-breasted grosbeak is the western counterpart of the Rose-breasted Grosbeak. The two species are closely related, despite their color differences, and interbreed where their ranges meet in the Great Plains. The Black-headed Grosbeak is aggressive on its breeding grounds, with both sexes fighting off intruders.

VOICE Call a *hwik*, similar to Rose-breasted Grosbeak, but flatter, "hollow," and less squeaky; song generally higher, faster, less fluid, and harsher.

NESTING Loose, open cup or platform, usually in deciduous sapling, not far above eye level; 3–5 eggs; 1–2 broods; May–September.

FEEDING Gleans insects and spiders; also eats seeds and fruit.

STREAMSIDE SONGSTER
Through much of its range, this species is common along riverine corridors containing a variety of trees.

SIMILAR SPECIES

CASSIN'S FINCH ♀ see p.340
smaller, dark bill
much smaller overall
lacks bold wing markings

ROSE-BREASTED GROSBEAK ♀ see p.414
pink bill
white belly
dense, thick streaking below

OCCURRENCE
Breeds in dense deciduous growth—old fields, hedgerows, woodlands along waterways, disturbed forests, and hillside thickets—from British Columbia and Saskatchewan, south to Baja California and central Mexico. Winters in interior, highland, and Pacific slope of Mexico.

Length **8½in (21cm)**	Wingspan **12½in (32cm)**	Weight **1 7/16–2oz (40–55g)**
Social **Solitary/Small flocks**	Lifespan **Up to 9 years**	Status **Secure**

DATE SEEN	WHERE	NOTES

Order **Passeriformes**	Family **Cardinalidae**	Species ***Passerina caerulea***

Blue Grosbeak

rufous wing bars
blue upperparts
MALE
IN FLIGHT

upperparts like adult male, but with brown patches
IMMATURE MALE (1ST SUMMER)

uniform dark indigo head
black patch between eye and bill
black streaks on shoulder feathers
rufous shoulder
MALE

tawny wing bars
huge bill
pale tan overall
FEMALE

FLIGHT: lightly undulating, fast, and direct.

Blue Grosbeaks, formerly seen only in the South, have expanded their range northward and westward in recent years, especially in the Great Plains. Nevertheless, they are not abundant anywhere and spotting one is a treat. In the East, dull-plumaged male Indigo Buntings with brown wing bars can be misidentified as Blue Grosbeaks in the spring. Features that help identification are the Blue Grosbeak's huge bill, uniformly dark plumage, black face, and reddish shoulder, which the buntings lack.

VOICE Call a loud, sharp, metallic *tchink*; similar to Indigo Bunting, but lower-pitched, louder, and burrier; song rambling, husky.

NESTING Compact cup placed low in deciduous tangle; 3–5 eggs; 1–2 broods; April–July.

FEEDING Eats seeds in winter, insects such as beetles, caterpillars, and grasshoppers in summer, and fruit.

TRUE INDIGO
The Blue Grosbeak is actually indigo in color, with rufous shoulders and wing bars.

OCCURRENCE
Breeds in dense undergrowth of disturbed habitats: old fields, hedgerows, and desert scrub across the southern US from California to New Jersey, and southward to northwestern Costa Rica; breeders are trans-Gulf migrants; winters from Mexico to Panama and West Indies.

Length **6¾in (17cm)**	Wingspan **11in (28cm)**	Weight **⅞–1¹⁄₁₆oz (25–30g)**
Social **Large flocks**	Lifespan **Up to 6 years**	Status **Secure**

DATE SEEN	WHERE	NOTES

Order **Passeriformes**	Family **Cardinalidae**	Species ***Passerina amoena***

Lazuli Bunting

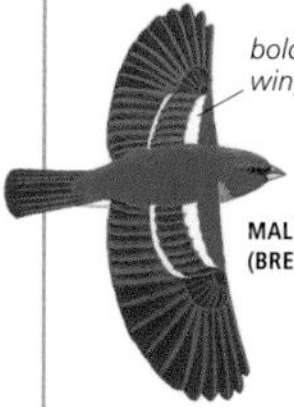
bold, white wing bars
MALE (BREEDING)
IN FLIGHT

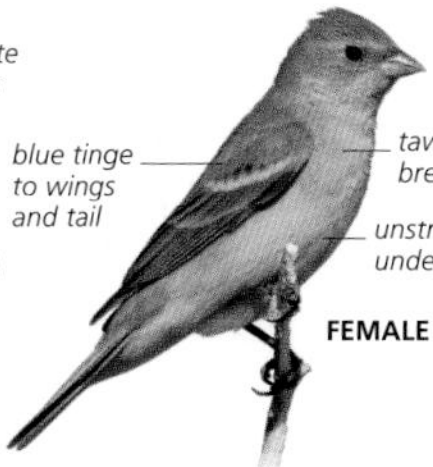
blue tinge to wings and tail
tawny breast
unstreaked underparts
FEMALE

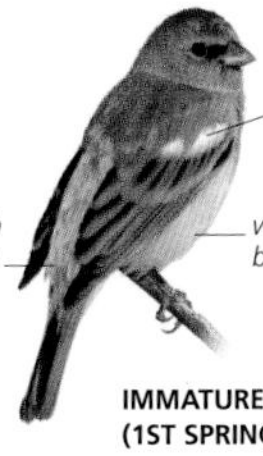
white shoulder
bluish rump
whitish belly
IMMATURE MALE (1ST SPRING)

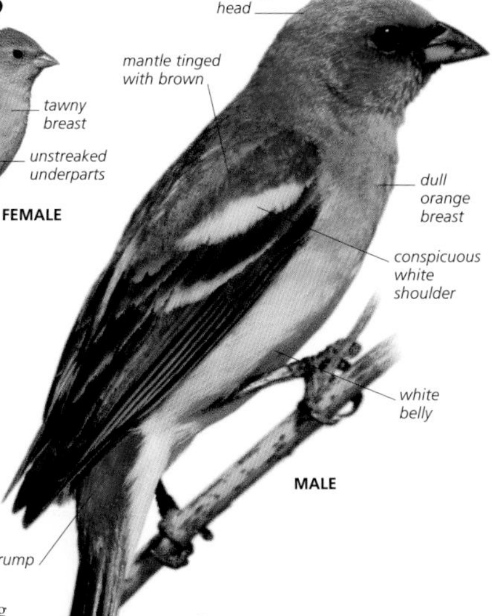
sky-blue head
mantle tinged with brown
dull orange breast
conspicuous white shoulder
white belly
MALE
sky-blue rump

Resembling a small bluebird, the dazzling Lazuli Bunting is the Indigo Bunting's western counterpart. The two species are closely related and hybrids are locally common where the two species meet on the Great Plains. Male hybrids are of two main types—the first resembles an Indigo Bunting with a white belly and wing bars, and the second resembles a dull Indigo Bunting with a brownish smudged back. Females may be impossible to identify. The Lazuli Bunting's common name is taken from the blue, semiprecious gemstone, lapis lazuli.

VOICE Call a sharp, dry, rattling *pik*! similar to Indigo Bunting; song a higher, faster, thinner, and with less repetition than Indigo Bunting.

NESTING Open cup above ground in dense tangle or shrub; 3–4 eggs; 1–2 broods; April–August.

FEEDING Eats seeds and fruits; insects if breeding.

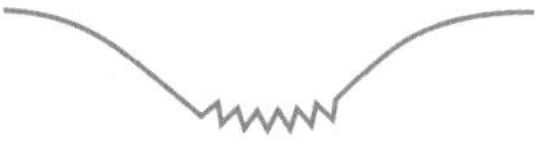

FLIGHT: lightly undulating, fast, and direct; erratic flights during territorial encounters.

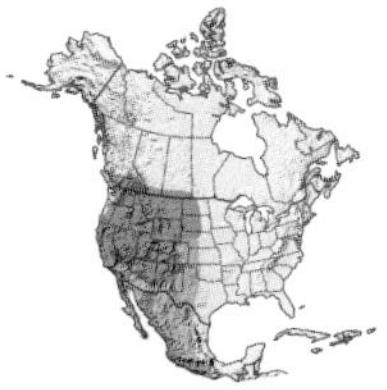

SIMILAR SPECIES

BLUE GROSBEAK ♀ see p.416

reddish rust on shoulder
larger overall
bigger bill

INDIGO BUNTING ♀ see p.469

lacks bold wing bars
streaking on breast

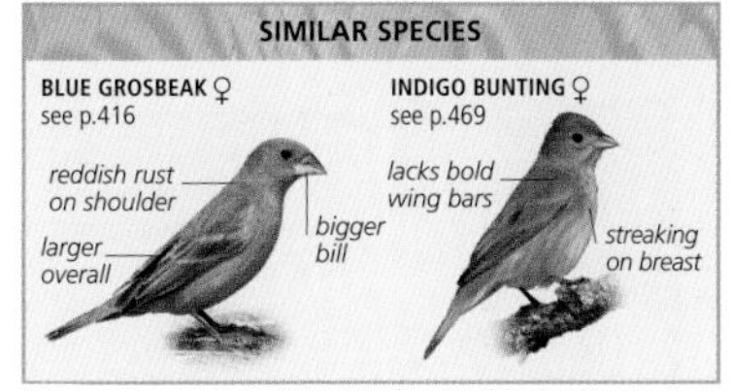

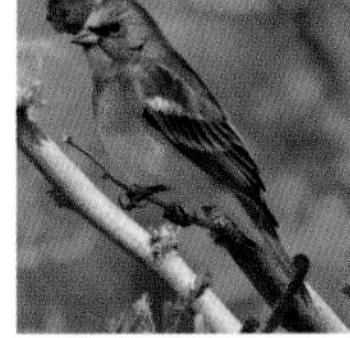

DAPPLED AND DAPPER Brightly colored males blend into their surroundings surprisingly well in dappled sunlight.

OCCURRENCE Breeds in various open, disturbed habitats, especially alongside waterways and in thickets from southern British Columbia and southern Saskatchewan to northern Baja California and northern New Mexico. Winters from southern Arizona to southwestern Mexico. Casual in the East.

Length **5½in (14cm)**	Wingspan **8½in (22cm)**	Weight **7/16–5/8oz (13–18g)**
Social **Large flocks**	Lifespan **Up to 10 years**	Status **Secure**

DATE SEEN	WHERE	NOTES

RARE SPECIES

Family **Odontophoridae** | Species ***Oreortyx pictus***

Mountain Quail

The most diagnostic field marks of this quail are its deep-gray body offset by a chestnut-colored throat and "zebra-striped" flanks edged in black and buff, and its thin, usually vertical head plumes. The largest quail found in the US, it is an adept runner, even uphill, and often prefers running to flying.

OCCURRENCE Resident in Washington, Oregon, California, Idaho, and Nevada; in mixed evergreen and oak forests at mid- to high elevations.

VOICE Males emit crowing *qu-ook* to attract mates; scattered coveys reunite using whistled *kow, kow*.

Length **9–11in (23–28cm)** | Wingspan **14–16in (35–41cm)**

Family **Odontophoridae** | Species ***Callipepla squamata***

Scaled Quail

Named for the scale-like appearance of its chest, neck, and belly feathers, this quail is also called the "Blue Quail," because of its bluish sheen in some lights, or "Cottontop," because of the fluffy white tip to its crest. Its population periodically experiences a "boom and bust" cycle that may be tied to rainfall and subsequent food shortages or abundance, but is also influenced by grazing practices.

OCCURRENCE Locally common in arid rangelands and semi deserts of western Texas, New Mexico, and eastern Arizona, preferring less dense vegetation than other quails.

VOICE Flushed or separated covey (flock) uses 2-syllable *CHE-kar* call to reunite.

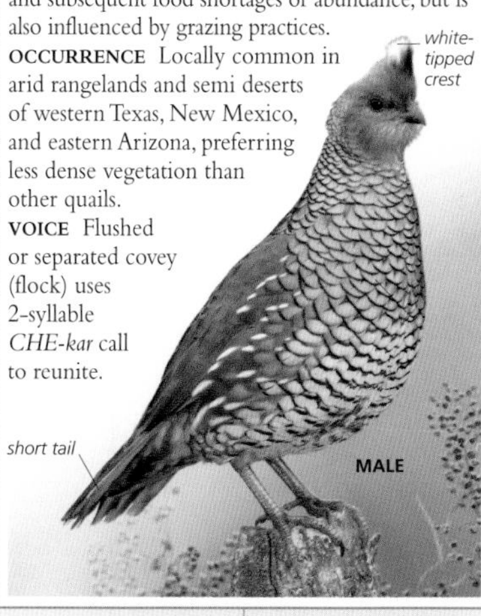

Length **10–12in (25–30cm)** | Wingspan **13–15in (33–38cm)**

Family **Odontophoridae** | Species ***Cyrtonyx montezumae***

Montezuma Quail

When seen, the male Montezuma Quail is unmistakable with its "clown-like" black-and-white face and white-spotted underparts, but its secretive nature makes this species difficult to spot. When threatened, it prefers to crouch, walk, and then run away, but it may also crouch and freeze in place, then suddenly burst into flight.

OCCURRENCE Habitat is a mixture of grassy and open pine-oak woodlands at 4,000–6,000ft (1,200–1,800m); also found in arid scrubland. Predominantly a Mexican species.

VOICE Males produce a loud, descending buzzy whistle *wheeerrr,* sometimes compared to the sound of a bomb falling; female emits low descending hoots.

Length **8½–9in (21–23cm)** | Wingspan **11–12in (28–30cm)**

Family **Odontophoridae** | Species ***Colinus virginianus***

Northern Bobwhite

This small, plump, chicken-like bird is loved by hunters. When flushed it erupts in "coveys" of 10 to 20 individuals, bursting from groundcover and dispersing in many directions. Large numbers are raised in captivity and released to supplement wild populations for hunting.

OCCURRENCE Widely distributed in much of the eastern US, and in Mexico, southward to Guatemala. Occurs in a patchwork of young forests, fields, and brushy hedges. Very local in the West; introduced in the Northwest and Colorado.

VOICE Characteristic *bob-WHITE* or *bob-bob-WHITE* whistled by males in breeding season; call to reunite flock includes *hoi-lee* and *hoi*.

Length **8–10in (20–25cm)** | Wingspan **11–14in (28–35cm)**

Family **Phasianidae** | Species ***Centrocercus urophasianus***

Greater Sage Grouse

The Greater Sage Grouse is the largest native North American grouse. Each spring, males gather on communal sites, known as "leks", where they compete for females with spectacular courtship displays. As many as 40 males may gather at a lek for these events. Once numerous, Greater Sage Grouse populations have declined, as human encroachment on sagebrush habitats has increased.

OCCURRENCE Present distribution in North America is a fraction of its formerly large range in the vast sagebrush plains of the West. Breeds in a variety of habitats, the ideal being composed of several sagebrush species of varying heights.

VOICE Clucks repeatedly when flushed; male makes odd popping sounds with throat sacs when displaying.

Length **19½–30in (50–76cm)** | Wingspan **32–39in (81–99cm)**

Family **Phasianidae** | Species ***Centrocercus minimus***

Gunnison Sage Grouse

In the 1990s, ornithologists discovered differences between the populations of the Gunnison Basin, Colorado, and other Sage Grouse populations. This led to the description of a new species, *minimus*, in 2001. Fewer than 10 breeding populations of *minimus* occur within this restricted area. Continuing loss of its habitat due to cultivation and development puts this species at risk of extinction.

OCCURRENCE Prefers areas of mixed, tall sagebrush with significant overhead cover and ground-based succulent plant foliage, especially in areas along river corridors. Also found where there is deciduous scrub and fruit-bearing trees.

VOICE Clucks repeatedly when flushed; male makes about nine booming sounds when displaying.

Length **21–23in (53–58cm)** | Wingspan **33–36in (83–91cm)**

Family **Phasianidae** | Species ***Tympanuchus pallidicinctus***

Lesser Prairie Chicken

Destruction of its native shortgrass prairie and oak scrub habitat has drastically reduced the range and numbers of the Lesser Prairie Chicken. The species is sensitive to fences, buildings, and power line towers, and females do not nest near such structures, further reducing its already restricted habitat.

OCCURRENCE Primarily native shortgrass prairie mixed with shrub woodlands; fallow fields; occasional agricultural properties.

VOICE Males "boom" or gobble in series of high, hooting notes during courtship display; females occasionally "boom" on lek.

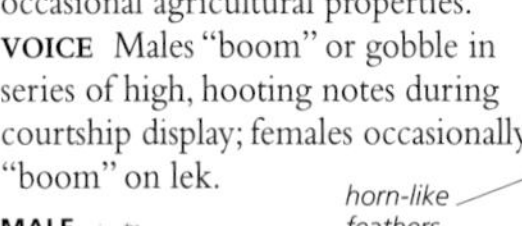

Length **15–17in (38–43cm)** | Wingspan **23–26in (58–66cm)**

Family **Phasianidae** | Species ***Tympanuchus cupido***

Greater Prairie Chicken

Once common in prairie and woodland areas across central North America, numbers of Greater Prairie Chickens have been greatly reduced as their native habitats have given way to agriculture. During the breeding season, males aggressively defend communal areas called "leks" and perform dramatic displays to entice females to mate with them.

OCCURRENCE Breeds in openings mixed with oak-forested river corridors with areas of native tallgrass prairie; resident year-round. Local in the west-central states.

VOICE During courtship, males emit "booming" sounds like a three-part low hoot; also cackling calls.

Length **15½–17½in (40–45cm)** | Wingspan **26–29in (66–74cm)**

Family **Phasianidae**	Species ***Tetraogallus himalayensis***

Himalayan Snowcock

Introduced from Asia in the 1960s to overcome Nevada's lack of upland gamebirds, it took the Himalayan Snowcock nearly 20 years to become successfully established. This large, wary species with its whitish head and brownish body appears gray when viewed from a distance. The very restricted range and high elevation habitat make this bird unlikely to be mistaken for anything else.

OCCURRENCE At high elevations near the snow line in the Ruby Mountains of northwestern Nevada.

VOICE Variety of low and high whistles; clucks, cackles, and chuckles to signal food, alarm, or mating.

Length **23½–29in (60–74cm)**	Wingspan **28–31in (71–79cm)**

Family **Anatidae**	Species ***Dendrocygna autumnalis***

Black-bellied Whistling-Duck

With its distinctive red bill, black belly, and long, pink legs, this Whistling-Duck is unmistakable. Unlike most other waterfowl, it has an upright posture when perched. Whistling-ducks are also known as "tree-ducks" because they perch on trees when roosting, and build their nests in tree holes.

OCCURRENCE Prefers shallow, freshwater habitats; rice fields are a common foraging habitat; also occurs along shorelines and mud bars. Casual west to southeastern California and occasionally east as far as Florida.

VOICE Soft wheezy series of 5–6 notes *pit pit weee do dew*; flight calls include a *chit-chit-chit.*

red bill
black belly
ADULT
pink legs

Length **18½–20in (47–51cm)**	Wingspan **34–36in (86–91cm)**

Family **Anatidae**	Species ***Dendrocygna bicolor***

Fulvous Whistling-Duck

Although sometimes thought of as dabbling ducks, whistling-ducks behave more like swans, as they form long-term pairs, but without elaborate courtship displays, and the males help to raise the brood. The Fulvous Whistling-Duck is widespread in tropical regions, but in the US it is found in coastal Texas, where it is associated with rice fields. The Fulvous Whistling-Duck is rare in California.

OCCURRENCE Permanent resident in southern Texas and Florida; range expands in summer to coastal Texas and Louisiana. Casual vagrant as far west as British Columbia and east as Nova Scotia.

VOICE High-pitched squeaky *pi-teeeew*; often calls in flight.

Length **16½–20in (42–51cm)**	Wingspan **33–37in (85–93cm)**

Family **Anatidae**	Species ***Anser canagicus***

Emperor Goose

With its white head, black throat, and scalloped silvery-gray body and wings, the Emperor Goose is a distinctive bird. During migration, they congregate to feed in large estuaries along the Alaska Peninsula. The Alaskan population of Emperor Geese declined drastically during the 1960s–80s, but has remained stable since then.

OCCURRENCE Breeds in Arctic and subarctic coastal salt marsh habitats in Alaska and eastern Russia. Majority winter along the Alaska Peninsula and on ice-free beaches in the Aleutian Islands.

VOICE Calls rapid high-pitched *kla-ha kla-ha kla-ha*, deep ringing *u-lugh u-lugh* when alarmed.

Length **26in (66cm)**	Wingspan **4ft (1.2m)**

Family **Anatidae** | Species ***Branta hutchinsii***

Cackling Goose

Arctic populations of the Canada Goose, long considered a subspecies, *Branta canadensis hutchinsii*, are now believed by many ornithologists to be a distinct but closely related species, *Branta hutchinsii*, the Cackling Goose. The populations breeding in the Aleutian Islands winter in California; those from the Canadian Arctic winter in the Great Plain and the Gulf Coast. Cackling Geese are smaller and thicker-necked than Canada Geese.
OCCURRENCE Breeds in rocky tundra from the Aleutians east to Baffin Island and Hudson Bay. Winters in pastures and agricultural fields; in the West, from British Columbia to California.
VOICE Male call a *honk* or *bark*; females have higher pitched *hrink*; also high-pitched yelps.

Length **21½–30in (55–75cm)** | Wingspan **4¼–5ft (1.3–1.5m)**

Family **Anatidae** | Species ***Cygnus buccinator***

Trumpeter Swan

North America's quintessential swan and heaviest waterfowl, the magnificent Trumpeter Swan has made a remarkable comeback after its numbers were severely reduced by hunting in the 1800s. By the mid-1930s, fewer than a hundred birds were known to exist. Successful reintroduction efforts were made in the upper Midwest and Ontario to re-establish the species to its former breeding range. Its typical far-reaching call is usually the best way to identify it.
OCCURRENCE Alaskan and northern Canadian breeders go south in winter; others remain year round at places such as Yellowstone National Park. Found on freshwater lakes and marshes with plenty of vegetation and on estuaries in winter.
VOICE Call nasal, resonant *oh-OH* reminiscent of French horn.

Length **4¼–5ft (1.3–1.5m)** | Wingspan **6½ft (2m)**

Family **Anatidae** | Species ***Aythya marila***

Greater Scaup

A great swimmer and diver, the Greater Scaup is the only diving duck of the genus *Aythya* that breeds both in North America and Eurasia. More restricted to coastal breeding and wintering habitats, it is less numerous in North America than its close relative, the Lesser Scaup. Greater Scaups can form large, often sexually segregated flocks outside the breeding season.
OCCURRENCE Most birds breed in western coastal Alaska on tundra wetlands; also in lower densities in northwestern and eastern Canada. Almost all birds winter offshore, along the Atlantic and Pacific coasts, or on the Great Lakes.
VOICE During courtship, male call a soft, fast, wheezy *week week wheew*; female gives a series of growled monotone *arrrr* notes.

Length **15–22in (38–56cm)** | Wingspan **28–31in (72–79cm)**

Family **Anatidae** | Species ***Polysticta stelleri***

Steller's Eider

With its steep forehead, flat crown, and the way it floats high on the water, Steller's Eider resembles a dabbling duck. Steller's Eiders are the synchronized swimmers of the duck clan. The Arctic and Pacific populations of this species have recently declined in numbers, and are classified as vulnerable.
OCCURRENCE Pacific population breeds mainly in Russia's far northeast; small numbers breed in Alaska. About half the Russian population molts and winters in large groups along the Alaska Peninsula and in the Aleutian Islands.
VOICE Female a rapid, harsh growling call; also loud *qua-haaa* or *cooay*; males growl but are rarely heard.

Length **17–18in (43–46cm)** | Wingspan **28–30in (70–76cm)**

Family **Anatidae** | Species ***Somateria fischeri***

Spectacled Eider

In order to see the striking Spectacled Eider one needs to travel to remote tundra in the far north of Alaska. Much of their life is spent offshore, with males spending up to 11 months of the year at sea. In flight, male Spectacled Eiders reveal more black extending up the breast than the other eiders, and the females have gray, rather than white, underwings.

OCCURRENCE Arctic coastal breeding sites are remote and isolated; most birds breed in northern Russia, few in Alaska. They winter in dense flocks in small ice-free areas in the Bering Sea.

VOICE Males a faint *ho HOOO* during display, otherwise silent; females a rapid clucking call *buckbuck buckbuck* with emphasis on second syllable; also guttural rolled *gow gow gow*.

Length **20½–22½in (52–57cm)** | Wingspan **33in (83cm)**

Family **Anatidae** | Species ***Somateria spectabilis***

King Eider

The scientific name of the King Eider, *spectabilis*, means "remarkable," and its gaudy marking and coloring around the head and bill make it hard to misidentify. Female King Eiders, however, can be hard to distinguish from female Common Eiders. King Eiders can dive down to 180ft (55m) when foraging for mollusks.

OCCURRENCE Nests along coasts and inland in the high Arctic, in a variety of habitats; prefers well-drained areas. During winter, found mostly in coastal waters along the southern edge of the ice pack.

VOICE Courting males give a repeated series of low, rolled dove-like *arrrooooo* calls, each rising, then falling, followed by softer *cooos*; females give grunts and croaks.

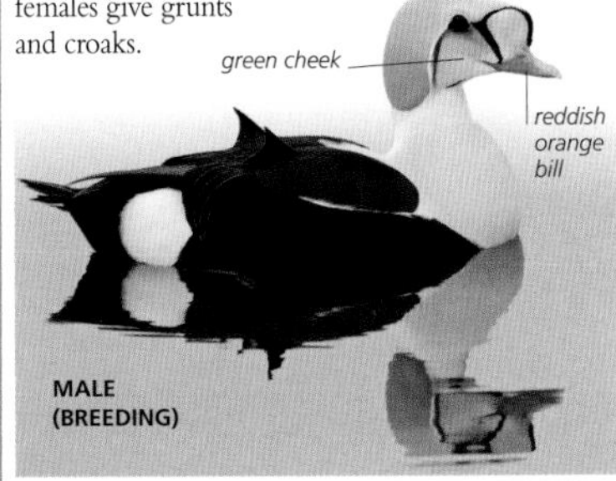

Length **18½–25in (47–64cm)** | Wingspan **37in (94cm)**

Family **Anatidae** | Species ***Somateria mollissima***

Common Eider

The Common Eider is the most numerous and widespread of the eiders. Males show considerable seasonal plumage changes, and do not acquire their striking adult plumage until their third year.

OCCURRENCE Arctic breeder on coastal islands and peninsulas. One population stays in the Hudson and James Bays region. Others winter in the Bering Sea, Hudson Bay, northern British Columbia, Gulf of St. Lawrence, and along the Atlantic Coast.

VOICE Repeated hoarse, grating notes *korr-korr-korr*, male's owl-like *ah-WOO-ooo*; female's low, gutteral notes *krrrr-krrrr-krrrr*.

Length **19½–28in (50–71cm)** | Wingspan **31–42in (80–108cm)**

Family **Diomedeidae** | Species ***Phoebastria nigripes***

Black-footed Albatross

The most frequently seen albatross in North American waters, this distinctive all-dark bird breeds mainly on the Hawaiian Islands, and regularly visits the Pacific Coast during the nonbreeding season. Unfortunately, a tendency to scavenge around fishing boats can cause them to drown when they are accidentally hooked on long lines or tangled in drift nets. This is a major conservation concern for this species.

OCCURRENCE Breeds on sandy beaches, almost exclusively on remote, uninhabited islands in Hawaii.

VOICE Generally silent outside the breeding season, but utters weak squeals while scavenging; makes a variety of noises during courtship.

Length **25–29in (64–74cm)** | Wingspan **6¼–7¼ft (1.9–2.2m)**

Family **Procellariidae** | Species ***Puffinus opisthomelas***

Black-vented Shearwater

An inshore feeder, the Black-vented Shearwater is one of the few species of tubenoses that can be seen easily from land. Flocks of hundreds can be observed from various points along the coast of California. Black-vented Shearwaters vary in color from ghostly pale beige to very dark.

OCCURRENCE Breeds on islands off Baja California, Mexico; spends August–January off the Pacific coast from southern California south to Mexico (as far as Oaxaca). Northernmost and southernmost extent of post-breeding range not well known.

VOICE Silent at sea; breeding ground vocalizations unknown.

Length **14in (36cm)** | Wingspan **34in (86cm)**

Family **Hydrobatidae** | Species ***Oceanodroma microsoma***

Least Storm-Petrel

The smallest storm-petrel in North American waters, the all-dark Least Storm-Petrel is numerous in flocks of tubenoses off the southern California coast in fall. These petrels are very susceptible to predation by introduced cats and rats on their Pacific nesting islands. The Least Storm-Petrel is dark and similar in appearance to the Black Storm-Petrel, but the latter flies with slower wing beats interrupted by glides.

OCCURRENCE Breeds on a small number of islands along the Pacific and Gulf coasts of Baja California, Mexico. After the breeding season, many birds disperse north to waters off southern California.

VOICE Silent at sea; whirring and purring at breeding sites.

Length **5½in (14cm)** | Wingspan **13in (33cm)**

Family **Hydrobatidae** | Species ***Oceanodroma melania***

Black Storm-Petrel

The Black Storm-Petrel, the largest storm-petrel occurring off the coast of southern California, breeds on islands free from predators such as rats, along the coasts of Baja California. After the breeding season, the population of the Black Storm-Petrel splits into two wintering populations—half head to the coast of Central and South America and half stay off the coasts of California and northern Mexico.

OCCURRENCE A warm-water species, breeding on a number of small islands off both the Pacific and Gulf Coasts of Baja California.

VOICE Silent at sea; in colonies, emits long, undulated, chattering and purring sounds.

Length **9in (23cm)** | Wingspan **19–21in (48–53cm)**

Family **Hydrobatidae** | Species ***Oceanodroma homochroa***

Ashy Storm-Petrel

The Ashy Storm-Petrel is one of four species of all-dark storm petrels that breed on islands in the waters of California and Baja California. In California, these islands include Farallon, San Miguel, Santa Barbara, Santa Clara, and Santa Cruz. Ashy Storm-Petrels molt during the breeding season, a double expenditure of energy. In flight, this species looks noticeably long-tailed.

OCCURRENCE Breeds on islands off the coast of California and northern Baja California. Post-breeding dispersal takes some birds north to waters off Humboldt County, others south to waters off central Baja California.

VOICE Usually silent at sea; coos and makes other calls at colonies.

Length **7½in (19cm)** | Wingspan **16–18in (41–46cm)**

Family **Ardeidae** | Species ***Ixobrychus exilis***

Least Bittern

The smallest species of heron in North America, the Least Bittern is also one of the most colorful, but its secretive nature makes it easy to overlook in its habitat of reeds and cattails. Widely distributed in the East, the Least Bittern is local in several western states, including Oregon, California, and Nevada.

OCCURRENCE Breeds in lowland freshwater marshes, occasionally brackish marshes. In winter in tropical American also found in saltwater marshes. Its breeding distribution ranges from eastern Canada through Central and South America, south to Argentina.

VOICE During courtship displays, a soft series of *ku, ku, ku, ku, ku* notes; calls are harsh and loud, *kak, kak, kak*.

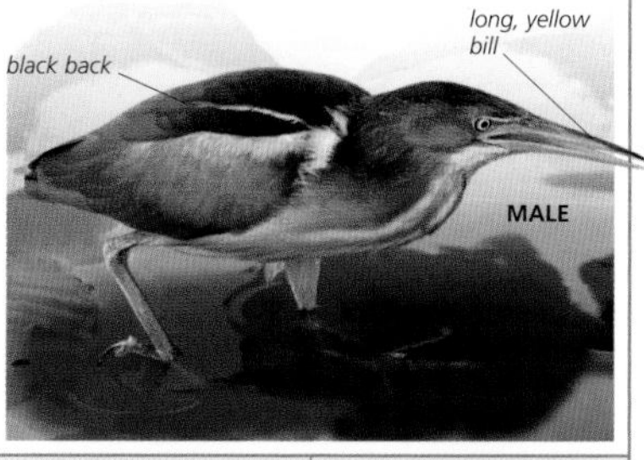

Length **11–14in (28–36cm)** | Wingspan **15½–18in (40–46cm)**

Family **Fregatidae** | Species ***Fregata magnificens***

Magnificent Frigatebird

One of North America's most-skilled aerialists, the Magnificent Frigatebird is not seen perched, except when nesting in mangroves or roosting on buoys. It is usually seen flying gracefully above bays, lagoons, or open ocean. This species is well known for its piratical behavior—it pursues birds such as boobies, making them disgorge their food.

OCCURRENCE Usually seen flying high in the sky over open water. In the West, rare along the coast of Southern California.

VOICE Male call consists of whirring, rattling, and drumming sounds, only at breeding sites.

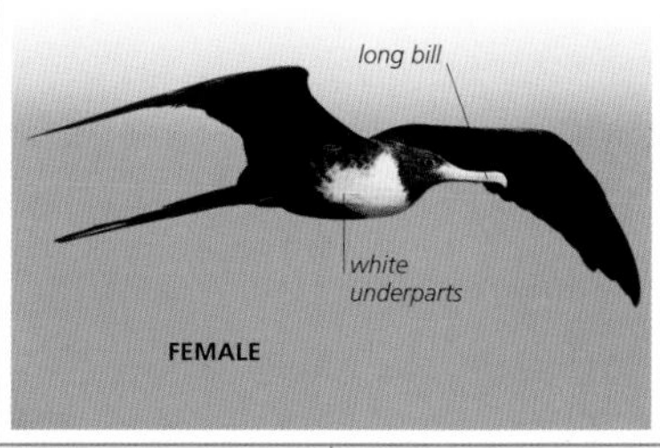

Length **3ft 3in (100cm)** | Wingspan **4½ft (1.4m)**

Family **Phalacrocoracidae** | Species ***Phalacrocorax brasilianus***

Neotropic Cormorant

The slender Neotropic Cormorant ranges widely in the Western Hemisphere. In the US, it breeds and winters along the Gulf Coast and in the lower Rio Grande Valley. In the west, it breeds locally in Arizona and New Mexico, and is a rare visitor to California.

OCCURRENCE Breeds in coastal marshes, swamps, and inland reservoirs from southeastern Texas and western Louisiana to the far south of South America; winters close inshore in protected bays, inlets, estuaries, and lagoons.

VOICE Series of low, pig-like grunts; croaks in alarm.

Length **24in (61cm)** | Wingspan **3¼ft (1m)**

Family **Phalacrocoracidae** | Species ***Phalacrocorax urile***

Red-faced Cormorant

The Red-faced Cormorant's breeding distribution stretches from the Aleutian Islands southward to British Columbia. Within this range, it occurs in small and isolated colonies on rocky outcrops and cliffs, usually in remote locations. The Red-faced Cormorant's bare facial skin varies from yellow to orange, and to red. Its crest is relatively prominent, even in nonbreeding birds.

OCCURRENCE Found in the Aleutian Islands and the Pacific Coast of Alaska. Nests on steep cliffs on rocky marine islands and headlands; seldom seen far out at sea.

VOICE Low groans and croaks; alarmed birds hiss.

Length **30in–3ft 3in (75–100cm)** | Wingspan **3½ft (1.1m)**

Family **Cathartidae**	Species ***Gymnogyps californianus***

California Condor

About 20,000 years ago, this vulture was widespread across the southern US. In the 20th century, shooting, low birthrate, and other factors, such as death from poisoned baits, all contributed to a steep reduction in the numbers of California Condors, and the species almost became extinct. However, recent breed-and-release programs in California and Arizona have succeeded and these magnificent birds can be seen flying again.

OCCURRENCE Released birds and their descendents occur in southern California and in Arizona.

VOICE Hisses and grunts.

naked orange skin

ADULT

shaggy black plumage

Length **3½–4¼ft (1.1–1.3m)**	Wingspan **8¼ft (2.5m)**

Family **Cathartidae**	Species ***Coragyps atratus***

Black Vulture

Common in southern and eastern states but rare in the West, the Black Vulture can be seen in large communal roosts in the evening. Maintaining long pair-bonds, these vultures remain together year-round. According to one study, parents will continue to feed their young for as long as eight months after fledging. When not feeding on roadkills along highways, they spend time soaring above the landscape, in search of carrion.

OCCURRENCE Breeds in dense woodlands, caves, old buildings; forages in open habitats, near roads and highways; found year-round throughout its range.

VOICE Usually silent; hisses and barks occasionally.

naked grayish skin

short tail

ADULT

Length **24–27in (61–68cm)**	Wingspan **4½–5ft (1.4–1.5m)**

Family **Falconidae**	Species ***Caracara cheriway***

Crested Caracara

In North America, the hawk-like Crested Caracara is only found in Texas, southern Arizona, and central Florida. Crested Caracara pairs are monogamous and highly territorial. Known locally as the "Mexican Buzzard," the Crested Caracara is actually a member of the falcon family, not the hawk family.

OCCURRENCE Ranges widely in Central and South America. Breeds and winters in open areas ranging from desert to grasslands with scattered tall trees. Has been recorded in California.

VOICE Adults disturbed at nest emit cackles, hollow rattles, and high-pitched screams; nestlings utter high-pitched screams and raspy *swee-swee* calls.

Length **24–27in (61–68cm)**	Wingspan **4½–5ft (1.4–1.5m)**

Family **Falconidae**	Species ***Falco rusticolus***

Gyrfalcon

The majestic Gyrfalcon breeds in the Arctic and the Subarctic in Eurasia and North America, and rarely occurs south of its breeding range, except during years with peaks in population numbers. For centuries, the Gyrfalcon has been sought by falconers for its power and gentle nature, and is the mascot of the US Air Force Academy. Variable in color, Gyrfalcons range from almost pure white to gray and dark forms.

OCCURRENCE Breeds across the North American Arctic, from Labrador and Québec westward to Alaska, the Yukon, and northwestern British Columbia.

VOICE Loud, harsh *KYHa-KYHa-KYHa.*

Length **22in (56cm)**	Wingspan **4ft (1.2m)**

Family **Accipitridae** | Species ***Ictinia mississippiensis***

Mississippi Kite

The locally abundant Mississippi Kite nests in colonies in the central and southern Great Plains. Foraging flocks of 25 or more birds are common, and groups of ten or more roost near nests. In the West, the species nests in urban habitats, including city parks and golf courses, westward to New Mexico, and, locally, in Arizona and Colorado. This graceful bird pursues and eats its insect prey in flight. Mississippi Kites are long-distance migrants, wintering in South America.

OCCURRENCE Western birds use both rural woodland and suburban or urban habitat.

VOICE High-pitched *phee-phew*; also multisyllabled *phee-ti-ti*.

orange-red eye

pale gray head with dark eye patch

long wings

SUBADULT

Length **13–15in (33–38cm)** | Wingspan **35in (89cm)**

Family **Accipitridae** | Species ***Buteogallus anthracinus***

Common Black-hawk

Although it is found in several US States (southwestern Utah, Arizona, New Mexico, and Texas), the Common Black-hawk is actually relatively uncommon north of Mexico. This long-legged, short-tailed, and broad-winged hawk is all black except for a broad white band across its tail. Almost always found near water, the Common Black-hawk is fond of frogs and fishes.

OCCURRENCE Mature woodlands of cottonwoods and willow along streams that offer hunting perches; US populations are migratory; resident in Central America and northern South America, and Cuba.

VOICE Complex, shrill calls when excited or alarmed; series of 8–14 piercing, whistle-sounding notes, increasing in speed.

Length **20–24in (50–60cm)** | Wingspan **4¼–5ft (1.3–1.7m)**

Family **Accipitridae** | Species ***Parabuteo unicinctus***

Harris's Hawk

Named by the renowned ornithologist John James Audubon in honor of his friend and patron, Edward Harris, Harris's Hawks nest in social units, unlike other North American birds of prey. These groups engage in cooperative hunting: members take turns leading the chase to wear down their prey and share in the kill. This species has become popular with falconers all over the world.

OCCURRENCE Forages and breeds year-round in semi-open desert scrub, savanna, grassland, and wetlands containing scattered larger trees and cacti. Occasionally appears in suburban areas. Essentially a Central and South American species, with a small range north of the Rio Grande.

VOICE Main territorial alarm call a prolonged, harsh growl lasting about 3 seconds; also chirps, croaks, and screams.

Length **18–23in (46–59cm)** | Wingspan **3½–4ft (1.1–1.2m)**

Family **Accipitridae** | Species ***Asturina nitida***

Gray Hawk

The elegant Gray Hawk is found from Mexico south to Argentina, but in North America is only seen in southwestern Texas and southeastern Arizona. The Gray Hawk's breeding system can include trios, one female and two males, all of whom cooperate with chick rearing. While only about 100 pairs breed in the US, their numbers are stable and possibly even increasing. Cottonwood and mesquite woodlands are key to their survival.

OCCURRENCE Breeds in riverine woodlands of mesquite and cottonwoods, especially along streams in the Gila River (Arizona) and Rio Grande (Texas) drainages. Little information exists about its winter habitats.

VOICE High-pitched whistled alarm, *creee*, rising and descending.

Length **16–17in (41–43cm)** | Wingspan **35in (89cm)**

Family **Accipitridae**	Species ***Buteo platypterus***

Broad-winged Hawk

A common species in the eastern US and Canada, the Broad-winged Hawk reaches British Columbia in the northwest, but otherwise is rare in the western US, usually in the fall. Broad-winged Hawks are a spectacular sight during fall migration at some eastern hawk-watching localities, when hundreds, and sometimes even thousands, of birds soar and glide in rising thermals. Most of these birds average 70 miles (110km) a day, and, after more than 4,000 miles (6,500km), reach their wintering quarters in Bolivia and Brazil.

OCCURRENCE Breeds across Canada (west to British Columbia) and the eastern US, in forested areas with clearings and water.

VOICE High-pitched *peeoweee* call, first note shorter and higher-pitched.

ADULT

one to two broad, white tail bands

black trailing wing edge

Length **13–17in (33–43cm)**	Wingspan **32–39in (81–100cm)**

Family **Accipitridae**	Species ***Buteo albonotatus***

Zone-tailed Hawk

Widely distributed in Central and South America, the Zone-tailed Hawk is more localized in the US, where it breeds in Arizona, New Mexico, and Texas, sharing its riverine woodland habitat with the Common Black-hawk. It has been suggested that the Zone-tailed Hawk "mimics" the Turkey Vulture. The hawk, like the vulture, has a long tail, and flies with its wings held up at an angle, called a dihedral. The hawk uses the vulture's ability to spot prey on the ground, but, unlike the vulture, it catches live prey.

OCCURRENCE Breeds in riverine woodland, desert uplands, and mixed-conifer forest in mountains. Winters in central South America. Found in South America southward to Paraguay.

VOICE Harsh *kreeee*; also another harsh 2-syllable *kreeee-arr.*

Length **17½–22in (45–56cm)**	Wingspan **4–4½ft (1.2–1.4m)**

Family **Rallidae**	Species ***Laterallus jamaicensis***

Black Rail

This tiny, mouse-sized rail is very secretive, with the result that its life history is still poorly known. Its presence is confirmed when it gives its territorial call during the breeding season, from the dense cover of its marshy habitat. Its distribution in the US is very local, except along the Eastern Seaboard. In the West, the Black Rail breeds in isolated populations in California, Arizona, Colorado, and Kansas.

OCCURRENCE Patchy distribution across the US in freshwater and brackish marshes or wet meadows; occurs locally in the West Indies, Central and South America.

VOICE Distinctive, 3-note *kik-kee-do* given by male, mostly at night, during breeding season; makes low growl when agitated.

Length **6in (15cm)**	Wingspan **9in (23cm)**

Family **Rallidae**	Species ***Rallus longirostris***

Clapper Rail

The Clapper Rail is common in tidal marshes along the entire seaboard of the Atlantic and Gulf coasts. In the West its distribution is more localized; it is found in coastal marshes of California and in freshwater marshes, inland, in Arizona. The Clapper Rail's loud, endlessly repeated "song" consists of sharp *kek, kek, kek...* notes that indicate its presence in dense marshes. It is rarely seen running across patches of marsh grass at low tide.

OCCURRENCE Breeds in saltwater and brackish marshes along the Atlantic Seaboard. Isolated populations are found in coastal California and inland in Arizona, along the lower Colorado River. Winters south of its breeding range.

VOICE Grunting calls; repeated loud *kek* notes.

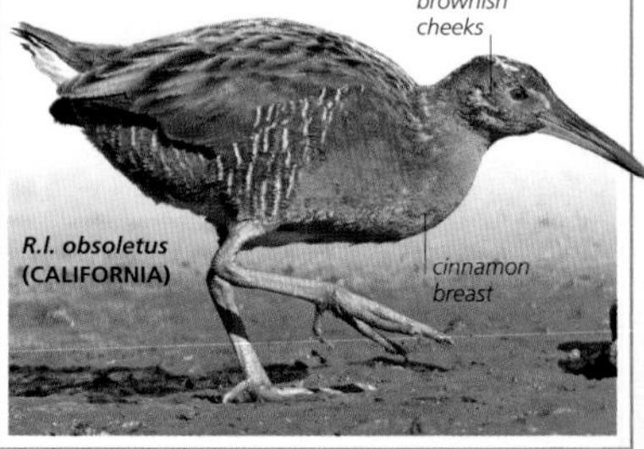

Length **14½in (37cm)**	Wingspan **19in (48cm)**

Family **Rallidae** | Species ***Rallus elegans***

King Rail

This chicken-sized marsh bird is the freshwater counterpart of the saltmarsh-dwelling Clapper Rail. The King Rail depends on freshwater marshes with tall, emergent reeds and cattails. Its distribution is centered on the eastern and southeastern US; in the West, local populations can be found in Kansas, Oklahoma, and Texas, but it is rare farther west. Like the Clapper Rail, the King is rarely seen and is most often detected by its loud calls.

OCCURRENCE Mostly freshwater marshes in the eastern US and in southern Ontario. Also found throughout the year along the southern coast of the US, including Florida, and in central Mexico and Cuba. Rare in the West.

VOICE Male call similar to Clapper Rail but lower; loud *kik kik kik* in breeding season.

Length **15in (38cm)** | Wingspan **20in (51cm)**

Family **Gruidae** | Species ***Grus americana***

Whooping Crane

The majestic Whooping Crane is one of the most compelling success stories that resulted from passing the US Endangered Species Act. The species has rebounded from just a few dozen birds in the mid-20th to hundreds of individuals in the early 21st century. It still remains endangered, however, because it reproduces slowly in a restricted area and migrates along a narrow corridor to winter in coastal Texas, risking mortality along the way.

OCCURRENCE Breeds in country with scattered ponds and prairies in a very small area of the Northwest Territories and Alberta; winters in coastal Texas; uses both agricultural fields and marshland on migration.

VOICE Piercing and trumpeting, *kerloo!* and *kerleeyew*; bugling calls during courtship dances.

Length **4–4½ft (1.2–1.4m)** | Wingspan **7¼ft (2.2m)**

Family **Haematopodidae** | Species ***Haematopus palliatus***

American Oystercatcher

This large, noisy, and conspicuous shorebird breeds along beaches and coastal dunes of the Atlantic and Gulf coasts. In the West, it is restricted to coastal southern California, and is replaced along the Pacific coast by the Black Oystercatcher. American Oystercatchers are social birds that can be observed in flocks, from a few birds to several hundred, especially in winter, at preferred feeding and roosting locations.

OCCURRENCE Saltwater coastal habitats, along the Atlantic Seaboard from Massachusetts to Argentina, and along the Pacific Seaboard from Baja California to Chile.

VOICE Whistled, loud, clear descending *wheeu* call; alarm call sharp *wheep*; flight display call several sharp whistles accelerating into a series of descending piping notes.

Length **15½–17½in (40–44cm)** | Wingspan **29–32in (73–81cm)**

Family **Charadriidae** | Species ***Pluvialis fulva***

Pacific Golden Plover

The Pacific Golden Plover and American Golden Plover were formerly considered to belong to the same species. The Pacific Golden Plover breeds in western Alaska and migrates over the ocean to wintering grounds on remote South Pacific Islands. Its nest is a shallow depression lined with lichens in the tundra.

OCCURRENCE Nests primarily in Arctic tundra; during migration and in winter, found in a variety of habitats, including prairies, pastures, mudflats, shorelines, mangroves, parks, lawns and gardens in urban areas, and roadsides. About 12 percent of the world's population nests in Alaska.

VOICE Flight call a clearly 2-syllabled *chu-EEt*, with emphasis on second note; breeding song a clear, haunting, low whistle *pEE-prr-EE*.

Length **9–10½in (23–27cm)** | Wingspan **21–24in (53–61cm)**

Family **Charadriidae** | Species ***Charadrius wilsonia***

Wilson's Plover

Slightly smaller than the well known Killdeer, Wilson's Plover is a coastal species, common in the East, but rare in the West. It has a relatively "heavy-looking" belly, which gives it a characteristic upright posture when it pauses after a run. This plover's populations may be declining; it was called a species of "high concern" in 2000.

OCCURRENCE Beaches, sand dunes, coastal lagoons, and saltwater flats along the Atlantic coast, south to Mexico, and in the West Indies; along the Pacific coast from Baja California southward to Peru.

VOICE Flight call a short *pip*, or *pi-dit*; alarm calls include slurred whistle *tweet*, and short whistled *peet*; common distraction call a descending buzzy rattle, given in series.

heavy, black bill

MALE

Length **6½–8in (16–20cm)** | Wingspan **15½–19½in (39–49cm)**

Family **Charadriidae** | Species ***Charadrius montanus***

Mountain Plover

Unlike most other North American shorebirds, this rather plain-looking plover is rarely found near water. Unusually wary by nature, the Mountain Plover often faces away from danger and squats motionless on the ground, virtually disappearing into the landscape and earning its nickname "Prairie Ghost." It is declining, and endangered because of habitat loss from overgrazing and pesticides.

OCCURRENCE Localized in west–central North America in dry, flat, short grass prairies and semi-desert areas with sparse vegetation; winters south to Mexico.

VOICE Generally silent; flight call grating *kirrp*; wintering birds in flight give short *kip* call; courtship song rolling, drawled, whistled *wee-wee*.

Length **8½–9½ in (21–24cm)** | Wingspan **21½–23½in (54–60cm)**

Family **Scolopacidae** | Species ***Limosa haemastica***

Hudsonian Godwit

This large sandpiper undertakes a remarkable annual migration from its tundra breeding grounds in Alaska and Canada all the way to extreme southern South America, a distance of at least 10,000 miles (16,000km) in one direction, with few stopovers. The number of breeding birds is unknown, but 30,000 to 40,000 birds have been counted in Tierra del Fuego. Hudsonian Godwits spend six months wintering, two breeding, and four flying between the two locations.

OCCURRENCE Breeds in the high Arctic in sedge meadows and bogs in tundra; locally found in flooded rice fields, pastures, and reservoirs in spring. Winters in extreme southern Chile and Argentina.

VOICE Flight call emphatic *peed-wid*; also high *peet* or *kwee*; display song *to-wida to-wida to-wida*, or *to-wit, to-wit, to-wit*.

Length **14–16in (35–41cm)** | Wingspan **27–31in (68–78cm)**

Family **Scolopacidae** | Species ***Limosa lapponica***

Bar-tailed Godwit

Primarily a Eurasian species, the Bar-tailed Godwit is a summer visitor to western Alaska. After breeding, it migrates a distance of over 7,000 miles (11,250km) to Australia and New Zealand, a non-stop overwater flight. Before this amazing journey, the Bar-tailed Godwit doubles its body weight with fat that will be used as fuel, and shrinks its digestive tract as a weight-saving measure. Almost 100,000 birds make this journey in September and early October.

OCCURRENCE Breeds in lowland tundra, coastal wetlands, foothills, and uplands of Arctic and sub-Arctic. Only Alaska in North America.

VOICE Flight call a slightly nasal *kirruc*, *kurruc* or *kirrik*; display song *ta-WEA, ta-WEA, ta-WEA*.

Length **14½–15½in (37–39cm)** | Wingspan **28–32in (72–81cm)**

Family **Scolopacidae**	Species ***Numenius tahitiensis***

Bristle-thighed Curlew

This rare and localized curlew is one of the world's most unusual shorebirds. It winters on oceanic islands, becomes flightless during its molting period on its wintering grounds, and uses "tools" when foraging, such as rocks to break open eggs. Nesting in only two areas of western Alaska, it migrates about 4,000 miles (6,500km) over the Pacific Ocean to reach its wintering grounds on South Pacific islands. The world population of Bristle-thighed Curlews may number as few as 3,000 pairs.

OCCURRENCE Breeds in hilly tundra with scattered vegetation in western Alaska; winters on remote South Pacific islands; occasional in California.

VOICE Flight call a clear whistle *ee-o-weet*; flight song a whistled phrase, *wiwiwi-chyooo*.

Length **16–17½in (41–45cm)**	Wingspan **30–35in (75–90cm)**

Family **Scolopacidae**	Species ***Bartramia longicauda***

Upland Sandpiper

Unlike other sandpipers, this graceful bird spends most of its life away from water. Its brownish coloration is a good camouflage in grasslands, especially when nesting. It is known for landing on fence posts and raising its wings while giving its tremulous, whistling call. Because of the disappearance of its grassland habitat the species has suffered substantial population losses, and is currently listed as endangered.

OCCURRENCE Breeds in tallgrass or mixed-grass prairies. During migration found in grazed pastures, turf farms, and cultivated fields. Uncommon along the west coast and inland in the Southwest. Winters in South America, south to Argentina.

VOICE Flight call a low *qui-pi-pi-pi*; song consists of gurgling notes followed by long, descending "wolf whistle" *whoooleeeeee, wheeelooooo*.

ADULT (BREEDING)

brownish, spotted back

straight, mostly yellow bill

Length **11–12½in (28–32cm)**	Wingspan **25–27in (64–68cm)**

Family **Scolopacidae**	Species ***Heteroscelus incanus***

Wandering Tattler

While "Wandering" refers to this species' remarkable migration, "tattler" highlights the loud songs it makes in its breeding haunts in Alaska and western Canada. The Wandering Tattler also breeds in eastern Siberia. The total population size of this species is small, of only about 10,000 to 25,000 birds. After long overwater flights, Wandering Tattlers spend the winter on Pacific islands, including the Galápagos and New Zealand.

OCCURRENCE Breeds in shrubby mountain tundra near water bodies. During migration and winter, uses rocky coastlines; also reefs, jetties, and piers along the California coast in fall and winter.

VOICE Flight call a ringing, trilled *dididididididi*; song a sharp, 3–4 note whistle *treea-treea-treea-tree*.

Length **10½–12in (27–30cm)**	Wingspan **20–22in (51–56cm)**

Family **Scolopacidae**	Species ***Calidris ptilocnemis***

Rock Sandpiper

Breeding in Siberia and western Alaska, and wintering along the Pacific coast south to California, the Rock Sandpiper is the western counterpart of the Purple Sandpiper. Both species are closely related to each other. In the winter, look for Rock Sandpipers along rocky shores, which they share with Surfbirds and Black Turnstones.

OCCURRENCE Breeds in Arctic coastal tundra and mountain tundra. During migration and in winter is common along rocky shores from Alaska south to southern California.

VOICE Call short squeaking *chreet*, *cheet*, or *cheerrt*; song *di-jerr, di-jerr, di-jerr* and more melodic *quida-se-quida-we-quida*.

Length **7¼–9½in (18.5–24cm)**	Wingspan **13–18½in (33–47cm)**

Family **Scolopacidae**	Species ***Tryngites subruficollis***

Buff-breasted Sandpiper

This sandpiper has a remarkable mating system. On the breeding grounds in the Arctic, each male flashes his white underwings to attract females for mating. After mating, the female leaves and performs all nest duties alone, while the male continues to display and mate with other females. Once nesting is over, the Buff-breasted Sandpiper leaves the Arctic and covers an astonishing 16,000 miles (26,000km) to winter in temperate South America.

OCCURRENCE Breeds in moist to wet, grassy, or sedge coastal tundra; during migration favors pastures, sod farms, meadows, rice fields, or farm lands. Winters in the pampas region of South America in short, wet grass habitats.

VOICE Flight call soft, short *gert*, or longer, rising *grriit*.

JUVENILE

Length **7¼–8in (18.5–20cm)**	Wingspan **17–18½in (43–47cm)**

Family **Scolopacidae**	Species ***Phalaropus fulicarius***

Red Phalarope

The Red Phalarope spends about ten months each year over deep ocean waters. Many Red Phalaropes winter in cold oceanic areas, with large concentrations in the Humboldt Current off Peru and Chile, and in the Benguela Current off southwestern Africa. During migration in Alaskan waters, flocks of Red Phalaropes feed on crustaceans in the mud plumes created by Gray and Bowhead Whales that forage on the ocean floor.

OCCURRENCE Breeds in coastal Arctic tundra in Canada and Alaska; small numbers are seen in coastal California in fall and winter. It is rare inland.

VOICE Flight call a sharp *psip* or *pseet*, often in rapid succession; alarm call a drawn-out, 2-syllabled *sweet*.

ADULT (NONBREEDING)

Length **8–8½in (20–22cm)**	Wingspan **16–17½in (41–44cm)**

Family **Laridae**	Species ***Larus livens***

Yellow-footed Gull

First described as a species in 1919, the Yellow-footed Gull was long considered to be a subspecies of the Western Gull. It is now thought to be related to the Kelp Gull of South America. It has yellow legs, but if its leg color is not visible, it is hard to distinguish from the Western Gull. The best place outside of the Sea of Cortez, Mexico, to see the Yellow-footed Gull is the Salton Sea in southern California.

OCCURRENCE Breeds in the Sea of Cortez, Mexico, on offshore islands and rocks; in the US, nonbreeders found at Salton Sea, June–September; occasional in Utah, Arizona, coastal California.

VOICE Call a *keow*, repeated in series, speeding up slightly towards the end.

ADULT

Length **21½–28in (55–72cm)**	Wingspan **5ft (1.5m)**

Family **Laridae**	Species ***Rhodostethia rosea***

Ross's Gull

Named for the great British Polar explorer, James Clark Ross, this small, delicate gull is unmistakable in adult breeding plumage. Dove-gray upperparts, pale-pink underparts, red legs, and a black collar contribute to make it elegant and beautiful. In winter it lacks the distinctive black neck ring and the delicate pink blush on the underside.

OCCURRENCE Siberian breeder found along Alaskan north coast in fall; expanded recently as a breeding bird to Arctic Canada; winter strays found across Canada, northeastern and northwestern US.

VOICE Rarely heard in winter; tern-like *kik-kik-kik* on the breeding grounds.

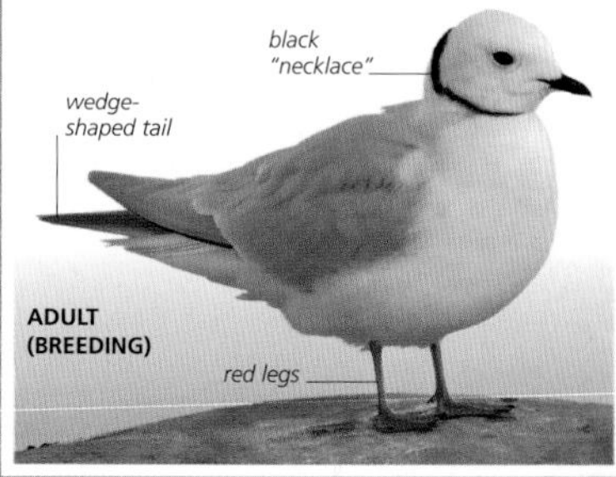

ADULT (BREEDING)

Length **11½–12in (29–31cm)**	Wingspan **35–39in (90–100cm)**

Family **Laridae** | Species ***Xema sabini***

Sabine's Gull

This striking looking gull has a distinctive black, white, and gray wing pattern and a notched tail, which make it unmistakable in all plumages—only juvenile kittiwakes are superficially similar. Previously thought to be related to the larger, but similarly patterned, Swallow-tailed Gull of the Galápagos, recent research indicates that Sabine's Gull is more closely related to the all-white Ivory Gull.

OCCURRENCE In the summer, breeds near the Arctic coast and on wet tundra in Arctic Canada and Alaska. Winters offshore in tropical and subtropical waters; widespread in Pacific and Atlantic oceans during migration

VOICE Raucous, harsh *kyeer, kyeer, kyeer*; tern-like.

Length **13–14in (33–36 cm)** | Wingspan **35–39in (90–100cm)**

Family **Laridae** | Species ***Rissa brevirostris***

Red-legged Kittiwake

Over 75 per cent of the world's Red-legged Kittiwake population nests on St. George Island, in the Pribilofs. Research has indicated that this species was once more widespread in the Aleutians than it is today. It is found accidentally south to Oregon. The Red-legged Kittiwake, when outside its normal range, can be mistaken for the Black-legged Kittiwake since the latter may also, occasionally, have red legs.

OCCURRENCE Spends life out at sea, mostly over deep waters. Restricted almost totally to the Bering Sea and vicinity.

VOICE Calls similar to Black-legged Kittiwake, but higher pitched; vocal at breeding colony, generally silent elsewhere.

Length **14–15½in (35–39cm)** | Wingspan **33–36in (84–92cm)**

Family **Laridae** | Species ***Sterna nilotica***

Gull-billed Tern

With its relatively heavy build, thick bill, and broad wings, the Gull-billed Tern is indeed more gull-like than other North American terns. Also, unlike many other terns, its diet is not restricted to fish, but also includes insects and lizards. It often nests in colonies with other tern species and with skimmers, and will occasionally hunt their chicks and steal their prey. During the 19th century, Gull-billed Terns were hunted ruthlessly for their eggs and feathers. Their numbers have now partially recovered.

OCCURRENCE Breeds on sandy beaches and barrier islands. Common along the East Coast; rare in California and Arizona. Worldwide in distribution.

VOICE Short, 2-note, nasal yapping, *kay-wek, kay-wek*.

Length **13–15in (33–38cm)** | Wingspan **3¼–4ft (1–1.2m)**

Family **Laridae** | Species ***Sterna elegans***

Elegant Tern

The Elegant Tern is not a geographically widespread species. By the mid-20th century its population had declined due to the demand for its eggs and the introduction of predators; at one point it was confined to only five nesting colonies. This bird nests in tight groups within colonies of Heermann's Gulls and Caspian Terns, taking advantage of the other birds' aggressive behavior toward predators. Elegant Terns nest in remarkable synchrony, most birds in a colony laying eggs within 24 hours of each other.

OCCURRENCE Southern California and Baja California; over 90 percent of world's population nest on one island, Isla Raza in the Gulf of California. After breeding, many fly to the coast of central California.

VOICE Nasal *karrreeek, karrreek*; very vocal at nesting colonies.

Length **15½–16½in (39–42cm)** | Wingspan **30–32in (76–81cm)**

Family **Laridae** | Species ***Sterna maxima***

Royal Tern

Royal Terns have a full black cap for only a very short time at the beginning of the breeding season; for most of the year, they have white foreheads. The color of a Royal Tern's bill is quite variable, ranging from yellowish orange to red. Some possess a reddish bill similar to that of the Caspian Tern, but the latter does not have a pure white forehead and its bill is thicker. Perhaps it was these red-billed Royal Terns that caused the renowned ornithologist, John James Audubon, to confuse the two species.

OCCURRENCE Breeds in dense colonies, often on barrier islands. Widespread along the Atlantic coast; in the West, southern California; occasional elsewhere.

VOICE Call *keer-reet*, usually during courtship; higher pitched and less raspy than Caspian Tern; more vocal around colonies.

black forehead and crown

ADULT (BREEDING)

Length **17½–19½in (45–50cm)** | Wingspan **4–4¼ft (1.2–1.3m)**

Family **Laridae** | Species ***Sterna paradisaea***

Arctic Tern

The majority of these remarkable migrants breed in the Arctic and subarctic, then migrate to the Antarctic pack-ice for the Southern Hemisphere summer before returning north. On this round-trip, Arctic Terns travel at least 25,000 miles (40,000km). Apart from migration periods, it spends its life in areas of near continuous daylight and rarely comes to land, except to nest. It looks similar to the Common Tern, but the Arctic has a comparatively smaller bill, shorter legs, and a shorter neck.

OCCURRENCE Breeds across North America in unforested areas near water and along coasts; generally migrates far offshore. Winters on edge of pack ice in Antarctica. Also breeds across northern Eurasia.

VOICE Descending call; nearly all calls similar to Common Tern, but higher-pitched and harsher.

Length **11–15½in (28–39cm)** | Wingspan **26–30in (65–75cm)**

Family **Laridae** | Species ***Sterna antillarum***

Least Tern

The Least Tern, the smallest of the North American terms, is, in addition, distinguished from them by its black cap, white forehead, and short yellow legs. In the 19th century the species suffered a dramatic decline, as its feathers were prized fashion accessories. Protected by the Migratory Bird Treaty of 1916, Least Tern numbers have increased, but continued protection is needed because of the loss of its breeding habitat due to development in coastal areas, especially sand dunes.

OCCURRENCE Breeds along beaches, in sand dunes and sandbars along sea coasts, rivers, lakes, reservoirs, and wetlands. Winters from Mexico to South America.

VOICE Extremely vocal during breeding; a high-pitched *ki-deek, ki-deek*; also a rapid, almost non-stop chatter.

Length **8½–9in (21–23cm)** | Wingspan **19–21in (48–53cm)**

Family **Laridae** | Species ***Sterna aleutica***

Aleutian Tern

The Aleutian Tern was the last North American tern to be described. Discovered on Kodiak Island in 1868, it was not found nesting there again until 1944. This tern received its scientific and English names from the assumption that it must nest somewhere in the Aleutian islands, although it was not actually found nesting there until the mid-20th century.

OCCURRENCE Breeds in coastal Alaska, in areas with low vegetation, marshes, meadows, sandy spits, lagoons, and tundra. Winter range is mostly unknown, but suspected to be in the southwestern Pacific. Migrants reported from Hong Kong and Indonesia. Also breeds in Siberia.

VOICE Vocal around colonies; no information elsewhere; shorebird-like 3-note whistle, unlike other tern species.

Length **12½–15in (32–38cm)** | Wingspan **30–31in (75–80cm)**

Family **Laridae** | Species ***Rynchops niger***

Black Skimmer

With its very long, orange-red and black bill, the Black Skimmer is unmistakable. Compressed laterally into a knife-like shape, the lower mandible is about 1in (2.5cm) longer than the upper mandible. This extraordinary bill allows Black Skimmers to "cut" the waters—they fly with the lower mandible in the water, then snap the bill shut when prey is caught.

OCCURRENCE East Coast from Massachusetts to Mexico; West Coast in southern California. Rarely found far from saltwater. Winters in Central America. Resident populations breed in South America.

VOICE Calls given by both sexes, more often at night; distinctive sound like the yapping of a small dog.

ADULT (BREEDING)

Length **15½–19½in (40–50cm)** | Wingspan **3½–4¼ft (1.1–1.3m)**

Family **Stercorariidae** | Species ***Stercorarius maccormicki***

South Polar Skua

A regular visitor to US waters, the Antarctic-breeding South Polar Skua is a large relative of the jaegers. It is a perpetual threat to penguins on their breeding grounds, patrolling around their colonies and waiting to pinch an egg or snatch a chick. Outside the breeding season, South Polar Skuas roam both the Atlantic and Pacific Oceans, reaching high latitudes in each.

OCCURRENCE Spends southern winters (northern summer) offshore in the North Atlantic and Pacific; breeds in the South Shetland Islands and along the coast and islands of the Antarctic.

VOICE Deep gull-like burbling; generally silent at sea.

IMMATURE

Length **21in (53cm)** | Wingspan **4¼ft (1.3m)**

Family **Alcidae** | Species ***Alle alle***

Dovekie

Also known as the Little Auk, the stocky and diminutive Dovekie is a bird of the high Arctic. Most Dovekies breed in Greenland in large, noisy, crowded colonies (some contain 15–20 million birds), others breed in northeastern Canada, and smaller numbers on a few islands in the Bering Sea off Alaska. On their breeding grounds in Greenland, both adult and immature Dovekies are hunted by Glaucous Gulls and Arctic Foxes.

OCCURRENCE Breeds on islands inside the Arctic Circle. Many birds remain south of the Arctic pack ice in the winter; others fly farther south to winter off the northeastern seaboard of North America. The wintering grounds of the Bering Sea population are still unknown.

VOICE Variety of calls at breeding colony, including high-pitched trilling that rises and falls; silent at sea.

ADULT (NONBREEDING)

Length **8½in (21cm)** | Wingspan **15in (38cm)**

Family **Alcidae** | Species ***Uria lomvia***

Thick-billed Murre

A large and robust auk, the Thick-billed Murre is one of the most abundant seabirds at high latitudes in Eurasia and North America. Some cliff colonies can number upwards of a million birds, breeding side by side on narrow ledges. Chicks leave the colony when their weight is only 25 per cent that of the adults, and they mature at sea, fed by the male parent. Thick-billed Murres can dive for fish and squid down to a depth of 600ft (180m).

OCCURRENCE Away from high Arctic colonies, Thick-billed Murres remain at sea off the Atlantic and Pacific coasts, usually far offshore. Regular off the coast of California in winter.

VOICE Roaring, groaning, insistent sounding *aoorrr*, lower-pitched than the Common Murre.

ADULT (BREEDING)

Length **18in (46cm)** | Wingspan **28in (70cm)**

Family **Alcidae** | Species ***Cepphus grylle***

Black Guillemot

The Black Guillemot, which is primarily a North Atlantic seabird found in both the Old and New Worlds, is largely replaced along the Pacific coast, from Alaska southward to California, by its close relative, and almost look-alike, the Pigeon Guillemot. Black Guillemots breed along the northern coast of Alaska, and occur in the Bering Sea during the winter. A Guillemot seen along the Pacific coast of North America is sure to be a Pigeon Guillemot.

OCCURRENCE Breeds in deep crevices on remote rocky islands. When foraging for food, prefers shallow waters close to shore.

VOICE Very high-pitched whistles and squeaks on land and water near nesting habitat that resonate like an echo.

Length **13in (33cm)** | Wingspan **21in (53cm)**

Family **Alcidae** | Species ***Brachyramphus brevirostris***

Kittlitz's Murrelet

This small, North Pacific-breeding auk was described by Vigors as *brevirostris* ("short-billed") in 1828, and later by Brandt as *kittlitzii*. Because of the rules of scientific names, the latter name was not retained, but Kittlitz's name remained in the vernacular. Little is known about it, other than that it does not breed in colonies, and lays its single egg hidden under a slab of rock, at inland locations high above the sea and far away from seashores.

OCCURRENCE Occurs where glaciers calve into the sea. When breeding feeds at sea around icebergs or close to coast; after breeding moves out to sea; winter location unknown. Breeds in the Bering Sea and along the Aleutian Island chain.

VOICE Quiet, low, groaning *urrrrn* call; also short quacking.

Length **9½in (24cm)** | Wingspan **17in (43cm)**

Family **Alcidae** | Species ***Synthliboramphus hypoleucus***

Xantus's Murrelet

The English name of this small seabird honors a colorful, Hungarian-born ornithologist, John Xantus. Among the world's most threatened seabird species, Xantus's Murrelets breed on islands in southern California and Baja California, but are rarely seen from shore. Two days after fledging, chicks leap into the water from cliffs as high as 200ft (60m). Parents then rear their young (usually only one per pair) in family groups offshore.

OCCURRENCE Nests in sheltered areas on California's and Baja California's islands, then, after breeding, disperses along the Pacific coast, offshore, northward as far as Washington State and, rarely, British Columbia.

VOICE Series of several high pitched *seeep* notes by southern Californian birds; Baja California birds give a rattling call.

Length **10in (25cm)** | Wingspan **15in (38cm)**

Family **Alcidae** | Species ***Synthliboramphus craveri***

Craveri's Murrelet

It was the German zoologist Johann Friedrich von Brandt (1802-1879) who gave such long scientific names to the tiny murrelets. The genus name, *Synthliboramphus,* actually simply means "compressed bill." Craveri's Murrelet breeds on a number of islands in the Gulf of California, Mexico, and wanders as far north as San Francisco afterwards. After breeding it forages offshore and is not normally seen from shorepoints. Craveri's Murrelet was named after Frederico Craveri, who discovered the bird.

OCCURRENCE Warm waters of the Gulf of California and the Pacific coast of Baja California during breeding season. Rare visitor, mostly from fall through spring, to pelagic waters off the coast of California.

VOICE Adult at sea gives high rattling or trilling *sreeeer*. Other calls unknown.

Length **9½in (24cm)** | Wingspan **15in (38cm)**

Family **Alcidae** | Species ***Aethia psittacula***

Parakeet Auklet

This robust, pot-bellied auklet has a bright orange, conical bill—a unique feature among alcids. Its range spans the North Pacific, the widest of any auklet species, but breeding is concentrated at colonies in the Bering Sea and the Aleutians. Like other auklets, Parakeet Auklets are monogamous, and pairs perform conspicuous vocal and visual courtship displays when breeding.

OCCURRENCE Breeds in rocky habitats on islands of the northern Gulf of Alaska and the Bering Sea.

VOICE Whinnying by males to attract a mate, followed by duet-whinnying by a mated pair during courtship; squeal calls when alarmed.

Length **10in (25cm)** | Wingspan **18in (46cm)**

Family **Alcidae** | Species ***Aethia pusilla***

Least Auklet

The smallest of the auklets, Least Auklets often form huge flocks, roosting on boulders along the edge of nesting islands. In the air, these flocks swirl around with great coordination. The Least Auklet's underparts vary individually from white to spotted or even solid gray—a possible status signal during the breeding season. The Least Auklet has a low survival rate compared to other auks. It is vulnerable to rats and foxes and sensitive to human disturbance.

OCCURRENCE Bering Sea islands and Aleutians; forages in areas with turbulent waters and concentrated food sources; winters at sea near breeding sites.

VOICE Pulsing series of high, grating trills, chirps, or chatters; silent at sea.

Length **6½in (16.5cm)** | Wingspan **12in (31cm)**

Family **Alcidae** | Species ***Aethia pygmaea***

Whiskered Auklet

This compact, dark-plumaged auklet lives along the outer islands of the Aleutian chain and in eastern Russia. Compared with other North Pacific auks, it is relatively scarce and lives in smaller colonies. During the nesting season, the birds become nocturnal, and huge numbers congregate after dark. The long head plumes help the birds feel their way to their underground nests. This nocturnal arrival keeps them safe from predatory birds such as large gulls and falcons, and crevice-nesting protects the eggs and chicks against predation in daylight hours.

OCCURRENCE Occurs locally in Alaska's Aleutian Islands. Forages in shallow waters off rocky coasts, especially in areas of rapid tidal currents.

VOICE Kitten-like *meew* and rapid, harp *beedeer, beedeer, beedeer* call; silent at sea.

Length **8in (20cm)** | Wingspan **14in (36cm)**

Family **Alcidae** | Species ***Aethia cristatella***

Crested Auklet

Male and female Crested Auklets have a forward-curling tuft of feathers on the forehead that varies in size among individuals. Both sexes prefer mates with large tufts. Pairs are typically monogamous and compete intensely for nest sites. Crested Auklets fly in large, tight flocks and are usually active only at night at the colonies. Like their close relative, the Whiskered Auklet, their plumage has a distinctive citrus-like odor.

OCCURRENCE Forages in turbulent waters around remote islands in the Bering Sea and the Aleutian Islands. Winters in the Gulf of Alaska. Very rare along Pacific coast south to California.

VOICE In colonies, variable barking *kyow* call, reminiscent of small dog; rapid series of honks; silent at sea.

Length **10½in (27cm)** | Wingspan **17in (43cm)**

Family **Alcidae**	Species ***Fratercula corniculata***

Horned Puffin

Similar to, but larger than, its close relative the Atlantic Puffin, the Horned Puffin lives in the North Pacific Ocean and Bering Sea, where it breeds on remote, rocky, offshore islands. Outside the breeding season, Horned Puffins spend much time far out at sea, hundreds of miles from the nearest land. Remarkably, when birds return to their breeding grounds, they go directly to the very same rock crevice they used the previous year.

OCCURRENCE Winters far from land in the North Pacific. Rare along Pacific coast, south to California.

VOICE Low-pitched, rumbling growls in rhythmic phrases.

Length **15in (38cm)**	Wingspan **23in (59cm)**

Family **Columbidae**	Species ***Streptopelia decaocto***

Eurasian Collared-Dove

A stocky bird, the Eurasian Collared-Dove can be identified by the black collar on the back of its neck and its pale body color. First released in the Bahamas in the mid-1970s, this species is now spreading rapidly across the mainland. Very tolerant of humans, it regularly nests and feeds in urban and suburban areas. Eurasian Collared-Doves have a high reproductive rate, as they raise several broods a year from March to November.

OCCURRENCE In North America south of the northern forest zone in suburban and urban areas; agricultural areas. In the West, less widespread, mostly in the Southwest and California.

VOICE Repeated 4-note *coo-hoo-HOO-cook* that is quick and low-pitched; also harsh, nasal *krreeew* in flight.

Length **11½–12in (29–30cm)**	Wingspan **14in (35cm)**

Family **Columbidae**	Species ***Columbina inca***

Inca Dove

A small, brownish gray dove that forages on the ground, the Inca Dove can be identified by the scaly pattern of its plumage. It has expanded its distribution northward to the US in the last 100 years, from its Central American and Mexican range. It now breeds in the Southwest from California, Nevada, and Arizona, eastward all the way to the Mississippi River. It is secretive, yet tame, and is often found in human settlements. Inca Doves commonly flush from almost underfoot, revealing the chestnut color of their wings.

OCCURRENCE Resident in cities, towns, and farms. Forages on lawns and in barnyards; occasionally near rivers and streams but favors drier areas in the south of its range.

VOICE Repeated 2-note chant, *pol-pah*, which can sound like the words "no hope;" sometimes low, trilling *coo*.

Length **7–9in (18–23cm)**	Wingspan **11in (28cm)**

Family **Columbidae**	Species ***Streptopelia chinensis***

Spotted-necked Dove

Originally from southern and eastern Asia, the Spotted-necked Dove was introduced to urban areas of California over a century ago. More chunky and with broader wings and tail than the Mourning Dove, this medium-sized species has grayish brown upperparts and pinkish brown underparts. A characteristic feature is a broad, black neck patch with white spots. The Spotted-necked Dove lives in parks, gardens, and suburbs.

OCCURRENCE Found in southern California from Santa Barbara and Bakersfield south to Baja California, uncommon.

VOICE Hoarse *coo-coo-croooo* call with emphasis on the middle and last notes.

Length **12in (30cm)**	Wingspan **19½in (50cm)**

Family **Columbidae** | Species ***Columbina passerina***

Common Ground-Dove

The Common Ground-Dove, the smallest of the North American doves, is only slightly larger than a sparrow. It retains its pair-bond throughout the year and tends not to form flocks: birds in a pair usually remain within a few yards of each other. Besides its diminutive size, the Common Ground-Dove is recognizable by prominent black spots on its reddish-looking wings, scaly underparts (seen when perched), and its square, blackish tail while in flight.

OCCURRENCE In the US, has a disjointed population in the Southwest, Texas, and Florida. Lives in dry, sandy areas with open vegetation and also shrubby habitats.

VOICE Simple, repeated, ascending double-note *wah-up* given every 2–3 seconds.

Length **6–7in (15–18cm)** | Wingspan **11in (28cm)**

Family **Columbidae** | Species ***Columbina talpacoti***

Ruddy Ground-Dove

The female Ruddy Ground-Dove is similar to the Common Ground-Dove with its black wing spots. It lacks the scaly neck pattern, however. Male Ruddy Ground-Doves are more colorful, with an overall rusty-red color and contrasting pale gray head. Common in tropical America north to Mexico, the Ruddy Ground-Dove is mostly a winter visitor to the US Southwest (Arizona) and southern California, but it occasionally breeds there.

OCCURRENCE Localized in California, Arizona, New Mexico, and Texas; occurs in woodlands, gardens, fields, forest edges, and shrubbery.

VOICE Monotonous, endlessly repeated 2-syllable *ca-whoop* given every second or so.

Length **6¾in (17cm)** | Wingspan **11in (28cm)**

Family **Cuculidae** | Species ***Crotophaga sulcirostris***

Groove-billed Ani

Anis, members of the cuckoo family, have black plumage, long tails, and high, narrow, blackish bills. They always appear dishevelled—as if their feathers were about to fall off. Two of their toes point forward and two backward. These social birds exhibit an unusual communal nesting behavior—several females lay eggs in the same nest, and both males and females share incubation duties.

OCCURRENCE Breeds along the Rio Grande Valley, but leaves the area in the winter. Widely distributed, and resident, from Mexico to South America.

VOICE Call a liquid *Tee-ho*, accented on first syllable, given in flight and when perched, chorus-like when many birds call together.

Length **13½in (34cm)** | Wingspan **17in (43cm)**

Family **Strigidae** | Species ***Otus asio***

Eastern Screech-Owl

This widespread little owl has adapted well to suburban areas, and its "rolled" trill is a familiar sound across the eastern US. In the West, it is replaced by the Western Screech-Owl, which has a different call, a series of hoots accelerating and descending in pitch.

OCCURRENCE Distribution reaches westward to Idaho in the North and western Texas in the South.

VOICE Most familiar call a descending whinny; also an even trill; occasional barks and screeches; female higher-pitched than male.

Length **6½–10in (16–25cm)** | Wingspan **19–24in (48–61cm)**

Family **Strigidae** | Species ***Otus trichopsis***

Whiskered Screech-Owl

The Whiskered Screech-Owl is more often heard than seen, and has a distinctive voice of hoots and trills. It can be heard on still nights in mountain canyons of southeastern Arizona and southwestern New Mexico. This small owl feeds largely on insects and insect larvae.

OCCURRENCE Resident at about 8,000ft (2,400m) in oak-pine woodlands in canyons, along rivers, deciduous woodlands. Ranges southward through Mexico to Nicaragua.

VOICE Series of toots and trills; also single hoots, barks, screeches; pairs may sing duets; female higher-pitched.

Length **6–7½in (15–19cm)** | Wingspan **17½in (44cm)**

Family **Strigidae** | Species ***Strix occidentalis***

Spotted Owl

In the Pacific Northwest, the Spotted Owl is threatened by competition from the Barred Owl and by habitat loss from clear cutting. Spotted Owls breed in old-growth forests, which the forestry industry covets, while conservationists argue that old-growth forests are not a renewable resource. These conflicting views have led to hot debates.

OCCURRENCE British Columbia, the US Pacific Northwest, California; Rocky Mountains south to Mexico. Breeds in forested areas.

VOICE Typical call of four notes, *whoo hoo-hoo hooo*, emphasis on the last syllable. Also whistles and barks.

Length **18–19in (46–48cm)** | Wingspan **3½ft (1.1m)**

Family **Strigidae** | Species ***Glaucidium brasilianum***

Ferruginous Pygmy-Owl

Quite widespread in the tropics, from Mexico to Argentina, this owl reaches the US only in Arizona and Texas, where it can be found close to rivers and in desert areas at lower elevations than the similar-looking Northern Pygmy-Owl. The Ferruginous species has an orange, not brown, tail, and its belly and crown are streaked, not spotted like the Northern Pygmy-Owl's.

OCCURRENCE Rare north of Mexico. Extreme southeastern Arizona and southern Texas. Occurs in riverine areas, and mesquite scrub; nests in cavities.

VOICE Call a quick series of repeated single rising notes.

Length **5½–7in (14–18cm)** | Wingspan **15in (38cm)**

Family **Strigidae** | Species ***Micrathene whitneyi***

Elf Owl

One of the smallest owls in the world, the Elf Owl is probably the commonest bird of prey in the deserts of the Southwest. Being strictly nocturnal, however, it is more often heard than seen, and its distinctive voice is easy to recognize once heard. Elf Owls defend their nests aggressively, and several can get together to mob an intruder.

OCCURRENCE Breeds in southern Nevada, Arizona, California, New Mexico, and Texas, and adjacent areas of Mexico. Occurs in thorn-scrub, woodlands along rivers, and suburban areas.

VOICE Call a loud chatter of 5–6 notes; also trills and barks.

Length **4¾–5½in (12–14cm)** | Wingspan **15in (38cm)**

Family **Caprimulgidae** | Species ***Chordeiles acutipennis***

Lesser Nighthawk

The Lesser Nighthawk is a wide-ranging airborne forager, and is well camouflaged while resting on the ground in daytime. Most active at dawn and dusk, it swoops low over water, bush, and desert in pursuit of insect prey, which it tracks with agile and abrupt changes in direction. This species was formerly known as the Trilling Nighthawk because of its distinctive call, which distinguishes it from the similar looking Common Nighthawk where the two species occur together.

OCCURRENCE Breeds in desert and open scrub and along watercourses. Occurs from the southern US to Central and South America as far south as Paraguay and Peru.

VOICE Low, trilled whistle lasting up to 12 seconds and resembling a calling toad.

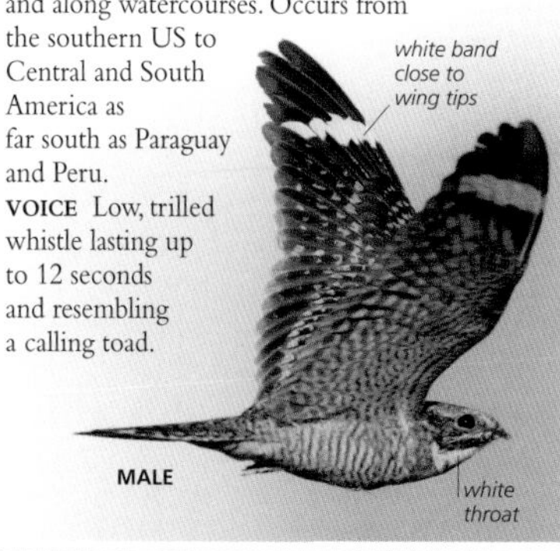

Length **8–9in (20–23cm)** | Wingspan **21–23in (53–58cm)**

Family **Caprimulgidae** | Species ***Caprimulgus carolinensis***

Chuck-will's-widow

The Chuck-will's-widow is the larger of the two species of North American nightjar. It is tolerant of human development and often nests in suburban and even urban areas. It captures its insect prey in flight, and has occasionally been observed chasing down and swallowing bats and small birds whole. Chuck-will's-widows hunt mostly at dawn and dusk, as well as being active during a full moon.

OCCURRENCE Breeds in forests composed of a mixture of deciduous and evergreen trees, and in open fields. Winters in Mexico and northern Central America.

VOICE Whistled *chuck-will's-wid-ow*; beginning softly, then increasing in volume, with emphasis on the two middle syllables.

Length **11–12½in (28–32cm)** | Wingspan **25–28in (63–70cm)**

Family **Caprimulgidae** | Species ***Caprimulgus vociferus***

Whip-poor-will

More often heard than seen, the Whip-poor-will's camouflage makes it extremely difficult to spot on the forest floor. It flies away only when an intruder is just a few feet away. This species has an unusual breeding pattern—the male feeds the first brood until fledging, while the female lays eggs for a second brood. Eggs from each brood may hatch simultaneously during a full moon, when there is most light at night, perhaps allowing the parents more time to forage for food.

OCCURRENCE Mixed mature forests with oaks and pines on dry upland sites. Breeds north to southern Canada and south to El Salvador. Eastern and southwestern populations are widely separated.

VOICE Loud, 3-syllable whistle *WHIP-perrr-WIIL.*

Length **9–10in (23–26cm)** | Wingspan **17–20in (43–51cm)**

Family **Apodidae** | Species ***Cypseloides niger***

Black Swift

The Black Swift is the largest of the North American swifts, and also the most enigmatic. It forages at high altitudes and nests on sea cliffs or behind waterfalls in mountains, meaning it can be difficult to observe. On cold and cloudy days, when aerial insect prey occurs closer to the ground, Black Swifts forage lower, and are easier to see.

OCCURRENCE Breeds from British Columbia in Canada south to Mexico, Costa Rica, and the West Indies. Found in mountains from May or June to early October. Wintering areas still largely unknown.

VOICE Generally silent, but gives twittering chips, sometimes in fast series, during interactions with other swifts; sharp *cheep* when approaching nest.

Length **7in (18cm)** | Wingspan **18in (46cm)**

Family **Apodidae** | Species ***Chaetura pelagica***

Chimney Swift

A familiar sight and sound during the summer months, Chimney Swifts race through the skies over town and country, their rolling twitters often very loud. These birds feed, drink, and bathe on the wing. Chimney Swifts used not to nest in tree holes, but have taken to many kinds of human structures. Although some populations have declined, they remain common in many places.

OCCURRENCE Widespread over many habitats; regular in summer in southern California. Winters in Amazonian South America.

VOICE High, rapid chips and twittering; notes from individuals in a flock run together into a rapid, descending chatter.

Length **5in (13cm)** | Wingspan **14in (36cm)**

Family **Trochilidae** | Species ***Cynanthus latirostris***

Broad-billed Hummingbird

The iridescent blue of an adult male Broad-billed Hummingbird qualifies it as one of North America's most beautiful birds. During courtship, males perform a pendulum-like display, accompanied by zinging wing beats and chattering calls. The bird's bill is broader at the base than that of many other hummingbird species.

OCCURRENCE Lives in dry shrubby washes and riverine areas. Winters in Mexico.

VOICE Common call dry *tch-chk*, sometimes with 1–3 syllables; chase call squeaky twittering; song short, rapid series of high *tsi* notes with buzzy ending.

Length **4in (10cm)** | Wingspan **5½in (14cm)**

Family **Trochilidae** | Species ***Amazilia violiceps***

Violet-crowned Hummingbird

Its white underparts, red bill, and violet-blue crown make the Violet-crowned Hummingbird the most distinctive hummingbird in North America. In the US, it is restricted to riverine sycamore woodlands in Arizona and New Mexico, which it leaves in winter. It is resident in its Mexican range.

OCCURRENCE Localized breeder in Arizona and New Mexico, vagrant in California and Texas. Resident breeder in Mexico.

VOICE Call a hard, dry *tek*, often in short series; chase call a squeaky series of *twi* notes; song a steady series of descending *chew* notes.

Length **4¼in (11cm)** | Wingspan **6in (15cm)**

Family **Trochilidae** | Species ***Amazilia beryllina***

Berylline Hummingbird

Named after the glittering green gemstone, this hummingbird lives up to its name, with extra colors added by its rufous wing patch and buff belly. This species is easy to identify in its limited North American range.

OCCURRENCE Rare in southeastern Arizona in summer; nests in very small numbers in high-elevation canyons and pine-oak woodlands; very rare in the mountains of western Texas. Its main range is in central Mexico.

VOICE Call rough, buzzy *tzrrr*; song a series of high-pitched, squeaky chips and twitters.

Length **4in (10cm** | Wingspan **5½in (14cm)**

Family **Trochilidae** | Species ***Lampornis clemenciae***

Blue-throated Hummingbird

The largest hummingbird in North America, the Blue-throated strikes an imposing figure when seen near one of its smaller relatives. Its large size and a two-striped facial pattern distinguish it from other hummingbirds in its range. It is a specialist of the isolated "sky island" mountaintops of the Southwest.

OCCURRENCE Breeds locally in Arizona, New Mexico, and Texas; winters in Mexico. Sometimes winters at feeding stations in the Southwest.

VOICE Call a loud, high squeak, *seep*; common song a steady, slow series of *seep* notes given by perched male; song a whisper of mechanical hissing notes.

Length **5in (13cm)** | Wingspan **8in (20cm)**

Family **Trochilidae** | Species ***Hylocharis leucotis***

White-eared Hummingbird

The bold black-and-white facial pattern of this species distinguishes it from other hummingbirds in its limited US range. A resident of Mexico, it did not establish itself in the US until 1989. It is aggressive even for a hummingbird defending its nectar sources and chasing away larger species. Males are very vocal during the breeding season.

OCCURRENCE Breeds in mountain forests of southeastern Arizona and southwestern New Mexico.

VOICE Call a metallic *tchink*, often doubled; chase call a rapid series of high chip notes; song a fast series of chips with upslurred rattles.

Length **3¾in (9.5cm)** | Wingspan **5½in (14cm)**

Family **Trochilidae** | Species ***Eugenes fulgens***

Magnificent Hummingbird

Although smaller than the showy Blue-throated Hummingbird, this species is more spectacular. Living in the "sky islands" of Arizona and New Mexico, it is less territorial and aggressive than other hummingbirds, often utilizing more nectar sites.

OCCURRENCE Breeds at mid altitudes in woodlands of the Southwest; forages and migrates in drier habitats away from breeding areas.

VOICE Call a loud, sharp *chip*; chase call an accelerating series of squeaky *dee* or *dik* notes; song a quiet, buzzy warbling.

Length **5in (13cm)** | Wingspan **7½in (19cm)**

Family **Trochilidae** | Species ***Calothorax lucifer***

Lucifer Hummingbird

A specialist of the Chihuahuan desert, the Lucifer Hummingbird can be recognized by its long, curved bill. Males perform an impressive display in front of females at the nest, diving repeatedly and producing a vibrating sound with their wings.

OCCURRENCE Breeding range barely reaches Arizona, New Mexico, and Texas. Resident in Mexico.

VOICE A dry, hard *chit*, often doubled or rolled into series when agitated; a sweeter *chi-chip* in territorial interactions; chase call a rapid series of sharp *chit* notes.

Length **3½in (9cm)** | Wingspan **4in (10cm)**

Family **Trochilidae** | Species ***Archilochus colubris***

Ruby-throated Hummingbird

The only hummingbird breeding east of the Mississippi River, this species can only be confused with other species during migration, when other species are present in its range. Before migration, these birds add about 1/16oz (2g) of fat to their weight; this provides enough fuel for their nonstop 800-mile (1,300km) flight across the Gulf of Mexico.
OCCURRENCE Occurs in a variety of woodlands and gardens; leaves breeding range by November, returns as early as February. The bulk of the population migrates to Central America.
VOICE A soft, thick *chic*, sometimes doubled; twittered notes in interactions; chase call a fast, slightly buzzy *tsi-tsi-tsi-tsi-tsi-tsi-*; soft, rattling song rarely heard.

orange-red throat

MALE

Length **3½in (9cm)** | Wingspan **4¼in (11cm)**

Family **Trochilidae** | Species ***Calypte costae***

Costa's Hummingbird

Costa's Hummingbird lives in the Sonoran and Mojave deserts, where it is common locally. The male Costa's Hummingbird performs an acrobatic dive display, which includes up to 40 narrow vertical loops, a whistled song, followed by a back-and-forth shuttle display in front of the female.
OCCURRENCE Found in desert scrub, sage scrub, and dense shrubs in southern California and adjacent areas of the Southwest. Most birds migrate to Mexico for the winter.
VOICE Call a soft, metallic *tik*; chase call rapid series of *tik*, often mixed with high, buzzy *tssrr* notes; song a thin, high-pitched, buzzing whistle *tseee-seeeeeeew*.

straight, black bill

MALE

Length **3¼in (8.5cm)** | Wingspan **4¾in (12cm)**

Family **Trogonidae** | Species ***Trogon elegans***

Elegant Trogon

Although widely distributed in Mexico and Central America, the well-named Elegant Trogon reaches the US only in the Southwest, where it occurs in wooded canyons. Rather sluggish, Elegant Trogons can remain perched for long periods.
OCCURRENCE Breeds in wooded canyons with pine-oak or oak-juniper; widely distributed in Mexico and Central America.
VOICE Alarm call a rapid, hoarse *bekekekekek*; varying croaking or *churr* notes; song a series of deep, croaking, *Ko-ah Ko-ah*.

Length **11½in (29cm)** | Wingspan **16in (41cm)**

Family **Alcedinidae** | Species ***Chloroceryle americana***

Green Kingfisher

The Green Kingfisher is identified by its small size, proportionately large bill, conspicuous white collar, and green underparts. This species is the smallest of the three North American kingfishers. It is found in small numbers in southern Arizona and southern Texas, but its range is vast, and reaches as far south as Chile and Argentina.
OCCURRENCE Breeds and winters near wooded shorelines of lakes, ponds, and streams; in southern Texas and Arizona in US, and from Mexico all the way to southern South America (Chile and Argentina).
VOICE Staccato "ticking" call; also a harsh, buzzy scold; quieter than other two North American kingfishers.

Length **8½in (22cm)** | Wingspan **11in (28cm)**

Family **Alcedinidae** | Species ***Megaceryle torquata***

Ringed Kingfisher

The largest of the three species of North American kingfishers, the Ringed Kingfisher is easily identified by its size and color. Although it is brightly colored, and perches conspicuously on trees and branches over the water, its shy nature makes it difficult to spot. It flies off at the least suspicion of intrusion, with a loud rattle signalling where it was. Like other kingfishers it nests in a burrow, which it digs in a muddy or sandy riverbank.

OCCURRENCE Ranges from southern Texas to southern South America. At northernmost part of range, in Texas, occurs along the Rio Grande Valley.

VOICE Loud rattle; also loud, double-syllabled *ktok-ktok* in flight.

Length **16in (41cm)** | Wingspan **25in (63cm)**

Family **Picidae** | Species ***Melanerpes erythrocephalus***

Red-headed Woodpecker

Widespread in the East, but rare west of the Great Plains, the Red-headed Woodpecker is the only member of its family, and its completely red head makes it easy to identify. It stores its food—insects and nuts—to eat at a later time. A truly North American species, the Red-headed Woodpecker does not occur south of the Rio Grande.

OCCURRENCE Occurs in deciduous woodlands, orchards, municipal parks, agricultural areas, forest edges, and forests affected by fire.

VOICE Primary call an extremely harsh and loud *churr*, also produces breeding call and alarm; no song; active drummer.

Length **8½–9½in (22–24cm)** | Wingspan **16–18in (41–46cm)**

Family **Picidae** | Species ***Melanerpes uropygialis***

Gila Woodpecker

The Gila Woodpecker has characteristic heavily barred upperparts, with a tan head and underparts—only the male has a red crown patch. It is a common inhabitant of southern Arizona's desert and semi-desert areas, which are covered sparsely with a variety of cactus species. Both male and female excavate a nest hole in a live cactus, but they may not use that hole until its walls have hardened.

OCCURRENCE From the southwestern US to central Mexico, this species is attracted to cacti and dead trees in riverine woodlands; it is also found in suburban areas.

VOICE Noisy, loud *churr-churr* and a series of *pip-pip* or *yip-yip* notes; drumming is prolonged.

tan-rust neck and underparts

MALE

Length **8–10in (20–25cm)** | Wingspan **16–17in (41–43cm)**

Family **Picidae** | Species ***Melanerpes aurifrons***

Golden-fronted Woodpecker

The yellow forehead, red crown, and bright orange nape give the male Golden-fronted Woodpecker a tricolored head pattern, while the female has only two color patches. This Mexican species reaches Texas and Oklahoma in the US, where it lives in a variety of open woodlands, including mesquite, riverine thickets, and subtropical scrub.

OCCURRENCE Southern Oklahoma and Texas in US, Mexico, and Central America, south to Nicaragua.

VOICE Call a noisy, basic *churr* closely resembling that of other *Melanerpes* woodpeckers, especially the Red-bellied, but harsher; a rather short "drum."

Length **10–12in (25–30cm)** | Wingspan **17in (43cm)**

Family **Picidae** | Species ***Melanerpes carolinus***

Red-bellied Woodpecker

A quintessentially eastern species, the Red-bellied Woodpecker is common from the Mississippi Valley eastward to the Atlantic Seaboard, north to Minnesota and New York, and south to eastern Texas and Florida. It has recently expanded its range both northward into Canada and westward towards the Rockies. Its English name, "Red-bellied Woodpecker" is misleading, as its belly is pale buff, not red. Its presence is often given away by its rolling call, which is similar to that of the Gray Tree Frog.

OCCURRENCE Eastern and southeastern US; forests, swamps, suburbs, and gardens.

VOICE Rather soft, clearly rolling, slightly quivering *krrurrr* call.

red forehead to nape

MALE

Length **9–10½in (23–27cm)** | Wingspan **16in (41cm)**

Family **Picidae** | Species ***Picoides nuttallii***

Nuttall's Woodpecker

Named for the famous British naturalist Thomas Nuttall, Nuttall's Woodpecker is resident in California. It resembles the Ladder-backed Woodpecker, with black-and-white barring on the back, and the male's red crown. Interestingly, although Nuttall's Woodpecker prefers oak woodlands, acorns are not part of its diet. It excavates a new nest cavity each year and it is likely that earlier nest sites are used by other species.

OCCURRENCE Mainly oak woodlands, but also pine-oak and woodlands near rivers; also willows, sycamores, maple, and pine trees; occasionally found in Oregon.

VOICE Two calls; single note contact call *pweek* and 2-note call *pir-it-pir-it-pir-it.*

white breast with dark spots

MALE

Length **7–7½in (18–19cm)** | Wingspan **16in (41cm)**

Family **Picidae** | Species ***Picoides arizonae***

Arizona Woodpecker

A resident of southeastern Arizona and southwestern New Mexico, the Arizona Woodpecker is the only brown-backed woodpecker species in North America. In addition, it has a conspicuous white neck patch, and brown-and-white spots and bars on its underparts. It inhabits inaccessible areas, is well camouflaged, and is remarkably secretive during the nesting period, which makes it difficult to observe. It uses quite a range of calls, except when nesting.

OCCURRENCE Oak and pine-oak woodlands, from 4,000–7,000ft (1,200–2,150m). Winters at lower elevations if food is scarce.

VOICE Main call long *peep*; also lengthy, loud, and harsh rattling call; also a *kweek* call.

short, thin, pointed bill

MALE

Length **7–8in (18–20cm)** | Wingspan **14in (36cm)**

Family **Picidae** | Species ***Colaptes chrysoides***

Gilded Flicker

The Gilded Flicker used to be considered a subspecies of the Northern Flicker. Where the ranges of these two species overlap, in parts of the Southwest, there is interbreeding between them. Gilded Flickers have golden undertail coverts, yellow underwing coverts, and a white rump. They have a preference for Saguaro Cacti as nesting sites.

OCCURRENCE Resident in deserts with giant cacti in Arizona and southeastern California. Also resident in Baja California and continental areas of northwestern Mexico.

VOICE Two common calls, loud *kew-kew-kew* with each note ascending at end, and softer *wicka-wicka-wicka.*

red "mustache"

MALE

Length **11–11½in (28–29cm)** | Wingspan **18–19in (46–48cm)**

Family **Cotingidae** | Species ***Pachyramphus aglaiae***

Rose-throated Becard

The Rose-throated Becard is a grayish or brownish bird with a large head. The male's pink throat and the female's charcoal cap and brown body are distinctive. Its roundish, foot-long nest hangs from a high tree limb, and is a reliable cue to its presence. It forages mainly on fruit and insects, sallying short distances from a perch.

OCCURRENCE This Central American species reaches southeastern Arizona and the lower Rio Grande Valley in Texas.

VOICE Plaintive *tseeeuuuu*, and *pik* or *pidik* calls; song repeated *see-cheew, wee-chew*.

Length **7¼in (18.5cm)** | Wingspan **12in (30cm)**

Family **Tyrannidae** | Species ***Camptostoma imberbe***

Northern Beardless-Tyrannulet

This tiny flycatcher is uncommon along streams in southeastern Arizona, southeastern New Mexico, and southern Texas. Its whistled calls often reveal its presence before it is seen. "Beardless" referes to the lack of bristles at the base of its bill, and "tyrannulet" to its diminutive size for a flycatcher.

OCCURRENCE Found especially in riverine vegetation, including sycamores and cottonwoods; local in Arizona, New Mexico, and Texas; more common from Mexico to Costa Rica.

VOICE Calls include clear, piping *peeeuuu* and *peeut di-i-i-i*; song *pee-pee-pee-pee*, a descending series of whistles given by males.

Length **4½–5½in (11.5–14cm)** | Wingspan **7in (18cm)**

Family **Tyrannidae** | Species ***Sayornis phoebe***

Eastern Phoebe

An early spring migrant, the Eastern Phoebe often nests under bridges and culverts, as well as on buildings. Not shy, it is also familiar because of its *fee-bee* vocalization and constant tail wagging. Ornithologist John James Audubon tied threads on several birds' legs and established that individuals return from the south to a previously used nest site.

OCCURRENCE Occurs in open woodlands, forest edges, and parks, often near water. Breeds across Canada and in the eastern half of the US. Winters in the southeastern US and Mexico.

VOICE Common call a clear, weak *chip*; song an emphatic *fee-bee* or *fee-b-be-bee*.

Length **5½–7in (14–17cm)** | Wingspan **10½in (27cm)**

Family **Tyrannidae** | Species ***Contopus pertinax***

Greater Pewee

First identified by its whistled song, the Greater Pewee, when seen, looks like a plain grayish flycatcher with a tufted crest. Primarily a Mexican and Central American species, it reaches Arizona and New Mexico across the US border. Greater Pewees vigorously defend their nests against potential predators like jays and squirrels. US breeders move south after breeding.

OCCURRENCE Breeds in open pine woodland with oak understory at elevations of 7,000–10,000ft (2,100–3,000m) along steep-sided canyons.

VOICE A repeated *pip, peep*, or *beep-beep*; male territorial song a plaintive *ho-say ma-ree-ah*.

tufted crest

ADULT

Length **7in (18cm)** | Wingspan **13in (33cm)**

Family **Tyrannidae** | Species ***Contopus virens***

Eastern Wood-pewee

The Eastern Wood-pewee, common in woodlands in the eastern US and southern Canada, is replaced in the West by the very similar Western Wood-pewee. Their ranges overlap slightly at the margins of their respective distributions. The Eastern Wood-pewee looks somewhat like the Eastern Phoebe, but does not flick its tail.
OCCURRENCE Woodlands in the eastern US and southern and eastern Canada; also along rivers in the Midwest. Winters in shrubby, second-growth forests of South America.
VOICE Call terse *chip*; song slurred *pee-ah-wee*, plaintive *wee-ooo*, or *wee-ur*, and slurred *ah di dee*.

Length **6in (15cm)** | Wingspan **9–10in (23–26cm)**

Family **Tyrannidae** | Species ***Empidonax fulvifrons***

Buff-breasted Flycatcher

The smallest of the genus *Empidonax*, the Buff-breasted Flycatcher has a rusty or buffy wash on its breast. The other *Empidonax* species are grayish or yellow below. A resident in Mexico and Central America, the Buff-breasted Flycatcher reaches the US locally in Arizona and Texas, where it lives at high elevations in pine-oak woodlands.
OCCURRENCE Southern Arizona and New Mexico to Mexico, and south to Honduras. US populations migratory, resident in Mexico and Central America.
VOICE Call *pit*, and alarm call *quit-quit-qui-r-r*; song on breeding grounds *chee-lick* or *chee-lick-chou* by both sexes.

Length **5in (13cm)** | Wingspan **8½in (22cm)**

Family **Tyrannidae** | Species ***Pyrocephalus rubinus***

Vermilion Flycatcher

Contrasting with all other North American species of flycatcher, the Vermilion Flycatcher well deserves its English name. Beware, however, that only the male is red; the female, brownish above and streaked below, is drab by comparison. Males advertise their territories during spectacular flight displays accompanied by loud vocalizations.
OCCURRENCE Breeds mostly along rivers, in woodlands with cottonwoods, willows, and sycamores. In the US, found only in the South; south of the border, occurs south to Argentina.
VOICE Contact call *peeent*; male song an excited *p-p-pik-zee*, *pit-a-zee*, or *ching-tink-a-link*.

Length **5–6in (13–15cm)** | Wingspan **10in (25cm)**

Family **Tyrannidae** | Species ***Myiodynastes luteiventris***

Sulphur-bellied Flycatcher

In North America, this large and boldly marked flycatcher breeds in the mountain canyons of southeastern Arizona. It is heavily streaked on both back and belly, its tail is rufous, and its loud squeaky calls are distinctive. Sulphur-bellied Flycatchers are cavity nesters, using holes in trees, or, occasionally, nest boxes.
OCCURRENCE Southeastern Arizona; widely distributed from Mexico to Costa Rica. Winters from Ecuador to Bolivia and Brazil.
VOICE Calls *p'p'pe-ya, p'p'p'pe-ya, weel-yum, weel-yum, chu-eer*; male song soft *tre-le-re-re, tre-le-re-re, chu-eer, chee-a-leet s-lik*.

Length **8–9in (20–23cm)** | Wingspan **14½in (37cm)**

Family **Tyrannidae** | Species ***Tyrannus melancholicus***

Tropical Kingbird

The Tropical Kingbird is another of the widespread tropical American species of flycatchers that barely reach the US as a breeder. It nests in open areas of southeastern Arizona, but can be seen as far north as British Columbia in the fall.

OCCURRENCE In the US, regularly found in residential areas, such as golf courses, farmland, and gardens. In the tropics breeds in a wide variety of habitats, including evergreen forest edges and mangroves.

VOICE Twittering calls given throughout the day and all year long; song tremulous *tere-ee-ee-tril-il-iil-l* or *tre-e-e-e-e-eip*.

Length **7–9in (18–23cm)** | Wingspan **14½in (37cm)**

Family **Tyrannidae** | Species ***Tyrannus crassirostris***

Thick-billed Kingbird

Though it is similar in size and color to other kingbirds of the western region, the Thick-billed Kingbird has a noticeably thicker bill, and a darker head, both of which give it a somewhat "beefy" look. In North America, Thick-billed Kingbirds breed locally in southern Arizona and New Mexico, mostly in sycamore groves along streams.

OCCURRENCE Prefers cottonwoods and sycamores in wooded canyons, close to water. Reported from California and Texas.

VOICE Harsh and raspy *tch tchee* and *tch-uhreeeE* calls; vocal through the day while breeding; dawn song consists of two phrases *T-t-t-t-t, t-T-tt-rwheeuh -t-t-t*, or a loud whistled *pwaareeet*.

Length **9–9½in (23–24cm)** | Wingspan **16in (41cm)**

Family **Tyrannidae** | Species ***Tyrannus forficatus***

Scissor-tailed Flycatcher

The long tail streamers of the Scissor-tailed Flycatcher are seen in all their glory when males display in flight over their breeding territory. Scissor-tailed Flycatchers often incorporate man-made debris into their nests, including pieces of string, cloth, or bits of wrapping. This flycatcher forms large pre-migratory roosts in late summer, often of more than 100, and even up to 1000 birds.

OCCURRENCE Breeds in open areas in south-central US states and adjacent Mexico. Reported widely in western North America. Winters from Mexico to Costa Rica.

VOICE Males vocalize in breeding territories and communal roosts; song a variable number of *pups* followed by *perleep* or *peroo*.

Length **9–15in (23–38cm)** | Wingspan **15in (38cm)**

Family **Tyrannidae** | Species ***Myiarchus tuberculifer***

Dusky-capped Flycatcher

One of four species of flycatchers of the genus *Myiarchus* found in North America, the Dusky-capped breeds in Arizona and New Mexico. It inhabits dense woodlands, where it forages for insects in the foliage below the canopy. As in other *Myiarchus* species, the sexes are similar, and juveniles are slightly darker than adults. The species is mainly silent, except when it sings at dawn.

OCCURRENCE Southeastern Arizona and southwestern New Mexico. Migrates to Mexico. Resident populations occur all the way south to South America.

VOICE Dawn song a *whit, peeur*, or *wheeeeu* alternated with *huit* notes.

Length **7¼in (18.5cm)** | Wingspan **10in (25cm)**

Family **Tyrannidae** | Species ***Myiarchus crinitus***

Great Crested Flycatcher

The only species of *Myiarchus* flycatchers breeding in the eastern region, the Great Crested Flycatcher occurs in the west only in Canada, where it reaches Alberta. However it is sometimes seen farther west and north in the fall, when it can be identified by the pale base of its bill and the sharp definition between its gray breast and yellow belly.

OCCURRENCE From Alberta eastward to the Maritimes in Canada, southward to Texas and Florida. Migrates to Mexico, Central America, and northern South America. Breeds in woodlands.

VOICE Main call a loud, abrupt *purr-it* given by both sexes; male song repeated *whee-eep*, occasionally *wheeyer.*

Length **7–8in (18–20cm)** | Wingspan **13in (33cm)**

Family **Tyrannidae** | Species ***Myiarchus tyrannulus***

Brown-crested Flycatcher

This is the largest of the three western *Myiarchus* species. It is a slender-looking, long-tailed flycatcher, with a thick bill and a ragged-looking, tan-brown crest. In flight, the rufous outer tail feathers are quite noticeable. Although mostly an insect catcher, it will sometimes pluck a hummingbird from a perch.

OCCURRENCE Found only in the southwestern US, north to Nevada and east to Texas; breeds in riverine woodlands. Migrates to Mexico and Guatemala, resident south to Honduras.

VOICE Call *huit* singly or repeated, also distinctive *rasp*; dawn song loud *come-here, come-here* or *whit-will-do, whit-will-do.*

Length **8½in (22cm)** | Wingspan **13in (33cm)**

Family **Vireonidae** | Species ***Vireo flavifrons***

Yellow-throated Vireo

This large and robust vireo of eastern US woodlands is usually found foraging and singing high in the canopy. It is distinctly patterned, with a bright yellow throat, breast, and "spectacles," and a white belly and flanks. The fragmentation of forests, spraying of insecticides, and cowbird parasitism have led to regional declines in its populations, but the bird's range, as a whole, has actually expanded.

OCCURRENCE Breeds in deciduous and mixed woodlands in the eastern half of the US, and extreme southern Canada. Winter range from wooded areas of southern Mexico to northern South America.

VOICE Scolding, hoarse, rapid calls; male song a slow, repetitive, 2- or 3-note phrase, separated by long pauses.

Length **5½in (14cm)** | Wingspan **9½in (24cm)**

Family **Vireonidae** | Species ***Vireo atricapilla***

Black-capped Vireo

The only vireo to show a sexually dimorphic (different) plumage, the Black-capped Vireo is restricted to central and southern Texas and Mexico. Despite its broad, white "spectacles" and a red eye, it is not easy to spot as it forages in dense shrubby vegetation. It sings persistently from near the top of bushes, often long into the day. Habitat changes and Brown-headed Cowbird parasitism have caused declines in the bird's population.

OCCURRENCE Breeds only in the hill country of central southern Texas and adjacent Mexico, casually in Oklahoma. Winters in the foothill country of western Mexico.

VOICE Calls are variable scolds; song an extensive repertoire of trills, whistles, chips, and squeaks, with individual variations.

Length **4½in (11.5cm)** | Wingspan **7½in (19cm)**

Family **Corvidae** | Species ***Cyanocitta cristata***

Blue Jay

One of the best-known birds in North America because of its abundance and beautiful plumage, the Blue Jay is largely an eastern species, although in Canada it occurs westward to Alberta and British Columbia. In the west, it is replaced by the equally spectacular Steller's Jay.

OCCURRENCE In the west, breeds in British Columbia, Alberta, Saskatchewan, and Montana. Rare elsewhere (California, Oregon, Washington) in winter. Found in a variety of woodlands, suburban areas, and gardens.

VOICE Harsh, screaming *jay! jay!*; other common call an odd ethereal, chortling *queedle-ee-dee;* soft clucks when feeding.

Length **9½–12in (24–30cm)** | Wingspan **16in (41cm)**

Family **Corvidae** | Species ***Aphelocoma ultramarina***

Mexican Jay

The bell-like calls from a flock of Mexican Jays can be heard in the pine-oak canyons of Mexico and adjacent Arizona, New Mexico, and Texas. These birds have a fascinating social system. Instead of territorial pairs, they form territorial flocks, within which females mate with several males. Nestlings are not fed only by their parents, but also by other members of the flock, including those that have failed to breed.

OCCURRENCE Occurs in mountains with rugged slopes, covered with oaks and pines.

VOICE Rapid-fire, ringing *wink, wink*; harsher and less bell-like in Texas population, which also gives rattle call similar to scrub-jays.

Length **11–12½in (28–32cm)** | Wingspan **19½in (50cm)**

Family **Corvidae** | Species ***Aphelocoma insularis***

Island Scrub-Jay

The Island Scrub-Jay, a close relative of the mainland's Western Scrub-Jay, is restricted to Santa Cruz Island off the coast of southern California. It has a thicker bill than the Western Scrub-Jay, and sports deep blue undertail feathers.

OCCURRENCE The only scrub-jay on Santa Cruz Island, one of southern California's Channel Islands, where its preferred habitat is oak thickets.

VOICE Wide range of calls, similar to those of the Western Scrub-Jay but louder, including harsh *shek-shek-shek* and various "rattles."

Length **12in (31cm)** | Wingspan **17in (43cm)**

Family **Corvidae** | Species ***Pica nuttalli***

Yellow-billed Magpie

Found only in California, where it is common locally, the Yellow-billed Magpie is very similar to the more widely distributed Black-billed Magpie. Its yellow bill, small bare yellow patch underneath the eye, and slightly different calls all help to distinguish it from the Black-billed Magpie. The Yellow-billed Magpie occasionally nests in loose colonies, but never with more than one pair to a tree.

OCCURRENCE Oak savannah, orchards, and other open habitats with widely spaced trees; also areas near rivers and streams.

VOICE Whining *mag* call; also a series of *kwah-kwah-kwah*; similar to Black-billed Magpie, but higher-pitched and less harsh.

Length **15–17½in (38–45cm)** | Wingspan **24in (61cm)**

Family **Corvidae** | Species ***Corvus caurinus***

Northwestern Crow

Very similar to the widespread American Crow, the Northwestern Crow's range is restricted to a coastal strip from Alaska to Washington State, where the American Crow does not appear to occur. Northwestern Crows often congregate in large flocks in tidal areas, where they dig for clams, pry open barnacles, chase crabs, and catch small fish in tidal pools, at low tide.

OCCURRENCE Coastal areas from Alaska to Washington state; avoids dense forests; along rivers at higher elevation inland.

VOICE Varied, but most common call a loud, familiar *caw!* lower, raspier, and more rapid than most American Crows.

Length **13–16in (33–41cm)** | Wingspan **34in (86cm)**

Family **Corvidae** | Species ***Corvus cryptoleucus***

Chihuahuan Raven

Smaller than the Common Raven but larger than the American Crow, the Chihuahuan Raven was previously called the White-necked Raven. This name alludes to its concealed white neck feathers, which may come into view in the bird's windswept habitat. A gregarious and vocal species, the Chihuahuan Raven may be seen wheeling about in flocks of hundreds of birds.

OCCURRENCE Breeds in south-central and southwestern US and in Mexico, in grasslands, scrub, and deserts. Northern populations winter in Mexico.

VOICE High-pitched croaks, less varied than the highly diverse repertoire of the Common Raven.

Length **17½–20in (44–51cm)** | Wingspan **3½ft (1.1m)**

Family **Ptilogonatidae** | Species ***Phainopepla nitens***

Phainopepla

The name Phainopepla, Greek for "shiny robe," refers to the species' glossy plumage. Phainopeplas like to perch high up in trees and shrubs, from which they sally to catch flying insects. When in flight, the conspicuous white wing patches contrast with the black of body and tail. The somewhat similar Northern Mockingbird also has white wing patches, but also has white in its tail, and is gray, not black.

OCCURRENCE Inhabits the southwestern US and adjacent Mexico, in a variety of dry to arid habitats, including oak scrub, open mesquite woodlands, and patches of juniper on rocky slopes.

VOICE Call a mellow *wurp*, with upward inflection; song a long series of short phrases, overall soft and halting delivery.

Length **7¾in (19.5cm)** | Wingspan **11in (28cm)**

Family **Paridae** | Species ***Parus carolinensis***

Carolina Chickadee

This eastern and southeastern species is very similar to the Black-capped Chickadee, which is widespread in the West. In parts of the central and eastern US, both species have adjacent ranges and hybridize locally. The western range of the Carolina Chickadee is limited to parts of Kansas, Oklahoma, and Texas, where the Black-capped does not normally occur. The Carolina's characteristic call is the easiest way to distinguish it from the Black-capped.

OCCURRENCE Mixed woodlands, orchards, gardens; often at feeders.

VOICE Fast *dee-dee-dee* call; song clear, whistled, 4-note sequence *wee-bee wee-bay*, second note lower in pitch.

Length **4¾in (12cm)** | Wingspan **7½in (19cm)**

Family **Paridae** | Species ***Parus sclateri***

Mexican Chickadee

Although widespread in the mountains of Mexico, the Mexican Chickadee's range in the US is restricted to mountaintops in southern Arizona and New Mexico, known as "sky islands." These high elevation habitats include forests of conifers separated from one another by valleys.

OCCURRENCE High-elevation coniferous forests of southeastern Arizona, and southwestern New Mexico; mountains of Mexico; occurs as high as 12,800ft (3,900m). Some move lower down in winter.

VOICE Variety of rapid warbles, including *tse-tse tse-tse tse-tse*; also harsh *churr-churr* notes.

Length **5in (13cm)** | Wingspan **8in (20cm)**

Family **Paridae** | Species ***Parus wollweberi***

Bridled Titmouse

This species, the smallest of the North American titmice, is especially agile, capable of acrobatics and of hanging upside down to catch insects. Its striking black-and-white facial marks and tall, dark crest distinguish it from other titmice. Its voice is also softer and more chickadee-like than those of other titmice. It forms flocks in fall and winter that include chickadees, nuthatches, and kinglets.

OCCURRENCE Primarily a Mexican species, in US lives in the mountain oak and pine-oak forests up to 7,200ft (2,130m) in southeastern Arizona and southwestern New Mexico. Winters at lower elevations.

VOICE High-pitched *cheer cheer cheer* call; song a fast series of whistled *peet peet peet* notes.

Length **5¼in (13.5cm)** | Wingspan **8in (20cm)**

Family **Paridae** | Species ***Parus inornatus***

Oak Titmouse

The Oak Titmouse and its look-alike relative, the Juniper Titmouse, are the least colorful species of titmice. The two species were previously united in a single species, the Plain Titmouse. The Oak Titmouse, as its English name suggests, favors a habitat where oaks are present, especially the Coast Live Oaks of California.

OCCURRENCE Year-round resident in oak or oak-pine woodlands on dry foothills of the Pacific slope.

VOICE Rough *see-see-see-chrr* or *tsicka-tsicka jeer-jeer* call; song a series of clear, whistled double notes, *peedle peedle peedle* or *pe-er pe-er pe-er*.

Length **5¾in (14.5cm)** | Wingspan **9in (23cm)**

Family **Paridae** | Species ***Parus atricristatus***

Black-crested Titmouse

Only found in Texas and southwestern Oklahoma in the US, where it is resident, the Black-crested Titmouse much resembles the Tufted Titmouse, except for its noticeably taller, black crest. Because of this striking difference, the two were once considered separate species, but as the two interbreed in a wide area of Texas, ornithologists merged them into a single species in 1983. Still later studies in 2002 suggested, once again, that they should be considered distinct.

OCCURRENCE Scrubby oak woodlands; frequents feeders in winter. Occurs as high as 6,000ft (2,000m) in the mountain forests of Mexico.

VOICE Call a rasping, scolding *jhree jhree jhree*; song a loud series of clear notes *pew, pew, pew*.

Length **6½in (16.5cm)** | Wingspan **10in (25cm)**

Family **Hirundinidae** | Species ***Petrochelidon fulva***

Cave Swallow

Its orange throat and rufous forehead distinguish the Cave Swallow from its close relative, the Cliff Swallow. This species breeds locally in parts of Arizona, New Mexico, Texas, and southern Florida. Cave Swallows cement their cup nests to the walls of caves, bridges, culverts, and buildings. This adaptation, of building nests on man-made structures, has led to the species' geographical and numerical expansion.
OCCURRENCE Breeds in arid areas, preferably near water. Also breeds in Mexico and the Greater Antilles.
VOICE Call a low *wheet*; song a series of bubbly sounds blending into warbling trill, ending in series of double-toned notes.

Length **5½in (14cm)** | Wingspan **13in (33cm)**

Family **Alaudidae** | Species ***Alauda arvensis***

Eurasian Sky Lark

The Eurasian Sky Lark was introduced to Vancouver Island, British Columbia in the 1900s, and still breeds there in small numbers. Wild individuals of an Asian subspecies are occasional visitors to islands in the Bering Sea Region of Alaska; and vagrants occur south to California. Eurasian Sky Larks are similar to pipits and American sparrows, but have a short crest, white outer tail feathers, and different calls.
OCCURRENCE Likes windswept, hilly, and grassy areas near the ocean; stays close to the ground and is hard to see unless flushed; fluttery flight.
VOICE Flight call a sudden *jeerup*; aerial song consists of endless trills and buzzes, heard only on the breeding grounds.

Length **7¼in (18.5cm)** | Wingspan **12–14in (30–36cm)**

Family **Sylviidae** | Species ***Phylloscopus borealis***

Arctic Warbler

The Arctic Warbler is a small, slender, olive-colored bird with a prominent buffy yellow eyestripe and a faint, single wing bar. Predominantly Eurasian, it occurs in North America in willow thickets in Alaska, where it breeds. Its biology in Alaska is not as well known as its habits are in Eurasia. Vagrant birds occur as far south as California.
OCCURRENCE Breeds in stands of dwarf willow, often along streams. Winters in open rainforests, grasslands, gardens, and mangroves in the Philippines and in Indonesia.
VOICE Alarm call a short hard metallic *dzik*; male's song a loud, vigorous, monotonous slow trill *chingingingingingingng*.

Length **4¼–5in (11–13cm)** | Wingspan **8in (20cm)**

Family **Timaliidae** | Species ***Chamaea fasciata***

Wrentit

Much easier to hear than to see, the Wrentit is neither a wren nor a chickadee. It is the sole New World representative of the large and diverse Old World babbler family. Wrentits are not especially sociable; pairs are rather aloof, guarding their territories, and rarely foraging with other birds. Affected by the destruction of coastal brushwood, their numbers have nevertheless increased locally where logging has opened up new habitats.
OCCURRENCE Pacific Coast and dense foothill shrubs with Chamise, Manzanita, Sagebrush, and Poison oak. Nonmigratory; generally stay close to their breeding areas.
VOICE Calls varied, agitated-sounding *jrrr, krrrrt*; sings a loud accelerating series all year long: *pip... pip... pip... pi'pi'pi'pi'pi'pi'pi'pi*.

Length **6½in (16cm)** | Wingspan **7in (17.5cm)**

Family **Troglodytidae** | Species ***Cistothorus platensis***

Sedge Wren

A shy bird, the Sedge Wren is difficult to see except when singing atop a sedge stalk or a shrub. If spotted, it flies a short distance away, drops down, and runs off through the vegetation. In the west, it reaches Alberta in western Canada, and northeastern Montana in the US. The male, like other species of wrens, builds up to 8–10 unlined "dummy" nests before the female builds the real, better-concealed, nest.

OCCURRENCE In North America, breeds in wet meadows and sedge marshes. Winters in drier habitats. Occurs south to South America.

VOICE Call a loud *chap*; song a dry, staccato two-part chatter: *cha cha cha cha ch'ch'ch ch'ch'ch'ch'*.

Length **4½in (11.5cm)** | Wingspan **5½–6in (14–15.5cm)**

Family **Troglodytidae** | Species ***Thryothorus ludovicianus***

Carolina Wren

The Carolina Wren is a popular and common suburban and backyard bird in much of its range. It is rarely still, often flicking its tail and looking around nervously. Harsh winters at the edge of its range in New England can cause a decline in numbers, as food resources dwindle. At such times, food and shelter from humans may aid survival.

OCCURRENCE Breeds in woodlands; parks and yards, from northeastern Mexico to the Great Lakes, northeastward to New England. A separate population is found from Mexico to Nicaragua.

VOICE Calls variable; often a sharp *chlip* or long, harsh chatter; song a loud, long, fast *whee'dle-dee whee'dle-dee whee'dle-dee*.

Length **5¼in (13.5cm)** | Wingspan **7½in (19cm)**

Family **Polioptilidae** | Species ***Polioptila californica***

California Gnatcatcher

Scarce and threatened in its patchy, localized habitat in southern California, this species is highly sought-after by birders. To spot it, listen for its odd "mewing" call and then wait patiently for it to fly between patches of sage scrub. Formerly classified together with the more widespread Black-tailed Gnatcatcher, the two were separated in 1989, on the basis of plumage, vocal, and molecular differences.

OCCURRENCE Year-round resident in Baja California, Mexico, and scattered breeding localities in coastal sage scrub in southern California. In Baja California, breeds in desert scrub and thorn thickets.

VOICE Characteristic call an odd "mewing" sound *wee-eeew*; *ch-ch-ch* when disturbed.

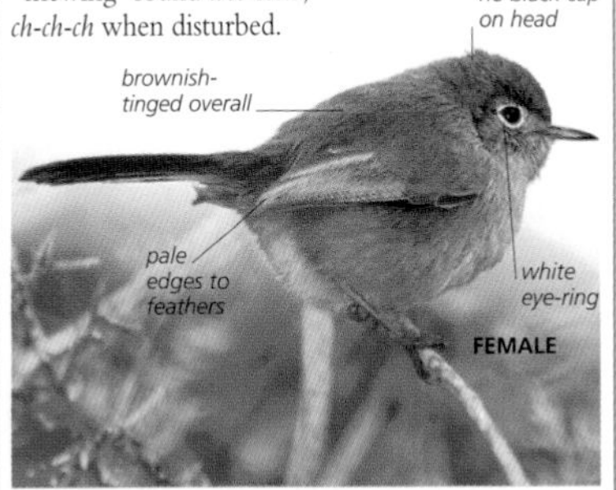

Length **4¼in (11cm)** | Wingspan **5½in (14cm)**

Family **Mimidae** | Species ***Toxostoma longirostre***

Long-billed Thrasher

In the US, this Mexican species is found only in southern Texas, where its habitat of semi-arid thickets and riverine woodlands has been much altered or destroyed by mechanized land-clearing practices. This habitat loss may be offset by the increase in area of invasive scrubby vegetation in other parts of its range.

OCCURRENCE Sedentary in scrubby vegetation in the lowlands along the Gulf of Mexico, along woodlands near the Rio Grande, and on the slopes of western mountains at up to 3,300ft (1,100m).

VOICE Call a harsh *tchek*; song a loud, harsh series of notes, usually repeated 2–4 times in succession.

Length **10–11in (25–28cm)** | Wingspan **12–13in (30–33cm)**

Family **Mimidae** | Species ***Toxostoma bendirei***

Bendire's Thrasher

This small and rather nondescript thrasher of southwestern US deserts was named in 1873 in honor of Charles Bendire, the US army officer who discovered it. In spite of its early discovery, much remains to be learned about this species, including the number of broods it can raise per season, and whether it winters in Baja California.

OCCURRENCE In the US, breeds in dry areas and sparse cover of cactus, thorn-scrub, and Joshua trees. Winters in Mexico; Mexican populations resident.

VOICE Call a hoarse *krrh*; song a clear, continuous series of notes, repeated 2–4 times, but not broken into distinct phrases.

Length **8–10in (20–25cm)** | Wingspan **11–13in (28–33cm)**

Family **Mimidae** | Species ***Toxostoma redivivum***

California Thrasher

This thrasher's Latin name, *redivivum*, means "resurrected." It was already known in the 16th century, but "rediscovered" in 1845. This is the largest of the North American thrashers, and a real Californian native. It likes the dense undergrowth of arid or semi-arid vegetation along the slopes of canyons, a habitat that is unfortunately used for suburban development, posing a threat to its survival.

OCCURRENCE Prefers arid to semi-arid, brushy canyons; also suburban parks and gardens; needs dense undergrowth vegetation.

VOICE Call a dry *tchek*; song a loud, clear series of repeated phrases; often includes songs of other species.

Length **11–13in (28–33cm)** | Wingspan **15–17in (38–43cm)**

Family **Mimidae** | Species ***Toxostoma crissale***

Crissal Thrasher

Although locally common, little is known about the life history of this secretive bird, which lives in dense mesquite thickets and shrubland. Its distinctive melodious songs set it apart from other, similar-looking southwestern thrashers. Its Latin name refers to the color of its undertail feathers in an otherwise pretty uniformly gray plumage. Although loss of habitat at lower elevations may restrict its numbers, its preference for high-elevation habitats insulate the species from much human encroachment.

OCCURRENCE Breeds in the arid southwestern US and Mexico, especially in dense shrubbery at mid-elevations, but can occur up to 6,500ft (2,000m).

VOICE Call a soft *Krrrt*; song a strong numerical note, or group of notes, with double repetitions, delivered softly.

Length **10–13in (25–33cm)** | Wingspan **13–16in (33–41cm)**

Family **Mimidae** | Species ***Toxostoma lecontei***

Le Conte's Thrasher

This species is the real desert thrasher, in terms of its habitat preference and sandy color, which is rather similar to its surroundings. Le Conte's Thrasher prefers a more open and sparsely vegetated habitat than any other member of its genus. This hardy and adaptable species regularly endures temperature extremes ranging from -4 to +133°F (-20 to +56°C). Increased irrigation of desert areas has caused loss of its habitat.

OCCURRENCE Resident in the southwestern US and Mexico, in sheltered areas along desert washes, with clumps of grass.

VOICE Call *ti-WHIP*; song a long, squeaky musical series of varied notes or phrases, often repeated two or three times.

Length **10–12in (25–30cm)** | Wingspan **12–14in (30–36cm)**

Family **Turdidae** | Species ***Sialia sialis***

Eastern Bluebird

The blue and chestnut Eastern Bluebird has made a remarkable comeback in the past 30 years. After much of the bird's habitat was eliminated by agriculture in the mid-1900s, nest boxes were readily accepted as alternatives to their tree cavities. The Eastern Bluebird's complex mating system involves multiple partners.

OCCURRENCE Found in clearings and woodland edges; occupies open habitats in rural, urban, and suburban areas; orchards, parks, and spacious lawns; westward to the 100th meridian.

VOICE Main song a melodious series of soft, whistled notes; *churr-wi* or *churr-li*.

Length **6–8in (15–20cm)** | Wingspan **10–13in (25–33cm)**

Family **Turdidae** | Species ***Catharus minimus***

Gray-cheeked Thrush

The Gray-cheeked Thrush breeds in remote areas of Canada, westward all the way to Alaska. During migration, this bird is more likely to be heard in flight at night than seen on the ground by birdwatchers.

OCCURRENCE Breeds in densely vegetated areas with small shrubs; prefers spruce forests in northern and western Canada and Alaska. Winters in northern South America.

VOICE Call a thin *kweer*, sometimes doubled; song flute-like, somewhat nasal, several notes ending on a lower pitch.

Length **6½–7in (16–18cm)** | Wingspan **11½–13½in (29–34cm)**

Family **Turdidae** | Species ***Hylocichla mustelina***

Wood Thrush

The Wood Thrush, an eastern breeder, has seen its populations decrease markedly over the past 30 years, largely due to forest destruction and fragmentation. Its susceptibility to parasitism by the Brown-headed Cowbird has also affected its numbers.

OCCURRENCE Hardwood forests in the East, from Texas and Florida to Minnesota and the Canadian Maritimes. Breeds in deciduous and mixed forests. Winters south through Central America to Panama. Rare in the West.

VOICE Rapid *pip-pippipip* or *rhuu-rhuu*; a three-part flute-like song—first part indistinct, second part loudest, third part trilled.

Length **7½–8½in (19–21cm)** | Wingspan **12–13½in (30–34cm)**

Family **Turdidae** | Species ***Turdus rufopalliatus***

Rufous-backed Robin

This secretive Mexican species is rare to uncommon in the southwestern US, especially in the winter. More colorful than the American Robin, it has a gray head, wings, and tail, reddish back and flanks, white abdomen, and long and thin dark streaks on its throat extending all the way to the breast.

OCCURRENCE Occurs in a variety of scrubby or woodland habitats in southern California, southern Arizona, southwest New Mexico, and western Texas.

VOICE Repeated warbling of cheery phrases; call is a *tche-tche-che*.

Length **8½–9½in (21–24cm)** | Wingspan **15in (38cm)**

Family **Turdidae** | Species ***Luscinia svecica***

Bluethroat

Widespread in Eurasia, the Bluethroat is found in North America only in Alaska and the Yukon. The male's iridescent blue throat adorned with a rufous spot is rarely seen because it spends most of its time in thick vegetation, except during its flight songs.
OCCURRENCE Breeds in willow thickets in the tundra of northern Alaska and the western Yukon.
VOICE Calls are sharp, dry *krak*, often repeated; also a soft *whooit*. Song is melodious, lengthy, and may include the calls of other bird species, as the Bluethroat is a gifted mimic.

Length **6in (15cm)** | Wingspan **9in (23cm)**

Family **Muscicapidae** | Species ***Oenanthe oenanthe***

Northern Wheatear

The largely Eurasian Northern Wheatear visits North America during a brief breeding season, and nests in the tundra of Alaska and northeastern Canada. The two subspecies breeding in North America, *O. o. leucorhoa* in the Northeast and *O. o. oenanthe* in the Northwest both migrate to wintering grounds in sub-Saharan Africa, but use different routes: *oenanthe* across Asia, and *leucorhoa* across the Atlantic.
OCCURRENCE Breeds in the Yukon (*O. o. oenanthe*) and the Arctic archipelago (*O. o. leucorhoa*).
VOICE Multiple calls, a sharp *tuc* or *tek* common; three types of songs—territorial, conversational, and perched—mixtures of sweet and harsh notes; imitates other species.

Length **5½–6in (14–15cm)** | Wingspan **10¾in (27cm)**

Family **Peucedramidae** | Species ***Peucedramus taeniatus***

Olive Warbler

Although its appearance and behavior are warbler-like, this orange-headed and black-masked species differs from warblers in the family Parulidae in its song, breeding habits, and genetic make-up. It is placed in its own family, the Peucedramidae, and lives at high elevations in coniferous forests.
OCCURRENCE Found in pine-oak woodlands, and forests with Ponderosa Pines and Douglas Firs. US birds winter in Mexico; Central American birds are resident.
VOICE Calls include a smack-like *bit* and a softer, bluebird-like *view*; song is a loud and repeated series of *peetar-peetar-peetar*, somewhat similar to the Tufted Titmouse.

Length **5¼in (13.5cm)** | Wingspan **9in (23cm)**

Family **Motacillidae** | Species ***Motacilla flava***

Yellow Wagtail

Like its relative the White Wagtail, the Yellow Wagtail is widely distributed in Eurasia, with a nesting foothold in Alaska and the Yukon. An extremely variable species geographically, it has about 17 subspecies. The Alaskan-Canadian population belongs to the subspecies *tschutschensis*, which was described as long ago as 1789, and also breeds in eastern Siberia.
OCCURRENCE In Western Alaska and extreme western Yukon found in tundra with scattered shrub, especially along watercourses. Winters in eastern Asia, south to Indonesia.
VOICE Call a short, "outgoing" *tzeep*!; song a thin, musical, *tzee-ouee-sir*, often in flight.

Length **5–7in (13–18cm)** | Wingspan **7–9in (18–23cm)**

Family **Motacillidae** | Species ***Motacilla alba***

White Wagtail

Only one (*M. a. ocularis*) of the 11 subspecies of the wide-ranging Eurasian White Wagtail breeds in North America, in a very small geographical area of northwestern Alaska and on St. Lawrence Island. It arrives in Alaska in late May or early June, and leaves after only about two months, in August, migrating to wintering areas in tropical southeast Asia.

OCCURRENCE Found near water, either coastal areas or along rivers; also commonly associated with human structures.

VOICE Call a single, sharp *tzzip* or double *tzzizzip*; song is an extension of its call, the notes blending into a warble.

ADULT

Length **6–8in (15–20cm)** | Wingspan **9–10in (23–25cm)**

Family **Motacillidae** | Species ***Anthus spragueii***

Sprague's Pipit

Sprague's is the only wholly North American pipit. Males perform an extraordinary fluttering display flight, circling high above the earth while singing an unending series of high-pitched calls, for periods up to an hour. The current decline in its population is quite likely the result of the conversion of tall-grass native prairie to extensive farmland.

OCCURRENCE Breeds along and across the US-Canada border, in dry, open, tall-grass habitat, especially native prairies in the northern part of the Great Plains; most birds winter in Mexico.

VOICE Call a high *squeeek*; song a high, repetitive series of *szee-szee-szee*, usually given during lengthy aerial displays.

ADULT

Length **4–6in (10–15cm)** | Wingspan **6–8in (15–20cm)**

Family **Motacilladae** | Species ***Anthus cervinus***

Red-throated Pipit

The heavily streaked upperparts, and pale legs of this rare Alaskan breeder help to distinguish it from the American Pipit. The extent of the red on the throat varies among individual birds from rusty brick red to tan. Nonbreeding birds are usually heavily streaked on the breast.

OCCURRENCE Tundra and low scrub along the coasts of northern and western Alaska. Occasionally along the coast of California in winter. Widespread in northern Eurasia, it winters in Africa and southeast Asia.

VOICE Two-syllable *tzee-zeep*, somewhat like White or Yellow Wagtails. Song is varied, musical, often in flight.

ADULT (BREEDING)

Length **5–7in (12–17cm)** | Wingspan **7–8in (20–23cm)**

Family **Fringillidae** | Species ***Carduelis lawrencei***

Lawrence's Goldfinch

John Cassin of Philadelphia's Academy of Natural Sciences described this species in 1850, to honor G.N. Lawrence, who worked on birds collected during the Pacific Railroad Surveys. The large yellow patches on the wings are characteristic of this species, which breeds in dry habitats like chaparral, grassy slopes, and open ranchland.

OCCURRENCE Breeds in open foothills and valleys of California at elevations up to 9,000ft (2,750m). Most migration is east and west rather than north and south.

VOICE Single, bell-like call notes and harsh *kee-urr*; song canary-like; may imitate other species.

MALE

Length **4–4¾in (10–12cm)** | Wingspan **6–6½in (15–16cm)**

Family **Fringillidae** | Species ***Carduelis hornemanni***

Hoary Redpoll

Closely related to the Common Redpoll, the Hoary Redpoll is more conspicuously white, has a stubbier bill, and looks more fluffy. These two species often breed in the same areas, but do not interbreed. The Hoary Redpoll is a bird of the high Arctic, breeding in extreme northern Canada westward to Alaska.

OCCURRENCE Breeds in low, scrubby trees of the open tundra, and winters in the boreal forest belt from the Canadian Maritimes to Alaska, south of the tundra.

VOICE Flight calls dry *zit-zit-zit-zit* and rattling *chirr*, also high *too-ee* call while perched; song series of rapid trills.

Length **5–5½in (12.5–14cm)** | Wingspan **8½–9¼in (21–23.5cm)**

Family **Fringillidae** | Species ***Leucosticte atrata***

Black Rosy-Finch

Actually deep-brown in color, this bird appears black when seen against its snowy background. Black Rosy-Finches, the darkest of the North American rosy-finch species, are nevertheless similar in appearance to the much more widely distributed Gray-crowned Rosy-Finch.

OCCURRENCE Found in Rocky Mountain and Great Basin mountaintop habitats above timberline. Breeds from central Idaho and southwestern Montana, south through northwestern Nevada and most of Utah. Winters at lower elevations.

VOICE Call a low, raspy *brrrt* and descending *peew*; song a long series of *peew* notes of variable composition and pitch.

Length **5½–6½in (14–16cm)** | Wingspan **13in (33cm)**

Family **Fringillidae** | Species ***Leucosticte australis***

Brown-capped Rosy-Finch

This southernmost member of the rosy-finch genus *Leucosticte* is more pink and less gray than the other two North American species. Despite its name, the "cap" of this species is almost black, similar to those of the other rosy-finches, and contrasts with the brown of the rest of the head and upper back.

OCCURRENCE Restricted to high elevations in the Medicine Bow range of Wyoming and the high mountains of Colorado and northern New Mexico. Lower down in winter.

VOICE High-pitched *peee*, raspy *brrt*, and descending and repeated *peew* calls.

Length **5½–6¾in (14–17cm)** | Wingspan **13in (33cm)**

Family **Parulidae** | Species ***Vermivora crissalis***

Colima Warbler

Big Bend National Park in Texas is home to the only breeding population of Colima Warblers in the US—up to 300 pairs may breed there. The scientific name, *crissalis*, refers to this bird's bright orange undertail coverts, or "crissum." The English name, Colima, indicates the area of Mexico where this warbler spends the winter.

OCCURRENCE Breeds in the Chisos Mountains and Mexico, in canyons with pine-oak woodland with brushy understory, normally above about 4,900ft (1,500m). Almost never detected on migration. Winters in similar but more humid habitats of southwestern Mexico.

VOICE Song a rapid trill, descending in pitch and ending with one or two emphatic motives *titititititi-tututu eet-choo eet-choo*.

Length **6in (15cm)** | Wingspan **8in (20cm)**

Family **Parulidae**	Species ***Vermivora luciae***

Lucy's Warbler

Named for Lucy Baird, daughter of the eminent ornithologist Spencer Fullerton Baird, this species, small and unassuming, lacks any yellow coloration and could be mistaken for a gnatcatcher, an immature Verdin, or a Bell's Vireo. It is locally common in mesquite woodlands near watercourses.

OCCURRENCE Breeds in riverine woodlands of the southwestern US and adjacent northern Mexico. Winters along the western seaboard of Mexico south to Oaxaca.

VOICE A sharp, metallic *vink*; flight call a soft *tsit*; song a loose trill, modulated in pitch and with variably emphatic ending.

Length **4¼in (11cm)**	Wingspan **7in (18cm)**

Family **Parulidae**	Species ***Dendroica pensylvanica***

Chestnut-sided Warbler

One of the few wood-warbler species that has benefited from deforestation, the Chestnut-sided Warbler depends on second-growth and forest edges for breeding. In all plumages, two conspicuous wing bars and a whitish belly are distinguishing characteristics. Its pleasant song has long been transcribed as *pleased pleased pleased to MEET'cha.*

OCCURRENCE Breeds in successional deciduous woodlands, from Alberta to the Great Lakes, New England, and the Appalachians. Winters in the West Indies, Mexico, and Central America.

VOICE Call a sweet *chip*; flight call a low, burry *brrrt*; song a series of fast, sweet notes, usually ending with an emphatic *WEET-chew*.

Length **5in (13cm)**	Wingspan **8in (20cm)**

Family **Parulidae**	Species ***Dendroica castanea***

Bay-breasted Warbler

A male Bay-breasted Warbler in breeding plumage is a striking sight. By contrast, fall females look very different with their dull greenish color. The Bay-breasted Warbler depends largely on outbreaks of spruce budworms (a moth larva) and its population fluctuations are related to those of this food source. Overall, Bay-breasted Warbler numbers have decreased in the last decade or so.

OCCURRENCE Breeds in mature spruce-fir-balsam forests from the Yukon east to the Maritimes, south to the Great Lakes and northern New England. Winters in wet forests in central America.

VOICE Call a somewhat upslurred *tsip*; flight call a high, buzzy, short, and sharp *tzzzt*; song of very high, thin notes, often ending on lower pitch: *wee-si wee-si wee-si wee*.

Length **5½in (14cm)**	Wingspan **9in (23cm)**

Family **Parulidae**	Species ***Dendroica fusca***

Blackburnian Warbler

Its brilliant orange throat makes this species one of the most beautiful members of the North American warblers. Blackburnian Warblers co-exist with other *Dendroica* warblers in the coniferous and mixed woodlands of the north and east, but exploit a slightly different niche for foraging—the treetops. They also seek the highest trees for nesting.

OCCURRENCE Breeds in coniferous and mixed forests of the eastern US and Canada, west to Alberta. Winters in wet forests in Costa Rica and Panama, and southward as far as Peru.

VOICE Call a slightly husky *chik*; flight-call a high, thin *zzee*; song variable, but always high-pitched; swirling series of lisps, spiraling upward to end in an almost inaudible trill.

black-and-orange facial pattern

MALE

Length **5in (13cm)**	Wingspan **8½in (21cm)**

Family **Parulidae**	Species ***Dendroica chrysoparia***

Golden-cheeked Warbler

The male of this beautiful species often sings throughout the day from conspicuous perches. It breeds in a restricted area of Texas, near, and on, the Edwards Plateau in woodlands where junipers are common. Habitat loss has made this scarce species even scarcer. It has been on the Endangered Species list since 1990.

OCCURRENCE Breeds in oak-juniper woodlands mixed with hardwood species like maple and ash. Winters in high-elevation pine-oak woodlands from Mexico to Nicaragua.

VOICE Dry *tsk* call; song a variable series of relatively low, buzzy notes, often ending on a high, clear note *zo zu zu zo zu zhray ZHEE*; another version ends at a lower pitch *ZOH zu ZO-ZOH zhray*.

Length **5in (13cm)**	Wingspan **8in (20cm)**

Family **Parulidae**	Species ***Dendroica graciae***

Grace's Warbler

Named for Grace Coues, sister of the well-known ornithologist Elliott Coues, this warbler is the western counterpart of the Yellow-throated Warbler. It lives in the tops of tall pines, and tends to have large territories, making it a difficult bird to spot and study. Its range has been expanding northward in recent years.

OCCURRENCE Breeds in mature, open pine and pine-oak mountain forests of the southwestern US and Mexico.

VOICE Call soft *chip*; flight call very high, thin *ssss*; song loose trill, louder toward the end and at times ending with a change in pitch: *chew chew chew chew chew CHEW CHEW CHEE-DEED-DEED-DEED.*

Length **5in (13cm)**	Wingspan **8in (20cm)**

Family **Parulidae**	Species ***Cardellina rubrifrons***

Red-faced Warbler

A dazzling-looking bird, with its red-and-black face and white nape, the Red-faced Warbler is a favorite of birdwatchers visiting mountains in the southwestern US. Because its closest relatives are uncertain at present, the Red-faced Warbler is placed by ornithologists in a separate genus, *Cardellina*.

OCCURRENCE Breeds in Arizona, New Mexico, and Mexico, in high-elevation fir, pine, and pine-oak forests. Winters in mountain pine-oak and pine forests from Mexico southward to Central America (Honduras).

VOICE Call a sharp *chik*; song a variable, sweet warble; often has emphatic ending: *swee-wee-wee tuh-wee-wee-wee WEE-chee-chew.*

Length **5½in (14cm)**	Wingspan **8½in (21cm)**

Family **Parulidae**	Species ***Myioborus pictus***

Painted Redstart

White, red, and black, the Painted Redstart (*pictus* means "painted" in Latin) is fairly common locally in the wooded canyons of Arizona, New Mexico, and western Texas. It flicks open its wings and tail, showing off white wing patches and undertail feathers, which has been interpreted as a behavior meant to flush out insect prey. Ten other species of *Myioborus* live from Mexico to South America.

OCCURRENCE Breeds at high elevations in oak and pine-oak forests in canyons of the southwestern US. Winters south of its breeding range in Mexico.

VOICE Call a distinctive, downslurred, bisyllabic *TSHEE-ew*; song a rich, whistled series of paired notes, at times with emphatic ending: *wee-dee wee-dee wee-dee chichi-chichi-tyew.*

Length **5¾in (14.5cm)**	Wingspan **8½in (22cm)**

Family **Icteridae**	Species ***Icterus spurius***

Orchard Oriole

The way Orchard Orioles flit among leaves when foraging for insects recalls the behavior of wood-warblers. In addition, and unlike other orioles, it flutters its tail. A late arrival in spring, it is also an early species to leave in the fall. The foothills of the Rocky Mountains correspond approximately to its range border in the West.

OCCURRENCE Breeds in open forest and woodland edges with a mixture of evergreen and deciduous trees; also found in parks and gardens. Winters in Mexico, Central America, and South America.

VOICE Fast, not very melodious, series of high warbling notes mixed with occasional shorter notes ending in slurred *shheere*.

Length **7–8in (18–20cm)**	Wingspan **9in (23cm)**

Family **Icteridae**	Species ***Icterus cucullatus***

Hooded Oriole

Tall palm trees in suburban gardens and urban parks, especially in California, have become popular nesting sites for the Hooded Oriole. Increasing numbers of palm trees, combined with the offerings of nectar intended for hummingbirds have contributed to the expansion of its range from California to the Southwest. By contrast, its numbers in Texas have been shrinking, in part because of its susceptibility to brood parasitism by Brown-headed and Bronzed Cowbirds.

OCCURRENCE Breeds in open woodlands along water courses, especially those containing palm trees. Winters in Mexico.

VOICE A harsh *weeek* call; song a weakly whined and rapid series of whistles where notes often run together; imitates other birds.

Length **7–8in (18–20cm)**	Wingspan **9–11in (23–28cm)**

Family **Icteridae**	Species ***Icterus galbula***

Baltimore Oriole

The brilliantly colored Baltimore Oriole, the eastern counterpart of the Bullock's Oriole, ranges westward in Canada to Alberta and, locally, eastern British Colombia. At the edge of their respective distributions, in the Great Plains, Baltimore and Bullock's Orioles interbreed. Ornithologists have, at times, considered them to be a single species.

OCCURRENCE A variety of woodlands, also parks and gardens. Most winter in Mexico, Colombia, and Venezuela.

VOICE Loud, clear, melodious song comprising several short notes in series, often of varying lengths.

Length **8–10in (20–26cm)**	Wingspan **10–12in (26–30cm)**

Family **Icteridae**	Species ***Molothrus aeneus***

Bronzed Cowbird

The range of this species has been expanding in the US ever since it was first recorded in the early 1900s. This could be the result of human clearing of native habitats and replacing them with agricultural crops. A brood parasite, it has been recorded to lay its eggs in the nests of more than 80 bird species, and their young have fledged from over 30 of these. The females may work cooperatively to identify and parasitize the nests of other birds.

OCCURRENCE Inhabits open fields, pastures, scattered scrub, and suburban parks. In the US occurs from California to Texas, from Mexico to Panama and Colombia.

VOICE High and metallic with short notes, can be described as *gug-gub-bub-tzee-pss-tzee*.

Length **8in (20cm)**	Wingspan **13–14in (33–36cm)**

Family **Icteridae** | Species ***Agelaius tricolor***

Tricolored Blackbird

A close relative of the widespread Red-winged Blackbird, the Tricolored occurs primarily in California, where it breeds in marshes in large colonies, sometimes containing more than 100,000 pairs. After breeding, flocks of Tricolored Blackbirds move to agricultural areas.

OCCURRENCE Found in cattail marshes, also in a variety of human altered upland and wetland habitats; found in western California, northward to Washington State and southward to Baja California.

VOICE Both sexes call a *chip*, *chuk*, and *chu-aah* when alarmed; male song a grave, nasal *kera-oooow* or *kerrrraaaa*.

Length **7–9½in (18–24cm)** | Wingspan **10–13in (26–33cm)**

Family **Emberizidae** | Species ***Calcarius mccownii***

McCown's Longspur

Named for Confederate Major-General John Porter McCown, this longspur inhabits native shortgrass prairies from Alberta and Saskatchewan southward to Nebraska and Colorado. In this windswept habitat males perform flight displays, hovering and floating, wings held in a "V" position, looking surprisingly dark against the pale sky.

OCCURRENCE Breeds in shortgrass prairies of the High Plains. Winters in grasslands from southeastern Colorado southward to Texas and westward to southeastern Arizona.

VOICE Flight call a short, liquid *rit-up*; also an abrupt *poink* and metallic *tink*; song melodious; high-pitched tinklings in flight.

rufous shoulder patch
black breast patch
MALE (BREEDING)

Length **6in (15cm)** | Wingspan **10–11in (25–28cm)**

Family **Emberizidae** | Species ***Calcarius pictus***

Smith's Longspur

With its pumpkin colored breast and black-and-white "helmet," Smith's Longspur in its breeding colors contrasts strongly with its drab winter plumage. On its Arctic breeding grounds and shortgrass prairie range in winter, this longspur remains hidden on the ground, and is hard to spot. Smith's Longspurs breeds communaly: males mate with several females; they, in turn, mate with several males.

OCCURRENCE Breeds along the tundra-taiga timberline from northern Alaska south and east to northern Ontario. Winters in open areas with shortgrass.

VOICE Flight call a mechanical, sharp rattle; also a nasal *nief* when squabbling; song a series of thin, sweet whistles.

Length **6–6½in (15–16cm)** | Wingspan **10–11½in (25–29cm)**

Family **Emberizidae** | Species ***Calcarius ornatus***

Chestnut-collared Longspur

Once quite common and widespread, the Chestnut-collared Longspur bred where huge herds of bison disturbed its prairie habitat. After the elimination of bison and the "farming" of the prairies, such areas were hard to find, and the longspur declined. A distinguishing feature of this species is the large amount of white on its outer tail feathers.

OCCURRENCE Breeds in shortgrass prairie in south-central Canada and central US. Winters in grasslands and other barren areas in the southern Great Plains.

VOICE Flight call a chortling *KTI-uhl-uh*, often in series; also a soft rattle and short *buzz*; song a sweet, rich, whistled series, in fluttering, circular flights over the prairies.

Length **5½–6in (14–15cm)** | Wingspan **10–10½in (25–27cm)**

Family **Emberizidae**	Species ***Plectrophenax hyperboreus***

McKay's Bunting

A close relative of the widespread and similar-looking Snow Bunting, with which it occasionally interbreeds, McKay's Bunting numbers fewer than 6,000 individuals, which breed on two isolated islands in the Bering Sea.

OCCURRENCE Breeds in rocky areas on Hall Island and St. Matthew Island in the Bering Sea. Occasional visitor to St. Lawrence Island and the Pribilof Islands.

VOICE Like Snow Bunting, flight call musical, liquid rattle; also *tyew* notes and short *buzz*; song squeaky repetitive whistle.

Length **6¾in (17cm)**	Wingspan **14in (36cm)**

Family **Emberizidae**	Species ***Zonotrichia querula***

Harris's Sparrow

The only North American species to breed only in Canada, Harris's Sparrow migrates southward and winters in the US Great Plains. Its scientific name, *querula*, was given because of the plaintive quality of its whistled song. Its nest was first discovered in 1907 in the Northwest Territories.

OCCURRENCE Breeds in scrub-tundra along the taiga–tundra timberline. Winters in the Great Plains from South Dakota and Iowa south to northern Texas. Nonbreeders are found in thickets and hedges. Casual to rare in East and West.

VOICE Call a sharp *weeek*; song a melancholy series of 2–4 whistles on the same pitch.

Length **6¾–7½in (17–19cm)**	Wingspan **10½–11in (27–28cm)**

Family **Emberizidae**	Species ***Junco phaeonotus***

Yellow-eyed Junco

This common and confident bird, the Mexican representative of the Dark-eyed Junco, lives at high elevations in pine and oak-pine forests from Arizona and New Mexico to south-central Mexico. Its "glaring" yellow eyes set off by a black mask are distinguishing characters. Yellow-eyed Juncos often forage for food under picnic tables.

OCCURRENCE Southeastern Arizona and southwestern New Mexico, and more widely in Mexico.

VOICE Loud *dip*, soft *dyew*; flight call a twittering, buzzy *zzeet*; song 2–3 whistles followed by various trills and buzzes.

Length **6½in (16cm)**	Wingspan **9½–10in (24–25cm)**

Family **Emberizidae**	Species ***Ammodramus nelsoni***

Nelson's Sharp-tailed Sparrow

This shy species was recently split from the Saltmarsh Sharp-tailed Sparrow. It includes three subspecies that differ in plumage, breeding habitat, and range. The brightly colored *A. n. nelsoni* is found from the Northwest Territories south to Wisconsin. The duller *A. n. subvirgatus* breeds in coastal Maine, the Maritimes, and along the St. Lawrence River. The intermediate *A. n. alterus* breeds along the southern and western coasts of Hudson Bay.

OCCURRENCE Breeds in a variety of marsh habitats across Canada and extreme north central North America.

VOICE Sharp *tik* call; song a husky *t-SHHHHEE-uhrr.*

Length **4¾in (12cm)**	Wingspan **7in (17.5cm)**

Family **Emberizidae** | Species ***Ammodramus bairdii***

Baird's Sparrow

The sweet, tinkling song of Baird's Sparrow is a sure sign of high-quality mixed-grass prairie in the Northern Plains. Its musical song and square, pale-edged tail are unique in its genus. Like other species that depend on native grasslands, it has not coped well with the intensive agriculture that has swept across the Northern Plains during the last century.

OCCURRENCE Breeds in light mixed-grass prairie of central US and adjacent Canada. Migrates through the High Plains. Winters in grasslands in Mexico.

VOICE Call soft, metallic *tsink*; flight call insect-like *tisk*; song *tsk tsk tsuck tsooweeeeee*.

Length **5½in (14cm)** | Wingspan **8½–8¾in (21–22.5cm)**

Family **Emberizidae** | Species ***Spizella pusilla***

Field Sparrow

The distinctive, accelerating trilled song of the Field Sparrow is a characteristic sound in shrubby fields and scrub of the eastern US and adjacent Canada. Westward, this species reaches Montana, the Dakotas, and Nebraska. The Field Sparrow's pink bill, rusty cheek patch, and pale eye-ring are good field marks. Western-most birds are paler than eastern ones.

OCCURRENCE Breeds in overgrown fields, woodland edges, roadsides. Casual in Atlantic Canada and along the Pacific Coast.

VOICE Call a sharp *tsik*; flight call a strongly descending *tsiiiu*; song a series of sweet, down-slurred whistles accelerating to a rapid trill.

Length **5½in (14cm)** | Wingspan **8in (20cm)**

Family **Emberizidae** | Species ***Spizella atrogularis***

Black-chinned Sparrow

This gray, yet elegant, bird is a locally common but secretive inhabitant of dense shrubbery on steep hillsides of the southwestern US and California. In the breeding season the loudly-singing and brightly-plumaged males are easy to spot, but in the winter their plumage is quite drab and they are not easy to see. The plumage pattern and pink bill of the Black-chinned Sparrow are reminiscent of those of juncos, but they are not closely related.

OCCURRENCE Breeds in California, southwestern Utah, and northeastern New Mexico southward to central Mexico.

VOICE Call a high *tsip*; song an accelerating, bouncy trill climaxing in a rapid, metallic, ascending echo.

Length **5¾in (14.5cm)** | Wingspan **7¾in (19.5cm)**

Family **Emberizidae** | Species ***Aimophila carpalis***

Rufous-winged Sparrow

This sparrow is very localized within its restricted US range, as it lives in grassland with thorn bushes, a habitat that has largely been lost to grazing. Rufous-winged Sparrows depend on the greening of their habitat that follows irregular rains. Male sparrows "respond" to this uncertainty by maintaining their territory all year-round, and are thus ready to breed as soon as the rains begin.

OCCURRENCE Resident in Sonoran Desert scrub and bunch grass from south-central Arizona southward to central Sinaloa, Mexico.

VOICE Call high, strident *tseeep*!; song a couple of *chips* or whistles followed by long, loose trill, or accelerating series of *chips*.

Length **5¾in (14.5cm)** | Wingspan **7½in (19cm)**

Family **Emberizidae** | Species ***Aimophila botterii***

Botteri's Sparrow

Essentially a bird of Mexican grasslands, Botteri's Sparrow reaches the US in two areas, coastal southern Texas and the Southwest. In Texas, its habitat includes gulf cordgrass, whereas in the Southwest it lives in grasslands and open mesquite woodlands with a grass understory. When alarmed, Botteri's Sparrows run rather than fly.

OCCURRENCE Breeds in grasslands of southeastern Arizona and southwestern New Mexico, and in coastal prairies of southern Texas. Winters in Mexico.

VOICE Call a *chip* or double *tsip*; song starts with stuttering, mechanical *chips* and ends in an accelerating trill.

Length **18–20in (46–51cm)** | Wingspan **27–38in (68–96cm)**

Family **Emberizidae** | Species ***Aimophila quinquestriata***

Five-striped Sparrow

The Five-striped Sparrow is one of the rarest of the breeding sparrows of North America, with perhaps as few as 100 pairs which are found only in southern Arizona. The Five-striped Sparrow is a large, handsome sparrow with gray underparts, olive-brown upperparts, a blackish head with the stripes for which it is named and eye crescents, a black central breast spot, and a long, thick bill.

OCCURRENCE Breeds on steep, arid mountain slopes, up to about 6,500ft (2,000m); locally in southern Arizona, and more commonly in Mexico, southward to Chihuahua and Sonora.

VOICE Call a low *turp*; song a series of musical chirps, tinklings, and trills interspersed with second-long pauses.

Length **6in (15cm)** | Wingspan **8in (20cm)**

Family **Emberizidae** | Species ***Pipilo crissalis***

California Towhee

This fairly large and grayish-colored towhee is common around human settlements, including suburban gardens, parks, and riverine woodlands, from northern California to Baja California. Once considered, together with the Canyon Towhee of the Southwest, to form a single species (the "Brown Towhee"), they are now split into separate species because of morphological and molecular differences.

OCCURRENCE Along California's Pacific Coast in a variety of bushy habitats with open areas for foraging and bush for cover.

VOICE Call a ringing, metallic *tink*; song an accelerating trill of ringing *chips*, occasionally ending with squeaky chatter.

Length **9in (23cm)** | Wingspan **11½in (29cm)**

Family **Emberizidae** | Species ***Pipilo aberti***

Abert's Towhee

Restricted to the southwestern US and adjacent Mexico, Abert's Towhee, named after Major James W. Abert, was originally found in the dense undergrowth of cottonwood-willow stands along the Colorado River and its tributaries. It has declined since its description in 1852, due to habitat destruction, overgrazing, and invasive plant species.

OCCURRENCE Resident in dense brush, remnant patches of mesquite woodland close to rivers and streams, and desert scrub; also suburban areas. Prefers the proximity of water, even small streams. Occurs up to about 3,280ft (1,000m).

VOICE Sharp *peek* call; song short, accelerating *peeks* followed by harsh, squeaky chatter; pairs often duet.

Length **9½in (24cm)** | Wingspan **11in (28cm)**

Family **Emberizidae** | Species ***Arremonops rufivirgatus***

Olive Sparrow

The rather drab and shy Olive Sparrow spends much of its time hopping in and out of the undergrowth of dense, tropical woodlands and thorn scrub. In the Lower Rio Grande Valley in winter, this tough-to-spot species does not sing at this time of the year, but its lisping calls will often lead to a birdfeeder, where tamer individuals may be observed at leisure.

OCCURRENCE From southern Texas and northwestern Mexico south to northwestern Costa Rica. Often found at backyard feeders in southern Texas in the winter.

VOICE Dry *chip* call, also a drawn-out *sreeeeee*; song a series of chips accelerating to a level.

Length **6½in (16cm)** | Wingspan **8in (20cm)**

Family **Thraupidae** | Species ***Piranga flava***

Hepatic Tanager

This species ranges widely in the Americas, from California (very locally) and Colorado south to Mexico, central America, and South America (to Argentina). In the US, the Hepatic Tanager is the western counterpart of the Summer Tanager, which it replaces at higher elevations in oak-pine woodlands. It is slightly more orange-colored than the Summer Tanager.

OCCURRENCE Found in southwestern US in mountain woodlands of pine and pine-oak. Winters away from US, except in extreme southeastern Arizona.

VOICE Single *chuk* or *chup* call; flight call an upslurred, slightly burry *veet*; song less burry than other tanagers, more robin-like.

Length **8in (20cm)** | Wingspan **12½in (32cm)**

Family **Cardinalidae** | Species ***Spiza americana***

Dickcissel

A tallgrass prairie resident, the Dickcissel seldom breeds outside this core range. Known for its spectacular seasonal movements, this bird winters in Venezuela, with flocks of tens of thousands ravaging rice fields and damaging seed crops, making it a notorious pest.

OCCURRENCE Breeds in tallgrass prairie, grasslands, hayfields, unmown roadsides, and untilled cropfields across the eastern central US. Casual in the West.

VOICE A flat *chik*; flight call a low, electric buzz *frrrrrrt*; song a short series of sharp, insect-like stutters followed by few longer chirps or trill *dick-dick-dick-SISS-SISS-suhl.*

Length **6½in (16cm)** | Wingspan **9½in (24cm)**

Family **Cardinalidae** | Species ***Cardinalis cardinalis***

Northern Cardinal

The state bird of seven different states in the US, the Northern Cardinal, or "redbird," is a familiar sight across the eastern US. In the west, it is restricted to Arizona, New Mexico, and Colorado.

OCCURRENCE Resident in thickets of various relatively moist habitats, such as deciduous woodland, scrub, desert washes, and backyards. Range spans across the eastern US, southernmost Canada, the extreme Southwest, and south into Mexico, northern Guatemala, and northern Belize.

VOICE Sharp, metallic *tik* call, also bubbly chatters; song a loud, variable, sweet, slurred whistle, *tsee-ew-tsee-ew-whoit-whoit-whoit-whoit-whoit.*

thick, orange-red bill

MALE

Length **8½in (22cm)** | Wingspan **12in (30cm)**

Family **Cardinalidae** | Species ***Cardinalis sinuatus***

Pyrrhuloxia

The "Pyro" is considered to be the Southwest's equivalent of the Northern Cardinal and was once known as the "Arizona Cardinal." Their ranges do overlap, and, although the two birds share very similar habits and vocalizations, they seem to tolerate each other's presence well.

OCCURRENCE Desert scrub of southwest US and Mexico. Where they occur together, prefers drier, more upland habitats than the Northern Cardinal, at elevations up to 6,500ft (2000m).

VOICE Call a distinctive dry, low *chik*, often accelerating into chatter; song generally higher, thinner, and less musical than the Northern Cardinal's.

Length **8½in (22cm)** | Wingspan **12in (30cm)**

Family **Cardinalidae** | Species ***Passerina cyanea***

Indigo Bunting

Brilliantly colored, this bird however is not really indigo but rather a vibrant, almost cyan-blue. Only a part of the male's head is colored indigo. Dependent on tree-falls within forests and the grassland-forest edge, they are specialists of disturbed habitats. Human activity has greatly benefited them with a radical increase in suitable habitats for their breeding.

OCCURRENCE Breeds in moist disturbed habitats, such as weedy fields, forest edges, and areas of heavy cultivation. Winters in small numbers along the Gulf Coast and in Florida.

VOICE Call a sharp, dry, rattling *pik*!; flight call a long *buzz* ; song a series of high-pitched "*fire*!-*fire*!, *where*?-*where*?, *there*!-*there*!, *put-it-out*!, *put-it-out*!"

Length **5½in (14cm)** | Wingspan **8in (20cm)**

Family **Cardinalidae** | Species ***Passerina versicolor***

Varied Bunting

It is the only purple-and-red songbird in North America. When seen in good light, males are a rich plum color with ruby-red napes and sparkling, sapphire-blue foreheads and rumps. The female, by contrast, is the dullest member of the Cardinalidae group. A Mexican species with a small US range, it is localized and hard to find.

OCCURRENCE Breeds in dense desert scrub in canyons and washes and in thorn forests of southwest US. In winter, most migrate to the coastal slopes of Mexico.

VOICE Call a sharp, dry, rattling *pik*!; song a pleasant, rambling burry warble.

Length **5½in (14cm)** | Wingspan **7½–8in (19–20cm)**

Family **Cardinalidae** | Species ***Passerina ciris***

Painted Bunting

With its violet-blue head, red underparts, and vibrant lime-green back, the adult male Painted Bunting is the most brightly-colored bunting in North America. The female is dull yet distinctive as one of the few truly green songbirds of the region. There are two populations that differ in molt pattern. Western birds molt after leaving the breeding grounds, while eastern molt before they depart for the winter.

OCCURRENCE Breeds in dense thickets, and other disturbed areas, across south central US and northern Mexico and along the East Coast. Western birds winter from tropical Mexico to western Panama.

VOICE A soft, ringing, upward slurred *pwip*!; flight call slurred, softer, and flatter than Indigo Bunting; song a sweet, relatively clear warble.

Length **5½in (14cm)** | Wingspan **8½in (22cm)**

VAGRANTS & ACCIDENTALS

THE LIST THAT FOLLOWS INCLUDES species that occur rarely in western North America (defined in this book as Canada and the continental United States *west* of the 100th Meridian). These species can reach North America from Eurasia, Central or South America, Africa, and even Oceania, and Antarctica. The US and Canada can receive birds that drift off course, during migration, from eastern Asia across the Pacific Ocean, or from Europe across the Atlantic. Western Alaska has a high concentration of "vagrants" because the southwesternmost tip of the state forms a series of islands, the Aleutians, that reach almost all the way across the Bering Sea to the Russian Far East.

The occurrence of "vagrant" species is classified by the American Birding Association, depending on their relative frequency, and this terminology is followed in the "status" column for each species. **Rare** species are reported every year in small numbers. **Casual** visitors have been reported at least a dozen times. **Accidental** species have been recorded no more than five times. However, because of climatological, biological, and other factors, the status of "vagrant" species is constantly changing.

COMMON NAME	SCIENTIFIC NAME	FAMILY NAME	STATUS
Waterfowl			
Eurasian Wigeon	*Anas penelope*	Anatidae	Rare visitor from Eurasia to West Coast
Garganey	*Anas querquedula*	Anatidae	Rare visitor from Eurasia to the Pribilofs; casual in California
Whooper Swan	*Cygnus cygnus*	Anatidae	Rare visitor from Eurasia to Aleutians, south to California
Tufted Duck	*Aythya fuligula*	Anatidae	Rare visitor from Eurasia to Alaska; casual along the West Coast
Smew	*Mergellus albellus*	Anatidae	Rare visitor from Eurasia to Alaska; casual to California
American Black Duck	*Anas rubripes*	Anatidae	Introduced to British Columbia and Washington state
Petrels, Shearwaters, and Storm-Petrels			
Cook's Petrel	*Pterodroma cookii*	Procellariidae	Regular visitor from New Zealand off the coast of California
Flesh-footed Shearwater	*Puffinus carneipes*	Procellariidae	Rare visitor from New Zealand and Australia to California
Wedge-rumped Storm-Petrel	*Oceonodroma tethys*	Hydrobatidae	Rare visitor to California coast; breeds on Galapagos and islands off Peru
Ibises and Herons			
Wood Stork	*Mycteria americana*	Ciconiidae	Accidental visitor from Mexico to California
Glossy Ibis	*Plegadis falcinellus*	Threskiornithidae	Casual visitor from the East or Central America to California
Yellow-crowned Night Heron	*Nyctanassa violacea*	Ardeidae	Casual visitor from Mexico to California
Reddish Egret	*Egretta rufescens*	Ardeidae	Rare visitor from Mexico to California
Tricolored Heron	*Egretta tricolor*	Ardeidae	Rare visitor from Mexico to southern California
Little Blue Heron	*Egretta caerulea*	Ardeidae	Rare visitor from Mexico to West Coast from California to British Columbia
Pelicans and Relatives			
Brown Booby	*Sula leucogaster*	Sulidae	Rare visitor to southern California
Eagles			
Steller's Sea Eagle	*Haliaeetus pelagicus*	Accipitridae	Casual visitor from eastern Asia to Alaska
Plovers and Sandpipers			
Common Ringed Plover	*Charadrius hiaticula*	Charadriidae	Casual visitor from Eurasia to the Aleutian and Pribilof Islands
Lesser Sand Plover/ Mongolian Plover	*Charadrius mongolus*	Charadriidae	Rare visitor from Asia to West Alaska and Pacific Coast
Wood Sandpiper	*Tringa glareola*	Scolopacidae	Rare visitor from Eurasia to Alaska and south to California
American Woodcock	*Scolopax minor*	Scolopacidae	Casual from the East to the West and Southwest
Black-tailed Godwit	*Limosa limosa*	Scolopacidae	Casual visitor from Eurasia to the Aleutian and Pribilof Islands
Common Sandpiper	*Actitis hypoleucos*	Scolopacidae	Casual visitor from Eurasia to western Alaska and the Aleutian Islands
Gray-tailed Tattler	*Heteroscelus brevipes*	Scolopacidae	Rare visitor from Asia to Alaska, southward to California

COMMON NAME	SCIENTIFIC NAME	FAMILY NAME	STATUS
Red-necked Stint	*Calidris ruficollis*	Scolopacidae	Rare visitor from Siberia to both coasts in summer and fall
Temminck's Stint	*Calidris temminckii*	Scolopacidae	Casual visitor from Eurasia to Alaska and Pacific Northwest
Long-toed Stint	*Calidris subminuta*	Scolopacidae	Rare visitor from Asia to Aleutians, Pribilofs, Pacific Coast to California
Sharp-tailed Sandpiper	*Calidris acuminuta*	Scolopacidae	Rare visitor from eastern Asia to Alaska and Pacific Coast to California
Curlew Sandpiper	*Calidris ferruginea*	Scolopacidae	Rare visitor from Eurasia in Alaska and Pacific Coast
Ruff	*Philomachus pugnax*	Scolopacidae	Rare visitor from Eurasia to Alaska and Pacific Coast
Gulls			
Great Black-backed Gull	*Larus marinus*	Laridae	Casual visitor from the East to several western states
Laughing Gull	*Larus atricilla*	Laridae	Rare from Mexico to SouthCalifornia; casual from the East to Colorado and West Texas
Slaty-backed Gull	*Larus schistisagus*	Laridae	Casual visitor from Asia to Alaska and West Coast
Ivory Gull	*Pagophila eburnea*	Laridae	Casual visitor from the Arctic to Colorado, California, and British Columbia
Cuckoos			
Common Cuckoo	*Cuculus canorus*	Cuculidae	Casual from Eurasia to islands off Alaska
Oriental Cuckoo	*Cuculus saturatus*	Cuculidae	Casual visitor from Asia to Aleutian and Pribilof Islands
Hummingbirds			
Xantus's Hummingbird	*Hylocharis xantusii*	Trochilidae	Accidental from Baja California to S California and British Columbia
Trogons			
Eared Quetzal	*Euptilotis neoxenus*	Trogonidae	Casual from Mexico to Southeast Arizona; may be resident
Chickadees			
Gray-headed Chickadee	*Poecile cincta*	Paridae	Eurasian species resident from northern Alaska to Northwest Yukon
Old World Warblers			
Willow Warbler	*Phylloscopus trochilus*	Sylviidae	Casual visitor from Eurasia to Alaska
Wrens			
Sinaloa Wren	*Thryothorus sinaloa*	Troglodytidae	Accidental from Mexico to Arizona
Mockingbirds and Thrashers			
Blue Mockingbird	*Melanotis caerulescens*	Mimidae	Casual visitor from Mexico to southeastern Arizona
Pipits			
Olive-backed Pipit	*Anthus hodgsoni*	Motacillidae	Rare visitor from eastern Asia to Alaska (Aleutians); accidental to California
Finches			
Brambling	*Fringilla montifringilla*	Fringillidae	Regular visitor to Alaska (Aleutians); casual in West Canada, south to California
Wood-warblers			
Golden-winged Warbler	*Vermivora chrysoptera*	Parulidae	Casual visitors from the East to many western states
Northern Parula	*Parula americana*	Parulidae	Rare from the East to the western states to California
Yellow-throated Warbler	*Dendoica dominica*	Parulidae	Casual visitor from the East to many western states
Prairie Warbler	*Dendroica discolor*	Parulidae	Casual to rare visitor from the East to California, also other western states
Pine Warbler	*Dendroica pinus*	Parulidae	Casual visitor from the East to California, also other western states
Louisiana Waterthrush	*Seirurus motacilla*	Parulidae	Casual to rare visitor from the East to Arizona and California
Hooded Warbler	*Wilsonia citrina*	Parulidae	Casual to rare visitor from the East to California and southwestern states
Rufous-capped Warbler	*Basileuterus rufifrons*	Parulidae	Casual visitor from Mexicoto Texas and Arizona
Slate-throated Redstart	*Myioborus miniatus*	Parulidae	Casual visitor from Mexico to the Southwest

GLOSSARY

Many terms defined here are illustrated in the general introduction (pp.10–21).

adult A fully developed, sexually mature bird. It is in its final plumage, which no longer changes pattern with age and remains the same after yearly molt, although it may change with season. *See also* **immature, juvenile.**
aerie The nest of birds of prey, like eagles or peregrine falcons, usually on a cliff, and often used by the same pair of adult birds in successive years.
alarm call A call made by a bird to signal danger. Alarm calls are often short and urgent in tone, and a few species use different calls to signify the precise nature of the threat. *See also* **call.**
allopreening Mutual preening between two birds, the main purpose of which is to reduce the instinctive aggression when birds come into close contact. In the breeding season, allopreening helps to strengthen the pair bond between the male and female. *See also* **preening.**
altitudinal migrant see vertical migrant
alula A small group of two to six feathers projecting from a bird's "thumb," at the bend of its wing that reduces turbulence when raised.
Audubon, John James (1785–1851) American naturalist and wildlife illustrator, whose best known work was his remarkable collection of prints, *Birds of North America*.
axillary A term describing feathers at the base of the underwing. Axillary feathers often form small patches, with coloration differing from the rest of the underwing.
barred With marks crossing the body, wing, or tail; the opposite of streaked. *See also* **streaks.**
bastard wing *see* **alula**
beak *see* **bill**
bill A bird's jaws. A bill is made of bone, with a hornlike outer covering of keratin.
bird of prey Any of the predatory birds in the orders Falconiformes (eagles, hawks, falcons, kites, buzzards, ospreys, and vultures) and Strigiformes (owls). They are characterized by their acute eyesight, powerful legs, strongly hooked bill, and sharp talons. These birds, particularly the Falconiformes, are also known as raptors. *See also* **talon, raptor.**
body feather *see* **contour feather**
booming A sound produced by bitterns and some species of grouse. The booming of male bitterns is a deep, resonant, hollow sound that can carry for several miles. The booming of male grouse is produced by wind from air pouches in the sides of the bird's neck.
brackish Containing a mixture of salt-water and freshwater.
breeding plumage A general term for the plumage worn by adult birds when they display and form breeding pairs. It is usually (but not always) worn in the spring and summer. *See also* **nonbreeding plumage.**
brood (noun) The young birds produced from a single clutch of eggs and incubated together. *See also* **clutch. (verb)** In birds, to sit on nestlings to keep them warm. Brooding is usually carried out by the adult female. See also incubate.
brood parasite A bird that lays its eggs in the nest of other birds. Some brood parasites always breed this way, while others do so only occasionally.
brood patch An area of bare skin on the belly of a parent bird, usually the female, that is richly supplied with blood vessels and thus helps keep the eggs warm during incubation. This area loses its feathers in readiness for the breeding season and is fully feathered at other times.
caged-bird A species of bird commonly kept in captivity.
call A sound produced by the vocal apparatus of a bird to communicate a variety of messages to other birds. Calls are often highly characteristic of individual species and can help to locate and identify birds in the field. Most bird calls are shorter and simpler than songs. *See also* **alarm call, booming, contact call, song.**
casque A bony extension on a bird's head.
cere A leathery patch of skin that covers the base of a bird's bill. It is found only in a few groups, including birds of prey, pigeons, and parrots.
claw In birds, the nail that prolongs their toes.
cloaca An opening toward the rear of a bird's belly. It is present in both sexes and is used in reproduction and excretion.
clutch The group of eggs in a single nest, usually laid by one female and incubated together.
cock A term sometimes used to describe the adult male in gamebirds and songbirds. *See also* **hen.**
collar The area around a bird's neck, which in some species is a prominent feature of its plumage pattern and can be used for identification.
color form One of two or more clearly defined plumage variations found in the same species. Also known as a color morph or phase, a color form may be restricted to part of a species's range or occur side by side with other color forms over the entire range. Adults of different color forms are able to interbreed, and these mixed pairings can produce young of either form.
comb A fleshy growth of bare skin usually above the eyes.
contact call A call made by a bird to give its location as a means of staying in touch with others of the same species. Contact calls are used by birds in flocks and by breeding pairs. Contact calls are crucial for nocturnal migrants. *See also* **call.**
contour feather A general term for any feather that covers the outer surface of a bird, including its wings and tail. Contour feathers are also known as body feathers, and help streamline the bird.
cooperative breeding A breeding system in which a pair of parent birds are helped in raising their young by several other birds, which are often related to them and may be young birds from previous broods.
courtship display Ritualized, showy behavior used in courtship by the male, and sometimes by the female, involving plumage, sound (vocal and non-vocal), and movements.
covert A small feather covering the base of a bird's flight feather. Together, coverts form a well-defined feather tract on the wing or at the base of the tail. *See also* **feather tract.**
creche A group of young birds of about the same age, produced by different parents but tightly packed together. One or more adults guards the entire creche.
crepuscular Relating to the period just before dawn, when many birds are active, especially during courtship. When used in connection with birds, the term is often used to refer to both dawn and twilight.
crest A group of elongated feathers on top of a bird's head, which may be raised during courtship or to indicate alarm.
crown The area on top of a bird's head. It is often a prominent plumage feature, with a different color from the feathers on the rest of the head.
dabble To feed in shallow water by sieving water and obtain food through comblike filters in the bill; used mostly for ducks (dabbling ducks or dabblers).
decurved A term describing a bird's bill that curves downward from the forehead toward the tip.
dimorphism *see* **sexual dimorphism**
display *see* **courtship display, distraction display, threat display**
distraction display A display in which a bird deliberately attempts to attract a predator's attention in order to lure it away from its nest or nestlings.
diurnal Active during the day.
down feather A soft, fluffy feather, lacking the system of barbs of contour or flight feathers, that provides good insulation. Young birds are covered by down feathers until they molt into their first juvenile plumage. Adult birds have a layer of down feathers under their contour feathers. *See also* **contour feather, juvenile.**
drake An adult male duck. The adult female is known as the duck.
drift The diversion of migrating birds from their normal migration route by strong winds.
dynamic soaring *see* **soaring**
ear tuft A distinct tuft of feathers on each side of a bird's forehead, with no connection to the true ears, which can be raised as a visual signal. Many owls have ear tufts.
echolocation A method of sensing nearby objects using pulses of high-frequency sound. Echoes bounce back from obstacles, enabling the sender to build up a "picture" of its surroundings.
eclipse plumage A female-like plumage worn in some birds, especially waterfowl, by adult males for a short period after the breeding season is over. The eclipse plumage helps camouflage them during their molt, when they are flightless.
elevational migrant *see* **vertical migrant**
endemic A species (or subspecies) native to a particular geographic area—such as an island, a forest patch, a mountain, or state, or country—and found nowhere else.
escape An individual bird that has escaped from a zoo or other collection to live in the wild. *See also* **exotic**
eye-ring A ring of color, usually narrow and well defined, around the eye of a bird.
eyestripe A stripe of color running as a line through the eye of a bird.
eyrie *see* **aerie**
exotic A bird found in a region from which it is not native. Some of these are escapees, or were originally, but now live as wild birds.
feather tract A well-defined area on a bird's skin where feathers grow, leaving patches of bare skin inbetween.
fledge In young birds, to leave the nest or acquire the first complete set of flight feathers. Known as fledglings, these birds may still remain dependent on their parents for some time. *See also* **flight feather.**
fledging period The average time taken by the young of a species to fledge, timed from the moment they hatch. Fledging periods in birds range from 11 days in some small songbirds to as long as 280 days in the Wandering Albatross.
fledgling *see* **fledge**
flight feather A collective term for a bird's wing and tail feathers, used in flight. More specifically, it refers to the largest feathers on the outer part of the wing, the primaries and secondaries.
forewing The front section of a bird's wing, including the primary coverts and secondary coverts. *See also* **hindwing.**
gamebird Generally, any bird that is legally hunted, including some doves and waterfowl. This name is generally used for members of the order Galliformes.
gular sac Also known as a gular pouch, it is a large, fleshy, extendable sac just below the bill of some birds, especially fish-eaters such as pelicans. It forms part of the throat.
habitat The geographical and ecological area where a particular organism usually lives.
hen A term sometimes used to describe the adult female in gamebirds, especially grouse and songbirds. *See also* **cock.**
hindwing The rear section of a bird's spread wing, including the secondary feathers, especially when it has a distinctive color or pattern. *See also* **forewing.**
hybrid The offspring produced when two species, sometimes from different genera, interbreed. Hybrids are usually rare in the wild. Among birds, they are most frequent in gamebirds and waterfowl, especially ducks. Hybrid progeny may or may not be fertile.
immature In birds, an individual that is not yet sexually mature or able to breed. Some birds pass through a series of immature plumages over several years before adopting their first adult plumage and sexual maturity. *See also* **adult, juvenile.**
incubate In birds, to sit on eggs to keep them warm, allowing the embryo inside to grow. Incubation is often carried out by the female. *See also* **brood.**
incubation period In birds, the period when a parent incubates its eggs. It may not start until the clutch is completed.
injury feigning *see* **distraction display.**
inner wing The inner part of the wing, comprising the secondaries and rows of coverts (typically marginal, lesser, median, and greater coverts).
introduced species A species that humans have accidentally or deliberately brought into an area where it does not normally occur.
iridescent plumage Plumage that shows brilliant, luminous colors, which seem to sparkle and change color when seen from different angles.
irruption A sporadic mass movement of animals outside their normal range. Irruptions are usually short-lived and occur in response to food shortage. Also called irruptive migration.
juvenile A term referring to the plumage worn by a young bird at the time it makes its first flight and until it begins its first molt. *See also* **adult, immature.**
keratin A tough but lightweight protein. In

birds, keratin is found in the claws, feathers, and outer part of the bill.
kleptoparasite A bird that gets much of its food by stealing it from other birds, usually by following them in flight and forcing them to disgorge their food.
lamellae Delicate, comblike structures on the sides of the bill of some birds used for filtering tiny food particles out of water.
leap-frog migration A pattern of migration in which some populations of a species travel much further than the other populations, by "leap-frogging" over the area where these sedentary (nonmigratory) birds are found. *See also* **migration**.
lek An area, often small, used by males as a communal display arena, where they show off special plumage features accompanied by vocal and non-vocal sounds, to attract females. Females wait along the lek and select the male or males that they will mate with.
lobed feet Feet with loose, fleshy lobes on the toes, adapted for swimming.
lore A small area between a bird's eye and the base of its upper bill.
mandible The upper or lower part of a bird's bill, known as the upper or lower mandible respectively.
mantle The loose term used to define the back of a bird, between its neck and rump.
migrant A species that regularly moves between geographical areas. Most migrants move on an annual basis between a breeding area and a wintering area. *See also* **partial migrant**, **sedentary**.
migration A journey to a different region, following a well-defined route. *See also* **leap-frog migration, partial migrant, reverse migration, sedentary, vertical migrant**.
mobbing A type of defensive behavior in which a group of birds gang up to harass a predator, such as a bird of prey or an owl, swooping repeatedly to drive it away.
molt In birds, to shed old feathers so that they can be replaced. Molting enables birds to keep their plumage in good condition, change their level of insulation, and change their coloration or markings so that they are ready to breed or display.
monogamous Mating with a single partner, either in a single breeding season or for life. *See also* **polygamous**.
morph *see* **color form**
nape The back of the neck.
nestling A young bird still in the nest.
New World The Americas, from Alaska to Cape Horn, including the Caribbean and offshore islands in the Pacific and Atlantic oceans. *See also* **Old World**.
nictitating membrane A transparent or semiopaque "third eyelid," which moves sideways across the eye. Waterbirds often use the membrane as an aid to vision when swimming underwater.
nocturnal Active at night.
nomadic Being almost constantly on the move. Birds of deserts, grasslands, and the coniferous forests of the far north are commonly nomadic.
nonbreeding plumage The plumage worn by adult birds outside the breeding season. In many species, particularly in temperate regions, it is also known as winter plumage. *See also* **breeding plumage**.
nonmigrant *see* **sedentary**
nonpasserine Any bird that is not a member of the order Passeriformes (or passerines). *See also* **passerine**.
oil gland Also called the preen gland, a gland at the base of a bird's tail that secretes oils that are spread over the feathers for waterproofing them during preening.
Old World Europe, Asia, Africa, and Australasia. *See also* **New World**.
orbital ring A thin, bare, fleshy ring around the eye, sometimes with a distinctive color. *See also* **eye-ring**.
outer wing The outer half of the wing, comprising the primaries, their coverts, and the alula (the "thumb").
partial migrant A species in which some populations migrate while others are sedentary. This situation is common in broadly distributed species that experience a wide range of climatic conditions. *See also* **migration, sedentary**.
passerine A bird belonging to the vast order Passeriformes (the passerines). This group contains more species than all other orders of birds combined. Passerines are also called songbirds or perching birds. *See also* **nonpasserine**.
pelagic Relating to the open ocean. Pelagic birds spend most of their life at sea and only come to land to nest.
phase *see* **color form**
polygamous Mating with two or more partners during the course of a single breeding season. *See also* **monogamous**.
population A group of individual birds of the same species living in a geographically and ecologically circumscribed area.
preening Routine behavior by which birds keep their feathers in good condition. A bird grasps a feather at its base and then "nibbles" upward toward the tip, and repeats the process with different feathers. This helps smooth and clean the plumage. Birds often also smear oil from their preen gland onto their feathers at the same time. *See also* **allopreening**.
primary feather One of the large outer wing feathers, growing from the digits of a bird's "hand." *See also* **secondary feather**.
race *see* **subspecies**
range A term to indicate the geographical distribution of a species or population
raptor A general name for birds belonging to the order Falconiformes, often used interchangeablely with bird of prey. *See also* **bird of prey**.
ratite A member of an ancient group of flightless birds that includes the ostrich, cassowaries, emus, rheas, and kiwis. In the past, the group was larger and more diverse.
resident *see* **sedentary**
reverse migration A phenomenon that occurs when birds from a migratory species mistakenly travel in the opposite direction from normal, causing birds to turn up in places far outside their normal range. *See also* **migration**.
roost A place where birds sleep, either at night or by day.
rump The area between a bird's back and the base of its upper tail coverts. In many species, the rump is a different color from the rest of the plumage and can be a useful diagnostic character for identification.
sally A feeding technique (sallying), used especially by tyrant flycatchers, in which a bird makes a short flight from a perch to catch an insect, often in midair, followed by a return to a perch, often the same one.
salt gland A gland located in a depression of the skull, just above the eye of some birds, particularly seabirds. This enables them to extract the fluids they need from saltwater and then expel the excess salts through the nostrils.
scapular Any one of a group of feathers on the "shoulder," forming a more or less oval patch on each side of the back, at the base of the wing.
scrape A simple nest that consists of a shallow depression in the ground, which may be unlined or lined with material such as feathers, bits of grass, or pebbles.
secondary feather One of the row of long, stiff feathers along the rear edge of a bird's wing, between the body and the primary feathers at the wingtip. *See also* **primary feather**.
sedentary Having a settled lifestyle that involves little or no geographic movement. Sedentary birds are also said to be resident or nonmigratory. *See also* **migration**.
semipalmated The condition in which two or more of the toes are partially joined by an incomplete membrane at their base.
sexual dimorphism The occurrence of physical differences between males and females. In birds, the most common differences are in size and plumage.
shorebird Also known as a wader, any member of several families in the order Charadriiformes, including plovers, sandpipers, godwits, snipe, avocets, stilts, oystercatchers, and curlews. Not all species actually wade in water and some live in dry habitats.
soaring In birds, flight without flapping of the wings. A soaring bird stays at the same height or gains height. Updraft soaring is a type of soaring in which a bird benefits from rising currents that form at cliffs or along mountain ridges. Seabirds are expert at dynamic soaring, repeatedly diving into the troughs between waves and then using the rising air deflected off the waves to wheel back up into the air.
song A vocal performance by a bird, usually the adult male, to attract and impress a potential mate, advertise ownership of a territory, or drive away rival birds. Songs are often highly characteristic of individual species and can be a major aid in locating and identifying birds in the field. *See also* **call**.
songbird A general term used to describe a member of the suborder Passeri (or oscines), a subdivision of the largest order of birds, the Passeriformes (passerines).
species A group of similar organisms that are capable of breeding among themselves in the wild and producing fertile offspring that resemble themselves, but that do not interbreed in the wild with individuals of another similar group, are called a species. *See also* **subspecies, superspecies**.
speculum A colorful patch on the wing of a duck, formed by the secondary feathers. *See also* **secondary feather**.
spur A sharply pointed, clawlike structure at the back of the leg of some birds, like the Wild Turkey.
staging ground A stopover area where migrant birds regularly pause while on migration, to rest and feed.
stoop A near-vertical and often very fast dive made by falcons and some other birds of prey when chasing prey in the air or on the ground.
streaks Marks that run lengthwise on feathers; opposite of bars.
subspecies When species show geographical variation in color, voice, or other characters, these differentiated populations are recognized by ornithologists as subspecies (formerly also called races). *See also* **species**.
superspecies Closely related species that have different geographical ranges. See also species
syrinx A modified section of a bird's trachea (windpipe), equivalent to the voicebox in humans, that enables birds to call and sing.
talon One of the sharp, hooked claws of a bird of prey.
territory An area that is defended by an animal, or a group of animals, against other members of the same species. Territories often include useful resources, such as good breeding sites or feeding areas, which help a male attract a mate.
tertial Any one of a small group of feathers, sometimes long and obvious, at the base of the wing adjacent to the inner secondaries.
thermal A rising bubble or column of warm air over land that soaring birds can use to gain height with little effort. *See also* **soaring**.
threat display A form of defense in which a bird adopts certain postures, sometimes accompanied by loud calls, to drive away a rival or a potential predator.
trachea The breathing tube in animals, also known as the windpipe.
tubenose A general term used to describe members of the order Procellariiformes, including albatrosses, petrels, and shearwaters; their nostrils form two tubes on the upper mandible.
underwing The underside of a bird's wing, usually visible only in flight or when a bird is preening, displaying, or swimming.
upperwing The upper surface of a bird's wing clearly exposed in flight but often mostly hidden when the bird is perched.
vagrant A bird that has strayed far from its normal range. Usually, vagrants are long-distance migrants that have been blown off course by storms, have overshot their intended destination due to strong winds, or have become disoriented.
vent Also called the crissum, the undertail feathers between the lower belly feathers and tail feathers, which in some species are differently colored from either belly or tail feathers. Can be helpful in identification.
vertical migrant A species that migrates up and down mountains, usually in response to changes in the weather or food supply. *See also* **migration**.
wader *see* **shorebird**.
waterfowl A collective term for members of the family Anatidae, including ducks, geese, and swans.
wattle A bare, fleshy growth that hangs loosely below the bill in some birds. It is often brightly colored, and may play a part in courtship.
wildfowl *see* **waterfowl**
Wilson, Alexander (1766–1813) A contemporary of J.J. Audubon, Wilson's seminal American Ornithology marks the start of scientific ornithology in the US.
wingbar A line or bar of color across the upper surface of a bird's wing. Wingbars can often be seen when a bird is on the ground or perched and its wings are in the closed position, but they are normally much more obvious in flight. Wingbars may be single or in groups of two or more.
wingspan The distance across a bird's outstretched wings and back, from one wingtip to the other.

INDEX

A

B

C

T

U

V

W

ACKNOWLEDGEMENTS

Dorling Kindersley would like to thank the following people for their help in compiling this book: Lucy Baker, Rachel Booth, Kim Bryan, Arti Finn, Peter Frances, Lynn Hassett, Riccie Janus, Megan Jones, Maxine Lea, Ruth O'Rourke, Himanshi Sharma, Catherine Thomas, Yen-Mai Tsang.

Producing such a comprehensive book would be impossible without the research and observations of hundreds of field and museum ornithologists and birdwatchers. The Editor-in-Chief would like to name four who have been especially inspirational and supportive over the years: the late Paul Géroudet, the late Ernst Mayr, Patricia Stryker Joseph, and Helen Hays. In addition, we acknowledge *Birds of North America Online*, edited by Alan Poole, a joint project of the American Ornithologists' Union and Cornell's Laboratory of Ornithology, and *The Howard and Moore Complete Checklist of the Birds of the World*, revised and enlarged 3rd edition, edited by Edward C. Dickinson and published by the Princeton University Press, as invaluable sources of information on the birds of North America.

The publisher would like to thank the following for their kind permission to reproduce their photographs:

Almost without exception, the birds featured in the profiles in this book were photographed in the wild.

(Key: a-above; b-below/bottom; c-centre; f-far; l-left; r-right; t-top)

Alamy Images: AfriPics.com 11cra; Derrick Alderman 18cl; Charles Melton 241fcla; All Canada Photos 186tr; blickwinkel 19cr; Rick & Nora Bowers 256cra, 350bc, 442tl, 460br; Bruce Coleman Inc. 14tr, 19br; Gay Bumgarner 18bc; Nancy Camel 19clb; Redmond Durrell 15cb; Elvele Images Ltd 18-19cb; David Hosking 13fcrb; Juniors Bildachiv 13tr; Don Kates 16cla; Renee Morris 418; Rolf Nussbaumer 16clb; Peter Arnold, Inc. 16cl; Robert Shantz 310cla; Stock Connection Blue 13cr; © tbkmedia.de 16-17c; **Ardea**: Ian Beames 11cr; **Doug Backlund**: 12-13ca, 27cb, 112crb, 117cra, 124tr, 171crb, 317cr, 325cla, 325cra, 325crb; **Photolibrary** Tim Zurowski 255cra; **The Barn Owl Centre, UK**: 199cl; **Corbis**: Tim Davis 2-3; Steve Kaufman 28cra; Joe McDonald 14cla, 102cla; **Mike Danzenbaker**: 72tc, 424tl, 77ca, 78cra, 79crb, 185ca, 185crb, 185tc, 188ca, 188crb, 188tc, 189tc, 218ca, 218crb, 218tc, 219cra, 219crb, 219tc, 245cb, 377tc, 424bl, 435br, 441bl, 443br, 465tl; **DK Images**: Robin Chittenden 67tr, 453bl; Chris Gomersall Photography 33crb, 33tr, 48ca, 48crb, 48tr, 51crb, 64crb, 94crb, 105ca, 105crb, 108cra, 108tc, 149crb, 152crb, 172cra, 183cla, 183cra, 191cra, 280cla, 320tc, 331cra, 331tc; David Tipling Photo Library 49ca, 67tc, 69tc, 82tc, 108crb, 132cla, 160cla, 172cla, 191cla, 298tc; Mark Hamblin 52ca, 71c, 200cra, 213cra, 422bl; Chris Knights 68crb; Mike Lane 33cla, 33cra, 37tc, 46ca, 62cla, 69tr, 83ca, 153cla, 159tc, 165tc, 177ca, 182cra, 182crb, 280ca, 436tl, 458tl; Gordon Langsbury 92cla, 134cra, 147cla, 161tr; Tim Loseby 52crb, 337cla; George McCarthy 34crb, 37tr, 90ca, 92cra, 149cra, 181ca; Natural History Museum, London 10cla, 12cl; Roger Tidman 45ca, 53tr, 58ca, 64ca, 69ca, 71tr, 149tc, 154tc, 163ca, 177crb, 180cra, 320cla, 386cla, 386tc, 432tr, 433bl, 435bl, 438tr, 458tr, 459bl; Steve Young 46tc, 53cr, 62cra, 62tr, 64tc, 64tr, 68ca, 68tc, 78crb, 78tc, 160tc, 165cla, 177tc, 177tr, 180tc, 182cla, 307ca, 386cra; **Dudley Edmondson**: 23cra, 27cl, 31tr, 420br, 34cla, 40b, 40cra, 40tl, 84ca, 84tc, 89cb, 97cla, 98cla, 98tr, 106ca, 110ca, 110cb, 110cla, 110tc, 112cla, 112cra, 112tc, 114crb, 116cla, 116cra, 117crb, 124crb, 127crb, 128tc, 129crb, 130ca, 131crb, 137ca, 430tr, 431tl, 148crb, 151cra, 158tc, 164cr, 166tr, 169cla, 169cr, 174crb, 179crb, 206tl, 207cb, 210cla, 210cra, 215crb, 230br, 236bc, 259crb, 275ca, 323bc, 376crb, 387ca, 388tc, 400cra, 450tl; **Tom Ennis**: 432tl; **Hanne & Jens Eriksen**: 109crb, 429br, 142crb, 176tc; **Neil Fletcher:** 39bc, 39ca, 40cla, 42tc, 44ca, 44cra, 46tr, 52tr, 54tc, 55crb, 55tr, 320cra, 331crb, 421br; **FLPA**: Tui De Roy/Minden Pictures 17ca; Goetz Eichhorn / Foto Natura 73fbl; John Hawkins 17cla; S Jonasson 74cra; Daphne Kinzler 17tr; S & D & K Maslowski 18clb; Roger Tidman 74tr; Winfried Wisniewski/Foto Natura 17cr; **Joe Fuhrman**: 100cra, 142ca, 255crb, 322bc, 426tl; **Getty Images**: Marc Moritsch 14-15b; Brad Sharp 18c; **Melvin Grey**: 49crb, 87bc, 87cra, 425tl, 91crb, 92crb, 93cla, 426br, 126cra, 133tr, 430tl, 137cra, 137crb, 137tr, 152ca, 153cra, 200crb, 430br, 435tr; Tom Grey: 76cr, 86crb, 89cra, 103crb, 105cra, 109tc, 113crb, 117cla, 126crb, 165cl, 176crb, 184ca, 184crb, 193ca, 202bc, 231bc, 244tc, 257bc, 279cra, 283tc, 287tc, 303crb, 376fcla, 376fcra, 381cla, 381cra, 394crb; **Martin Hale**: 79ca; **Josef Hlasek**: 163crb; **Barry Hughes**: 183crb; **justbirds.org**: 427tr; **Arto Juvonen**: 36tc, 119cra; **Kevin T. Karlson**: 27cra, 28tc, 61ca, 61crb, 72ca, 139cr, 139cra, 139crb, 139fcla, 428tl, 430bl; **Garth McElroy**: 15cl, 25tc, 43cla, 60tc, 61tc, 62ca, 63tc, 65cla, 66crb, 73tc, 83tc, 84cla, 90tr, 91cla, 93tc, 94ca, 95cra, 95tc, 100crb, 100tc, 100tl, 101crb, 123cra, 123crb, 129ca, 429bl, 133cra, 134cla, 134crb, 135ca, 136cla, 136crb, 138cr, 138tc, 139ca, 140tr, 144ca, 144cra, 144crb, 145cra, 146crb, 147cra, 148fcl, 148cr, 150ca, 150crb, 151crb, 153crb, 153tr, 154cb, 156tc, 157crb, 157tc, 158ca, 164crb, 166ca, 170crb, 170tc, 170tl, 173cra, 195cra, 196crb, 205cr, 209crb, 211crb, 212cla, 213bc, 213tc, 225cra, 239cb, 239cla, 239cra, 247crb, 251cla, 251crb, 254crb, 259ca, 270crb, 272bc, 273cla, 273cra, 273crb, 275crb, 282cla, 282cra, 282tc, 283cla, 284crb, 286bc, 286ca, 286crb, 289ca, 291ca, 291crb, 294cra, 296bc, 296ca, 296crb, 298cr, 299crb, 301c, 301t, 304tr, 307bc, 309tc, 311crb, 313cra, 313crb, 314bc, 314cra, 315cb, 315crb, 318bc, 321b, 326cb, 326tc, 327cb, 327crb, 328cb, 328tc, 329crb, 329tc, 330crb, 332cra, 333tr, 334crb, 335cra, 335tc, 337bc, 339cb, 339cra, 339tc, 342cra, 342crb, 343cr, 344cra, 344crb, 344tc, 345bc, 345ca, 349bc, 461tr, 352cra, 352tc, 353cla, 353crb, 353tc, 357cra, 361cb, 361cra, 362bl, 363ca, 363crb, 364crb, 366crb, 368cra, 368crb, 370cb, 373cra, 377crb, 377tr, 379bc, 380tr, 383crb, 383tc, 388crb, 389bc, 390ca, 391tc, 393cla, 393crb, 393tc, 395c, 398cra, 399cra, 400crb, 400tc, 401ca, 403ca, 407cla, 408ca, 408cb, 408crb, 410cb, 410tc, 413cra, 414cra, 417tr, 434bl, 439tl, 457tl, 464tl, 465br; **Bob Moul**: 83cla, 135crb, 368tc, 379cla, 426bl; **Alan Murphy**: 23cl, 419tr, 81ca, 96tr, 427tl, 121tr, 428br, 190b, 195b, 195cl, 197crb, 198crb, 214tr, 217b, 217cl, 226bl, 226br, 227ca, 227cb, 228l, 231cla, 243tr, 254cla, 269crb, 281cr, 284ca, 346b, 351cla, 372b, 462tl; **Tomi Muukonen:** 46crb, 70cl, 82tr, 111tr, 119cla, 172fcla, 175cla, 175crb, 385crb, 386crb, 434tr, 454tr; **naturepl.com**: Barry Mansell 38c; Vincent Munier 10-11c; Nigel Marven 186ca; Tom Vezo 17crb; **NHPA/Photoshot**: Bill Coster 80bc, 128bc; Dhritiman Mukherjee 421tl; Mike Lane 439tr; Kevin Schafer 74cb; **Wayne Nicholas**: 429tr; **Judd Patterson**: 22, 30cra, 30tc, 96bc, 201cra, 261cra, 425tr; **E. J. Peiker**: 25cla, 26cl, 41cra, 45tc, 47cb, 49tc, 50ca, 50tr, 53cla, 53cra, 54ca, 54crb, 54tr, 55ca, 55cb, 55tc, 56cb, 56crb, 57ca, 57crb, 65crb, 66tc, 70tr, 72crb, 73crb, 85crb, 87cl, 88cra, 93cra, 94cra, 98fcla, 100fcra, 104ca, 104cla, 115c, 118cla, 118crb, 125tc, 128cr, 130crb, 131ca, 131cra, 132cra, 132crb, 136cra, 140tc, 143ca, 147crb, 149ca, 161cr, 164ca, 168crb, 175cra, 433tr, 178tr, 189cra, 189crb, 193bc, 194crb, 200cla, 200tc, 204cra, 220tr, 221tr, 228br, 230cra, 230tc, 232cb, 243cl, 244cra, 256crb, 258cb, 260cra, 274tc, 275cra, 275tr, 277crb, 283cra, 285crb, 285tc, 287bc, 289crb, 292cla, 300c, 300crb, 301b, 302crb, 308bc, 319bc, 335tr, 336crb, 341crb, 341tr, 348cla, 351crb, 348tc, 371bc, 372tr, 374bc, 375tr, 380bc, 380tc, 382bc, 384br, 384cla, 402crb, 404ca, 405crb, 411crb, 411tc, 414bc, 417cla, 421tr, 421bl, 427bl, 438br, 444bl, 445bl, 446bl, 449bl, 451tr, 452tr, 453tr, 460bl,468tl, 469tl; **Jari Peltomäki**: 34tc, 36cra, 39cra, 62crb, 70bc, 102bc, 120ca, 120cra, 120crb, 125cla, 125cra, 194crb, 191crb, 199b, 206cb, 263crb, 290cra, 290crb, 333cla, 385cra, **David Plummer**: 445br; **Eric Preston**: 77crb; **Mike Read**: 35bc, 75crb, 107crb; **Robert Royse**: 28cla, 29cla, 34cra, 42crb, 60ca, 85ca, 429tl, 142cra, 144cla, 145ca, 152tr, 157ca, 170cra, 176ca, 176tr, 196cra, 223ca, 251cra, 265cb, 265crb, 288crb, 306cra, 308tc, 310crb, 317crb, 321ca, 360cra, 365crb, 365tr, 366cla, 386tr, 387crb, 397ca, 397crb, 401crb, 405cra, 407cra, 423tl, 429br, 431br, 452br, 456tl, 458bl, 461tl, 462tr, 464bl, 465bl, 466tl, 466tr, 469bl; **Chris Schenk**: 62fcla; **Bill Schmoker**: 29crb, 43cra, 44tc, 75cr, 76ca, 76crb, 76tr, 84crb, 89ca, 106crb, 117tc, 118cr, 118cra, 192crb, 262ca, 419tl, 420tr, 422tl, 441br, 443tr; **Brian E. Small**: 1c, 11fcra, 24tc, 24tr, 28cra, 29tr, 31crb, 32cla, 32cra, 32crb, 42ca, 47ca, 47tc, 52tc, 56ca, 56tc, 57tc, 59tc, 60tr, 63ca, 66ca, 71ca, 72cla, 80tr, 95cla, 97cra, 98cra, 99cla, 99crb, 103ca, 103tc, 109cra, 110cra, 111ca, 113cra, 115bc, 122ca, 122crb, 127c, 127cla, 132tc, 133tc, 136tc, 141ca, 141tc, 143cra, 145cla, 146ca, 147ca, 151ca,

151tr, 152tc, 154ca, 155ca, 155cra, 156tr, 163fcla, 166cra, 167cra, 169ca, 169tr, 171ca, 171cla, 171cra, 174tr, 178ca, 179ca, 192ca, 193tc, 194ca, 197ca, 197cra, 198ca, 201cla, 201crb, 202ca, 204cla, 205ca, 205cra, 206cra, 207cla, 207cra, 208cb, 209cra, 214cl, 216ca, 220cla, 220crb, 221cra, 222cla, 222cra, 223bc, 224tr, 225cla, 226t, 227cra, 227tr, 228cra, 229cla, 232cla, 232cra, 233cb, 233cla, 233cra, 234tc, 235cra, 235tc, 237cb, 237cla, 237cra, 240cb, 241ca, 241cra, 242cla, 242cra, 244crb, 245ca, 246ca, 247cra, 247tc, 249cra, 250ca, 250crb, 252ca, 252crb, 253crb, 259cra, 260crb, 260tc, 261cla, 262crb, 264crb, 265ca, 267ca, 267crb, 268ca, 268crb, 269tr, 270cra, 271ca, 271crb, 272ca, 273tc, 274cra, 276ca, 276cra, 278ca, 278cra, 283crb, 288ca, 290ca, 293cra, 294crb, 295ca, 297ca, 298tr, 299bc, 299cra, 300cla, 302ca, 305crb, 306crb, 309ca, 310cra, 311bc, 311ca, 312cra, 312tc, 313cla, 315ca, 316ca, 316crb, 316tc, 319cra, 322cra, 322tc, 323tc, 324ca, 324cra, 324tr, 326ca, 327tc, 327cra, 328cla, 328cra, 332tc, 334ca, 335cla, 337cra, 338tc, 340ca, 340crb, 342cla, 342tc, 343ca, 343cra, 343tl, 346tr, 347cra, 347tc, 348crb, 349tr, 350cra, 350crb, 351cra, 352crb, 353tr, 354cra, 354crb, 354tc, 356cra, 356crb, 356tc, 357tc, 358cra, 358tc, 359cra, 359tc, 360bc, 360cla, 360tc, 361cla, 362cra, 362tc, 364ca, 365ca, 366tc, 366tr, 367cra, 367crb, 369ca, 369tc, 370tc, 371ca, 371tc, 375tc, 376cra, 378crb, 379ca, 379cra, 380ca, 381bc, 382cra, 382tc, 383cla, 383cra, 384tr, 387tr, 388tr, 389cra, 390crb, 391cra, 391crb, 392cla, 392cra, 392crb, 392tc, 393cra, 394cla, 395cra, 395crb, 395fcla, 395tc, 396tr, 398ca, 400cla, 403cra, 404tc, 405cla, 406bc, 406crb, 410ca, 411ca, 412ca, 412cla, 412cra, 412crb, 412tr, 413cr, 413tc, 414cl, 414cla, 414tc, 415cla, 415cra, 415crb, 415tc, 416bc, 416cla, 416tr, , 417bc, 417tc, 419br, 419bl, 420bl, 422tr, 423br, 426tr, 427br, 428tr, 428bl, 431br, 432bl, 433tl, 433br, 434tl, 435tl, 439bl, 439br, 440tl, 441tl, 440bl, 440br, 442tr, 442bl, 443tl, 443bl, 444tr, 445tl, 445tr, 445br, 446br, 446tr, 447tl, 447tr, 447br, 448tl, 448bl, 448br, 449tl, 449tr, 449br, 450tl, 450tr, 450br, 450bl, 451bl, 453bl, 453br, 454br, 455tl, 455tr, 455bl, 455br, 456tr, 456br, 457br, 457tr, 457bl, 459tr, 459br, 460tr, 461bl, 461br, 462bl, 463tr, 463bl, 463br, 463tl, 464tr, 464br, 465tr, 466bl, 466br, 467tl, 467tr, 467bl, 467br, 468tr, 468bl, 468br, 469tr, 469br; **Bob Steele**: 13cb, 24cla, 24crb, 26cla, 27cla, 30cla, 32tc, 35ca, 39cla, 40tc, 41cla, 41crb, 43crb, 44crb, 45tr, 47crb, 48tc, 49tr, 50crb, 57tr, 59crb, 59tr, 63crb, 65tc, 66tr, 73tr, 75ca, 81crb, 81tc, 85tc, 86ca, 86cb, 88cla, 88tr, 90crb, 92tc, 97tc, 98crb, 99cra, 101cra, 101tc, 104tr, 111cra, 113ca, 115tc, 116bc, 116ca, 116tr, 118tr, 119crb, 121b, 121t, 123cla, 124ca, 124tc, 126cla, 127cra, 129cra, 130bl, 130cra, 130tc, 131cla, 133ca, 134tc, 137cr, 140ca, 140crb, 141crb, 143crb, 145crb, 146tc, 148tc, 150cra, 155crb, 155tr, 156ca, 156crb, 158crb, 159bc, 240ca, 160cra, 161bc, 161ca, 162ca, 162crb, 162tc, 162tr, 163fcra, 164tr, 165cra, 165crb, 166cla, 166crb, 166tc, 167cla, 167cr, 167crb, 167tr, 168cla, 168cra, 168tc, 168tr, 169cra, 169crb, 172crb, 172tc, 173cla, 173tc, 174ca, 178crb, 178tc, 179tc, 180bc, 180fcla, 182tc, 184tc, 198cb, 199tr, 203cra, 203tc, 204cb, 208cra, 208tc, 209cla, 211cra, 211tc, 212crb, 214crb, 214b, 215ca, 216crb, 217t, 220tc, 221ca, 221crb, 222cb, 222crb, 223cla, 223cr, 224cra, 224crb, 225cb, 225crb, 229cra, 229fclb, 229fcrb, 230bl, 231ca, 231cra, 234cla, 234cra, 234crb, 235bc, 236ca, 236tr, 238bc, 238ca, 238cla, 238cra, 240cla, 240cra, 243b, 245crb, 246crb, 249crb, 253cla, 253cra, 254cra, 257ca, 258ca, 258cra, 258crb, 261b, 262cra, 263tc, 264ca, 266ca, 266cb, 266crb, 270tc, 272crb, 274cb, 276crb, 277ca, 278crb, 279ca, 279crb, 452tl, 280crb, 281b, 285cb, 285cra, 287cra, 287crb, 289cra, 291cra, 291tr, 292cra, 292crb, 293crb, 293tc, 294tc, 295crb, 295tc, 296tc, 297crb, 297tc, 297tr, 298bc, 298cla, 299tc, 300bc, 300tr, 302cb, 302cra, 303cra, 304crb, 305cra, 306bc, 306ca, 308cra, 309crb, 312crb, 313ca, 317ca, 318ca, 320fcla, 321cra, 322crb, 323cla, 323cra, 324cb, 325tc, 329cla, 329cra, 330cla, 330tr, 332crb, 333b, 334cb, 336cla, 336cra, 336tc, 337cl, 337tc, 338cla, 338cra, 338crb, 340tc, 341cla, 341cra, 345cra, 346cl, 347cla, 347crb, 348cra, 349cla, 350tc, 351tc, 352cla, 348cl, 348cra, 357crb, 358crb, 359crb, 361crb, 362bc, 362cla, 367tc, 369cb, 369crb, 370ca, 370crb, 372cr, 373bc, 373cl, 373tc, 374ca, 374cra, 374tr, 375crb, 376cla, 376tr, 377cla, 378cra, 378tc, 382cla, 384bl, 387cra, 388cla, 388cr, 389cl, 394cra, 394tc, 396crb, 396tc, 398crb, 399cla, 399crb, 399tc, 402ca, 402cb, 403bc, 404bc, 405bc, 406ca, 406cra, 407crb, 409ca, 409crb, 410crb, 413bc, 413ca, 413crb, 416tc, 420tl, 425br, 431tr, 431bl, 435br, 437tl, 437tr, 437br, 438tl, 438bl, 440tr, 441tr, 442br, 444tl, 446tl, 447bl, 448tr, 451br, 452bl, 453tl, 454bl, 458br, 462br; **Andy & Gill Swash**: 75tr, 88crb, 91cra, 97crb, 304cb, 425bl; **Glen Tepke**: 187tc, 436tr, 437bl; **Markus Varesvuo**: 4–5c, 12–13bl, 23cb, 33ca, 36crb, 37cra, 37fbr, 38cra, 39crb, 51ca, 51cb, 51tr, 58cb, 58crb, 58tc, 60crb, 65ca, 67ca, 67crb, 71crb, 73ca, 73cb, 80cl, 82ca, 82crb, 83crb, 107cla, 111crb, 114cra, 114tr, 119ca, 119tr, 160crb, 181crb, 181tc, 183tc, 186fbl, 187crb; 203crb, 212cra, 263cra, 282crb, 307crb, 320crb, 343crb, 385cla, 385tc, 422br, 423tr, 436bl, 460tl; Rick and Nora Bowers 296fbl, 458tl; Herbert Clarke 79bc, 424br; Robert L. Pitman 187ca, Don Roberson 186bc, 436br; Doug Wechsler 459tl; **Peter S Weber**: 25crb, 26crb, 30crb, 41tc, 59ca, 91tr, 93ca, 95crb, 98tc, 190cla, 192cr, 210crb, 215tr, 232fcla, 235cla, 236tc, 242clb, **Roger Wilmshurst**: 107cra.

Jacket images: *Front:* **Garth McElroy.** *Back:* **Garth McElroy:** tr, **Brian E. Small:** cr (female & male), crb (birds at nest hole), fcr. *Spine:* **Garth McElroy**